TEACHER'S GUIDE TO

A HISTORY OF
THE UNITED STATES

Daniel J. Boorstin
Brooks Mather Kelley

with

Ruth Frankel Boorstin

GINN AND COMPANY

Teacher's Guide Author

Henry Thomas Van Dyke taught social studies for many years at Ramsey (New Jersey) High School. He also wrote a weekly column for a newspaper in his area. Mr. Van Dyke is the author of *Youth and the Drug Problem* and *Juvenile Delinquency* in Ginn's Youth and the Law series. And he is the editor of another Ginn paperback, *Our Environment: Pathways to Solution*.

© Copyright, 1981, by Ginn and Company (Xerox Corporation)
All Rights Reserved

Home Office: Lexington, Massachusetts 02173

0-663-37422-7

Contents

Overview 4
Features and Organization of the Text 4
Features of the Teacher's Guide 5
General Teaching Hints 6
Audiovisual Correlation with the Text 8
Learning Objectives and Teaching Suggestions 17

1 What Europeans Found: the American Surprise 17
2 An Assortment of Colonies 21
3 New Ways in a New World 25
4 The Road to Revolution and Victory 29
5 From Confederation to Nation 34
6 The United States Begins 38
7 Jefferson in Power 42
8 Struggles of a Young Nation 47
9 The Jacksonian Era 51
10 The Flourishing Land 56
11 Reforming and Expanding 60
12 The Failure of the Politicians 65
13 The Civil War 71
14 To Punish or Forgive? 76
15 The Passing of the Frontier 82
16 The Nation Transformed 87
17 The Challenge of the Cities 92
18 Politics in the Gilded Age 99
19 The United States and the World 106
20 The Progressive Era 110
21 The United States and World War I 116
22 Return to Normalcy, 1918–1929 121
23 The Coming of the Great Depression 127
24 "Nothing to Fear but Fear Itself" 132
25 Reshaping American Life 139
26 Clouds of War 144
27 A World Conflict 152
28 Truman: Neither War nor Peace 160
29 Eisenhower: Moderate Republican 167
30 Mobile People and Magic Machines 172
31 Years of Hope and Promise 177
32 Lyndon B. Johnson—from Success to Failure 183
33 The Rise and Fall of Richard Nixon 189
34 A New World of Competition 193
35 Changing Leaders in Washington 198

Epilogue: The Mysterious Future 202

Bibliographies for Outside Reading 203

Handout Facsimiles 215

Outline Map Facsimiles 271

Unit and Final Tests 280

Answer Key to Tests 319

Overview

Features and Organization of the Text

Numerous features of this new American history text make it an appealing and useful learning tool.

1 *High interest level:* Above all, this text captures the student's interest. The narrative brings both famous and little-known history makers to life. Accounts of political, economic, and social developments come into sharp focus with vivid description—from colonial smuggling to civil-rights protest marches, from the failure of silk production in the Georgia colony to wagon towns moving west.

2 *Lively, prize-winning prose:* The craftsmanship that helped to bring the Bancroft, Parkman, and Pulitzer prizes for Dr. Boorstin's trilogy *The Americans* is a hallmark of this textbook. This model of writing excellence comes along at a time when the public is calling for student competency in writing skills.

3 *Interpretive history:* Students encounter two frank, thoughtful, and creative historical minds. While recognizing and explaining underlying social and economic forces as "causes" of particular developments, the authors time and again remind the reader that individuals and groups make history and can change history. Character and personality count. Prejudice, vanity, timidity, and greed affect the course of public affairs. So do courage, resoluteness, vision, and goodwill.

4 *Broad coverage:* The full span of American history is here—from European background of discovery to the latest presidential administration. Yet this is no encyclopedia. The drama of the unexpected, the foibles of the mighty, the vision of uncommon men and women, the impatience of reformers, the bravado of steamboat captains—all these are skillfully woven into the narrative.

5 *Narrative, chronological approach:* While the authors do not hesitate to use flashbacks, in the main the account is chronological. Such an approach helps students to see how events are interrelated—to see causes and results. At the same time, when it is appropriate to study some topic in depth, the relevant parts of the subject can be found in the index.

6 *Regional, as well as national, emphasis:* Events and people from every part of the land get attention. The narrative begins properly with New Spain and the Spanish borderlands, and the scene often shifts from west to east and from east to west. In addition, the chapter-end exercises called "Your Region in History" continually remind students that their locality played a part in our history.

7 *Her story as well as his story:* From Isabella supporting Columbus—and Freydis (Leif Ericsson's bold half-sister) rallying the Norse explorers—to Rosalynn Carter and Betty Friedan, this text in both narrative and illustrations recognizes the roles of women in our history.

8 *Multi-racial and multi-ethnic:* Students of all racial and ethnic groups can take pride—and feel anguish—as they read about their own group's contribution to the building of our country and about the special handicaps suffered.

9 *Illustration program:* The rich variety of illustrations, many in full color, includes paintings, lithographs, photos, cartoons, trade bills, broadsides, and song-sheet covers. All illustrations are authentic to the period being studied. They show the period as it was, not as some later artist imagined it. In addition to commentaries on American art that appear in the narrative and in picture captions, an essay on American art and artists appears in the appendix—along with a state-by-state listing of many local museums.

10 *Map program:* More than 80 colorful maps, including an atlas of the world today, complement the narrative.

11 *Basic documents explained in detail:* The Declaration of Independence and the Constitution of the United States contain the exact wording and historical spelling of the original documents. Accompanying each of these documents are detailed explanations of why particular parts were written ("Origins") and how certain phrases and clauses were later applied or interpreted ("Afterlife").

12 *Learning exercises:* Each chapter is divided into sections that are generally suitable in length for daily reading and discussion assignments. Each section ends with a set of review exercises tied directly to the text to help students master facts and improve their reading comprehension.

The Chapter Review in every case consists of four types of learning exercises: (a) discussion questions that go beyond mere recall and often cut across various chapter sections, (b) questions that relate chapter content to present-day issues and events, (c) questions and activities that relate chapter content to the student's own region, state, or locality, and (d) a variety of skill-building activities, which frequently require students to use or interpret material in the chapter.

Features of the Teacher's Guide

Above all, this Guide is not a static, prescriptive manual. Instead it is a collection of ideas for adding variety in day-to-day use of the text. The key to its use is *selectivity:* choosing ideas and activities that fit your teaching style and the interests and abilities of your students.

1 *Instructional objectives:* Learning objectives are provided for each chapter section (or occasionally for two brief consecutive sections). The objectives are primarily of the cognitive type and geared to the text narrative. However, you can easily adapt and add to the listed objectives, particularly by providing additional affective and skill-development goals that your own course of study recommends.

2 *Teaching suggestions:* Several ideas are provided for teaching each chapter section: topics for student reports, audiovisual recommendations, questions to use in studying maps and illustrations, anecdotes and other elaboration of the text narrative, notes for brief teacher lectures, chalkboard and/or notebook diagrams for mastering text content, supplementary questions to use in class discussion, etc.

3 *Handout lessons and outline maps:* Ordinarily one or two of the "Teaching Suggestions" per chapter will call for use of duplicable pages of the Guide containing (a) narrative that supplements the text, (b) excerpts from original sources, (c) vocabulary and reading comprehension exercises, (d) graphs or diagrams to make, complete, and/or interpret, (e) chronologies, and (f) writing exercises.

Several duplicable outline maps are provided for map-study activities.

4 *Competency exercises:* Ordinarily one or more of the "Teaching Suggestions" per chapter provides practice in basic competencies that have been identified as such in the "minimum competency testing movement."

5 *"Introducing the Chapter":* This feature appears at the beginning of each chapter "lesson plan." It provides either an activity to get students into the chapter (as in Chapter 1) or a brief commentary on the chapter—its relationship to previous or upcoming chapters and sometimes a word of advice on finding out students' retained information (and misinformation) from earlier history courses.

6 *Answers to "Chapter Review":* Suggested answers and/or tips on finding answers are provided for the exercises called "Meeting Our Earlier Selves" and "Questions for Today" in the end-of-chapter exercises in the text. Answers to a few of the skill exercises are also provided.

7 *"General Teaching Hints":* In this Overview of the Guide we have provided some general suggestions on using the text. Many of the techniques can be used over and over; they appear in the Overview to avoid repetition in the teaching suggestions provided for each chapter section.

8 *Audiovisual correlation:* A list of films, filmstrips, and records keyed to the 12 units of the text appears at the end of this Overview.

9 *Bibliographies:* A list of books for outside reading and independent study is provided for each unit of the text. A page of General Bibliography suggests books that can be useful throughout the course. Bibliography pages can be removed from the Guide and duplicated for student use.

10 *Unit and final tests:* Each test consists of multiple-choice, matching, and other short-answer items. Teachers are urged to add essay items to fill out each test. The tests appear at the end of the Guide on duplicable pages.

The *Answer Key to Tests,* following the Final Test, can be removed and kept in a secure place.

General Teaching Hints

The following teaching suggestions are provided "up front" because they are the kinds of techniques that can be used again and again.

1 Using the "Section Review" Exercises: Items that tell students to identify, explain, or locate, as well as the questions in the Section Review, are generally arranged in the order in which the answers appear in the text.

These review exercises can be used in a variety of ways: (a) In a class discussion or recitation period students may answer the questions orally. As a variation the teacher may occasionally ask a student to find and read aloud the sentence (or sentences) which best answers a question. (b) Students may be asked to write brief answers to the questions in their notebooks. If such a lesson is assigned as homework, you should collect the papers frequently for spot-checking. (c) Brief quizzes based on the questions may be used to encourage proper lesson preparation.

2 Using "Chapter Review" Exercises: Before the class finishes its work on one chapter, look ahead to "Questions for Today" and "Your Region in History" in the following chapter to see if there are items that ought to be assigned ahead of time so that student reports can be ready to present in class at the appropriate time.

Some of the discussion items in "Meeting Our Earlier Selves" and in "Questions for Today" relate to a particular chapter section. Ordinarily these items can best be used when the relevant topic is being discussed in class. (The "Teaching Suggestions" in this Guide frequently call attention to items that can be used most effectively with a particular chapter section.) Other items in the Chapter Review are based on the chapter as a whole. Such items, of course, are best used after students have studied the entire chapter.

3 Discussing Issues: Questions posed by the text, the Guide, the teacher, and students may sometimes arouse strong feelings. When this happens, you have a fine chance to use the *"feed-back"* technique suggested by psychologist Carl Rogers. It is an excellent device for developing skill in listening. As soon as discussion warms up on some controversial topic, stop it momentarily to suggest that the class try the following experiment: *Each person can speak up only after he or she has first restated the ideas and feelings of the previous speaker accurately and to that speaker's satisfaction.* As the rule is given, write it on the chalkboard as a reminder. Allow several minutes before the class period ends for an analysis of the effect of this rule on the preceding discussion. Students may decide to use it again when a controversial issue is discussed.

Brainstorming: Some topics and questions are best discussed by having students speculate, or give tentative answers: "What might have happened if . . ." "Why might the President have wanted to . . ." "What were some probable effects of . . ." If a wide range of responses seem possible, tell students to begin "brainstorming." Ask them to come up with any plausible answers—one per student at a time. As responses are made, write them (or the gist) on the chalkboard without making any evaluations until the responses stop. Then students can decide if any of the responses ought to be eliminated or modified.

If a topic has several facets to consider, divide the class into two, three, or more small groups for a five-minute brainstorming session. One member of the group can take down the responses and report them to the rest of the class.

4 Time Schedule: In the absence of a prescribed course of study which sets the time for dealing with various topics, you will have to decide the relative merits of "completing the book" and emphasizing particular aspects of the subject.

The 35 chapters plus Epilogue suggest a time schedule of one chapter per week. If you need to spend more than a week on particular chapters, simply spend a day or two on certain other ones. The Publisher sincerely believes that the high interest level of this book makes every text chapter worth reading.

In most cases a chapter section makes a convenient study assignment.

5 Using Text Maps and Illustrations: To ensure that students *use* maps and illustrations as tools and not simply as pictures to be passed over lightly, spend a few minutes in class probing students' ability to make connections between maps, illustrations, and the text content.

Maps: Make sure that students understand the purpose of the map by asking for a brief description. Insist on an accurate statement that includes the major elements which are portrayed (time period, geographic limits, and other features). On maps which have an abundance of details, probe by asking students to construct generalizations which they can draw from the maps. For example, for the Colonial Settlement map on page 49, you might ask students to describe the initial pattern of settlement and then state how that pattern grew and changed in the next 115 years. Following these statements, you might ask students to hypothesize about the relationship between settlement patterns and geographic features such as rivers (which would encourage settlement) and mountains (which would discourage settlement). Ask students to compute distances using the distance scales so that they can understand communication and transportation problems that the nation faced. Finally, encourage students to use more than one map in the text to make comparisons and to increase their comprehension about the relationships between political and social phenomena and the natural terrain of the United States.

Illustrations: Many of the illustrations in the text offer a number of opportunities to glean additional information about the period under study. Have students determine the basic nature of the illustration and its purpose (portrait, trade card, song sheet, broadside, etc.). Encouraging students to examine details within the illustration will often bring to light many additional questions on which fruitful discussion can be based. Many of the portraits contain revealing symbols of their time, and the broadsides yield significant information which students should investigate. Where possible, try to relate illustrations in the text to those which students might see in magazines or on television by asking them to point out the similarities and differences between past and present.

6 **Vocabulary Development:** One way to determine the words that students find difficult or unfamiliar is to ask them directly. But since few students will admit that they don't know their vocabulary, here is a non-threatening method to elicit those words. As a homework assignment or in class, ask students to skim the chapter or the section under study and list the words which they feel might be difficult for *other students in the class.* Collect the lists, and sort for the words most frequently mentioned. Use this new list as your basis for vocabulary development. In reality the students have probably answered for themselves rather than for their peers. In any case, the method—and variations of it you can easily design—will produce a list of vocabulary words that require some extra attention.

7 **Handout Lessons:** Teachers in schools that have purchased the text in classroom lots have the Publisher's permission to duplicate the copyrighted Handouts that appear at the back of this Guide. Suggestions on how and where to use the Handouts appear in the chapter-section "Teaching Suggestions."

Create additional handouts to supplement (or replace) those provided in this Guide. Perhaps you would like to share a successful handout or worksheet with other teachers using this text. The Publisher would welcome the opportunity to consider your idea(s) for inclusion in a revised edition of this Guide—with acknowledgment, of course. Send such handouts to the Social Studies Department, Ginn and Company, 191 Spring Street, Lexington, MA 02173.

8 **Outside Reading and Reports on Reading:** The most obvious way to challenge average and able students is to encourage them to read a substantial amount of American history beyond the text. Most students, of course, will need the incentive of earning extra credit on their grades for the course. Two typical ways of doing this are (a) to require x-number of pages to earn a B or A in the grading period and (b) to add points toward a grade for a satisfactory reading report.

Reluctant readers, of course, should be encouraged to read, but other opportunities should also be provided for them to earn extra credit—interviewing, collecting, drawing, displaying, etc., as suggested throughout this guide.

A sample reading report form that may be duplicated (or adapted) appears at the end of the duplicable Outline Maps in the back of this Guide.

The Bibliographies should be adapted to fit your needs and the resources locally available. Save pupil time by crossing out items that are not suitable or available. Add others. Encourage students to find other useful readings, but require them to get approval before submitting reports for extra credit.

The Bibliographies appear on Guide pages 203–214. They can be removed and duplicated—one unit or two at a time—and handed out to students.

9 **Using Films and Filmstrips:** On the following pages is a list of films and filmstrips selected to correlate with the text. These audiovisual aids are available from major film distribution centers at a reasonable rental cost. A key to the abbreviations of distributors' names follows the list.

New and updated films appear each year. Keep a file of promising titles.

In the "Teaching Suggestions" in this Guide many more films are recommended than can profitably be used. One key to effective film and filmstrip use is selectivity. Will the film add to the text and class discussion in some important way? Can you obtain and use the film at just the right time? For teaching concepts, filmstrips are often more useful than films.

Here are a few tips on using films:

• Always try to preview a film before you use it. Decide for yourself whether the film is appropriate for the particular lesson.

• Study the instructional guide furnished by the producer so that you can benefit from suggestions on how to use the film.

• Select questions to point out the aspects of the film you want to emphasize. Write them on the board before showing the film.

• Make clear to the students why you are showing the film. Keep before them the fact that the film is a part of a lesson and not merely entertainment.

• Prepare everything you can in advance. Have the film ready to run when the class enters the room.

• Do not leave the projector unattended while a film is being shown. Check the operation of the projector from time to time during projection. Unusual noise from the projector may mean film damage or improper threading.

• Discuss the film with the students. Answer questions and correct misconceptions.

• Keep a record of the films you use along with a note on the effectiveness of each one. Use this record for future reference.

10 Oral History: Outside Speakers and Interviews: Keep a file of the names of people in the community who are willing and able to share their special interests and expertise with the class by appearing in person or by granting interviews.

Working people are often too busy to make return visits or to grant repeated interviews. Some sessions may be well worth taping for use with other classes and in other years.

Plan for guest speakers well in advance through proper administrative channels. Have students share in the activity by preparing questions in advance for the speaker or performer. Later, have students evaluate the activity. Discuss what was learned that supplemented the text and the class discussion.

11 Field Trips: The Appendix of the text contains a state-by-state selected list of museums, art galleries, and historic sites. Use it as a starting point for compiling your own list of places that are within field-trip range. In addition to historic sites, museums, and galleries, there may be contemporary institutions worthy of a visit because they show industrial methods, commercial developments, the results of reform, or a persistent problem.

Few activities stir up as much enthusiasm as a field trip. Convert this into a meaningful experience by telling students in advance what the objectives of the trip are and what is expected from them in the form of a written assignment. Provide a focus so that students will know what to look for and why. After the trip, take time for an evaluation.

Maps and floor plans prepared in advance can help students orient themselves quickly.

If the site is large, assign student teams to gather information and report their findings to the class.

All schools, of course, have definite procedures for teachers and students to follow on planning and taking field trips.

12 Evaluating student achievement: As an aid in evaluation, this Guide contains 12 unit tests and a final examination that can be removed and copied for student use. Test items include multiple choice, identification, completion, sequence, cause and effect, and other types of short-answer items. (An answer key is provided.) Essay questions can be added from among those given in the Chapter Review or from supplementary questions provided in this Guide.

In constructing chapter tests, here are a few useful rules: (a) avoid determiners such as *always* or *never;* (b) avoid more than one plausible response; (c) use true-false questions sparingly; (d) change the textbook wording enough that rote memorization is discouraged.

Remember that *testing* in social studies is only one approach to student evaluation. The activities of this Guide will aid in providing additional evaluation means: class participation, projects, research papers, oral and written reports, role playing, interviewing, making and interpreting graphs, and a variety of writing exercises.

Audiovisual Correlation with the Text

UNIT 1—CHAPTERS 1–3

Films

Age of Discovery (MGHT) 15 min. color.

American Indians before European Settlement (CORF) 11 min. color/b&w.

Captain John Smith, Founder of Virginia (EBEC) 20 min. b&w.

Colonial America, 1620–1690 (XEROXF) 20 min. color.

Colonial America: the Beginnings (MGHT) 25 min. color.

Colonial Economy (MGHT) 25 min. color.
Colonial Expansion (EBEC) 11 min. color.
Colonial Expansion of European Nations (CORF) 14 min. color/b&w.
English and Dutch Explorers (EBEC) 11 min. color/b&w.
First Americans, The (FI) 53 min. color.
Folksongs of American History (CORF) 14 min. color.
French and Indian War (CORF) 11 min. color/b&w.
French and Indian War—Seven Years' War in America (EBEC) 16 min. color/b&w.
French Explorers, The (EBEC) 11 min. color/b&w.
Heritage of Slavery (BFA) 53 min. color.
Into the New World—Discovery and Exploration, 1492–1763 (GRACUR) 24 min. color/b&w.
Jamestown (EBEC) 22 min. color/b&w.
Pilgrim Adventure, The (MGHT) 54 min. color.
Puritan Experience: Forsaking England (LCOA) 28 min. color.
Puritan Experience: Making a New World (LCOA) 31 min. color.
Spanish Conquest of the New World, The (CORF) 11 min. color/b&w.
Spanish Explorers, The (EBEC) 14 min. color/b&w.
Spanish in the Southwest (BFA) 14 min. color
Vikings and Their Explorations (CORF) 11 min. color/b&w.
Who Discovered America? (FI) 14 min. color.

Filmstrips

Age of Exploration (LIFE) 52 fr. color.
Colonial America (MGHT) Set of 5; 40–48 fr. each.
Colonial Cities, 1700–1750 (POPSCI) 43 fr. color.
Crusades and Early Trade Routes (HANDY) 17 fr. color.
Discovery and Exploration (MGHT) Set of 5; 60 fr. each. color/sound.
French Colonization (EBEC) 49 fr. color.
Indian Cultures of the Americas (EBEC) Set of 6; 44–53 fr. color.
Jamestown (USPA) 42 fr. b&w.
New England Colonization (EBEC) 48 fr. color.

UNIT 2—CHAPTERS 4–6

Films

America: Inventing a Nation (TIMLIF) Pts. 1–2, 26 min. each. color.
America: Making a Revolution (TIMLIF) Pts. 1–2, 26 min. each. color. These two "America" titles are from Alistair Cooke's *America* series.
American Revolution (EBEC) 16 min. color/b&w.
American Revolution—Background Period (CORF) 11 min. color/b&w.
American Revolution—War Years (CORF) 11 min. color/b&w.
Benjamin Franklin (EBEC) 17 min. b&w.
Boston Massacre (MGHT) 27 min. b&w.
Boston Tea Party (MGHT) 27 min. b&w.
Constitution—The Compromise That Made a Nation (LCOA) 27 min. color.
Constitutional Convention—Conflict and Compromise (FI) 30 min. b&w.
Critical Period—Articles of Confederation to the Constitution (NF) 30 min. b&w.
Dawn of the American Revolution: A Lexington Family (CORF) 16 min. color/b&w.
Deborah Sampson: A Woman in the Revolution (BFA) 15 min. color.
Economic Impact of the Revolution (FI) 30 min. b&w.
George Washington (EBEC) 20 min. b&w.
George Washington: Man and Myth (NET) 30 min. b&w.
Launching the New Government, 1789–1800 (CORF) 14 min. color/b&w.
Meet George Washington (NBCTV) 51 min. color.
Paul Revere's Ride (BFA) 22 min. color.
Putting the New Constitution to Work (NET) 29 min. b&w.
Valley Forge: No Food, No Soldier (CORF) 13 min. color.
Winning Our Independence (IU) 37 min. b&w.
World Turned Upside Down (FI) 52 min. color.

Filmstrips

America: Colonization to Constitution (NGS) Set of 5; 52–59 fr. color.
American Revolution (EBEC) Set of 6; 48–57 fr. color.
American Revolution (GA) 2 parts; 70, 82 fr. color. sound/record.
Benjamin Franklin: Symbol of the American Revolution (GA) 2 parts; 95, 94 fr. color. sound/record.
Black People in the Revolution (EBEC) 55 fr. color.
Revolution (MGHT) Set of 5; 34–46 fr. color.
Your Bill of Rights (POPSCI) 40 fr. color.

Records

Ballads of the American Revolution (FRSC) 2 records.
Oscar Brand's Songs of '76: A Folk Singer's History of the Revolution (MILLER) 4 records.

UNIT 3—CHAPTERS 7–9

Films

Age of Andrew Jackson, The (NET) 29 min. b&w.
Alexander Hamilton (EBEC) 18 min. b&w.
Andrew Jackson (EBEC) 18 min. b&w.
Emergence of a Nation, 1800–1817 (GRACUR) 24 min. color.
Era of Good Feelings—1817–1828 (GRACUR) 24 min. color/b&w.

Era of the Common Man—The Age of Jackson, 1828–1848 (GRACUR) 24 min. color/b&w.
Hamilton-Burr Duel, The (MGHT) 27 min. b&w.
Jackson Years: The New Americans (LCOA) 27 min. color.
John Marshall (EBEC) 18 min. b&w.
Lewis and Clark Journey (CORF) 16 min. color/b&w.
Life of James Madison (NET) 29 min.
Louisiana Purchase: Key to a Continent (EBEC) 16 min. b&w.
Thomas Jefferson (EBEC) 18 min. b&w.
Thomas Jefferson (HANDEL) 28 min. color.
War of 1812 (CORF) 14 min. color/b&w.

Filmstrips

Alexander Hamilton—Nation Maker (POPSCI) 40 fr. color.
Era of Good Feelings (MLA) 26 fr. color.
Federalists versus Republicans, Response to Change, 1789–1815 (EAV) 25 fr. color. sound/record.
James Madison and James Monroe (EGH) 40 fr. color.
John Adams and Thomas Jefferson (EGH) 44 fr. color.
Lewis and Clark Expedition (EAV) 45 fr. color.
Louisiana Purchase (EAV) 45 fr. color.
Thomas Jefferson (MGHT) 45 fr. color.

Records

Ballads of the War of 1812 (FRSC) 2 records.

UNIT 4—CHAPTERS 10–12

Films

Abraham Lincoln (EBEC) 19 min. b&w.
Abraham Lincoln: A Background Study (CORF) 16 min. color/b&w.
Background of the Civil War (BFA) 21 min. color/b&w.
Civil War: Background Issues, 1820-1860 (CORF) 16 min. color/b&w.
Civil War: Its Background and Causes (MGHT) 16 min. color/b&w.
Great Debate: Lincoln vs. Douglas (EBEC) 30 min. color/b&w.
Industrial Revolution—Beginnings in the United States (EBEC) 23 min. color.
Nomination of Abraham Lincoln, The (BFA) 22 min. color.
Oregon Trail, The (BFA) 31 min. color.
Prelude to the Civil War: A House Divided (GRACUR) 24 min. color.
Revolution (WILEYJ) 10 min. color. John Brown's views.
Texas and the Mexican War (EBEC) 18 min. color.
United States Expansion—California (CORF) 16 min. color.
United States Expansion—The Oregon Country (CORF) 14 min. color/b&w.
United States Expansion—Texas and the Far Southwest (CORF) 14 min. color/b&w.

Wagons West (HF) 14 min. b&w.
Westward Expansion (MGHT) 25 min. color.

Filmstrips

Black People in the Free North, 1850 (EBEC) 62 fr. color. sound/record.
Black People in the Slave South, 1850 (EBEC) 53 fr. color. sound/record.
Election of 1860 (EBEC) 89 fr. color. sound/record.
Erie Canal Opens the West (POPSCI) 40 fr. color.
King Cotton (EGH) 24 fr. color.
Sam Houston: The Tallest Texan (EAV) 45 fr. color.
Westward Expansion—U.S. (ELKINS): Mexican Cession and Gadsden Purchase 43 fr. Oregon Territory 31 fr. Texas 31 fr.

UNIT 5—CHAPTERS 13–15

Films

Abraham Lincoln and the Emancipation Proclamation (AMEDFL) 20 min. color.
Andrew Johnson (IQFILM) 48 min. b&w.
Assassination of Lincoln (FI) 28 min. color.
Civil War, The (EBEC) 16 min. color/b&w.
Civil War: First Two Years (CORF) 16 min. color/b&w.
Civil War: 1863–1865 (CORF) 16 min. color/b&w.
Civil War: Postwar Period (CORF) 16 min. color/b&w.
Grant vs. Lee (FI) 25 min. b&w.
Invisible Empire—Ku Klux Klan (ADL) 45 min. color.
Lincoln's Last Day (ABCTV) 27 min. color.
Meet Mr. Lincoln (FI) 27 min. b&w.
Reconstruction: A Changing Nation—1865–1880 (GRACUR) 24 min. color.
Robert E. Lee: A Background Study (CORF) 16 min. color/b&w.
1619–1860: Out of Slavery (MGHT) 20 min. b&w.
Westward Movement: Settling of the Great Plains (EBEC) 17 min. color/b&w.
Westward Movement: The Gold Rush (EBEC) 23 min. color/b&w.

Filmstrips

Black American, The—Civil War and Reconstruction (ALPHA) 48 fr. color. sound/record
Black People in the Civil War (EBEC) 62 fr. color. sound/record.
Civil War—As It Happened (SCOTED) Set of 6; 30-55 fr. color. sound/record.
Cowboys, Homesteaders, and Outlaws (LIFE) 65 fr. color.
Folk Songs and Cowboys (SCHLAT) Set of 2; 68, 70 fr. b&w. sound/record
Picture History of the Civil War (EBEC) Set of 8; 42-52 fr. color.

Robert E. Lee, Military Leader of the South (EGH) 25 fr. color.

Ulysses S. Grant (EGH) 41 fr. color.

Records

Ballads of the Civil War, Vol. 1—1831–1861; Vol. 2—1861–1865 (FRSC)

Confederacy (COLUMBIA). Songs of the Confederacy.

Lonesome Train, The (DECCA). Trip of Lincoln's funeral train set to music.

Union (COLUMBIA). Songs sung by the Union side in the Civil War.

UNIT 6—CHAPTERS 16–18

Films

Andrew Carnegie: The Gospel of Wealth (LCOA) 26 min. color.

1876: Labor and Violence (FI) 22 min. color.

Grover Cleveland (IQFILM) 50 min. color.

Growth of Farming in America 1865–1900 (CORF) 14 min. b&w.

Had You Lived Then: Life in a Midwestern Small Town, 1910 (PARACO) 15 min. color.

Immigrant Experience: A Long, Long Journey (LCOA) 31 min. color. Story of a Polish family in America.

Immigrants in the Cities (FI) color.

Industrial Revolution: Beginnings in the United States (EBEC) 23 min. color.

Inventions in America's Growth, 1850–1910 (CORF) 11 min. color/b&w

Labor Movement: Beginnings and Growth in America (CORF) 14 min. color/b&w.

Mark Twain's America (MGHT) 54 min. b&w.

Millions of New Americans (NET) 29 min. b&w.

Rise of Organized Labor (MGHT) 18 min. b&w.

Toward the Gilded Age: Inventions and Big Business, 1876–1898 (GRACUR) 24 min. color/b&w.

Filmstrips

Alexander Graham Bell (MGHT) 37 fr. color.

Changes in American Life, 1865–1900 (SVE) 53 fr. color.

Creation of Modern Industrial America, 1870–1900 (SVE) 57 fr. color.

Emergence of Industrial America (MGHT) 45 fr. color.

Growth of the Labor Movement, Pt. 1 (GA) 100 fr. color. sound/record.

Industry Changes America (MES) 44 fr. color.

Jane Addams (MGHT) 44 fr. color.

Records

Cross of Gold Speech by William J. Bryan (ENRICHMENT).

Songs of the Suffragettes (FRSC).

UNIT 7—CHAPTERS 19–21

Films

Admiral Dewey's Victory at Manila (MGHT) 27 min. b&w.

Boxer Rebellion (TFC) 21 min. color.

Causes and Immediate Effects of the First World War (IGP) 23 min. b&w.

End of Innocence: World War I, 1914–1920 (GRACUR) 24 min. color/b&w.

Home Front, 1917–1919—War Transforms American Life (FI) 17 min. b&w.

Innocent Years—1910–1914 (MGHT) 52 min. b&w.

Life and Times of Teddy Roosevelt (MGHT) 26 min. b&w.

Progressives, The (MGHT) 25 min. color.

Puerto Rico—Its Past, Present, and Promise (EBEC) color.

Sinking of the Lusitania—Unrestricted Submarine Warfare (FI) 17 min. b&w.

Women Get the Vote (MGHT) 27 min. b&w.

Woodrow Wilson (MGHT) 26 min. b&w.

Woodrow Wilson—The Fight for a League of Nations (AMEDFL) 20 min. color.

World War I (MGHT) 25 min. color.

World War I—The Background (CORF) 14 min. b&w.

World War I—The War Years (CORF) 14 min. b&w.

World War I—Building the Peace (CORF) 11 min. b&w.

Filmstrips

Causes of World War I—How War Came (EAV) 88 fr. color. sound/record.

Emerging Giant—the U.S. in 1900 (ME) 76 fr. b&w.

Hawaii—50th State (LIFE) 79 fr. color.

Progressive Era, The (EAV) 97 fr. color.

Spanish-American War (MULTED) 81 fr. color. sound/audio tape.

Theodore Roosevelt (EGH) 45 fr. color.

U.S. Becomes a World Power (EBEC) Set of 6; 60 fr. each. color.

U.S. Becomes a World Power (MGHT) 45 fr. color.

Woodrow Wilson (EGH) 42 fr. color.

Record

Pack Up Your Troubles—Songs of Two World Wars (RCA).

UNIT 8—CHAPTERS 22–23

Films

After the War—The Prosperous 20's (PATHE) 25 min. color. Highlights of the 1920s in newsreel form.

America—The Automobile Age (MTP) 38 min. color.

Automobile in America (HEARST) 14 min. b&w.

Boom or Bust—Between the Wars, 1925–1935 (GRACUR) 24 min. color/b&w.

Charles Lindbergh (SF) 26 min. b&w.

Herbert Hoover (FI) 55 min. b&w. Hoover himself discusses his career and views on public affairs.

Jazz Age (MGHT) 52 min. b&w. Fred Allen narrates.

Lindbergh vs. the Atlantic (FI) 25 min. b&w.

Twenties, The (MGHT) 25 min. color. Describes the conflicts caused by postwar changes.

Twenty-Nine Boom and the 30's Depression (MGHT) 14 min. b&w.

Filmstrips

Changing Role of Women (SED) Set of 2; 106, 111 fr. color. sound/audio tape.

Crash, The (FSH) 60 fr. b&w. sound/record.

Herbert C. Hoover (EGH) 47 fr. color.

Nineteen Twenties and the Depression (SCHLAT) 74 fr. color. sound/record.

Prosperity and Panic (USNAC) Set of 2; 52, 49 fr. color.

Warren G. Harding and Calvin Coolidge (EGH) 39 fr. color.

Record

I Can Hear It Now, Vol. III (COLUMBIA). Events from 1919 to 1932.

UNIT 9—CHAPTERS 24–27

Films

Bank Holiday Crisis of 1933 (MGHT) 27 min. b&w.

D Day (MGHT) 27 min. b&w.

December 7, 1941 (MGHT) 27 min. b&w.

Decision to Drop the Bomb (FI) 35 min. b&w.

Dust Bowl (MGHT) 26 min. b&w.

Eleanor Roosevelt (SF) 26 min. b&w.

Failure of American Neutrality, 1933–1939, The (FI) 17 min. b&w.

Fascist Revolution (IU) 29 min. b&w.

Franklin Delano Roosevelt, Part 1, *The New Deal* (MGHT) 26 min. b&w.

Franklin Delano Roosevelt, Part 2, *The Wars Years* (MGHT) 26 min. b&w.

Gaudalcanal (GRACUR) 30 min. b&w.

Hundred Days, The (FI) 19 min. b&w.

Labor Comes of Age (FI) 19 min. b&w.

Road to World War II (MGHT) 19 in. b&w.

Roosevelt and U.S. History (CENTRO) 32 min. b&w.

Storm Over the Supreme Court (CAROUF) 31 min. b&w.

Twisted Cross, The (MGHT) 55 min. b&w. Rise and fall of Nazi Germany.

World War II: Background and Causes (CORF) 16 min. b&w.

World War II—1939–1941 (CORF) 16 min. b&w.

World War II—1942–1945 (CORF) 16 min. b&w.

World War II—Prologue USA (EBEC) 29 min. b&w.

Filmstrips

Black Man in the Depression (EAV) 62 fr. color.

Causes of World War II (EVA) 72 fr. color. sound/record.

Folk Songs in the Great Depression (SCHLAT) Set of 2; 60, 61 fr. color. sound/record.

Franklin D. Roosevelt: The Years That Changed the Nation (GA) Set of 2; 114, 115 fr. color/b&w. sound/record.

Grapes of Wrath and the 1930s, The (EAV) Set of 2; 100, 107 fr. color. sound/record.

Negro Fights for the Four Freedoms, The (MGHT) 41 fr. color.

New Deal, The (MULTED) 63 fr. color. sound/audio tape.

New Deal, The (FSH) 68 fr. b&w. sound/record.

Organized Labor in Today's America (CAF) 44 fr. color.

United States as World Leader: The Gathering Storm, 1933–1941 (EAV) 79 fr. color. sound/record.

World War II (MGHT) Set of 5; 70 fr. each. color.

Records

Finest Hours, The (MERCURY) 2 records. World War II and the speeches of Winston Churchill.

Songs from the Depression (FRSC).

World War II (AMERICAN HERITAGE). Includes FDR and Churchill.

UNIT 10—CHAPTERS 28–30

Films

Aftermath of World War II—Prologue to the Cold War (MGHT) 25 min. b&w.

Age of Specialization (MGHT) 13 min. b&w.

American Foreign Policy: Confrontation 1945–1953 (FI) 32 min. b&w.

American Foreign Policy since Pearl Harbor (MGHT) 43 min. color.

Automation: What It Is and What It Does (CORF) 14 min. color/b&w.

Berlin Airlift (TFC) 20 min. b&w.

Changing City, The (CF) 16 min. color.

Charge and Countercharge (PH) 43 min. b&w. Activities of McCarthy.

Cold War: Early Period, 1947–1954 (MGHT) 18 min. b&w.

Dwight David Eisenhower (MGHT) 26 min. b&w.

Eisenhower Years, The (TFC) 21 min. b&w.

Harry S. Truman (MGHT) 54 min. b&w.

I Have a Dream—The Life of Martin Luther King (BFA) 35 min. b&w.

Joseph McCarthy (MGHT) 26 min. b&w.

Korea: 38th Parallel (FI) 50 min. b&w.

MacArthur vs. Truman (FI) 25 min. b&w.

Not So Long Ago—1945–1950 (MGHT) 52 min. b&w. Bob Hope narrates.

Space Age: From Dr. Goddard to Project Apollo (VAS) 27 min. color/b&w.

Truman and the Cold War (LCOA) 16 min. b&w.
Truman Years, The (TFC) 19 min. b&w.
Warren Years: The Great Decisions (IU) 24 min. b&w.

Filmstrips

Black Odyssey: Migration to the Cities (GA) color.
D Day to Reelection of Eisenhower (DAVCO) 55 fr. color.
Korea—A Crisis in the Cold War (QED) 53 fr. color/b&w.
Race to Outer Space, The (STA) 43 fr. b&w.
United Nations Today (MGHT) Set of 6; 34–39 fr. color.
United States as a World Leader: The Burden of Responsibility, 1945–1953 (EAV) 72 fr. color. sound/record.
United States as a World Leader: The Uneasy Coexistence, 1953–1963 (EAV) 71 fr. color. sound/record.

Record

I Can Hear It Now (COLUMBIA) No. 2. Postwar events.

UNIT 11—CHAPTERS 31–33

Films

Age of Kennedy: The Presidency (MGHT) 52 min. b&w.
America on the Moon—Apollo 11 (CASTLE) 9 min. color/b&w.
American Tragedy—The Death of President Kennedy (HEARST) 21 min. b&w.
Berlin—Test for the West (EBEC) 19 min. b&w.
Cuba: Bay of Pigs (FI) 29 min. b&w.
Essay on Watergate—Bill Moyer's Journal (IU) 59 min. color.
John Fitzgerald Kennedy: 1917–1963 (FI) 21 min. b&w.
John Glenn Story, The (NASA) 30 min. color.
Journey of Lyndon Johnson (FI) 51 min. color.
Kennedy: What Is Remembered Is Never Lost (FI) 25 min. b&w.
Kennedy vs. Khrushchev (PMI) 25 min. b&w. Cuban missile crisis.
Last Reflections of a War (IU) 44 min. b&w. Vietnam War.
Making of a President 1960 (FI) 80 min. b&w.
Making of a President 1964 (FI) 80 min. b&w.
Making of a President 1968 (FI) 83 min. color.
Making of a President 1972 (TIMLIF) 80 min. color.
Mission of Discovery, A (USNAC) 28 min. color. About the Peace Corps.
Nixon: Checkers to Watergate (PFP) 20 min. color.
Silent Spring of Rachel Carson (MGHT) 54 min. b&w.
Urban Rebellions—The Crisis from 1964–1968 (HRAW) 30 min. color.
Vietnam: An Historical Document (CAROUF) 56 min. color.
Vietnam Epilogue (HEARST) 15 min. color. Chronology of U.S. involvement.
Watts—Riot or Revolt (ADL) 60 min. color. A CBS Report.

Filmstrips

Black American, The: Struggle for Civil and Human Rights (ALPHA) 52 fr. color. sound/record.
John Fitzgerald Kennedy (SVE) 70 fr. b&w. sound/record.
The 1960s: A Decade of Hope and Despair (GA) Set of 2; color. sound/audio tape.
War Against Poverty, The (NYT) 53 fr. b&w.
Youth Scene—Unrest, Rebellion, and Drugs (CAF) 63 fr. color. sound/record.

Records

Making of a President 1960 (UNIT. ART) 2 records.
John F. Kennedy—The Presidential Years—1960–1963 (TWCF).
John Fitzgerald Kennedy—A Memorial Album (PREMIER).

UNIT 12—CHAPTERS 34–35, Epilogue

Films

America: The Huddled Masses (TIMLIF) 52 min. color/b&w. Alistair Cooke series.
American Indian Speaks, The (AIM) 47 min. color.
Bill of Rights in Action—De Facto Segregation (BFA) 22 min. color; *—Equal Opportunity* (BFA) 22 min. color.
Black Woman, The (IU) 52 min. color.
California, 2000 A.D. (TIMLIF) 40 min. b&w. Examines revolutionary technology.
Future Shock (MGHT) 42 min. color.
Futurists, The (MGHT) 25 min. color. Ten leaders give their views of the future.
Island in America, An (ADL) 28 min. color. Puerto Ricans in the U.S.
Mexican Americans: A Quest for Equality (ADL) 29 min. b&w.
Nation of Immigrants, A (FI) 53 min. b&w.
Our Immigrant Heritage (MGHT) 32 min. color.
Strangers in Their Own Land—The Puerto Ricans (ABCMED) 14 min. color.
Take This Woman (NBCEE) 25 min. color.
Woman's Place (XEROXF) 58 min. color.
Women's Liberation (XEROXF) 23 min. color.
Women's Prejudice Film (BARR) 19 min. color.

Filmstrips

American Indian: A Dispossessed People (GA) 105 fr. color. sound/record.
Desegregation: How It Works in the Schools (ADL) 54 fr. color.
Native Americans: Yesterday and Today (FI) 77 fr. color.
Portrait of a Minority: Spanish-Speaking Americans (SED) 188 fr. color. sound/record.
Women in an Era of Change (VEC) 35 fr. color.

Directory of Producers and Distributors

ABCTV
American Broadcasting Co., TV
1330 Avenue of the Americas
New York, NY 10019

ADL
Anti-Defamation League
6505 Wilshire Blvd., Suite 814
Los Angeles, CA 90048

AIM
Associated Instructional Materials
600 Madison Avenue
New York, NY 10022

ALPHA
Alpha Film Productions
520 N. Michigan Avenue
Chicago, IL 60611

AMEDFL
American Educational Films
132 Lasky Drive
Beverly Hills, CA 90212

AMERICAN HERITAGE
American Heritage Pub. Co.
551 Fifth Avenue
New York, NY 10017

BFA
BFA Educational Media
2211 Michigan Avenue
PO Box 1795
Santa Monica, CA 90406

BRR
Barr Films
3490 E. Foothill Blvd.
Pasadena, CA 91107

CAF
Current Affairs Films
24 Danbury Road
Wilton, CT 06897

CAROUF
Carousel Films, Inc.
1501 Broadway
New York, NY 10036

CASTLE
Castle Films
404 Park Avenue, South
New York, NY 10016

CENTRO
Centron Educational Films
1621 W. 9th Street
Lawrence, KS 66044

CF
Churchill Films
662 N. Robertson Blvd.
Los Angeles, CA 90069

CORF
Coronet Instructional Media
65 E. South Water Street
Chicago, IL 60601

EAV
Educational Audio-Visual Inc.
29 Marble Avenue
Pleasantville, NY 10570

EBEC
Encyclopedia Britannica
 Educational Corporation
425 N. Michigan Avenue
Chicago, IL 60611

EGH
Eye Gate House
146–01 Archer Avenue
Jamaica, NY 11435

ELKINS
Herbert M. Elkins Co.
10031 Commerce Avenue
Tujunga, CA 91042

ENRICHMENT
Enrichment Materials, Inc.
c/o Scholastic Magazine
50 W. 44th Street
New York, NY 10036

FI
Films, Inc.
733 Green Bay Road
Wilmette, IL 60091

FSH
Filmstrip House
United Learning
6633 W. Howard Street
Niles, IL 60648

FRSC
Folkway Records
165 W. 46th Street
New York, NY 10036

GA
Guidance Associates
P.O. Box 300
White Plains, NY 10602

GRACUR
Graphic Curriculum, Inc.
P.O. Box 565
Lenox Hill Station
New York, NY 10021

HANDEL
Handel Film Corporation
8730 Sunset Blvd.
W. Hollywood, CA 90069

HANDY
Prentice-Hall, Inc.
Route 9W
Englewood Cliffs, NJ 07632

HEARST
Hearst Metrotone News
235 E. 45th Street
New York, NY 10017

HF
Harvest Films, Inc.
309 Fifth Avenue
New York, NY 10016

HRAW
Holt, Rinehart & Winston
383 Madison Avenue
New York, NY 10017

IGP
International Geographic Pictures
1776 Broadway
New York, NY 10019

IQFILM
IQ Films
P.O. Box 326
Wappinger Falls, NY 12590

IU
See NET

LCOA
Learning Corp. of America
1350 Avenue of the Americas
New York, NY 10019

LIFE
Life Filmstrips
Time and Life Building
9 Rockefeller Plaza
New York, NY 10020

ME
Multimedia Education Corp.
2530 Kemper Lane
Cincinnati, OH 45206

MES
Museum Extension Service
80 West 40th Street
New York, NY 10018

MGHT
McGraw-Hill Films
110 15th Street
Del Mar, CA 92014

MLA
Modern Learning Aid Division
 of Ward's Natural Science
Box 1712
Rochester, NY 14603

MTP
Modern Talking Picture Service
2323 New Hyde Park Road
New Hyde Park, NY 11040

NASA
National Aeronautics and Space
 Administration
400 Maryland Avenue, SW
Washington, DC 20546

NBCEE
NBC Educational Enterprises
30 Rockefeller Plaza
New York, NY 10020

NET
National Educational
Television Film Service
Audio-Visual Center
Indiana University
Bloomington, IN 47401

NF
Norwood Films
P.O. Box 1894, Wheaton P.O.
Silver Springs, MD 20902

NGS
National Geographic Society
17 and M Streets, NW
Washington, DC 20036

NYT
New York Times
2 Kisco Plaza, Times Square
Mt. Kisco, NY 10549

PARACO
Paramount Communications
5451 Marathon Street
Hollywood, CA 90038

PATHE
Pathe News, Inc.
835 Broadway
New York, NY 10003

PFP
Pyramid Films
P.O. Box 1048
Santa Monica, CA 90406

PH
Prentice-Hall Media
150 White Plains Road
Tarrytown, NY 10591

PMI
Public Media, Inc.
1144 Wilmette Avenue
Wilmette, IL 60091

POPSCI
Denoyer-Geppert Audio-Visuals
Times Mirror
5235 Ravenswood Avenue
Chicago, IL 60640

QED
Q-Ed Productions Division
 of Cathedral Films
2921 Almeda Avenue
Burbank, CA 91507

RCA
RCA Educational Service
Front and Cooper Streets
Camden, NJ 08108

SCHLAT
Warren Schloat Productions
Prentice-Hall Media
150 White Plains Road
Tarrytown, NY 10591

SED
Scott Education Division
104 Lower Westfield Road
Holyoke, MA 01040

SF
Sterling Educational Films
241 E. 34th Street
New York, NY 10016

STA
Stenbow Productions, Inc.
4 Broadway
Valhalla, NY 10595

SVE
Society for Visual Education, Inc.
1345 Diversey Parkway
Chicago, IL 60614

TFC
Teaching Film Custodians
25 West 43rd St.
New York, NY 10036

TIMLIF
Time-Life Films
43 West 16th Street
New York, NY 10011

TWCF
Twentieth-Century-Fox Film Corp.
10201 W. Pico Blvd.
Beverly Hills, CA 90213

USNAC
U.S. National Audiovisual Center
National Archives and Records Service
Washington, DC 20409

USPA
U.S. Publishers' Association
46 Lafayette Avenue
New Rochelle, NY 10801

VAS
Visual Aids Studio
Box 1759, 2121 Normal Park
Huntsville, TX 77340

VEC
Visual Education Consultants, Inc.
2066 Helena Street
Madison, WI 53701

WILEYJ
John Wiley & Sons, Inc.,
605 Third Avenue
New York, NY 10016

XEROXF
Xerox Films
245 Long Hill Road
Middletown, CT 06457

CHAPTER 1

What Europeans Found: the American Surprise

Introducing the Chapter This chapter, more than most others, covers subject matter that many students have gone over two or three times. Yet there is likely to be fresh material here too. Here is one way to set the stage:

- Draw two 6 to 10 foot timelines on the board similar to the ones at the foot of this page.

  Assign each page of the chapter to a different student. He/she should jot down any date and its event found on this page. Then as you read each time span, have students call out the date and event. Write as many events as possible at the appropriate place on the line. Ask students to make some generalizations from this exercise. For example:

1. Humans occupied the Western Hemisphere long before the Europeans came.
2. Norse explorations were not followed up by other Europeans.
3. Columbus's first voyage led quickly to many other expeditions.

Section 1 (pp. 4–8)
Christopher Columbus: Who He Was and Why He Came

Instructional Objectives Students will be able to

1. Show how Columbus's experiences and character traits fitted him for the role of explorer.
2. Describe the handicaps that Columbus had to overcome to begin and to complete his first voyage of discovery.
3. Explain the significance of Columbus's first voyage.

Teaching Suggestions The chapter begins with the story of Columbus not just because it is the traditional beginning of American history but because the authors want to convey the excitement of their account and interpretation of our nation's history right at the start. The lesson needs no teacher introduction. Simply have the students read the story for enjoyment. Then, before using the Section Review, you may want to obtain some reactions to the story by asking questions like these:

1. How does this account of the Columbus story differ from others that you have read?
2. What new things did you learn about Columbus?
3. Find a sentence that helps you picture (a) Columbus, (b) Europe in the 1480s, or (c) the voyage to America.

- Samuel Eliot Morison's *Admiral of the Ocean Sea* is loaded with fascinating details about Columbus and his voyages.

- You may want to supplement the Section Review items with these questions:

1. Why was it so difficult for Columbus to get a sponsor for his first expedition? (high risk, royal advisers opposed it, etc.)
2. Why wasn't Columbus accorded the honor due him? (hadn't reached his objective; died before the significance of his discovery was known)

Section 2 (pp. 8–11)
Before Discovery

Instructional Objectives Students will be able to

1. Trace the probable migration of peoples from Asia to North America.
2. Locate the Mayans, Incas, and Aztecs and name distinctive aspects of their cultures.
3. Identify by tribal name some Indians of the Southwest and Eastern Woodlands.
4. Locate places mentioned in this section on maps of North America and South America.

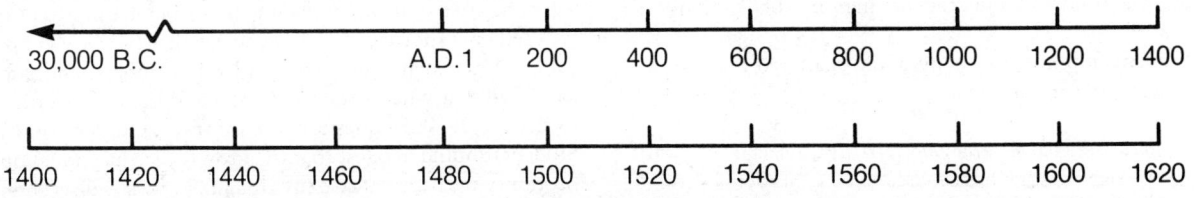

Chapter 1

17

Teaching Suggestions The chief purpose of this lesson is to provide a *framework for review* of what students are likely to have studied in the past about pre-Columbian native peoples and their cultures in the Americas. Unless your course of study, or your own preference, calls for two days to a week on this topic, you will need to focus on only one or two of many possible activities. (After all, Indians are discussed many times in succeeding lessons.)

• List on the board (preferably before the class assembles) the following place names mentioned in this section.

Bering Strait	Cuzco
Siberia	Mexico City
Alaska	Arizona
Strait of Magellan	New Mexico
Guatemala	California
Belize	Great Plains
Honduras	New York (state)
Mexico	Virginia
Peru	Mississippi (state)

Using wall maps, desk outline maps, or the atlas maps on text pages 744–755, have students locate each place.

• Use the map on text page 11 to locate Indian tribes mentioned in Section 2. Also have students find the names of tribes that lived in your general region. Are there Indians still living within 50 to 100 miles of your school? Are they descendants of the original inhabitants of the region? If not, where was their original homeland?

• After using the review exercises, focus attention on similarities and differences in the cultures of North American Indians (chiefly those within present U.S. boundaries) by having students suggest items for the following headings:

North American Indian Cultures

Traits of nearly all cultures in 1492

Traits of particular cultures in 1492

Traits resulting from contact with Europeans

Under column 1, students might suggest such traits as (1) nature worship, (2) belief in unity of humans with nature, (3) stone tools and weapons, (4) no written language, etc.

Under column 2, a large number of words and phrases can be listed. You may want to indicate in parentheses the tribe or general class (Plains, etc.) to which the trait applied. Examples: (1) tribal federation (Iroquois), (2) buffalo hunting (Plains), (3) sand paintings (Pueblo), etc.

The text suggests two items for column 3 (slavery—for some; use of horses), but students may be able to think of others.

Students might keep a copy of the chart and make additions to it later in the course.

• *Competency exercise—copying correctly:* Select a two- to four-sentence paragraph from Section 2. Students should copy it correctly with no mistakes in spelling, punctuation, or wording.

• Extending the lesson: Students can prepare brief reports on some particular aspect of Indian culture. The report can be descriptive of one tribe or group of tribes, or it can compare and contrast several tribes. Topic examples are (1) Iroquois League, (2) Tribal Federations, (3) Role of Women, (4) Art, (5) Agriculture, (6) Food Gathering and Hunting, (7) Childrearing, etc.

Section 3 (pp. 12–14)
Why Europeans Went Exploring

Instructional Objectives Students will be able to

1. Name at least three differences between the feudal states of Europe and the rising nation-states of the 1400s.

2. Explain how each of the following helped to bring about the voyages of discovery: rise of trade, printing press, Crusades, Renaissance, rise of nation-states, the Portuguese navigators.

3. Locate ten cities, states, or countries, given their location in latitude and longitude.

Teaching Suggestions In the few pages available for European background the text can only touch on the highlights. As with Section 2, this lesson provides opportunity to review what should be familiar subject matter, particularly if students have had a recent course in world or European history. Teachers may need to provide detail on topics where students lack background information.

• If students are likely to need help with unfamiliar words in this section, use Teaching Hint 6 on page 7.

• Point out that, besides Columbus, a number of explorers named later in the chapter (Vespucci, Cabot, Verrazano) were Italians. Yet they all sailed for other countries. Ask students to speculate why. The discussion should lead to explanation of the term "nation-state." Provide a brief description of Italy around 1500, and then of Portugal, Spain, France, and England.

• Along with the Section Review, use item 2 of *Meeting Our Earlier Selves* in the Chapter Review with this lesson.

• *Handout lesson.* Distribute *Handout 1.* Some teachers may wish to make a transparency, masking out the questions, to use with an overhead projector during the class discussion. Prior to general discussion, ask students to answer the first two questions on the handout using one or two sentences for each. Check to see that the answers include all pertinent information (dates, numbers, and subjects) and that what is stated is accurate. Next ask students to answer the third question in a short paragraph or orally. Students should suggest that the growth of educational opportunity may indicate a growth in literacy as well as an increasing desire to gain knowledge about the world. The sharp increase in printing houses suggests that knowledge about discoveries could be quite rapidly disseminated throughout Europe and that knowledge of the New World would, in turn, stimulate additional efforts to explore.

- *Competency exercise—using latitude and longitude:*

1. Using the maps on text pages 744–755, write correctly a line of latitude and a line of longitude which are shown crossing each of these countries:

    Example: Angola 10°S, 20°E
    - (a) Nigeria
    - (b) Kenya
    - (c) Spain
    - (d) West Germany
    - (e) Romania
    - (f) Paraguay
    - (g) Cuba
    - (h) Ecuador

2. Write the name of the city located at each of these lines:
    - (i) 41°45″N, 87°40″W
    - (j) 30°0″N, 90°5″W
    - (k) 61°10″N, 149°50″W
    - (l) 34°0″N, 118°10″W
    - (m) 39°45″N, 105°0″W
    - (n) 40°0″N, 75°10″W
    - (o) 19°20″N, 99°10″W
    - (p) 12°0″S, 77°0″W
    - (q) 38°42″N, 9°10″W
    - (r) 36°50″N, 10°11″E
    - (s) 59°55″N, 30°20″E
    - (t) 30°1″N, 31°14″E

Answers: (a) 10°N, 10°E; (b) 0°, 40°E; (c) 40°N, 5°W; (d) 50°N, 10°E; (e) 45°N, 25°E; (f) 20°S, 60°W; (g) 20°N, 80°W; (h) 0°, 80°W; (i) Chicago; (j) New Orleans; (k) Anchorage; (l) Los Angeles; (m) Denver; (n) Philadelphia; (o) Mexico City; (q) Lisbon; (r) Tunis; (s) Leningrad; (t) Cairo.

Section 4 (pp.14–22)
Spanish Adventurers

Instructional Objectives Students will be able to

1. Identify at least six Spanish explorers by naming the main achievement of each and explaining its significance.
2. Name some contribution made by each of the following to the Spanish explorations: Pope Alexander VI, Charles V, blacks, Indians.
3. Explain why historians credit Columbus instead of Ericson with the discovery of America.
4. Identify two chief motives for the Spanish explorations.
5. Demonstrate appreciation of, and skill in using, vivid language in a brief written account of a Spanish expedition.

Teaching Suggestions Except for the brief interlude on the Norse explorers, this lesson focuses on a relatively short time span of 50 years—from 1493 after Columbus's first voyage to 1543 at the end of DeSoto's expedition. The Spanish settlement of New Spain from Mexico southward was well under way by 1543, but Spanish colonial policy lies outside the scope of this lesson.

- To help students visualize the time span, have them draw a 6-inch vertical timeline on the left side of a notebook page. Mark off one-inch segments and label them to the left of the line 1490, 1500, 1510, etc., starting at the top. The year 1550 will be at the bottom. At the proper point on the right-hand side of the timeline, have students write each significant event of this time period given in the text and any others that you want to add.

Point out that the text can deal with only a third or less of the known Spanish expeditions to and in the New World. Using an encyclopedia of American history or other source, you can provide thumbnail descriptions of some of the others. Then ask the class to suggest some generalizations about the Spanish exploratory efforts, such as the following:

1. Expeditions originated both in Spain and in the New World (especially from Hispaniola and Mexico).
2. Members of one expedition often took part in succeeding ones.
3. Ideas of where to explore came from members of previous expeditions who were now on another one, from word-of-mouth accounts by the explorers and from their letters and other written accounts, and from advice and stories told by Indians.

- Using Outline Map 2, students can draw the routes of the Spanish expeditions shown on page 20 of the text.

- *Competency exercise—using vivid language:* Perhaps students have already discovered that the writing in their textbook differs from others they have used. One reason is the authors' use of simple yet vivid, colorful words and phrases. Call attention to some examples like these from the story of Columbus in Section 1:

". . . a money-making project . . . where Queen Isabella had a mind of her own . . . the gamble was worth the risk . . . reached the verge of mutiny . . . winds were the engine that took you there and back . . . loaded him with honors . . . reaped only misfortune and disgrace."

Provide students with a copy of the following dull, matter-of-fact account of the expedition of another Spanish explorer. Ask them to rewrite it using at least 10 vivid, colorful words and phrases.

Juan Rodriguez Cabrillo came to Mexico in 1520. He was in a company of soldiers sent from Cuba to Mexico. There he joined up with Cortes and took part in the conquest of Mexico. In 1541 the viceroy of New Spain sent Cabrillo with two ships to explore the Pacific coast of North America. In June 1542 the ships left from a port on the west coast of Mexico. Cabrillo and his crew were the first Europeans to see San Diego Harbor, Santa Catalina Island, Monterey Bay, and other places along the coast of California as far as Point Reyes north of San Francisco Bay. On the return trip Cabrillo fell from the mast of his ship. His crew spent several weeks on the Santa Barbara Islands east of Los Angeles. There Cabrillo died from an infection that had developed from his wounds. In February 1543 his chief pilot took the ships north again, perhaps as far as the Oregon coast.

Section 5 (pp. 22–25)
French and English Exploration

Instructional Objectives Students will be able to

1. Name the main achievements of Cabot, Verrazano, and Cartier and tell their significance.

2. Name the motives of the English and French explorations.

3. Indicate the relation of one place to another on a map by using compass direction symbols and language.

Teaching Suggestions Students will understand the lag in English and French exploration better if you provide a brief explanation of the internal situation in England and France in the early 1500s.

• Have students add the English and French expeditions to the timeline made for Section 4.

• The large number of place names in this lesson provides a good opportunity to review place geography. Use a wall map to locate Genoa, Newfoundland, Brittany, Bristol, Lyon, Cape Fear, Cape Hatteras, Pamlico Sound, Chesapeake Bay, Delaware Bay, Long Island, Narragansett Bay, Newport Harbor, Nantucket Sound, Cape Cod, Gulf of St. Lawrence, Quebec, and others as needed.

Here is one way to get student participation: Draw on the chalkboard a direction finder like that shown here.

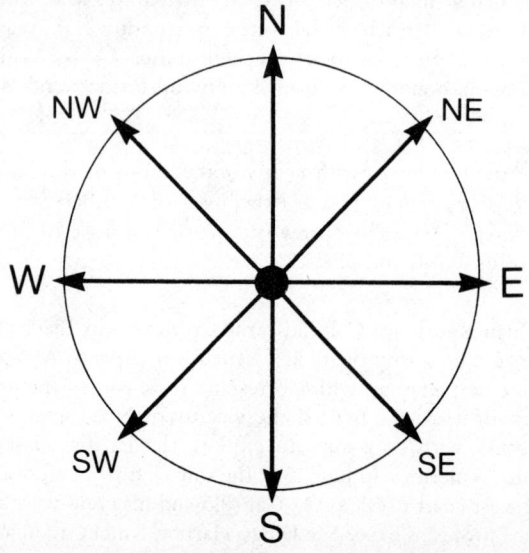

Then point to one of the places named in this lesson (Quebec, for example) and ask, "What city is here?" When it has been identified, ask the direction to reach, say, Cape Cod. Continue to ask the direction from one place to another until all places in your list have been located. (For more precise directions add to the direction finder NNE, ENE, ESE, etc.)

• Students can add the routes of Cabot, Verrazano, and Cartier to their outline map of explorations.

• Items 3–5 of *Meeting Our Earlier Selves* can be used to conclude this lesson.

CHAPTER REVIEW

Meeting Our Earlier Selves

1. Many of the early explorations—especially the sea voyages—were aimed at finding a water passage to the Indies. But—by accident—islands, continents, bays, and rivers were discovered instead. Accidents in the form of storms, Indian attacks, drownings, and disease stopped exploring parties from continuing on intended paths and sometimes sent them on detours. By chance (accident) an exploring party might have a member of a previous expedition to serve as guide—or might have stumbled across friendly natives to serve as guides. Rumors of wealth or "northwest passages" or other wished-for goals were obtained from Indians and from other exploring parties.

2. Rise of nation-states, invention of printing, advances in navigation, the spread of knowledge about the Near East (via the Crusades, for example) and the Far East, advances in knowledge of astronomy—all the developments named in Section 3—stimulated the age of exploration.

3. National rivalries spurred the powerful European countries to make land claims and to exploit the resources of the Western Hemisphere.

4. Correlate discussion of this item with skill exercise 2.

5. Explorers were willing to take great risks because the chances for wealth, fame, and power were always there. Some explorers were driven by religious motives; others were seeking escape from boredom or "trouble" back home. Most of the motives that drive people today to take great risks were present among the explorers.

Questions for Today

1. Have students look in encyclopedias under Antarctica and Space Exploration (or Space Law). In 1959 twelve nations signed a 30-year treaty forbidding further Antarctica land claims and for free scientific, but no military, use of the continent. UN agreements provide that no nation may claim sovereignty in outer space or to a celestial body.

2. Space exploration differs from early New World exploration in that (a) required resources are far vaster; (b) much use of unmanned craft; (c) intensive training for explorers; (d) economic rewards in the form of spin-offs from technological developments rather than any direct eco-

nomic gains; (e) no intention to claim territory; (f) planning extends to the smallest details—nothing left to chance; (g) constant contact with home base; (h) explorers start out with much knowledge about their objectives; etc.

Space explorers are chosen on the basis of rigid tests and prior training in specialized fields. Leaders of early exploring parties won sponsorship on the basis of their proven navigation skills, their prior exploring experience, sometimes their ability to supply part of the needed material resources, and their power to persuade sponsors. Lesser members of exploring parties were picked for their specialized skills or sometimes their simple willingness to go along.

3. This exercise might be handled as student reports on selected inventions and discoveries.

4. Use up-to-date encyclopedias of American history and world history to help students compile a list of events.

CHAPTER 2

An Assortment of Colonies

Introducing the Chapter Most students will know less about the founding of the Spanish settlements than of the English colonies. After an overview of the Spanish Empire, this chapter analyzes the particular character of the Spanish approach to colonization. As students proceed through the chapter they can compare the Spanish colonies with those of the English, Dutch, and French.

The early English failures are noted. You might emphasize how remarkable it was that the English succeeded in the face of their early setbacks.

A timeline on the chalkboard or in the student's notebooks will put the settlements in a clear perspective. As each section is studied, indicate on the timeline (a) the dates of the settlements and the nations involved and (b) other significant events.

Section 1 (pp. 27–30)
The Spanish Empire

Instructional Objectives Students will be able to

1. Locate the Spanish settlements in North America.
2. Analyze the framework of Spanish colonial government.
3. Give examples of the influence of religion and the missions in developing Spanish colonies.
4. Compare the Spanish attitude towards colonization, Indians, and slaves with that of the English colonies.
5. Describe and evaluate the Spanish contributions to our culture.

Teaching Suggestions Students who have lived in or visited the Spanish borderlands might identify places that have retained Spanish names. Also ask them what other signs of the Spanish heritage can be found in Florida, the Southwest, and California. Remind students that the old borderlands contain some of the largest concentrations of Spanish-speaking people in our country today, but most of these people are recent immigrants—Cubans in Florida and Mexicans in Texas, New Mexico, Arizona, and California. So the Hispanic culture in these areas is a blend of the old and the new.

• Using the map of the Spanish borderlands on page 28, locate the Spanish settlements in what is now the United States. Emphasize that these settlements were chiefly colonial outposts set up (a) to defend the main settlements in the Caribbean and in Mexico and (b) to convert the native population. Thus these settlements were mainly forts and missions. *Handout 2* provides a chronology that can be used to help students understand when and why particular settlements were started.

• Because the borderland settlements were chiefly defense and mission outposts and because most of them were founded relatively late in the Spanish colonial period, the *encomienda* system did not apply. Some vast ranches (*haciendas*) were carved out in the Southwest and in California, but even here the major type of landholding and Indian control was that of the missions.

• Ask the class to find newspaper and magazine stories and advertisements that reflect Spanish influence—names of foods and drinks, dances, songs, etc. Ask for volunteers (for extra credit!) to make a bulletin board display on the theme "Spain in America."

• Students can write a letter in the role of Father Serra to friends back in Spain explaining the importance of religion and missions in the New World. Find at least four activities of the missions and weave these into the letter. (religious services, education, building, farming, protection of the Indians)

Section 2 (pp. 30–33)
A Great and Victorious England

Instructional Objectives   Students will be able to

1. Explain why Philip II of Spain was eager to conquer England.

2. Point out the significance of the defeat of the Spanish Armada.

3. Describe how Gilbert, Raleigh, and Hakluyt set the stage for the founding of English colonies in North America.

4. Locate and tell the story of Raleigh's "Lost Colony."

Teaching Suggestions   You may want to supply additional detail on sixteenth-century England, including more facts about Henry VIII's break with the Roman Catholic church and Philip II's quarrels with England.

Students will be interested in trying to locate the lost colony of Roanoke. Tell them that it may have been located at Manteo, North Carolina, where each summer a play, "The Lost Colony," is presented. Roanoke Island lies between Albemarle Sound and Pamlico Sound.

• Pick a student to be Queen Elizabeth, and assign five advisers to help her question Gilbert, who also has five advisers. Have them discuss the question, "Should we build settlements in the New World?" Have Elizabeth ask such questions as "Why do you think we should support this expedition?" Have Gilbert's group justify the expedition. Let the remaining class members vote for or against granting the expedition and explain their vote.

• Help students to see that the early colonization efforts of Gilbert and Raleigh came before the defeat of the Spanish Armada. Have students put these dates on their timeline: 1578—Gilbert gets first colonial charter. 1583—Gilbert lost at sea after second attempt to found colony. 1585—first Roanoke colony. 1587—second Roanoke colony. 1588—defeat of Spanish Armada. 1590—Roanoke found abandoned.

Section 3 (pp. 33–37)
The Planting of Virginia

Instructional Objectives   Students will be able to

1. State five or more reasons why the English government wanted to establish colonies in North America.

2. Locate Jamestown and point out its disadvantage as a site for settlement.

3. Relate the early hardships of the Jamestown settlers and John Smith's role in keeping the colony going.

4. Name three important events of 1619 and tell the significance of each.

Teaching Suggestions   Have students imagine that they are young men and women in England in 1606 when the Virginia Company began to recruit settlers for what would become the Jamestown Colony. Have them suggest sentences or phrases from a "sales pitch" that they might hear from a Virginia Company recruiting agent. Then have them suppose that they are half-convinced to join the expedition. What objections are they likely to hear from family and friends?

• Individuals or groups can prepare posters or broadsides designed to recruit settlers for the Jamestown Colony.

• Have students assume the role of a London journalist reporting that King James I has just given a colonial charter to the Virginia Company. The news story can point out that the king took the action on the advice of certain members of his court. They urged various reasons for England to go all-out in colony building in America. The news story should include five or more of the reasons given in the text. When finished, students can exchange papers and check them for content, grammar, and spelling.

• Here are some suggested entries for the chapter timeline: 1603—James I becomes king of England. 1607—Jamestown Colony founded. 1612—John Rolfe grows tobacco in Virginia. 1619—Virginia House of Burgesses meets; black laborers arrive in Jamestown.

• The film *Jamestown* (22 min) provides a good re-enactment of the settlers' problems.

• Have the class simulate a meeting of the Jamestown settlers called by Captain John Smith. He asks, "What are your complaints?" Have the class list from the text the "gripes" of the settlers. A role-playing session can then follow, with Smith basing his replies on the theme of "work or starve." How can he reply to those who complain that they are ill?

• Pick a student to be the newly arrived English governor in Jamestown in 1619. Two students can serve as aides representing the "London" point of view. The rest of the class can be members of the House of Burgesses. Have them discuss with the governor what strict rules should be abolished or changed.

• Fifteen minutes or more can profitably be spent using the illustration on page 36. Explain that the cost columns are pounds (li), shillings (s), and pence (d). One shilling was equal to 12 pence, and one pound equalled 20 shillings. Spanish silver dollars circulated widely in the colonies (and in Europe) and were valued at around 5 shillings. Thus £ sterling was worth about $4 in Spanish currency.

Next, you can help students read the unfamiliar print. Don't worry if particular words and phrases remain unclear —for example, what is "one suite of frize"? Most of the material is readable if students recognize that the small "s" often looks like our "f" and that the letter "u" can be either "u" or "v."

Here are some questions to stimulate interest in the broadside:

1. If your vessel was shipwrecked, which items would you save first? last? Why?
2. You plan to take a group of twelve persons including yourself. Approximately how much money will you need to invest in your trip? (Sums given for one person will have to be multiplied by 12; sums given for six persons are multiplied by 2.)
3. Can you think of any other items that ought to be added to this list?

Section 4 (pp. 38–42)
The Puritans Come to New England

Instructional Objectives Students will be able to

1. Locate the New England colonies on a map.
2. Distinguish between the Pilgrims and Puritans, and indicate what role each group played in the settlement of New England.
3. Identify the Mayflower Compact as the first American constitution.
4. Tell how the Pilgrims were befriended by the Indians.
5. List reasons why the Puritans were more suited than other colonists for successful settlement in the wilderness.
6. Explain how non-Puritan groups founded colonies outside of Massachusetts.

Teaching Suggestions Most students already know the story about the legendary Thanksgiving feast shared by the Pilgrims and Indians. This section probes more deeply than in earlier grades into the essential motivations to succeed in the New England colonies, with emphasis on the influence of religious faith in the overcoming of hardships. You might stress the overall theme question, "In what ways were the Puritans extraordinary people?"

• Put the dates of settlement of the various New England colonies on the chapter timeline.

• Title parallel columns on the chalkboard PILGRIMS and PURITANS. For each column have students supply words and phrases for each of the following items: (a) Reason for name; (b) Attitude toward Church of England; (c) Reason for leaving England; (d) Location of original land grant; (e) Growth of colony; (f) Prominent leaders.

• With the text as a guide, have each student write three questions to ask Governor John Winthrop in a simulated interview. For example, "Why do you believe the Massachusetts Bay Colony will be a success?" Write the questions on the chalkboard (omitting duplicates). For homework, select five "best" questions for students to answer in writing, using the text for fact or inference.

• *Handout lesson:* Use *Handout 3* for skill development in finding pertinent facts and presenting them in correct, succinct form. Tell students that a major highway near New York City is the Hutchinson River Parkway, named after Anne Hutchinson. Say that you would like some of the students to write a tribute to her in 40 to 50 words. They are to be engraved on a plaque to be placed along the highway. Remind students that grammar and spelling must be perfect, since there must be no mistakes in bronze!

You may wish to divide the class into four or more groups, giving each one a different person named in this chapter. Then have a student from each group put his or her inscription on the chalkboard for review of content and accuracy.

Section 5 (pp. 42–43)
Other Europeans in North America

Instructional Objectives Students will be able to

1. Name three nations besides England and Spain that founded settlements in North America and locate these settlements.
2. Explain how the French and Dutch settlements differed from the English.
3. Tell the importance of at least three French and Dutch colonial leaders.

Teaching Suggestions Sections 5 and 6 can be handled by most students as a single reading assignment, but learning activities and chapter review can easily occupy two class periods.

The story of the French in America resumes in Chapter 3. The map of New France in Chapter 3 is useful for this lesson too.

Handout 4, prepared for use with Section 6, provides further information on the Dutch and Swedish settlements.

• Place the non-English settlements, along with their dates, on the chapter timeline.

• Item 3 in the Section Review deserves special attention.

• Notice that the text gives three reasons for the fall of New Netherland: (a) its position between New England and the southern colonies, (b) the imminent outbreak of war between Holland and England in Europe, and (c), by inference, the unwillingness of the Manhattan merchants to put up a fight. In addition you might want to remind students of the *patroon system.* This feudal landholding system along the Hudson was hardly the kind to inspire loyalty or to develop the fierce spirit of independence that developed among small farmers in the English colonies.

Section 6 (pp. 43–46)
The Proprietary Colonies

Instructional Objectives   Students will be able to

1. Define the term "proprietary colony."
2. Name and locate the proprietary colonies.
3. Discuss the role of William Penn and the Quakers in Pennsylvania.
4. Show how the ill-laid plans of the Georgia founders retarded the colony's development.

Teaching Suggestions   You may want to supplement the fascinating stories about Pennsylvania and Georgia with some additional highlights on the Jerseys, Delaware, Maryland, and the Carolinas. *Handout 4,* which provides information about these colonies, can be used in a variety of ways, including the following competency exercise.

- *Competency exercise—selecting pertinent information and using it in a paragraph:* Give students *Handout 4,* "A Chronology for Selected Proprietary Colonies." Have students write a coherent paragraph about one of these colonies: New Jersey, Delaware, Maryland, North Carolina, South Carolina. Assign so that all colonies receive attention.

  Of course, you can make this a more demanding exercise by having students write on two or more colonies.

  A less demanding exercise would have students simply rearrange the items under the names of the various colonies.

- Students of Dutch, Swedish, Finnish, or French Huguenot descent might be particularly interested in investigating and reporting on the settlements of these people.

- The class would enjoy hearing from the teacher or a student some detail about the governorship of New Sweden's Johan Printz, a seven-foot, 400-pound giant.

- Have students put selected events from the text and *Handout 4* on the chapter timeline.

- Have half of the class write a Pennsylvania political speech entitled "Why the Quakers Should No Longer Govern Us," and the other students write one from the Quaker viewpoint entitled "Why the Quakers Should Continue to Govern Pennsylvania."

- Role-play a group of Georgia settlers airing their complaints to a visiting trustee of the company.

- *Handout lesson:* As part of the chapter review, use *Handout 5* as a vocabulary skills exercise. It will also illustrate the contributions of the Spanish, French, Dutch, and Germans to the American language. Perhaps students can think of other words to add to the list. (See Albert H. Marckwardt's *American English* for background on the early growth of language in America.)

CHAPTER REVIEW
Meeting Our Earlier Selves

1. Use the text for information on the four comparison items.

2. Rise of the strong Tudor ruling family in England; activity of the English "sea dogs"; persistence of English settlers in the face of enormous hardships; inflation in Spain resulting from the rapid increase of specie (gold and silver); and, of course, the defeat of the Spanish Armada.

3. False advertising helped colonizers to recruit settlers. Rumors of the chance to get rich in America also stimulated recruitment. But rumors of dangers must have deterred many would-be settlers from leaving Europe. Settlers who left Europe because of religious or political persecution must have been less influenced by advertising and rumor than those who came chiefly for economic reasons. The topic "The unknown land" in Section 3 provides examples of advertising and rumors.

4. *Good planning:* The Puritans of Massachusetts Bay were obviously well organized; so were the Quakers in Pennsylvania; other examples might be cited. *Bad planning:* the Georgia colony; Locke's elaborate scheme of government for the Carolinas; etc. *Good luck:* the arrival of Squanto; help from Indians in various localities; Rolfe's finding of tobacco as a "money crop" (luck and enterprise); the lucky presence of outstanding leaders (like John Smith); etc. *Bad luck:* fight with Spain delaying help for Roanoke colony; swampy ground at Jamestown (luck plus lack of foresight); outbreak of infectious diseases; hostility of Indians in some places (some luck but mostly resulting from attitudes and actions of the settlers); etc.

5. Most New England colonies: religion helped shape the pattern of settlement around the church meetinghouse; government—congregational-style town meeting and leadership of the clergy; education—to enable everyone to read the Bible and religious tracts; the Puritan ethic of hard work and individual enterprise; etc.

Rhode Island: all of the above plus the idea of religious liberty.

Pennsylvania: among other things, the Quaker philosophy affected the institution of public safety and defense (against Indian attacks).

Maryland: the mixture of Catholics and Protestants forced the adoption of religious toleration.

New Spain: immigration policy (Protestants excluded); state-supported religion; Indian relations (conversion, education, some protection); church control of education.

New France: most of influences characteristic of New Spain applied here; immigration policy had even more effect here.

Questions for Today

1. Religious dissent implies the existence of a powerful religious establishment—usually supported by the government. Taken in this literal sense, it would be impossible to name dissenting groups in the United States today. Still, in the recent past the Jehovah's Witnesses clashed with civil authorities on the issue of the flag salute in schools, but court cases were decided in their favor. Even today we hear of clashes between members of this sect and the authorities on the issue of blood transfusions.

If religious dissent is interpreted broadly to cover hostility toward or estrangement from the prevailing religious thought and activity, any number of groups can be cited. "Treatment" of such dissenters includes ostracism (simply being left out), expulsion from an organized religious group, and various kinds of private harassment.

2. Nations can become more powerful today through trade, including the use of boycotts against "enemies" and favorable arrangements with "friends"; through loans and gifts to less powerful nations in the hope of making and keeping friendly relations; through alliances (in unity there is strength); through diverting productive resources to armaments; through lending armed assistance to others (Vietnam, Afghanistan, etc.).

In our day the United Nations was designed to deter military aggression and to provide instrumentalities for international cooperation. Its relative weakness has promoted the formation of alliances designed to deter aggression (NATO, for example). The European Common Market—and less successful arrangements elsewhere—serve to suppress rivalry and promote international cooperation.

CHAPTER 3

New Ways in a New World

Introducing the Chapter This chapter provides a fine opportunity to compare living in the colonial days with that of the present. You may want to go beyond the broad descriptions in the text and devote additional time on the background of your own state if it had colonial settlements by 1765.

Section 1 (pp. 47–57)
Many Kinds of Americans

Instructional Objectives Students will be able to

1. Identify at least six non-English peoples who settled in the English colonies and locate where two of these groups settled in large numbers.
2. Name the chief commodities involved in the triangular trade and trace the routes on a map.
3. Show how geography affects the economy and lifestyles of people by pointing out appropriate contrasts between New England and the southern colonies.
4. Compare the roles of colonial parents and children with those of the present.
5. Cite three examples to show colonial interest in education.
6. Show by example that colonial art tended to emphasize the practical.

Teaching Suggestions This section offers a vivid survey of the peoples who settled here for reasons of adventure, trade, religion, necessity, or slavery. The colonies expand rapidly with energetic settlers. The patterns of American identity can be recognized even as the people retain their ties to the Old World. But slavery casts a growing shadow on freedom and opportunity in the colonies.

• Conduct a survey of the national or ethnic origins of class members (many students will be able to name two or more) and record these on the chalkboard. How many of the groups named were numerous in colonial America? Remind students that subsequent waves of immigration will be studied too. Students having some tie to a nationality or ethnic group that had a role in our colonial development can be encouraged to investigate and report on that group's settlements, distinctive features, and contributions.

• List at least six non-English peoples who settled in the colonies. Using the map on page 49, locate where these people settled. Where were the areas of largest concentration? Why?

• Interesting colonial trade statistics in *Historical Statistics of the United States* can be used to help students study the map "Colonial Trade about 1750." The table showing colonial exports in 1770 is particularly relevant. It shows, for example, that

— Over half of the exports (in pounds sterling) went to Great Britain, 25% to the West Indies, and 20% to southern Europe.

— Tobacco was the chief export (26% of the total value), and almost all of it went to Great Britain.

— Other leading exports, their approximate percent of the total value, and their chief destinations:
  Bread and flour (15%) to West Indies, southern Europe.
  Dried fish (11%) to southern Europe, West Indies.

Rice (10%) to England, West Indies, southern Europe.
Furs and deer skins (4%) to England.
Indigo (4%) to England.
Wheat (4%) to southern Europe, Ireland.
Whale oil and fins (3%) to England.

— Among other big exports to the West Indies were candles (409,000 lbs.), Indian corn (403,000 bu.), lumber (36 million bd. ft.), and barrel staves and hoops (15 million pieces).

— Nearly 293,000 gallons of New England rum (84% of rum exports) went to Africa.

• Tell students that ever since the rise of big cities and large-scale business, some Americans have sought escape in the simple life. The rejection of modern technology perhaps reached a new peak in the 1960s with the establishment of rural communes and with individuals and families seeking a life akin to that of the colonists.

Have the class prepare a list of the conveniences (phones, electric stoves, sweepers, refrigerators, autos, etc.) and services (hospitals, libraries, etc.) that the colonists had to do without. Then list the things *they* had that are now often denied to us (pollution-free air, etc.). What are the virtues of the back-to-nature movement? What fruits of modern science and technology are the modern "pioneers" least willing to give up?

• Obtain present-day maps, such as auto travel maps, of several of the states included among the original colonies. Affix these to the rail above the chalkboard or spread on desks or tables. Divide the class into groups to examine each map. Have them report in turn on their assigned state as follows:

1. What were the homelands of the earliest settlers? How can you tell?

2. What evidence, if any, is there of Indian settlement? (place names, rivers, mountains, etc.)

3. Where are the largest cities located? Would the colonists have anticipated these and their locations? Why?

4. What map changes have taken place in this state since colonial days? (highways, railroads, state parks, etc.)

If your school is in one of the original thirteen states, you may want to concentrate on it.

• Ask students to look at the illustrations in this chapter section and write 3 to 5 inference statements about colonial life in the 1700s. To help students get a start, write on the board: "From the illustrations on text pages 48–57 we can infer (guess) the following about life in the colonies:"
Then have students turn to a particular picture. Write a sample inference statement on the board based on student responses. When students understand what they are to do, have them complete the assignment.

• Prepare a list of outcomes that colonists hoped to achieve through their support of education.

• Extending the lesson: Many creative activities may be encouraged in this section, such as the making of model sailing ships, pioneer implements or wagons (Conestoga, e.g.), salt-box farm houses, or colonial costumes.

Independent study projects can be suggested, such as an inquiry into the impact of French customs, law, or language on the development of America as we know it. One topical area and one nation would be enough for any student.

Section 2 (pp. 58–61)
The Colonists Govern Themselves

Instructional Objectives Students will be able to

1. Show how the changes in English parliamentary history affected the colonies.

2. Explain the acceptance of smuggling.

3. Show how distance and poor communication promoted a spirit of independence in the colonies.

4. Trace the steps leading to colonial self-government.

5. Write a 150–200 word summary of one of the topics in the text.

Teaching Suggestions Troubles in England benefit the colonies. Students who have never had a course in English or European history may be bewildered by the kings and the changes in England, so some review may be necessary.

• The steps leading to colonial self-government may be indicated through the responses or attitudes expressed by the colonists to the terms or persons listed below. Have students find evidence in the text to support their answers.

(a) Navigation laws
(b) Privateering
(c) English kings
(d) Royal governors
(e) Dominion of New England

Colonial Response or Attitude

(a) (ignored or violated them)
(b) (encouraged, and profited from, it)
(c) (declining loyalty to them)
(d) (varying states of disobedience)
(e) (resisted it; existed in name only)

• Assume that you are a member of a prominent colonial family. A relative in England has written you a letter condemning your activities as a smuggler. Write a letter in reply.

• Write a news story from the viewpoint of an English newspaper correspondent in which you list at least five activities of the colonists that indicate a rebellious attitude and forebode a movement towards independence. (smuggling, buying stolen goods from privateers, coining own money, ignoring Navigation Acts, banning Anglican church, hanging Quakers in violation of English law, harassing royal governors)

- A brief review of English history can be helpful during the study of this section. Even a listing of the rulers on the chalkboard will help the class retain a time perspective:

Charles I	1625–1649
Council of State (dominated by Cromwell)	1649
Protectorate	
Oliver Cromwell	1653–1658
Richard Cromwell	1658–1659
Charles II	1660–1685
James II	1685–1688
William III (of Orange) and Mary	1689–1702

This activity may spark interest in the role of the monarch in England today with focus on Elizabeth II. Here is a chance to "humanize" the kings and queens. If students want to pursue this subject, suggest Robert Lacey's *Majesty —Elizabeth II and the House of Windsor*.

- Reenact a town meeting in Massachusetts Bay in which the citizens express their opinions on the following items of business:

1. Should the king's name be on our legal forms?
2. Who should have the right to vote in this town?
3. Should we go on public record as being in support of or against the recent hanging of a Quaker on Boston Common?
4. What should we say in our letter to the governor expressing our opinion about the Navigation Acts?
5. Our town hall is greatly in need of about 100 chairs for our meetings. We learn from one of our citizens who is a friend of a New York merchant-privateer that we can get these chairs cheaply if we pay a little "protection money" to the right officials. Should we do this?

- *Competency exercise—summarizing:* Divide the class into five groups and assign students in each group one of the five topics in this chapter section. Have each student write a summary of his or her topic. You may want to suggest length limits, such as 10 to 12 sentences or 150 to 200 words. After you have selected a "best" model, have the author read it to the class for discussion of its merits.

Section 3 (pp. 61–65)
Britain against France

Instructional Objectives Students will be able to

1. Show sensitivity toward colonial anti-Indian attitudes by relating the story of the Deerfield Massacre.
2. Explain why the Albany Congress met and why its Plan of Union failed to win acceptance.
3. Relate highlights of the French and Indian War.
4. Describe and explain the land transfers in the Peace of Paris.

Teaching Suggestions This section has many of the ingredients that motivate student interest in history: a brief but realistic portrayal of an Indian raid on a New England village; and, on a larger scale, a frontier-type war between two nations locked in a bitter struggle for power in North America. In addition, we see the first stirrings of colonial unification. This is a good time to show a film, such as *French and Indian War* (11 min). Students will understand the films better if they study the section *first*.

- Ask the students to prepare an oral or a written summary of the film that is seen. Evaluate the film, using as guidelines questions prepared in advance. Are there any differences in interpretation of historic events between the film and the text?

- Have students rewrite the story of the Deerfield Massacre from the viewpoint of a French soldier as he might have told it in a letter home. He should explain why the French and Indians are attacking English settlers and what his feelings were during and after the attack on Deerfield.

- An alternative is to have the class discuss the event from the viewpoints of both the settlers and the French soldier. The morality of war might be discussed, as well as the question of obedience to orders in the military.

- Have students act as English newspaper reporters interviewing Benjamin Franklin when he was in London as a colonial agent (text page 64). Ask him about the details and meaning of the Albany Plan of Union and about the attitudes of the colonists towards England. Pick one of the better students to be Franklin (and give him or her an "adviser"). The class should write down the questions before the interview. Here are several that may be given to students having difficulty thinking of a question:

1. Mr. Franklin, what was the purpose of the Albany Plan of Union?
2. What were the proposals contained in the plan?
3. Why did the colonial legislatures turn down the plan?
4. What do you think will be the future of Canada?
5. Are the colonists ever going to unite against England? Why, or why not?

- Have students make a time chart of the period relating to the French and Indian War. Using the text as a guide, place the following dates in the date column: 1745, 1754, 1755, 1757, 1758, 1759, 1763. Then record the events and results opposite the dates.

      DATE   EVENT   RESULT

CHAPTER REVIEW

Meeting Our Earlier Selves

1. The varied population produced a ferment of change. The English language was enriched. The dominant group in any locality or colony had to learn to make concessions to minorities in their midst. The special craft skills, farming techniques, cooking recipes, and social customs of one group were picked up—and perhaps adapted—by their neighbors. People were forced out of old ruts and learned to accept change. This development was reflected in the "new" American's willingness to strike out on new paths.

2. Plantation owners turned to slave labor because the Indians could not be induced to supply labor service and it was almost impossible to recruit agricultural labor from Europe. With the abundance of free or low-cost land, why should an immigrant work for someone else except to learn a trade or to pay for passage to America! Even if a white person promised to work on a plantation for a period of time, it must have been easy to run away. Immigrants tended to go the northern colonies, where common people could make it on their own and not be beholden to the big landowners. Northern immigrants encouraged friends and relatives in Europe to join them, thus accelerating the flow to the northern colonies.

3. Lacking photography, colonists could preserve their likenesses only by patronizing painters. Enterprising Americans who could afford landscapes, for example, would want the family pictures but could find better uses for their money than investing it in luxury paintings, since the colonies were short on capital as well as labor.

4. The simple design of furniture, silverware, etc., reflected the practicality necessary in the lives of the people. Other things were made for use—not just to admire—quilts, guns, woodenware. Yet crafting such articles artistically brought emotional satisfaction too. There was occasional imitation of the more ornate European styles among the wealthy, especially the southern "leisure class."

5. Long before fighting broke out, the colonists asserted economic and political independence by resisting the Navigation Acts, patronizing privateers, resisting the royal governors, coining their own money, banning the Anglican church in Massachusetts, etc. Even more important, perhaps, was the social revolution: the breaking of Old World ties, the making of the "new American" and a distinctive American culture.

6. Discuss the term "salutary neglect." Lack of rigid enforcement of the Navigation Acts and other aspects of the mercantile system permitted the colonies to thrive economically—and England reaped much of the benefit.

7. Various wars involving England, France, and Spain were shared by the colonists on both land and sea. These wars gave the colonists military and naval training, dictated the location of forts, exacerbated hostility toward the Indians, etc.

Questions for Today

1. While the American culture has been enriched very substantially by the presence of non-British population stock, the continued predominance of English culture remains. The importance of language and legal tradition to a culture should be emphasized. The class can also use the occasion to specify some non-English influences.

2. Training took place in the family—plus in the workshop for apprentices. Schooling was meager and was concerned largely with literacy, but the religious emphasis in the schools did buttress the teaching in the home in the area of morals. Schools today, of course, put much emphasis on vocational guidance and training and on civic responsibility.

3. To the extent that nations use protective tariffs and put other restrictions on international trade, there is a resemblance to mercantilism. Some people continue to believe that a nation is better off if exports exceed imports with the balance coming in the form of gold or other forms of money.

Differences: Colonies have largely vanished, and where they exist they may operate at a net loss for the parent country—being held chiefly for strategic purposes or out of a sense of responsibility. Most people today realize that trade is a two-way street. Also the developed nations today tend to support industrialization in the less-developed nations as a means to promote stability in the world.

Your Region in History

1. The Peace of Paris spelled the decline of French influence in the trans-Appalachian region and the continued dominance of English culture on the East Coast. It affected the whole nation by making Canada an English neighbor rather than a French one.

2. This question suggests a museum trip and/or a special report.

Skills to Make Our Past Vivid

1. The letters might reveal stirrings of independence in the colonies and describe changes in the economy. But since the economy and social structure of the southern colonies were more static than in the North, the letters might not reveal much about the "new American."

The diary would be most informative because it would likely tell of meetings with all kinds of people and provide observations of a variety of lifestyles.

The eyewitness account at Albany would focus on political problems. To the extent that it described participants, it could throw light on the "new American."

2. Presuming that the Quaker lived on the East Coast, he or she would probably pass through Providence (Rhode Island), New Haven (Connecticut), New York City (New York), and Jersey (just founded—no major town).

CHAPTER 4

The Road to Revolution and Victory

Introducing the Chapter Does any period in our history offer such a dramatic setting as this one? You might teach it from the viewpoint of the underdog Americans facing the apparently overwhelming strength of the British Empire. We were surrounded on three sides—from the sea, the north, and the west. At one point—Valley Forge—Washington's army was so small that it could have been seated in a modern convention hall. And yet, remarkably, we won our independence.

Throughout the chapter, you will note that our history hinges upon "ifs": would the colonies have revolted if Parliament had granted them representation? And once the war began, would the British have won if they had not made mistakes or omissions in their strategy? The study of history affords hindsight—encourage your students to rewrite the American Revolution as it might have been!

Good films exist on the American Revolution: *Dawn of the American Revolution: A Lexington Family* (11 min) and *The American Revolution* (16 min). See the unit audiovisual list for other films and filmstrips, and the bibliography for a number of fascinating novels and biographies about this period.

Section 1 (pp. 68–76)
The British Take a Collision Course

Instructional Objectives Students will be able to

1. Indicate on a map the Proclamation Line of 1763 and the land claims in North America according to the Peace of Paris.
2. List and explain British and colonial actions and reactions in 1763–1774 leading to the First Continental Congress.
3. Describe the role of propagandists like Sam Adams in the movement toward independence.

Teaching Suggestions The thrust of this section is to set the stage for the American Revolution by describing the oppressive legislation that stirred hostility in the colonies. Where possible, compare the British and American viewpoints. Encourage students from time to time to take the Tory (British sympathizer) position and at other times the patriot position.

- Distribute copies of Outline Map 3 of North America for students to show the territorial claims after 1763 and the Proclamation Line of 1763.

- Use skill exercise 1 in the Chapter Review with this lesson. The "action" column should have these events with their dates: Proclamation Line of 1763, Sugar Act, Stamp Act, Declaratory Act, Townshend Acts, tea monopoly (Tea Act, 1773), Intolerable Acts, Quebec Act. Ask: Which of these laws were most objectionable to the colonists? Why?

- *Competency exercise—writing a "letter to the editor":* Write to the editor of the *Pennsylvania Journal* protesting the Stamp Act, giving at least two objections to the tax. When the class is finished, ask several students to read their letters aloud, and list the objections on the chalkboard. Ask for other objections not already given. Then try to reach a consensus on the three or four best objections.

- *Handout lesson:* Using *Handout 6,* pick a good student reader to be Benjamin Franklin appearing before a committee of the British House of Commons. Ask several other students to take turns reading the questions. When the testimony is finished, ask questions like these:

1. What taxes paid in Franklin's day no longer exist today?
2. What did the colonies contribute to the French and Indian War?
3. According to Franklin, what was the only way by which the stamp tax could be collected?
4. Describe the attitude of the colonists toward England before 1763.
5. Name five reasons for a change of attitude toward England in the colonies by 1766.
6. What did Franklin think would happen in the colonies if the Stamp Act was not repealed?

- Ask students to pretend that they have listened to a street-corner speech by Sam Adams in Boston. Have them write what they think he might have said to inflame public opinion against the British. Ask them to suppose that two English soldiers are standing in the back of the crowd. What might they murmur to each other about Adams's remarks on the Boston Massacre?

- Have the class list five Intolerable Acts in the order in which they think Bostonians objected to them, putting the most objectionable first, etc. Then try to get a class consensus on the most objectionable act. What are the reasons for this choice?

- Simulate a meeting to organize the Boston Tea Party. Pick a persuasive student to be Sam Adams urging that a group disguised as Indians board the tea ships and dump the tea into the harbor. Have the class raise objections to Adams's plan. What would Adams say in reply?

When news of the Tea Party spread through the colonies, people reacted in various ways. How might a Tory (Loyalist) have responded? a Patriot opposed to mob action?

- Extending the lesson: Offer students extra credit for preparing oral or written reports on (a) Pontiac—Leader of the Ottawas, (b) Samuel Adams—Master Propagandist, or (c) Crispus Attucks—First Black to Die in the Revolution.

Section 2 (pp. 76–81)
Declaring Independence

Instructional Objectives Students will be able to

1. List the activities and recommendations of the First and Second Continental Congresses, and show how these led finally to the Declaration of Independence.

2. Describe and explain the significance of the battles at Lexington, Concord, and Bunker Hill.

3. Discuss the American offer of peace and the British reaction to it.

4. Describe France's support of the American cause in the early part of the war.

5. Summarize the principles in the preamble of the Declaration of Independence and list some accusations against the king.

Teaching Suggestions The highlight of this section is the Declaration of Independence—its significance in the Revolution and its impact on subsequent world history. You may want to extend the lesson by having students read the document itself (pp. 756–759) and the explanations accompanying it. If you read it aloud, stop often to ask for an interpretation. This is also a good opportunity for vocabulary building. See General Hint 6 on page 7.

- Some of the items in the Section Review for this lesson go beyond a simple matching of question with the text narrative.

In item 1 the match-ups are (a) Galloway—First Continental Congress, (b) Revere—Dawes, (c) *Common Sense*—Paine, (d) Howe—Tories.

The dates for item 2 are Lexington (April 19, 1775), Bunker Hill (June 17, 1775), and Ticonderoga (May 10, 1775). A Lexington minuteman might easily have fought at nearby Bunker Hill. But he could only have been at Ticonderoga too if news of that coming attack had reached him in time (highly improbable). Also Ticonderoga was largely an operation of Ethan Allen and his Vermont Green Mountain Boys, while the fighting around Boston was chiefly by the Massachusetts militia—probably with some help from Connecticut, Rhode Island, and New Hampshire. It was too early in the war to have much mixture of the militias.

Item 4: The shot at Lexington was "heard 'round the world" in the sense that it began a war for independence that would later influence independence movements and popular revolutions throughout the world.

Item 5 is answered in the last paragraph of the topic "The Battle of Bunker Hill."

- Have students refer to the map "The American Revolution" and locate Lexington, Concord, and Bunker Hill. Procure a modern map of Massachusetts (an automobile road map will be fine) and trace the routes of Revere and Dawes from Boston to Lexington and Concord. How do the routes today differ from similar ones in Revere's day? What would be some obstacles today to traveling Revere's route on horseback?

- Read Longfellow's "Paul Revere's Ride" to the class or make a stencil and distribute copies for class reading. If you do the latter, ask a number of students to read a stanza at a time. Then discuss the following: (a) How does Revere find out what the British plan to do? (b) What is the time of day? (c) When at last Revere gets the signal, what is it and what does it mean? (d) How many hours does his journey take? (e) What was the result of Paul Revere's ride?

- Have students locate Bunker Hill on the map "The American Revolution." For more details and a map of the battle, see *Battles of the American Revolution* (1968 reprint), available in many libraries. Then discuss what happened at Bunker Hill, including the following: (a) What was the primary problem of the colonials during the battle? (b) Why were the losses so heavy, especially among the British? (c) Why weren't the British accustomed to this type of fighting? (d) Why did George Washington say, "The country is safe"?

- Ask the students to turn to the excerpt from the declaration of war on page 78. Suppose that King George had accepted the Olive Branch Petition and had agreed to negotiate. Ask the students to rewrite the war declaration into a statement of willingness to discuss peace negotiations. What would the Americans ask for? What would they be willing to concede? If this had actually happened and revolution had been avoided later, what would the United States be like today? What form of government would we have?

- Silas Dean returns to America from France. Have the students write a brief report in which Dean tells the Congress about the help we may expect from France and the reasons why he is sure that we will get it.

- *Competency exercise—summarizing:* Have students write the gist of the preamble of the Declaration of Independence in around 100–125 words.

Here is a sample that might be used in follow-up evaluation and discussion:

Whenever a group of people decide to break away and set up their own government, they should state their reasons. We believe in human equality in the enjoyment of life, liberty, and the pursuit of the good life. A government answerable to the people must guarantee these rights. If it fails to do so, the people have the right to change or abolish it—and set up a new government. Such drastic action should be based on very substantial abuses. We have suffered such abuses, and herein list them for the world to see.

- *Competency exercise—paraphrasing:* Have each student rephrase ten of the listed abuses in the Declaration of Independence. Begin by writing two or three examples on the chalkboard. For example:

1. He has refused to sign laws needed for the general welfare.

2. Our governors may not put laws into effect until he has signed them. Then he neglects to study and sign them.

    Notice that a number of abuses need to begin with a phrase like "He has allowed Parliament to pass laws on . . ."

- In addition to using these competency exercises—or handling them as part of the class discussion— here are other questions to use in teaching the Declaration of Independence:

1. How many men signed the Declaration?
2. Which colony provided the most signers?
3. Why was Washington not a signer?
4. Why would the king consider the signers to be traitors?
5. What risk were the signers taking?
6. Today we hear "Put your John Hancock here." What does this mean? Why not say "Thomas Jefferson"?
7. From the signers came two Presidents and three Vice-Presidents. Who are they? (See table on text page 804.)
8. What are some examples of the influence of the Declaration of Independence on the later history of the world?

Section 3 (pp. 82–92)
How British Power Was Overthrown

Instructional Objectives Students will be able to

1. Compare European and American styles of warfare in the 1770s.
2. Identify and discuss the roles of at least five important American and three British figures in the War of Independence.
3. Trace and summarize the chief campaigns and battles of the war.

4. Explain why some colonists became patriots and others remained loyal to Great Britain.
5. Discuss the contributions of women, blacks, and Europeans to the American cause during the war.
6. Give the terms of the Treaty of Paris of 1783.
7. State at least four reasons why the Americans won and four reasons why the British lost the war.

Teaching Suggestions You will need to decide how to allocate class time among (a) campaigns and battles, (b) the other text material on the nature of warfare, armies and their recruitment, the home front, etc., and (c) the peace treaty.

- Notice that the map "The American Revolution" provides a rough time framework for tracing the course of the war with the bold-face numbers (1 to 7) and titles. For a quick checkup, have students identify battles (and their significance) for each of the seven main titles on the map. Notice that the map names a few more battles than those described in the text narrative.

- *Handout lesson:* Use *Handout 7* as a timeline for studying the war. It can be used in conjunction with the map.

    For extra credit, encourage students to write one or two paragraphs about one of the engagements listed on the handout.

    One or more students might accept an assignment to find and write brief additions to the handout—the names, dates, and one-sentence summaries of two to five other engagements.

- Skills session—understanding basic terms associated with the American Revolution: Have students define and use each of the following terms in a sentence relating to the Revolution: rebel, patriot, Loyalist, protest, confrontation, resistance, riot, rebellion, revolution, independence.

- On the chalkboard make two columns—one titled EUROPEAN and the other AMERICAN. To the left, write these topics for comparison: (1) Rules of battle and styles of fighting; (2) Casualty rate; (3) Description of soldiers; (4) Soldier recruitment; (5) Degree of patriotism; (6) Dependability of armies. Have students suggest words and phrases to complete the chart, using the text as a guide.

- Have students use the text and *Handout 7* to list George Washington's activities in the war. Then ask: Why is Washington called "first in war" in spite of the reverses suffered by troops he personally commanded? (creating the Continental Army, providing overall direction in the war, paying expenses out of his own funds, inspiring the troops and the home front, etc.)

- Ask students to prepare a 40–50 word description of the military participation of the five American figures (other than Washington) that they consider most important to the success of the American Revolution. Have the students do the same for the three British figures who contributed most to their cause. After the class has finished, tabulate the results on the chalkboard. How can Benedict Arnold be considered? Should his early contributions to the American cause be separated from his becoming a traitor? Why?

• Draw the diagram below on the chalkboard. Have the students locate Albany and the planned movements of the British on the map on page 85. Have the class list the reasons why each British plan failed. Which one of these failures was most significant? Why? What would have happened thereafter had all aspects of the plan succeeded?

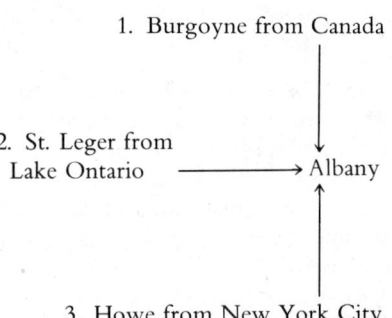

• *Handout lesson.* Use *Handout 3,* "Writing Historical Inscriptions," again. This time the inscription could be for a battle site, beginning "On this spot . . ." or "Near this spot . . ."

Sites can be selected according to local interest (any military action in the Revolution near your school?) or from *Handout 7,* "Important Engagements in the American Revolution." The handout, of course, can also be used to memorialize a hero/heroine of the war.

• Cast four or more girls in the roles of the following: Margaret Corbin, Molly Pitcher, Deborah Sampson, Betsy Ross, Abigail Adams, Martha Washington, and/or others. Have a TV "Talk Show" on the topic "My Role in the Revolutionary War," and have each historic character tell about herself. An emcee can ask questions, and the class can participate also. Adequate preparation (research) by the participants is necessary for a successful lesson. If you prefer, ask the students to give oral reports to the class instead of having a TV show.

• Use the article "The Sentiments of an American Woman" on page 89 by having students do the following:

1. Copy three sentences or phrases that illustrate how women have shown acts of courage in battle.

2. Copy the sentence in which the author tells what women are willing to offer as their contribution to the war.

3. List some of the sacrifices that, according to the author, women have already made in the war.

4. Summarize the article in five original sentences.

• Most students are aware that drummers and fife players are popular participants in Independence Day parades. Ask why these musicians symbolize the soldiers of the Revolution. Discuss the music and songs of the Revolution, beginning with "Yankee Doodle." Perhaps some recorded Revolutionary War music and songs can be obtained from your school's media center. Why was music important to the colonial soldier? What were some of the settings in which songs and ballads were sung in colonial days? (See Commager and Morrison, *The Spirit of 'Seventy Six,* Chapter 22, "Songs and Ballads of the Revolution," and the reading list for this unit.)

• A colorful bulletin board display can be made with the flags of the Revolutionary period. Ask art-minded volunteers to make flags out of tagboard. Begin with the drawing and coloring of the first American flag used by George Washington for the Continental Army. Suggest that students use encyclopedia references under "Flags" in the media center or library. The role of Betsy Ross may also be explored in the making of early flags.

• Ask students to refer to the map on page 90. Have them list the terms of the Treaty of Paris in 1783. Why did we fail to obtain Canada? What caused the French to be surprised at England's generosity?

CHAPTER REVIEW

Meeting Our Earlier Selves

1. Defend: British leaders, such as Chancellor Grenville, never having been in the colonies, thought that the people would be grateful to Great Britain for having protected them from the French and Indians during the recent war (1763). Hence the colonists would gladly pay taxes like those on sugar. Also, Parliament had little conception of the growing spirit of independence in the colonies, and felt that it could treat the people in a manner similar to that extended in Great Britain—i.e., with little consideration. Thus the leaders of Parliament did not think that they were unduly imposing taxes on the colonies.

Challenge: As early as 1766, Benjamin Franklin went to England and testified directly to the House of Commons that the colonies would not tolerate oppressive taxes. London merchants, because of a decline in trade, also well knew the colonial attitude. The fact was that the British leaders could not accept the increasing spirit of self-government in the colonies.

2. True. The Americans, being mostly of English blood, fought for their principles rather than against a foreign foe. Also, ideas survive better than the people who support them, so that losses did not deter the Americans from continuing the war—such as during the dark days of Valley Forge.

3. True. As the text indicates, the Americans fought the war mostly as a "people's" army of militia, often ill-trained and poorly disciplined. By contrast, the British soldiers were professionals who had a job to do and felt no particular hatred towards the Americans. And the Hessians—20,000 of them according to the text—were merely mercenaries soldiering for money.

4. Agree: (a) From the defeat, Britain may have learned something about controlling colonies. (b) Later clashes might have proved inevitable—with the British losses much heavier. (c) Would Napoleon have sold Louisiana to Great Britain? (d) The strong U.S. that emerged over the years actually benefited the British about as much as if they had kept political control—enormous help in two world wars, for example. Etc.

Disagree: A British Empire dominating North America would have made Great Britain an even more dominant power than it was in the nineteenth century. Napoleon might not have challenged Britain. Would Germany have "started" two world wars and thereby challenged a powerful Anglo-American empire? Would the imperialism of the late nineteenth century have been more benign? Would slavery have been halted earlier? Etc.

Questions for Today

1. A colonial people—or a suppressed minority seeking independence—might adapt the preamble to their own situation and then spell out their own list of complaints. The philosophy of the preamble—human equality, unalienable rights, regard for world public opinion—remains relevant today.

2. Many modern revolutions seem to be led by a dedicated minority (often Communists), by a military clique, or by a charismatic leader (often, it appears, one seeking personal power and rewards). Their strategy is to manipulate apathetic masses to the desired political end. A small group can more easily "go underground" to gather arms, carry on terrorist activities, and spread their propaganda to the masses.

3. Wars of the twentieth century have touched the whole population in that wars are economic efforts. The work force must be converted to military production. The daily television reports of war activity, such as during the Vietnam War, also cause civilians to feel that they are participants in a war.

The Revolutionary War was economically, politically, and militarily a minority war (witness the starvation at Valley Forge while the nearby civilian population remained well-fed). Also, the Revolutionary War had very poor communication devices, so that sometimes months passed before news came across the sea or traveled from one end of the colonies to another. This prevented bringing the war home to all of the people at any given moment.

4. The non-English colonists gradually adopted English laws, ways, and language. Their European ties were broken, and they became Americans. The English colonists were proud of their English heritage as late as 1766, according to Benjamin Franklin. Their motives towards independence were thus primarily inspired by political and economic oppression—not having representation and being taxed unfairly, etc.

Skills to Make Our Past Vivid

1. See the teaching suggestions for Section 1.

2. Various replies—could have participated in the French and Indian War as an enlisted soldier. If in trade, British legislation could have affected business directly. Stamp Act could have been oppressive to printers, etc. Even a home owner could have been affected by the quartering of British soldiers. In short, almost everyone in the Boston area could have been affected by the various events.

3. Poster would emphasize hardships of soldiers and the need to donate medicine, blankets, shoes, clothing, and food to the patriots' cause. Emphasis too upon creating a feeling of shame that people lived so well but that only 20–30 miles away soldiers experienced great hardships.

CHAPTER 5

From Confederation to Nation

Introducing the Chapter Perhaps more than any other chapter in the text, this one will require diligent study and patient teaching. Students will retain interest in the story of our constitutional development so long as they do not become confused. Your students may have difficulty realizing that early loyalties were given to states rather than to a federal government and that the executive branch represented a form of tyranny to many people. Emphasize that unity came only through a willingness to compromise, thus creating one of the most remarkable documents in history.

Section 1 (pp. 93–96)
New State Governments

Instructional Objectives Students will be able to

1. Indicate how the original states went about creating new written constitutions.
2. List the basic political principles reflected in the first state constitutions.
3. Explain why legislatures were strong and governors weak in the early governments.
4. Trace the abolition of slavery in the states.

Teaching Suggestions This section prepares students for our national experience of acting cooperatively to create effective governmental authority. The first constitution of your own state—especially if written before 1850 or so—may be examined in an extended lesson as an introduction to the attitudes and problems of the early days.

- Have students list in a left-hand column the following phrases relating to early state constitutions, and in a right-hand column define or describe them: Concord constitutional plan, rights retained by people, two-house legislature, Pennsylvania legislature, power of governor, Pennsylvania attitude toward governor, posts changed from appointive to elective, voting qualifications, representation in legislatures, early attitudes towards slavery.

- Or review the text material by having each of seven small groups report to the whole class on one of the following topics: (1) Why independence was a state rather than a national feeling. (2) The reasons for and against calling a special constitutional convention in a state. (3) The general framework of the state constitutions. (4) What was different about Pennsylvania's constitution? (5) Why the powers of the governor were weakened in state constitutions. (6) Ways in which people were treated unequally in the states. (7) How slavery was gradually abolished in some states.

- Many school and community libraries have a section of books related to the history of the state. Have a committee report on the history of your state's constitutions. What main changes were made each time, especially in the executive branch? (In New Jersey, for example, the constitution of 1776 gave the governor a one-year term; that of 1844, a three-year term; and that of 1947, a four-year term. What does this lengthened term—and possibility of being re-elected—indicate?)

Section 2 (pp. 96–98)
The Continental Congress

Instructional Objectives Students will be able to

1. Explain the activities of the Second Continental Congress.
2. Identify at least six members of the Congress.
3. Evaluate the successes and failures of the Continental Congress.

Teaching Suggestions Remind students that the First Continental Congress met only briefly (about 7 weeks) in 1774. So "Congress" in the text refers to the Second Continental Congress. This brief section will provide the student with a background of some of the governmental problems preceding the Articles of Confederation, and specifically illustrate the need for a strong central government. You may want to combine this lesson with the next one on the period under the Articles of Confederation.

- In parallel columns have students list POWERS OF THE CONTINENTAL CONGRESS and POWERS DENIED CONGRESS. Have students use the text to find facts for each column.

- Ask the students to list at least six members of the Continental Congress, along with their states of origin. Then have them answer these questions about the Congress as a whole: (1) What was the principal age group of the members? (2) What were their occupations? (3) What economic class or classes did they represent?

- On the chalkboard draw a vertical timeline for the period 1777–1789 as illustrated below. Or have the students do the same in their notebooks. Use the timeline to record the events in this chapter dealing with the development of our national government. Start with "Congress approves Articles of Confederation." Be sure to include treaties and ordinances.

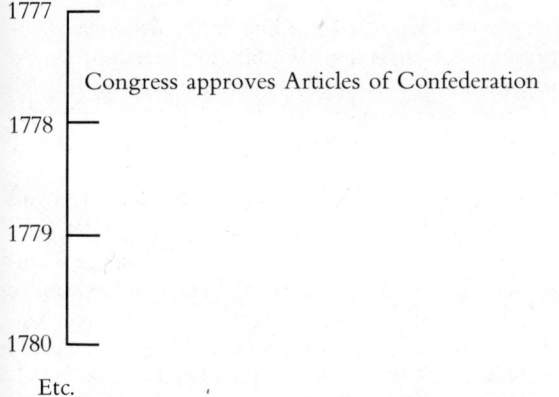

Section 3 (pp. 98–104)
A Weak Confederation

Instructional Objectives   Students will be able to

1. Explain the principles of the Articles of Confederation.
2. Show how the Land Ordinance of 1785 and the Northwest Ordinance of 1787 facilitated western settlement.
3. Indicate how our difficulties with foreign nations continued after the Revolutionary War.
4. Describe the problems of debtors that led to Shays's Rebellion.

Teaching Suggestions   The United States begins to expand to the west. You might compare land values of 1785 with those of today after the class reads the topic "New Englanders settle along the Ohio." Also explore the motivations of the pioneers who moved to the West.

• Have the students continue the timeline of the development of the national government and the Constitution.

• Have students make a chart titled "The Articles of Confederation." Label one column "Strengths" and another "Weaknesses." Use items from the chart on the powers of Congress suggested for Section 2. Then have students find other items from information provided in Section 3.

• Ask students to refer to the map on page 100 and note the areas constituting the western claims of the various original states. Then have them discuss the following:

1. What was the importance of the western lands to the U.S. at this time?
2. What role did speculators play?
3. Which state had the largest claims?
4. What were the complaints of the "land-poor" states that had no claims?
5. What caused Virginia to compromise on her claims?
6. Which present-day states contain land that was claimed by one or more of the original states in 1784?

• Use the map and diagrams on page 101 to help students see the importance of land surveys to orderly settlement and to visualize certain common land measurements. Explain that any tract of land in the Northwest Territory could be positively identified by its location in a particular section of a particular township, which in turn could be located by reference to its range and its distance from a particular base line. Have students speculate on the importance of precise knowledge of land boundaries. (Ownership disputes less likely to arise and more easily settled.)

If your school is in a county that is divided into civil townships, students can compare the size of their township to a congressional (land-survey) township. For further help in visualizing the size of a township, ask the class to imagine that their school lies in one corner of a township— say, the southeast corner. What landmark would be six miles directly north? six miles directly west? Or if the school were in the precise center of a township, what are some landmarks three miles distant to the east, west, north, and south?

To help students visualize an acre of ground, find out the acreage of your school property. Or have an interested student measure off an acre of land on the school grounds.

• After students have read the topic "New Englanders settle along the Ohio," ask them to assume that they are living in New England in 1787 and have a chance to head west with General Putnam to form a new settlement in Ohio. Poll the class to find out who would go and who would remain behind. Have several students explain their decision, giving special emphasis to the rewards and the dangers involved in going west. To what degree was life in New England easier and more pleasant than it had been 100 years before? Explain.

• Ask students to imagine that they live in one of the thirteen original states. Have them write a letter to their state's Continental Congress members asking them to vote against a treaty with Spain giving up our right to the Mississippi for 25 years. The letter should give the reasons for requesting such a vote.

• Explain that the expression "not worth a Continental" came about because the currency issued by the Continental Congress was worth ony two cents on the dollar at the end of the war. Then ask the students to put themselves in the financial position of the farmers—many of whom were ex-soldiers in the Continental Army—who joined Daniel Shays as "shotgun reformers."

1. What did these men hope to gain by preventing debt collection and threatening violence?
2. Were they justified in acting as they did?

3. What were their alternatives?

Then ask the students to assume the role of a merchant trying to collect a debt.

1. Was he justified in giving support to the militia to stop Shays and his men?
2. From the viewpoint of the merchant, what would be a fair sentence for Shays and his men after they were caught, tried, and found guilty?

After discussing these questions, tell the students that Governor John Hancock of Massachusetts pardoned Shays and 13 of his men after they had been sentenced to death. Shays had meanwhile escaped to Vermont.

Section 4 (pp. 104–109)
Writing a Nation's Constitution

Instructional Objectives Students will be able to

1. Tell how the Constitutional Convention came about.
2. Discuss the roles of leading members at the Convention.
3. Describe three compromises in the Convention.
4. Indicate how the Constitution corrected the defects in the Articles of Confederation.

Teaching Suggestions Students may need some help in trying to be spectators at the Constitutional Convention. Without extensive research, students may find role playing in class too demanding. A good film may be more satisfactory. For enrichment, suggest that students read such books as Carl Van Doren's *The Great Rehearsal*.

• Have students continue the timeline of the development of the national government and the Constitution.

• *Competency exercise—writing sentences:* Ask students to define the following terms and use each in a sentence: convention, delegates, amendments, sovereign, federal, treaty, compromise, levy, export, revenue.

• Divide the class into two groups. Have one group write a brief newspaper report on the activities of the delegates at Annapolis. Have the other group write a brief report on the Philadelphia meeting, emphasizing who attended and what was the purpose of the meeting. Ask the groups to exchange papers after they have finished in order to check the correctness of the facts.

• Ask students to read the names of the signers of the Constitution. If your school is in one of the original states, get volunteers—for extra credit—to prepare a report on the signers from your state. What were the backgrounds of these men, and why were they chosen to go to the convention? Of the 55 delegates who came to the convention, only 39 signed the Constitution. Why did some of the delegates not sign? (Facts useful to understanding the delegates: youngest delegate—Jonathan Dayton, 27; oldest, Benjamin Franklin, 81; average age 42; only 11 delegates past 50; 31 delegates with some college education; there were two university presidents and three professors.)

• Tell the students that according to the delegates at the Constitutional Convention, Washington remained almost silent during the proceedings. Franklin at 81 frequently fell asleep during the meetings. Yet each played a most important role. Discuss what this was.

• Extending the lesson: Hold a mock Constitutional Convention. Have students role-play the principal delegates and research what their contributions were. George Washington will have to introduce the delegates and explain to them the rules of procedure and the areas of agreement. Have the Virginia delegation present their plan, followed by the New Jersey Plan. Discuss the advantages and disadvantages of each plan. Then present the Connecticut Plan and discuss the issues involved. Have the delegates reach a compromise and accept this last plan.

• Ask students to read carefully the last paragraph of Section 4 on changes made in the Constitution to correct particular defects in the Articles of Confederation. Which changes are working most successfully today? What further changes are needed? (If the students need prodding, remind them that critics contend that the House of Representatives with 431 members is an unwieldy body.)

• The Appendix contains the "official" (National Archives) version of the Constitution along with substantial explanations of the documents, "Origins" and "Afterlife."

Section 5 (pp. 109–112)
The States Ratify

Instructional Objectives Students will be able to

1. Describe the procedure by which the Constitution was ratified to become the law of the land.
2. Name the principal supporters of the Constitution and identify the role each played.
3. Explain why a Bill of Rights was added to the Constitution.
4. Explain these features of our constitutional system: popular sovereignty, limited government, federalism, national supremacy, judicial review, separation of powers, checks and balances, and the amending process.

Teaching Suggestions In this last section, the student will realize two important points (a) that at the time of ratification there were many persons who still supported the idea of state autonomy, and (b) that the Federalists won because of their respected leaders and their willingness to compromise. After you have introduced these points, you might ask what our future would have been like if the Constitution had not been ratified.

- Divide the class into two groups. Call one "Federalists" and the other "Anti-Federalists." Ask the students to line up as many arguments as they can find for their side. Then compare these. Which are still valid today? Can they be identified with any of today's political parties?

- To illustrate that the Constitution affects our lives today on a daily basis, have the students peruse metropolitan newspapers for several days for articles that relate events, legislation, or court cases relating to the Constitution. Ask the students to clip out these articles and bring them to class. Assign a committee to make a bulletin board display. Discuss the significance of the articles with the students before taking down the display.

- *Handout lesson:* Five pages of text and charts on "Chief Features of the American Constitutional System" are available as *Handout 8.* You may want to require students to keep these pages as part of their history notebook.

Since the text and charts in this handout can provide only terse summaries, you may want to augment the explanation of certain of the constitutional principles with additional explanation and examples.

Or divide the class into groups, each one to study and report on one of the "features." Suggest, for example, that they find in American government textbooks an explanation of their assigned feature and report to the class on (a) divergent or expanded explanations, (b) examples of the constitutional principle in practice, and (c) differing ways of showing the principle in diagram form.

CHAPTER REVIEW

Meeting Our Earlier Selves

1. Reasons for relatively lengthy state constitutions: (a) States are responsible for a wide range of activities—education, family law, contracts, property rights, welfare programs, etc.—whereas the federal Constitution puts fairly narrow limits on Congress. (b) The federal Constitution does not say how state governments must be organized, but state constitutions must deal—often at length—with the organization and powers of local government units. (c) Because state governments affect daily life so closely, citizens may prefer that "changes in the rules" do not take place too easily—at the whim of legislators and other public officials.

The big advantage of a relatively short constitution is that it is not loaded with details that need to change with the changing times. Many decisions are best left to legislative bodies.

2. The old constitution may be full of workable parts that ought not to be cast aside. Starting from "scratch" carries the risk of introducing all kinds of new governmental problems.

3. Various abuses cited in the Declaration of Independence get specific attention in the Constitution, especially in the Bill of Rights. The Declaration implied too much centralization of authority in the king, and the Constitution carefully provides for separation of powers. The Declaration said that governments should not be changed for light and transient reasons; the Constitution allows for change but does not make the amending process "too easy." Both the Declaration and the Constitution honor the principle of popular sovereignty—final authority resting with the people.

4. Forces for separatism: (a) Each colony had its separate history. (b) State officials would not want to relinquish their power. (c) Some states had economic interests that collided with those of other states. (d) Rival claims to western land—and the jealousies of land-poor states. (e) Transportation and communication were primitive, thus isolating the states from each other. (f) Fear of the unknown—what will happen to our way of life if we join in a closer union?

Forces for unity: (a) Need to defeat and then make common peace arrangements with the British. (b) Need for mutual defense against Indian attacks. (c) The breakdown of interstate commerce as each state sought its own narrow advantage. (d) The need for a uniform money system. (e) Threats of internal disorder like Shays's Rebellion. (f) Surrender of western land claims to Congress.

Questions for Today

1. By 1980 more than half the state legislatures had sent to Congress resolutions calling for a convention to propose an amendment that would (a) require a balanced budget or (b) put other limits on federal spending.

Arguments for the convention method: (a) Delegates would be chosen for that specific purpose, whereas members of Congress are selected for their views on a wide range of contemporary issues. (b) Convention could propose changes that might be opposed by Congress because they would infringe on congressional privileges and prerogatives.

Arguments against: (a) A convention meeting to propose a single amendment might open a floodgate of proposals. (b) Amendments that cannot win two-thirds support in Congress are not likely to be good amendments, some critics would argue.

2. The *Congressional Quarterly* is perhaps the best source of information for this activity.

Skills to Make Our Past Vivid

1. A simple way to match place names in your state with signers of the Constitution is to arrange the names of the signers in alphabetical order (see signers on text pages 783–784) and then match this list with a list of counties and a list of cities and towns.

2. (a) Art. I, sec. 8; (b) Art. II, sec. 1; (c) Art. II, sec. 2; (d) Art. IV, sec. 3; (e) 26th Amendment; (f) First Amendment; (g) 25th Amendment; (h) Sixth Amendment; (i) 20th Amendment; (j) Fourth Amendment.

CHAPTER 6

The United States Begins

Introducing the Chapter Although this chapter begins with an overview of American society in the 1790s, it is Washington the man and President who soon commands our attention. The space allotted in the text may not be enough for your students to understand and appreciate Washington's place in history as "the father of our country." You may want to broaden your students' perspectives of Washington with a film or filmstrip.

Section 1 (pp. 114–117)
The Nation in the 1790s

Instructional Objectives Students will be able to

1. Locate and indicate the size of the nation's largest cities in 1790.

2. Describe the chief modes of transportation in the 1790s.

3. Locate the chief area of trans-Appalachian settlement in 1790 and explain the importance of rivers to that settlement area.

4. Compare English and American social classes and social mobility in the late 18th century.

Teaching Suggestions This section will help students visualize America in the 1790s, with particular emphasis on the problems of travel and communication in a rural society. You may want to extend the lesson to include a look at your own community or area some two hundred years ago. If you have not already taken your students on a field trip, this is a good time to visit nearby historic houses.

• Use the map on page 115 to estimate travel times. If a stagecoach trip from New York to Philadelphia took two days in 1790, have the students estimate how many days it would take to travel by land from Philadelphia to the following cities: Boston, Charleston, Savannah. How could the trip be made to New Orleans, and approximately how long would it take? Then ask the students to estimate the times for similar trips by automobile and airplane today.

• Suggest a student report—for extra credit—on Daniel Boone as a folk hero of the frontier. The report should include Boone's travels, how he dressed, how he survived while on the trail, and what his subsequent career was. What motivated men like Boone? See Bakeless's *Daniel Boone* or a similar book.

• A description of John Fitch's first steamboat—or better still a drawing or tagboard model of it—will interest your students in early modes of transportation. Ask students who like to draw or make models to do some encyclopedic research or refer to such books as Flexner's *Steamboats Come True: American Inventors in Action*. What were the objections to Fitch's invention? Why couldn't he find commercial backers?

• Write the following on the chalkboard:

OCCUPATIONS SURVIVING
FROM 1790 TO TODAY

Ask the students to prepare such a list, using the text as a guide. Then discuss the following:

1. Which jobs related to our period will survive for another 200 years? Which will become obsolete? Why?

2. Under what circumstances would a worker be unemployed in 1790? How have these conditions changed?

• *Handout lesson: Handout 9* is a reading comprehension exercise designed to provide additional detail on frontier life with special emphasis on the log cabin. Before students begin reading the selection, have them find Lancaster on the map on page 115.
Tell students to read the handout selection and then mark the statements that follow—according to the directions given. If students are likely to need help in recognizing inferences, you can spend a little time prior to the reading for explanation.

• Beginning with the most important factor, have students list in descending order the aspects of American life in 1790 that related to one's position on the social ladder.

Section 2 (pp. 118–124)
George Washington Sets the Course

Instructional Objectives Students will be able to

1. Describe George Washington and his background, and identify significant events of his Presidency.

2. Explain the contribution of Alexander Hamilton as first Secretary of the Treasury to our national development.

3. Identify our first two political parties and explain why they developed.

Teaching Suggestions The transition from state sovereignty to federal supremacy is clearly established in this section, along with the concept of the need for a strong executive as an elective part of the American system. You might discuss with your class how much the shaping of early American political tradition was due to the image of George Washington and how much to the leadership of Alexander Hamilton.

- Share with the class some details on Washington's first inaugural (below). Then have them point out contrasts in contemporary inaugurations: date, place, dress, size of audience, media coverage, Inaugural Day events, etc.

Washington was inaugurated April 30, 1789, from the balcony of Federal Hall at the corner of Broad and Wall Streets in New York City. Probably he could be heard by only a small group, and seen by several hundred persons. He rested his hand on a Bible, and was somewhat flustered and overcome with emotion as he took the oath of office. As a result, he read his address poorly. He wore a dark-brown suit of American manufacture, along with white silk stockings and a steel-hilted sword. In the fashion of the day, his hair was powdered and worn in a queue.

- Pick a student to be Alexander Hamilton. Assign him or her a number of "advisers." Have them study the chapter so that they know Hamilton's views. Then have the rest of the students conduct an interview with Hamilton, using the text as a source of questions. For students who need help, here are some suggested questions:

1. Why do you think Congress does not want close ties with Cabinet members?
2. Why don't you have faith in the common people?
3. Why do you feel that the federal government should assume state debts?
4. Why did you make a deal to locate the city of Washington on the Potomac River?
5. Do you believe that the wealthy people should run the country? Should the poorer people be allowed to hold office?
6. Why do you favor a national bank?
7. Why are you in favor of a "broad" interpretation of the Constitution?
8. Although the French supported us in our war with England, you now support England in its war with France. Why?
9. Why do you support Washington for a second term?
10. Are you hopeful of being President yourself someday? (You might suggest that the Constitution has the answer: Hamilton, being foreign-born, was not eligible to be President.)

- Have students prepare a chart comparing the views of the Federalists and the Republicans. Write the following on the chalkboard or have the students write this in their notebooks:

ATTITUDES | FEDERALISTS | REPUBLICANS

Then in a vertical column under ATTITUDES list the following: payment of state debts, National Bank, interpretation of Constitution, manufacturing and industry, tariffs, agricultural society, strong central government. With the text as a guide, have the students complete the views for each category.

Section 3 (pp. 124–130)
Foreign Affairs for a New Nation

Instructional Objectives Students will be able to

1. Explain our problems in 1796–1800 with England, France, Spain, and the Indians and the treaties that resolved these problems.
2. Describe the activities of Citizen Genêt and their impact on the United States.
3. State the cause and the outcome of the Whiskey Rebellion.
4. Summarize topics in this lesson in two to five sentences each.

Teaching Suggestions The text topic "Troubles with France" provides a thumbnail account of the French Revolution as background for understanding French-U.S. relations. You may wish to provide some further detail on how the French Revolution produced widespread instability in Europe and frightened the wealthy and powerful everywhere.

- On the chalkboard or in their notebooks, have students fill in a chart like the one shown below.

	Jay's Treaty	Pinckney's Treaty	Treaty of Greenville
TREATIES IN WASHINGTON'S ADMINISTRATION			
ISSUES			
TERMS			

The map on text page 249 can be used to clarify our border problems with Spain. The east-west border line

Chapter 6

between Alabama and Florida is 31 north latitude. Thus a strip of present-day southern Georgia was acknowledged as Spanish territory under Pinckney's Treaty.

- You might tell the class that Genêt never did return to France. By the time our government asked the French to recall Genêt, a radical faction (the Jacobins) had gained control in France. His disgrace at being recalled would have meant death by the guillotine. So Genêt asked for, and was granted, political asylum. He became an American citizen, later married the daughter of Governor George Clinton of New York, and settled along the Hudson.

- Use the account of the Whiskey Rebellion to remind students that their families buy goods and services on which the producers paid the federal government an excise tax: gasoline, auto tires, airline tickets, telephone service, alcohol, and tobacco, for example. Gasoline and various auto excises are collected as kind of a direct payment for federal outlays on highways. The excises on alcoholic beverages and tobacco are sometimes justified as a way to raise the cost of unneeded or harmful consumption goods. Although the federal government collected over $18 billion in excise taxes in a recent year, that was less than 4 percent of total revenue. The $383,000 collected in 1793 (the year before the Rebellion) was about 8 percent of that year's revenue; nearly all the rest came from customs duties.

The Whiskey Rebellion can also be cited as perhaps the first large-scale protest demonstration after the government was organized under the Constitution. Ask students how they think a group might protest against "unfair" taxes today.

- *Competency exercise—summarizing:* Assign or have students select two topics in this chapter section for written summaries. Tell students to write the gist of each topic in two to five sentences. Insist on complete, error-free sentences. After collecting the papers for evaluation, select at random a few samples and read them without identifying the writers. Invite the class to suggest improvements.

- To help students understand the election of 1796, tell students that the electors chosen in each state meet in their state capital to cast their electoral ballots. Divide the class into four groups, each representing one of the 16 states that existed in 1796. Two of the states (A and B) have chosen Federalist electors; the other two (C and D) have Republican electors. Select a chairperson for each state. Tell Chairperson A to persuade his/her colleagues to write the names of John Adams and Thomas Pinckney (the agreed-on Federalist candidates) on their ballots. Tell Chairperson B to persuade Group B to vote for John Adams and a second Federalist other than Pinckney (Oliver Ellsworth received 11 votes, so his might be the second name). Chairpersons C and D should persuade their colleagues to put Thomas Jefferson's name first on their ballots and then a second Republican (among those receiving votes were Aaron Burr, Samuel Adams, and George Clinton).

The four groups should NOT be of uniform size. Remind students that each state has as many electors as it has members of Congress. Arrange for Groups A and B to have, together, at least two more electors than Groups C and D, so that Adams wins by two or three votes.

When the ballots have been marked, have the students take their regular seats and imagine that they are the Senate, meeting to count the electoral votes. As the President of the Senate reads the ballots, a Clerk can put the results on the chalkboard.

Section 4 (pp. 130–134)
John Adams and the Rise of Parties

Instructional Objectives   Students will be able to

1. Point out highlights of the Presidency of John Adams.
2. Explain the impact of the XYZ Affair in bringing us close to war with France.
3. Clarify values on waging war for "national honor."
4. State the purpose and effect of the Alien and Sedition Acts.
5. Show how the election of 1800 led to the Twelfth Amendment.

Teaching Suggestions   Some additional detail on the Directory (1795–1799) may help students better understand the renewed troubles with France in the Adams administration. See any world history or modern European history textbook.

- Have students draw a timeline for the period 1789–1800, listing events discussed in Chapter 6.

- *Handout lesson: Handout 10* provides further detail on the new city of Washington, especially the White House, and can be used as an exercise in reading comprehension. After students have read the adapted letter from Abigail Adams to her daughter, have them answer the questions at the end of the handout.

- In discussing the topics dealing with troubles with France, ask students to specify actions of the French government which some Americans regarded as serious enough to justify war. Follow up with questions like these:

1. Would similar actions by one nation toward another lead to serious talk of war today?
2. What alternatives to outright war did the Adams administration employ?
3. Would these measures be regarded as appropriate today? What other kinds of responses might be used in our day?

Discussion of these and similar questions can lead to some useful understandings about modern war and diplomacy. For example, (a) The destructiveness of modern weapons makes war over "insulting behavior" or for "national honor" unreasonable. (b) Irrational rulers do appear on the world stage even in modern times (Hitler, Idi Amin, Khomeini, and others). (c) Though imperfect, instruments for resolution of tensions between countries do exist today—the United Nations particularly.

- The following questions might be used to check on and deepen understanding of the Alien and Sedition Acts and the Virginia and Kentucky Resolutions:

1. How did our troubles with France provide the Federalists an excuse to pass the Alien Act? (The country was on the verge of war with France, and the law would empower the President to deport enemy aliens.)

2. What was the chief reason for passing the Alien and Sedition Acts? (to maintain Federalist party supremacy by stemming the flow of immigrants to the Republicans and halting criticism of the Federalist officeholders)

3. Why was the Sedition Act especially offensive? (clearly unconstitutional—First Amendment)

4. How, according to Jefferson and Madison, could the Alien and Sedition Acts be overturned? (nullification by state legislatures)

5. What was dangerous about this idea? (threat to whole federal system)

CHAPTER REVIEW

Meeting Our Earlier Selves

1. A Federalist might have proposed (a) federal subsidies to the states for building roads and canals, (b) expansion of the postal system, (c) federal registration of steamboats using navigable waters—in order to sidestep harmful state controls, (d) protective tariff to stimulate industry.

2. Answers will vary.

3. The War of Independence had to be fought with borrowed money—borrowed by Congress and by the states. Hamilton and others argued that the war debts of the states were really a national obligation.

Paying the debt in full was necessary for establishing the credit of the United States. Lenders are wary of borrowers who fail to pay their debts in full. On the other hand, payment in full rewarded speculators. Many people who had loaned the government money received from speculators only a few cents on the dollar.

4. The Constitution said little or nothing about: (a) dignity of the presidential office/George Washington set precedents; (b) personal rights and liberties/Congress proposed a Bill of Rights; (c) federal prosecutors and federal police/Congress established office of United States Attorney and United States Marshal; (d) nature of lower federal courts and court procedure/provided in Judiciary Act of 1789; (e) the number and nature of executive departments/new departments set up by Congress; (f) relationship of executive departments and Congress/Congress rejected close ties; (g) how Senate should advise President on treaties/Senate turned down chance to advise; (h) the war debt/assumption of state debts and full payment of public debt; (i) manner of collecting revenue and safekeeping federal funds/establishing the national bank. Other things can be named, such as location of the capital, the existence of political parties, holdover of Cabinet officials from one administration to the next, and possibly others.

5. See especially pages 122, 124 on the contrasting views of Hamilton and Jefferson.

6. In both sections the Indians anticipated less white settlement of the land if it remained under British or Spanish control. It was clear that Americans wanted the land and were moving in ever-increasing numbers to occupy Indian hunting grounds.

7. The claim arose over the passage of the Alien and Sedition Acts—particularly the Sedition Act—and it was voiced in the Virginia and Kentucky Resolutions. Nullification was a dangerous view because it meant state supremacy rather than national supremacy.

Questions for Today

1. Consumer protection laws; pollution controls; any business regulation not dealing directly with the movement of goods across state lines; federal subsidies (grants-in-aid) to the states for all manner of activities such as education, welfare, health care, etc.; federal drug control laws; and many other kinds of laws based on the implied powers of Congress.

2. A tax revolt movement would probably be organized and would be aimed at changing the tax law or amending state and federal constitutions to limit the taxing power of legislative bodies. Such a movement does exist. Individuals or small groups might also stage protest demonstrations. Tax evasion would probably increase.

3. Display of presidential shield; playing "Hail to the Chief"; use of the title "Mr. President"; special limousines and aircraft; presidential libraries for the papers and mementos of former Presidents; Camp David retreat; etc. His critics charged Richard Nixon with operating an "imperial Presidency." On the other hand, Jimmy Carter—particularly early in his Presidency—rejected much ceremony and tried to appear as "a man of the people."

4. Opinions differ on the advisability of widely divergent political philosophies in the Cabinet. Modern Presidents expect some differences of viewpoints—and may encourage the expression of dissent while public policy is being formulated. But once a policy has been made, Cabinet support for it is expected. Presidents today tend to pick Cabinet members and other advisers who are in tune with the President's own philosophy—and then to ask for the resignation of advisers who show up as "too divergent."

Your Region in History

2. *Historical Statistics of the United States* has a table showing the apportionment of members in the House from 1789 to the date of the volume's publication.

Skills to Make Our Past Vivid

1. A traveler by land might very well have gone some stretches by riverboat. The overland route would be 850 to over 1000 miles depending on the starting place in western Kentucky, the straightness of the trails and roads, and the choice of using "roads" or "paths." A trip by boat down the Mississippi and by ship to Philadelphia would be 2500 miles or so. Yet the water route might be faster and less dangerous.

2. Point out that some timeline items will be nonpartisan in nature.

CHAPTER 7

Jefferson in Power

Introducing the Chapter This chapter surveys the second of the early Presidents considered by historians to be among the "great" Presidents. However, unlike the revered Washington, Jefferson has his detractors as well as supporters. You might "humanize" Jefferson by going beyond his political views and presidential activities to examine his contributions to the arts and sciences. A filmstrip, such as *Thomas Jefferson* (45 fr), may provide encouragement to read one of the many interesting biographies or lead to a desire to visit Monticello and the University of Virginia someday. Perhaps some of your students have visited both places.

Acquisition of the Louisiana Territory introduces the student to a vast unexplored area that emphasizes once more our movement westward. Your school may be in a state which was part of the Louisiana Purchase. You may want to extend the lesson to survey some early impacts of the Purchase on your state or local history.

Section 1 (pp. 139–144)
The Man and His Policies

Instructional Objectives Students will be able to

1. Describe the new capital of Washington.

2. Summarize the life and accomplishments of Thomas Jefferson.

3. State Jefferson's political philosophy as indicated in his Inaugural Address.

4. Explain why the Barbary pirates were an international and an American problem and tell what Jefferson did about it.

Teaching Suggestions When a number of winners of the Nobel Prize were invited to the White House in 1961, President Kennedy described them as "the most extraordinary collection of talent, of human knowledge, that has ever been gathered at the White House, with the possible exception of when Thomas Jefferson dined alone." With the text as a guide, have students find evidence to support Kennedy's statement about Jefferson's talent and knowledge.

• Have a student (or committee) report on various aspects of Jefferson's life and career, such as: boyhood and student days at William and Mary College, marriage and family life, building of home at Monticello (with descriptions of Monticello today), inventor and scientist, farmer, musician, career before becoming President, life in retirement.

As part of this lesson, show the film *Thomas Jefferson* (18 min). Ask for an evaluation of the film, particularly a response to what the film contributed beyond the text and the reports.

• Jefferson wrote his own epitaph: "Here lies Thomas Jefferson, Author of the American Declaration of Independence, of the Statute of Virginia for Religious Freedom, and Father of the University of Virginia." Ask students to write another twenty-five to fifty words to add to this epitaph.

• On notebook paper have students list the six *promises* in Jefferson's inaugural address. The second column can be headed *Fulfillment*. As students read each chapter section have them fill in the *Fulfillment* column, noting failures as well as successes. When this assignment has been finished with the study of Section 4, use it in the discussion of the first exercise in the Chapter Review.

• Tell students that historians consider that both Jefferson and Hamilton were great men. Yet they were rivals with contrasting political philosophies. Ask students to write a one-page composition titled "Jefferson or Hamilton— Which I Would Rather Have Been—and Why." Remind students to list the virtues and accomplishments they most admire in the statesman they select. Chidsey's *Mr. Hamilton and Mr. Jefferson* provides interesting contrasts.

- Using the map on page 143, have students locate the North African countries that harassed our ships. Then discuss (a) what type of trade brought our ships to the Mediterranean, (b) why we didn't stay out of the area altogether to avoid pirates, (c) what circumstances, if any, justify appeasement and bribery as an alternative to war, (d) the role of Stephen Decatur in stopping the piracy, (e) the role of the Marines in Tripoli, etc. (You might point out that the Marine's Hymn includes the words, "From the halls of Montezuma to the shores of Tripoli.")

- Tell the class that on March 16, 1802, the Military Academy at West Point was established by an Act of Congress. The first training school was opened July 4 of that year. Then discuss the following:

1. Although Jefferson said, "Peace is our passion," the Academy was begun during his administration. Was this a wise decision? Why?
2. What role has the Military Academy played in our history?
3. Has modern warfare made the "West Point" system of education obsolete, especially the emphasis on tactics and strategy? (Ask the students if they would like to be West Point cadets. Have them defend their answers.)

Section 2 (pp. 144–150)
Buying Louisiana

Instructional Objectives Students will be able to

1. Explain how Napoleon's military difficulties caused him to offer to sell Louisiana.
2. Link Toussaint's Haitian revolt to our obtaining Louisiana.
3. Discuss the reasons why Jefferson decided to buy Louisiana, despite protests.
4. Trace the route and summarize the experiences of the Lewis and Clark expedition.
5. Explain the Aaron Burr conspiracy and his treason trial.

Teaching Suggestions This section describes the expansion of the nation into areas almost unknown to those who were asked to approve of its purchase. Your students will have difficulty, however, in imagining that anyone would ever oppose the acquisition of land at four cents an acre! You might spend more time than usual with map work, particularly if your school is in one of the thirteen states formed out of the Louisiana Territory.

- Have students locate Haiti on the map on page 177. Then ask:

1. Why did Napoleon consider French possession of Haiti important?
2. Why did the French arrest Toussaint?
3. What factors prevented the French from subjugating Haiti?
4. Why did Napoleon decide to sell the Louisiana Territory to the United States?

- On the chalkboard write:

LOUISIANA PURCHASE
Arguments for   Arguments against

Have students list appropriate arguments in each column. Then use the following questions for discussion:

1. What was the importance of the Louisiana Territory for future settlement? for trade? for military security?
2. What problems might the country have faced if France had continued to own this territory?
3. On what basis did the Federalists argue that the territory was useless?
4. How did the Constitution enter into the dispute over the Purchase?

- Use the maps on pages 147, 148, and 249 for further study of the Louisiana Territory. Here are some questions to use:

1. What thirteen states were formed wholly or in part out of the Louisiana Territory?
2. What chief rivers draining the territory flow into the Mississippi?
3. Why is the site of New Orleans important?
4. Why did Lewis and Clark depend chiefly on river instead of land transportation?
5. What is the "Great Divide"?
6. How did the Lewis and Clark expedition give our nation claims to the Oregon country?
7. What was the importance of the expedition?

- Have the students read *Handout 11,* in which Senator White in 1803 opposes the Louisiana Purchase. After they have finished, have them answer the questions that follow. Discuss these. Explain that the resettlement of Indians mentioned by the senator will be studied in Chapter 15.

Another approach to this activity is to ask the students to write a brief speech in reply to Senator White supporting the Louisiana Purchase. After the students have finished the speeches, read several aloud in class. What would the senator say in rebuttal to these?

- Ask for student reports on the expeditions of Lewis and Clark and of Zebulon Pike. Books such as Bakeless's *Lewis and Clark: Partners in Discovery* and Baker's *Pike of Pikes Peak* will be helpful. During the presentation of the reports, use a wall map to follow the routes of the expeditions. Emphasize the physical hardships faced and the help given to the exploring parties by the Indians, particularly Sacajawea.

- Show the film *Louisiana Purchase: Key to a Continent* (16 min) or the filmstrip *Louisiana Purchase* (45 fr). Then ask the students to imagine that these visual materials could have been shown to the senators debating the Louisiana Purchase treaty. Discuss (a) what the senators would have learned that they didn't know before; (b) how the film would have influenced the vote. Also ask the students for their own reactions. What did the film or filmstrip add to their knowledge of the Louisiana Purchase?

- Ask a student to take the role of Alexander Hamilton and another of Aaron Burr. Give each several advisers. Divide the rest of the class into two groups—one to interview Hamilton on the day before his duel, the other to interview Burr.

For those students who may need some help, here are some guideline questions for Hamilton:

1. Why do you think that Burr hates you?
2. Why as a Federalist did you prefer Jefferson to Burr as President?
3. Do you think dueling should be made illegal?
4. Since you've already lost your son in a duel (Philip was killed more than two years before), why don't you withdraw from this one?
5. Do you intend to shoot to kill Burr?

Questions for Burr:

1. Why did you challenge Hamilton to a duel?
2. Why do you suppose that Hamilton supported Jefferson rather than you in the election of 1800?
3. Why did you change political parties?
4. Would you help break up the Union by joining a northern confederacy?
5. Do you intend to shoot to kill Hamilton?

After the interview, tell the class that according to Morison and Commager's *Growth of the American Republic,* Vol. 1, p. 395, ". . . Hamilton went to his doom, resolved to prove his courage and yet not to kill: to reserve and throw away his first fire, in the hope that Burr would miss and honor be satisfied." However, ". . . Burr raised his arm slowly, took deliberate aim, and fired."

- Have a student or a committee report on the life and tragedy of Aaron Burr, emphasizing (1) Burr's contribution to his country, (2) the cause and result of the duel with Hamilton, (3) the Burr conspiracy in the West, and (4) Burr's exile and decline. Discuss the statement, "Historians generally have condemned Burr, while most of his biographers have sided with him". (Current et al, *American History: A Survey,* 1961, pp. 192) E.g., Abernethy's *The Burr Conspiracy* asserts that Burr was guilty, while Schachner's *Aaron Burr: A Biography* acquits Burr. Does this indicate that Burr's personal charm influenced not only his associates but also his biographers?

Section 3 (pp. 151–154)
Jefferson, Marshall, and the Courts

Instructional Objectives Students will be able to

1. State the principle of judicial review as derived from *Marbury v. Madison*.
2. Explain the impeachment process.
3. Discuss the issues and results of the election of 1804.

Teaching Suggestions This section introduces the principle of judicial review. Be sure that students understand that the Supreme Court does not on its own initiative review acts of Congress or of executive officials. Some party must bring a case into a lower federal court and argue that the law—or some provision of it—is contrary to the Constitution. Most laws are not challenged in court on constitutional grounds.

See also that students understand that the Court rarely overturns a federal law, but it often declares state laws—or portions of them—to be unconstitutional.

Also be sure that students see that this section is chiefly a flashback to the closing days (hours) of the Adams administration and to the time when Jefferson first took over the presidential office.

- Have a student give a report on Chief Justice Marshall—with emphasis on how he shaped the role of the Court in our history. See Corwin's *John Marshall and the Constitution*. Background details may be found in the *Dictionary of American Biography* or in an encyclopedia. Then discuss (a) why Marshall felt it was "the duty of the court to say what the law is" and (b) why he believed that the Constitution and not the statute "must govern the case to which they both apply."

Show the film *John Marshall* (18 min) following the student report. Evaluate the film's analysis of Marshall's influence.

- The events in this lesson fit into a party-rivalry framework. Tell the class that in the election of 1800 the Federalists lost not only the Presidency but their majority in both houses of Congress. In the House in 1800 there were 64 Federalists to 42 Republicans, but the new Congress of 1801–1803 had 69 Republicans to 36 Federalists. (The party makeup of Congress can be found in *Historical Statistics,* Series Y.) With the legislative and executive branches going out of their control, the Federalists made a last-gasp effort to retain their influence—through the judicial branch.

Following are some questions that direct attention to the party-rivalry aspect of the events in this lesson:

1. What advantage did the Federalists expect to obtain from the Judiciary Act of 1801? (New judgeships—16 in all—and some minor judicial offices—clerks, etc.—to be filled by Federalists. You may need to explain that, under the arrangement that existed until the 1930s, congressmen defeated in November returned in December for another session of Congress. So these "lame duck" Federalists had ample time to get the Judiciary Act passed and signed by Adams before he left office.)

2. How would a Federalist-dominated court system help the Federalist party? (Provide lifetime jobs for some party members; might restrain attempts of Republicans to "get even" with Federalists through legal action; might assure a Federalist—broad construction—interpretation of the Constitution.)

3. When the *Marbury v. Madison* case reached the Supreme Court, Marshall and his Federalist colleagues could have ruled that Republican Madison must deliver the commission (the authority to serve as justice of the peace) to Federalist Marbury. Speculate on why the Federalist Supreme Court turned down this victory for their party. (The "victory" would have been too trivial. Marshall seized the opportunity to strengthen the role of the Court by firmly establishing its power of judicial review. In the future, of course, the Court could interpret the Constitution according to Federalist views so long as Federalists comprised a majority on the Court.)

4. How did the outcome of the impeachment cases strengthen the two-party system in our country? (Students should cite the last two sentences of the topic on impeachment on page 153.)

• You may need to review the impeachment process. The House of Representatives accuses (brings charges against) a federal official; this is impeachment. (Good chance here for students to add the word "impeach" in its nontechnical sense to their vocabulary.) The Senate tries the case—with the senators acting as the jury and their presiding officer, the Vice-President, sitting as judge. If the President is on trial, the Chief Justice presides.

Section 4 (pp. 154–158)
Trouble on the Seas

Instructional Objectives Students will be able to

1. Explain how the war between England and France in 1803 affected our country.

2. Relate the *Chesapeake* affair and other instances of impressment to increasing support for war with Britain.

3. Explain the advantages and disadvantages of a trade embargo as a diplomatic tool.

Teaching Suggestions Two issues of contemporary significance stand out in this lesson. Foremost is the embargo as a weapon in international relations. Another issue is the right of persons to leave their native land to seek a better life elsewhere.

• Draw a timeline on the chalkboard from the election of 1800 to that of 1808. Students should use the entire chapter as a guide to list the events and achievements of Jefferson's two terms. Have students decide which term Jefferson would want to be remembered by—and discuss why.

• As headings for three columns on the chalkboard, write:

ACTION | EFFECT ON U.S. | U.S. REACTION

Under the first heading list (a) British Orders, (b) French decrees, (c) *Chesapeake* affair, (d) impressment, and (e) Canning's reply. Have students use the text to supply facts for the other two columns.

• Students might write a one-page report from Captain Barron of the *Chesapeake* defending his action in striking his colors and not resisting the British boarding party. Then discuss (a) what alternatives were open to Captain Barron, and (b) what action, if any, the Navy Department should take against the captain.

• Have students role-play a House committee that is meeting to recommend that the Embargo bill be brought to the floor for a vote. Have two-thirds of the committee (as Republicans) support the bill. The other third (as Federalists) should oppose the bill. Each side should choose a spokesperson to present its views. Areas to discuss include (a) the probable consequences of the Embargo Act on the American economy and on the British and French; (b) alternatives, possibly war; and (c) the probable impact of the Embargo Act on the election of 1808.

Then discuss what happened after the Embargo Act was passed by Congress, particularly (a) why the embargo was quickly repealed, (b) what Jefferson had failed to anticipate, and (c) who was hurt most by the law.

• *Competency exercise—sentence writing:* The following phrases refer to events in the Jefferson administration. Choose ten of these phrases and write a sentence about each, pointing out what Jefferson or his administration did. Write complete sentences with correct grammar, spelling, and punctuation.

> national debt
> naturalization act
> Barbary pirates
> Louisiana Purchase
> Embargo Act
> excise tax repeal
> modern budget system
> cut in armed-services budget
> Lewis and Clark expedition
> repeal of Judiciary Act of 1801
> urging conviction of Chase
> barring Federalist appointees from office

- Use appropriate Chapter Review exercises that have not been introduced earlier. Items 1 and 5 in *Meeting Our Earlier Selves* are particularly useful for making connections between the several chapter sections.

- Skills session: In your school or community library or media center find an evaluation of Jefferson that mostly praises him and another that is mostly critical. List the facts that are used by the authors to support their over-all judgment. What criteria would you use to evaluate the authors themselves?

CHAPTER REVIEW

Meeting Our Earlier Selves

1. Promises made before an election may seem unwise once a President takes office. Some Presidents may not have enough legislative support (e.g., Carter's unsuccessful gas-rationing plan in 1979). Unanticipated problems may arise. Presidents may be constrained by policies of their predecessors.

Jefferson shifted his views concerning strict interpretation of the Constitution when he seized the opportunity to purchase the Louisiana Territory. Also, after opposing the patronage implicit in Adam's "midnight judges," Jefferson created his own patronage. Also the Bank of the United States was allowed to continue.

2. With American control on the east side of the Mississippi River, and French control on the west side, conflicts over trade and customs rights would have brought tensions possibly unresolvable except through war. Trade to the north with England was more a matter of exchange of goods than of competition for markets. Also, as Canada has learned to this day, the problem of two languages creates misunderstanding and disharmony in relationships.

3. In leaving Washington without welcoming Jefferson, Adams was petty, and hurt the national interest as well as his party. Burr was self-serving in switching to the Federalist party to seek the governorship of New York. His killing of Hamilton in a duel was personally vindictive and a great loss to the country. Burr's ambition overruled his loyalty in whatever he planned in the "conspiracy" in the West. Jefferson may have been personal in his motives in seeking the impeachment of Justice Samuel Chase.

Jefferson knew the personal and party risks in ordering the purchase of the Louisiana Territory. Hamilton put national interest ahead of that of party when he supported Jefferson over Burr and later campaigned to defeat Burr in New York.

4. (a) Probably not, although the timing of the principle of judicial review (1803) and the national prestige of Marshall were important. Had this decision come later, the role of the Supreme Court might have been less strong thereafter.

(b) Jurists believe that the conviction of Chase would have weakened and might possibly have destroyed the independence of the courts.

5. Professor Thomas Bailey, in his *Presidential Greatness* (1966), says that Jefferson "could more easily rank among the five greatest Americans of all time than among the five greatest Presidents." It is difficult, for example, to disassociate the President from the author of the Declaration of Independence. Jefferson's achievements, in suggested order of importance, include "The Revolution of 1800"—his leadership as the spokesman for democracy as opposed to control by the Federalists as the party of economic privilege; the acquisition of the Louisiana Territory; and his standing up to the Barbary pirates, giving the nation a respectable image on the international scene.

Jefferson's failures and mistakes include the unsuccessful Embargo Act, his economizing in national defense needs so that Great Britain had no fear in provoking us into the War of 1812, and his failure to encourage the development of American industry and manufacturing during his two terms.

Questions for Today

1. Look in text chapters dealing with contemporary events. Keep a file of significant cases for use in handling this exercise from year to year.

2. (a) Five months in 1973–1974 as opposed to about 15 months (1808 to March 1809). (b) No export of oil to the United States from Arab nations. No merchandise exports from U.S. to France or Britain, and most manufactured goods from England denied U.S. entry. (c) Increasing fuel shortages in U.S.; much higher fuel prices followed the embargo; Arabs not hurt much because any temporary losses were made up by rises in the price of oil. Under Jefferson's embargo, U.S. exports dropped from $108 million in 1807 to $22 million in 1808. Imports also dropped sharply. Much unemployment and discontent.

Conclusions: the embargo was ineffective in Jefferson's time because nations could "make do" with substitutes. In the present day, an embargo is not likely to be effective unless it involves some commodity vital to the welfare of the "enemy" and not obtainable in sufficient quantity elsewhere and unless it hurts the "enemy" more than the nation applying the embargo. Then even powerful nations such as the United States can be intimidated in international relations.

Your Region in History

2. Coastal manufacturing and seafaring states, particularly in New England, were hurt most by the embargo. Other states were affected to the extent that they normally sold surplus crops abroad and received needed goods in return. The interior states, more agrarian and self-sufficient, were hurt much less.

Skills to Make Our Past Vivid

1. Dayton—Miami River; Indianapolis—White River; Nashville—Cumberland River; Greenwood—Tallahaga River.

CHAPTER 8

Struggles of a Young Nation

Introducing the Chapter The paradox of sectionalism within a larger framework of patriotism and nationalism becomes quite evident in this chapter. You might clarify the definitions of these terms with your students. They will see the emergence of the provincial, boastful American who feels confident that he can win every battle and will never lose a war. You might ask about the changes that have entered into our national thinking as a result of modern wars, particularly the conflict in Vietnam.

Section 1 (pp. 159–168)
The War of 1812

Instructional Objectives Students will be able to

1. Explain several "causes" of the War of 1812.
2. Point out distinctive features of the war.
3. Trace the leading events of the war.
4. Show why New England Federalists opposed the war.

Teaching Suggestions Ten chief engagements of the war appear in chronological order on the map on page 165. After students have read the entire lesson, give each student a number from 0 to 11 and tell the students with numbers 1 to 11 to find their number on the map and to review quickly what the text says about their particular "battle." Students assigned 0 should report on the Battle of Tippecanoe; those assigned 11 can report on the war at sea. After five minutes or so, go through the engagements in order. Have the student(s) assigned a number tell what happened and the significance of their "battle."

• Following are several techniques for teaching the causes of the war.

— On the chalkboard write "The United States went to war with Great Britain in 1812 because:" As students supply reasons based on their reading of the text, write several completions to the opening statement. Follow this with a brief lecture that supplies other factors and/or interpretations.

— A day or two in advance, pick two or four students to simulate a congressional debate on the resolution declaring war on Great Britain. The affirmative debater or team should, of course, give a reasoned listing of grievances and war aims. The negative side should point to exaggerations in the complaints, predict fearful outcomes, and suggest other ways of handling the grievances. The other students should come to class with lists of reasons for and against the war based on their reading of the text. Urge the debaters to use additional resources (textbooks and special works) to prepare their presentations.

— Divide the class into four groups representing the following people in 1812: (a) frontier farmers, (b) New England manufacturers, (c) sailors in our merchant fleet, and (d) Pennsylvania Quakers. Ask each group to prepare a five-minute speech (or write an editorial) on the topic, "Should We Go to War with Great Britain?"

• *Handout lesson:* Have students read *Handout 12*, following the directions closely. After students have read Madison's message, have them answer the questions that follow, and vote for or against the war before they read Randolph's speech. Then have them read Randolph and answer the questions that follow. After the students have finished, use the last question (#4) as the basis for a class discussion on the following questions:

1. Why is it important to understand all sides of an issue before taking a stand?
2. What role does emotion play in influencing our judgment on national issues?
3. Why does the Constitution require a confirming vote in Congress before there can be a declaration of war?

After discussion of the causes, events, and results of the war, have students turn again to the section introduction on page 159. Read aloud, one by one, sentences 2–5, and have students explain each one. Then read sentence 6 and have students speculate about how the nation could emerge from the war "a prouder, stronger, and more unified nation." Afterwards have them read the 3-paragraph introduction to Section 2 for help in dealing with sentence 6.

• Extending the lesson: Offer extra credit for oral or written reports on such topics as: (a) the War Hawks, (b) Tecumseh and the Prophet, (c) the *Constitution*—"Old Ironsides," (d) William Henry Harrison, (e) the burning of Washington, (f) "The Star-Spangled Banner," (g) blacks in the war, (h) Dolley Madison, (i) the early career of Andrew Jackson—to the Battle of New Orleans.

• The film *The War of 1812* (14 min) provides a good summary. Have students evaluate it by pointing out how it added to understandings gained from the text, from student reports, and from class discussion.

• In this section—and in the rest of the chapter—call attention to the illustrations. Have students point out examples of national sentiment.

Section 2 (pp. 169–173)
Madison and Monroe

Instructional Objectives Students will be able to

1. Point out changes noticeable in America after the War of 1812.
2. Explain why the East, the South, and the West either supported or opposed (a) protective tariffs, (b) a national bank, (c) internal improvements.
3. Speculate on whether Monroe's administration deserved to be called an "Era of Good Feelings."
4. Locate boundary adjustments with England and Spain and identify the treaties or agreements involved.
5. Show how decisions of the Supreme Court under John Marshall strengthened the national government.
6. On an outline map show the states that comprised the East, the South, and the West around 1820—and explain the difficulty of applying sectional labels rigidly.

Teaching Suggestions While North-South and East-West sectional differences had emerged earlier in our history, they begin to move onto center stage in this lesson. Students may need some help in understanding the tariff and the national bank as sectional issues whereas the concept of internal improvements—while a new term—is relatively simple.

This section deals with two other major topics. One —territorial expansion and boundary adjustments—requires use of maps. The other—Supreme Court decisions strengthening the national government—may need some teacher input.

• Focus on Madison's annual message of 1815 by challenging students to reduce Madison's seven points to five without omitting anything. (Items 1–3 can simply be labeled "Strengthening national defense.")

You can dismiss the minor point about "assumption of some state debts" by pointing out that these were state militia expenses in the War of 1812. Still, assumption in a small way contributed to the spirit of nationalism by recognizing defense as a national responsibility.

To help students understand southern opposition to the tariff of 1816, remind students of the earlier text discussion of how the ocean tied the southern plantation economy to England (pp. 50–51). Planters did not want to pay higher prices for English and other European imports. Cotton exports were booming, and two-way trade with Europe would help the South. You may want to tell students that Calhoun would soon become a vigorous opponent of the tariff, but at this stage of his career he was an ardent nationalist. He also hoped that tariff protection would stimulate industrialization in South Carolina. Strangely enough, Daniel Webster—among other New Englanders—opposed the tariff of 1816, because commerce rather than manufacturing was seen as that region's primary interest. Soon Webster—and New England—would be strongly in favor of protective tariffs. The tariff was less an issue in the West, where people's livelihood depended less on trade than in the other sections.

You might point out that one reason for lively western interest in the bank issue was that the rise of state banks made it easier to buy and sell land.

• The first skills exercise in the Chapter Review can be used with this lesson. A list of states with their admission dates appears in the Appendix of the text. Where did "the West" begin? A reasonable boundary is the eastern borders of Ohio, Kentucky, Tennessee, and Alabama. One way to solve the dilemma of how to classify Alabama, Mississippi, and Louisiana is to show them in alternate stripes of the colors for South and West. Remind students (a) that Virginia included West Virginia and (b) that the sections had no rigid boundaries. For example, western Pennsylvanians may have thought of themselves more as "westerners" than "northerners."

• The map on text page 249 can be used with the topics "Adjustments with Great Britain" and "Spain Cedes Florida" on page 172.

• To understand how the Supreme Court under John Marshall contributed to the rise of nationalism, students must see how the five cases cited on pages 172–173 blocked state power in one way or another.

As the text points out, *Martin* v. *Hunter's Lessee* and *Cohens* v. *Virginia* clearly established the right of the United States Supreme Court to review decisions of the state courts when a state court was ruling on a matter arising under the federal Constitution. If the Constitution and federal laws and treaties were to be supreme, they could not be left to the whim of state judges. You might point out that the *Martin* case involved the peace treaty of 1783. In that treaty the United States guaranteed that a state would not interfere with the collection of debts owed to British creditors. A state court had interfered with that right, but the United States Supreme Court did not permit that action to stand. *Cohens* v. *Virginia* is a complicated case involving a lawsuit over property rights.

In the *Dartmouth College* case the Supreme Court served as the protector of contracts against action of a state legislature. The Court asserted its right to set aside state laws if they were contrary to the Constitution.

McCulloch v. *Maryland* is important for two reasons: (a) It protected a federal agency from state interference. (b) It served to expand the powers of Congress by giving the "implied powers" clause a broad construction. You might point out that James McCulloch was cashier of the Baltimore branch of the Bank of the United States. He ignored the Maryland tax on the bank's notes. Maryland sued, and the state courts upheld the tax. But McCulloch then appealed to the United States Supreme Court. Five other states had enacted taxes to drive out the Bank, but the Maryland case served to nullify their efforts as well.

Gibbons v. *Ogden* is important, of course, for clearly establishing the power of Congress to regulate interstate commerce without state interference.

- Items 1 and 2 in *Meeting Our Earlier Selves* (p. 180) can be used with this chapter section.

- Madison performed other roles with great distinction, but historians rank him as only an "average" President. Have students recall other great achievements of Madison. What personal qualities made him a success in certain roles but not others? A student report on Madison would be useful at this point.

Section 3 (pp. 174–176)
The Missouri Compromise

Instructional Objectives Students will be able to

1. Show how the invention of the cotton gin promoted the continuance of slavery in the South.

2. Explain the Missouri Compromise as a temporary solution to the issue of the balance between slave and free states.

Teaching Suggestions You may wish to combine this short reading assignment with the next one on the Monroe Doctrine.

- Have an individual or a committee prepare a report on the life of Eli Whitney, with emphasis on what the invention of the cotton gin meant to the South. The report should include a response to the contention that since the cotton gin added greatly to the profits of cotton culture—thus making slaves indispensable—the invention of the cotton gin made the Civil War inevitable. Helpful will be such books as Green's *Eli Whitney and the Birth of American Technology* and Mirsky and Nevins' *The World of Eli Whitney*, along with encyclopedic references available in the school library or media center.

After the report is given, show *Eli Whitney Invents the Cotton Gin* (27 min). Evaluate the film by asking what it added to the report and the text.

- Have students turn to the map of the Missouri Compromise on page 174 and name the eleven free and the eleven slave states. Then discuss the following:

1. Why did Missouri become a focal point in the slavery issue at this time?

2. How did southerners link the slavery question to the depression of 1819?

3. Why was the Missouri Compromise more of a truce than a compromise?

4. Why do you suppose that Jefferson and John Quincy Adams were alarmed with the Missouri Compromise?

- Item 4 in *Meeting Our Earlier Selves* (p. 180) can be used with this lesson.

Section 4 (pp. 176–177)
The Monroe Doctrine

Instructional Objectives Students will be able to

1. State four ideas that comprise the Monroe Doctrine.

2. Show how the effectiveness of the Monroe Doctrine depended on British foreign policy.

3. Discuss the significance of the Monroe Doctrine in the present day.

Teaching Suggestions Some additional background on the situation in Europe and on the independence movement in Latin America would be useful. If some of your students have taken the world history course, invite them to supply some background details.

- Students might be asked to rephrase the four points in the Monroe Doctrine, pretending that Monroe is talking face to face with the European rulers and making "You shall" and "We shall" statements. For example, "You shall make no further attempt to establish or reestablish colonies in the Western Hemisphere." "We shall regard it as an unfriendly act if you try to set up any monarchy in the Western Hemisphere." Etc.

- Following are additional questions to clarify and extend understanding of the Monroe Doctrine:

1. How might European interference in Latin America hurt our national security?

2. Why would Great Britain want to keep other European nations out of the Western Hemisphere? (threat to its Caribbean holdings and to Canada)

3. Speculate on the advantages and risks of rejecting the option of having a joint U.S.-British proclamation.

4. Has any European power in recent years tried to extend its influence and/or system to Latin America? (the Soviet Union in Cuba—and perhaps elsewhere)

5. Has the United States kept a "hands off" position in regard to Europe? (obviously not, since we are in NATO and have troops in Europe)

6. Since 1933 we have preferred to call the Monroe Doctrine a "Pan-American Doctrine," meaning that Western Hemisphere defense is a joint responsibility of the American nations. What is the advantage of this change of emphasis? (Latin Americans tend to resent the "big brother" image of the United States.)

- Remind students that the Monroe Doctrine will come up again in their American history course.

- Using the map on page 177, have students point out changes in the political boundaries in the Western Hemisphere since 1823.

Section 5 (pp. 178–180)
A National Spirit

Instructional Objectives   Students will be able to

1. Prove that a national spirit flourished in the 1820s by citing appropriate evidence.
2. Show how our public education system contributed to the national spirit even though it was state controlled.

Teaching Suggestions   If your students are studying American literature this year, be sure to have them point out how American writers influenced, and were influenced by, the rising spirit of nationalism in this period. Perhaps some joint activity with the English Department can be worked out.

- Select details from this section and have students tell how each provides evidence that a national spirit was alive in the years after the War of 1812. For example: (a) Lafayette's visit / welcomed as a hero throughout the land; (b) adding new stars to flag / each new state would feel that it was part of the Union; (c) bald eagle symbol / used throughout the land; (d) Constitution / became revered symbol for whole nation; (e) slogans and heroes / glorified the nation rather than a particular section; etc.

- Students who have attended school in some other state —particularly since the 7th grade—might try to think of differences between the two states, such as curriculum, compulsory age, etc. Also share your own observations about differences. Then ask students to consider areas where national uniformity in education would be desirable. Finally, share with students your knowledge of forces that contribute to a great deal of similarity in public education from state to state: U.S. Department of Education regulations on spending federal aid; use of textbooks, audiovisual aids, and other learning materials published for the national market; national professional education organizations of many kinds; regional accrediting associations, which consult with similar groups elsewhere; common requirements for college admittance; etc.

CHAPTER REVIEW

Meeting Our Earlier Selves

1. War of 1812 sparked nationalism by uniting people from all sections against a common enemy; by producing national heroes, slogans, and a poem that would become the national anthem. But the war also fanned sectionalism in the North, chiefly because the British blockade hurt trade.

The Hartford Convention was the culmination of the sectional feeling in New England against the War of 1812.

The Tariff of 1816 promoted sectionalism in that it seemed to favor the North over the South.

The second Bank of the U.S. promoted nationalism—for a while at least—by providing a national currency.

Supreme Court decisions under Marshall promoted nationalism by increasing the powers of the federal government versus the states.

2. 1817—Rush-Bagot Agreement on unfortified borders with Canada; 1818—agreement with Great Britain on our northern boundaries and joint occupation of Oregon; 1819—Adams-Onís Treaty with Spain. Our border disputes and the fortification issue with Britain were easy to compromise or were in the interests of both parties. The Florida issue found Spain in no position to wage war, the area would have been difficult to govern, and the U.S. was willing to buy rather than fight. In each case, then, one side or both decided that the rewards were too small to fight over.

3. Madison: (a) what to do about the embargo / decided to lift it against France but enforce it against Britain. (b) whether to ask for declaration of war on Britain / decided to ask for war. (c) whether to sign the Bonus bill / decided to veto it.

Monroe: (a) whether to support or disavow and apologize for Jackson's aggressive acts in Florida / decided to support Jackson and send Spain an ultimatum. (b) whether to support a hands-off doctrine for Latin America alone or by a joint declaration with Great Britain / decided to make it an American doctrine.

4. The moral position would make it very difficult to vote for the Missouri Compromise. Only if an equally or more compelling moral issue were involved in "saving the Union through compromise" could a congressman compromise his moral position on slavery. In 1820 it would have been hard to find such a competing moral issue.

5. National symbols and slogans inspire national feelings. We may not all stand in respect when "Dixie" is played, but we do for "The Star-Spangled Banner." Among important national symbols are the flag, the national anthem, certain other national patriotic songs, the bald eagle, and various slogans mentioned in the text.

Questions for Today

1. Sectional issues included slavery, the tariff, internal improvements, the Bank of the United States, the Indian danger, and others. None of these is really an issue at all today except perhaps the tariff, and it has no special sectional overtones. Almost every part of the nation is now both industrial and agricultural. There is wide recognition throughout the country today that we cannot rely much on tariff protection if we want to trade with other countries. Federal aid for internal improvements is taken for granted today, and all sections share in it. The other matters —slavery, the national bank, defense against Indians— are no longer political issues.

Identifying regional political conflicts today is difficult. Most regions have a mix of economic enterprises. Nevertheless, the heavily populated urban, industrialized Northeast (including the Great Lakes states) will tend to vote differently from the predominantly agricultural states on aid to cities, farm price supports, and a few other issues. Regions where unions are strong vote differently from those where unions are weaker. In general, however, Americans divide on political issues not so much on the basis of where they live as on how they make a living, educational level, religious beliefs (abortion, for example), age level, etc.

2. "Flag waving," use of patriotic slogans, hero worship —these seem less pronounced than in the past. Often the playing of the national anthem and reciting the pledge of allegiance seem to be done by rote rather than with real feeling. Feelings of nationalism are noticeably aroused in our day in international sports competition, by insults of foreigners (hostage taking in Iran, anti-American demonstrations), and to some extent in national election campaigns.

Students might speculate on whether nationalism is diluted in our day by special attachment to racial and ethnic groups.

3. The Tecumseh strategy was to form a confederation —with a single objective of blocking further advance of whites into Indian territory. Today we have some national Indian organizations and local groups of tribes organized to achieve particular objectives. In legal battles to obtain compensation for broken treaties much of the effort is by individual tribes. United Indian action is an appropriate research topic.

4. The two generals are Andrew Jackson and William Henry Harrison. Since World War II, Eisenhower is the outstanding example. J.F. Kennedy's war heroism (p. 644) helped form his attractive political image. A good military record is usually an influential factor for candidates seeking public office.

Skills to Make Our Past Vivid

1. See an activity suggested for Section 2 for help on this exercise.

CHAPTER 9

The Jacksonian Era

Introducing the Chapter The chapter introduction sets the tone. You might read it aloud—or have a good student reader do so. Then ask students to recall two earlier encounters with Andrew Jackson in the text (War of 1812 and the East Florida campaign). Have students speculate about how Jackson would differ from the previous Presidents.

You may also want to point out that Section 2 departs from the sequence of presidential administrations to discuss the development of popular participation in government— through public elections—from late colonial times to about the middle of the 19th century.

Section 1 (pp. 181–184)

A Second Adams in the White House

Instructional Objectives Students will be able to

1. Show how the presidential candidates of 1824 reflected sectional interests.

2. Identify the "Corrupt Bargain" and point out its significance.

3. Evaluate the Presidency of John Quincy Adams.

Teaching Suggestions This section sets the stage for the coming of Andrew Jackson. Adams can be portrayed as the last of the Presidents who could remain aloof from the people. Tell students that again an election for President will be decided in the House of Representatives. Ask them to recall the earlier occasion (Chapter 6, Section 4).

• In discussing the election of 1824, you might begin by having students recall why there was no opposition party to the Republicans. Then have students speculate why such a situation would result in having a half dozen or so presidential candidates.

Students may need some help in understanding the congressional caucus system for nominating candidates.

To focus on the candidates in 1824, you might list their names on the board in a vertical column. In a second column write the state of origin of each as students supply the information. For a third and fourth column students can supply phrases that tell about the advantages and disadvantages of each candidate. Then provide a fifth column for the electoral vote received by each candidate.

When the chart is completed, use questions like the following for discussion:

1. Why did the caucus system break down?

2. How did the bitterness of the campaign reflect sectional interests?

3. Could Calhoun's tactic of switching from the presidential race to seek the Vice-Presidency be repeated in a modern election? Explain. (Today, candidates for President and Vice-President run as a team, and national conventions choose the candidate for Vice-President who is endorsed by the party's candidate for President.)

4. The text speaks of "grave disadvantages to not being a popularly elected President." What are these?

5. Why did Jackson attack Clay as "the Judas of the West"?

6. Do you consider Clay's bargain with Adams to be "corrupt"? Explain.

• Use the first item in the Chapter Review (p. 201) to probe understanding of the text topic "A national program." Discussion might lead to consideration of the dilemma facing a President who "knows" what the country needs but lacks popular support for his proposals.

• If you have not done so earlier, you might explain the nature of a 19th century tariff act to help students better understand the Tariff of Abominations. The law might permit some kinds of merchandise to be imported free of duty (the free list). All other imports would be taxed, but each kind of item would have its own rate. For example, if tea were taxed at 10%, a merchant importing tea would have to pay $10 tariff for each $100 worth of tea. If the tariff on wine was 30%, a wine merchant would pay $30 for each $100 worth of wine imported. Consumers of tea and wine would pay more for these products than if they were on the free list. In each of these two cases the purpose of the tax is to raise revenue for the federal government.

But a tariff law may put some very high rates on certain items not to raise revenue but to discourage their entering the country and competing with the same products grown or manufactured here. This is the protective feature of a tariff. (Make it clear that most tariff laws have both revenue and protective features.) For example, woolen goods might be taxed at 60% to protect domestic woolen manufacturers. Consumers who wanted fine English woolens would thus have to pay heavily for them.

Now you can explain that in the tariff of 1828 (the Tariff of Abominations) Congress tinkered with the rates—not generally for sensible economic reasons but for political ones.

• Have a student report on the life and contributions of John Quincy Adams, with emphasis upon his Presidency. Bemis's *John Quincy Adams and the Union* or the *Dictionary of American Biography* will provide background. After the report, discuss (a) whether he was helped or hindered in being the son of a President; (b) whether a candidate with his personality could be elected to the Presidency today; (c) his motives in appointing Clay to be his Secretary of State; (d) an evaluation of his rank among the Presidents (considered "average"); (e) why he had more failures than successes despite his proven abilities as Secretary of State under Monroe; (f) his motives in returning to Washington after his term ended as President to serve for sixteen years in the House of Representatives. (If it is not mentioned in the report, you might tell the students that Adams "died with his boots on." In 1848, at age 80, he collapsed at his desk and died in the Speaker's office.)

• On a wall outline map or on desk outline maps, have students locate the states that supported Jackson and those won by Adams in 1828. Discuss (a) the reasons for Adams's defeat in seeking reelection; (b) the changes in America that brought a "westerner" into the Presidency for the first time.

Section 2 (pp. 184–188)
The New Politics

Instructional Objectives   Students will be able to

1. Explain changes in the electoral system between 1800 and 1830 with respect to (a) voter qualifications, (b) the voting process, and (c) nominations.

2. Describe the new-type politician, using Jackson as an example.

3. Discuss the origins, advantages, and disadvantages of the spoils system.

Teaching Suggestions   This section provides perspective on the evolution of our system of voting. It also gives graphic examples of frontier-type behavior that became particularly American. You might ask your students if these influences can still be observed today.

• *Handout lesson:* Give students *Handout 13*. Have them read the description of Jackson's inauguration and then answer the questions that follow.

• Ask students to imagine that the next state/national elections will be held under rules and procedures that prevailed in the mid-1820s. Elicit from students statements that describe how the election will differ from what they are accustomed to. As students respond, write their statements on the board. Following are some possible responses:

1. Women will not show up to vote.

2. Black persons will not vote.

3. No voters under age 21.

4. No voting machines.

5. Different colored ballots for different parties.

6. Candidates chosen in conventions, not by direct primaries.

7. No distance limit on campaigning at polling place.

8. Few or no limits on vote watchers.

9. All male election officials.

10. No female candidates.

Tell students that Andrew Jackson's wife, Rachel, died of a heart attack shortly after the election of 1828. Believing that slander killed her, the President-elect in turn killed Charles Dickinson in a duel related to slander. Ask a student to report upon the happiness and the tragedy of Jackson's marriage to Rachel Donelson. Stone's novel *The President's Lady* gives many of the details.

• Divide the class into two groups. Have one use the text to find the *advantages* of the spoils system, applicable both in Jackson's and the present day. Ask the other group to list the *disadvantages* of the spoils system. Use the chalkboard to compare lists. Then discuss the following:

1. In the late 1970s nearly 21 million persons were on the government payroll in local, county, state, and national employment. Which kinds of jobs, if any, should be filled as patronage?

2. In 1883 the first Civil Service Act was passed, leading to merit system examinations as a requirement for federal government employment. Is this system still desirable today? Why?

3. To what extent are government jobs in your state and locality filled by the merit system?

4. To what degree should government employees be protected in their jobs by seniority and tenure? (You may first have to explain these terms to your students.)

5. Should special consideration be given to minorities or other particular groups, or quotas be established, in filling government jobs?

6. Under what circumstances should government employees be dismissed? What rights should they have in the dismissal process?

7. Are there any non-elective posts—aside from judges—that should be appointive and remain so (the President's Cabinet, e.g.)?

Section 3 (pp. 189–196)
Jackson Takes Command

Instructional Objectives Students will be able to

1. Describe the social attitudes of the Jackson era as indicated by the Eaton affair.

2. Explain the motives of the southern states, and Vice-President Calhoun in particular, in advocating the doctrine of "nullification."

3. State the principal arguments in the Webster-Hayne debate on state rights.

4. Cite the Indian wars and treaties as examples of our national policies towards the Indians during the Jacksonian period.

5. Tell how Jackson handled the threat of nullification.

Teaching Suggestions In this section, students may show greatest interest in the dramatic personal relationship topics—Jackson's dueling, the Eaton affair, the Jackson-Calhoun toast confrontation. Relate these to the bigger topics by asking the students how personal relationships sometimes affect major public decisions. For example, if the Eaton affair halted Calhoun's march to the Presidency, did this setback embitter him enough that thereafter he spoke more strongly for nullification at the expense of his loyalty to the Union? You might also compare the impact of oratory in Jackson's day with the present as students learn about Daniel Webster.

• *Competency exercise—writing a paragraph:* Have students write a paragraph on the Peggy Eaton affair. Suggest an appropriate topic sentence like the following: "Soon after Andrew Jackson became President, a minor problem arose that upset his administration." After students have finished, have them exchange papers to check facts, spelling, and grammar.

• Have a student in the role of a northern manufacturer state the case for a protective tariff in the 1830s. Have another student in the role of a cotton planter give the southerners' rebuttal.

• Re-create the scene in the Senate in 1830 of the Webster-Hayne debate. Have students look at the reproduction of Healy's famous painting of Webster's reply to Hayne on page 192. Tell them that Webster's speech was hours long and filled 73 printed pages. Ask one of your better students to read the closing paragraphs of Webster's oration to the class. (See Butterfield's *The American Past,* Chapter 3.) After the reading, and with the text as a guide, discuss (a) the key point made by Webster; (b) the principal arguments of both Hayne and Webster; (c) the importance of oratory in Webster's day; and (d) why oratory has less of an impact in the present day.

• Have students role-play the Jefferson Day toasts of Jackson and Calhoun. Then discuss the following:

1. What were the issues involved?

2. Why was Calhoun so upset by Jackson's toast?

3. What was the effect of Jackson's toast on the country?

4. Why did Jackson have such a dislike for Calhoun? (You might tell the students that many years later Jackson was asked if he had any regrets in his life. He admitted to two: that he had been unable to shoot Henry Clay or to hang John C. Calhoun.)

• Write these headings on the chalkboard:

JACKSON'S INDIAN POLICY

Policy towards   Action   Indian reaction

Under *Policy,* list the following: Indians in general, Black Hawk's tribes, Seminoles, Cherokees. Using the text as a guide, have the students complete the chart in the appropriate columns. After they have finished, discuss:

1. How would Jackson have justified his policy towards the Indians?
2. From today's viewpoint, what would be the public reaction to Jackson's treatment of the Indians?
3. What policy alternatives did Jackson have?
4. Do you agree with Marshall or Jackson in the *Worcester v. Georgia* case? Defend your answer.

If your school is in a state that experienced Indian relocation in the 1830s, solicit oral or written reports on the treaties, tribes, and leaders involved. Pearson's *The Indian in American History* will provide an overview, and local sources the details.

• Tell the class that the best known of the "black conspiracies" against slavery was that of Nat Turner and his followers in Virginia in 1831. Ironically, Turner helped perpetuate the memory of the rebellion. A semi-educated preacher-reformer, he was induced—while in irons—to write a "confession" before he was hanged. Ask a student to prepare a report on Nat Turner based upon Styron's *The Confessions of Nat Turner* (1967). After the report, discuss the following:

1. One historian speaks of Turner's rebellion as producing only "senseless slaughter" of blacks and whites. Do you agree? Why?
2. Considering the fact that there were nearly three million slaves by 1850, why were there relatively few slave revolts?
3. What was the impact of the Turner rebellion on the South?

• Discussion of the South Carolina nullification convention and its aftermath offers another chance to discuss the importance of compromise in making and altering public policy. Perhaps students can identify some current policy issues at the federal, state, or local level. To what extent is compromise possible?

This topic also brings out the importance of symbolic victories and other face-saving techniques in human relations. Was the South Carolina convention's nullification of the "Force Bill" helpful in any way?

Section 4 (pp. 196–200)
Banks and Money

Instructional Objectives Students will be able to

1. State how Jackson destroyed the second Bank of the United States.
2. Link the unwise banking practices of the "pet banks" with the onset of the Panic of 1837.

3. Explain the origin and purpose of the new Whig party
4. Show how economic depression affected the Presidency of Martin Van Buren.
5. Illustrate how and why the election of 1840 was the firs of the modern-type campaigns.

Teaching Suggestions Although Jackson's war with the Bank of the United States can be discussed chiefly to clarify the politics involved, a brief lecture on the money situation in our early history would be useful.

• One way to present the money and banking problems is to make contrasts with today.

You might begin by having students name four kinds of "money" they and their families use to make purchases coins, paper currency, bank checks, and credit cards. (Travelers' checks are a fifth kind.)

By contrast, Americans in 1830 had to depend on (a) gold and silver coins and (b) bank notes. Explain that specie (coin) was scarce. There was not nearly enough to carry on trade even though there was much foreign coin in circulation. So, much business had to be carried on with bank notes. A $100 bank note was a bank's promise to pay the bearer $100 in gold or silver coin.

Then explain that when a person in 1830 borrowed from a bank—say, $1000—the bank would give the borrower the money in bank notes. (Today a bank would ordinarily just add $1000 to the borrower's checking account.)

Our paper currency today consists almost entirely of Federal Reserve notes. These, too, are bank notes, but their issue is carefully regulated by an agency of the federal government, and they are our official paper currency. By contrast, the bank notes of the 1830s circulated with little or no government regulation. And the value of the notes fluctuated wildly from bank to bank, depending on public confidence in the ability of the issuing bank to repay in specie as promised.

The notes of the Bank of the United States circulated at par—their stated value. Thus its notes were more acceptable than those of most state banks. The existence of national bank notes helped to keep the state banks in line. In addition, the Bank of the United States acted as "regulator of the currency" by regularly redeeming state bank notes that it received in day-to-day transactions.

Yet, in spite of the useful services it provided the nation, the Bank of the United States was open to criticism: (a) It tended to drain specie (gold and silver coin) from the South and West to the North. (b) It enjoyed a monopoly of government business. (c) It could and did show favoritism in the granting of loans. And (d) it did meddle in politics.

• Encourage students to read one of the many interesting biographies on the life of Jackson. See the reading list for this unit. Give extra credit for oral or written reports. Tell students that Nashville, Tennessee, is famous for more than its music. Jackson's home, *The Hermitage,* is open to the public. One of the most beautiful national shrines in the country, it is furnished with original pieces.

- Show the film *Age of Jackson* (29 min) after the students have heard a report on Jackson's life and Presidency. Ask the students what the film has contributed to their understanding and knowledge of Jackson. Then evaluate his place in American history. (Historians rank him at the top of the "near great.") Discuss the following:

1. What were Jackson's greatest achievements? failures?

2. The text speaks of Jackson's "strong prejudices." What examples of these may be found in the text? Should a President have these? Why?

3. Jackson's enemies called him "King Andrew." What is the difference between strong leadership and being dictatorial?

4. Before he was elected to the Presidency, Woodrow Wilson said that "Americans of the present day shudder at the recollection of Jackson." Would that statement be true today? How popular would a candidate like Jackson be today?

5. Despite some of the present-day criticism of Jackson, the evidence indicates that he left the White House more popular than when he entered. How can we account for this?

- Have a student report on the life and Presidency of Martin Van Buren. Curtis's *The Fox at Bay* is a recent biography; the *Dictionary of American Biography* also provides background. Tell students that as Jackson's hand-picked successor, Van Buren is rated "average" among the Presidents by historians. After the report, discuss the following points:

1. Whether a four-year term, such as Van Buren's, is enough to provide a fair evaluation of a President.

2. The source of Van Buren's nickname, "The Red Fox of Kinderhook."

3. Why workers have reason to be grateful to Van Buren.

4. Apparently Van Buren believed that he could do little about the depression that followed the Panic of 1837. From present-day experience and viewpoint, what could he have done?

- Have students draw a timeline for Chapter 9, covering the events of the period from 1824 to 1840.

CHAPTER REVIEW
Meeting Our Earlier Selves

1. Students should cite sentences and phrases from the topic "A national program," such as: "Adams would not retreat." "He preferred ideals and principles to the compromises of political parties." ". . . did not mend his political fences . . . ignored his followers . . ."

2. Factors included the rising political strength of the West, where aristocrats had no foothold; the decline of property requirements for voting; and the rise of party nominating conventions.

3. Jackson was strongly prejudiced against aristocrats and aristocratic behavior that could be interpreted as insulting. These feelings led him to fight a duel in 1806 and later to meet with a "Kitchen Cabinet" instead of his regular Cabinet. These feelings also soured his relationships with Calhoun.

Jackson's anti-Indian prejudices contributed to his Indian-removal policy. His money-and-banking prejudices led him to reject the rechartering of the Bank of the United States, to deposit federal funds in state banks, and to issue the Specie Circular. His pro-common-man feelings lent support to the spoils system.

4a. Settlement of the West spurred the decline of property qualifications for voting. (Everyone was a property owner, so why make it a voting qualification.) **(b)** The Webster-Hayne debate was directly concerned with the opening of public land in the West. **(c)** Indian removal was designed to open the trans-Appalachian land to unrestricted white settlement. **(d)** The Bank was a restraining force on western land speculation.

Questions for Today

1. See the listing of voting practices on Guide page 52. Most students, of course, will regard the changes as improvements because they promote democratic participation and fairness.

2. Jackson is quoted on text page 188. He believed general intelligence was qualification enough. Today many appointive offices call for specialized training (in accounting, law, public administration) and often practical experience (in management, for example). In addition, appointive (and elective officials) ought to have broad general education to provide perspective and to sharpen communication skills.

3. The booming voice, the use of classical and biblical allusions, the histrionics, and the long speeches that are associated with old-fashioned oratory seem out of place today. Radio and TV have accustomed people to a more conversational style of communication.

Skills to Make Our Past Vivid

1. Jackson: popular vote, 56%; electoral vote, 68%. Adams: popular vote, 44%; electoral vote, 32%. The electoral majority is larger because of the winner-take-all rule in the electoral college system.

2. Some of the rise in voter participation can be explained by the repeal of property qualifications, although most states had taken that legal step before 1824. But it often takes a while for newly enfranchised voters to exercise their voting rights. Probably between 1824 and 1828 some new voters got used to the idea of being part of the electorate. The rise of paper ballots and the spread of party conventions may also have stimulated voter participation.

CHAPTER 10

The Flourishing Land

Introducing the Chapter All five sections of this chapter are distinctive in themselves and can be so treated. Yet all are interrelated. The development of canals, steamboats, roads, and railroads provided access to the growing markets for the output of the Industrial Revolution. Immigrants were needed to supply labor for the factories and settlers for the open lands. The impact of transportation improvements and technology upon the growth of the cotton kingdom can be linked to the ominous shadow of the dispute over slavery.

Section 1 (pp. 204–212)
Drawing the People Together

Instructional Objectives Students will be able to

1. Locate on the map the first turnpikes and national roads, and discuss their impact on American expansion.
2. Point out the location and significance of the Erie Canal.
3. Describe the importance of the steamboat in the development of American commerce.
4. Identify peculiarly American features of railroad building and explain how railroads united East and West.
5. Describe the contributions of Morse and Fields in communication.

Teaching Suggestions If your locality was settled before the Civil War, consider emphasizing a nearby aspect of the transportation revolution. Are there remnants of old turnpikes or canals near your community? Is there a river that once thrived with riverboat commerce? If a railroad goes through town, what is its history? Are there any abandoned spur lines? Special reports can be shared with the class.

• Have students compare the map on page 205 with the one on page 115 to get a generalized picture of road building in the 60 years to 1850. Tell students that some roads were called "turnpikes" because toll roads in the Middle Ages had barriers called "turnepikes." The following questions might be used in discussing the topic of roads and turnpikes:

1. Where did the National Road cross the Appalachians? (Cumberland Gap) Why? (one of the easiest ways across the mountains)
2. How do you think roads were surfaced? (dirt until after War of 1812; then gravel and macadam)
3. Why were tolls high? (costs up to $13,000 per mile to clear forests and/or to resurface local roads)
4. What are the advantages and disadvantages of financing modern superhighways by means of tolls?
5. How are most highways in our Interstate System (map, p. 630) financed? Is this a fair financing system?
6. How might a good highway system benefit you even if you were unable to travel by automobile?

• Dramatize the length of the Erie Canal (363 miles) by writing BUFFALO on the chalkboard. With a noticeable drop in pitch, draw a line nearly 73 inches long to a point labeled ALBANY, representing a scale of five miles to the inch. Then select a familiar place about 360 miles from your school so that students can visualize the distance.

Have students locate the Erie Canal on the map on page 207—along with Albany, Buffalo, Cleveland, Toledo, and Chicago. Point out that because of the different altitudes, a drop of 571 feet in the canal was controlled by 82 locks. Ask students to explain the principles involved. Discuss the following:

1. How were barges moved through the canal? (towed by horses or mules walking on a path alongside the canal)
2. Why was the canal a financial success despite low rates (see text) and slow movement (two miles per hour)? (high volume of freight because no suitable alternative)
3. Why did the canals become outmoded? (chiefly because of railroad competition)

Other questions can be generated by showing a film or filmstrip on the canals.

• The topic on steamboats affords an occasion for simple pleasure reading. You can supplement it by reading excerpts from Mark Twain's *Life on the Mississippi*. But remind students that, while some western steamboats were "racers," the majority of steamboats on the western rivers were freight carriers. They played a big role in opening the Mississippi Valley to settlement.

• Have students turn to the map "Railroads 1850–1860" on page 210. Locate the railroad lines as of 1850 and then of 1860. The maps on page 345 show railroad building after the Civil War and the land grants. Discuss:

1. How did the railroads make the canals obsolete?
2. Why was the growth of railroads so phenomenal in the decade of the 1850s?

3. How did methods of building railroads in the United States differ from those in Europe?

4. Why was the middle of the train the safest place for passengers?

• Write CHARACTERISTICS OF AMERICAN RAILROADS on the chalkboard. In a vertical column on the left, have the students complete the items that follow, using the text as a guide: (a) peak building years, (b) miles of track built, (c) financed by, (d) why expensive to build, (e) how different from European railroads, (f) changes brought by growth of railroads.

• *Handout lesson:* Have students read *Handout 14,* Charles Dickens's version of a short American train ride in 1842. After the students finish reading Dickens's report, have them answer the questions at the end of the handout.

• Extending the lesson: Subjects for oral or written reports include (a) steamboat inventors, (b) early steamboat rivalry, (c) a particular pre-Civil War canal or railroad, (d) Morse's telegraph network, (e) laying the Atlantic cable, (f) earliest U.S. postage stamps.

Section 2 (pp. 214–218)
The Industrial Revolution

Instructional Objectives Students will be able to

1. Define "Industrial Revolution" and describe its impact on the United States.

2. Explain the Lowell labor system and its provision of employment for women.

3. Tell how Eli Whitney introduced mass production to the United States.

Teaching Suggestions Although the United States is indebted to England for the origins of the Industrial Revolution, this section illustrates how quickly we developed characteristics all our own. You might emphasize these, including the specialization of labor in mass production. Again, the inventor Eli Whitney plays an important role, but there are others. You might ask if we are a nation of mechanics, and what factors explain our inventiveness. Some controversial matters can be examined too, such as the exploitation of the labor of women and children.

• Present, or have a student report, additional details on Samuel Slater. Discuss whether or not Slater was unethical in violating English law in using secret designs for the machinery of American factories. This may lead to a discussion of the definition of business ethics and of the broad question, "What should we do about a bad law?"

• *Handout lesson:* Have students read *Handout 15* about working in a Lowell factory in 1845. Then have them respond to the generalized statements that follow, finding evidence in the testimony or in the text that agrees or disagrees with the statements in the handout. Discuss these, so that all students have learned how to locate the relevant statements. (1,2,4,5,6,7, and 10 are *agree;* 3,8, and 9 are *disagree* statements.)

• Encourage students to read and report on some other pre-Civil War manufacturing industry besides textiles and guns. Who were some leaders? What part did invention play? What mass-production techniques were used? Where were the chief industrial sites? How was labor recruited? Etc.

Section 3 (pp. 219–222)
America's Leading Import: People

Instructional Objectives Students will be able to

1. Explain the chief reasons for pre-Civil War immigration.

2. Identify some contributions of the Irish and German immigrants.

3. Show U.S. immigration 1820–1860 on bar and line graphs.

Teaching Suggestions This section takes a particular look at the immigration of the Irish and the Germans from 1820 to 1860. If possible, link population growth in your state/locality to the immigration of this period.

• Constructing a bar graph: Have students draw a graph outline similar to the one shown below. Then have them

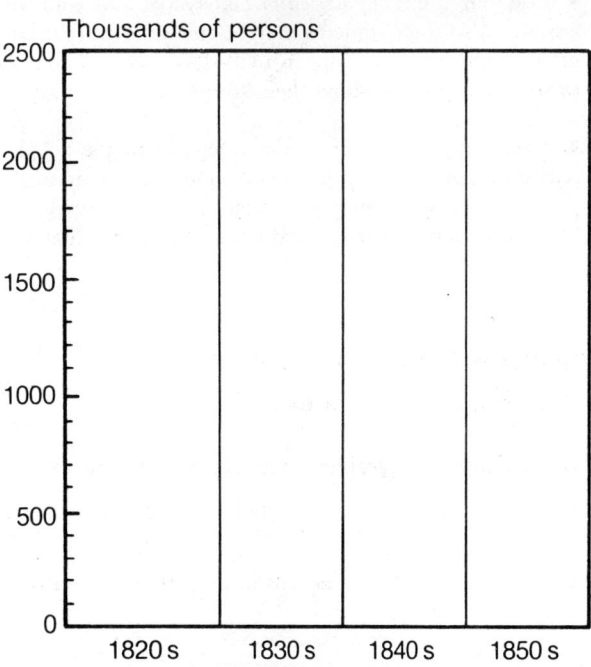

U.S. Immigration, 1820-1860

Chapter 10

complete the bars using the following data: 1820s, 143,439; 1830s, 599,125; 1840s, 1,713,251; 1850s, 2,598,214.

When the graphs are finished, ask questions like these:

1. What factors help account for the rise of immigration in this 40-year span?

2. About how many times did immigration rise each decade over the preceding one? (1830s, four times; 1840s, three times; 1850s, 1 1/2 times)

3. According to the text, where did many of these immigrants settle in the United States?

• *Handout lesson:* Handout 16 provides further practice in graphing while focusing on the countries of origin of the immigrants in 1820–1860. Circulate around the class to offer help, if needed, as students complete the graph. If colored pencils are available, they might be used in place of the suggested symbols.

When students have finished the graph, you might use some class time for comparing this graph with the one on total immigration suggested above. Students might compute the percent of total immigration accounted for by Great Britain, Ireland, and Germany in each of these four decades.

• Divide the class into four groups. Have one group write letters to relatives in Ireland giving reasons for coming to America. Ask another group to write from Ireland with reasons for leaving the homeland. Similarly, have the other two groups write to and from Germany. After the letters are finished, ask students to exchange letters. Read a few aloud in class. Do they reflect mostly economic, political, or social viewpoints? Encourage students to read such books as Wittke's *The Irish in America* and his *Refugees of Revolution: The German Forty-Eighters in America*.

• Use item 3 in *Your Region in History* (p. 228) with this lesson. Also some students may be able to identify immigrant forebearers who came in 1820–1860. Invite students to share information about their "roots" with the class.

• Extending the lesson: Student reports might be presented on particular immigrants of note who came in the period under study and on special elements of Irish and German culture that influenced life in the United States.

Section 4 (pp. 222–225)
The Rise of the West

Instructional Objectives Students will be able to

1. Describe the activities of settlers as they populated the Midwest.

2. Illustrate how the Americans improved home construction techniques.

Teaching Suggestions Sections 3 and 4 might be combined as a single reading assignment. Section 4 provides further descriptions of "the making of an American." You might secure illustrations of the types of houses and construction that distinguish American and English styles. Life's *American Arts and Skills* will provide illustrations of the balloon frame (p. 112) to show to students. Students in woodshop might display a small 2 × 4 frame and a mortise-and-tenon joint.

• Today's average American moves a number of times during a lifetime. Ask the students to make a comparison of the motives for moving during the first half of the nineteenth century with those of today. What are the similarities? What problems did homeowners face then that are no longer a problem, and vice versa?

• Have the students turn to the map of present-day United States (pp. 752–753) and locate the "instant cities" mentioned on text page 222. Ask them to estimate the population rank of these cities today, based on the apparent desirability of geographic location. Then inform the students of the actual population rank. The 1970 figures: Chicago—3,369,359 (2nd); Detroit—1,514,063 (5th); Cleveland—750,879 (10th); Memphis—623,530 (17th); St. Louis—622,236 (18th); Pittsburgh—520,089 (24th); Buffalo—462,768 (28th); Cincinnati—451,410 (30th); Minneapolis—434,400 (32nd); Louisville—361,706 (38th); Omaha—354,389 (41st); St. Paul—309,866 (46th); Des Moines—201,404 (64th); Davenport—98,469 (160th). Then ask:

1. Why do Chicago, Detroit, Cleveland, Memphis, and St. Louis still rank in the top twenty?

2. What waterways are still important to the above cities?

3. Are highways more important today to the above cities than railroads? Why?

Section 5 (pp. 225–228)
The Cotton Kingdom

Instructional Objectives Students will be able to

1. Compare the northern and southern viewpoints on slavery.

2. Trace the roots of the slaves brought to the United States.

3. Describe the life and treatment of slaves in the South.

4. Indicate the effects of slavery on the South.

Teaching Suggestions Recent interest in the problem of slavery in American literature and particularly in the television media should help motivate student interest in the origins of the problem that brought the North and the South into conflict. This section offers a good opportunity to understand slavery as an institution, especially from the Southern point of view.

• Show the filmstrip series, *Black People in the North, 1850* and *Black People in the South, 1850.* Have students compare life for the blacks during this period in the North with that in the South. Discuss why slavery was economically undesirable in the North and why the South was so dependent upon it.

• Ask for a student report on the experiences of slaves before they reached the United States—how they were obtained in Africa, how they fared aboard ship, etc. Haley's novel *Roots* has some vivid descriptions.

• Suggest that a student give an oral book report on Styron's *The Confessions of Nat Turner,* describing the Virginia rebellion in 1831. Who was Nat Turner, and what motivated him to lead the revolt? What happened after the revolt to the insurgents and to Turner?

• On the chalkboard write this title:

EFFECTS OF SLAVERY

Political   Economic   Social

Then with the text as a guide, have students list the effects in vertical columns under the appropriate category. Discuss these. Ask students to indicate which effects they consider desirable and which undesirable.

CHAPTER REVIEW

Meeting Our Earlier Selves

1. The Erie Canal (a) would lower the cost of shipping wheat from northern Ohio to the East Coast and would tend to raise the price of wheat in Ohio because local surpluses could be marketed more readily; (b) a big increase in potential buyers (travelers and the local populations, since Buffalo grew rapidly when the canal was completed) and lower freight costs on his merchandise; (c) speedier and lower cost travel to Michigan from an East Coast port, probably New York City; (d) rising patronage because of increased travel through Albany.

2. Local roads were public ways built by the states and localities or by landowners with some government aid. The national government provided funds for the building of the National Road. The turnpikes were generally built and operated by private companies but with state governments often buying substantial amounts of shares in a company.

Canals were state enterprises financed by selling state bonds, and several states failed to pay off the bonds.

Railroads were chiefly private undertakings, although a few states actually built the railways. Government aid by states tended to be in the form of land grants (much of it donated by the federal government and then transferred to the railroad companies), direct loans to the companies, and purchase of railroad stock. Cities and counties also made similar contributions. Federal aid was in the form of land grants to the states.

Private companies sought aid from government because the enterprises were highly speculative and, they argued, because benefits would reach the general public, not just the investors.

It can be argued that government aid stimulated the free enterprise system by providing facilities needed for growth of the private sector. The alternative was state ownership and control of most transportation facilities—or pitifully slow economic growth for lack of good transportation.

3. Slater, Lowell, and Whitney are good choices if one depends on the text and focuses on the factory system. Many other persons, however, might be named, including pioneers in the transportation field.

4. See text pages 219–221 for information for comparisons.

5. See the first paragraph on page 226 for ways that white Southerners defended slavery. Abolitionists could be expected to rely heavily on moral, religious, and humanitarian arguments against slavery: (a) All humans are equal in the sight of God. (b) Deprival of freedom is degrading. (c) Sale of humans is offensive and degrading. (d) Split-up of families is morally wrong. Other abolitionist arguments might have focused on the harm to character and personality: dulling of initiative, destruction of feelings of self-worth, etc. Economic arguments might also have been used: slavery retarded industrialization, inhibited the flow of immigrants, tied up large amounts of capital, promoted a static rather than a dynamic economy, etc.

Questions for Today

1. Assembling and erecting the frame, attaching siding, laying subflooring and plank roof—these steps would be similar. Differences would arise in the use of power tools, perhaps vinyl siding, plywood, composition roofing, electrical and plumbing installations—and heavy use of other finished components made in factories.

2. Laotian, Vietnamese, Cuban, and Haitian refugees have fled poverty, war, and political repression.

3. Urge students to be as specific as possible in making comparisons.

Skills to Make Our Past Vivid

1. Have students use the map on page 207 and urge them to find additional cities to put on the map.

2. The poster would omit mention of long hours, hazardous conditions, monotony, poor ventilation, etc.

CHAPTER 11

Reforming and Expanding

Introducing the Chapter Like the previous chapter, this one has no clear-cut starting and closing date. And like the previous chapter, it takes a look at some particular developments in the 30 to 40 years before the outbreak of the Civil War.

Both Chapters 10 and 11 help to set the stage for the critical political developments of the 1850s that led to the Civil War.

Section 1 (pp. 229–235)
An Age of Reform

Instructional Objectives Students will be able to

1. Describe religious trends before the Civil War.

2. Identify characteristics and leaders of pre-Civil War reform movements in education, care of the mentally ill and retarded, and women's rights.

Teaching Suggestions The purpose of this lesson is to indicate the many changes in thought and attitude that marked a period of searching for national improvement and reform. Encourage students to probe into a particular reform that interests them most, including a study of the motives and backgrounds of the individuals who sought the reforms.

• The 1800 to 1860 entries in the "Religion" section of Morris's *Encyclopedia of American History* might be used to supplement the text topic "A religious age." Encourage students to report on particular sects, developments, or religious leaders of the period.

Several modern-day religious groups besides the Unitarians had their origin in this period: the United Brethren in Christ and the Evangelical Church (merged in 1946; then later merged with Methodists); Disciples of Christ; Latter-Day Saints, or Mormons; Adventists and Seventh-Day Adventists (Millerites); and various independent churches organized by blacks, including the African Methodist Episcopal Church. Encourage students who have family ties with any of these groups to trace the early history. Other students might investigate 1800–1860 developments in some older religious body. For example, the Congregational Church was not disestablished until 1818 in Connecticut and 1833 in Massachusetts.

• If your students are studying American literature this semester, perhaps a joint lesson or cooperative activities on Transcendentalism can be arranged with the English Department.

• In discussing Thoreau, you might raise questions like these:

1. Why, do you suppose, Thoreau went to live at Walden Pond?

2. Have you heard of people following his example of solitude in our time? Explain.

3. What uses of tax revenue might Thoreau protest if he lived today?

4. What grounds, according to Thoreau, justified civil disobedience? (major injustice, not personal dislike or inconvenience)

5. What other ways do we have to protest injustice? How do they compare in effectiveness to civil disobedience?

6. How does Thoreau exemplify the Transcendentalist stress on individualism?

• Notice that several of the Chapter Review exercises relate specifically to topics in this chapter section.

• *Handout lesson:* Handout 17 provides a slightly shortened and adapted version of the Seneca Falls Declaration of Women's Rights. You might want to have students compare the language and format with the Declaration of Independence.

Section 2 (pp. 235–237)
The Abolition Movement

Instructional Objectives Students will be able to

1. Trace the development of the abolition movement in the North.

2. Describe the southern antislavery movement and debates, particularly in Virginia.

3. Explain how abolition became an emotional issue leading to violence and the growing separation of North and South.

4. Analyze the role of such leading figures as Weld, Garrison, and Lovejoy on the abolition movement.

5. Define and use specific words related to abolition and slavery.

Teaching Suggestions Help students to see that this lesson continues the previous section's discussion of the pre-Civil War reform movements. After students have read the text, you might begin the discussion by raising this question: "In what ways was slavery a more difficult 'reform problem' than education, treatment of the mentally handicapped, and women's rights?" Discussion can lead to observations like these: (a) Slavery did not lend itself to small, gradual "improvements." (b) The moral issue of slavery ruled out compromises. (c) The financial burden of abolition would rest heavily on a small group of people —the slaveowners—rather than being assumed by the public generally. (d) The slavery issue pitted one section of the country against another; the other problems were national in scope. (3) Both abolition and the granting of equal rights to women threatened the existing social order, but it would have been easier to make gradual adjustments in the case of women's rights.

- You may want to point out that the American Colonization Society represented a mixture of good will and deep racial prejudice. Some donors to the cause, no doubt, sincerely subscribed to the belief that freed blacks would be happier in Africa. And some believed fervently in the Society's stated goal of using freed American blacks in the Christianization of pagan Africa. But much of the support for colonization must have come from whites who did not want to face up to the problems of racial relations in this country. Point out that leaders among the free blacks— living in the North, of course—vigorously opposed colonization. "America is as much our country as it is yours" was a common response. One black Philadelphia minister in a Fourth of July oration declared, "We are NATIVES of this country, we ask only to be treated as well as FOREIGNERS."

- *Competency exercise—defining words and writing sentences:* Have students locate and write definitions of the following words in Section 2: abolition, prejudice, slavery, institution, assimilated, virtue, crusade, martyr. Then have students write original sentences using each term.

- Re-create a meeting of the Virginia legislature as they debate a bill which proposes to abolish slavery gradually in the state. Divide the class into two groups, with the pro-slavery group larger than that advocating abolition. Using the text as a guide, have each group prepare a statement supporting its position. Ask a student from each side to present this position. Have an open debate on the bill. Then have the class vote according to the Virginia ratio.

Section 3 (pp. 238–243)
Westward Ho!

Instructional Objectives Students will be able to

1. Tell how Americans settled in Texas, New Mexico, Oregon, and California, and describe the difficulties they faced.

2. Identify the leading figures in the westward movement before the Civil War.

3. Explain who the Mormons were and why they settled in Utah.

4. Use a map to locate the routes to the various settlements in Texas, New Mexico, Oregon, and California.

Teaching Suggestions This section explains how the American settlements in the West paved the way for our acquisition of much of the territory comprising the western states of today. At the start, you may want to elaborate on the first sentence of the section introduction, pointing out that getting more land in the West would raise the critical issue of whether slavery would be permitted there.

- Have the students turn to the map on page 240 to locate the Sante Fe Trail, Santa Fe, Albuquerque, Oregon Trail, Astoria, Whitman Mission, California Trail, Sutter's Fort, San Francisco, San Diego, Independence, and Great Salt Lake. Using the map on page 244, point out that Austin's colony was on the Gulf of Mexico from San Jacinto westward to about the "o" on *Refugio* and northward to a little beyond *Washington on the Brazos*.

- Assign one of the places (Texas, New Mexico, Oregon, California, Utah) to each student and tell them to write 3 to 5 factual statements about the early settlement of the assigned place. Then taking the places in order, have each student read one of his/her statements (without simply repeating an earlier response). When the written responses —for Texas, for example—are exhausted, see if the class agrees that the main facts have been named. If not, invite students to add other statements.

- Have students write a poster-type advertisement for eastern newspapers in which Stephen Austin seeks to lure settlers to his Texas grants. Suggest an opening heading, such as OPPORTUNITIES FOR TEXAS SETTLEMENT. The ad should contain not fewer than 100 words. Select the most imaginative posters for display.

- *Handout lesson:* Have students read *Handout 18,* "A Day on the Oregon Trail in 1843" and answer the questions that follow the reading. You might extend the lesson by showing *The Oregon Trail* (31 min). Evaluate the film by asking the students (a) what the film added to what has already been learned from the text and the handout, and (b) what was the best part of the film and why.

Section 4 (pp. 243–247)
Texas and Oregon

Instructional Objectives Students will be able to

1. Describe how Texas broke away from Mexico and declared its independence.

2. Show how (a) Texas and (b) the "gag rule" were linked to the slavery issue.

3. Tell how Tyler and then Polk came to the Presidency.

4. Define "manifest destiny."

5. Explain why and how Polk avoided war with Great Britain over Oregon.

Teaching Suggestions Students might be interested in some additional detail on the troubled political situation in Mexico following Mexico's independence from Spain up to the Texas Revolution. It is interesting to speculate how long even a stable Mexican government could have kept control of Texas.

• You might tell the class that historians have expressed disagreement about the wisdom of the attempt to defend the Alamo with fewer than 200 Texans against Santa Anna's army of 4000. Earlier, Colonel William B. Travis had received orders from General Sam Houston to destroy and abandon the Alamo. But when Santa Anna arrived and ordered the Texans to surrender, Travis refused, and reported to Houston, "I answered them with a cannon shot." Later, in his last defiant message requesting help, Travis wrote: *"I shall never surrender or retreat. . . . I am determined to die like a soldier. Victory or death!"*

• After you have told the above story to your students, you might discuss the following:

1. Was Travis responsible for the death of his men?

2. If Travis had lived, how should his disobedience have been handled by General Houston?

3. Travis paraded his men in single file before him and challenged them to die with him. Since soldiers are not eager to die, why did all men but one join Travis?

4. What would you have done if you had been Colonel Travis?

5. Mexican General Santa Anna said of the Alamo battle, "It was but a small affair." Why would Texans disagree?

   You might tell students that later in the Battle of San Jacinto, Santa Anna fled in a private's uniform, but was recognized and captured. Despite pleas by Houston's troops that Santa Anna be hanged, the hero of Texas spared Santa Anna's life.

• Show the filmstrip *Sam Houston: the Tallest Texan* (45 fr). After the showing, discuss (a) why Sam Houston is considered the "tallest Texan"; (b) how he conquered Santa Anna and gained independence for Texas; (c) why the new republic continued slavery; (d) why some northerners opposed the request of Texas to join the Union.

• You might tell students that up to 1980 William Henry Harrison at age 68 was the oldest candidate ever elected to the Presidency. He also served the shortest period of time: one month. Disdaining a hat or overcoat during a bitterly cold March 4, 1841, inaugural, Harrison spoke for nearly two hours and caught cold as a result. Pneumonia developed because of the damp, almost unheated White House. Following medical practice of the day—little advanced from the time in 1799 when Washington died—physicians blistered and bled the dying President as they dosed him with opium, camphor, and brandy. When this did not work, they forced him to swallow Indian remedies, including oils and snakeweed. After this treatment, the hero of Tippecanoe expired, leading an observer to remark that Tecumseh had had his revenge at last.

After telling the above story, you might ask:

1. Should we put an age limit on presidential candidates?

2. Should presidential candidates be required to take a thorough physical exam and have the results made public record?

3. What circumstances and arrangements make repetition of the Harrison incident unlikely?

• Ask one of your better students to play the role of President John Tyler. Give him or her several "advisers." Wellman's *The House Divides* has several chapters detailing Tyler's activities as President. Have the remaining students use the text as a guide to prepare questions for an interview with the President that takes place early in 1844. For those students needing help, the following questions might be suggested:

1. Why have you opposed the Whigs, the party that chose you for the Vice-Presidency?

2. You have been bitterly denounced by the Whigs and you have few friends among the Democrats. Do you think you have a chance to be renominated by any party in 1844?

3. Why do you want to annex Texas?

4. If you are not nominated in 1844, what do you plan to do about Texas?

5. Are you willing to risk war with Mexico in order to add Texas to the Union?

• Use the map on page 247 in discussion of the Oregon boundary settlement. Point out that President Tyler had opened negotiations with Great Britain in 1844. He proposed the 49th parallel as the U.S.-Canadian border—just as John Q. Adams had earlier—but the British turned this down. They wanted the Columbia River as the border. Fort Vancouver on the north bank of the Columbia opposite the site of Portland was a Hudson's Bay Company fur-trading post. And by 1844 there were around 700 British subjects north of the Columbia compared to only a handful of Americans. While Polk was an expansionist eager to stretch U.S. boundaries to the limit, one must wonder if his demand for all of Oregon (to 54°40′) was designed to give U.S. negotiators some bargaining power.

Students might turn to the map of the Mississippi River Basin on page 147 to see that the Continental Divide marked the Oregon country's eastern boundary.

Then have students turn to the map on page 249 to see what states and parts of states were created in whole (Washington, Oregon, Idaho) and in part (Montana, Wyoming) from the Oregon country.

Section 5 (pp. 247–250)
War with Mexico

Instructional Objectives Students will be able to

1. Explain how the United States went to war with Mexico in 1846.
2. Trace the events of the war, including the Bear Flag Republic in California.
3. State the terms of the Webster-Ashburton Treaty of 1842, the Treaty of Guadalupe-Hidalgo in 1848, and the Gadsden Purchase in 1853.
4. Use maps to categorize American territorial acquisitions to 1853.

Teaching Suggestions In this section, you might illustrate how unpopular the Mexican War was with part of the population by telling the class that Abe Lincoln as a Whig member of Congress supported his party in stating that "the war was unnecessarily and unconstitutionally commenced by the President." Yet our "manifest destiny" was in full sway, and you might ask whether it could be stopped. Maps will be a most useful aid in teaching this lesson.

• If you want students to learn more details on the Mexican War, prepare a brief lecture for notetaking as students follow the course of the war on the map on page 248. Or assign particular engagements or campaigns for brief student reports.

Following are some questions to use in class discussion:

1. Why did Mexico refuse to sell New Mexico and California?
2. What reason did Polk give for going to war against Mexico?
3. Why did Thoreau (Section 1), James Russell Lowell, Emerson, and other New England figures oppose the Mexican War?
4. What does the Mexican War illustrate about the President's war-making powers?
5. Some expansionists were not satisfied with our acquisitions from the Mexican War. They demanded the whole of Mexico. Polk refused. Which view would you have supported? Why?
6. How did the Mexican War alter the boundaries of the United States?

• Show the film *United States Expansion: California* (16 min). Have students evaluate it, with particular emphasis upon how well the film expanded the text's explanation of the acquisition of California. Then discuss (a) why Polk and other expansionists were so determined to obtain California; (b) the role of Frémont in creating the Bear Flag Republic; (c) whether or not it was inevitable that California become part of the U.S.

You might tell the class that when Colonel Kearny reached California he had authority to take over the government. However, Captain Frémont had already "conquered" California and was reluctant to surrender authority to Kearny, who then arrested Frémont and sent him back to Washington to be court-martialed for mutiny and misconduct. Frémont was found guilty and was dismissed from the army. President Polk's offer of pardon was rejected by a stubborn Frémont. Ten years later (1856), Frémont would become the first presidential candidate of the newly formed Republican party.

• Have the students draw and fill in a timeline for the expansionist period 1821–1853 from Austin's Texas settlement to the Gadsden Purchase in 1853, using Sections 3–5 as a guide.

• *Competency exercise—categorizing:* Using the map on page 249, students can arrange the first 48 states into a variety of categories:

1. States acquired in whole or part (a) before 1820; (b) after 1840. (Tell students that the Webster-Ashburton Treaty of 1842 covered both northern Maine and northeastern Minnesota.)
2. States acquired wholly by a single treaty or agreement; states acquired in two or more treaties/agreements.
3. States acquired wholly or in part (a) through war or threat of war; (b) by peaceful negotiation, including purchase.
4. States acquired wholly or in part from (a) Great Britain, (b) France, (c) Spain, (d) Mexico.

For a quicker exercise, write the names of 10 to 15 states on the chalkboard; then have students arrange these selected states according to one or more of the category exercises suggested here.

CHAPTER REVIEW

Meeting Our Earlier Selves

1. Denominations and sects included Baptists, Congregationalists, Episcopalians, Presbyterians, Lutherans, Methodists, Quakers, Moravians, Amish, Rappites, Shakers, Adventists, Unitarians, etc. Then later there were divisions into northern and southern bodies of some of the mainline churches. The variety may have added to the total religious commitment of Americans by affording a style and set of beliefs for nearly everyone; a united Protestant church might have "turned off" large numbers—thus failing to give them moral guidance and spiritual comfort. On the other hand, a united Protestantism might have had a strong influence on public affairs—for good or ill.

2. Changes included rising immigration, growth of cities, industrialization, and extension of the suffrage. Educational reform was concerned with Americanization

of immigrants, literacy for the rising number of voters, the ability of workers to communicate in a common language, the training of young people for the increasing variety of occupations, and the greater need for formal education in an industrialized, urban society.

3. Violations included slavery, unequal treatment of females, lack of appreciation of learning differences in the schools, and wretched confinement of the mentally handicapped. Related reforms: abolition, schools for women and girls, improved teacher training and school facilities, and the establishment of mental hospitals.

4. Social reformers were motivated—at least in part—by religious and humanitarian sentiments that inevitably led to a condemnation of slavery.

5. Some people who would have eagerly supported expansion (manifest destiny) had their enthusiasm dampened by the fear of the extension of slavery into the new territories.

6. Cooperation—not individualism—had to be the rule on the western wagon trains to prevent and ward off Indian attacks and to make satisfactory daily progress.

Questions for Today

1. Today's women's movement, compared to the mid-1840s, (a) probably has more male support; (b) operates with a base of political power—women can vote and hold public office; (c) has a very strong economic and social orientation rather than political; (d) is made up of a coalition of women's groups; etc. In both cases, women experienced ridicule and failed to get full female support. In both cases there was a supreme goal: women's suffrage in the 1800s; the Equal Rights Amendment in our day.

2. Reform movements in the last few years, besides women's rights, have been concerned with civil rights, Indian compensation, equality for the handicapped, environmental quality, consumer safety, among others. Women's rights and treatment of the mentally handicapped are extensions of earlier movements. Equality (equal rights and equal justice) is the watchword today whereas humanitarianism, uplift, helping the downtrodden pervaded the earlier movements.

3. Chances of a major party "dark horse" seem very unlikely today because most delegates go to their convention committed to a candidate who has been running for the nomination for months.

4. Civil disobedience was practiced by black people beginning in the late 1950s with the violation of segregation laws. The resulting confrontations were widely publicized and helped to crystallize public opinion in support of civil rights legislation. Much voluntary desegregation also took place. More recently, anti-nuclear protestors have blocked traffic and broken other laws at power-plant sites. Their activities may have contributed to a slowdown in plant construction.

5. This question offers students a chance to suggest educational changes. Challenge students to speculate why a Horace Mann might or might not support the suggested changes.

Skills to Make Our Past Vivid

1. Outline Map 4 in this Guide can be duplicated for use with this activity. Be sure that students understand that northern Maine and northeastern Minnesota (shown on the map on page 249 as "By Treaty with Great Britain") came with the Webster-Ashburton Treaty of 1842.

2. Other categories besides food and tools might be home furnishings, clothing, weapons, medical supplies—and, for a few things difficult to categorize, "Miscellaneous." Remind students that a family would have to take the barest minimum—or risk having to discard "unnecessaries" along the way.

CHAPTER 12

The Failure of the Politicians

Introducing the Chapter Although the events of this chapter occurred more than a century ago, your students may still reflect sectional interests in their responses to the learning activities. You can convey the span of time during which the slavery issue develops by pointing out that Clay and Calhoun, young War Hawk expansionists several chapters back, are now aging and ailing statesmen. Again you can propound the question in retrospect: "Was there any way that the Civil War could have been prevented?"

Section 1 (pp. 251–258)
The Compromise of 1850

Instructional Objectives Students will be able to

1. Show how the California gold rush hastened the development of the West.
2. Identify three positions on the issue of the extension of slavery.
3. Compare the elections of 1848 and 1852.
4. Explain how Clay's Compromise of 1850 settled the slavery issue only temporarily.
5. Link the Fugitive Slave Act to the Underground Railroad.
6. Consider the impact of *Uncle Tom's Cabin* upon the slavery issue.

Teaching Suggestions Your students might be fascinated by the stories of the California gold rush, the adventurous overland travel, and the speedy clipper ships. Link these related stories to the slavery issue and the Compromise of 1850 as California seeks admission to the Union as a free state.

- Have students review the map on page 240 and use a Western Hemisphere wall map to locate the following: inland routes to the West Coast and California, Sutter's Fort, Isthmus of Panama, and route of the clipper ships from New York to San Francisco. Then discuss the following:

1. What was the safest route? the most dangerous? the unhealthiest? (Take a poll of the class concerning which route most of the students would have taken.)
2. Describe the types of people most likely to join the gold rush.
3. Why were the recently arrived California residents eager to join the Union as a free state?

- *Competency exercise—word recognition and sentence writing:* Use *Handout 19* to teach some less-familiar words found in this chapter. The answers are:

1. fugitive
2. concoct
3. avenge
4. wary
5. prejudice
6. involuntary
7. rational
8. anarchy
9. sovereignty
10. dilemma
11. incitement
12. reckoning
13. defy
14. inevitable
15. martyr
16. forebodings
17. optimist
18. travesty
19. servile
20. patronage

- Use the illustrations on page 252 and display reproductions of paintings of clipper ships (see *Life History*, Volume 5, p. 48). Tell them that these ships were the fastest sailing vessels ever built—the clipper *Lightning* once sailed 500 miles in a single day. The ships required large crews to handle the great spread of sail, with masts up to 200 feet high. Yet the years of glory were short—from 1845 to 1860. You might ask why. (They were a response to the development of the steamship, which was easily beaten in trip time at first, but gradually forged ahead. The steamship was also less dependent on the weather, and promised a more regular schedule.) If students want to learn more, suggest such books as Chapelle's *The History of American Sailing Ships*.

Student artists might draw reproductions of clipper ships for bulletin board display. (See reference above.)

- Write this heading on the chalkboard: VIEWS ON SLAVERY IN TERRITORIES IN 1840s. Below this title write: *Proslavery, Middle Ground, Antislavery*. Have students state the position of each group, using the text as a guide. Then discuss the following questions:

1. How did the Mexican War complicate the problem of the expansion of slavery?
2. Why could antislavery forces get the Wilmot Proviso through the House but not the Senate? (Southerners were minority in House but had equality in Senate.)
3. Some members of Congress wanted to compromise the expansion issue. What arguments would you expect them to use? (Let's not risk a breakup of the Union over this issue. Slavery unlikely to succeed in West. Etc.)

- Have students point out some similarities and differences in the elections of 1848 and 1852, such as:

SIMILARITIES

1. Incumbent President not nominated.
2. Military heroes nominated.
3. Democrats and Whigs still the major parties.
4. Both parties supported Compromise of 1850 as "final."
5. Democrats each time chose a Northerner, while Whigs picked a person of southern background.

DIFFERENCES

1. Whigs won in 1848 and lost in 1852.
2. Close election in 1848 but not in 1852.
3. Third party a major factor in 1848.

• Write this heading on the chalkboard: COMPROMISE OF 1850. Below this, write the following terms across the board: *Provisions, Supported by, Opposed by, Significance.* Have students fill in the details in the appropriate columns, using the text as a guide. After they have finished, discuss the following:

1. Does the title of the chapter, "The Failure of the Politicians," apply also to the Compromise of 1850? Why?
2. Would you have supported the views of Seward, Calhoun, or Clay? Explain.
3. What was the most important provision of the Compromise? Why?
4. Why did Webster turn on the abolitionists?
5. Why was the Compromise only a temporary solution to the slavery issue?
6. What did the Compromise achieve?

• Extending the lesson: Have individual students or committees prepare brief reports on the following: the California gold rush; the last years of Clay, Calhoun, and Webster; Harriet Tubman; and Harriet Beecher Stowe. Use the following for further discussion:

1. How was gold obtained by an individual miner?
2. Why did Clay, Calhoun, and Webster fail in their ambition to reach the Presidency? What was the greatest achievement of each?
3. What did the terms "passengers," "stations," and "conductors" mean on the Underground Railroad?
4. The Underground Railroad made effective propaganda for both the North and the South. How could this be?
5. As an escaped slave, Tubman had a $12,000 bounty on her head in the South. Yet she returned 19 times, and led more than 300 slaves to freedom. How did she manage all this without capture?
6. What experiences in Stowe's life led to the writing of *Uncle Tom's Cabin*?
7. Why was the book so popular?
8. Was Lincoln right in his assessment that *Uncle Tom's Cabin* "made a great war"? Explain.

Section 2 (pp. 258–262)
How the Compromise Collapsed

Instructional Objectives   Students will be able to

1. Show how the Ostend Manifesto was an expression of both nationalism and sectionalism.
2. Explain how the Kansas-Nebraska Act intensified the slavery issue and led to the formation of the Republican party.
3. Identify the Know-Nothing party as an illustration of the impact of minor parties in the United States.
4. Indicate how "Bleeding Kansas" afforded a preview of the Civil War.
5. Describe the Sumner-Brooks affair in the Senate as an example of the emotional intensity dividing the North and South.

Teaching Suggestions   This brief section describes certain unpraiseworthy aspects of our history. They cast ominous shadows on the future. Were the personal motives of Douglas responsible for the bloodshed in Kansas? How did hate and prejudice help to shape our national destiny at this time? Can we rise above our personal feelings in deciding great issues? You might explore these disturbing questions with your students. Remind them that emotions have had more than a hundred years to cool.

• Have students turn to the map on page 439 to locate Cuba. Have them respond to the following:

1. What is the approximate length of Cuba from east to west?
2. How far is Cuba from our mainland?
3. Would you have supported the Ostend Manifesto? Why? What would have been (a) the advantages and (b) the disadvantages of our annexation of Cuba in the 1850s?

• Have students turn to the map on page 262 to locate the following: Kansas Territory, Lawrence, and Pottawatomie Creek. Have them answer the following:

1. What were Senator Douglas's motives in sponsoring the Kansas-Nebraska Act?
2. What were its provisions?
3. What was unusual about the bitterness surrounding the passage of the Kansas-Nebraska Act?
4. How did popular sovereignty lead to violence in Kansas?

5. What were the reasons for and against carrying "Beecher's Bibles"?

6. Was John Brown justified in seeking revenge? Defend your answer.

• Have individuals or committees prepare reports on the founding of the Republican and the Know-Nothing parties. Moos's *The Republicans: A History of Their Party* and encyclopedia articles will be helpful. After the reports, discuss the following:

1. Why was the Republican party founded?

2. What elements of other parties joined it?

3. What were the principles of the Know-Nothing party?

4. How could members of Congress be members of both of these parties?

5. Why do new political parties sometimes appear and disappear so quickly?

• Tell your students that at a time when feelings were tense in Washington, Senator Sumner's remark that his elderly colleague, Senator Butler of South Carolina, must have chosen "the harlot, Slavery," to be his "mistress" was intolerable to the South's code of honor and had to be avenged. Congressman Brooks seems to have intended to kill Sumner by beating him on his bare head with a heavy gutta-percha cane. Caught by surprise, Sumner became entangled around his desk, which was fastened to the floor, and thus could not escape the blows. Brooks battered Sumner's skull until the cane broke. Some Democratic senators standing near by, including Douglas, laughed at the almost-tragic beating, and made no effort to interfere. While Sumner slowly recovered, Brooks was fined $300 in a Washington court. Southern admirers sent him scores of canes and whips to use on other abolitionists.

After you have told the above, discuss the following:

1. Must one's "honor" be avenged? Why?

2. Is personal violence ever justified? When? Why?

3. Should fellow senators have interfered and prevented the beating?

4. A resolution to expel Brooks from the House of Representatives failed by a few votes. Would you have voted *for* or *against* this resolution? Why?

Section 3 (pp. 262–266)
The Nation Comes Apart

Instructional Objectives Students will be able to

1. Describe the remarkable showing of the Republican party in the election of 1856.

2. Point out how the Supreme Court decision on the *Dred Scott* case widened the gulf between the North and South.

3. Tell how Lincoln, in debating Douglas, became a nationally prominent political figure.

4. State the purpose of John Brown's plan to invade the South, and describe its impact on both the North and South.

Teaching Suggestions Students may be more interested in the persons of Lincoln, Douglas, and John Brown than in the issues involving these men. Interrelate the human side with the developing events and issues.

• In discussing the election of 1856, you might point out that even though there were still 15 slave states and 15 free states, the free states had 169 electoral votes to 120 for the slave states (see *Historical Statistics*). Therefore, by carrying all, or nearly all, the free states a Republican or other antislavery candidate could win the election. But a Democrat depending chiefly on southern support would have to carry some free states. Ask students to identify the Democratic presidential candidates of 1848, 1852, and 1856 and the home state of each. Then ask: What good reason did the Democrats have for picking a Northerner to lead their ticket in each of these elections?

• Tell your students that Dred Scott became one of the best known slaves in our history by sheer chance. Unable to read or write, he was chosen by abolitionists to become a test case on the principle that, having lived for four years on free soil, he was entitled to be free. The case went on for years before it reached the Supreme Court, and even then might not have caused much stir if Chief Justice Taney had merely denied Scott's appeal for freedom. Instead, Taney broadened the case to include all slaves and slavery itself, declaring (a) that Scott as a slave was not a citizen but a piece of property and (b) that all legislation excluding slavery was unconstitutional because the Fifth Amendment prohibited Congress from depriving any person of ". . . property, without due process of law." In essence, implied Taney, the Constitution was made by and for white people.

This great legal victory for the South caused the antislavery forces of the North to vow that they would win the election of 1860 in order to reverse the Dred Scott decision by packing the Supreme Court with new members unsympathetic to slavery.

Ironically, after being set free by his owner shortly after the Supreme Court decision, Scott died of tuberculosis within a year.

If students would like to know more about the Dred Scott case, one excellent source is Latham's *The Dred Scott Decision*.

• You might tell students that a poll of 75 historians ranked Polk among the "near great" Presidents, possibly because not much was expected of him as a "dark-horse." Instead, according to Professor Thomas A. Bailey in his *Presidential Greatness* (page 282), Polk "was clearly the strongest President between Jackson and Lincoln"—in part because of his expansionist program. Taylor, Fillmore, Pierce, and Buchanan are rated "below average" for various reasons, chiefly because they showed weak leadership in facing great problems.

You might want to have reports on the backgrounds of these Presidents. There are numerous biographies available (see reading list for Unit 4).

• In discussing the Lincoln-Douglas debates, tell students that in the fall election of 1858 the voters of Illinois would be voting for United States Representatives and for members of the state legislature (and perhaps other state and local officials) but not for a United States Senator. The new state legislature would elect Douglas or Lincoln to represent Illinois in the United States Senate. The debates, therefore, were held chiefly to influence the voters on their choice of state legislators. We can imagine that at Freeport, for example, the legislative candidates from that area were on the platform along with the two speakers. Lincoln would have urged the audience to vote for Republican state senators and representatives, and Douglas would have done the same for the Democratic candidates.

The following questions might be used to discuss the debates:

1. How did Douglas wiggle out of Lincoln's trap—could the people of a territory lawfully exclude slavery prior to the formation of a state constitution? (By not saying "yes" or "no." Instead, he maintained that by failing to pass laws protecting slavery—through inaction—the legislature could exclude slavery.)

2. On what did Lincoln and Douglas agree? (non-interference with slavery in the states where it was already established)

3. Although Douglas tried to support the Dred Scott decision, it was really a blow to his doctrine of "popular sovereignty." Why? (meant that the territories had no legal choice but to accept slavery)

4. What point in the debates apparently won the Senate election for Douglas? (Historians suggest that the Freeport Doctrine was most persuasive—the belief that, if we fail to face or act on a problem, it will fade away. On the other hand, Lincoln's support of the Republican policy of seeking to override the Supreme Court decision and outlaw slavery in the territories was a harbinger of war.)

• Have a report on the background of Abraham Lincoln up to the election of 1860. Sandburg's *Abraham Lincoln: The Prairie Years* will provide much background. Lorant's *Lincoln, a Picture Story of His Life* contains many illustrations.

You might want to compare Lincoln's background with that of Stephen Douglas. Johannsen's *Stephen Douglas* will be helpful. Following the reports, the showing of films such as *Abraham Lincoln* (19 min) will provide additional perspective.

• Have a committee arrange a bulletin board display on the life of Lincoln. The school library or media center may have a collection of mounted photographs or illustrations which may be borrowed. The display will also be useful during the study of Chapter 13 on the Civil War.

• *Competency exercise—sentence writing and summarizing:* Using the text as a guide, write five sentences which might be used in a TV newscast or newspaper story on John Brown's raid at Harpers Ferry up to the capture of the surviving raiders. The sentences must be original and written with correct spelling and punctuation. (Remind students that a reporter includes the who, where, when, why, and how of the event somewhere in the account.)

After the papers have been checked for correct form and fact, a committee might select model sentences for a complete newscast or news story.

• You might continue the above exercise by having the students review the text description of John Brown's trial. Tell your students that this took place only eight days after Brown's capture. The wounded defendant lay on a cot in a little courthouse crowded with lawyers, reporters, and politicians. When hanged, Brown showed no fear or remorse. Many thought him insane, although his last statements and letters are concise and coherent. The film *Revolution* (10 min) dramatizes the trial and inquires about Brown's views on revolution.

To extend the above lessons, discuss the following:

1. Why were the blacks, including Frederick Douglass, reluctant to join John Brown in his raid?

2. A historian points out that Brown is a "supreme example of the doctrine that the end justifies the means." What are the arguments for and against this doctrine?

3. If Brown were tried in a modern court, what might be the outcome of the trial?

4. Although church bells tolled throughout the North on the day of Brown's execution, both Lincoln and Douglas condemned his actions. Why would they oppose popular sentiment on this issue?

5. Was the impact of John Brown's raid greater in the North or the South? Explain.

Section 4 (pp. 266–271)
The Election of 1860

Instructional Objectives Students will be able to

1. Describe the election of 1860 and explain why it was the most significant in our history.

2. Tell about Lincoln's background.

3. Show how the southern states seceded despite compromise attempts to prevent civil war, and identify these states.

4. Relate how Lincoln's decision not to give up Fort Sumter began the Civil War.

5. Locate Fort Sumter on the map.

Teaching Suggestions The election of 1860 led directly to secession, and Lincoln's determination to save the Union meant Civil War. So it is reasonable to call the election of 1860 the most fateful in our history. You may, however, want to raise the question of whether the war had to be fought at one time or another. Was the war inevitable?

• *Handout lesson:* Have students read *Handout 20* on Lincoln's nomination. After they finish, have them answer the questions that follow. Discuss these, or assign them for completion as homework.

• Tell your students that, despite its importance, the campaign of 1860 was conducted in the customary way of the period, except by Douglas. Lincoln stayed in Springfield, and remained silent. Bell made one non-political trip from Nashville. Breckinridge made a single appearance at a barbecue. Douglas, however, decided to campaign in his own behalf because the Democratic party lacked funds and was poorly organized. Ostensibly to see his mother, he went to New York State. But he took a month to get there, making speeches along the way. He also made two trips to the South. His campaigning ended when he lost his voice.

After you have related the above to your students, discuss the following:

1. Why was this election the most significant in our history?

2. What evidence is there that most voters in the South were not in favor of secession at the time of the election? (Breckinridge received fewer votes than Douglas and Bell combined.)

3. What is the evidence that Lincoln would have lost to the Democrats if the latter had not split? (The combined vote for Douglas and Breckinridge was greater than the vote received by Lincoln.)

4. Lincoln won despite having a minority of the popular vote. Explain.

5. Suppose that Douglas had won the election. Would the southern states have seceded? Explain.

6. What would be the fate today of a candidate who would conduct a "front porch" campaign and make no speeches? Explain.

• Tell your students that Lincoln grew a beard for the first time the month before he was to leave Springfield, Illinois, for the White House. He gave no explanations, although legend persists that he obliged a girl from New York who had written him a letter asking him to grow a beard.

Prior to his departure, Lincoln roped his trunks himself, and fastened cards addressed "A. Lincoln, The White House, Washington, D. C."

Students will be impressed by Lincoln's farewell speech from the observation car of the train at the railway station. See Sandburg's *Abraham Lincoln—The Prairie Years* or Sherwood's play *Abe Lincoln in Illinois*.

• Divide your students into two groups. Have one group list the *Causes of the Civil War* (political, economic, social) from the viewpoint of the North, and the other group from that of the South. Have them use the text as a guide. Use the chalkboard to list the responses.

Another approach might be to show the film *The Civil War: Background Issues, 1820–1860* (16 min), and then ask the students to do the above exercise, aided by the text.

• Have students prepare a timeline of the events described in Chapter 12 from the election of 1848 to the surrender of Fort Sumter in 1861, using the text as a guide.

• Have students turn to the map on page 281 to locate the states that seceded from the Union. Then have them locate Fort Sumter. What was the significance of this fort to each side? Why did Lincoln decide to attempt to supply and defend it?

• Ask your students to write one of two letters: Either from the viewpoint of (a) a South Carolina college student to his parents explaining why he approves of secession and will join the Confederate Army as soon as possible; or (b) a New England student who has joined an abolitionist group and wants to serve the Union. Read several of the letters aloud from each group to the class to compare views.

• Have some students write an editorial on the topic, "Is It Too Late?" It should summarize the reasons for secession and then evaluate the possibilities for peace if the Crittenden amendments are adopted. Was Lincoln right in opposing this compromise? After the students have finished, read several editorials aloud and have the students discuss them.

Other students can write an editorial on Lincoln's decision to defend Fort Sumter. Was he right in deciding not to give up Fort Sumter peacefully? Had he done so, could the Union have been saved through further compromise and without bloodshed?

CHAPTER REVIEW

Meeting Our Earlier Selves

1. The Fugitive Slave Act was unacceptable to abolitionists; popular sovereignty on slavery in Utah and New Mexico territories planted the seeds for further conflict over slavery.

2. Slaves would be a threat to northern jobs and wage rates. Slavery rested on a different kind of social system that would clash with their own democratic system. But, perhaps most important, many northerners had racial prejudices—as pointed out on page 260.

3. Students might divide into committees to review a particular election and report the slavery influences.

4. Mexican Cession and Wilmot Proviso—opened question of extension of slavery to former Mexican lands; Fugitive Slave Act—further aroused northern abolitionists who were helping slaves to escape; *Uncle Tom's Cabin*—helped to win uncommitted persons to the abolitionist position; Ostend Manifesto—firmly identified slavery with expansion; raids in Kansas—violence superceded discussion on the slavery extension issue; attack on Charles Sumner—more violence; Dred Scott decision—enraged the antislavery movement by suggesting that legal remedies were not available; Lecompton Constitution—the fraud may have alienated some people, and the problem cast doubt on the efficacy of popular sovereignty; John Brown's raid—convinced Southerners that abolitionists would stop at nothing to end slavery.

Questions for Today

1. The desegregation issue comes to mind, of course. Other very emotional issues include abortion, nuclear power, and in some places the Equal Rights Amendment. The pace of desegregation offered some room for compromise. Class discussion may show the difficulty of compromise on the other issues. Political protest on some of these issues has led to violent confrontations.

2. Today's major parties continue to try to assure national appeal—perhaps chiefly in the wording of the party platform. Also the party's presidential candidate may pick a running mate from another region than his own. When elected, the party's candidates may support bills and take other action that show concern for a particular region's problems. Political observers today, however, point to the decline of party influence in elections and in public affairs and the rising influence of single-interest groups like environmentalists, Right-to-Life, and others.

Skills to Make Our Past Vivid

3. Remind students that some events might appear on both sides of the timeline. For example, the first vote on the Lecompton Constitution would cheer the proslavery forces, and the second would be good news for the antislavery cause. And the Ostend Manifesto would be good news to the proslavery people, and the uproar over it would be welcomed by the antislavery side.

4. The cartoon on page 259 is subject to conflicting interpretations. It may be that the cartoonist is praising Douglas as a giant rightfully carrying off a deserved prize, the Presidency. Or it may be a critical statement about the inordinate political influence of Douglas. Douglas was known as the "Little Giant," so his giant size is symbolic of his nickname. The White House is symbolic of the Presidency—or simply of enormous political power and influence. The cartoonist also appears to be using the symbolism of Gulliver and the Lilliputians.

The cartoon on page 270 appears to be sympathetic toward Lincoln, who is symbolized as a cabinetmaker faced with the job of restoring the Union (symbolized as a cabinet). We can only guess what the cartoonist had in mind as the "union glue"?

CHAPTER 13
The Civil War

Introducing the Chapter Only an overview of the Civil War can be given within the restrictions of a single chapter in this text. Nonetheless, you might extend the lessons in the areas in which your students show the greatest interest. If your school is located near scenes once part of the movement or clash of armies, emphasis can be placed upon their relationship to the war as a whole, perhaps through field trips. Some of the battles, such as at Gettysburg, are commemorated by national memorials that are visited by thousands of persons each year. The literature of the war, both fiction and nonfiction, is almost limitless, and there is something for every student to read. In the study of this chapter—perhaps more than in any other—the numerous available films will help your students envision the vivid drama of long ago.

Section 1 (pp. 274–282)
A New Kind of War

Instructional Objectives Students will be able to

1. Compare the military and economic advantages and disadvantages of the Union and the Confederacy.
2. Explain why many in the North thought that the war would be short.
3. Describe the changes in styles of warfare as developed in the Civil War.
4. Show how the Civil War was also a "people's war" that included the contributions of women.
5. Examine Lincoln's motives in delaying the emancipation of slaves in the border states.
6. Tell how the western movement of Americans continued during the Civil War.

Teaching Suggestions This section establishes perspective for the Civil War before examining the military aspects: some of the motivations for fighting the war, particularly in the South; the changes in weapons and methods of waging war; the importance of railroads in military movement; and the role of civilians, especially women, in supporting the war. You might compare most of these categories with their counterparts in war during modern times.

- Have students turn to the map on page 281 to locate the Union, Confederate, and Border states. Write the following headings across the chalkboard:

    CATEGORY   NORTH   SOUTH

In the first column list the following: *Number of states; Population; Railroad miles; Type of crops; Type of labor; Comparative economic assets (factories, etc.); Use of blacks; Motives for war.* Have students fill in the appropriate columns, using the map and the text as a guide, and place a check (√) in the appropriate category and column to signify whether the North or the South had the *advantage*. After they have finished, discuss the answers to reach a consensus. Then discuss the following:

1. Were there any advantages or disadvantages for either side not listed in the above chart?
2. Was the North's attitude that the war would be a short one an advantage or disadvantage? Explain.
3. How were slaves both an advantage and a disadvantage to the South?

- Tell students that as the Civil War began, most persons in the North believed that the war would be over in a few months. Even President Lincoln's proclamation, issued a few hours after the fall of Fort Sumter, called for 75,000 militia to serve for only three months to suppress the "rebellion." In Galena, Illinois, a former West Point soldier named Ulysses S. Grant had no idea that some two years later he would become commander of all the Union armies. Instead, in a letter to his father, he wrote: "My own opinion is that this war will be of short duration. . . . A few decisive victories in some of the Southern parts will send the secession army howling, and the leaders in the rebellion will flee this country." (Woodward, *Meet General Grant*, 1928, page 178.)

Ask your students to list possible reasons why both Lincoln and Grant believed as they did and why they were so wrong.

- Some of your students will express an interest in the weapons carried and used in the Civil War, particularly by the infantrymen. Encourage reports which will promote student interest and understanding. Do not, however, permit the bringing in of weapons of any kind into the classroom. The problem—from the author's experience—is not the display of these collector's weapons inside the classroom, but the carrying and demonstration of them *outside* the classroom. A better approach might be to use community resource persons who may have Civil War weapons, uniforms, insignia, etc., to display and explain.

Another approach is a student report that features the showing of illustrations from such books as *The American Heritage Picture History of the Civil War* (2 vols.) and Buchanan's *A Pictorial History of the Confederacy*.

- As the population figures in the text indicate, most persons in the North and the South remained at home as civilians despite four bitter years of war. Yet almost every home was touched by the war because the ratio of soldiers to civilians—and the casualties which necessitated fresh replacements—was relatively high compared with other American wars. Geographically, there were areas—particularly in key Confederate cities and along railroads—which were destroyed by the war. On the other hand, extensive rural areas remained unscathed on both sides.

    Some of your students may want to read more or give reports on the nonmilitary aspects of the war. Many novels touch on this, the best known being Mitchell's *Gone With the Wind*. Numbers of diaries are also available. See the reading list for Unit 5.

- Survey the class for photography enthusiasts. Ask for a report on the contribution to the history of the Civil War (and to photography) of the remarkable Mathew Brady. Many of his photographs are available in various pictorial histories of the war. Suggest also such books as Meredith's *Mr. Lincoln's Camera Man*.

    Tell students that there are few photographs showing action scenes because of the slowness of the photographic process at that time—basically the making of a direct positive image on a silver plate.

- Encourage a student to role-play President Lincoln in a press conference. Give him/her a number of "advisers." Suggest that these students consult histories of the Civil War (available in the school library) to add to the explanation in the text concerning the attitudes and problems of the border states, and how Lincoln attempted to handle them to the advantage of the Union. Ask the remaining students to prepare questions to ask Lincoln during a press conference, using the text as a guide. For those students needing help in preparing possible questions, suggest the following:

1. Mr. President, why did you suspend constitutional rights in Maryland and impose martial law?
2. Why did you ignore the opinion of Chief Justice Taney concerning the Merryman case?
3. Why did you have the federal government move swiftly in Missouri but slowly in Kentucky?
4. Although you maintained in your debates with Douglas that slavery was a moral wrong, you overruled the freeing of slaves in Missouri by General Frémont. Why did you do this?
5. Why are the border states important to the Union cause?

Section 2 (pp. 282–288)
The First Year: 1861–1862

Instructional Objectives Students will be able to

1. Tell how the overconfident Union forces suffered defeat in the first Battle of Bull Run.
2. Explain the significance of the war in the West and the activities of General Grant.
3. Describe the clash between the *Monitor* and the *Merrimac* to illustrate the change in naval warfare.
4. Characterize Robert E. Lee as the South's foremost military leader.

Teaching Suggestions In this section, you have the option of teaching the progress of the war through the study of the military aspects of the campaigns or through the eyes of the leading generals. Whichever approach is followed, use of the maps in the text will be essential.

- Have students turn to the map on page 283 to locate Manassas Junction (Bull Run). Have them note the 35-mile distance from Washington, along with the symbol denoting a Confederate victory. Have the students use the text as a guide to answer the following:

1. Why did the North attack at Bull Run before the army was ready?
2. What was General Scott's "anaconda" policy?
3. Historians agree with General "Stonewall" Jackson that the Confederates could have entered Washington after their victory at Bull Run. What prevented them from doing this?
4. Confederate General Johnston believed that the Union army was helped more by defeat than they would have been by victory at Bull Run. Why was this so?

- Use the map on page 285 to locate Fort Henry, Fort Donelson, Pittsburg Landing (Shiloh), Vicksburg, and New Orleans. Then discuss the following:

1. What was the significance of these strategic locations to each side?
2. How did the Union Navy help gain the victory at Forts Henry and Donelson?
3. What military lessons did Grant's forces learn at Shiloh?
4. Why was Shiloh so costly to the Confederates despite their victory?
5. How did Farragut succeed in capturing New Orleans by ignoring orders?
6. Why was the loss of New Orleans a great blow to the Confederacy?

- Obtain photographs of ironclad ships of the Civil War in various pictorial histories. *Life History of the United States*, Vol. 6, page 43, has a painting depicting the clash between the *Monitor* and the *Merrimac*. Over a thousand Confederate workers worked around the clock to create a slow-moving monster out of flattened railroad tracks that would be impervious to any shell from an ordinary warship. (There had been no need earlier to design an armor-piercing shell.) But the North knew all about the *Merrimac*, nd hastily had towed its own ironclad *Monitor* from New York to the Chesapeake area just in time to engage the *Merrimac* in battle.

As the text indicates, the fight was indecisive. Interestingly, the *Merrimac* was eventually scuttled, being too unseaworthy to go out into the open seas. With little industrial capacity, the South could build and repair only a few more ironclads, one of which, the *Tennessee*, singlehandedly took on Farragut's entire fleet in Mobile Bay in 1864. Authorities agree that had the South had the North's manufacturing capacity to build additional ironclads, the war would have taken a different turn.

Perhaps some of your students would be interested in making cardboard or plastic models of the *Monitor* and the *Merrimac* for extra credit in lieu of a written report.

Encourage students to choose some Civil War officer for a special report. Be sure that both Grant and Lee are included. See the reading list for useful biographies. You might also show the film *Robert E. Lee* (15 min).

Point out that Lee's estate on the Potomac became the site of Arlington National Cemetery.

Have your students write a TV newscast-type story summarizing the highlights of the first year of the war. These might include (a) the victories for each side, (b) the activities of the outstanding generals, (c) the changing aspects of naval warfare, and (d) which side seemed to be winning.

Section 3 (pp. 288–293)
The Widening Conflict

Instructional Objectives Students will be able to

- Analyze Lincoln's position and actions on emancipation.
- Explain the impact of the Emancipation Proclamation on the North, the South, and Europe.
- Describe the contributions of blacks to the North and the South during the war.
- Tell how the Union financed the war and created a national banking system.
- Trace developments in the trans-Mississippi West in the war years.

Teaching Suggestions This section explains the significance of Lincoln's Emancipation Proclamation to the war. Removed by time and distance from it, your students may not feel the Proclamation's emotional impact as experienced so differently on each side. In discussing it, you have a chance to explore the contributions of blacks to the North and the South.

Write these headings on the chalkboard:

IMPACT OF EMANCIPATION PROCLAMATION
North   South   Europe

Have the students use the text as a guide to fill in the appropriate columns. After they have finished, discuss the following:

1. What impact did the Battle of Antietam have on emancipation?
2. Should Lincoln have issued an Emancipation Proclamation at the start of the war? Why?
3. Since blacks were already free in the North, what actual changes did the Proclamation bring?
4. Why was the Emancipation Proclamation written to exclude the loyal slave states, occupied New Orleans, and occupied parts of Virginia?
5. Speculate on why many northern newspapers wrote critical editorials about the Proclamation.
6. How did nations in Europe react to the Proclamation?

You might extend the lesson by showing the film *Abraham Lincoln and the Emancipation Proclamation* (20 min).

An individual or committee report might be used to enlarge on the contributions of blacks to the war in the North and the South. Quarles's *The Negro in the Civil War* or the references in various histories of the Civil War will be helpful. You might also use the filmstrip *Black People in the Civil War* in the series *Chains of Slavery*.

Students can speculate on the outcome of the war had the Confederacy actively recruited and used black troops for combat duty. (Not until the war was about to end did President Jefferson Davis sign a bill calling on the states to provide 300,000 more troops without regard to color. Of course, there was no time to carry out this program.)

- *Handout lesson:* Have students read *Handout 21* to learn more about the use of the draft. Use the questions for a writing exercise and/or class discussion. For more information on religious objections to the war, see Wright's *Conscientious Objectors in the Civil War.*

- A most significant result of the Civil War was its impact on the nation's financial system. The concise text discussion of war financing merits elaboration—particularly for your more able students. Consider the following points:

— War costs: Federal expenditures in 1861-1865 exceeded total federal spending from 1789 to 1860. A Treasury official in 1869 estimated direct Union war costs to be about $4.2 billion—and total costs including veteran pensions and property destruction (North and South) at $9 billion, or "three times as much as the slave property of the country was ever worth." While these costs seem insignificant in terms of today's federal budget and public debt, they were enormous at that time.

— Taxes: Prior to the war, customs duties and receipts from the sale of public land had largely financed the federal government. By the end of the war, internal revenue (excises and the income tax) was more than double the tariff receipts. The income tax proved effective but was abolished in 1872.

— Greenbacks: Although interest-bearing Treasury notes in large denominations had been issued in earlier times of stress and had a small circulation as currency, the United States notes (greenbacks) were really the federal government's first paper currency. This printing-press money would become a major public issue in the postwar era.

People tended to hoard metal currency (because of its greater value), so the government issued fractional paper currency in denominations as low as three cents.

— National banking system: Despite persistent banking problems after the war, this was a major advance. The banks provided an orderly way for the Union to sell its bonds. And the system provided the country with a stable uniform currency to replace the bank notes issued by some 1600 state banks. In 1865 the government drove state bank notes out of existence by placing a 10% annual tax on them.

— Inflation: The war brought a rise in demand for products of all kinds, so prices rose rapidly. Inflation was also kindled by the rapid increase in the supply of currency—especially the greenbacks. One of the legacies of the war was the 30-year fight by debtor groups to prevent a contraction of the money supply. Farmers and other producers had borrowed heavily during the war to increase their production. They naturally wanted to pay off these debts with money no more valuable than what they had borrowed, but in the postwar era the government adopted a policy of contracting the currency and resuming the redemption of the paper currency with gold and silver, or specie.

• The topic on the trans-Mississippi West (p. 292) can be a reminder to relate the war to developments in your own locality. If your locality was settled, what was the "home front" like?

Section 4 (pp. 294–298)
Gettysburg to Appomattox, 1863–1865

Instructional Objectives   Students will be able to

1. Summarize the Battle of Gettysburg and explain its significance in the war.
2. Explain the importance of the Union victories in the West.
3. Tell how and why Lincoln won reelection in 1864.
4. Show how Sherman's "march to the sea" and through South Carolina ravaged the Confederacy and led to the end of the war.
5. Describe the end of the war and the terms given by Grant to Lee.

Teaching Suggestions   The need in this section to describe the last two years of the war permits only a brief survey of the many events and the changing American scene.

You might want to extend the lesson through readings (such as Sandburg's description of Gettysburg in *Abraham Lincoln: The War Years*), emphasis on the Gettysburg Address itself (see *Handout*), use of one of the many available films or filmstrips (see lists), or the playing of records (see activity related to songs of the Civil War).

• Have students turn to the map on page 295 to locate Gettysburg, the routes taken by the armies to get there, and the scene of Pickett's charge. Tell your students that in this most terrible battle on American soil, more than 7000 soldiers were killed. The Union forces had about 20,000 wounded and missing, and the Confederates over 24,000. Lee lost nearly a third of his whole army. Thus he had little choice other than to retreat. Military historians state that had Meade been bolder, he could have destroyed Lee's army, but "Meade was too cautious to try to force another battle on Lee north of the Potomac." (Catton, *Short History of the Civil War,* page 140.)

Tell students that Gettysburg National Military Park, commemorated by Lincoln, has more than 35 miles of roads passing through 3500 acres of fighting areas. More than 1200 monuments, markers, and tablets of granite and bronze dot the landscape, along with 400 cannon in battle positions.

Visitors may tour the area, and from a 75-foot tower on the adjoining retirement farm of former President Eisenhower see more of the battlefield than was possible for any of the participants. A huge electric map also portrays the battle.

Students may read more about the battle in such books as Catton's *Gettysburg: The Final Fury*. Williams's Civil War novel *A House Divided* takes the reader to Gettysburg.

• *Handout lesson: Handout 22* provides background on and the text of the Gettysburg Address. After students have finished reading the handout, have them answer the questions that follow.

• Have students turn to the map on page 285 to locate Vicksburg, Port Hudson, Chattanooga, Lookout Mountain, and Missionary Ridge. Discuss (a) the significance of the battles at each of these places; (b) the role played by General Grant.

• Have the students turn to the map on page 297 to locate the route of Sherman's march from Chattanooga to Atlanta and then to Raleigh. Discuss the following:

1. How did General Sherman's march to the sea and then through South Carolina contribute to the approaching end of the war?
2. A great historian (Morison) points out that whereas "Lee was the finest general of a Napoleonic age that was passing; Sherman was the first general of an age that was coming." What methods link Sherman to modern warfare?
3. What is the justification in war for inflicting damage upon the countryside to make the civilians suffer?

Use the text narrative and the map on page 297 to locate Petersburg, Richmond, and Appomattox and to discuss these questions:

1. What was the strategy of Grant and Sherman that convinced Lee of "the hopelessness of further resistance"?

2. Why did Grant and Lee show respect and kindness to each other rather than bitterness and hatred?

3. Historians point out that some Southern generals believed that Lee should not have surrendered but should have set his troops loose to carry on guerrilla warfare "as long as there was a Yankee south of the Mason and Dixon Line." What would have been the consequences had Lee done this?

4. Some Northerners wanted Lee and other leading Southerners, including President Davis, hanged. However, Lincoln supported moderation towards the vanquished. Which view would you have supported? Explain.

• Refer to *National Geographic,* April 1965, "Appomattox," pages 435–469. Use the article by Ulysses S. Grant III to extend the lesson on the ending of the war. Use an opaque projector to show the numerous illustrations and photographs in the article.

Tell your students that Lincoln was so uncertain of reelection in 1864 that he asked his Cabinet to sign in advance a note indicating their willingness to cooperate with a new President. The war seemed stalemated, there was resistance to the draft, and the Democratic candidate, General McClellan, surprisingly agreed to a platform that called the war a failure and sought a cessation of hostilities. Some Union victories at the right time, along with the President's reminder to voters that it was "not best to swap horses in the middle of a stream" helped Lincoln defeat McClellan.

No war produced so many songs as the Civil War. Play the albums *Union* and *Confederacy* or Burl Ives's *Songs of the North and the South*. If these are not available, take your students to the music room and have a student pianist play such songs as "Battle Hymn of the Republic," "Dixie," "Tenting on the Old Camp Ground," "The Battle Cry of Freedom" and others, available in most books of favorite songs.

Some students may be interested in drawing reproductions of Union and Confederate uniforms for display. Pictorial histories like *The American Destiny* (Vol. 7, pages 30–32) contain paintings in color of the uniforms of the Blue and the Gray.

Allan Pinkerton—later known for his detective agency—provided information to General Grant. Confederate spies infiltrated Washington. Among other reasons, Lincoln suspended the writ of habeas corpus so that suspected Southern agents would not be released after arrest. Such books as Foley's *Famous American Spies* and Bakeless's *Spies of the Confederacy* may interest your students.

• *Competency exercise—writing sentences:* Have the students write one-sentence identifications of five to ten persons studied in this chapter. Give them an example, such as "She served as Superintendent of Nurses for the Union Army." (Dorothea Dix.) Be sure that the answer is included.

To extend the lesson, use the descriptions for a quiz contest. Sort out the answers so that there is no repetition. Then have four of your better students participate in a "Name the Person" contest. Ask a student with good leadership ability to act as moderator. This activity can also be used as a "warm-up" before a chapter quiz.

• Have students prepare a timeline of the war from the fall of Fort Sumter in 1861 to the surrender at Appomattox Court House in 1865.

CHAPTER REVIEW

Meeting Our Earlier Selves

1. Rifle as standard weapon; use of instant forts for defense; fighting from trenches; use of railroads for supply; destroying railroads for defense; destruction of enemy's resources, not merely armies; etc.

2. See pages 278–280.

3. See page 292.

4. Anaconda plan: naval blockade of South plus seizure of New Orleans and control of Mississippi River. Engagements: at Fort Henry, Fort Donelson, Nashville, and Pittsburg Landing (Shiloh). Farragut's seizure of New Orleans; defense of the blockade by the *Monitor.*

5. This item might be used for a student report.

6. He delayed to keep the support of the border states. He finally issued the Proclamation in the belief that the North needed this moral issue to shore up its support of the war; his own feelings against slavery may have helped to persuade him that the North needed this goal.

Emancipation was limited to any state or part of a state still in rebellion on January 1, 1863.

The last question in this item calls for a value judgment. It would be hard to deny, however, that Lincoln played a crucial role in emancipation.

Questions for Today

1. Today women would serve in uniform—filling thousands of noncombat positions at least. Nurses would be uniformed armed forces personnel. As in the Civil War, women would perform a wide variety of home-front roles but in larger numbers of persons and roles. Unlike the 1860s, today's women would photograph and report the war. Etc.

2. Today one would expect the draft to be used immediately; a large force of reserves would be called to active duty; no chance to buy a draft substitute; active recruitment of women; no bounties—as such—for volunteering; etc.

CHAPTER 14

To Punish or Forgive?

Introducing the Chapter This chapter offers another "if" opportunity—to imagine how Reconstruction would have turned out if Lincoln had lived to finish his second term. You might point out that in recent decades "revisionist" historians have disagreed with earlier ones about the impact of "Radical rule" on the South, contending that it may have been more democratic than any rule the South had known before (see Stampp, *The Era of Reconstruction 1865–1877*). With your students, you might examine other controversial aspects of the whole period, including the activities of the Ku Klux Klan and the treatment of the blacks.

Section 1 (pp. 300–303)
"With Malice toward None"

Instructional Objectives Students will be able to

1. State Lincoln's (and Johnson's) Reconstruction plan.

2. Describe the Radical views of Reconstruction, particularly those of Stevens and Sumner.

3. Analyze the Wade-Davis plan and tell why Lincoln vetoed it.

4. Tell the circumstances of Lincoln's assassination.

Teaching Suggestions Lincoln's direct role as President, but certainly not his impact on our history, ends with this section. You might be tempted to extend the lesson in relating the details of the assassination. Yet the comparative plans of Lincoln and the Wade-Davis bill probably should be assessed first. Your students will also be interested in evaluating Lincoln's rank among the Presidents.

Write these headings on the chalkboard:

RECONSTRUCTION

Lincoln Plan   Wade-Davis Plan

In the appropriate vertical column for each plan, have students summarize the details given in the text. Then discuss the following:

1. Which plan was most workable for returning southern states to the Union? Why?

2. Why did Lincoln's plan not satisfy the Radical Republicans?

3. In deciding to pocket veto the Wade-Davis bill, what alternatives did Lincoln have in mind? (If necessary, explain pocket veto: If the President fails within ten days of the adjournment of Congress to sign or return a bill—in effect keeping it in his "pocket"—he has "killed" it since the adjournment prevents Congress from passing the bill over the veto.)

• Point out that the Wade-Davis bill nearly defeated Lincoln's bid for reelection in 1864. After the pocket veto of the bill, the Radical Republicans started a movement to hold another convention in late September to select a candidate to replace Lincoln. The President's nomination was saved and the movement fell apart after the Democrats became a "peace" party and also because the country was cheered by Union victories.

• Have individuals or committees prepare reports on Thaddeus Stevens and Charles Sumner, with emphasis on their "Radical" philosophy on Reconstruction. Williams' *Lincoln and the Radicals,* along with articles in the *Dictionary of American Biography,* will provide adequate background. After the reports, discuss the following:

1. How had both Stevens and Sumner been harmed by white Southerners? (Stevens lost property—page 301; Sumner beaten by Brooks—page 261)

2. Stevens believed that the South should be treated as "conquered province" and that the estates of "leading rebels" should be divided into 40-acre farms and sold to the former slaves at $10 an acre. What results would you expect if this plan had been carried out?

3. President Andrew Johnson called Stevens and Sumner "traitors" for their harsh Reconstruction views. What description do you think fits them best? Explain.

• *Competency exercise—reporting an event:* Have students use the text as a guide to a TV-type newscast of at least one page describing the circumstances of the assassination of President Lincoln. Remind them again of the who, what, where, when, why, and how of a good story. After they have finished, have them read aloud a number of the stories.

Suggest books that discuss the details of Lincoln's assassination, such as Bishop's *The Day Lincoln Was Shot.* Stern's biography of John Wilkes Booth tells the story from the assassin's viewpoint.

• Point out that in death Lincoln became an American legend. After more than 25,000 persons filed silently past the coffin in the East Room of the White House and funeral services were held, a 1700-mile long procession began as Lincoln's "Lonesome Train" carried the body over much of the route by which the President-elect had come from Illinois four years and two months before. In sunshine and darkness, blue sky and spring rain, crowds of somber mourners gathered at railway stations and crossroads along the way until at last the procession stopped at Oak Ridge Cemetery in Springfield.

Suggest to your students that they read Chapter 69, "Vast Pageant, Then Great Quiet" in Sandburg's *Abraham Lincoln: The War Years.* You might read aloud portions of Walt Whitman's "When Lilacs Last in the Dooryard Bloomed."

• In the various polls of presidential rank, historians rate Lincoln as the greatest of our Presidents. They consider him one of the strongest leaders in a time of crisis, a great person in character, and unyielding in his ideal of preserving the Union. Find, or ask students to find, brief characterizations of Lincoln as President to read to the class. For example, see Johnson's *The Oxford Companion to American History.*

Section 2 (pp. 304–308)
Andrew Johnson and the Radicals

Instructional Objectives   Students will be able to

1. Compare President Andrew Johnson with Lincoln as to background and personal traits.
2. Explain how southern states angered Northerners in the early months of Johnson's Presidency.
3. Describe the activities of the Freedmen's Bureau.
4. State the provisions of the Fourteenth Amendment and tell how the South reacted to it.

Teaching Suggestions   In retrospect it is interesting to contemplate "what might have been" (a) if Lincoln had been at the helm in the early months of Reconstruction and (b) if southern leaders had acted with more caution until their states were safely back in the Union and their senators and representatives were back in Congress.

• Ask students to use the text to find specific actions of Andrew Johnson that were likely to anger Northerners—and especially the Radical Republican leaders in Congress. As students respond, write the actions (in chronological order) on the chalkboard. The list should look something like this:

— Refuses to call Congress into special session.

— Suggests, but does not insist on, conditions for southern state conventions to meet in applying for readmittance to the Union.

— Pardons former Confederates elected to Congress instead of opposing their election.

— Vetoes the new Freedmen's Bureau bill.

— Declares that Congress should pass no legislation until southern members are seated.

— Vetoes Civil Rights bill and a second Freedmen's Bureau bill.

— Tries to form new party of Democrats and moderate Republicans for congressional elections of 1866.

You might ask students to imagine that they are either a southern or a northern moderate, eager to see the Union restored. Then ask: "Which of Johnson's actions would you approve? disapprove? Why?"

• You might point out that the severity of the Black Codes varied with the ratio of blacks to whites in the population. They were most severe in the Deep South where blacks outnumbered whites; they were mild in Virginia and North Carolina, and were not imposed in Tennessee.

White Southerners and their champions viewed the Black Codes as critical safety measures to handle potentially unruly, unproductive hordes of people who were unused to freedom and lacked self-discipline. At the other extreme, blacks and their northern champions viewed the Codes as a shabby attempt to reinstitute slavery. Does the truth lie somewhere between?

Students might speculate on measures that southern people of good will might have taken to handle their problem of relations with the former slaves.

• Write FREEDMEN'S BUREAU on the chalkboard. Below it in a vertical column list *Purpose, Achievements, Why vetoed.* Have students supply appropriate responses. Then ask:

1. What link do you see between the Civil Rights bill and Johnson's veto of the Freedmen's Bureau bill? (Freedmen's Bureau bill would have bypassed local southern courts in protecting the rights of blacks, and Civil Rights bill did so as well.)

2. What link do you see between the Civil Rights bill and the Black Codes? (Black Codes were depriving former slaves of their civil rights.)

3. How did both the Freedmen's Bureau bill and the Civil Rights bill become law when both were vetoed? (passed over the veto by Congress).

• Have the students read the Fourteenth Amendment and the accompanying explanations on text pages 790–791. After they have finished, have them answer the following questions using the Amendment and the text as a guide:

1. What factors determine citizenship in the United States?

2. What penalty is to be imposed on a state that denies the right to vote to any citizen who is entitled to do so?

3. What disability was imposed on those who had fought for the Confederacy? How could this disability be removed?

4. Payment of what debt was guaranteed? What debt was rejected?

You might point out that President Johnson could have urged the former Confederate states to accept the Fourteenth Amendment and get back their representation in Congress. But he distrusted the Radicals and believed they had no intention of admitting the Southerners until Republican rule in the South was assured—through suffrage for the blacks.

Section 3 (pp. 308–323)
"Black Reconstruction"

Instructional Objectives Students will be able to

1. Describe the system of military Reconstruction imposed on the South.

2. Explain why and how impeachment proceedings against President Johnson took place.

3. Summarize the election of 1868 and state why Grant won.

4. Analyze the "myth and reality" of black Reconstruction.

5. Explain the origins of terrorism in the South as a reaction to federal Reconstruction practices.

Teaching Suggestions This section discusses the only presidential impeachment trial in our history. You might encourage student interest by comparing Johnson's trial with what might have been the experience of President Nixon had he not resigned. The issues of Johnson's impeachment may not excite the feelings of today's student, but the tension and the drama of the single vote that cleared the President can be felt by every generation.

- Write the following headings on the chalkboard:

   MILITARY RECONSTRUCTION

   Advantages   Disadvantages

Have the students fill in the appropriate vertical columns, using the text as a guide. Then discuss (a) why military districts were used to rule the South; (b) possible reasons why Johnson vetoed the Military Reconstruction Act; (c) who could and who could not vote in the South.

- *Handout lesson:* After students have read the text account of Johnson's impeachment and trial, have them read *Handout 23,* which provides some description of the trial, particularly the pressures put on Senator Ross of Kansas. Questions like the following might be used in class discussion:

1. What are the two chief steps in the removal of a federal official by impeachment? (impeachment by the House—the voting of accusations; trial by the Senate)

2. Why is it appropriate that the Chief Justice preside at the impeachment trial of a President? (As President of the Senate, the Vice-President of the United States should have no part in a trial that might result in his becoming President of the United States. Of course, there was no Vice-President when Johnson was tried, since the office was vacant. However, under the Presidential Succession Act of 1792, which was in effect in 1868, the President pro tem of the Senate was next in line after the Vice-President. Thus President pro tem Benjamin Wade of Ohio, one of the authors of the Wade-Davis bill, was next in line to the Presidency in 1868.)

3. What was unfair about the impeachment and trial? (Congress trapped Johnson by passing the Tenure of Office Act; the pressures put on senators to vote against Johnson.)

4. Was the failure to remove Johnson good for the country? Why? ("Good" in that impeachment for political purposes might have been encouraged. Also "good" because of the unfairness of the proceedings.)

- To extend the lesson on Johnson's impeachment and trial, show the film *Andrew Johnson* (48 min). Ask students what additional insights the film gave them on (a) Johnson and (b) the trial.

   Call students' attention to—or read portions in class from—the essay on Senator Ross in John F. Kennedy's *Profiles in Courage.* Tell students that Ross failed to win re-election, so he paid a price for voting his convictions.

- *Competency exercise—vocabulary building:* Have students turn to pages 789–791 and read Articles XIII, XIV, and XV of the Constitution. Then have them define the following words, using the dictionary if necessary: abridge, apportioned, appropriate, duly, emancipation, incurred, inhabitant, immunities, insurrection, involuntary, jurisdiction, naturalized, rebellion, servitude, validity. Then have the students use any ten of the words in sentences (but not those of the Constitution).

   Another approach is to have students rewrite the three amendments in their own words. Have students work in teams to agree on suitable versions. Then ask a number of students to read aloud what they have written.

- Discussion of the election of 1868 might be focused on (a) presidential qualifications and (b) the Fifteenth Amendment. The text describes Seymour as "a man of decency and moderation" and as "honest." Did Grant also share these qualities? What crucial qualification did Grant lack? (political knowledge and experience) Why is this important?

- Write KU KLUX KLAN on the chalkboard. Below, to the left, list the following in a vertical column: *Origin of name; Where located; Purpose; How dressed; Leaders; Activities; Impact on blacks; Southern attitude; Federal reaction.* Have students complete the chart, using the text as a guide. After they have finished, go over the answers to reach a consensus.

- *Handout lesson: Handout 24* provides excerpts from a federal grand jury report on the Klan. The handout questions can be used as a writing exercise or for class discussion.

To extend the lesson on the Klan, show the film *The Invisible Empire—Ku Klux Klan* (45 min). For additional reading on the Klan, see Horn's *Invisible Empire: The Story of the Ku Klux Klan, 1866–1871.*

• Tell students that the troubled Andrew Johnson is rated "low average" by the historians. Stubborn and often tactless, he failed as an "accidental" President to carry out Lincoln's Reconstruction program. It is also a historical burden to be the only President ever brought to trial on impeachment.

Section 4 (pp. 313–317)
The North Withdraws

Instructional Objectives
Students will be able to

1. Describe and give examples of the corruption prevalent in government after the Civil War.
2. Explain why the period of prosperity ended, creating the panic of 1873.
3. Describe the controversy that clouded the election of 1876.
4. Summarize how President Hayes ended federal Reconstruction in 1877.

Teaching Suggestions
In this section, you might use the tribulations of President Grant (and his later business failures) as an illustration of the moral collapse of the "Gilded Age." You also have an opportunity to teach the economics of the business cycle.

• Tell your students that Horace Greeley, often remembered in the present day only for his "Go West, young man," is a good example of the rise to success of a number of nineteenth century Americans. Born on a New England farm, poorly educated, he became a successful newspaper publisher through ability, hard work, and his promotion of social reforms. Yet his quest for the Presidency ended not only in failure but also in tragedy—the death of his wife shortly before the election of 1872, and then his own insanity.

• Have an individual or committee provide further details on the scandals of the Grant era. Facts can be found in Loth's *Public Plunder: A History of Graft in America* or in any detailed history of the period. Then discuss the following:

1. Why was there so much corruption in the post-Civil War period?
2. Why was the nation in no mood for reform?
3. Greeley was a reformer; Grant was not. Would it have made a difference if Greeley had been elected in 1872?
4. What was the connection between the corruption of the period and the economic depression that followed?

• Tell your students that in a poll 75 historians rated Grant a "failure." You might discuss the reasons. (According to Professor Thomas A. Bailey in *Presidential Greatness,* "Grant was an ignorant and confused President," who appointed incompetent cronies to important offices and relied too heavily on party bosses.)

Grant's last years were sad ones. He lost all his savings and property after being cheated by his Wall Street partner, Ferdinand Ward (who later was sent to prison for ten years for his crimes). Rescued financially by Mark Twain, who published Grant's *Memoirs,* the ailing former President died of throat cancer before the book was published. The generous Twain, soon to be in financial difficulties himself, paid royalties of $400,000 to the Grant family.

• The panic of 1873 began the most serious depression in our history up to that time. Here is a logical place to teach the business cycle. You might draw the following diagram on the chalkboard.

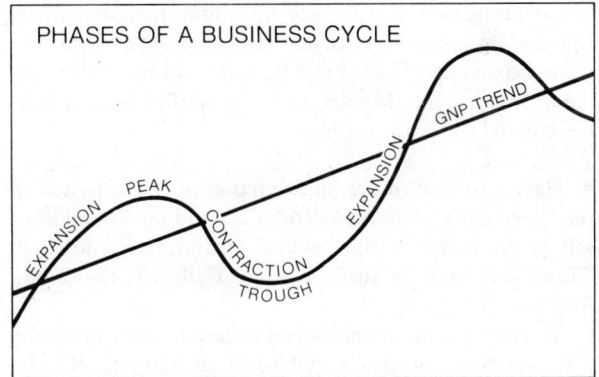

If any of your students are taking—or have studied—a course in economics, try to include them in the explanation of the diagram.

The GNP TREND line can be omitted if you think it introduces complexities. But it is useful in pointing out that gross national product (total output of goods and services in a year) has a long-term upward tendency. The chief signal of a recession is a pause in the upward GNP trend, and in a severe recession GNP actually declines.

Starting at the left of the wavy line, *expansion* is the month-by-month increase in production and usually jobs. This is prosperity. Prices tend to rise. Optimism spreads throughout the economy. New business firms get started, and existing firms expand production. This new capital spending requires borrowing. The prosperity preceding the panic of 1873 was based on large increases in production in the North during the war and in the immediate postwar years and especially a huge expansion of the railroads—accomplished, of course, with borrowed money.

Sooner or later the economy stops expanding—the business cycle has reached the *peak.* Rising prices (and interest rates) choke off demand for goods and borrowed funds. Banks reach their lending capacity. Rising costs of production (for raw materials and labor) squeeze profits. Borrowers finding the need to repay debts must save more —and therefore buy less.

The combination of circumstances that bring expansion to a peak start the *contraction,* or downturn. Major construction projects taper off (railroad building, perhaps, by 1873), and nothing replaces them; so construction workers are laid off. Other industries lay off workers as orders stop coming in at the former pace. Businesses all over the land tighten their operations to save money in the hope of protecting profits or stave off losses.

Typically in the 1900s (and not likely today because of banking reforms) the contraction was speeded by a financial *panic.* Perhaps a big banking house (Jay Cooke's firm in 1873) has overextended credit and collapses. People worried about their bank deposits may start a run on the banks (see text page 435). The collapse of the financial system hastens business collapse in other parts of the economy. As people are laid off, the demand for goods drops sharply—and more unemployment results. (Make it clear that the panic of 1873 merely hastened the contraction and, as the text points out, led to a five-year depression.)

Eventually the contraction reaches bottom—the *trough*—and business begins to pick up a little here and there. Business optimism spreads; new firms start up and old ones begin expanding again. Employment picks up, and the increased wages stimulate demand. Again the business cycle has entered the *expansion* phase.

- Have a student or committee report on the activities of the "Tweed Ring" in New York City and on Tweed himself as the leader of the political organization known as "Tammany Hall." Such books as Callow's *The Tweed Ring* will be helpful.

To supplement the cartoon on page 316, show others by Thomas Nast, originally published in *Harper's Weekly,* which helped break up the Tweed Ring. Some of these may be found in Butterfield's *The American Past,* Chapter 5.

Tell students that eventually Tweed was arrested, tried, and convicted on various felony charges. He died in prison in 1878.

- The following questions might be used to supplement the Section Review on the election of 1876:

1. Why was there a dispute over the electoral votes? (The Republican and Democratic election boards in three southern states both claimed to have won the popular vote and thereby the electoral votes, so these three states sent in two sets of returns—one set showing Republican electors voting for Hayes; the other set showing Democratic electors voting for Tilden. Tell students that evidence shows considerable fraud by both Republicans and Democrats in the voting in these states.)

2. Does the makeup of the electoral commission seem fair? ("Yes"—the five Supreme Court justices might reasonably have been expected to be guided by the evidence, not by party loyalty. "No"—Congress should have made a determined effort to assure an independent electoral commission.)

3. Which of the four "favors" for the South in the compromise of 1877 would please white Southerners? black Southerners? Explain. (All would please the whites, but only the internal improvements would benefit blacks—by helping the entire economy of the South. The other "favors" were clearly for the benefit of whites. The removal of federal troops was most offensive to blacks, since it assured the end of black political power in the South.)

4. After reading about this election, would you support the election of President by popular vote and the elimination of the electoral college? Why? (Any election where the "will of the people" is frustrated suggests the need for change. Yet, it can be argued that the situation in 1876 was unique and therefore not a proper basis for changing the system.)

Section 5 (pp. 317–319)
Abandoning the Blacks

Instructional Objectives   Students will be able to

1. Explain that racism in the South did not end with the freeing of the slaves.

2. Describe and give examples of "Jim Crow" laws.

3. Summarize the "separate but equal" *Plessy* v. *Ferguson* decision.

4. Evaluate the impact of Radical Reconstruction on the South.

Teaching Suggestions   In this section we see the disappearance of important gains made by blacks in the South during Reconstruction. During the fight for desegregation after 1954 some opponents of civil rights laws were fond of saying that "the law" was not the right instrument for dealing with racial relationships. Yet the informal segregation that developed after Reconstruction was soon buttressed by law—the Jim Crow laws. It was this framework of legal segregation that had to be swept away before other gains could be made in racial relations.

- The text points out that the term "Jim Crow" as applied to forced segregation originated in a popular old minstrel song. This song of the 1830s included these lines:

> I came from ole Kentucky
> Long time ago,
> Where I first larn to wheel about
> An' jump Jim Crow.
> Wheel about and turn about,
> And do jes' so,
> Every time I wheel about
> I jump Jim Crow.

- Various pictorial histories contain illustrations that show Jim Crow laws in practice. Ask an individual or committee to prepare a report on Jim Crow laws. Woodward's *The Strange Career of Jim Crow* or the section "Jim Crow in the South" in Morison's *Oxford History of the American People* will provide details.

- While the focus of this lesson is on "abandoning the blacks" in the South, you may want to remind students that segregation and other forms of racial discrimination, sometimes buttressed by law, existed in the North too. If yours is a non-southern community, you might look at its racial discrimination—particularly before the 1960s.

- Have students supply responses to complete the following chalkboard chart. Have them use the topic "Black Reconstruction—myth or reality" on page 311 as well as the last topic of Section 5.

RECONSTRUCTION SCORECARD

Achievements   *Failures*

Point out that a "balance sheet" on Reconstruction remains a challenging problem for historians—in part because of disagreement over the role of the northern "carpetbaggers" and the southern "scalawags." Early portrayal of the imposition of harsh military rule in the South amid much corruption has been "revised" to reflect the moral idealism of the Radicals and their contributions to the restoration of the southern economy and the protection of the rights of the freedmen. You might also point out that conditions varied from state to state, making overall judgment difficult.

If your students would like to read more about this "tragic era," refer them to the reading list for Unit 5. The film *Reconstruction: A Changing Nation—1865–1880* (24 min) surveys the period.

Another approach is to read from—or have students investigate—summaries of Reconstruction in textbooks of the 1950s and of today.

- Tell your students that Hayes is rated as "average" by the historians. An honest man in a corrupt period, he struggled against a Democratic House during his entire term. Nonetheless, he pioneered in urging civil service reform. On a humorous note, Mrs. Hayes was known as "Lemonade Lucy." She banned wine and liquor from the White House and served fruit juices instead. Several biographies tell the story of the Ohio-born Civil War general who became President.

CHAPTER REVIEW

Meeting Our Earlier Selves

1(a). Vengeance as a motivation is suggested by the feelings of Stevens and Sumner—revenge for loss of property by Stevens and bodily injury by Sumner—and by severe limits put on former Confederate leaders and army officers. **(b)** Concern for blacks shows up in the Freedmen's Bureau, in the Civil Rights Act of 1866, and in efforts to enfranchise the blacks. **(c)** Party advantage for the Republicans can be seen as a motive in virtually the entire Reconstruction program.

2. A model Reconstruction Act might have begun with Lincoln's plan for readmitting the states; contained some kind of civil rights protection for blacks; set up educational and work-training programs for freedmen; helped southern states to finance internal improvements; helped blacks acquire land and tools; etc. Discussion should bring out the fact that even if Congress had been motivated by a spirit of generosity and good will, it could not have moved in ways that it might today: There were constitutional obstacles, and the federal government's enormous revenue-collecting apparatus had not yet been invented.

3. Excluding the old leaders seems like a natural reaction. Yet there were vast differences among them. Some, like Lee, could have had enormous influence for good. Some historians argue that as a whole the planter class would have been more magnaminous in helping blacks to assume a dignified and productive place in the southern economy than did the poorer whites who rose to political power in the South.

4. The term Radical came to refer to congressional Republicans who were determined to punish the South and institute Republican control there. The Radicals' program for the South was "Radical Reconstruction." It harmed Southerners by delaying their readmittance, by failing to win the cooperation of the moderate white element in the South, and by generating long-term animosity in the South toward the North. It helped black Southerners to get some political experience, and numerous laws and programs enacted by the Reconstruction governments were beneficial.

5. Similar in that blacks occupied an inferior social position and had relatively little opportunity for economic advancement. They remained disfranchised—but by tricks and intimidation. They remained in peonage—a debt peonage in 1890. Differences: could escape from peonage somewhat more easily; could marry and raise families; had some educational opportunity; but lacked the economic security provided under slavery.

Questions for Today

1. The two most important are *Brown* v. *Board of Education* (pp. 612–613), the 1954 school desegregation case; and the Civil Rights Act of 1964 (p.662), which swept away discriminatory service in hotels, restaurants, theaters, and other businesses serving the public.

2. We can only guess, of course. One clue, however, is to look at racial relations in northern cities in this century: residential segregation, employment discrimination, all-white clubs, limited social contacts between blacks and whites, etc. Efforts of blacks to win equality would have been met with even more intimidation, including false arrest and more severe penalties than those given whites for similar offenses. With whites having to depend chiefly on intimidation to "keep blacks in their place," one might reasonably expect more outbreaks of violence in the form of race riots. Without legalized segregation, black leaders might have focused their civil rights efforts earlier and more strenuously on voting rights and economic inequalities.

CHAPTER 15

The Passing of the Frontier

Introducing the Chapter The chapter introduction provides a lyrical overview that you might well read aloud as students look at the maps entitled "The Vanishing Western Frontier" on page 339. First call attention to the term "settled area" at the foot of the maps. Point out that "frontier" means unsettled wilderness land beyond the settled areas—and that an area was called "settled" when it had two or more persons per square mile. Also, tell students that "frontier" in the historical context used here means *land in the process of settlement and under the control of a particular society*—in this instance the dominant white society. Thus any occupation of the land by a native population is ignored so far as the definition of "frontier" is concerned.

Section 1 (pp. 320–326)
Indian Wars and Resettlement

Instructional Objectives Students will be able to

1. Interpret maps showing natural vegetation and annual precipitation on the Great Plains by showing how these two features are related.
2. Locate and describe the Indian wars of the Great Plains.
3. Tell how national policy towards the Indians changed as white settlers moved westward.
4. Identify leading figures of the Indian wars and summarize the roles they played.
5. Explain how and why buffalo nearly disappeared from the Great Plains.
6. Describe Indian policy reforms and identify the individuals sponsoring them.

Teaching Suggestions Audiovisual aids, including maps, will be most helpful in teaching this section. Amid the conflicting points of view concerning our Indian policy, *Handout 25* provides actual quotations that should stimulate discussion. Invite students to suggest what would have been an equitable policy.

• Have students turn to the maps on page 321 to locate the states of the prairies and Great Plains. Point out that experts consider 40–45 inches to be an ideal rainfall for growing purposes in a temperate climate.

These maps can be used again with Section 4, "The Farmers' Frontier," but in this first lesson focus on (a) how the Indian culture was adapted to the Great Plains habitat and (b) why "Great American Desert" was a misnomer.

Call attention to map details and review some elementary principles of geography with questions like these:

1. About how much annual rainfall is needed for woodlands (forest)? (over 35 inches)
2. Why are there fingers of woodland along the rivers? (Trees can grow along river banks—and on the sides of creeks flowing into the rivers—because their roots can reach the water in the subsoil.)
3. How does average rainfall affect grassland? (shorter grass in drier areas)
4. What do the Rocky Mountains have to do with rainfall on the Great Plains? (Rain clouds moving west to east drop most of their moisture on west side of the mountains.)
5. Which part of the Great Plains comes closest to being desert? (western belt).

• Have students identify highlights of Indian policy using these dates as benchmarks: 1820–1850, 1850–1867, 1867–1868, 1871–1886, 1887–1934. A chalkboard summary might look like this:

1820–1850: Push eastern Indians west of the Mississippi, where they would occupy the land along with the Plains tribes.

1850–1867: Treaty making with tribes to allow settlers to pass safely through Indian land—or treaties to give up land and move farther west. Forts built and troops kept in West to protect settlers moving through Indian lands and to enforce treaties.

1867–1868: Creation of large reservations that were to be free of white interference.

1871–1886: End of treaty making; Indians to be treated as wards of the government; smaller reservations; forced settlement on the reservations.

1887–1934: Division of reservation land into individual plots; efforts to break up tribes; eventual citizenship for Indians.

As each shift in policy is noted on the chalkboard, ask students to tell how the Indians reacted. Be sure that students note that one reaction to the pushing of new tribes onto land used by earlier claimants led to inter-tribal warfare.

In connection with the review of Indian policy, use the map on page 324 for students to identify places where Indians lost and gained reservation land after 1875.

- Have individual or committee reports on Chief Crazy Horse, Chief Sitting Bull, and Chief Joseph. Such books as Joseph's *The Patriot Chiefs: A Chronicle of American Resistance* and Brown's *Bury My Heart at Wounded Knee* will provide vivid details.

  Instead of reports, you might show the film *End of the Trail: The American Plains Indian* (53 min). After the reports or the showing of the film, have the students read and answer the questions on *Handout 25* for viewpoints of the Indian problem.

- Tell students that as the youngest general in the Union Army, George A. Custer compiled a stellar war record and was present when Lee surrendered at Appomattox. Custer's record thereafter became controversial, however. In 1868 he was accused of abandoning men who were then wiped out by Cheyenne Indians in the battle of the Washita. In 1876 Custer decided to attack an Indian encampment on the Little Bighorn River without realizing that he was outnumbered. All of Custer's men were massacred and scalped by the Sioux; later, they were buried where they fell. (The battlefield is now a national monument in Montana.) Out of respect for Custer, the Sioux did not scalp him; later, he was buried as a military hero at West Point.

  You might show paintings of the battle on the Little Bighorn, including an Indian version. See American Heritage's *History of the Great West,* pages 364–367.

- Some students will enjoy reading more about or by Helen Hunt Jackson and Sarah Winnemucca. Of the books mentioned in the text, only Jackson's novel *Ramona* may be commonly available in local libraries. It tells how Ramona, a half-Scots, half-Indian girl, elopes with an Indian. Thereafter they are harassed by whites until the Indian is killed and Ramona is forced to flee with her family to Mexico.

  Sarah Winnemucca, born "Shell Flower," added Sarah to her tribal name after childhood contact with whites. Disturbed later by the treatment of the Paiutes on a reservation in Oregon, she lectured throughout the country seeking help for her fellow Indians. A forceful speaker, she was influential in securing passage of the Dawes Act in 1887. (See Life's *Remarkable American Women,* page 39, and various encyclopedias and Indian histories for further details on Sarah Winnemucca.)

- *Competency exercise—vocabulary building and sentence writing:* List the following words from the chapter on the chalkboard: barrage, domain, eluded, era, folklore, foraging, ingenuity, integration, optimistic, outlandish, plagued, remnants, searing, siege, stampede, tactic, technology, trailblazer, wards, wresting. Go through this list with your students, and have them define as many words as possible without using a dictionary. Then have them look up the meaning of the remaining words.

  After all of the words have been defined, have the students use any ten of the words in original sentences. Collect and grade the papers, or have the students exchange and check each other's papers in class.

Section 2 (pp. 326–330)
Seeking Gold and Silver

Instructional Objectives Students will be able to

1. Locate the early western mining towns on the map.
2. Describe the uncertainties that led to success for some miners and failure for others.
3. Describe lawmaking in the mining communities.
4. Summarize the significance of mining in our national development.

Teaching Suggestions This section portrays the colorful West of long ago. Your students will recall the films and the television shows they have seen. In that vein, you might supplement the text with audiovisual materials. Encourage students to share their screen-acquired knowledge of mining and frontier life.

- Point out that towns grew up in the West to serve cattle ranchers and farmers, but these people did not generally live "in town." Where miners went, however, they set up "instant towns." Have students speculate why. (Miners not self-sufficient—needed supplies and services they could not provide for themselves. They had to live near the "diggings," and a discovery of precious metal would draw people to a relatively small area by the hundreds and thousands. Wealth obtained from mining was available for home construction and other amenities.)

- Point out that Mark Twain, one of America's favorite authors, went to Nevada to seek a fortune in gold or silver, as described in *Roughing It* (1872). Then known as Samuel L. Clemens, he wrote to his brother in 1862 that he owned an eighth of a Humboldt (Nevada) claim, and "money won't buy a foot of it; because I know it to contain our fortune." A year or two would "find all our earthly wishes satisfied, so far as money is concerned." But it was not to be, as thousands of others found out. Mark Twain was soon broke, and had to accept a job as a newspaper reporter in Virginia City for $25 a week.

  Another well-known American writer, Bret Harte, wrote of the life of miners in a short story, "The Luck of Roaring Camp."

- Tell students that many frontier towns attracted not only eager miners and cowboys, most of whom were law-abiding, but also (as Mark Twain listed them) "desperadoes, gamblers, sharpers, thieves, and murderers." At times the usual law-enforcement agencies—the U.S. marshal and his deputies—seemed inadequate to the need for "quick justice."

  According to legend, two desperadoes were arrested in one of the mining communities after allegedly murdering a shopkeeper. A revenge-seeking mob soon gathered and shouted down the mayor, who urged calmness until the case could be tried in the courts. One William T. Coleman, a local merchant, angrily replied, "We will not leave it to the courts. The people have no confidence in the execution of the law by its officers. I propose that the people here present form themselves into a court [and] that the prisoners be brought before it. If the prisoners be found innocent, let them be freed; but if guilty, let them be hanged!"

Thus perhaps the first vigilantes began executing justice. Sometimes, unfortunately, mob violence took over. They did not hesitate to order a death sentence; many communities had a favorite "hanging tree."

- To students who would like to read more about vigilance committees, suggest such books as Gard's *Frontier Justice* and Madison's *Vigilantism in America*.

  After relating the above, discuss (a) the dangers involved in this form of justice; (b) whether there is ever a need for "vigilance" committees in modern society; and (c) how these committees can be controlled if and when they are formed.

- Tell students that a number of women achieved fame and notoriety in the mining towns and "cow towns" of the "Wild West." Annie Oakley became well-known after she joined Buffalo Bill's Wild West Show as a rifle sharpshooter. Later, she toured the world and met Queen Victoria in England. Irving Berlin based his musical comedy *Annie Get Your Gun* on Annie Oakley.

  Calamity Jane, born Martha Jane Canary, gained her nickname by telling men who offended her that they were courting "calamity." Usually dressed like a man, she nonetheless had a number of husbands, including Wild Bill Hickok. (See Life's *Remarkable American Women, 1776–1976*, pages 32–33.)

- Items 2 and 6 in *Meeting Our Earlier Selves* (page 341) can be used with this chapter section.

Section 3 (pp. 331–335)
The Cattle Kingdom

Instructional Objectives Students will be able to

1. Locate the early cattle trails on the map.
2. Explain the hardships of living on the western frontier, particularly for women.
3. Tell about the era of the "cowboy" and the herding of cattle along trails from Texas to railheads in Kansas and other states.
4. Describe the early "cow towns" of the West.
5. Explain why the open range ended.

Teaching Suggestions Compare student stereotypes of the cowboy with versions available in the primary sources, such as Adams's *The Log of a Cowboy*. An excellent cultural approach in this section might be a showing of paintings of the Old West by Charles M. Russell, Frederic Remington, and others.

- In discussing the long drive and cow towns, use the map on page 334. Here are some questions to direct attention to details of the map and the text narrative:

1. About how many miles was the drive from Bandera to Ogallala? (between 1300 and 1400 miles) from San Antonio to Ellsworth? (around 1000 miles)

2. If the herd averaged 10 miles a day along the Chisholm Trail, how long was the trip from Austin to Abilene? (100 days)

3. If Goodnight lost 222 of his 3000 cattle along the trail, what was his gross income at Cheyenne? (3000 × $36 = $108,000; 222 × 36 = $7992. Gross income = $100,008) What expenses would have to be deducted to find his profit? (supplies and pay for cowboys)

4. About how many horses were needed for his trip? (160–180)

5. Why did the cowboys have to learn hand signals?

6. Why did the cowboys prefer to be "pointers" rather than "drags"? (Bringing up the rear was assigned to beginners because it was the hardest and dustiest work.)

7. Why were the cowboys afraid of a stampede?

8. Note that some of the trails led through Indian reservations. Were the Indians justified in asking for some cattle as payment for the trespassing? Why?

- Have the students write a one-page composition on the topic, "The Cowboy—Our Most Romantic Folk Hero." Suggest that the following might be helpful:

1. What conception of the cowboy has been created by our "western" or "dime" novels, "horse opera" motion pictures, and television shows?

2. Did the cowboy defend women, truth, and honor? What made him romantic? ("Why not the sheepherder?" asks historian Morison, who believes that riding on a horse made all of the difference.)

3. What songs did he sing along the trail? Why?

4. Was he a free, independent spirit who defied not only the Indians but also rejected the confinements and comforts of civilization?

5. Did he end the long trail ride by celebrating in the saloons and dance halls until his money was all spent?

6. What was life like in a cowboy town? Was a gun needed for self-protection?

After the students have finished, discuss the above questions. Then ask: what is a *stereotype*? (A simplified and standardized conception having special meaning and held in common by members of a group. For example, the belief that Indians were savages; that cowboys were romantics who sang ballads on the trail.)

Tell the class that according to Furnas's *The Americans* (page 685), the cowboy was usually quite different from our conception of him. He seldom had the opportunity to bath or wash his clothing; there were usually vermin in the bunkhouses of the ranch. On the trail, his diet consisted principally of "beans, grease, and tough meat."

The trail boss got up first, usually at 3 A.M. Then the cook would boil the coffee "until a pistol would float on it" while he prepared breakfast. The average working day began before dawn and ended after sunset.

The average cowboy's wage was $25 a month, often spent in a few days in a cow town at the end of a long trip. Then the cycle of much work and little fun would begin all over again.

Show the section "The Cowboy Legend: Fact and Fiction" in Life History, Volume 7, *The Age of Steel and Steam* (pages 60–71). Some of the paintings are by the noted artists Charles M. Russell and Frederic Remington, who had been cowboys themselves.

To students who may want to read more about cowboy life, suggest such books as Frantz and Choate's *The American Cowboy, the Myth and the Reality*, or Hough's classic *The Story of the Cowboy*.

- Have students with guitar or harmonica-playing ability or musical interests prepare a report or brief program on the songs of the cowboy and the Old West. (The guitar, not so commonly played as in today's "country and western" music, gradually became popular as it was brought north from Mexico.) Suggest songs as "The Dying Cowboy," "The Old Chisholm Trail," and "Good-by, Old Paint." The latter may be the oldest cowboy song of all. It was sometimes played at the end of a square dances instead of "Goodnight, Ladies." ("Paint" was a cowboy term for a pinto horse.)

Many of these songs are contained in Lomax's *Cowboy Songs and Other Ballads* and in Botkin's *A Treasury of American Folklore*. They may also be heard on two sound filmstrips entitled *Folk Songs and Cowboys*.

- "The Cattle Kingdom" in Walter Prescott Webb's *The Great Plains* provides vivid details on the forces that brought an end to cattle raising on the open range.

- Tell your students that the hunters, miners, cowboys, ranchers, and gamblers of the early West—as did other pioneers—contributed to the making of the "American" language. To illustrate, ask students if they know what a *maverick* is (besides being a name for an automobile), or the meaning of the expression, *to pass the buck*.

Tell them that in the days when cattle were not fenced in, a yearling calf belonged to anyone who could rope it. To protect their property, ranchers began to brand their cattle. Over 5000 brands were subsequently registered. However, Sam Maverick of Texas refused to brand his cattle. To this day, a *maverick* is a nonconformist who refuses to be branded with party labels.

To pass the buck is a card players' term. One who did not care to deal in a game would pass on an object to the next player—usually a knife with handles made from the horn of a buck. In modern usage, one who "passes the buck" avoids having to make a decision. President Truman made the expression famous in 1945 when he had a sign on his desk that read, "The buck stops here."

Other such expressions still in use include breaking a string, bite the dust, pan out, strike it rich, piker, call his bluff, hot under the collar, and long time no see.

To students interested in reading more about terms surviving from western frontier days, suggest Dillard's *American Talk* or Mencken's *The American Language*.

Section 4 (pp. 335–341)
The Farmer's Frontier

Instructional Objectives   Students will be able to

1. Explain why pioneer farm settlers lived in sod houses on the Great Plains.

2. Describe the problems of living on a farm on the Great Plains.

3. Tell how a citizen could get free land under the terms of the Homestead Act of 1862.

4. Show the importance of barbed wire and windmills to the rise of farming on the Great Plains.

5. Describe and explain population growth of the West between 1870 and 1890.

Teaching Suggestions   The location of your school will determine how closely your students will relate to the saga of pioneer farming in the Great Plains. Yet all students can understand the challenge of overcoming a harsh environment and the rewards of accomplishment.

- Suggest to your students that a number of novels portray the pioneer farm days in the prairies and the Great Plains. Rolvaag's *Giants in the Earth* (see text) depicts the struggle of European immigrants to gain a foothold in the new land; it includes the building of a large sod house. Willa Cather lived with her family on a farm in Nebraska, and later wrote stories dealing with the struggles of prairie women, as in *My Antonia*.

- *Handout lesson:* After students have read about the sod house in the text and studied the picture on page 336, use *Handout 26* for additional information. Following are questions to guide discussion:

1. What were the sod houses's advantages and disadvantages?

2. Why were sod houses so inexpensive to construct?

3. What comforts available to you were lacking in a sod house?

4. Why was friendship and cooperation with neighbors so important in the pioneer days?

5. Imagine that you could be transported back to 1877 and had to live in a sod house. What would be the most difficult adjustment you would have to make?

- Under the heading HOMESTEAD ACT on the chalkboard, write *Terms, Advantages, Disadvantages*. Have students fill in the items using the text as a guide. After they finish, discuss the following:

1. What motivated settlers to apply for a homestead?

2. What was the importance of the railroads to the homesteaders?

3. Prior to 1890, the United States government awarded title to 48,225,000 acres of land to homesteaders. If each received 160 acres, how many homesteaders benefited from the provisions of the Homestead Act? (301,406. Thousands, of course, abandoned their claims.)

4. Some historians contend that the Homestead policy "was never suited to the needs of the landless workingman or immigrant." What reasons support this statement? (Because there were so many difficulties to overcome: moving the family to the West; building a house; buying farm equipment; waiting for crops and money to come in; facing extremes of climate. Also, a 160-acre farm was too small to be profitable.)

The map of railroad land grants on page 345 can be used in the discussion of homesteading.

- Tell your students that "natural" fences, such as Osage Orange, not only grew relatively slowly and were never quite tight enough, as the text indicates, but also required water to survive. Hence the need for wire. But ordinary fence wire did not work well in the West, since cattle could easily shoulder it aside. The barbed wire of Glidden and others prevented this.

A salesman named John W. Gates dramatized the value of barbed wire. In San Antonio, Texas, he used barbed wire to convert a town plaza into a corral, herded cattle into it, and then challenged observers to stampede the cattle over, under, or through the wire. The barbs soon kept the animals at a respectful distance from the wire.

See also the discussion of barbed wire in Webb's *The Great Plains*.

- Urge an interested student to provide further detail on "dry farming" in an oral report.

- Remind students that Section 4 of Chapter 10 described the growth of "instant cities" in the West. Oklahoma repeated this in 1889 in Oklahoma City and Guthrie. It was, in fact, an "instant" state. Have the students turn to the map on page 324 to locate the area supposedly set aside in perpetuity for the Indians, but two million acres of which were opened on April 22, 1889, to whites in a great land rush of settlers from everywhere. (On the evening of the first day, a roll call in Guthrie indicated the presence of people from 32 states, 3 territories, and 6 foreign countries.) Show the illustrations in Time-Life's *The South Central States*, "The saga of early Oklahoma," pages 67–73. Then discuss the following:

1. If much of the Indian territory was purchased for white settlement, what became of the Indians already on the land? (They were confined even more on their reservations. Oklahoma still has 65,000 Indians, exceeded only by Arizona among the states.)

2. How were the "Sooners" rewarded for breaking the law? Was this fair? Why?

3. Claims were often defended by gunfire; it took years to straighten out the land titles. What would have been a better way of distributing the land?

To students who would like to read more about the Oklahoma land rush, suggest one of the numerous histories of the state. Edna Ferber's epic novel *Cimarron* has a vivid description of the land rush.

CHAPTER REVIEW

Meeting Our Earlier Selves

1. It would have been much easier, of course, in the 1830s when the western lands were considered not very suitable for settlement. If a big-reservation policy had been accompanied by federal safeguarding of Indian rights on the land, we would have to assume a much slower economic development of the West. Where development occurred on reservation lands, the tribes involved could have received a big share of the rewards. Indian pride might well have been enhanced—and Indian-white conflict substantially reduced.

2. The text mentions laws (a) on the size, staking, and defense of mining claims and (b) on deciding what was a crime and how it was to be punished. Presumably the mining-claim law would include procedures for settling disputes over claims. Other laws needed quickly would have to deal with procedures for settling other types of disputes. There would be laws needed on town operation, on buying and selling of town lots, and perhaps laws (regulations) designed to protect public health and safety.

3. In eastern markets the supply of cattle was relatively low because farmers, presumably, could get the best return from their land and labor by raising other things besides cattle; and demand for beef was relatively high because of the substantial urban population to be fed.

In Texas thousands of wild cattle were there for the taking, or cattle could be bought cheaply because owners had little money tied up in investment. Demand for beef in Texas was low because the population was sparse—and the people there could raise or hunt their own meat supply.

4. The land grants benefited (a) the *railroad stockholders* by increasing greatly the value of their investment and by freeing capital for use in laying track and buying rolling stock; (b) *farmers and ranchers* by making transportation available with the result that their agricultural output became more valuable because it could be marketed—and in the process their own land became more valuable; (c) the *nation* in that railroad expansion contributed to economic growth. Also part of the deal on land grants was rate discounts for the federal government; over the years these rate discounts greatly exceeded the worth of the land.

5. The buffalo provided the Plains Indians with food, clothing, shelter, and fuel. Probe for specifics.

6. The map on page 329 identifies some mining boom towns. These towns differed from those on the East Coast by the absence of paved streets, sidewalks, parks, etc., and by the relative lack of variety of stores and shops, cultural attractions, and service establishments.

Questions for Today

1. *Policy A*—set up reservations. *Policy B*—remove the natives to camps where they would be maintained and trained until they could move into the mainstream of Brazilian society. *Policy C*—push the natives deeper into the rain forest and permit development only in the vacated areas. *Policy D*—forbid development of any populated forest land until the natives freely give consent for development, and gradually provide the natives with training to handle their own affairs in a modernized environment. *Policy E*—stop all development. Etc.

Business groups, adventurers, and would-be settlers would favor B,C, and A—probably in that order depending on details. Anthropologists, human-rights proponents, and environmentalists could be expected to favor E and D in that order.

3. Farm life on the Great Plains can still be relatively lonely, and be subject to natural disasters such as droughts, dust storms, tornadoes, and insects. The auto brings neighbors closer, and radio and TV bring entertainment, news, and education. Modern household appliances and farm machinery reduce the drudgery. Housing is modernized. Etc.

CHAPTER 16

The Nation Transformed

Introducing the Chapter This is the third of five chapters dealing chiefly with events in the 35 years after the Civil War. Help students to get a sense of the time span by pointing out that a 17-year-old in 1865 would be age 52 in 1900. You might ask students to imagine that their 17th birthday occurred in January 1865. They would be age 20 during Andrew Johnson's impeachment trial; age 25 when the Crédit Mobilier scandal became news and when the panic of 1873 hit the land; age 26 during Custer's last stand; and in their early thirties at the peak of the buffalo slaughter. (Other events from Chapters 14–15 might be added.) Now ask students quickly to find a significant date in Chapter 16 and determine how old they would be at the time. Arrange for some students to look in Section 1, others in Section 2, and so on. As students respond, the class will get a quick preview of the chapter.

Another way of putting the events in Chapters 14–18 in a time perspective is to have students begin a timeline of significant events from 1865 to 1900. Specify (or have students choose) major events from Chapters 14 and 15. Then during the study of Chapter 16 have students add items to their timeline.

Section 1 (pp. 344–350)
Railroads and Big Business

Instructional Objectives Students will be able to

1. Describe the growth of the railroads from 1865 to 1900.

2. Identify the standard time zones and the reasons for them.

3. Explain the importance of standard gauge railroad track.

4. Evaluate the roles of John D. Rockefeller, J.P. Morgan, and Andrew Carnegie in American business.

Teaching Suggestions Some students may be "railroad buffs." Encourage them to share their knowledge of past and present railroading, using the text maps as a guide. Perhaps models of steam locomotives can be shown.

The tycoons of American business and industry are interesting subjects for reports and extra reading. The senior text author, Daniel J. Boorstin, has written extensively of "The Go-Getters" in his *The Americans: The Democratic Experience* (1973).

• Have students turn to the maps on page 345 for help in visualizing the expansion of railroads from 1870 to 1890 and the pattern of the land grants. To focus attention, ask questions like these:

1. What places could a traveler reach much more easily in 1890 than in 1870?

2. How might a person have gone from Chicago to Portland, Oregon, in 1870? in 1890?

3. How would the railroad expansion have affected:

   (a) Montana sheep raisers? (better outlets for wool and mutton)

(b) a Nevada silver mining company? (easier to get mining machinery)

(c) East Coast beef consumers? (better selection of meat and lower prices)

(d) an Ohio cattle raiser? (probably drop in prices from western competition)

(e) an eastern manufacturer? (extension of market area)

Students may need help beyond that provided on the map to understand the railroad land grants. Point out that the lines showing the grants provide an approximate measure of land actually received. Railroads received alternate square-mile sections of land on each side of the track, typically five miles on each side. The land was worth little without the railroads there. In return for federal aid, the government got reduced fares and freight rates that amounted over the years to much more than the estimated value of the land at the time of the grants.

• The railroad-growth map also shows the time zones as adopted in 1883. It will be useful to have a map showing current time zones in the classroom for comparisons. Students living near the borders of today's time zones will be able to explain the need to remember about time zone changes when they plan visits "across the border." Ask students how time zones help others besides the railroads today.

• Draw two parallel lines exactly 56 1/2 inches apart on the chalkboard. Have students review the text to tell how this particular gauge came about. Then discuss the following:

1. Why is the standard gauge better than a narrow gauge? (Railroad cars can be wider and thus carry more; safety because cars tip less easily.)

2. What are the advantages of having a standard-gauge track throughout the nation? (Freight cars can switch from one track or line to another without transferring loads; lines can exchange freight cars; freight costs reduced; shipments speeded up.)

For students interested in reading more about the improvement of railroad equipment and facilities, suggest pages 343–457 in Furnas's *The Americans: A Social History of the United States—1587–1914*.

• In the Chapter Review, item 4 of *Meeting Our Earlier Selves* and items 1 and 2 of *Questions for Today* can be used with this lesson.

• Extending the lesson: Encourage student reports on other Go-Getters associated with the building of the railroads or the rise of the trusts.

Forms of business organization may interest some students. Suggest that they report on the nature and legal status of the trust, holding company, pool, and cartel. A separate report could explain how business mergers are typically accomplished today.

Section 2 (pp. 350–352)
Rock Oil Lights Up the World

Instructional Objectives Students will be able to

1. Trace the discovery and significance of rock oil in Pennsylvania.

2. Explain how Rockefeller's Standard Oil Company became the largest oil company in the country.

Teaching Suggestions The discovery of rock oil for lighting purposes will be even more interesting to the students if you demonstrate an oil lamp to them.

• *Handout lesson:* Give the students *Handout 27*, in which Andrew Carnegie records early observations of an oil town in Pennsylvania. After they have finished reading it, have them answer the questions that follow, using the other side of the handout for writing. Then discuss the replies.

• In discussing this lesson you can point out that a petroleum product, *petrolatum* (trade name *Vaseline*), has medicinal uses in ointments and dressings even today.

Be sure that students notice that in the early days of the oil industry the two chief uses of the refined product were kerosene for lighting and oil for lubricating machinery. It would be many years before the sale of gasoline for motor vehicles and the sale of oil for heating would become paramount.

The story of the break-up of the trusts comes later, but students may be interested to learn that the original oil trust was Standard Oil of Ohio. It was formed in 1882, but soon Ohio and other states began to pass antimonopoly legislation. In 1890 the courts of Ohio broke up the Standard Oil Trust into 20 companies. Trust certificates were replaced by proportionate shares of stock in the new companies.

Rockefeller tried again to bring all his oil companies together by forming Standard Oil of New Jersey in 1899 as a holding company. In 1911 the Supreme Court ordered the holding company dissolved, but the various companies remained loosely tied together through interlocking directorates. Standard Oil of New Jersey (now Exxon) remained as one of the operating companies. In 1979 it was the largest U.S. industrial corporation (moving well ahead of long-time leader General Motors in total sales and net income), according to *Fortune* magazine's annual listing of 500 top companies. Seven other oil companies (including Standard Oil of California and Standard Oil of Indiana) were in the top 15 companies in annual sales.

• Use the skill exercise at the end of the Chapter Review. After students have answered the questions, you may want to have further discussion on the petroleum situation in the nation today. (Text chapters dealing with the 1970s, of course, discuss the current oil crisis.) Recent data on United States oil production, consumption, and trade can be found in the current edition of the *Statistical Abstract*. Here are some observations to make about the past and the present:

1. The United States was importing crude oil in significant amounts as early as the 1920s—from Mexico, for example. But exports—chiefly of petroleum products—were greater in value (dollar amounts) until around 1950.

2. By 1969 United States imports of petroleum accounted for 16% of our oil consumption; the 1977 the figure had risen to 46%.

Sections 3–4 (pp. 353–357)
City Goods for Country Customers / Buyers' Palaces

Instructional Objectives Students will be able to

1. Explain the origins and business practices of the large mail-order companies.
2. Describe the impact of the department store on consumer buying in the cities.
3. Compare the early mail-order houses and department stores with those of today.

Teaching Suggestions Most classes can handle these two sections as a single daily assignment. If possible, have both an early Sears' or Ward's catalog (reprints have been published) and a contemporary one to show the class. Show six to ten double-page spreads from each catalog. Ask students to name differences between the two. Then tell students that these two mail-order companies are much different in other ways than they were 80 to 100 years ago. Have students speculate on other changes (retail stores; enormous size, especially Sears; serving an urban population even more than the rural people; etc.).

If only a contemporary catalog is available, show it and have students speculate on differences they would expect to find in looking at a catalog of 80 to 100 years ago.

• *Competency exercise—writing a business letter of complaint:* Choose an item (or have each student choose one) from a current catalog of any mail order firm. Have students assume that they have received their merchandise and found it unsatisfactory in some specific respect(s). Students are to write a covering letter to send back with the merchandise. Require students to use a standard business letter form with correct spelling, punctuation, and grammar.

• Have individuals or a committee prepare reports on Montgomery Ward and/or Richard Sears. Interesting background stories—in addition to those in the text—may be found in Boorstin's *The Americans: The Democratic Experience*. For further details, suggest Baker's *Big Catalog, the Life of Aaron Montgomery Ward*, and Emmet and Jeuck's *Catalogs and Counters: A History of Sears, Roebuck and Company*. Also available in bookstores and libraries are reprints of early mail-order catalogs. They offer comparisons of goods and prices with those in current catalogs sent to the homes of students. Collect catalogs to use in class.

After the reports and the examining of catalogs, discuss the following:

1. What factors were (and are) necessary for a successful mail-order business? (adequate mail service, confidence of customers, quality and variety of merchandise, presses able to print large catalogs, sufficient income among customers—particularly farmers, etc.)

2. What previously unsatisfied needs were met by mail-order purchasing through catalogs? (convenience of home delivery for those not near stores, awareness of new products, broadening of cultural horizons, etc.)

3. Why were the Sears and the Ward catalogs called the "farmer's bible" and "wishing books" for many years? (They served as guides to satisfy material needs of farmers as Bibles did the religious needs; also, in looking at catalogs, customers "wished" they could own the goods depicted.)

• Have students bring in full-page newspaper ads of leading department stores in your area. Ask them to compare the modern stores with those of a hundred years ago as described in the text—particularly those built by James Bogardus. To students who would like to read more, suggest Pasadermadjian's *The Department Store: Its Origins, Evolution and Economics* or Mahoney and Sloane's *The Great Merchants, America's Foremost Retail Institutions and the People Who Made Them Great*.

Then discuss the following:

1. Before department stores became popular, customers went to small "shops" to buy goods. What were the advantages and disadvantages of the small shops? (personal service; knew reputation of shopkeeper; could buy on credit; but less variety and perhaps higher prices)

2. What chief advantages came with the department store? (brought democracy to shopping—everybody welcome; prices the same for all; wider selection of goods)

• Tell your students that a good example of American know-how and merchandising during the post-Civil War period was provided by Gail Borden, whose firm is still known as a distributor of milk and cheese products. Before the Civil War, milk was usually sold in the cities by dipping into large cans with a ladle and pouring the milk —often quite warm—into the family's jug. There was a high sickness and mortality rate from this practice. After much experimentation, Borden learned how to purify milk by boiling and condensing it. Put into cans (also a new process), the milk kept indefinitely. Later, Borden also put sanitary fresh milk into bottles shortly before Louis Pasteur in France taught the world how to "pasteurize" milk, a major step in halting the spread of tuberculosis.

The advances in the canning and processing of vegetables and meats opened up new markets for American goods throughout the country and the world. If students would like to read more about the above phase of our national development, suggest Frantz's *Gail Borden: Dairyman to a Nation*, Boorstin's *The Americans: The Democratic Experience*, and various encyclopedia articles about other food processors such as Gustavus Swift, Philip Armour, and Clarence Birdseye.

- Point out that other retail businesses became well known during the second half of the nineteenth century. George F. Gilman and Huntington Hartford featured low-priced tea in their small New York store, which they named "The Great Atlantic and Pacific Tea Company." It grew to become one of the nation's largest grocery chain stores.

From a small upstate New York variety store, F.W. Woolworth expanded his idea of a "Five and Ten Cent Store" to a nationwide "poor man's department store" business. He built the Woolworth Building in New York, famous for a long time as the tallest habitable building in the world.

Section 5 (pp. 357–360)
Things by the Millions

Instructional Objectives Students will be able to

1. Point out the significance of the Centennial Exposition of 1876.
2. Tell about the improvements in industrial production and efficiency.
3. Show how a repetitive task can be performed efficiently by listing the steps involved.
4. Describe the contributions of Thomas A. Edison to the advancement and application of scientific invention.

Teaching Suggestions Some teachers may choose to combine this relatively brief section with the next one as a single reading assignment. But we will treat them here as separate lessons.

- Mitchell Wilson's *American Science and Invention: A Pictorial History* provides excellent pictures of the 1876 Exposition, including Machinery Hall. See Part V of this volume for these pictures and commentary and for material on machine tools.

- To reinforce understanding and appreciation of the importance of standardization and other aspects of scientific management, have each student write the steps involved in some repetitive job. Students with work experience can select a task that they have actually worked at (servicing a car, manning a post at a carwash, bagging groceries, operating a cash register, etc.). Other students can (a) observe a worker at a repetitive task and write the steps involved; (b) interview a worker; or (c) identify a familiar task that could be managed efficiently and list the steps involved (baking cookies, washing windows, mowing lawns, preparing a hundred ham-and-cheese sandwiches, etc.).

Conclude the activity with class discussion of the benefits and drawbacks of standardized, highly efficient work procedures, including the following: *Benefits:* lower unit production costs are likely to result in some combination of higher profits, higher wages, and lower consumer prices; easier to assure uniform high quality of product; lower unit costs give nation an advantage in world trade; easier to train workers for specialized tasks; etc.

Drawbacks: monotony of work; perhaps loss of pride in workmanship.

- Ask one of your science-minded students to role-play Thomas A. Edison. Give him or her a number of "advisers." Have this group research how Edison invented the electric light bulb, the phonograph, and the motion picture. Various biographies, including those of Tate, Josephson, and Silverberg, will provide details, as will Wilson's *American Science and Invention.*

Have the rest of the class use the text as a source for questions to ask in a press interview. Suggest that each student ask a question. For those needing help, offer the following:

1. What was your early background?
2. You hold over 1000 patents. Which of your inventions do you consider most important, and why?
3. Is there something about this country that encourages invention? Would you have succeeded elsewhere?
4. You have described yourself as a good inventor but a poor manufacturer. Explain.

Section 6 (pp. 360–363)
Labor Begins to Organize

Instructional Objectives Students will be able to

1. Describe the slow growth of early labor unions.
2. Explain why the Knights of Labor rose and fell in public esteem so quickly.
3. Tell why and how Samuel Gompers organized the American Federation of Labor.

Teaching Suggestions Review with students developments described in previous sections of this chapter that would stimulate efforts to organize and strengthen labor unions, especially separation of ownership and management (last paragraph of Section 1); giant trusts controlling whole industries and driving uncooperative producers out of business (Section 2); pressure on workers to boost output and the fear of loss of jobs (Section 5).

- Show a film like *The Rise of Organized Labor* (18 min) and have students identify (a) information found both in the text and the film; (b) information on labor unions up to about 1900 that goes beyond the text.

- The National Trades Union was founded by delegates from six cities in 1834 but collapsed only three years later with the Panic of 1837. Have students speculate how a business recession doomed the union. (cuts in production as people reduced their buying led to worker layoffs; employers likely to layoff the "troublemakers" first)

Ask: How would a business recession affect labor unions today? (loss of dues income as workers are laid off; no membership growth; harder for union to win concessions in bargaining; but laws protect workers against management reprisal for union activity).

• Extending the lesson: Suggest the following topics for individual or group reports:

1. The life of a nineteenth-century labor leader, such as Gompers, Eugene V. Debs, Terence Powderly, or other.

2. A particular strike in the period 1865–1900.

3. Wages, hours, and working conditions in the 1880s and 1890s.

4. The influence of European radical movements, such as socialism, on the American labor movement.

• *Handout lesson:* As part of the chapter review give students *Handout 28* on naming causes and results. You might see how many items students can complete without using the text, and then permit use of the text to finish the exercise. Or assign the handout for homework. When the writing is completed, have students respond orally so that they can see the variety of possible answers.

CHAPTER REVIEW

Meeting Our Earlier Selves

1. Hamilton would have celebrated because he envisioned the United States as a powerful commerical/industrial nation—with agriculture important but not necessarily predominant. By 1900 the United States had become a ranking industrial nation. Jefferson would have wept because he envisioned a nation of mainly small independent farmers, artisans, and tradesmen.

2. Inventions of new products and gadgets would have small pay-offs lacking the means to manufacture the products efficiently—and thus sell them cheaply. Standardization was all-important in driving down unit costs. Standard procedures, for example, boosted steel production and lowered per-ton costs, thereby permitting the thousands of products using steel to be sold at reasonable prices. Telephones could not have been used widely without standardized production of phones and other equipment, without standard procedures for making wire and stringing it across the land, etc.

3. Refer to the text for ways in which each of these developments transformed the nation.

4. The early captains of industry tended to be aggressive, imaginative, daring—willing to take big risks, dedicated (workaholics), persuasive, well-organized, etc. In most respects the business leaders of today have the traits that characterize leadership in any age, but any tendencies toward aggressiveness and ruthlessness in dealing with competitors and employees have to be suppressed today to conform to the laws and to accepted business practices.

Questions for Today

1. Time zones help radio/TV in program planning; telephone industry by informing users on practical times to make long-distance calls; airlines in arranging schedules; bus lines in arranging schedules; etc.

2. Highway transportation is aided by general uniformity in traffic signals, road markers, traffic lanes, no-passing zones, etc. Some traffic experts advocate more uniformity in driver qualifications, speed limits, car inspections, certain traffic rules, auto insurance requirements, accident reporting, and so on. New rules and procedures often cause problems—at least temporary problems—for drivers, pedestrians, and officials who are accustomed to the old ways. New rules on auto inspection or auto insurance might raise the cost of driving for some people. Other uniform rules or facilities might require higher taxes or fees.

3. Among twentieth-century innovations in merchandising are discount stores, supermarkets, shopping malls, credit-card buying, drive-in establishments, plastic wrappings, price stickers on packages, etc.

Skills to Make Our Past Vivid

1. The 18.2 increase in 1889–1890; the 89% increase in 1873–1874 (11.9 − 6.3 = 5.6) (5.6 ÷ 6.3 = 88.8%).

2. 1870 (.09 × 42 gals. per barrel = 3.78); 1876; 1884; 1892.

3. Much less use for illumination (kerosene) and vast increases for gasoline and diesel fuel in transportation, for heating oil, for fuel oil in powering electric-generating plants, and for oil in making synthetic products of all kinds.

4. The other 6 cents had to cover refining, transportation, and selling costs—with something left over for profit.

5. In most years, when production climbed, the price of oil at the well declined.

6. Production and price both rose in 1889–1890, in 1895–1896, and in 1899–1900. In these years the oil trust might have been able to force prices upward. Or perhaps in these years the demand rose faster than the supply. Also notice that a drop in production did not always lead to rise in price. Remind students that supply and demand both figure into price changes.

7. One would get the impression that oil production rose continuously between 1870 and 1900, when in fact there were production declines. One might also think that prices dropped regularly between 1870 and 1890. Use this question to impress students with the need to base judgments on adequate evidence.

CHAPTER 17

The Challenge of the Cities

Introducing the Chapter Despite the immensity of our open spaces, we see our cities becoming crowded with immigrants who seek fulfillment of the American dream. You can relate the problems of the cities of the turn of the century with those of today. American know-how and engineering skills in constructing bridges and skyscrapers will attract students more interested in technology than in political affairs. The introductions for this chapter and the next one (p. 385) explain the term "Gilded Age." It may be useful to have students look at both explanations at this time.

Section 1 (pp. 365–373)
The Growth of an Urban Nation

Instructional Objectives Students will be able to

1. Explain the growth of American cities during the second half of the nineteenth century.

2. Give reasons why millions of immigrants came to this country.

3. Describe the conditions and problems created by city slums.

4. Explain the role of bosses and political machines in controlling city government.

5. Summarize the movement to restrict immigration, particularly of the "undesirables."

Teaching Suggestions Your approach to teaching this section may depend on the nearness of your school to a large city. A field trip to observe slum conditions and ethnic areas will be more effective than even films or filmstrips. Your students can react to the growth of prejudice towards newcomers, and evaluate the legislation seeking to restrict them.

• Have students turn to the maps on page 368 to note the big increase in urbanization. Have students locate and name one city of more than 100,000 population by 1900 in each of the following regions: New England, Middle West, Far West, South. For each city, point out its link to a major transportation route: river(s), railroad(s), lake or ocean port. After they have finished, discuss the following, using the text as a guide:

1. Why did the Northeast experience the greatest growth during this period? (nearness to ports of entry; factories with jobs for unskilled labor; desire to be near ethnic centers already established; shortage of funds to travel or buy land; etc.)

2. Why did New York become the nation's largest city?

3. Why did some of the New England villages, once thriving, become "ghost villages"?

• Have students rearrange the cities in the list that follows according to numerical rank by listing them in two parallel vertical columns, the first headed *1860* and the second *1910*. (The first figure after each city is the population for 1860; the second for 1910.)

Baltimore: 212,418—558,485; Boston: 177,812—670,585; Buffalo: 81,129—423,715; Chicago: 109,260—2,185,283; Cleveland: 43,417—560,663; Detroit: 45,619—465,766; New York: 1,174,779—4,766,883; Philadelphia: 562,529—1,549,008; Pittsburgh: 77,919—533,905; St. Louis: 160,773—687,029. (1860: New York, Philadelphia, Baltimore, Boston, St. Louis, Chicago, Buffalo, Pittsburgh, Detroit, Cleveland. 1910: New York, Chicago, Philadelphia, St. Louis, Boston, Cleveland, Baltimore, Pittsburgh, Detroit, Buffalo.) Then have students answer the following questions:

1. Which city had the largest total population increase? (New York) the smallest increase? (Buffalo)

2. Which cities rose in rank? (Chicago, St. Louis, Cleveland) What collective reasons explain this? (important rail centers, port facilities, job opportunities for unskilled labor, ethnic centers)

3. Which cities fell in rank? (Philadelphia, Baltimore, Boston, Buffalo) Why? (various answers, but mostly because growth opportunities were greater in other cities)

4. What geographic factors do all of these cities share? (located in northeastern quadrant of country and have temperate climate, port facilities, and rail links)

• *Handout lesson:* Distribute copies of *Handout 29*. It provides data on 100 years of immigration. The wave from around 1840 to the 1870s is often called the "old immigration," and the wave beginning around 1880 and continuing to the 1920s is known as the "new immigration." Besides providing practice in graphing, the exercise is designed to help students see why immigration restriction became a lively political issue in the late 19th century.

This activity demonstrates the problem of graphing data when the range is very wide—from thousands to millions. Point out that this is the reason that the first set of bars covers three decades instead of one. Even so, it is almost impossible to show the southern/eastern immigration because the total for the 30 years was around 14,000 while the northern/western was almost 2,200,000.

The designation "northern and western" includes the British Isles, Norway, Sweden, Denmark, Germany, France, Switzerland, Belgium, Holland, and Luxembourg. "Southern and eastern" takes in the rest of Europe.

The following questions might be used with the graph.

1. In what two ways did immigration change around 1880? (almost double any previous decade; start of big wave from southern and eastern Europe)

2. Why did each of these developments worry some native-born Americans? (Large numbers: job and wage pressures, housing shortages, rapid city growth with its attendant problems. Southern/eastern Europeans: cultural threat; mostly Catholic, Orthodox, or Jewish; low literacy rates; etc.)

3. How did the "new immigration" enrich American culture?

- *Handout lesson:* For students who are interested in drawing a family tree, provide *Handout 30*. Be sure to make it clear that this is an optional activity. Tell them that the results can be used to obtain an "immigration profile" of the class.

Following are directions for filling in the diagram:

1. Put your own name on the first line (to the left). Below this line put your place of birth—and, if you wish, your year of birth in parentheses.

2. On the top line under "Parents" put your father's name. Below this line put his place of birth (state or country) and, if you wish, his year of birth. If he was born abroad, write "Immigrated" and the date. You may also put other information, such as *occupation*.

3. On the bottom line under "Parents" write your mother's *maiden* name. Add other information as you did for your father.

4. Fill in as many of the remaining lines as you can in a similar way. For this activity we are particularly interested in the national origin and approximate immigration date of any immigrant ancestor.

5. If you are able, and willing, to trace your geneology beyond one or more of your great-grandparents, ask for additional copies of the handout. Put the great-grandparent's name on the first line—and continue the diagram.

After students have had a day or two to obtain readily available information, you can poll the students about their immigrant ancestors. Provide small slips of paper, using one for each immigrant ancestor and on which the student should list the relationship, country of origin, and approximate immigration date. For example: Mother/Sweden/1969. Great-grandfather/Italy/1905. Collect the slips, and have a student sort them by country of origin. On the chalkboard put the country names followed by dates of entry.

- Tell students that the immigrants' hardships usually began *before* they arrived here. In the years before 1860 an ocean crossing by sail took from one to three months, during which conditions aboard crowded ships caused much illness and a high mortality rate. A cholera outbreak in 1866 was fortunately the last of its kind.

Although the change to steamships reduced crossing time to New York to about ten days, conditions in the crowded steerage of the ship's hold were usually barely tolerable. There was no privacy, and cleanliness was impossible. Nerves became frayed, especially when rough weather prevented passengers from going up to the deck for exercise and fresh air. Hence a physical and mental examination for immigrants was necessary on arrival at Castle Garden in New York, and after 1892, at Ellis Island.

Reformers got Congress to enact the Passenger Act in 1882 to improve the squalor aboard ships, but the law made little change in conditions, primarily because European governments were little interested in the prevention of overcrowding or the inspection of ships before departure.

Arrival in the United States did not end the immigrants' problems. As the text indicates, living conditions in slum neighborhoods offered little improvement from those of steerage. Jacob Riis, in *How the Other Half Lives* (1890), described "dark hallways and filthy cellars . . . crowded with dirty children." Handlin's *The Uprooted* and Wittke's *We Who Built America* are two of many books that describe immigrant life. See the reading list for Unit 6.

Useful films are *The Immigrant Experience* (31 min) and *Millions of New Americans* (29 min).

- Tell your students that an interesting aspect of the "Americanization" of immigrants is what happens to surnames. According to the Social Security Administration, the 25 most common surnames are Smith, Johnson, Brown, Williams, Miller, Jones, Davis, Anderson, Wilson, Taylor, Thomas, Moore, White, Martin, Thompson, Jackson, Harris, Lewis, Allen, Hall, Green, Robinson, Baker, King, and Nelson. These and other English names became the models for Anglicizing difficult-to-pronounce names from other languages. A good example is that of the Marciszewski family that came from Poland in 1903. One of their descendants is Edmund Muskie of Maine. Other examples of name changes include Kucharz—Cook, Krawiec—Taylor, Pulkinnen—Polk, and Chisefsky—Chase.

According to the American Council of Learned Societies, "One in every eighty-eight Americans is now a Smith, but only a little better than half could trace their ancestry to the British Isles." The other Smiths turn out to be German Schmidts, Scandinavian Smeds, Czech Kovars, Hungarian Kovacs, Polish Kowalczyks, French Ferriers, Italian Ferraros, and Russian Kuznetzovs. No wonder the Smiths now total nearly 1 1/2 million in the Social Security files!

- Have several volunteers look in other history texts for topics comparable to "Boss rule" and "The immigrant and the politician" (pp. 370–371). Have them report on similarities and differences in the accounts. Follow the reports with questions like these:

1. How are the social services that were handed out by the machine politician supplied today? (public welfare offices; U.S. Employment Service; some short-term aid by charities, perhaps funded by United Fund; and, here and there, some direct aid from politicians may still exist)

2. What are the advantages of tax-supported and government-administered social services? (broad sharing of costs; costs out in the open; more likelihood of fair treatment, etc.)

3. Did the politician-supplied services have any advantage? Explain. (no red tape; low administrative costs; helped people too proud, too ignorant, or too fearful of dealing with the bureaucracy)

4. Does the aid to immigrants justify the graft?

On the last point, you might want to point out that New York City paid dearly for whatever services the Tweed Ring performed for residents. To illustrate, New York paid a bill of $1,826,278 for the plastering of one city building; and $170,729 for 40 chairs and tables. These amounts are even huge for today when construction and manufacturing costs are many times what they were a century ago. Such huge sums make understandable Tweed's offer of $5 million to the *New York Times* and $500,000 to cartoonist Thomas Nast of *Harper's Weekly* to stop attacking him in the press.

• The text's explanation of the Turner thesis should not be interpreted as endorsement. In his "Bibliographical Notes," Part Three, of *The Americans: the National Experience,* Daniel Boorstin derides the romanticism attached to the frontiersman. "Such romanticism attained academic status through the appeal of the writings of Frederick Jackson Turner," Boorstin declares.

Able students can be encouraged to find a dissent on the Turner thesis in a college textbook—and then explain the analysis to the class.

• Use Section Review item 6 (p. 373) and *Meeting Our Earlier Selves* item 4 (p. 384) to structure class discussion on the topics dealing with immigration restriction. Begin by reminding students that in the 1850s the main plank of the Know-Nothing party was immigration restriction. Ask: What was happening in the late 1840s and the 1850s to stir up anti-immigrant prejudices? (the big jump in immigration, particularly from Ireland and Germany—almost totally Irish Catholics and many German Catholics)

Next solicit, and put on the chalkboard, responses to WHY restrictionist sentiments emerged again by the 1880s. For example:

1. The big increase in *number* of immigrants—increasing the competition for jobs and available housing.

2. Big rise in Catholic and Jewish population—seen as threat to Protestant dominance.

3. Cultures of southern and eastern Europeans seemed more strange and threatening—less easy to "Americanize" than were the northwestern Europeans.

4. Political threat: Oldcomers losing control of state and city governments.

5. Rising costs of government—more schools and other services.

6. Immigrants infusing the labor movement with radical ideas—socialism.

7. Easy to associate rising crime rates and other problems with the "foreigners."

Then review the HOW of immigration restriction: organization of Immigration Restriction League; push for literacy test; "Gentlemen's Agreement."

Section 2 (pp. 373–375)
Reformers and Self-helpers

Instructional Objectives Students will be able to

1. Identify problems needing reform in 1880–1900.

2. Tell about the contributions to reform of Jane Addams, Frances Willard, Ida B. Wells-Barnett, and others.

3. Describe the function of settlement houses in slum areas.

4. Explain where and why women first gained the vote in the West.

Teaching Suggestions This brief section might be combined with the next one as a single reading assignment. The activities of settlement houses can be compared with the services of present-day social welfare agencies.

• Point out that before 1900 there were relatively few municipal services or agencies to take care of the urban problems most visible in the slums: poverty, epidemic-type diseases related to poor sanitation and overcrowding, crime, prostitution, public drunkenness, and illiteracy, among others. Stirred to indignation and then action, Jane Addams and other young social workers sought to alleviate some of the problems by setting up neighborhood settlement houses like Hull House in Chicago, South End House in Boston, and the Henry Street Settlement House in New York. These were maintained by charitable contributions from the more fortunate citizens, and staffed by dedicated middle-class volunteers.

Further background on settlement houses may be found in Davis's *Spearheads for Reform* and various encyclopedias.

• If your school is in a community large enough to maintain an extensive program of social services, assign a committee to find out what these are and what services they perform. The local telephone book is a good place to start for names and addresses of services.

After the reports, discuss the following:

1. According to the text, what services and activities were available at Hull House? What agencies provide these services today?

2. What changes in our attitudes toward social reform may be noted since the turn of the century?

3. Should helping the poor and needy be a function of government or of private charitable organizations? Explain.

- Have a student report on the life and contributions of Jane Addams. The story is well told in her autobiographies *Twenty Years at Hull House* and *The Second Twenty Years at Hull House*. Or after suggesting the reading of the above books for extra credit, tell students that Jane Addams became world famous for her activities in social reform. She became a leader in the woman suffrage and the pacifist movements. In 1931 she received the Nobel Peace Prize.

- Have a student report on the life and contributions of Frances Elizabeth Willard (not to be confused with the pioneer educator Emma Willard, 1787–1870). Good biographies are by Earhart and Gates.

  Or you might add to the text's discussion of Willard by pointing out that her activities in leading the Women's Christian Temperance Union after 1879 played a significant role in the campaign against alcohol that led to the passage of the Eighteenth Amendment in 1919 (see Chapter 22).

- Tell students that Ida B. Wells-Barnett was born in 1862 shortly before Lincoln issued his Emancipation Proclamation. Overcoming many obstacles, she attended college and taught in a one-room school. At age 21 she became well known when as a railroad passenger in Tennessee she refused to sit in a section reserved for blacks only. Removed by force, she sued the railroad for violation of her rights and won her case (subsequently overturned by the state supreme court). Later, after writing articles critical of white lynchers, she carried a gun to protect herself. However, this did not prevent her enemies from destroying the newspaper office in Memphis where she worked. Her reputation as a courageous crusader spread until she became the national figure described in the text.

- Have students assume that they are living in Wyoming in 1869. The territory has the chance to become the first in the nation to introduce woman suffrage. Have the students write an editorial for one of the local newspapers on the topic "Why Wyoming Should Be First (or Should Not Be First) to Grant the Vote to Women," stating reasons in support of the position taken. Then discuss:

1. Why did women first get the right to vote in the West rather than in the more settled and educated East? (appreciation of the pioneer women; their smaller numbers made them less a threat; frontier tended to be more democratic; etc.)

2. Why was the vote for women so slow in coming on a national basis? (It was not granted nationally until the passage of the Nineteenth Amendment in 1920.)

3. Do women vote independently, or do they follow their father, husband, or other respected male? Explain. (Point out that in the 1976 election the male vote was 52% for Carter and 48% for Ford. The vote by women showed exactly the same percentage.) Ask: What does this similarity indicate?

Section 3 (pp. 375–378)
The Spread of Learning

Instructional Objectives   Students will be able to

1. Show the importance of the schools in the Americanization of immigrants and the reduction of illiteracy.

2. Describe the impact of the Morrill Act of 1862 on the growth of state colleges.

3. Categorize the founding and growth of women's colleges during the 1865–1900 period.

4. Tell about the growth of educational facilities for blacks, particularly through the efforts of Booker T. Washington.

5. Explain the basic disagreement between Booker T. Washington and W.E.B. Du Bois concerning the advancement of blacks.

Teaching Suggestions   In stressing the growth of learning during the closing years of nineteenth century America, this section offers an opportunity for you to examine the development of any educational institutions related to your community or area. If you are near a long-established college, particularly a land-grant or women's college, you can trace its history to illustrate growth in general.

Draw this chart on the chalkboard:

GROWTH OF EDUCATION -- U.S.				
	1870	1900	1960	1985
Elementary Enrollment	7 Mil.	15M	32.5M	48M(Est.)
Cost per Pupil	$15	$23	$472	$2500
Illiteracy Rate	17%	11%	3%	2%

Or, you might give the above facts to the students, and then have them prepare simple graphs for each of the three categories and four dates listed above.

After you have drawn the chart, or the students have completed the graph activity, discuss the following, using the chart and the text as guides:

1. If the total population in 1870 was 40 million, and census estimates for 1985 are for 230 million, how will the ratios of elementary population (see chart) to total population have changed from 1870 to 1985? (from 1 out of every 5.7 persons to 1—4.8 persons) What is the significance of this change? (reflects broader opportunities of schooling for all; also, impact of compulsory attendance laws; etc.)

2. What factors explain the steady rise in cost per pupil? (more costly schools, greater maintenance expenses, higher teacher salaries, more services and facilities, longer school year, inflation, etc.)

3. What needs were satisfied by the schools in the 1870–1900 period? How have these needs changed?

4. Point out that the growth of high school enrollment has been even more dramatic than that of the elementary schools. From 94,883 high school graduates in 1900, we climbed to 3,153,000 in 1975–1976. What factors explain this rise?

• Appoint a committee to prepare a report surveying the land-grant colleges in your section of the country (currently a total of 70 in the nation). Your guidance department will have helpful college guides from which students can secure the following information: (a) the origin of the colleges; (b) what programs they offer; (c) a comparison of their tuition and academic rank with that of private colleges.

After the report, discuss the following:

1. The Morrill Act is acknowledged as "the single most important piece of education legislation ever enacted in the United States." What evidence supports this statement? (At present, land-grant colleges award 99% of all agricultural and 40% of all engineering degrees in the U.S.)

2. What was the original purpose of the Morrill Act? Has this need been met through the years? Explain.

3. A provision of the Morrill Act is that every land-grant college establish a military training program (now part of the Reserve Officers' Training Corps on an elective basis). What are the arguments for and against such a military program in the state colleges?

• *Competency exercise—correcting writing errors:* Have students read Handout 31, "Letter from a Polish Immigrant." After they have finished, have them rewrite the letter, making corrections in grammar, capitalization, and punctuation (the spelling has already been corrected). If the work is done in class, give any necessary help to individual students.

After they have finished, students may be interested in discussing current problems of immigrants, particularly those for whom English is a second language. Perhaps there are teaching specialists in your school or community who can provide additional information.

• Put the following table on the chalkboard. Use it and the text to structure the discussion of the rise of educational opportunities for women.

COLLEGE GRADUATES—U.S.

	Men	Women
1900	22,173	5,237
1920	31,980	16,642
1940	109,546	76,954
1960	254,063	138,377
1980 (est.)	580,000	450,000

1. What changes have taken place during this century in the ratio of men/women college graduates?

2. Should women's colleges admit male students in our day? Why? (In recent years, they generally do. To illustrate, Vassar's enrollment in 1978 consisted of 794 men and 1430 women. Wellesley, however, had only 5 men and 1985 women.)

3. How have the opportunities for women changed since the days of Matthew Vassar?

• Have students prepare successive reports (so that contrasting views can be compared) on the lives and philosophies of Booker T. Washington and William E.B. Du Bois. Washington's *Up from Slavery* and Du Bois's *The Souls of Black Folks* provide excellent resource materials, as do numerous biographies and encyclopedia references.

After the reports, discuss the following, using the text as a guide:

1. What were the basic differences between Washington and Du Bois as to how blacks could advance and reach equality with whites? Whose views do you support? Explain.

2. Why were Washington's views more acceptable to whites than those of Du Bois?

3. Are job-training institutes such as Tuskegee still needed? Explain. (Point out that Tuskegee has remained a successful institution; in 1978 it had an enrollment of 1594 men and 1716 women.)

• Tell students that educational opportunities and facilities for blacks remained limited after Reconstruction (see Chapter 14). Segregation laws (Jim Crow) were maintained by the *Plessy* v. *Ferguson* (1896) case which upheld the constitutionality of "separate but equal" facilities for blacks. Improvement came with the *Brown* v. *Topeka* decision, which ruled that segregation in public school is "inherently unequal." Yet progress was slow. By the fall of 1972, only 44% of the black students in the South, and 30% in the North, were in predominantly white schools. Suggest Green's *Racial Crisis in American Education* or Konvitz's *A Century of Civil Rights* to students who would like to read further about the educational progress of blacks.

Sections 4–5 (pp. 378–382)
Bridge-Building Heroes / Going Up! Elevators and Skyscrapers

Instructional Objectives Students will be able to

1. Summarize the achievements of James B. Eads and the Roeblings in bridge building.

2. Tell what Otis, Bogardus, Jenney, and Bessemer each contributed to the construction of skyscrapers.

3. Point out the significance of bridges and skyscrapers.

Teaching Suggestions These two short sections can be handled as a single reading assignment. The learning objectives are simple, so you can tell students to read the material for sheer pleasure.

- Have students identify long and/or high bridges in or at the edge of a familiar large city. Ask how the absence—or collapse—of a particular bridge would affect the city—and its influence in the region. What adjustments would have to be made?

- The location and configuration of stores and offices in the 19th century and today are good topics for a review of economic principles. Point out (or use questions to elicit the facts) that most expansion of shopping facilities has occurred at the edge of cities rather than downtown. Have students speculate why. (downtown land too scarce—and therefore costly—for free parking facilities and for spread-out stores preferred by modern shoppers and required for self-service stores where shopping carts are used; self-service retailing is a response to high labor costs) Widespread car ownership, of course, promoted the changes in retail marketing. Have students explain why multistoried buildings were used for retail expansion in the 19th century (high land costs plus dependence on public transportation—streetcars, elevated railcars, and subways).

Next point out what is happening in office construction: both new and bigger downtown skyscrapers and two- to ten-story buildings on the city fringes. Have students speculate on why these twin developments are occurring. (high downtown rents because of scarce—valuable—land and high city taxes mean building higher and/or moving to cheaper land; need of certain downtown business people to have face-to-face contacts and easy message delivery dictates their preference for a downtown location, etc.)

- Point out that New York City adopted Building Zone Resolutions as early as 1916 to establish city control over the height and planning of skyscrapers relative to health, fire hazards, and the need for adequate light and air.

The tallest skyscraper currently is the 110-story Sears Tower in Chicago (1454 feet), with an additional 350 feet television antenna on top. In New York, the highest building is the World Trade Center (110 stories, 1350 feet).

To those who might like to read more about skyscrapers, suggest Condit's *The Rise of the Skyscraper* and Shultz's *Offices in the Sky*.

Section 6 (pp. 382–384)
New Towns in the Country

Instructional Objectives Students will be able to

1. Explain the purpose and construction of company towns in the 1880–1900 period.
2. Tell what problems developed in the company towns.
3. Describe the purpose and characteristics of garden cities.
4. Give examples of company towns and garden cities.

Teaching Suggestions Analysis of similarities and differences in suburban development a century ago and today can be interesting and enlightening. One focus, of course, should be on transportation: the influence of railroads—and after 1895 some electric railroads—on 19th century suburban development and the influence of the auto in our day.

- On the chalkboard under the titles COMPANY TOWNS and GARDEN CITIES write student reponses to the *Purposes* and *Features* of each. Then have students identify which features were advantages for residents and which were disadvantages. Follow with questions like these:

1. Do the advantages of a company town outweigh the disadvantages? Explain.

2. Although we have retained some of our early "garden cities," and have created Reston and Greenbelt, Maryland; Greendale, Wisconsin; and Greenhills, Ohio, our planned communities seem few and far between at the present time. What are some reasons for this? (Americans are individualistic; our tradition is to have freedom of choice as to when, where, and how to build our homes; having ample space, we have had little need to plan; we are unconcerned because we are a very mobile population. Etc.)

3. Many company towns have either been abandoned or combined with nearby municipal communities. Does this indicate that Americans have outgrown the need for company towns? Explain.

4. Does the increased cost of building single-family homes indicate that "cluster" homes and shared services within planned garden communities will be part of our future housing development? Explain.

- If you are within field-trip distance of a company town and/or a planned community, a tour of these areas will be most enlightening to your students. Encourage the taking of notes and photographs. Announce in advance that a written report will be required.

- Have individuals or a committee prepare reports on planned communities. Such books as Osborne's *Green-Belt Cities* and Creese's *The Search for Environment* will provide interesting background material. Howard's *Garden Cities of Tomorrow,* mentioned in the text, is available as a reprint paperback.

CHAPTER REVIEW

Meeting Our Earlier Selves

1. Rural villages provided farm families with one or more retail stores, church, and probably a bank, school(s), doctor's office, blacksmith, sometimes a lawyer, etc. Towns and cities supplied these services, plus others, in

more variety, and they had newspaper(s), mills and factories, and offices serving a larger market area.

2. Rural immigrant colonies could cling to old-country ways easier and longer because there was less pressure to conform to the American culture. Children especially were shielded from what parents considered deviant behavior influences. There was less pressure in the rural colony to give up the old-country language. Etc.

3. These municipal services included water supply, sewerage, gas lines (and later telephone and electric lines), street building and maintenance, public transportation, hospitals, police and fire protection, schools, etc. City-supplied services were open to corruption in the awarding of building contracts, in land acquisition, in payroll padding, in granting building permits, in protection of vice, etc. Where private enterprise supplied a public service under monopoly conditions—natural monopolies like water, gas, electric power, and public transportation—there was often graft in the awarding of franchises.

4. Changes easy to blame on Newcomers included rising crime rates, strikes involving alien workers, higher taxes for public services, rise of slums, low wages (foreigners willing to work for less), etc. Some Oldcomers would be disturbed by the rising influence of Catholics and Jews—and by an increase in interfaith marriages, especially if it meant one's own son or daughter. To the extent that the Newcomers contributed to crowding, to disease, and to noise, they could be blamed for these conditions as well.

5. The professional and clerical jobs requiring formal education were overwhelmingly in the cities. The growth of cities meant more job openings for people with formal training.

Questions for Today

1. The key is the wide availability of private transportation by the 1930s vs. the dependence on public transportation—or being within walking distance of work—in the pre-automobile era. The early garden-town suburbs were chiefly for the well-to-do who could afford the cost of commuting.

2. The big change is from private charity to tax-supported social agencies. Causes include (a) the growing belief that social services are a public obligation, (b) the effect of income and estate taxes on private fortunes, and (c) the general rise in income levels making it relatively easy to collect the taxes. A related change is that public schools more and more came to supply guidance, health education, and other "fringes" beyond mere academic training. Also the big decline in immigration after World War I reduced the need for the kinds of services performed by settlement houses.

3. Lax enforcement of codes; even well-built houses can be poorly maintained and become dilapidated; easier to check on construction than on maintenance, and many cities have weak or nonexistent housing codes—as distinct from building codes; where legal remedies for poor housing maintenance exist, they may be obstructed by crowded court calendars and long-drawn-out procedures.

CHAPTER 18

Politics in the Gilded Age

Introducing the Chapter Perhaps in introducing the last chapter you had students look at the definition of "Gilded Age" in the Chapter 18 introduction as well. Have them read it again. Then focus on the next-to-last sentence: "That glitter covered a multitude of sins." Ask: What "sins" did the authors uncover in the preceding chapter? After students have responded, ask them to turn the pages of this chapter and look at the topic headings for clues to other "sins" of the Gilded Age.

Section 1 (pp. 385–389)
Parties in Balance

Instructional Objectives Students will be able to

1. State that the close party balance in 1876–1892 made for an age of timid Presidents.
2. Explain the effect of Hayes's announcement that he would not seek a second term.
3. Define *deflation* and *inflation,* and explain how these economic conditions were affected by the supply of gold and silver currency.
4. Summarize the election of 1880.
5. Relate the circumstances of Garfield's assassination.
6. Describe the provisions of the Pendleton Act.
7. Evaluate President Arthur and his administration.

Teaching Suggestions You might begin discussion of this lesson by calling attention to the section title and asking, "What evidence does the text provide to show that the two major parties were in balance between 1876 and 1892?" (the close votes in presidential elections and the lack of one-party control of Congress) Then ask: "What effect, according to the authors, did this party balance have on government?" (made for an age of timid Presidents)

You may want to follow this with other questions like these:

1. How would a forceful President differ from a timid one?
2. Would you expect some voters to favor a timid President over a forceful one? (Yes, if the forceful one advocated policies opposed by the voter.)
3. How did the party balance in 1880 affect the party platforms? (Both parties avoided difficult issues.)
4. While the parties were in balance nationally, this was not true regionally. Where was one party absolutely dominant? (South) Why? (reaction to Republican Reconstruction)

• Three Presidents pass quickly in review in this lesson. Garfield's four-month period in office before being shot is too short to judge his worth as President. Both Hayes and Arthur have been ranked as "average" by a panel of historians. You might point out that of the eleven Presidents ranked above average by the panel, only two (John Adams and J.K. Polk) were one-term Presidents. Thus length of Presidency obviously has something to do with achievement.

Following are questions that might be used to evaluate Hayes and Arthur:

1. What are three main problems that faced Hayes as President? What did he do about each?
2. How did his announcement of serving only one term hurt his effectiveness?
3. Why could he accomplish little in his last two years in office?
4. Name at least four accomplishments of Arthur as President.
5. What did Arthur's administration show about the influence of the office of President on the person who occupies the office?

• Have students write a TV news report from the 1880 Republican convention explaining how "dark horse" candidate James A. Garfield was chosen. Use the text as a guide. After they have finished, discuss the following:

1. Why were the Republicans divided? How did the views of the "Stalwarts" and the "Half-breeds" differ?
2. Why did Conkling fail to support Blaine? (Conkling was a Stalwart; Blaine a Half-breed. However, the real reason was that in 1866 Blaine had made a slighting personal remark about Conkling, so that they were enemies thereafter. See reference in text.)
3. Why was Garfield an acceptable candidate to all delegates?

• Tell students that the railway strike in July 1877 was the most violent labor disturbance in our history. The B&O had cut the wages of its employees twice before, so that a 10% cut on July 16 brought the total to a 30% reduction. The strike that followed became violent in Baltimore when the militia fired on a hostile crowd, killing twelve people.

In Pittsburgh, where the Pennsylvania Railroad had similarly cut wages, 57 strikers and soldiers were killed, and 126 locomotives destroyed in a wall of fire three miles long. The use of federal troops by President Hayes in five states prevented interference with the trains and ended the strike. See Life History's *The Age of Steel and Steam*, Volume 7, pages 86–87, for illustrations, and Bruce's *1877: Year of Violence* for details.

The following quotations about the strike might also be presented.

1. A worker of the 1870s said: "When a man is steady and sober, and finds himself in debt for a common living, then something must be wrong."
2. Jay Gould, railroad tycoon, said: "I can hire one half of the working class to kill the other half."
3. Eugene Debs, leader of the Brotherhood of Locomotive Firemen, said: "Those who engage in force and violence are our real enemies."
4. According to a contemporary newspaper: "It is wrong to call this a strike; it is labor revolution."
5. Said another worker: "We seek an honest day's wages for an honest day's work."
6. Headline in New York *Herald*: "Pittsburgh Sacked—City Completely in the Power of a Howling Mob."

Then you might ask: On the basis of what you have read and heard so far about the great railway strike, on which side do your sympathies lie? Why?

Follow this question with a reminder that students have expressed judgments on the basis of incomplete evidence. Ask: "What other kinds of facts would be useful to know before making a judgment on the strike?" (railroad profits or losses; cost-of-living changes; wages and wage changes in other industries at the same time; effect of the strike on the country and on particular users; etc.)

• The "Skills" exercise on page 401 can be used with this lesson. One of its chief objectives is to show that the connection between inflation (and deflation) and money supply is quite complex and that therefore the calls for cheap money in the Gilded Age were simplistic.

A second major objective is to introduce or provide further practice in the reading of index numbers. Help students to see that the figures in parentheses (1910–14 = 100) in the table mean that wholesale prices of 1860–1890 are being compared with those of 1910–14. For example, the wholesale price index for "All Products" in 1880 was the same as in 1910–14—that is, the average wholesale price of a selected group of products was the same in these two periods. In 1860 wholesale prices of "All Products" were 7 percent lower than in 1910–14 (and 1880); in 1875 they were 18 percent higher. Another way to explain the figures is to point out that commodities that cost $100 in 1910–14 (or 1880) could be bought for $93 in 1860 but would have cost $118 in 1875. (But make clear that the numbers refer to average prices of many products and cannot be used to tell what happened to the price of any particular product or small group of products.)

Suggested answers to the questions follow:

1. Prices of both "All Products" and "Farm Products" just about doubled between 1860 and 1865 (the war years). But the currency supply went up 2 1/2 times.
2. Wholesale prices returned to their prewar (1860) level somewhere between 1880 and 1885.
3. Currency supply went back up to its 1865 level by 1880.
4. Several conclusions are possible: (a) A big rise in currency supply in a relatively short time period is likely to produce a rise in prices. (b) Changes in currency supply may or may not produce significant changes in price levels. (c) The table does not supply enough data to make *sound* judgments about the link between money supply and prices. This last conclusion is the most important.

In support of this last conclusion you may wish to point out that by at least 1870 more and more of the nation's money supply consisted of demand deposits in commercial banks (checking account money) because payments for goods and services were being made increasingly with bank checks. Today, currency makes up only 25–30 percent of what economists call "the money stock." (See "Money supply" in the *Statistical Abstract*.)

• Ask students to assume that they are members of Congress in 1883 and have been asked by a newspaper reporter how they are going to vote on the Pendleton (civil service) bill. Have them write out their answers, giving reasons for their vote. Use the text as a guide. After they have finished, discuss the following:

1. What provisions of the Pendleton Act are still in effect? (the use of competitive examinations and the classification of jobs)
2. Why should the Civil Service Commission be nonpartisan? (so that members will not be influenced by party considerations and will not vote along party lines)
3. What positions should be political appointments excluded from civil service regulations? (persons in sensitive policymaking positions such as department heads, their chief assistants, members of regulatory boards and commissions, etc.)

• Have students analyze the cartoons on pages 386–387. Ask questions like these about the railroad cartoon:

1. Why was railroad building a "natural" symbol for the cartoonist to use in 1878? (tremendous railroad building at that time)
2. What does the railway (rails and ties) symbolize? (the President's policies)
3. What is the "bloody-shirt radicalism" that Hayes is rejecting? (the stirring-up of ill will toward the South and the linking of Democrats with the Civil War)

4. Where else in this chapter section is there reference to the "bloody shirt"? (p. 388, col. 1)

5. Who is Mr. Blaine? What does the cartoon tell you about Blaine? (eager to wave the "bloody shirt" for political advantage; working against, rather than with, the President)

6. What does the locomotive symbolize? (federal government; notice US on front of engine) What do the railroad cars symbolize? (the states)

7. What statement does the cartoon as a whole make? (Hayes is going to see that the nation runs smoothly on solid conservative policies.)

The use of the term "conservative" seems strange when linked to the words "reform" and "new measures" that appear on the railroad ties. But in this post-Civil War era, "conservative" Republicans were those who opposed the Radicals, who were now coming to be called the Stalwarts. Also, despite favoring civil service reform, Hayes was basically a conservative in political ideology.

Before asking questions like the following about the cartoon on page 387, you may need to read the bottom line aloud:

Conkling—"Well, just at this moment, I feel as though I was a bigger man than old Hayes!"

1. Was this cartoon drawn in the earlier or later stages of the customhouse battle? How can you tell? (earlier, because Conkling is still dominant)

2. In what sense was Conkling more powerful than Hayes? (controlled customhouse patronage and could block Hayes in the Senate)

3. How does the cartoonist show Conkling's power? (one foot on customhouse and the other on the Senate; towering over everything in the cartoon)

4. What is the building in the background? (the Capitol—the seat of Congress)

5. Speculate on the meaning of "door-keeper." (may allude to Conkling's influence over bills that pass/fail in Congress—and/or to his patronage power)

Section 2 (pp. 389–394)
The Democrats Come and Go

Instructional Objectives Students will be able to

1. Compare the elections of 1884 and 1888.

2. Explain the provisions and significance of the Interstate Commerce Act of 1887.

3. State the views of the political parties on the tariff issue.

4. Explain the purpose of the Sherman Antitrust Act.

Teaching Suggestions This section is a "political" one that describes two presidential elections of the Gilded Age and two important laws (Interstate Commerce Act and Sherman Antitrust Act) that are still important in the regulation of American commerce.

• Both Cleveland and Blaine made interesting candidates in 1884. Have students give reports on the backgrounds and personal aspects of these men that caused the campaign to be filled with charges of scandal and bitter invective. Nevins's *Grover Cleveland: A Study in Courage* and the section on Blaine in Stone's *They Also Ran* will be excellent sources. You might also show the film *Grover Cleveland* (50 min).

Or you might tell the students that since presidential candidates are human they have the strengths and weaknesses of ordinary people. The Republicans gleefully spread the story that bachelor Cleveland was the father of a son born to a Buffalo widow. Republican processions chanted, "Ma! Ma! Where's my pa? Gone to the White House, Ha! Ha! Ha!" Cleveland blunted the charge by admitting the facts, explaining that he had made arrangements to take care of the child.

Meanwhile, the Democrats hurled the charge "Burn this letter" at the Republicans, a reference to the "Mulligan" letters that implicated Blaine in the sale of worthless bonds at a high price to the Union Pacific Railroad, ostensibly in return for legislative favors. A note in Blaine's own hand urging the recipient to "Burn this letter" did not help the senator's cause.

The voters followed the advice given by a Mugwump: "Mr. Cleveland has shown high character and great capacity in public life, but in private life his conduct has been open to question; while, on the other hand, Mr. Blaine in public life has been weak and dishonest while he seems to have been an admirable husband and father. The conclusion I draw . . . is that we should elect Mr. Cleveland to the public office which he is so admirably qualified to fill and remand Mr. Blaine to the private life he is so eminently fitted to adorn."

• Write these headings on the chalkboard:

INTERSTATE COMMERCE ACT—1887

Purpose—

Provisions—

Have students complete the chart by filling in the appropriate spaces to the right of *Purpose* and *Provisions,* using the text as a guide. Then discuss the following:

1. Why did the railroad owners oppose the Interstate Commerce Act?

2. Many industrialists and financiers of the period believed that government should practice a "laissez-faire" ("let business alone") attitude. Do you agree? Explain.

3. Although the Interstate Commerce Commission was first intended to prevent exorbitant railroad rates, it has since then broadened its jurisdiction through other legislation (Hepburn Act, 1903; Mann-Elkins Act, 1940; etc.)

What are some of the areas supervised by the I.C.C. today? (ferries, terminal facilities, express companies, pipelines, buses, trucks, water-born carriers, freight forwarders) The safety functions of the ICC were transferred in 1966 to the newly created Department of Transportation.)

• In discussing pension legislation under Cleveland (p. 390) and Harrison (p. 393), help students to see that the bill vetoed by Cleveland (about two months before he left office) was promptly passed again by Congress and became law when the new President signed it.

You might point out that pensions had been offered as a way to spur enlistments in the colonial wars and the Revolution, and Congress had passed some general pension laws as early as 1818. A Civil War pension law had been passed in 1862 providing payments for Union veterans who suffered service-connected disabilities and for their widows and children. The big change in the 1887 law was that now pensions would pay for any disability. The new law was, in part, a response to the problem raised by the increasing introduction of *private* pension bills sponsored by members of Congress as favors to constituents.

If you care to pursue the pension issue, you might raise questions like these:

1. Does the government have more of an obligation to pay for service-connected disabilities than for other kinds? Why?

2. Should needy veterans get more protection from the government than needy non-veterans? Why?

3. Should society supply special benefits for ex-servicemen and women regardless of whether they served in combat?

4. How do veterans' benefits today differ from those offered in the 19th century?

• Analysis of the cartoon on page 391 can help students see why tariffs and trusts were twin political issues in the late 1880s—and to focus on the "evil" inherent in both, namely, their role in softening competition. Help students identify the trusts represented as the heads of the hydra. Ask them to identify some of the symbols used: gas meter, rubber boot, anvil, etc. The trusts, of course, were organized to reduce competition among firms operating in the United States. But some producers still had to worry about competition from abroad, so they favored high tariff rates on goods that competed with their own. Thus Keppler shows the trusts thriving on the hydra's body, the "war tariffs." Tell students that "war" here refers to the fact that tariffs rates had gone up substantially during the 1860s—the Civil War and postwar years.

• You might remind students that the tariff had been a hot political issue in the late 1820s (the Tariff of Abominations of 1828), producing the nullification controversy of the early 1830s. It was also a divisive sectional issue—with the industrial Northeast favoring high rates (protection) and the South wanting low tariffs, since its agricultural products did not need protection and because a protective tariff raised the cost of manufactured goods purchased by Southerners.

It is significant that tariff rates rose sharply in the 1860 when northern Republicans controlled Congress. But i the 1880s, with the southern Democrats again a force i Congress and with the parties in balance on the nationa scene, the tariff once more becomes a partisan (and sec tional) issue. And it will continue to be so for the next fift years—to the 1930s.

The foregoing can serve as background for the tariff dis cussion in this lesson. Cleveland, the first Democrati President (omitting Andrew Johnson) since James Bu chanan in 1857–1861, opposes high tariff rates on principl but also conforms to traditional Democratic doctrine When the Republicans win with Harrison, they proceed t work for higher rates in the McKinley tariff. And now th sectional aspects of the tariff show up. Protectionist north ern Republicans had to have help in getting the McKinle bill passed, so they turned to the Westerners, who had n strong sectional interest in the tariff because they were les affected by foreign trade. So the Westerners were willin to trade support for the tariff in return for Republican sup port on the silver issue.

• Have the students point out some similarities and differ ences in the elections of 1884 and 1888, such as:

SIMILARITIES

Cleveland a candidate in both campaigns.

Cleveland won popular vote in both campaigns.

New York the decisive state in both elections.

Irish city vote important in both elections.

DIFFERENCES

Democrats won in 1884 and lost in 1888.

Incumbent President not nominated in 1884; lost election i 1888.

Personal smear campaign in 1884; not in 1888.

Although the decisive state in both elections, N.Y. wen Democratic in 1884 and Republican in 1888.

Irish voted against Republicans in 1884 but not in 1888.

• If you passed over the trusts quickly in Chapter 16, thi lesson is a good place to review the trust as a form of busi ness organization, to explain other kinds of business combi nations designed to lessen competition (merger, holding company, cartel, etc.), and to describe other "restraints o trade." Following are some questions that can be used t guide discussion:

1. What is a business monopoly? (a single firm or combina tion of firms controlling a particular market. Examples all steel mills in the nation run by one firm—or by a group of firms who agree to divide the market and no

compete; a single phone company serving a state or a city; one taxi company in a town; etc.)

2. Why might most producers like to enjoy a monopoly? (could charge the price that would bring in the highest net income)

3. Why do buyers prefer competition (competitive market conditions)? (better prices, product quality, and customer service can be expected)

4. Do monopolies ever serve the public interest? Explain. (Some businesses, chiefly public utilities, are called natural monopolies because they could hardly exist with direct competition. Two or three sets of power lines or gas mains in the same city would be too wasteful, so we permit some businesses to operate as monopolies but under fairly strict regulation. Firms whose products are protected by patents or copyrights enjoy a limited monopoly, which seems desirable as an incentive for creative effort.)

5. The Sherman Antitrust Act was passed to break up and stop the formation of business combinations (trusts, mergers, etc.) that would lessen competition. (Point out that the terms "trust" and "antitrust" continued in use with reference to business monopolies even after the formal "trust" arrangement had been outlawed.) The Sherman Act also forbade other "restraint of trade or commerce." What kinds of practices might be covered by this phrase? (railroad rebates, price fixing and/or dividing market territory among competitors, identical bidding on government contracts, and others)

6. Why was the Sherman Antitrust Act ineffective for some years? (see text)

Section 3 (pp. 394–399)
The Farmers' Revolt

Instructional Objectives Students will be able to

- Identify problems facing the farmers.
- Trace the organization of the farmers that led to the Granger laws and the founding of the Populist party.
- Summarize the election of 1892, emphasizing the role of the Populist party.
- Compare Cleveland's second term with his first and evaluate his Presidency.

Teaching Suggestions This section offers a chance to examine the problems of rural America. You might also note that the promise of the frontier is challenged by forces the farmers feel they cannot control, so they turn to a third party for help. Some of its goals seem so modern that you can relate them to the present day.

Competency exercise—letter writing: Using the text as a guide, write a letter from a farmer in the West to a brother who works in an eastern city, telling about the problems of the western farmer. Remind students that the sentences must be original and written with correct spelling and punctuation.

After the letters have been checked for correct form and fact, select several for reading aloud to the class.

- For a quick review of the farmers' revolt write these items on the chalkboard in a vertical column: Patrons of Husbandry, Granger laws, *Munn* v. *Illinois,* Farmers' Alliances, Populist party. In an adjoining column write responses as students tell how the listed item helped or tried to help farmers. Follow with questions like these:

1. The "farm problem" was low prices and high costs. Why had prices dropped? (wartime demand dropped; mechanization produced crop surpluses)

2. What high or rising costs particularly inflamed the farmers? (high mortages and other borrowing contracted when prices were relatively high; railroad freight rates; grain elevator rates)

3. How did cooperatives help farmers?

4. Why were the Granger laws relatively ineffective?

5. Which of the Populist party planks do you consider sound? unsound? Why?

- The film *Growth of Farming in America, 1865–1900* (14 min) is useful for this lesson.

- Tell your students that Mary Elizabeth Lease was widely known as Mary Ellen and then Mary "Yellin" Lease because of her flamboyant style of oratory. Of Irish background, she became a lawyer in Kansas, and soon an advocate of Populism.

Tom Watson spoke not only for Populism, but was a prominent anti-Catholic author and speaker. He was indicted three times for libel, but never convicted.

James B. Weaver was a frontier lawyer in Iowa before rising from the rank of private to that of general in the Union army. Although unsuccessful as a minor party candidate seeking the Presidency, he and the Populists contributed much to the progressive legislation passed at the turn of the century.

- A persistent problem in teaching American history in high school is how much time and attention to give to the monetary issues of the late 19th century. Clearly, the less-able students will do well to see some connection between money supply and prices, to understand that the growth of the money supply was inadequate for the needs of the time, and to know that paper money can be (a) a promise to pay the bearer in metal—gold or silver—or (b) a certificate having no specific exchange value.

In addition, more-able students should learn the meaning of "gold standard" and get some insight into the difficulties of tying money to some metallic standard.

But is trying to teach *bimetallism* worth the effort? Probably only insofar as it contributes to an understanding of the political events of the late 19th century. Perhaps it is enough to point out that Congress legally adopted a bimetallic system in 1792 but that the system worked for only a short time at the beginning. Gold and silver kept getting off the fixed (legal) ratio, such as 16 to 1. If gold went up in value so that commercial buyers demanded 17 oz. of silver for one of gold, people would take their silver to the Treasury and exchange 16 oz. for 1 oz. of gold—and people would hoard their gold. If silver increased in value relative to gold (say, 15 to 1), people would turn in gold to the Treasury (or spend their gold coins and hoard their silver), getting 16 oz. from the Treasury and earning 1 oz. of silver for each ounce of gold turned in. (The transactions actually involved getting coins for bullion.)

Another problem arises in teaching "free coinage of silver." The term "free coinage" means that people could bring gold or silver to the Treasury and have it coined. (In effect, they exchanged bullion for coins.) In 1873 Congress had ended the free coinage of silver—chiefly, it seems, because silver hadn't been coming in ever since the gold rush of 1849 and later (when gold dropped in value relative to silver—and people thus hoarded their silver). At about this same time a number of European countries went on the gold standard and limited the coinage of silver. Huge amounts of silver bullion flooded the market, and silver dropped in value. Then rich supplies of silver were found in Nevada (Chapter 15), further depressing the price of silver. Now suddenly people (especially the western mining interests) wanted to bring in their 90-cent silver and get coins worth a dollar. The Populists, including the farmers and other debtors, also had an interest in "free coinage of silver" because this would add to the currency supply and promote inflation.

• Some of the foregoing explanation may be required for students to understand the "drain on gold" problem that faced the Cleveland administration in the 1890s.

• Tell the class that Coxey's Army made one of the first prolonged "protest marches" in our history. A ragged group carrying food and blankets on their shoulders, Coxey's followers hiked slowly along dusty roads for a month until they reached Washington. Their Populist program called for the hiring of the unemployed to work on government projects, such as the improvement of roads (a preview of the New Deal work programs in the 1930s).

Neither Cleveland nor Congress would see Coxey. The "army" marched to the Capitol steps, where policemen and a large crowd waited. Coxey began to read a petition, and was arrested for walking on the grass. The crowd and the "army" then dispersed, and no more was heard of Coxey thereafter.

Section 4 (pp. 399–401)
Our Money: Gold versus Silver

Instructional Objectives Students will be able to

1. Tell about William Jennings Bryan and his oratory at the Democratic convention in 1896.

2. Describe the candidates, issues, and results of the election of 1896.

Teaching Suggestions This brief section introduces William Jennings Bryan, one of the most colorful figures in our political history, and a presidential candidate at 36 years of age. Students will be more interested in stories about his oratory than in his views. Bryan was also the first of the modern campaigners as he criss-crossed the country. Yet he was beaten by a "front porch" opponent. Here is a chance to explore the merits of the various approaches to campaigning and factors that help elect a candidate. *Handout 32* provides further description of the campaign.

• Have reports on the background of Bryan and McKinley up to the election of 1896. Koenig's *Bryan: A Political Biography* and Stone's *They Also Ran* will be helpful for Bryan, while Leech's *In the Days of McKinley* tells not only about McKinley but describes his whole era.

The famous "Cross of Gold" speech is found in *A Treasury of the World's Great Speeches*.

Ask students to imagine speaking to a crowd without the use of amplification. Bryan faced a noisy crowd of 20,000, quieted them, and reportedly was heard by everyone in the Chicago convention hall. After the reports, discuss the following:

1. Professor Houston Peterson says that Bryan's speech was "the most effective convention speech of all time." How can this statement be supported? (Bryan had a powerful voice; this was an age when listeners were moved by high-flown oratory; the convention listeners were emotionally "ready" for this type of speech. Since then, audiences have become more sophisticated and are less easily impressed.)

2. To whom did Bryan appeal with his demand for "free silver"? (western farmers, debtors, workers in East, Populists, the "common" people)

3. Why was Mark Hanna considered more important to McKinley's success than the candidate himself? (because of his skillful management of the campaign and his influence with powerful and rich party supporters)

4. Why did Bryan lose, even though he polled more than any previous winning candidate? (two million more votes in 1896 than in 1892, so that figures are relative; Bryan's single issue—silver; his youth and inexperience; some voters who preferred Bryan may have been intimidated to vote for McKinley; the Republican slogan of "a full dinner pail" had a wide appeal)

• *Handout lesson:* After students have read *Handout 32*, have them respond orally or in writing to the following questions:

1. Which candidate impressed the writer the most? Why?

2. Why did Bryan get "silver" roses? Why was the McKinley delegation wearing "yellow"? (playing up the silver vs. gold issue)

3. Would a candidate today depend on a front-porch campaign? Why?

4. What does the writer think of American audiences?

• Have students draw a timeline for the period 1877 to 1896, using Chapter 18 as a guide. Then discuss the following:

1. Which election during this period do you consider most important? Why?

2. Which of the Presidents of this period impressed you most? Why?

3. What was the most important law passed at this time in terms of our present day? Why?

4. Which party would you have belonged to at this time? Why?

CHAPTER REVIEW

Meeting Our Earlier Selves

1. Twelve years of Republicans in the White House and eight years of Democratic rule; several years of divided party control of Congress. Party balance made Presidents fearful of taking strong initiatives out of fear of losing current support, and a divided Congress—or a Congress dominated by the opposing party—would block presidential initiatives. With the balance between the major parties, the Populists had a reasonable chance of winning some elections—particularly for seats in Congress. Also the party balance made both parties timid on the issues, and thus induced the "radicals" to form their own party.

2. Presidency forces the incumbent to view problems in a broader perspective. Actions of predecessors (and existing law) put constraints on what President can accomplish. At least some Presidents are concerned about their place in history and therefore become "statesmen" instead of merely "partisans," etc.

3. (a) Would favor "sound money" because inflation would erode their savings; (b) would favor "cheap money" as a way to boost farm prices, thus making it easier to pay off debts; (c) on the fence because "cheap money" *might* bring wage increases but would almost certainly raise the cost of living; (d) "cheap money" because of merchant's dependence on farm prosperity; (e) "sound money" because bank wants to have its loans repaid with money at least as valuable as the dollars it lent.

4. Failed to guide Congress on Interstate Commerce Act; vetoed pensions to save money; opposed higher tariff with "unnecessary taxation" argument; allowed Wilson-Gorman tariff to become law without his signature; but did take fairly strong stands and action on "sound money" issues. Ideally it would be best to have a good manager *and* a strong political leader. But the latter seems more important in a President. The President must be a leader but can pick good managers. Time spent on management is not available for leadership activities.

Questions for Today

1. Much of the desegregation that has been accomplished in the past thirty years might have occurred earlier, and perhaps less segregation would have developed. Blacks would have attained political power, and the battle over voting rights would have occurred earlier or been avoided. One can visualize much more equal education for blacks over the years, which along with other avenues for upward mobility would have lessened some of the black-white economic inequality. One must recognize, of course, that in spite of having political rights and access to education, a "poor white" class grew up in the South—and in other parts of the nation. Yet it was far easier for a "poor white" to achieve distinction than for a black person.

2. The chance for a political appointment still motivates some people today—as does the chance to win an elective office. Many people become politically involved because of their general interest in good government or because they have a strong attachment to particular public issues (minority rights, antinuclear power, abortion, etc.). Also, despite tremendous advances in the management of public finance, opportunities still exist for personal enrichment.

Skills to Make Our Past Vivid

See teaching suggestions and answers on Guide page 100.

CHAPTER 19

The United States and the World

Introducing the Chapter Remind students that, since Chapter 9, the text has focused on the domestic achievements and problems of the United States except for foreign relations with Mexico and Great Britian over territorial expansion in the West. Now we go back nearly to the Monroe Doctrine and pick up the thread of our diplomatic history. Then you might have students speculate on why our foreign relations from around 1830 (Andrew Jackson) to 1890 (Benjamin Harrison)—outside of the Mexican War and the Oregon issue—assumed a fairly minor place in public affairs. Then ask: What developments that we have studied in the past three chapters about the post-Civil War period might you expect would lead to greater involvement in world affairs?

Section 1 (pp. 404–407)
Looking Outward

Instructional Objectives Students will be able to

1. Tell how we became involved with the Far East, particularly through the efforts of Commodore Perry.

2. Evaluate the significance of the acquisition of Alaska.

3. State what the *Alabama* claims were and how we settled them with Great Britain.

4. Describe our opposition to the establishment of a French empire in Mexico.

5. Explain our problems with Chile.

Teaching Suggestions Early efforts to annex Hawaii are described in this lesson—and later ones in the next section. This first section would be an appropriate place to provide (or have student reports on) enrichment materials dealing with early contacts of traders and missionaries with the Hawaiian people.

- Use the map on page 414 for help in locating some of the places mentioned in this lesson and for learning some distances in the Pacific. Using a strip of paper (or a compass) students can find some approximate equal distances: for example, San Francisco to Hawaii = Hawaii to Wake Island = San Francisco to Detroit = Wake Island nearly to Philippines, etc. Or, Maine coast to San Francisco = San Franciso to Midway Island = Midway nearly to Philippines, etc.

- The Treaty of Wanghia introduces the term "most favored nation." For a long time a most-favored-nation clause has been a standard provison in most commercial treaties. It promises that the signers will treat each other as well as they treat anyone else. ("If we have given country X some privilege, we give it to you too.") It does not mean, "We are giving some special privileges to you alone." You might also point out that although the Treaty of Wanghia followed close on the heels of the Opium War, the privileges gained had nothing to do with trade in opium.

- Have a student report on Commodore Matthew C. Perry and his opening of Japan to American trade. Barrows's *The Great Commodore* or the *Dictionary of American Biography* will be helpful.

Or tell the class that Matthew Perry was a younger brother of Oliver Perry of Lake Erie fame in the War of 1812. Matthew performed the delicate task of opening Japan to western trade without starting a war. He did this with a combination of seven steam-propelled black warships of a kind that the Japanese had never seen before and gifts of a telegraph instrument and a small steam locomotive that could travel twenty miles an hour. Soon further imports of western products helped end Japanese isolation.

- *Competency exercise—sentence and paragraph writing:* Write the following facts about Alaska on the chalkboard. Then direct students to use the facts to write a paragraph on the geography of Alaska. Insist on complete sentences with correct spelling, grammar, and punctuation.

THE GEOGRAPHY OF ALASKA

Area: 589,757 sq. mi.; larger than next three states (Texas, Calif., Mont.) combined.

Topography: very mountainous with thousands of glaciers; Mt. McKinley is highest point in N. America. Broad central plateau.

Climate: extremely varied; moist and mild in SE; dry, cold winters and mild summers in parts of central plateau; far north very cold and dry; long summer days and winter nights.

Chief economic resources: oil and natural gas; forests; fish.

- Write ALABAMA CLAIMS on the chalkboard. Below and to the left, list in a vertical column: *Countries involved, Claims made, Method of settlement, Terms of settlement.* Have students complete the chart by filling in appropriate responses. Then discuss the following:

1. Was the arbitration decision fair to both sides? Why?

2. Would the U.S. and Great Britain become involved in similar problems in the present day? Explain.

3. What kinds of international problems are most suitably handled by an international tribunal? Why?

• Point out that Napoleon III's Mexican venture, besides being a violation of the Monroe Doctrine, posed another serious post-Civil War problem for the United States. Not all Confederate troops laid down their arms. Cavalry General Jo Shelby marched an "Iron Brigade" of 1000 ex-Confederate troops to Mexico City in the summer of 1865, offering them as support for Emperor Maximilian and promising to recruit more thousands of troops. Fearful of the consequences, Maximilian rejected the offer. He offered land grants for settlement instead. Some 500 Americans took up the offer, naming their new town "Carlota" after Maximilian's wife. However, with the evacuation of the French army and Maximilian's execution, the hope for a confederacy away from home vanished. Soon most of the settlers returned to their southern U.S. hometowns.

After you have related the above, and students have reviewed the text, discuss the following:

1. If the French entry into Mexico was a violation of the Monroe Doctrine, why didn't we prevent the French from coming in the first place?

2. Why didn't Maximilian go back to France while he had the chance?

3. Suppose that enough ex-Confederate soldiers had gone to Mexico to enable Maximilian to hold on to the Mexican throne. What would—or should—the United States have done? Explain.

• Have students turn to the map on page 751 to locate Chile. Have them note the other South American countries. Have them also review "Problems with Chile" in the text. Then discuss the following:

1. Why did the United States periodically have diplomatic problems with Latin American countries? (specific incidents of relationship, such as the one described in the text; trade, military, or ideological differences; dissatisfaction with our role as "big brother"; etc.)

2. How would a modern American President handle a problem similar to that faced by President Harrison? Explain. (would be less inclined to go to war; would use offices of OAS and UN; etc.)

3. Do you think that our early conception of the Monroe Doctrine should still apply to our relationships with our southern neighbors? Should we become involved if they are threatened by a Communist takeover, for example? Explain.

Point out that since 1948 the U.S. and Latin American countries have cooperated in the solution of numerous hemispheric problems as members of the Organization of American States.

Section 2 (pp. 407–410)
Expanding on the Seas

Instructional Objectives Students will be able to

1. Explain and evaluate the Mahan theory that sea power determines the military strength of a nation.

2. Tell why and how the United States annexed Hawaii.

3. Describe our involvement in the Venezuela-British Guiana boundary dispute.

Teaching Suggestions Students may express some skepticism as to the significance of sea power in a nuclear age. Encourage debate on this topic. The acquisition of Hawaii offers the opportunity to examine its geography, ethnic groupings, and relationships with the United States. And the Venezuelan incident brings an important extension of the Monroe Doctrine.

• A brief lecture on the "new imperialism" that developed in the latter half of the 19th century seems appropriate at this point. Among points that might be covered are these:

1. The "old imperialism" that had begun in the late 1400s came to a halt around 1800 with Britain's loss of the American colonies, the French Revolution and Napoleonic wars upsetting Europe, then Spain's loss of its American colonies, and all the while European preoccupation with the Industrial Revolution.

2. The Industrial Revolution was the major force behind the "new imperialism": (a) vast populations of Asia and Africa seen as customers for the growing factory surpluses, and political control by a rival power could lead to trade restrictions; (b) the ever-growing need for secure sources of raw materials; (c) with surplus of capital rising in Europe—and interest rates falling—overseas investment became more and more attractive, but safety of investment seemed to require political control.

3. Rising world trade was linked—by Mahan and others—with sea power: to establish and protect colonies and spheres of influence, to keep trade routes open, and to protect merchant fleets.

4. Political considerations of world power and prestige augmented the economic arguments.

5. To the above factors we must add the "white man's burden" appeal of "civilizing" and Christianizing "backward" peoples. It was a sincere belief held by many people, and it was a rationalization used by others to cloak selfish motives.

6. The United States was a late entrant in the "new imperialism"—both for idealistic reasons (cherishing of liberty) and because of the big national market for goods and the relative abundance of our raw materials.

• Item 2 in *Meeting Our Earlier Selves* might be used in connection with the above lecture/discussion.

- "To what extent, if any, has air power reduced the importance of sea power for a strong nation today?" This question might be posed to begin a discussion leading to a deeper understanding of Mahan's thesis and its applicability today. To get at this broad question, it will be useful to raise some subsidiary questions:

1. What tasks performed by navies a hundred years ago are still naval tasks today? What new tasks do modern navies perform? (carrying aircraft, chiefly)

2. How do modern navies differ from those of a century ago?

3. What basic change(s) in the climate of international affairs has taken place in the past hundred years that affects sea power? (imperialism is universally condemned)

- Follow up a lecture or student reports on early contacts between Americans and Hawaiians with teacher or student presentations of the details surrounding the annexation of Hawaii by the United States.

- Have students turn to the maps of South America on pages 177 and 751 to locate Venezuela. Have them also review "The Venezuelan boundary dispute" in the text. Then discuss the following:

1. Under the Monroe Doctrine, does the United States have the right to intervene in boundary disputes as well as threats against American lives in Latin America? Explain.

2. Do you agree with the point of view of Olney or Salisbury? Explain.

3. Is there ever a time, as urged by Theodore Roosevelt, when "this country needs a war"? Explain.

Section 3 (pp. 410–418)
War with Spain

Instructional Objectives Students will be able to

1. Explain how and why we went to war with Spain over Cuba.

2. Describe the impact of the "Yellow Press" and the sinking of the *Maine* in molding American opinion against Spain.

3. Summarize the events and the results of the Spanish-American War.

4. Name some anti-imperialists and summarize their views.

5. Describe our postwar relations with the Philippines, Cuba, and Puerto Rico.

6. Explain how the United States became involved with China.

Teaching Suggestions This section explores more than the military events of the Spanish-American War—the influencing of American public opinion by the press, the inability of a weak President to stem the tide of war, the spread of our imperialism to the Philippines, and the participation of American troops in Chinese affairs.

- Write SPANISH-AMERICAN WAR on the chalkboard. Below and to the left, list the following in a vertical column: *Cuban problems, Reasons for American entry, Naval engagements, Army activities, Results of Spanish defeat*. Using the text and the map on page 412 as a guide, have students complete the chart. After they have finished, discuss:

1. Why was possession of Cuba naturally attractive to Americans?

2. Why did we have sympathy for the Cuban people?

3. What role did the press play in our going to war with Spain? (Publisher William Randolph Hearst was reported to have cabled to artist Frederic Remington: "You furnish the pictures and I'll furnish the war.")

4. Why might American business firms have wanted the war? (investments in sugar; also point out that Senator John M. Thurston of Nebraska said: "War with Spain would increase the business and earnings of every American railroad, it would increase the output of every American factory, it would stimulate every branch of industry and domestic commerce.")

5. Why were there so many "jingoes" at this time? (had not had a war for a long time; the nation was in an imperialist mood; Spain posed no serious challenge; etc.)

6. Was the navy or the army more significant to our victory in the war? Explain.

7. Were the terms of the Platt Amendment fair to Cuba? Explain.

- *Competency exercise—sentence writing:* Use skill exercise 2 on page 418. When you assign the exercise, you might call attention to the line "Other deaths" and say that most of these arose from various diseases brought on by unsanitary camps, spoiled food, and polluted water. Many of the needed medicines never reached the camps; soldiers labeled their canned meats "embalmed beef"; and the water was not boiled or purified.

- The following questions might be used to compare and contrast the policy of the United States government in the Philippines, Puerto Rico, and Cuba:

1. How did the United States acquire Puerto Rico? (granted by Spain as part of peace treaty) the Philippines? (purchased)

2. Why did the U.S. not acquire Cuba? (Teller Amendment)

3. How was American acquisition regarded by the Puerto Ricans? the Filipinos?

4. How did the United States keep a "presence" in Cuba? (coaling or naval stations; mention Guantanamo Bay)

5. What other conditions did the United States make for getting out of Cuba?

6. How were these conditions forced on the Cubans?

7. What similarities were there in the postwar treatment of Puerto Rico, the Philippines, and Cuba? What were some of the differences?

8. If American statesmen in 1898–1900 could have "read" the future, which of the following policies do you think they would have adopted? Why?
   a. Much the same policies as they did adopt.
   b. Rapid independence and self-government for all three territories.
   c. Acquisition, territorial self-government, and eventual statehood for all three territories.
   d. Independence for Cuba and retention of Puerto Rico and Philippines by Spain.
   e. Other. Explain.

- If you have any Puerto Rican students in your classes, you might have them prepare reports on the people, history, geography, and government of Puerto Rico. Many helpful books are also available, such as Golding's *A Short History of Puerto Rico*. You might also discuss the continuing nationalist campaign for independence (in 1967 Puerto Ricans voted to retain the status quo).

- Have students use the map on page 417 plus the text to answer these questions about our involvement in the Far East around 1900:

1. How had the United States become intimately involved in the Far East by 1900? (acquisition of Philippines)

2. About how far are the Philippines from the coast of China? (400–500 miles)

3. What three nations had the largest spheres of influence in China at this time? Why was their presence in China "logical"? (all held territory bordering China)

4. What nation controlled Macao? Hong Kong? Indochina? Korea?

5. Where did Russian and Japanese influence overlap? (Manchuria)

6. Why would the United States want an "Open Door" in China?

7. Why did the United States take part in putting down the Boxer Rebellion?

8. What actions by the United States at this time would you expect the Chinese government and people to regard favorably? Why? (both the Open Door policy and the return of Boxer Rebellion indemnity)

- Have students prepare a timeline of key events of the chapter beginning with Perry's entry into Japanese ports in 1852.

CHAPTER REVIEW

Meeting Our Earlier Selves

1. In spite of our growing population and the resulting big national market, American business (and agriculture) was eager for even broader markets. Some businesses would also be concerned about secure supplies of raw materials or cheaper supplies than were available in the U.S.

2. The territorial grabs by the European powers made some Americans envious—and eager for the United States to get "its share." Anti-imperialists could point to European expansion as activity unbefitting liberty-loving Americans.

3. See pages 405–406 on Seward's hopes that the purchase of Alaska might lead to the annexation of Canada.

4. The Monroe Doctrine was involved (a) in the Maximilian affair in that France was interfering with the independence of an American nation; (b) in the Venezuelan boundary dispute in that President Cleveland chose to interpret British pressure on Venezuela as interference; and (c) in the Platt Amendment in that it required Cuba to promise not to forfeit its independence to any foreign power (other than the United States, of course).

5. Overseas territories (with the possible exception of Hawaii) were not obtained for settlement. Some of the smaller territories were governed directly by officials sent out from Washington; others were allowed limited self-government. At the time of their acquisition there seems to have been little consideration of eventual statehood.

6. Nations are most likely to arbitrate boundary and financial disputes, since the stakes are relatively low compared with what the costs might be in fighting and because the issues lend themselves to compromise solutions. Disputes over political control of a large territory instead of just a boundary line or over insults to national honor may be harder to settle by compromise.

Questions for Today

1. Probably not, since a large proportion of the public depends on TV and radio for news and opinion. Some poeple might argue that the public—with its higher average educational levels—is less susceptible to "slanted news" today. Also the news media today are not dominated by a couple of giants like Hearst and Pulitzer.

2. A notable recent example is Carter's influence in the Israeli-Egyptian peace accord.

3. Recent relations with Cuba stand out. The links with the past are complex, but it is safe to say that developments in Cuba that led to the Castro-led revolution had some roots in our protectorate over Cuba; moreover, our naval base at Guantanamo Bay has remained a sore spot.

Our touchy relations with the Philippines from time to time may have some link to the development of that land under our tutelage. The political status of Puerto Rico is a persistent problem.

CHAPTER 20

The Progressive Era

Introducing the Chapter The five sections of this chapter cover a broad range of topics—including the enactment of numerous laws still pertinent today—so that special care will be needed in picking out subject matter for elaboration in order to stay on a reasonable time schedule.

You might begin by reading the chapter introduction aloud—or having a good student reader do so. Then ask, "What era, or age, have we just finished studying?" (the Gilded Age) Follow with: "Why is it not surprising that a Gilded Age was followed by a Progressive Era, a period of reform?" After hearing responses, you might conclude by reminding students that historical eras, or ages, are inventions of historians and often do not have clear-cut starting and ending points.

Section 1 (pp. 419–425)
Theodore Roosevelt's Square Deal

Instructional Objectives Students will be able to

1. Describe McKinley's assassination.
2. Tell about the background and philosophy of President Theodore Roosevelt.
3. Summarize Roosevelt's intervention in the coal strike and his "trust-busting" activities.
4. Describe the reform and conservation legislation of the Roosevelt administration.

Teaching Suggestions By describing the background and characteristics of Theodore Roosevelt, this section features a President once worshipped as a hero, then considered passé, and now popularized again (see *Newsweek*, August 6, 1979, "The Saga of Teddy"). Some of the reforms summarized can be examined in terms of their current application. Link Roosevelt's pioneer conservation efforts to our modern environmental protection movement.

• To your students, the ease with which Leon Czolgosz stood in line, concealed a handkerchief around his hand, and shot President McKinley may seen incredible in light of the security now given the President. However, according to Margaret Leech's *In the Days of McKinley*, "It was a hot day, and handkerchiefs were much in evidence" (and thus were ignored).

Even more difficult to believe is why no use was made of one of the new X-ray machines at the nearby Buffalo Exposition. Perhaps the surgeons were skeptical of its value to locate a bullet buried deep in the abdomen of a weakened patient. Failing to locate the bullet, surgeons closed up the wound without drainage, hoping the President's sturdy constitution would resist infection. For a little while, McKinley rallied, but then worsened as gangrene set in. Within a few days he was dead. You might ask how modern surgeons would have handled this case—would the President have survived? (Aided by X-rays, modern physicians would have removed the bullet, drained the wound, and used antibiotics. McKinley would have had a good chance of survival.)

• Tell students that McKinley is rated "average" by the historians. Although considered more able than many Presidents, McKinley seemed to lack courage in resisting the cries for war against Spain (a belief perpetuated by an alleged statement by T.R. that McKinley had "no more backbone than a chocolate eclair"). A much admired and respected President during his term of office, McKinley has faded somewhat as anti-imperialism has grown as a national philosophy during recent decades.

• Call attention to the photograph of TR on page 420 and the cartoon on page 430. If possible, show other pictures and cartoons of him. Ask: "How do the pictures support the description of Teddy Roosevelt in the text?" Then: "Do any of the pictures or cartoons give you different or additional impressions about TR?"

• Remind students that TR was another of our "accidental" Presidents, rising to the office as a result of the death of the President. Ask students to imagine that McKinley had served out his second term and then retired. "Would the Republican convention in 1904 have picked Vice-President Roosevelt as their new candidate for President?" Use such a device to have students examine the character and personality traits and the background of TR as provided by the text (and by other material you may present) for those traits and experiences that would have persuaded the convention delegates to pick Roosevelt as the presidential candidate. Ask: "Do you see any traits that might have caused the delegates to choose someone else?" (too outspoken and forceful? lacking in dignity?)

• Use the song "Sixteen Tons," popularized by Tennessee Ernie Ford, to impress on students some of the coal miners' complaints that led to the strike of 1902. Read the words, play a record, or have a student vocalist sing the song. Then have students repeat phrases that link complaints or implied complaints in the song to the conditions described in the text.

You might have students express views, or try to formulate a view, on labor-dispute conditions that call for government intervention. You can start with the conditions described in the text that led Roosevelt to intervene. Then ask: "Under what other kinds of situations should a President, governor, or other official step into a labor dispute to force a resolution of the conflict?"

You might conclude discussion of the coal strike by pointing out that it lasted 163 days and cost close to $100 million in lost wages and business income. The miners received a 10 percent increase in wages.

- While the details of holding-company organization are not needed to understand the Northern Securities case, a simple diagram of a holding company drawn on the chalkboard can be useful. Perhaps you can find a diagram—plus useful description—in a high school economics textbook. You might tell students that the American Telephone and Telegraph Company (AT&T) has been a holding company for the various regional Bell Telephone Companies and for Western Electric Company, producer of phone equipment. AT&T was also an operating company for long-distance service. (Reorganization in 1980 changed AT&T's structure somewhat.)

The following questions might be used to supplement Section Review item 4 on the Northern Securities trust case:

1. How does a holding company differ from a trust? (In a trust all the stock of the subsidiary, or operating, companies was exchanged for trust certificates; a holding company acquires by purchase or exchange of stock simply a controlling ownership interest in the operating companies—but could own up to 100% in some cases—and control may be achieved by, say, as little as 15% of the stock if the rest is widely dispersed.)

2. Why are holding companies sometimes called trusts? ("Trust" and "antitrust" have become common terms to refer to any business monopoly or near monopoly.)

3. What had happened to the Sherman Antitrust Act that required revival by TR? (text page 393)

4. Was Roosevelt naive in trying to distinguish between "good" and "bad" trusts? (Presumably a trust—a monopoly or near monopoly—is formed to get rid of competition or at least to soften competition, so to the extent that a trust "restrains trade" it can hardly be considered "good." On the other hand, it is possible to identify giant corporations that *dominate* an industry largely because they are efficient and turn out quality goods at satisfactory prices. Sometimes early dominance is achieved through patents—a kind of monopoly—as with Xerox, Polaroid, IBM, etc.)

5. Why might Republican leaders be frightened by Roosevelt's statement that the government must be "the senior partner in every business?" How do you evaluate that position? (Answers should lead to recognition that such a position is not consistent with a belief in free enterprise and that such a remark contributed to the fears of people who saw TR as a "socialist." Students should also distinguish between government as a "senior part-

ner" and as an "umpire" seeing that business plays according to the rules of the game.)

- Have a student report on the impact of Sinclair's novel *The Jungle* in 1906 on the reform movement. Or tell students that Sinclair's vivid descriptions of the meat-packing industry at work and the life of the Slavic immigrants in Chicago probably achieved more in its social and moral impact than any novel since *Uncle Tom's Cabin*.

Sinclair as a muckraking author can be combined with other authors in a report in the next section.

Write these headings on the chalkboard:

ROOSEVELT'S REFORM LEGISLATION

Act   Date   Provisions

Under *Act*, list the following in a vertical column: Hepburn Act, Meat Inspection Act, Pure Food and Drug Act, Employers' Liability Act, Newlands Reclamation Act. Have students complete the chart in the appropriate columns, using the text as a guide. After they have finished, discuss the following:

1. Which of these laws do you think was the most important of Roosevelt's achievements in terms of the future? (At least one historian—Morison—thinks it was the conservation of natural resources. Relate each of these laws to the present for purposes of comparison and evaluation.)

2. What factors help explain why 1906 was a "banner" year for reform? (strong leadership by Roosevelt; growth of Progressive movement; reforms were long overdue; impact of muckraking authors; etc.)

3. Would you have voted for Roosevelt in 1904? Explain.

- Have an individual or committee report on the conservation movement beginning with the pioneer efforts of Theodore Roosevelt and Gifford Pinchot. Because the subject is so broad, you might want to limit the research to the conservation and reclamation of our forests to the present. (Evaluate the present situation: about a fifth of all standing timber in the U.S. today is held by the federal government.) Helpful source material can be found in such books as Graham's *Man's Dominion: The Story of Conservation in America*. Current references under "Conservation" may be found in the *Readers' Guide*.

Section 2 (pp. 425–428)
Middle-class Reformers

Instructional Objectives   Students will be able to

1. Summarize the city and state political reforms of the Progressive Era.

2. Define the Progressives as a group, and identify some of the leaders.

3. Describe the 17th and the 19th amendments.

4. Identify the "muckraking" publications and authors and tell about their activities.

5. Evaluate Theodore Roosevelt and his administration.

Teaching Suggestions Query students to see that they have not overlooked the two main points about the Progressives made in the section introduction: (a) basically middle-class support; (b) general goal for government to be more than an umpire in economic affairs. While the section deals chiefly with Progressive political reforms, a number of state laws dealing with business regulations are described. The last sentence of the introduction talks about the government as "guardian" of the people against business. Compare this term with "senior partner in every business" attributed to T. Roosevelt. If not done earlier, you might point out here that the issue of government as "umpire" vs. government as "guardian" is a persistent one in American politics. And the protagonists today are "conservatives" vs. "liberals."

- *Competency exercise—categorizing:* On paper have students title one vertical column *Political Reforms* and a second column *Economic Reforms*. Using the following list on the chalkboard, students should write each item in one column or the other: commission plan, workmen's compensation, women's suffrage, initiative, wage and hour laws for women, recall, direct primary, public utility regulation, compulsory insurance, city manager plan, direct election of senators, referendum, child-labor laws, restrictions on lobbying. (Note: lobbying might go in either column or in both.)

- Extend the above lesson by assigning each student one of the terms to define or explain concisely. As students respond orally, invite the rest of the class to suggest improvements in wording where needed—and then to copy the edited versions in their notebook.
  Then have students look at the two columns—*Political Reforms* and *Economic Reforms* once more to pick out the top three in significance in each column. Have several students defend their top choice in one column or the other.

- Invite "mini-reports" on some of the Progressive leaders and muckraking authors, including Sam "Golden Rule" Jones, Robert M. La Follette, Lincoln Steffens, Ida Tarbell, Upton Sinclair, Frank Norris, and Theodore Dreiser. The *Dictionary of American Biography* and various encyclopedias and American literary histories will provide details. You might also display some of the works mentioned in the text, and suggest that they be read by your students for extra credit.
  In addition, some of your students may be interested in the art of the Progressive period. Ask someone to prepare a report on the significance of the "ashcan school" of American artists. See Eliot's *Three Hundred Years of American Painting,* Chapter VI, "The Ashcan School," for reproductions of some of the artists' works.

Section 3 (pp. 428–433)
Taft in the White House

Instructional Objectives Students will be able to

1. Characterize President William Howard Taft and summarize the events of his administration.

2. Explain why Theodore Roosevelt entered the presidential arena once more.

3. Describe the three-way presidential race among Taft, Roosevelt, and Wilson in 1912.

Teaching Suggestions This section highlights the election of 1912, one of the most colorful in our varied history. You might extend the lesson by reading aloud some descriptions of the campaign, including the raucous Republican convention that split the party, the crusade-like formation of the Progressive party, the attempt on Roosevelt's life, and the skill with which the scholar Woodrow Wilson handled his campaign.

- Tell students that historians believe that Roosevelt could easily have been reelected in 1908. Yet he had said that "under no circumstances" would he consent to be a candidate to succeed himself. As much as he regretted the statement, he could not undo it. The best he could do was to handpick his successor. Yet Taft, at 300 pounds, was as lethargic as Roosevelt was energetic, and really did not want to be President. For quite a while, it is said, whenever Taft heard someone say, "Mr. President," he would turn around and look for Roosevelt.
  By 1910, across the seas, Roosevelt began to hear a little ditty popular in the U.S.:

  Teddy, come blow your horn,
  The sheep's in the meadow, the cow's in the corn,
  The boy you left to tend the sheep
  Is under the haystack fast asleep.

  By the time Roosevelt returned home, he indicated that he was "ready and eager to do my part" in contributing to the fulfillment of American life. Gradually, as he called Taft "utterly hopeless" and "a flub-dub with a streak of the second-rate and common in him" and as Taft warned against "political emotionalists" and "neurotics," the Republican party became divided beyond reconciliation. The stage was set for one of the most dramatic campaigns in our history.

- Have a student report on the background and life of William Howard Taft. Biographies such as Pringle's *Life and Times of William Howard Taft* will be helpful. Lorant's *The Glorious Burden* contains illustrations of Taft and his family (and also of Roosevelt and Wilson).

- Have students write a newspaper editorial on the topic, "Why Roosevelt Is Unhappy with Taft." Have them use the text as a guide. Include the Ballinger-Pinchot disagreement, Taft's indictment of U.S. Steel, and the reforms sought by the Progressives (which Roosevelt favored and felt that Taft had not achieved). Then discuss:

1. Would Roosevelt have been happy with any Republican President other than himself? Explain. (To all indications, he would not. He was so desirous of running again that he was willing to split his party in order to head the ticket—thus making certain its defeat.)

2. If Roosevelt was so popular with the people, why did Taft win the Republican nomination in 1912? (There is an old political adage: the President controls the machinery of his party, and can have the nomination if he wants it.)

• After finding that students understand the personalities and issues of the 1912 conventions and campaigns, you might use the following questions for discussion.

1. The Progressives adopted the symbol of a bull moose. Why? What were (and are) the Republican and Democratic symbols? (elephant and donkey) What is the value of such symbols? (easier recognition of party, particularly in campaign advertising; qualities of symbol may be transferred to the party; etc.)

2. The text indicates that Bryan urged his supporters to vote for Wilson, thus giving him the nomination. Why, do you suppose, Bryan—three times a contender—decided to do this at the 1912 convention? (Bryan had already been picked three times, and knew that he could no longer win the nomination; he disliked Clark, and felt that Wilson was a better man. Wilson later rewarded Bryan by appointing him Secretary of State.)

3. Would Wilson have won had not the Republican party split? (Probably not; he received only 42 percent of the popular vote. Had Roosevelt been the Republican candidate—and received most of the Progressive vote—his total could have been as high as 7 1/2 million votes to Wilson's 6 million plus.)

• Tell the students that during the campaign of 1912 an anti-third-term assassin named John Schrank tried to kill Theodore Roosevelt in front of a Milwaukee hotel. Fortunately, the bullet passed through the folded copy of Roosevelt's speech and his glasses case, resulting in a superficial chest wound. "There is a bullet in my body, but it takes more than that to kill a Bull Moose," Teddy cried out. After first-aid treatment he went on with his speech. Such heroics of course endeared him to his followers.

• You might extend the lesson of the dramatic 1912 campaign by reading aloud to your students some of the details from such books as Rosewater's *Backstage in 1912,* Warren's *The Battle for the Presidency,* or Martin's *Ballots & Bandwagons.* Your reading may encourage students to read the books—or sections of them—for extra credit.

• The 46 ballots needed to pick a winner in the 1912 Democratic convention provide a particularly sharp contrast with national party conventions over the past 30 years or so. This was the era before the "invention" and rising influence of presidential primaries in delegate selection, and the Democratic party still had its "two-thirds rule" for winning the nomination.

Section 4 (pp. 434–437)
Woodrow Wilson and the New Freedom

Instructional Objectives   Students will be able to

1. Describe the background of Woodrow Wilson before he became President.

2. Name and explain various reforms of the Wilson administration.

3. Summarize the provisions of the Federal Reserve Act.

Teaching Suggestions   Students looking ahead to their college years will be interested in Woodrow Wilson, the only college professor besides Garfield to reach the Presidency. Encourage biographical reports that describe Wilson's early days. (Save the war leadership and the tragic later years for the next chapter.) Relate the Federal Reserve Act to present-day banking activities.

• Have an individual or committee report on the life of Woodrow Wilson before he became President. Many biographies are available, although those of one volume, such as by Garraty, provide the best introduction to the scholar destined to lead the nation into its first world war. Or show the film *Woodrow Wilson* (26 min). After the report or the film, discuss the following:

1. Wilson had only two years of governmental experience before becoming President. Was this enough? Explain. Should we have job-holding standards for Presidents? Explain.

2. What did Wilson mean by the "New Freedom?" (Reform policies which would return political control to the people and free them from the domination of special interests.)

• Write these headings on the chalkboard:

WILSON'S REFORMS

Purpose   Provisions

Below and to the left of *Purpose,* list the following: Underwood-Simmons Tariff Act, Federal Reserve Act, Clayton Antitrust Act, Federal Trade Commission Act. Have students complete the chart by filling in the appropriate columns, using the text as a guide. After they have finished, review the responses so as to reach a consensus. Then discuss the following:

1. Why was the country divided into twelve Federal Reserve districts? (so that the "local" problems of banks

could be handled by regional banks; the needs of one part of the country differed from those of another part; etc.)

2. What panic-producing weakness in our financial structure did the Federal Reserve System intend to correct? (local member banks could borrow from the nearest F.R. bank to slow up or prevent a run on deposits)

3. In subsequent years, the Clayton Act became well known because of its provision that labor unions could not be brought to court as combinations in restraint of trade—labor was thus not a commodity. Does this give an unfair advantage to labor over business? Explain. (Wilson opposed special privileges to any group such as labor, but gave in to the demand so as to ensure the party vote for the Clayton Act.)

4. The worker's day gradually changed from "sunrise to sunset" (in early New England factories) to ten and then to eight hours during Wilson's administration—a figure that has generally remained over the years since then. What are the reasons for this? (Workers can earn maximum pay within physically tolerable limits; tradition; allows factories to run three equal shifts. In recent years, unions have negotiated coffee and other "breaks" within the eight-hour day so that the time worked is actually closer to seven hours; workers now commonly have a five-day week.)

• While providing tremendous improvements in the nation's banking system, the Federal Reserve Act of 1913 was not able to stop the bank collapse in 1933. New Deal banking laws in 1933 and 1935 brought major improvements, including deposit insurance; and some other changes were made even before 1933. Thus the Federal Reserve System operates in certain important respects differently than the 1913 law provided. So if you use *current* descriptions of the FRS to augment what the text tells, remind students that you are describing today's system, including changes made since 1913.

The function of the Federal Reserve in providing an elastic currency and credit system is fairly complex but may be worth reviewing with able students. See a high school economics text for help with the details.

Section 5 (pp. 437–442)
Seeking a World Role

Instructional Objectives Students will be able to

1. Explain our continued involvement in Far Eastern affairs, and particularly Roosevelt's role in the Russo-Japanese War.

2. Tell how the United States completed the Panama Canal.

3. Define the Roosevelt Corollary, Taft's "dollar diplomacy," and Wilson's "moral" foreign policy.

4. Summarize Wilson's problems with Mexico.

Teaching Suggestions The story of the building of the Panama Canal will interest all students. You might approach the topic from various aspects—the historical and military significance, the engineering feats, the conquest of malaria and yellow fever, and the significance of the canal to the United States at the present time (the U.S. turned over control of the canal to Panama in 1979).

• Have students again use the map on page 417 to locate the areas of conflict in the Far East over which Russia and Japan fought, including Manchuria and Korea. After these have been located, you might discuss the long-term implications of TR's mediation in the Russo-Japanese War ending with the peace treaty at Portsmouth, N.H., in 1905. Point out that some historians question the "wisdom" of the treaty. Have students speculate why. (It merely substituted Japan for Russia in Manchuria, thus committing us to the support of Japan had France or Germany decided to support Russia. In the power politics of the time, Roosevelt led the American people into possible foreign commitments they might not have wanted to accept. The treaty also enabled Japan to become the dominant sea power in the Pacific, for which we would pay a heavy price in 1941.)

On the other hand, TR's diplomatic efforts must be judged in the climate of the time. Here is a good place to emphasize the important concept of "balance of power" in a world where there were several power centers.

• Have students turn to the map on page 439 to locate the area in Latin America where we built the Panama Canal. Individuals or committees might report on particular aspects of the project, including (a) difficulties met by the French company; (b) the contributions to the building of the canal by Colonel George W. Goethals; (c) the physical details of the canal; (d) the conquest of malaria and yellow fever, beginning in Cuba; (e) the administration of the canal today, including the turning over of control by the United States to Panama in 1979.

To extend the lesson, you might have students read aloud portions of Sidney Howard's play *Yellow Jack,* dealing with the attempts to prove that mosquitoes were the carriers of the dreaded disease.

Or tell students that the Panama Canal, begun in 1904, was officially declared open in 1920. It is 51 miles long between channel entrances of the Atlantic and Pacific oceans. The minimum depth is 41 feet. From the Atlantic a ship is raised by a series of locks to an elevation of 85 feet, then after a crossing of Gatun Lake is lowered by locks once more to sea level. Although modernization has taken place through the years, permitting increased two-way traffic, the largest of the modern merchant and naval vessels cannot use the canal.

• After checking to see if students can explain and give examples of the Roosevelt Corollary, Taft's "dollar diplomacy," and Wilson's "moral" foreign policy, use items from the Chapter Review relating to this chapter section and questions like the following:

1. How did the Roosevelt Corollary go beyond Cleveland's

extension of the Monroe Doctrine (p. 409)? (U.S. could step in to avert European intervention even before a real threat of intervention occurred.)

2. Taft urged U.S. business firms to invest in foreign lands, and by the late 1970s direct business investment by U.S. corporations in foreign countries totaled $168 billion (and foreign investment in the U.S. was $40 billion). Should our government help, hinder, or remain neutral in this flow of American capital to other lands? Explain. If you support foreign investment as being good for the American economy—and thus the country, what grounds are there for criticizing Taft's "dollar diplomacy"? (can be criticized on ground of promises or implied promises to provide protection, leading to potential costly intervention)

3. Under what circumstances, if any, would you want the United States to withhold recognition (not exchange ambassadors) of a foreign government? Why?

• Taking into consideration both domestic and foreign policies, historians have ranked T. Roosevelt as "near great" and Taft as "average" as President. Ask students: "Based on your study of these two Presidents, do these assessments seem fair and reasonable? Why?"

CHAPTER REVIEW
Meeting Our Earlier Selves

1. Interest in nature (conservation movement); development of wide range of interests; persistence; forcefulness; pride (keeping blindness in one eye a secret, and later showing his self-assertiveness on many occasions, including his opposition to paying Colombia for Panama "with regrets"); energy (officials had to join him on his strenuous walks or miss meeting with him); etc.

2. Workers: long working day, low wages, strikebreaking, unsafe working conditions, dishonest counting of worker output, payment of miners' wages in scrip to be cashed at company stores, lack of insurance for on-the-job accidents and health hazards, child labor, horrible conditions in merchant marine.
Consumers: high prices because of monopoly practices by business, rotten meat, impure foods and drugs, false labeling, poor quality of services by public utilities.
Business competitors: killing off or forcing small businesses to join a trust, railroad rebates, other kinds of price discrimination; also see business abuses affecting consumers (above), since such abuses were often a form of unfair competition.

Other victims: *businesses* having to buy from price-fixing monopolists; *taxpayers* to the extent that business abuses raised the cost of government; the *general public* from the denuding of public lands.

3. Vigorous competition would be particularly effective in reducing abuses having to do with "jacked up" prices and poor quality goods and services (if poor quality resulted from a monopoly situation).

4. The press—and today other media—plays a very significant role in reform efforts. Intolerable conditions will not arouse public opinion—and in turn the politicians—unless they are widely known.

5. TR carried a big stick in the coal strike, the Northern Securities case, in getting the Hepburn bill passed, etc. He did so also in getting the canal built in Panama, in intervening in the Dominican Republic, and in showing off the navy in the Pacific. TR's outspokeness on many, many occasions belies the first part of his motto. Yet he can hardly be accused of blustering.

6. These interventions were examples of a "big brother" policy that came to be highly resented in Latin America, so their long-term effect may have been harmful. One must distinguish between (a) providing help at a neighbor's request and (b) forcing a neighbor to accept help. In recent years the United States (and the Soviet Union as well) has supplied advisers—technical and military—to a number of foreign governments. The question is whether the "advisers" are forced on the recipient government. Another problem in providing help to a foreign government is determining whether you are bolstering an unpopular regime (as the U.S. did in Iran for many years). Another aspect of the problem is national security: is the chaos in another land a real threat to one's own security?

Questions for Today

2. Some critics would point to unwon battles on the conservation front, over consumer protection, and perhaps other issues. Other observers are shocked at the extent of business regulation—the high cost of trying to protect against all hazards to consumers and to workers, for example. The over-regulation of railroads, trucks, etc., has recently led to deregulation. Some critics also say that political reform has gone "too far," that political leaders have lost the power to lead.

3. The United States could do so only by abandoning its long-term Good Neighbor policy and by inviting the condemnation of world opinion. One of the frustrations of policymakers today is that the United States has enormous military power but the constraints of the age (including the fear of the outbreak of nuclear warfare) put severe limits on the use of that power.

CHAPTER 21

The United States and World War I

Introducing the Chapter Before beginning this chapter, find out what students know about the European backgound of the war; then fill in needed facts. The map on page 444 can be used to identify the opposing alliances. A wall map of the world in 1914 would be useful to see the worldwide empires of some of the European nations.

Section 1 (pp. 443–451)
A Spark Ignites Europe

Instructional Objectives Students will be able to

1. Give reasons for the outbreak of World War I.
2. Explain why Americans tended to favor the Allies.
3. Describe the shipping rights of neutrals and belligerents under international law.
4. Tell how both Great Britain and Germany violated America's neutral rights.
5. Describe Wilson's efforts to maintain the trading rights of the United States.
6. Summarize our increasing trade involvement with the Allies and the preparedness program of 1915–1916.
7. Describe the campaign and election of 1916.
8. Explain the events of early 1917 that led to America's entry into the war.

Teaching Suggestions This section provides a concise explanation of the factors and events leading to the outbreak of the war. If your students have had a course in world history or modern European history, have them help fill in some details. Keep in mind, however, that a thorough understanding of the European background will be time consuming to achieve and will contribute relatively little to the understanding of our nation's growing involvement and eventual entry into the war.

• Four major factors often used to analyze the origins of the war are *nationalism, imperialism, militarism,* and *alliances.* Put these terms on the board and have students help explain how each was involved in the outbreak of the war. Ask them to find sentences and phrases on pages 443–445 that allude to these terms. Use the map on page 444 with this activity.

• If their own community existed in 1915, students might speculate on pro-Allied and anti-Allied sentiment that might have existed based on the ethnic composition of the community at that time. Or they might speculate on the sentiments of a particular ancestor living at that time.

• Point out that the text reference to a peace ship chartered by automaker Henry Ford had its origins when Rosika Schwimmer, a Hungarian pacifist, met Ford, who was opposed to the war. It is said that both former Secretary of State William Jennings Bryan and Thomas Edison rejected the opportunity to join the 168 Americans who sailed aboard the *Oscar II* on December 4, 1915, for Norway. The press ridiculed Ford's optimistic contention that "We're going to try to get the boys out of the trenches before Christmas," and renamed the *Oscar II* "the ship of fools."

• *Handout lesson:* After students read the text and *Handout 33* on the sinking of the *Lusitania,* have them give written or oral responses to the following questions:

1. Were the Germans justified in sinking the ship after giving the warning in newspapers? Explain.
2. What "law of the sea" did the sinking of the *Lusitania* violate? (supposed to give warning, to see that passengers were safe, and do everything else reasonable to save civilian lives)
3. What violations did the owners of the *Lusitania* make? (flying neutral flag; carrying ammunition)
4. In what respects does the newspaper report of the sinking differ from the submarine captain's log and the text narrative?

• If you have an AFS (American Field Service) chapter in your school, your students will be interested in the origin of this exchange program whereby foreign students come here and American students go abroad. When World War I began, a former Harvard professor named Piatt Andrew volunteered to drive an ambulance for the American hospital in Paris. Soon other volunteers, using mostly Model T Fords as their transport, went to the front to bring back wounded soldiers. When America entered the war, the AFS became part of the army's ambulance corps.

With the war's end, the AFS became a fellowship program for American students at French universities, and after World War II a high school exchange program.

• Tell the class that despite Wilson's reforms and the slogan "He kept us out of war," the 1916 race was surprisingly close, perhaps because many Bull Moose followers of Theodore Roosevelt crept back into the Republican fold to vote for Hughes. So confident was Hughes—an Easterner

—that he had won the election that a reporter who tried to call him well after midnight was told, "The President cannot be disturbed." Replied the reporter: "When he wakes up, just tell him he isn't President." Wilson had finally won in California by 4000 votes, giving him the electoral victory.

- In discussing U.S. entry into the war, use Section Review item 6 and items 1 and 2 of *Meeting Our Earlier Selves* (p. 465). You might have students judge which, if any, of the following reasons (and perhaps others) were justifications for entering the war:

1. Violation of America's neutral rights on the sea.
2. German connivance with Mexico as demonstrated in the Zimmermann note.
3. Unrestricted German submarine warfare killing civilians.
4. To make the world safe for democracy by crushing the autocratic European powers.
5. To preserve British sea power as security for the U.S.

- You might read portions of Wilson's war message and of Senator Norris's speech given two days later in opposition. Both appear in a number of documentary histories including *A Documentary History of the American People* by Craven, Johnson, and Dunn (Ginn, 1951).

- Suggest that the text discusses Wilson's Fourteen Points in conjunction with the war message—even though they came months later—because they illustrate Wilson's idealism as a factor in calling for the declaration of war. Point out that eight of the points had to do with particular nations—chiefly with the adjustment of national borders to allow all people to govern themselves. Six general points dealt with (a) open covenants—no secret diplomacy; (b) freedom of the seas; (c) removal of economic barriers "so far as possible"; (d) armament reduction; (e) impartial adjustment of all colonial claims; and (f) the League of Nations.

Section 2 (pp. 451–454)
Helping to Win the War

Instructional Objectives Students will be able to

1. Describe what war was like on the western front in Europe.
2. Tell why World War I was the bloodiest war in the world's history.
3. Explain the role of the American Expeditionary Force in helping to win the war.

Teaching Suggestions The incredible loss in human lives will be difficult to explain in this lesson. Besides films, you might show illustrations of trench warfare, the destruction of French towns by artillery fire, and the use of gas warfare.

- To avoid letting the narrative get bogged down in the complex military campaigns of 1914–1917, the authors quickly summarize the action and then the long stalemate on the western front in Belgium and northern France. To show that this really was a world war, you may want to review (or have students report on) the other major fronts: eastern, Italian, Balkan, Turkey and the Near East (Lawrence of Arabia). Several major naval engagements took place. And the British, French, South Africans, Australians, and New Zealanders rather quickly took over Germany's colonies in Africa and the Pacific.

Russia's role in the war and the Bolshevik takeover in November 1917 deserve some attention. The presence of the tsarist Russian autocracy on the Allied side weakened the credibility of Wilson's war aim to make "the world safe for democracy." With Russia's withdrawal at the end of 1917, Wilson could more convincingly tell Congress and the world his vision of a peace settlement—the Fourteen Points (text page 451).

Students might speculate on the following aspects of the war:

1. Lacking the concentrated and massive bombing of World War II, why was loss of life so heavy in World War I? (artillery more advanced than earlier; machine guns had come into use; but especially the absence of the wonder drugs we know today)

2. With air power, how could armies be massed month after month in the trenches? (airplanes very primitive in W. W. I; not suitable for heavy bombing; valuable chiefly for observation; air fighting was mostly one-on-one or small group "dog fights")

3. Why was poison gas used in this war and not in W. W. II? (soon found to be too big a risk—shifting winds blowing it back on attackers—and it invited retaliation; its use had invited worldwide condemnation; armies more mobile in W. W. II; gas was stored and available in W. W. II but apparently neither side wanted to be the first to use it).

- Show pictures of trench and barbed-wire warfare. Terraine's *The Great War—1914–1918—A Pictorial History* or *The American Heritage History of World War I* will be helpful. Point out that besides the introduction of airplanes and poison gas, tanks made their appearance. The British sent 42 tanks into the battle of the Somme in 1916. However, tanks did not play a major role in the war because they were too few in number and too lightly armored to withstand heavy shelling. Also, tank movements had little significance unless followed by waves of infantry.

- Have a student report on the airplanes used in World War I and on some of the "ace" pilots of the war, including the American Eddie Rickenbacker (26 German planes) and the German "Red Baron" Manfred von Richthofen (80 Allied planes).

Or tell students that the flimsy frame and uncertain qualities of airplanes in World War I placed great emphasis on the individual skill and daring of the pilots. Richthofen was shot down in April 1918; Rickenbacker survived the war, and was incredibly a hero at age 53 in World War II when in the Pacific he assumed command of a raft whose survivors waited 22 days before being rescued.

For those who would like to read more about the pilot-heroes of World War I, suggest such books as Rickenbacker's *Fighting in the Flying Circus* or Reynold's *They Fought for the Sky*.

- Call attention to the black soldiers in the upper-left picture on page 453. Point out that of the 4.8 million enlistees, draftees, and National Guard members who served in the American armed forces in World War I approximately 371,000 were blacks. Prejudice and discrimination in the military kept black units separated from white ones. The 10,000 blacks in the navy were assigned to noncombat duties as were most of the 200,000 black troops sent to Europe. A regiment from the all-black Ninety-Third Division was among the first units to drive across the Rhine River. Seventy of their members won the Distinguished Service Cross.

Section 3 (pp. 455–461)
The Home Front

Instructional Objectives Students will be able to

1. Explain how the draft was used to mobilize military forces in World War I.
2. Describe government controls on and inducements given to business, agriculture, labor, and consumers to help win the war.
3. Show how the war was financed.
4. Describe government efforts to win popular support for the war.
5. Evaluate the wartime restrictions put on civil liberties.

Teaching Suggestions Call attention to the words "mobilize" and "mobilization." Have students try to determine the meaning from the root word "mobile." Then point out that besides the general meanings of "mobilize" (to put into movement or circulation; to marshal resources for action), the word has a special wartime meaning: to assemble and make ready for war duty. Conclude by asking: "What are some things that have to be mobilized—that have to be done to put a nation on a wartime footing?"

- Students might speculate on why the 1917–1918 draft operated smoothly while the Civil War draft was the occasion for riots. Besides the absence of a provision for paying for a substitute, you might point out that provisions for exemptions and deferments seemed fair, that the law was administered through regional civilian boards (who would consider local needs and circumstances), and that enthusiasm for the war was relatively high.

Tell students that as the war spirit grew, there were occasional vigilante raids in the cities to "track down slackers," and any man without a draft card in his possession was led off to the nearest police station to be questioned further. Although many were thus arrested, few turned out to be "draft dodgers."

- Point out that the text statement that the navy "was in better shape than the army" may be explained with a number of reasons. In peacetime, navies usually retain full crew strength aboard ships, whereas armies may be reduced to skeletal organizations. Navies are thus made "combat ready" rather easily, while armies have to be built up and trained—mostly with draftees.

You might point out that until American Admiral Sims "insisted that all ships headed across the Atlantic should travel in convoys," the Allies had not used this system to protect merchant ships, with the result that German U-boats were sinking more than 500,000 tons of Allied shipping per month. Once cruisers and destroyers began escorting convoys, Allied losses were cut drastically. The navy also helped close the North Sea to enemy submarines by laying down vast numbers of underwater mines.

- Tell students that the most important of the German vessels seized by the United States when the war began was the passenger liner *Vaterland,* which later as the *Leviathan* made frequent trips across the Atlantic as a troop ship carrying 12,000 American soldiers on each voyage.

- Students might recite the words or sing such popular World War I songs as "Over There," "Keep the Home Fires Burning," "Pack Up Your Troubles," and "There's a Long, Long Trail."

- Encourage art students in your classes to draw World War I posters for a bulletin board display. Have students collect slogans for their poster, such as "Food Will Win the War," "Wheatless Monday," "Meatless Tuesday," "Blood or Bread—Give," "Light Consumes Coal—Save Light—Save Coal," "Can Vegetables, Fruit and the Kaiser Too."

- *Competency exercise—speech writing:* Tell students that to raise money for World War I, the Treasury enlisted the help of famous personalities of the day, such as Charlie Chaplin and Mary Pickford, to sell "Liberty Bonds." These persons and thousands of others were known as "four-minute speakers." Have students write a brief, informal "speech" convincing listeners to buy bonds and giving some reasons why. After students have finished, have some of them read their speeches aloud. Then collect the papers for evaluation.

- Tell students that the Committee on Public Information under George Creel distributed over 100 million pieces of literature, and promoted 75,000 "four-minute" speeches in public meetings throughout the nation. Meanwhile, there were 1500 prosecutions under the Espionage and Sedition laws, including Eugene V. Debs, who would poll a million votes for President while in jail in 1920. Interestingly, although Wilson asserted that we were fighting for democracy in the world, he refused to pardon Debs or reduce his sentence after the war. It remained for the easy-going and forgiving President Warren G. Harding to do that.

To extend the lesson, read aloud the following statement by Justice Oliver Wendell Holmes on the need to curtail civil liberties in wartime: "When a nation is at war, many things that might be said in time of peace are such a hindrance to its effort that their utterance will not be endured . . . and no court could regard them as protected by any constitutional right." Have students reply in the form of a newspaper editorial agreeing with or opposing Justice Holmes's statement, giving reasons for the viewpoint. Read aloud several editorials reflecting approval or disapproval. Collect the papers for evaluation.

Section 4 (pp. 461–465)
Losing the Peace

Instructional Objectives Students will be able to

1. Summarize the terms of the Versailles Treaty.

2. Explain the opposition to the League of Nations in the United States.

3. Describe Wilson's unsuccessful efforts to win acceptance of the League of Nations.

Teaching Suggestions The tragic drama of Wilson's defeat and physical collapse in urging the nation to join the League of Nations highlights this section. You might read aloud excerpts from Wilson's speeches on the League of Nations issue. Survey your students as to whether they would have supported President Wilson or the Borah-Lodge view. Perhaps your students can anticipate the consequence of losing the peace.

- Write VERSAILLES TREATY—1919 on the chalkboard. Below and to the left, list the following in a vertical column: *Big Four leaders, Main provisions, Attitudes in U. S. Senate, Wilson's reply, Final result.* Have students complete the chart by filling in the appropriate spaces, using the text as a guide. After they have finished, discuss the following:

1. Why was Wilson "irritating" to the other leaders? (preachy; spoke for all mankind rather than selfishly just for his own nation)

2. Which of Wilson's Fourteen Points (page 451) was violated? ("Open covenants openly arrived at.")

3. What mistake had Wilson made in picking the American peace commissioners? (failed to pick prominent Republicans so as to gain bipartisan support)

4. Why did the Republicans in the Senate oppose Article 10 of the treaty? (seemed to obligate U. S. to support other nations in war, thus violating the power of Congress alone "to declare war")

5. What was Wilson's last big mistake? (refusal to compromise with Senator Lodge and other Republicans and instead make the League an election issue)

- Tell students that Wilson refused to compromise on the League because be believed that he spoke for people throughout the world who supported his views. When he had gone to Europe in December 1918, he was cheered everywhere by millions as savior of mankind. He had also been greeted by large crowds on his return to New York. Thus he could not understand rejection by the Senate.

Earlier, Senator Lodge had favored a League of Nations, but then opposed it when Wilson became the sponsor. Each man hated the other, and stubbornly refused to compromise. After Wilson's collapse and return to Washington, his pro-League adviser, Senator Gilbert M. Hitchcock of Nebraska, suggested that ratification of the treaty was still possible if the President would compromise and accept the Lodge amendment that kept the war-making power in the hands of Congress. "Let Lodge compromise!" Wilson protested. "Better a thousand times to go down fighting than to dip your colors to dishonorable compromise." And with that, Wilson went down to defeat as the Senate rejected the treaty.

- Read to students a description of the last speech given by President Wilson during his tour of the West in 1919. Smith's *When the Cheering Stopped,* pages 80–81, and Garraty's *Woodrow Wilson,* pages 177–180, provide vivid descriptions.

Or tell students that Wilson's physical breakdown was no surprise to those around him. From September 3 to September 25 he delivered forty speeches. Meanwhile, unable to sleep well, particularly on trains, the President experienced great fatigue and painful headaches. In Pueblo, Colorado, he began to hesitate while speaking, but went on to the finish. Finally ordered by his doctor to return to Washington, Wilson collapsed that night on the train. He had suffered a stroke, from which he never recovered fully.

- Historians rate Wilson among the "great" Presidents, a position sustained in the Wells Poll of 1979. Yet historians who point out Wilson's superior record as a reformer and wartime leader also are quick to list his weaknesses: a too-narrow approach to right and wrong, and a stubbornness that made compromise impossible. Perhaps, as the decades go by and the nation forgets Wilson's frailties, his stirring words as a spokesperson for democracy will live on.

CHAPTER REVIEW

Meeting Our Earlier Selves

1. Some people—see item 2—interpreted Germany's unrestricted submarine warfare as a necessary defensive effort and not as war on the United States. The moral appeal might have been seen as useful in getting support in Congress for declaring war—and in drumming up support in the nation once we had entered.

2. The text mentions our "soft" protests on British seizure of cargo in the early part of the war; Wilson's insistence that Americans be allowed to travel on British ships and into the war zone; enormous trade with the Allies; loans to the Allies. In addition, Senator Norris pointed out that the United States had kept its vessels out of the British-declared war zone but not out of the German zone, and that we could have placed an embargo on both nations, but did not.

3. Other "winners" were (a) organized labor—see page 460; (b) farmers—higher prices; (c) women—new job opportunities; (d) blacks—new jobs, boost to northern migration. "Losers" were (a) people on fixed incomes hurt by inflation; (b) German-speaking aliens and citizens—by persecution and taunts; (c) pacifists and other opponents of the war—by persecution and prosecution; (d) families suffering war casualties, etc.

4. Freedoms curtailed: speech, press, assembly (in connection with free speech), plus numerous restrictions on economic freedoms, such as right to strike, rationing, loss of owner control of certain businesses like the railroads. Probably most people would say the limits on economic freedom were most necessary (justifiable) because of the crucial importance of economic mobilization in modern warfare. Limits on freedom of speech, press, and assembly may be regarded as least necessary, since the words are so often not linked directly to identifiable action. Where speech directly incites to obstruction of the war effort, the issue becomes more difficult. Some people would argue that the obstruction should be punished, not the speech.

5. Future Presidents could learn to get bipartisan support during the making of policy, to give special attention to sensitive powerful leaders, to consult with—not preach at—people whose support is needed, to compromise negotiable points if necessary to achieve a broad objective, and so on.

Questions for Today

1. This is a research exercise. The decisions include the promise of a homeland for the Jews in Palestine, the formation of certain Arab states, the support of particular Arab rulers, etc.

Other recent conflicts having roots in World War I and the treaties include South Africa's hold on Namibia (former German Southwest Africa), Soviet Union hostility and suspiciousness of the West insofar as it related to Allied intervention in Russia (p. 468), persistent Greek-Turkish animosity. Also, insofar as W. W. II was a legacy of the First World War and the Versailles Treaty, many of the problems that grew out of World War II and persist to the 1970s–1980s can be linked to World War I.

2. Examples under Carter include SALT II, the Panama Canal treaties, energy conservation, wage and price restraints to curtail inflation, etc. Almost every government agency has its public relations department to boost agency activities. Techniques include the publishing of a voluminous "information" literature, presidential press conferences and TV addresses, addresses by public officials at conventions of special interest groups, and even commercial advertising (for armed services recruits, for example).

CHAPTER 22

Return to Normalcy, 1918–1929

Introducing the Chapter One of the most colorful periods of our history is described in this chapter. You might explore with your students why disillusionment followed a war for a "noble" cause. Photographs and other illustrations, along with films, will help students understand the 1920s as the introductory decade of the present age.

Section 1 (pp. 468–473)
The Postwar Reaction

Instructional Objectives Students will be able to

1. Describe and account for the fear of postwar radicalism in the United States and evaluate the responses to it.

2. Point out the significance of the Sacco-Vanzetti case.

3. Identify major American writers of the 1920s.

4. Explain the factors leading to the adoption of the 18th and 19th amendments.

Teaching Suggestions You may find it difficult to convey the narrowness of attitudes on the one hand towards certain ideas and the liberation of manners and morals at the same time during the 1920s. Helpful will be readings from such books as Allen's *Only Yesterday* describing specific changes and the reactions to them. Encourage reports on specific topics, such as "The Impact of Motion Pictures in the 1920s."

• Have students turn to the map on page 748 to locate Murmansk and Arkhangel'sk (Archangel), where a token force of about 5000 American infantrymen from Michigan and Wisconsin joined Allied units from Japan and England. Their assignment was to "guard military stores" and help 45,000 Czechs (released soldier-prisoners) fight their way north along the Trans-Siberian railroad to Vladivostok (from where they hoped eventually to get to the western front). Wilson had had some misgivings about our Siberian venture, but agreed to it to please the British and the French.

Our intervention soon proved to be a mistake. According to former American Ambassador to the Soviet Union George Kennan, "the American forces had scarcely arrived in Russia when history invalidated at a single stroke almost every reason Washington had conceived for their being there." With the armistice, there were no Germans to fight; the Czechs did not need us; we were fighting Bolsheviks instead, a historic venture that the Soviet people have never been allowed to forget. Although the American troops were recalled during 1919 and 1920, Soviet distrust and the American "Red Scare" at home chilled relations between the two countries for more than a decade.

After telling the above to the students, have them review "Allied intervention in Russia" and "A. Mitchell Palmer pursues the Bolsheviks" in the text. Then discuss the following:

1. Would it have been possible to carry out Winston Churchill's wish to "strangle Bolshevism at its birth"? Why? Would you have favored our joining such an attempt? Explain.

2. It is reported that at his first Cabinet meeting after his stroke, President Wilson said to his Attorney General, "Palmer, do not let this country see red!" Must Wilson, therefore, share responsibility for the "Red Scare"? What would have been your attitude towards the radicals?

• You may want to emphasize the legacy of the war as a factor in the "Red Scare." The text points out that the Creel Committee had made Americans suspicious of anything un-American. The war had also stirred up aggressive tendencies (against "the enemy") that did not subside overnight. And the Communists provided a very visible target: (a) Communists were leaders of some strikes and were ready to exploit any sign of unrest in the country; with 4 million workers on strike in 1919 (see text), it was easy to see a Communist conspiracy at work; (b) world Communist leaders in March 1919 formed the Third International and announced their aim of world revolution; (c) the danger of a Communist takeover in Germany and in some other European countries seemed real.

Even though their numbers were small in the United States, their presence scared many people because a Bolshevik minority had seized control in Russia. Moreover, people tended to label any radical activity as "Communist." Socialists were tarred with the Communist brush because both advocated public ownership of productive facilities. Anarchists were often called "reds" because they usually advocated revolution—or saw revolution as the only way to overturn the existing order. Also the Communist philosophy promised that government would wither away (the anarchist ideal) once socialism was firmly established.

• You might tell students that Attorney General Palmer had been a typical Progressive—a suppporter of the League of Nations and of progressive legislation. At first he tried to resist the public outcry against the radical aliens—even after his own home was bombed—but then gave in to pressures from Congress and the press and apparently came to believe that a real danger existed. An interesting sidelight is that in August 1919 Palmer set up a General Intelligence Division in the Department of Justice to gather information on radical activities. As head of the Division he appointed a young man just three years out of George Washington University. His name was J. Edgar Hoover.

• For students who would like to read more on the "Red Scare," suggest Murray's *Red Scare: A Study in National Hysteria: 1919–1920.*

• Living in an era when unionization of public employees is widespread and strikes are not uncommon, students should be reminded that even aside from the disorder that arose out of the Boston police strike the event was upsetting because the prevailing view was strongly against unionization of public employees. Some beginnings had been made, however; and police in 37 cities were affiliated with the AF of L. The police had walked out in Boston because the police commissioner refused to allow them to unionize.

• *Competency exercise—writing a "letter to the editor":* Ask students to write a letter of six to ten sentences either supporting or opposing the granting of unionization rights to the Boston police in 1919.

• Tell students that some of the most vivid reporting of the Chicago race riots in 1919 was written by Carl Sandburg, the great biographer of Abraham Lincoln. Reporting for the *Chicago Daily News,* Sandburg drew national attention to the tragic riots. The dispute mentioned in the text began when a black youth using a railroad tie as a raft at a Lake Michigan bathing beach crossed an "imaginary" line separating blacks from whites. White youths on the beach then pelted the black with stones, causing him to let go of the railroad tie and drown. Feelings soon became tense. Beach-front fighting spread to violence in the streets, causing many injuries and deaths. Pedestrians were assaulted; trolley cars derailed; houses set afire. Sniper fire came from buildings; incendiary fires swept through whole blocks. The coming of the state militia and a timely rainfall during successive evenings encouraged many people to stay in their homes, and tensions began to ease.

According to a subsequent (1922) report by the Chicago Commission on Race Relations, "Despite the community's failure to deal firmly with those who contributed to the reign of lawlessness, there is evidence that the riot aroused many citizens of both races to a quickened sense of the suffering and disgrace which has come and might again come to the city."

After you have related the above and students have reviewed "Urban riots" in the text, discuss the following:

1. Did the beach incident "cause" the riot? (would expect discussion of how one incident can be the "last straw" of accumulated injustices)
2. What are some motives of people participating in a riot once one gets under way?
3. What urban riot have you witnessed or heard about? What triggered it? What were some costs? Did it lead to any "good" results?
4. Can urban riots be prevented? How?
5. Have race relations in cities improved since the 1920s? Explain.

• Students should understand that the "new" Ku Klux Klan had no organizational ties to the old Klan of the Reconstruction era. The new Klan was organized in Georgia in 1915 but grew partly in response to the postwar turmoil. While both the old and new Klan were white supremacist, the new Klan was also a nativist organization. In the South especially the new Klan thrived on the hostility engendered by the new opportunities that the war had given to blacks. In the Midwest and West the hostility was directed more against foreigners, Catholics, and Jews. Klan members posed as guardians of public morality and enemies of nonconformist behavior. Rivalry among Klan leaders, misuse of Klan funds, and the outrageous behavior of some groups contributed to the rapid decline in membership in the late 1920s.

• Encourage students to choose an author mentioned in "The disillusioned writers" (p. 473) for a brief written or oral report on how that writer reflected the 1920s. You might elaborate on the disillusionment of the intellectuals: (a) the war and its aftermath had upset old values; (b) the excesses of the "Red Scare" and the Klan, and the efforts of Prohibitionists and religious fundamentalists to foist a narrow conformity on the American people; (c) the materialism of the business class; (d) the blasted hopes of Wilson's idealism; etc.

• Students should see that temperance and women's suffrage were reform movements of long standing that got their final push from the wartime situation as the text reports.

You might point out that in the 1920 presidential election, held about three months after final ratification of the Nineteenth Amendment, about one-third of the females of voting age went to the polls. In 1948 still less than half of voting-age women voted. But by 1976 the proportion of males and females voting was nearly equal: an estimated 59% for women and 60% for men. (Note that male suffrage for the country as a whole has rarely exceeded 70%.)

In contrast to the relatively slow effects of the Nineteenth Amendment, some dramatic effects of the Eighteenth Amendment appeared almost at once. (Notice that the Prohibition Amendment was to take effect one year after final ratification—time for distillers and dealers to make adjustments.) A film, lecture, or student reports on the problems of enforcing Prohibition and the links between Prohibition and organized crime, political corruption, and youthful rebellion are of enduring interest.

• Tell students that historians usually link the expansion of organized crime as a national problem with the coming of Prohibition. Most notorious of the "gangsters" of the day was Al "Scarface" Capone in Chicago, whose income, according to the I.R.S., was $105 million in 1927 alone. During the decade, there were some 500 gangland murders in Chicago. Most spectacular were those of the 1927 Valentine's Day massacre in which gangsters in police uniforms burst into a garage and killed six members of a rival gang. Allsop's *The Bootleggers and Their Era* will provide further details.

Section 2 (pp. 473–477)
Searching for the Good Old Days

Instructional Objectives Students will be able to

1. Tell why the Republicans chose Warren G. Harding as their candidate for President.

2. Summarize the results of the Washington Naval Conference of 1921–1922.

3. Evaluate the domestic program of the Harding administration.

4. Describe the Harding scandals.

Teaching Suggestions Students will express interest in the rise of a man of ordinary abilities—with a weakness for women—to the Presidency. Some discretion is advised in what is told about Harding's personal life. If you familiarize yourself with Russell's *The Shadow of Blooming Grove—Warren G. Harding in His Times,* you will be able to separate fact from rumor concerning Harding's life and the scandals.

• Use the picture of Harding on page 474 along with the paragraph on his background to initiate discussion of qualifications desired in a President. Ask such questions as these:

1. What facts or inferences about Harding (from the first paragraph in the topic "Warren G. Harding" and from the picture) mark him as an attractive candidate for President?

2. Is physical attractiveness an important asset for a would-be presidential nominee today? Explain. (perhaps more than ever because of TV exposure)

3. What traits of Harding damaged his Presidency? (easy-goingness, cronyism)

4. Can voters make a reliable judgment about the probable success of a President by looking at the candidate's record of experience and watching campaign performance? Explain. (No, because weaknesses do not always show up and because many factors besides personal ability affect presidential success. Yet, voters should feel obligated to make a judgment on the best available knowledge—not blindly.)

• Tell students that the text reference that Harding "died suddenly and mysteriously" stems from the contradictory medical reports relating to his illness and death. His physician, Charles E. Sawyer, at first diagnosed "ptomaine poisoning" from bad sea food, then gave the cause of death as a cerebral hemorrhage. Dr. Samuel A. Levine was convinced that Harding suffered an "acute coronary thrombosis." Mrs. Harding refused to permit an autopsy. Since then, although historians have researched various theories as to how and why Harding died—including suicide—the death remains a mystery.

• Avoid efforts to have students memorize details of the Washington Naval Conference treaties. It is probably enough to remember that the conference involved nine world powers with interests in the Far East, that the leading naval powers agreed on some limits on size of navies and respect for the Pacific possessions of each, that all the nations involved pledged to respect the Open Door policy in China, and that the treaties provided no means for enforcement. (You might point out, of course, that treaties seldom have reliable enforcement provisions. One of their chief functions is to get agreement on policy for the near future so that the parties involved are not just groping in the dark.)

• Ask students to assume that they were members of Congress during the Harding administration. Have them review the three topics starting with "Harding's domestic program." Then have them vote for or against the following domestic proposals: Budget and Accounting Act, emergency tariff (to exclude Canadian farm goods), Fordney-McCumber tariff, repeal of excess profits tax on industry, reduction of income tax, bonus bill for veterans, and bill to cancel foreign war debts.

After they have finished voting, tally the votes. Compare these with the actual results. Ask: What changes have taken place in our political attitudes since Harding's administration? (various answers: lowering of tariffs, tax cuts tied to economic conditions, generous aid to veterans, and generous foreign aid)

• Tell students that historians are generally critical of Harding and rate him (along with Grant) as a "failure." This judgment reflects a negative view of Harding's personal life but especially of his poor judgment in appointments. The administration itself is given credit for the Washington Naval Conference, for improved relations wtih Latin American countries—particularly Mexico; and for legislation that helped expand prosperity and employment.

Section 3 (pp. 478–481)
"Keeping Cool with Coolidge"

Instructional Objectives Students will be able to

1. Describe Coolidge's background and philosophy.

2. List highlights of the 1924 and 1928 elections.

3. Show how the Coolidge administration helped business and failed to help farmers.

Teaching Suggestions One of the most unusual political conventions in our history—that of the Democrats in 1924—can be explored in some depth in this section. Why were there 103 ballots? What was the impact of the Ku Klux Klan? The contrast between the sociable Harding and "Silent Cal" Coolidge will interest students, as will a close look at Al Smith, the first Roman Catholic presidential candidate of one of the major parties.

• Have students list the Coolidge statements as quoted in the text (except for "I do not choose to run."). Then discuss the following:

1. With which of these statements do you agree? Why?

2. Both Jefferson and Coolidge believed that the best government is one that governs least. Do you agree? Explain.

• The Harding-Coolidge era provides another fine opportunity to teach (and evaluate) the role of government in a free enterprise economy. Free-market advocates (like Milton Friedman, for example) acknowledge the need of a strong government *to enforce vigorous competition*. Competition tends to weed out the inefficient producers and thus to lead to the most economical use of productive resources. Coolidge seems to have understood the value of competition in farming—and farm productivity was growing spectacularly with the rising use of tractors, other mechanized equipment, commercial fertilizers, etc. But farmers were in no position to control output and thereby influence prices. Coolidge was willing to let the free-market forces work in agriculture. But he (and Hoover, Mellon, and others in the administration) in a seemingly consistent hands-off policy towards business was actually permitting large producers to get larger and condoning (even encouraging) cooperation among producers instead of vigorous competition. As a result, industrial firms were able to control output and fix prices to some extent.

One must wonder, if practical ways had been found for farmers to organize to control production and fix prices, whether the Republican administrations in the 1920s would have helped such efforts just as they did help industries to cooperate.

• In discussing the election of 1924, you might remind students that the Ku Klux Klan had about reached a peak in that year and was influential in both parties but perhaps especially so with the Democrats because of that party's hold on the "solid South."

Ask questions like these:

1. Why would some delegates to the Democratic convention insist on a platform plank condemning the Klan? (matter of principle; lack of condemnation would suggest approval; heavy anti-Klan sentiment in their state required condemnation if the Democrats were to carry the state)

2. Why would other delegates oppose such a plank? (some were Klan members or had Klan support; in their states condemnation would be interpreted as Democratic softness on "100 percent Americanism"; etc.)

3. Which candidate—McAdoo or Smith—would Klan supporters favor? Why? (McAdoo—regardless of his own sentiments toward the Klan—because Smith was a Roman Catholic, a "wet," and a big-city figure.)

• Tell students that the long, disorderly 1924 Democratic convention was the first to be heard by radio, and it did not give listeners a favorable picture of the Democrats.

An inspiring note was the return of Franklin D. Roosevelt to politics after a crippling siege of polio. He made his way on crutches to the podium and presented Al Smith to the convention as "the Happy Warrior."

William Jennings Bryan's political career ended sadly as he tried to address the raucous delegates and they yelled "louder" to the once-peerless voice. Within the year he would be dead. The choice of Bryan's brother Charles as nominee for Vice-President was an attempt to attract the remnants of the followers of the "Great Commoner."

Further details concerning this convention can be found in Murray's *The 103rd Ballot—Democrats and the Disaster in Madison Square Garden.*

• Tell students that Coolidge's decision not to run again in 1928—despite predictions of an easy victory—is usually attributed by historians to sadness over the death of Calvin Coolidge, Jr. After stepping on a nail while playing tennis, young Calvin died of blood poisoning. Later, Coolidge wrote: "I do not know why such a price was exacted for occupying the White House." He wanted to go back to Vermont—"a state I love." Ross's *Grace Coolidge and Her Era* will interest students who would like to read about an unpretentious first family.

• You might tell students that although there was more bigotry in the 1928 campaign than in any since the attacks on Jackson's alleged bigamy a hundred years earlier, both candidates in 1928 condemned it. Hoover said of his opponent later: "Governor Alfred E. Smith . . . was a natural-born gentleman. . . . During the campaign he said no word and engaged in no action that did not comport with the highest levels." Of his own campaign, Hoover said: "Religious questions have no part in this campaign. I have repeatedly said that neither I nor the Republican party want support on that basis."

Yet Smith, as a Roman Catholic and a "wet" on the Prohibition issue, was the subject of many attacks and rumors. The most serious and scholarly contention appeared in *The Atlantic Monthly,* stating that according to papal church law in any conflict between the civil and the secular "the jurisdiction of the church prevails and that of the state is excluded." Smith replied in a classic statement that should have put the matter to rest: "I believe that no tribunal of any church has any power to make any decree in the law of the land, other than to establish the status of its own communicants within its own church. I believe in the support of the public school as one of the cornerstones of American liberty. I recognize no power in the institution of my church to interfere with the operations of the Constitution of the United States or the enforcement of the law of the land. I believe in absolute freedom of conscience for all men, and in equality of all churches, all sects before the law as a matter of right."

After the election, comedian Will Rogers jokingly told the Pope to unpack. (There had been rumors that the Pope would have an office in the White House if Smith were elected.) Outside of the South, Smith had won only in the strongly Roman Catholic states of Massachusetts and Rhode Island.

You might ask for student reaction to the Smith statement on religion in government.

Not all historians agree that religion was the dominant issue in Smith's defeat. Professor William F. Ogburn, studying 173 counties in northern states, concluded that "prohibition sentiment was three times more decisive an influence . . . than the religious issue."

Section 4 (pp. 482–485)
Life in the Jazz Age

Instructional Objectives Students will be able to

1. Tell about the changes brought about in the 1920s by the automobile, movies, radio, phonograph, and other products.

2. List some of the changes in education during the 1920s.

3. Explain how hero-worship reached its peak in Charles A. Lindbergh's solo nonstop flight to Paris.

4. Evaluate the impact of advertising and credit on American life during the 1920s.

Teaching Suggestions This section offers an excellent opportunity to have each student research and report on one of the many aspects of life and the changing standards of the 1920s. Topics suggested by the text (movies, radio, phonographs, sports, jazz, etc.) can be augmented with vivid detail and can be subdivided so that each student has a distinctive topic. Add other topics not covered directly in the text, such as "Airplane Progress in the '20s" "Fashions of the '20s" "The Florida Land Boom," and so on. Fill out the list of topics with famous personalities. See the bibliography for Unit 8 for a wide variety of references.

• *Handout lesson:* On the chalkboard put the title "Impact of the Automobile on American Life in the 1920s." Tell students that they will begin to list influences of the automobile after reading extracts from *Middletown,* a sociological study of a small American city (Muncie, Indiana) made by Robert and Helen Lynd in the 1920s. Distribute *Handout 34.* After students have read it, call for responses to put under the title on the chalkboard. Tell students to look for inferences as well as for direct statements of influences. Expected responses include (a) less dependence on neighborhood shops; (b) wider range of recreational opportunities; (c) increased commuting to jobs; (d) less supervised dating; (e) decline of church attendance; (f) rise of credit buying; (g) decline of saving; (h) new source of parent-youth conflict; etc.

When students have exhausted the possibilities of the handout, ask for other "impacts." Confine responses to the 1920s (not outdoor movies and superhighways, for example).

At the start of this activity you may want to tell students that autos in use in the United States grew from 7 million in 1918 to 26 million in 1929. So some of the influences had begun earlier, but it was the swift rise in car ownership that caused the auto to have such a profound impact on American life in the 1920s.

• Students who are "car buffs" may have models or photographs of the automobiles of the 1920s which they will show or display to the class. Posters can be used for a bulletin board display.

• *Competency exercise—interviewing:* Ask students to prepare for an interview (whether or not they actually complete it) with one or more persons who can recall the 1920s. (The interviewees should have been at least age 3 to 5 in 1920 perhaps.) The task is to prepare a 2- or 3-sentence introduction explaining the purpose of the interview along with introducing oneself. Then to write some minimum number of questions to ask in the interview.

Encourage students to focus on one or two aspects of the period rather than trying to cover recollections of everything.

• The competency exercise suggested above has a very specific objective: to sharpen interviewing skills. After performing this initial task—the *writing* of a precise introduction and questions—you might arrange for several students to demonstrate (and practice) oral delivery in a role-playing situation.

Some students may be willing to take part in an *oral history* project by arranging to tape record their interview.

• Ask a committee to examine in your school library all available pictorial histories of the 1920s, such as *The American Destiny,* Volume 13, "The Twenties," to locate advertisements of the period. Show these to the students and read aloud some of the slogans. Then write these headings on the chalkboard:

ADVERTISING IN THE 1920s (AND NOW)

Desirable aspects—

Undesirable aspects—

CREDIT IN THE 1920s (AND NOW)

Desirable aspects—

Undesirable aspects—

Have students complete the chart in the appropriate places, using the text as a guide. After the students have finished, discuss the responses to reach a consensus.

Chapter 22

- The John Held magazine cover on page 483 somewhat exaggerates the dress fashions of the '20s. Supplement it with other pictures of popular dress and grooming fashions of the era—including, of course, the raccoon coats. According to fashion experts, you might point out, the apparel of the well-dressed woman changed from a total of twenty yards of material at the beginning of the decade to seven in 1929, and the hemline from scraping the ground to reaching the knee. Also, the use of lipstick and rouge became acceptable. For those who would like to read more, suggest Allen's *Only Yesterday*.

CHAPTER REVIEW

Meeting Our Earlier Selves

1. Disturbing changes: strikes, race riots, sudden inflation, cross burnings by Klan, women and blacks resisting a return to former roles, etc. Agreeable changes: radio, phonographs, new mobility from auto, refrigerators, machines easing farm labor. (See other disturbing and agreeable changes in the list worked out on the impact of the automobile.) In general, changes directly associated with technological progress are easier to accept than those having to do with changing roles and social relationships. Note that in the area of changing morals and manners the older generation is most likely to be disturbed.

2. Victims of the hysteria included aliens and recent immigrant citizens—especially from southern and eastern Europe; Catholics; Jews; blacks—especially those trying to cast off old restrictions; union members; nonconformists—particularly in Klan-dominated rural and small-town environments; and perhaps others. Sufferings included expulsion, beatings, threats, loss of jobs, housing restrictions, lack of job openings, but mostly ridicule and other signs of contempt including ethnic slurs. Prejudice (including stereotypes) was at the root of the problem.

3. *Anarchists:* largest measure of personal freedom possible; government replaced by agencies of voluntary cooperation; often see revolution as only means to replace existing order. *Socialists:* public ownership of major productive facilities—to be attained (and sustained) by democratic means. *Communists:* public ownership attained through revolution; "dictatorship of the proletariat," but actually of Communist party leaders.

Anarchists with their philosophical attachment to personal freedom tended to be poorly organized, but their fanaticism sometimes resulted in irrational behavior like bomb throwing. Socialists by and large believed in peaceful change. Communists were generally highly organized and dedicated to revolution.

4. Leaders after World War II were aware of the damage done by reparations. Also it quickly became clear after W. W. II that it was in the best interests of the U. S. to help Western Europe rebuild as a protection against communism and the Soviet Union. A strong West Germany and Japan as close U. S. allies represents a better situation than having them as resentful enemies or to have seen them collapse and become ripe for dictatorship.

5. Students can use their text and other accounts to find parallels and differences in the Grant and Harding scandals.

6. The text suggests that the government did not pursue antitrust enforcement vigorously but did encourage trade associations to draw up rules of fair competition (see col. 1, page 480).

Questions for Today

1. This text explains the SALT agreements briefly. Refer students to the text (see index) and to the *Readers' Guide* for magazine articles giving further information.

2. Religious affiliation has not been a significant issue since J. F. Kennedy ran in 1960. Edward Kennedy's run for the nomination in 1980 foundered for other reasons than religion. The Kennedy election in 1960 seems to have put the Catholic issue to rest.

Skills to Make Our Past Vivid

1. Suggest that students list the two kinds of changes in parallel columns. Remind them to consider changes mentioned in class discussion as well as those named or inferred in the text.

2. Examples: (a) The roar of the assembly line is suggested by the picture on page 484. (b) Imagine the roar of the Packard engine on page 485.

CHAPTER 23

The Coming of the Great Depression

Introducing the Chapter Ask students to think of some adjustments their own family, and their own city or nearest city, would have to make if a recession were to hit them in the next few months. Tell them that a quarter to a third of the wage earners, including those in their own family, would be laid off. There is no unemployment insurance, and only the most needy can expect to get any help from the local government. There is no federal welfare program. (Some students may be willing to describe adjustments that their own family has actually made when faced by loss of job or other big cut in income.)

Section 1 (pp. 487–489)
A Prosperous Nation

Instructional Objectives Students will be able to

1. Tell about the background and philosophy of President Herbert Hoover.
2. Describe the stock market boom during the last half of the 1920s.
3. Define "margin," and explain how such loans generated great activity and high prices on the stock market.

Teaching Suggestions To prepare students for the clash of political philosophies in the election of 1932, get their reactions to Hoover's "rugged individualism" beliefs. The stock market boom—particularly the use of brokers' loans—will require careful explanations. A film such as *The '29 Boom and the '30's Depression* (14 min) will help provide visualization of what happened and prepare the way for the crash described in the next section.

- Write the following stock market prices on the chalkboard as an illustration of what happened during the boom, or "bull" market:

	1927	1929
General Electric	128	396
American Tel. & Tel.	179	335
Montgomery Ward	132	466
R.C.A.	94	505

Point out that these are prices in dollars for one share of stock. Then explain that many of the transactions involved buying on "margin" (loans from brokers—thus, credit) in which the collateral (or backing) for the transaction was the stock itself. As the 1920s ended, loans for such transactions grew from $3 1/2 billion in June 1927 to $8 billion in September 1929. In many instances, an investor would buy shares of stock with little or no down payment, hoping that he could sell at a higher price within a few weeks or months. With the sale of the stock, the broker would collect interest for the loans plus commissions.

So long as stock prices continued to climb, there were immense "paper" profits (usually, little money would pass hands—the speculative investor would simply buy more stock). However, with a drop in stock prices, the lenders would call for "margin," meaning a payment to "cover" the difference between the decreased value of the stock and the amount of the loan. Since the stockholders usually had no ready cash available, they would have to cover their loan by selling their stock (or the broker would do it to protect himself), and the losses would of course be sustained by the investor. Thus, successful trading was dependent on rising prices. As will be explained further in the next chapter section, losses could be disastrous to traders.

Engel's *How to Buy Stocks* or any economics book dealing with the stock market will provide additional explanation of the techniques of investing and trading.

- Explain that the "mania" for investing in the stock market was based on the hope that prices would continue to go up, that the prosperity of the late '20s would continue indefinitely. In a campaign speech in 1928, Hoover said: "We in America today are nearer to the final triumph over poverty than ever before in the history of any land. The poorhouse is vanishing from among us. We have not reached the goal, but given a chance to go forward with the policies of the last eight years, we shall soon, with the help of God, be in sight of the day when poverty will be banished from this nation." Al Smith's campaign manager John J. Raskob, vice-president of General Motors, wrote a widely reprinted article for the *Ladies' Home Journal* entitled "Everybody Ought To Be Rich." In his inaugural address, Hoover said, "I have no fears for the future of our country. It is bright with hope."

Soon, however, there were ominous signs in the economy. By the summer of 1929, residential construction had fallen more than a billion dollars from that of the year before, consumer spending had dropped, business inventories were very heavy, and unemployment was growing. As the text indicates, with the end of summer in 1929 a wave of uncertainty began to undermine the confidence of investors, and reportedly "those in the know" began to sell.

- *Competency exercise—paragraph writing:* Have students write a brief editorial entitled "Hoover Will Make a Good

President," explaining to the readers why Hoover's experience and political philosophy indicated a prosperous four years ahead as he took office. Use the text as a guide.

After students have finished, have them read several editorials aloud. Then collect papers for evaluation purposes.

Section 2 (pp. 490–496)
The Big Crash

Instructional Objectives Students will be able to

1. Describe the stock market crash of October 1929.

2. Explain factors that caused the collapse of the stock market and the nation's economy.

3. Name steps that President Hoover took to restore prosperity.

4. Explain the collapse of the banking system.

5. Describe the extent of, and reactions to, the Great Depression.

Teaching Suggestions From the distance of a half century, the story of the collapse of our economy and the onset of the depression of the 1930s may seem unreal to students. You might expand the lesson with readings and visual aids. Encourage students to explore family history—interviewing grandparents or other relatives—for accounts of how the depression affected them.

• Read aloud descriptions of the stock market crash, such as from the chapter "The Stock Market Crash" in Allen's *Only Yesterday* or from Galbraith's *The Big Crash*. Or show a film, such as *The '29 Boom and the '30's Depression* (14 min) or a filmstrip *Prosperity and Panic, Part II, 1928–32*.

Following the above activities, have students review Section 2 up to "Hoover takes action." Then write this heading on the chalkboard:

REASONS FOR THE CRASH
AND THE DEPRESSION

Below this, have students list the reasons in a vertical column, using the text and other information presented in class as a guide.

• Have students identify and explain the measures taken by the Hoover administration to deal with the depression. You may need to tell students that our present-day techniques for dealing with a serious downturn in business—in fact even a mild recession—simply were not economic orthodoxy in the early 1930s. Even Roosevelt in the 1932 election campaign talked about balancing the budget. Not even conservatives in our day would prescribe that kind of medicine. Use item 2 of *Meeting Our Earlier Selves* (p. 501) as part of this discussion.

• In using the pictures on pages 493–494—and others you can find to show—ask students to look for indications (a) that the depression's impact differed from family to family and (b) that there were offsetting factors that helped people to adjust. For example, the billboard on page 493 and the well-dressed apple buyer on page 494 suggest the uneven impact of the depression. The "mush & milk 5¢" sign and the offer to sell a good-looking car for $100 tell something about the drop in the price level that eased adjustment to hard times. Also the fact that government tolerated shanties instead of rigorously enforcing housing codes might be pointed out.

On the other hand, you might mention that while millions of families weathered the depression with only minor hardship—if any—thousands of people who remained employed took wage cuts or worked fewer hours per week or both, and some felt obligated to help family members who had lost a job.

• Have a student report on the Bonus Army of 1932. Or tell students that in the spring of 1932, a group of veterans in Portland, Oregon, decided to "march" to Washington to seek immediate payment of a bonus for wartime service (a 20-year paid-up insurance policy) that had been approved by Congress for payment in 1945. Picking up other veterans and their wives and children en route, the marchers overcame many hardships and much resistance until they reached Washington, where they set up cardboard and tin shacks and soup kitchens along the Anacostia River.

Later, while 10,000 veterans waited on the steps of the Capitol, the Senate voted "no" to the immediate payment of a bonus that would have averaged $1000 per veteran. Disappointed, many of the veterans left to return home. Those that stayed in their encampment through the summer still hoped that Congress would do something for them. But nothing happened until a small riot broke out when some veterans were ordered to vacate their living quarters in abandoned buildings.

President Hoover approved calling out federal troops under General Douglas MacArthur (with Major Dwight D. Eisenhower as his aide). The troops dispersed the veterans and burned their shacks. The nation reacted apathetically; there were so many other problems to think about.

• Tell students that no President ever worked harder than Hoover. He labored from breakfast to eleven at night, often talking on the telephone for hours (he was the first President to have a telephone on his desk). Gradually he became grim from fatigue. "There was always a frown on his face and a look of worry," said Chief White House usher Ike Hoover (no relation).

Although the President had little sense of humor, the oppressed of the nation did. In addition to the Hooverville shantytowns mentioned in the text, there were "Hoover blankets" (newspapers used for warmth), "Hoover hogs" (jackrabbits shot by hunters and eaten in stew), and "Hoover wagons" (automobiles that like the economy had broken down and were used for shelter in city dumps).

• *Handout lesson:* Use *Handout 35* to enlarge on discussion of the topic "The unequal distribution of wealth" on page 491. You might have students write brief answers to the questions—or particular ones—and then go over their responses in class discussion. Or simply use the questions orally as the entire class studies the graphs. Suggested answers follow:

1. Too little income went to the lower income groups to buy the output of industry. The very rich, frightened by the stock-market crash, stopped spending and investing. (The decline of investment is a key point; see item 7.)

2. One would assume that income taxes went up sharply, and of course they did in the Revenue Act of 1935 (p. 516) and particularly during World War II. Notice the term "soak the rich taxes" on page 516. Emphasize the role of high graduated tax rates on incomes and estates in the redistribution of income.

3. *Dividends*—income from ownership of shares of business corporations. *Rent*—income from ownership of land, from resources on or under the surface of land, and from buildings and other improvements on the land. *Interest* represents income from property in the form of money (lendable funds).

4. The 82% figure on dividends shows the concentration of corporation ownership by the rich in the late 1920s. Thousands and thousands of people lower on the income ladder were starting to dabble in stocks in the late 1920s, but their small number of shares hardly made a dent in the huge amounts held by the top 5%. Have students notice that by 1948 stock ownership had become somewhat less concentrated. But the big interest in stocks by the "little people" was still in the future; by the 1960s stock-market executives and brokers were fond of the term "people's capitalism" in reference to the widening ownership of corporation stock. Today, huge amounts of stocks are held by institutions—charitable foundations, pension funds, and the like.

5. Interest income: saving accounts, paid-up life insurance policies, corporation bonds, government bonds, U.S. Treasury notes, personal loans, etc. Rental income: building rents, land rents, royalties on oil or coal obtained from one's land, etc. Rent is net income (gross income minus expenses). A chief reason for asking this question is to have students see that many people of modest means have some income in the form of interest and/or rent.

6. Both graphs show a significant shift of income shares from the top 5% and top 20% to the people lower on the income scale—but still considerable concentration of wealth at the top. Here would be a good place to point out that the 1977 "income pie" was vastly larger than that of 1929. Thus millions of people were getting a little bigger share of a much bigger pie. Ask students how this idea could be shown in a graph. (By showing the 1929 distribution in a small pie graph, or circle graph, and the 1977 distribution in a larger one—scaled to the actual difference in size.)

7. Economists point to two major benefits: (a) Somewhat large differences in income seem to be needed to spur initiative, risk-taking, hard work, etc. (b) More money is probably available for investment than if income were equalized; the rich can't possibly spend all their income, so it is available for investment. If that extra income were spread around, much of it would be spent for consumer goods—not capital goods.

Economists also point out that where wealth is simply inherited and does not represent risk-taking and hard work and where wealth is hoarded (or kept in nonproductive gold and jewels), the society suffers from big inequalities in wealth and income.

8. The bottom 40% might become more productive (if the sharing didn't come in the form of handouts); their higher incomes would stimulate the output of housing and all kinds of consumer goods and services.

Section 3 (pp. 496–498)
Foreign Affairs in a Gloomy World

Instructional Objectives Students will be able to

1. Describe the Kellogg-Briand Pact and other international efforts to maintain peace.

2. Summarize our Latin American relationships during the Coolidge and Hoover years.

3. Tell how peace ended with the Japanese aggression in Manchuria and the rise of Mussolini in Italy and Hitler in Germany.

Teaching Suggestions You may want to combine this brief section with the next one for a single reading assignment.

To guide their reading of this section, you might have students look for answers to these overriding questions:

1. How were foreign affairs in the late 1920s and early 1930s linked to the depression?

2. What events in this period foreshadowed the outbeak of World War II?

3. How did our relations with Latin America improve in this period?

• *Competency exercise—vocabulary development:* Write the following *ten* words from Section 3 on the chalkboard in a vertical column: moratorium, defaulting, renounce, belligerent, fascism, escalator, guerrillas, expropriation, collaboration, sanctions. Have students copy these and write a definition for each word from the text or the dictionary. Then have them use any *five* words in original sentences. Go over the meanings to reach a consensus. Collect the papers for evaluation.

• Point out that the seizure of power in Italy in 1922 by Mussolini did not disturb the democratic nations at the time. Winston Churchill saw some "positive aspects in it." Those who feared communism saw in anti-democratic fascism an acceptable counter-balance. Later, as fascist Italy joined Nazi Germany in moving towards war, the democratic nations realized that they had misjudged the threat of fascism to world peace.

Tell students that a more detailed story of Mussolini and Hitler comes in Chapter 26, Section 1.

• Point out that the Kellogg-Briand Pact was approved by the United States Senate by a vote of 81 to 1. Ask students to speculate on what kinds of pro and con arguments might have been presented during the ratification debate. (Examples: Pro—(a) "Pact can't do any harm, and may do some good." (b) "We must support our Secretary of State in this peace effort." (c) "Refusal to ratify will tell the world that the U.S. does not want to settle disputes peaceably." Etc. Con—(a) "Will lull the world into a false sense of security." (b) "Warlike nations will sign with no intention of obeying the pledge." Etc.

You might tell students that when the war crimes trials were held after World War II, one legal justification for the trials was that German and Japanese leaders had broken the pledge made by their nation in the Kellogg-Briand Pact.

• Tell students that Franklin Roosevelt in 1933 announced a Good Neighbor policy in our relations with Latin America (p. 540). Ask: "To what extent should Coolidge and Hoover share the credit for the Good Neighbor policy?" Have students list specific steps taken by the Coolidge and Hoover administrations to improve relations with Latin America—steps that appeared to renounce our role as "big brother."

• Be sure that students notice the emphasis in the text on the significance that the authors attach to the failure to apply sanctions against Japan for its aggression in China in 1931–1932. You might relate this situation to Carter's sanctions against the Soviet Union (including the 1980 Olympic boycott) for its aggression in Afghanistan, his efforts to get worldwide cooperation, and the extent of support he received in the United States.

Section 4 (pp. 498–500)
The Election of 1932

Instructional Objectives Students will be able to

1. Judge the fairness of the blame put on Hoover for the Great Depression.
2. Describe the appeals that Hoover and Roosevelt made to voters during the campaign of 1932.
3. Show that the outcome of the 1932 election was a landslide for the Democrats.

Teaching Suggestions Next to the 1860 election, the one in 1932 may have been the most significant in our history. Franklin D. Roosevelt became one of our most loved and yet hated of Presidents. Be sure to have your students listen to Roosevelt's persuasive voice on film or record.

• Tell students that although Roosevelt was the leading candidate at the Democratic convention in 1932, a *New York Times* survey showed that he was 200 votes short of the necessary two-thirds needed for victory. Al Smith told a press conference that "I am here to get myself nominated." Some leading "bosses," such as Mayor Frank Hague of Jersey City, backed Smith. Said Hague, "Roosevelt, if nominated, has no chance of winning." Another candidate was Speaker of the House John N. Garner of Texas, who was supported by the powerful newspaper publisher, William Randolph Hearst.

By the fourth ballot, Roosevelt's advisers realized that he could not win without gaining support from another candidate. They agreed to name Garner as the vice-presidential candidate in return for a switch of the Texan's delegates to Roosevelt. William G. McAdoo made the dramatic announcement for California as the Smith delegates were caught by surprise: "California casts forty-four votes for Franklin D. Roosevelt." Soon all other candidates except Smith fell into line.

In starting a new tradition whereby the winning candidate addresses the convention, Roosevelt decided on the difficult flight (for those days) from Albany to Chicago. Flying through stormy weather, the plane had to refuel twice en route. Two hours late, Roosevelt at last confidently faced the tired but curious delegates: "I pledge you," he cried in a ringing voice, "I pledge myself, to a new deal for the American people."

Amid the roar of the crowd, the band played "Happy Days Are Here Again," and millions of listeners wondered what the confident candidate could do to restore the spirit of the American people.

• Raise the question "Was it fair to blame Hoover for the depression?" Note that the Democrats did so in 1932, and they continued to remind voters of the Hoover depression in election after election in the years that followed. Ask subsidiary questions like these:

1. How do the authors of the text respond to this issue? (They point out that he was the "handiest person to blame, even though the depression had actually begun almost before he had moved into the White House." The authors, however, do report Hoover's failure to support proposed remedies and his inclination to let the business cycle run its course.)

2. To what extent should Presidents get credit for "good times" and blame for "bad times"? (Credit and blame is often unfair because of circumstances over which the President has no control. Yet it seems reasonable for voters to ask whether the President responded effectively (and consistently) to the economic situation; whether he exerted the leadership—over Congress especially—that he might have; etc.)

3. Is the consensus of historians that Hoover was "average" as a President a reasonable judgment? Why?

- Point out that Roosevelt's health as a polio victim was an issue during the campaign, although it was never mentioned by Hoover. To those who said that an immobile Roosevelt would be handicapped as President, Garner replied, "For the Presidency you run on a record and not on your legs."

The physical appearance of the candidates may have influenced many voters. The unsmiling Hoover soberly predicted that if Roosevelt were elected, grass would grow "in the streets of a hundred cities, a thousand towns; the weeds will overrun the fields of millions of farms." Roosevelt, by contrast, smiled a lot, spoke with enthusiasm, and in the words of historian Foster Dulles, "had almost irresistible charm." Call attention to the photos on pages 500 and 505.

CHAPTER REVIEW

Meeting Our Earlier Selves

1. "Buying on margin" increased the risk because of the amounts involved and because a forced sale to cover the margin may leave the investor with nothing, whereas paying cash allows you to sell at your own discretion.

Investment implies concern about protecting the money invested, willingness to accept moderate rewards, and—usually—intention to stick with the purchase for a while. Gambling implies taking big risks for big, quick gains.

2. Temporary adjustments: (a) tax cuts, (b) loans to farm cooperatives, (c) higher tariffs, (d) farm price supports, (e) limited program of public works, (f) aid to business through RFC, (g) home mortgage protection, (h) drought aid to farmers.

Like many economists at the time, Hoover believed that free-market forces would soon start the economy moving upward again. A little push by government, chiefly to relieve business distress, should be enough. In fact, the remedies accepted by Hoover went further than his beliefs dictated.

3. The crash signaled producers to cut back. Layoffs cut consumer buying, entailing further layoffs in affected industries. Additional layoffs signaled other producers to reduce production, thus adding to the unemployment rolls. When the auto industry made cuts, the parts suppliers like the tire makers had to do so too; then firms supplying the tire makers had to make cuts; etc.

4. The Kellogg-Briand Pact helped to provide a false sense of security, providing willingness—for example—to reduce naval power. Japan used the occasion to get special concessions in the Pacific area. Together the various treaties were unable to prevent the outbreak of World War II and earlier aggressions by Italy, Japan, and Germany) because they made no provision for cooperative action to stop aggression. And the false security engendered by the pacts told potential aggressors that there was little to fear by going to war to achieve national ambitions.

Questions for Today

1. Hoover and Eisenhower had established their reputations as forceful administrators in nonpartisan public service areas (war relief; army and NATO commander).

You will need to look around to see if there is anyone today fitting a similar description. Or is there someone who has served with distinction under both a Republican and Democratic President without having held a partisan elective office?

Both parties have to try to attract the vast number of middle-of-the-road Americans.

2. This is a value judgment question. One of the problems of agreeing with the credo is that for a generation now Americans have been hearing that the race is not equal, that public education—despite all the equality efforts—does not give the contestants an equal start. Another problem is visualizing the government as simply an umpire—presumably seeing that the race is run fairly (whistling the fouls). This role does not square with government as champion of affirmative action.

3. Students are probably familiar with unemployment insurance, job referrals by the Employment Service, Supplementary Unemployment Benefits (SUB) in some union contracts, food stamps, etc.

Skills to Make Our Past Vivid

1. Probably item G because the level of unemployment reflects the entire economy whereas other items relate to particular segments of the economy.

2. Items A, C, and E. A drop in farm income (cash receipts) is likely to be reflected in a drop in farm production expenses (spending for fertilizer). And since agriculture has long been a major contributor to our exports, the decline in exports contributed to the drop in farm income.

3. The drop in spending for new housing brought drops in lumber production because housing is a chief market for lumber.

4. Workers who kept their jobs saw pay levels decline. How seriously they were hurt depends also on what happened to the cost of living, so cost-of-living figures (changes in the Consumer Price Index) would be useful to know. Also you would want to know if the lower average weekly earnings reflect an average shorter working week. If so, the workers were trading some lost dollars for more leisure.

5. Given Hoover's and the Republicans' attachment to a balanced budget—and knowing that federal budget receipts must have declined from the tax cut and from probable reduced income from excises and tariff duties—the rise in government expenditures might be surprising. (Today we expect government spending to rise at the merest hint of recession.) Yet knowing the extent of economic distress and the pressure on public officials "to do something," it should not be surprising that government expenditures did indeed rise between 1929 and 1932. The surprise for someone familiar with government today is how little the spending went up in face of the disaster.

CHAPTER 24

"Nothing to Fear but Fear Itself"

Introducing the Chapter   After a summary of the background of Franklin D. Roosevelt, this three-section chapter examines the wide-ranging measures of the New Deal. Whenever possible, you might relate these to federal programs existing today. While much of the New Deal has become engrained, areas of controversy remain. Encourage the expression of opinions. Illustrations and films will aid students in visualizing some of the problems faced and solutions offered in the 1930s.

Section 1 (pp. 504–513)
Franklin D. Roosevelt's New Deal

Instructional Objectives   Students will be able to

1. Describe the background and political philosophy of Franklin D. Roosevelt.

2. Identify the "Brain Trust" and their roles in the New Deal.

3. Summarize the New Deal measures dealing with banking, currency, securities, conservation, housing, agriculture, business, and work relief.

4. Evaluate the achievements of the New Deal in Roosevelt's first term.

5. Interpret the map of the Tennessee Valley Authority.

Teaching Suggestions   This section names and describes a large number of laws and programs enacted in Roosevelt's first term. You may want to add others. Avoid memorization as an objective. It will be useful, however, for students to list the laws and programs in chart form in their notebook. Then they can refer to the legislation easily in class discussion. (Notice that the first two items in the Chapter Review on page 522 call for such a list.)

In charting the legislation, students might divide the page into one-third and two-thirds segments. Use the left column to name the law or program, and on the right jot down phrases that succinctly describe the legislation. Then a horizontal line can be drawn before listing the next item.

Point out that, while the measures named and described in this chapter section were enacted or promulgated in the first two years of the New Deal, they are not in chronological order.

- To help students understand the mood and the problems to be faced by the nation in 1933 as Roosevelt took office, show a film that includes part of the inaugural address, such as *The American Parade: F.D.R.—The Man Who Changed America* (29 min), or play parts of the album *I Can Hear It Now*.

Or you might tell students that Saturday, March 4, 1933, was a cold, gray day. A despairing Hoover had said, "We are at the end of the string." A somber and undemonstrative crowd listened as Roosevelt began his address in a ringing voice: "This is a day of national consecration." Not until he reached the end of his address did he smile warmly to the crowd below. Then he shook hands with the departing Hoover. An administration that would last longer than that of any other President was about to begin.

- Tell students that Roosevelt was nearly assassinated before he became President. On February 15, 1933, FDR left a vacation yacht to ride in an open car to a reception in Miami. With him was Mayor Anton Cermak of Chicago. The car stopped and FDR addressed the crowd briefly. Then from a distance of about thirty feet a short man on a box began firing a pistol wildly at the car. FDR escaped unharmed, thanks to a woman who deflected the assassin's arm, but five persons were wounded, including Mayor Cermak, who later died from his wound.

The assassin, an unemployed bricklayer, explained that he had "always hated the rich and powerful." He had, in fact, tried unsuccessfully to kill King Victor Emmanuel of Italy ten years earlier.

(Slightly more than a year before, Winston Churchill, destined to join Roosevelt during World War II as one of the leaders of the free world, was knocked down but not seriously injured by a taxi in New York City. So history is sometimes determined by a matter of inches.)

- Ask for volunteers to choose the name of one of FDR's advisers named in the topic "The Brain Trust" for about a two-minute report focusing particularly on that person's contribution to the New Deal. Follow the reports with questions like these:

1. "The country is being run by a group of college professors," complained Senator Hatfield of West Virginia. Why would politicians react this way to Brain Trusters? (jealousy of those with higher education; fear of their lack of government experience; considered more idealistic than practical)

2. Some of Roosevelt's close advisers were personal friends. What are the advantages and disadvantages of selecting friends? (advantages: loyalty, compatibility, awareness of abilities; disadvantages: may not be most qualified, may take advantage of friendship, President may overlook their weaknesses)

- Students should note that FDR was the last President to take office on March 4. It may be hard to think of another time in our history when a prompt takeover of the government by a new President was needed. You might ask: "Was Roosevelt acting in the public interest in refusing to support Hoover's efforts to deal with the depression during Hoover's last months in office?"

You might have students read the 20th Amendment on pages 793–794. Sections 1 and 2 are pertinent to this lesson. The "lame duck" aspect of the Presidency is easy enough to understand. Hoover lost the election in early November 1932, but he remained as President for another four months. The 20th Amendment cut this "lame duck" period to about 2 1/2 months beginning with the 1936 election for President.

The "lame duck" situation with Congress will be more difficult to explain. Remind students that congressional elections are held every even-numbered year. For example, there was a congressional election in November 1930. Then Congress convened a month later in December 1930, but it was the old Congress. It had to adjourn on or before noon, March 4, 1931, when its term expired. (This was known as the "short session" of Congress; it was always scheduled to start on the first Monday of December in even-numbered years.) The next regular meeting of Congress (for holdovers and for new members elected in November 1930) would then start in December 1931. It would generally remain in session until the next summer—say, July 1932 in our example. (This was the "long session," starting in December of every odd-numbered year.) The members of Congress would then go home for the congressional (and presidential) election of 1932 and return a month later, whether reelected or not, for their short session of December 1932 to March 4, 1933.

So when FDR took the oath of office on March 4, 1933, Congress had adjourned. And the new Congress was not scheduled to meet until the following December—*13 months after the 1932 election!* Like many other new Presidents just taking office, however, FDR called the new Congress into *special session*.

It was this new Congress—now heavily Democratic—that would work with the new President to give the country "a fresh start."

- To help students see why Roosevelt had to act quickly to prevent the complete collapse of the banking system of the country, show the film *The Bank Holiday Crisis of 1933* (27 min). Point out that by March 4, 1933, the day of Roosevelt's inauguration, bank holidays had already been declared in 38 states, including New York and Illinois before dawn on that very day. The New York Stock Exchange and the Chicago Board of Trade were also closed. Thus FDR had little choice but to make the closing of the banks for a holiday his first official act.

- Help students begin the aforementioned chart on New Deal laws and programs by listing the banking and currency measures: Emergency Banking Act, Glass-Steagall Act, and Gold Reserve Act. (Tell students that among its other provisions the Emergency Banking Act had given the Secretary of the Treasury authority to call in all gold and gold certificates in the country in exchange for Federal Reserve notes.)

Students should see that, besides the immediate objective of getting the banks reopened, the chief goals of the banking and currency measures were (a) deposit protection to end the runs on banks—FDIC, and (b) inflation (stopping deflation).

- Tell students that John Maynard Keynes's famous treatise, *The General Theory of Employment, Interest and Money* appeared in 1936. Therefore, although it had a little influence on the later years of the New Deal, Keynes's theory was scarcely known when FDR took office. As the text points out, FDR subscribed to the economic orthodoxy of the time—the balanced budget with perhaps some pump-priming to get things moving again. Thus the New Deal deficit spending, at least in the beginning, was not designed to apply some grand theory but was simply a response to the need to get people back to work. Even economic conservatives today accept the need for budget deficits in a recession, but they are more likely to advocate tax cuts in place of rising government spending. Incidentally, you should also probably tell students that Keynes proposed budget surpluses in times of prosperity. This aspect of Keynesian theory is much harder to apply because it is not popular to reduce spending or to raise taxes.

Ask: "How did the Economy Act go against Keynesian theory?" (provided for cutting rather than increasing federal spending) Then you might point out that the beer-wine legalization measure was not simply an inducement for Congress to pass the Economy Act but was designed to raise revenue by taxing the sale of beer and wine. So it was also a budget-balancing measure—and directly counter to Keynesian theory.

- Tell students that the CCC was probably the most popular of the New Deal programs, in part because it brought a big return for the money expended. More than 2.5 million unemployed single young men (500,000 in 1935 alone) worked in over 2600 camps. They were paid $30 a month, of which $25 was sent to their family.

Although the contribution of the CCC was significant —planting 1.5 billion trees in four years, for example—not everyone was pleased with the idea. The camps were run by army officers, and when Assistant Secretary of War Harry H. Woodring made an unfortunate remark that the CCC youths could be organized as "economic storm troops," some critics linked that future possibility to the Nazi youth camps being developed by Hitler in Germany. With the coming of World War II, interest in the CCC began to wane, and Congress abolished the agency in 1942. Horan's *The Desperate Years,* pages 103–107, or any pictorial history of the period, will provide illustrations and details. After you have related the above, and students have reviewed references to the CCC in the text, discuss the following:

1. Would a CCC be desirable today? Why? Who would be enrolled?

2. Roosevelt once said that every boy ought to have the chance to go into the woods for six months. Do you agree? Why?

3. Some sociologists have advocated that short-term inmates of delinquency centers and reformatories be placed in CCC-type work camps in rural areas. Do you agree? Why?

• *Competency exercise—map reading:* Have students use the TVA map on page 514 to answer the following questions:

1. Which seven states are served by TVA? (Tennessee, Kentucky, Virginia, North Carolina, Georgia, Alabama, Mississippi)

2. Where does the Tennessee River begin and end? (From the junction of the Holston and the French rivers in Tennessee it flows to the Ohio River at Paducah, Kentucky.)

3. In what direction is the river flowing as it nears the Ohio River? (north)

4. What is the approximate length of the Tennessee River? (650 miles)

5. Where would you expect the elevation of the river to be higher—at Knoxville or at Muscle Shoals? (at Knoxville because it "runs downhill" from the Appalachian Mountains to the Ohio River)

• Point out that one of the sixteen large dams built to control the Tennessee River was named for Senator George W. Norris of Nebraska, who had unsuccessfully proposed the TVA project in the 1920s.

• The first paragraph under "Help for housing" illustrates an interesting feature of the New Deal: an emergency program to deal with a critical need followed by the creation of a successor program with longer-term objectives. HOLC offered direct help on mortgage refinancing for home buyers struggling with relatively high interest loans and short payback periods (say, 10 years instead of 20 or 30). When HOLC ended its activities three years later in June 1936, it had made loans covering 1 million mortgages. Meanwhile the government went about working out a long-term program (FHA mortgages for new construction and home remodeling and rehabilitation) for private lending institutions to provide the loans under a loan-insurance program. The mortgage insurance meant that lenders could offer housing loans at interest rates below conventional mortgages.

The United States Housing Authority (Walter-Steagall Act) illustrates another technique that bypassed direct federal activity in the economic system: loans to cities and states to do a particular job. Much of the federal government's subsequent social-welfare spending was in the form of loans and grants to states and localities (called *grants-in-aid* today).

The Resettlement Administration was another emergency agency. In 1937 it was turned over to the Department of Agriculture and became the Farm Security Administration. An interesting experiment in the resettlement program was the movement of some 200 families from the Midwest to Alaska's Matanuska Valley, where the colony built up a flourishing business of grain, vegetable, and dairy farms.

• If you want to handle New Deal farm measures without interruption, have students read the passages on agriculture on pages 517, 521, and 524–528.

In discussing agriculture, review the items dealing with farming in the table on page 501. Tell students that farm cash receipts nearly doubled between 1932 and 1937, reaching $9,200 million in 1937.

• Give students some idea of the hoopla that was part of the NRA. Point out that the NRA stamp or poster with its "Blue Eagle" symbol—shown in the cartoon on page 511—was posted conspicuously by offices and factories and on store and shop windows as a sign that the firm had accepted the NRA code for its industry. Giant rallies in support of the NRA codes were held in cities throughout the nation; 250,000 people paraded in New York to the music of 200 bands. Some 700 codes for particular branches of business and industry were prepared, affecting nearly 25 million workers.

If you want to complete the story of the NRA at this point, have students read about the death blow struck by the Supreme Court (*Schecter* v. *United States*) in column 2 of page 515. It is called the "Sick Chicken Case" because Schecter was a Brooklyn poultry dealer who was convicted of violating the "Live Poultry Code" by selling an unfit chicken to a butcher and by breaking the code in other ways. Schecter appealed his conviction, and the Court accepted his case for review from among many appeals. (Violations of the codes had appeared almost at once as owners of small businesses found the regulations incomprehensible and confusing or contrary to their own established procedures or because the owners wanted to get a competitive edge on rivals.) Unlike the numerous close decisions on New Deal measures, in this instance the Court struck down the NRA by a 9-0 vote. Two chief grounds were (a) that Congress had wrongly delegated its legislative power to the President and (b) that in this case—and by inference in others—the federal government was regulating intrastate, not interstate, commerce.

The NRA, of course, was the very antithesis of free enterprise.

Whatever gains labor had made under the NRA would soon be guaranteed more effectively under the Wagner Act (NLRB) and the Fair Labor Standards Act.

• Point out that in many areas relief, recovery, and reform necessarily meant that the first governmental step was to give direct aid to the starving and homeless. In some communities—such as several stranded coal towns in Illinois—this meant that 95 percent of the people were on relief.

Thereafter, over a period of years and under one program or another, workers created 650,000 miles of roads and built 35,000 schools and other public buildings. Within your area there may be a number of municipal parks, schools, or post offices that were constructed as part of a federal works program. Appoint a committee to identify these projects by contacting local, county, or state officials. Such information may also be obtained from local libraries.

Less measurable was the contribution to the nation's educational and cultural growth. The National Youth Administration helped a million students continue their schooling. Under various programs, thousands of unemployed writers, actors, and artists were aided (see the next section).

Section 2 (pp. 513–520)
From Recovery to Reform

Instructional Objectives Students will be able to

1. Describe and evaluate the Works Progress Administration including the NYA.

2. Identify and explain sources of criticism against the New Deal that developed in the second half of FDR's first term.

3. Name and explain the key provisions of the Social Security Act and the National Labor Relations Act.

4. Point out the significance of the Revenue Act of 1935 and the Public Utility Holding Company Act.

5. Show how the Supreme Court obstructed the New Deal and describe FDR's response.

6. Describe the 1936 election and point out its significance.

Teaching Suggestions Try to help students capture the mood of the country during FDR's second two years in office. Despair had changed to hope as recovery was well under way. But the welter of laws and the proliferation of alphabetical agencies provided abundant opportunities for criticism.

• While emphasis in FDR's second two years was on reform, it soon became apparent that business recovery would not soon bring unemployment down to acceptable levels; so an even bigger work-relief program got under way. Ask any old-timer about memories of the New Deal, and the question will almost certainly quickly elicit the letters WPA. Appreciation of its achievements tended to come in later years. Pleasure over WPA-built sidewalks, bridges, parks, schools, and the like during construction seemed to be overmatched by displeasure at the leisurely work pace ("leaning on shovels half the day") and at "boondoggling." (This word may have been coined by a scoutmaster named Link who kept the Boy Scouts busy weaving cords of plaited leather to wear around the neck. Hence, to "boondoggle" meant to do work of little or no practical value.) One of the problems of keeping local workers busy was that the project could not compete with private industry or replace regular public works projects employing union labor. Hence, project managers sometimes resorted to "leaf raking" projects to keep men busy.

• Do your students know the political terms *Right, right-wing, Left,* and *left-wing?*

In addition to left-wing opponents like Huey Long and Dr. Townsend, who are often labeled Populists, there were naturally the Socialists and Communists. FDR, of course, had stolen much of the Socialists' thunder; but he hadn't gone far enough to suit many of them. Following Eugene Debs, their perennial candidate for President was Norman Thomas. He had received almost 900,000 votes in 1932 but dropped to under 188,000 in 1936.

Charles E. Coughlin is harder to classify. In effect he wanted to socialize the banks. Government should issue currency directly, not through the Federal Reserve System. He was a free-silver and paper-money man like Bryan and the late 19th century Populists. But his rabid anti-Semitism (Wall Street controlled the country, and the Jews owned Wall Street, he charged) and his increasing approval of fascism stamped him as a right-winger.

This Canadian-born priest became one of the most famous radio personalities of all time. Attracting as many as five million listeners each Sunday afternoon, Coughlin drew more mail—containing up to $25,000 per week in donations—than anyone else in the country, including FDR. He supported Roosevelt in 1932 with the slogan "Roosevelt or ruin." In the summer of 1933 over 100 members of Congress signed a petition to FDR to send Coughlin as an "adviser" to the American delegation going to the London Economic Conference that had been arranged to bring some order into the chaotic worldwide monetary situation. However, as the text notes, Coughlin quickly became disenchanted with FDR and the New Deal. He finally lost his national following when his superiors ordered him off the air and postal authorities banned his magazine *Social Justice* from the mails for violation of the Espionage Act. He continued his parish duties until his death in 1979.

• General discussion of the Supreme Court's decisions on New Deal measures could be postponed until students read about the court-packing plan in the next section. But to check up on student understanding of how cases reach the Supreme Court, you can ask them to speculate on why measures passed in mid-1933 (AAA and NRA) were not declared unconstitutional until 1935 and 1936. (The law first has to be challenged in a lower court by someone directly affected by it; then the dissatisfied party must prepare an appeal to a higher court; the Supreme Court takes some time deciding which few of many appeals it will actually accept; then there is a drawn-out hearing and decision process. The *Schecter* case, described earlier, provides an example: It took time for drawing up the Live Poultry Code and then for someone to complain about Schecter's violations. More time passed as officials drew up charges against Schecter and as the case was tried in a United States district court. Then the appeals process took time.)

• The amount of attention given to the Social Security Act should depend in part on the emphasis it receives in other social studies courses which all, or most, students take. If you elect to describe the programs as they evolved over the years, the following points can be made:

1. The law was amended and extended 15 times in its first 40 years—extending the number of people covered, adding new benefits, raising the level of monthly benefits to keep pace with rising prices and incomes, and increasing the taxes to pay for the higher benefits and wider coverage.

2. In 1939 survivors insurance was added to pay monthly benefits to a deceased worker's spouse and dependent children; so OAI (old-age insurance) became OASI (old-age and survivors insurance).

3. In 1956 disability insurance was added (then OASDI) to provide monthly benefits to severely disabled workers and their dependents.

4. In 1965 health insurance for the aged (Medicare) was added (now OASDHI).

5. Originally OAI covered only employees in business establishments, but over the years coverage was extended to the self-employed, farmers and farm workers, members of the armed services, domestic help, and government employees not covered by separate systems. Today nine out of ten workers are covered.

6. From the 1940s on, Congress nearly every two years raised the monthly benefit levels (and tax contributions) until in 1972 it added automatic cost-of-living increases. By 1980 the rising benefits—and especially the cost-of-living escalator—put the financing of the system on a precarious basis.

7. For details on OASDI today, you may obtain a free pamphlet, *Your Social Security,* from your local Social Security Administration office.

8. The level of benefits and the eligibility requirements for unemployment compensation differ from state to state but must conform to federal standards. Over the years, of course, the level of benefits has gone up.

9. Originally designed to help the needy aged, blind, and disabled who were not eligible for Social Security (OAI), public assistance has become essentially a welfare program of Aid to Families with Dependent Children (AFDC). In 1974 the existing programs for the needy aged, blind, and disabled were replaced by a new Supplemental Security Income (SSI) program administered by the Social Security Administration and financed out of general federal revenues.

• Public assistance (now chiefly AFDC) is a complicated and volatile issue which might better be postponed for elaboration until students study the 1960s "war on poverty" or some other more recent development.

• *Competency exercise—reading a table:* Obtain a class set of *Your Social Security* (see item 7 above) and have students turn to a table showing typical monthly benefits. Prepare a series of examples for students to find or compute the applicable monthly benefit. You might also find a current tax table for students to compute the total annual tax that people at specified wage/salary levels would pay.

• It is useful for students to learn about the National Labor Relations Act in this chapter section because it was an important element of FDR's emphasis on reform in the last two years of his first term. But any elaboration of the topic might well be postponed until students study Section 4, "The Struggles of Labor," in the next chapter.

• Remind students that third parties seldom had been a decisive factor in presidential elections. So it was in 1936 when the followers of Father Coughlin, Huey Long, and Dr. Townsend formed the "Union" party, referred to by skeptics as an "unholy alliance." With a platform calling for limitations on income and inheritance, cheap money, and stringent controls on big business, the party chose in William Lemke of North Dakota a colorless member of Congress who had spent most of his political career in obscurity. Someone nicknamed him "Liberty Bell Bill," but this became a source of embarrassment for the candidate when hecklers reminded him that the Liberty Bell was cracked. Despite the millions of votes predicted—especially by Coughlin—Lemke polled only 891,000 votes and did not win a single state.

• Tell students that although FDR's campaign manager James A. Farley correctly predicted that the President "will carry every state in the nation except Maine and Vermont," other observers and pollsters were not so accurate. A widely read magazine, the *Literary Digest,* using only automobile and telephone registrations for their straw poll, predicted a substantial Landon victory. Thereafter, more scientific polls, such as those of Gallup and of Roper, gave more accurate predictions of the vote.

• Ask students to describe the televised press conference of the present day. Then point out that FDR's press conferences were quite different. In an informal fashion, reporters would gather around his desk, and he would "captivate the reporters . . . with his joshing and fun-making, his swift repartee, his sense of the dramatic, his use of first names and easy geniality." (Burns, *Roosevelt: The Lion and the Fox,* 1956, page 205.)

Section 3 (pp. 520–522)
The End of the New Deal

Instructional Objectives   Students will be able to

1. Analyze Roosevelt's major defeat on the Supreme Court "packing" issue.

2. Tell why the nation experienced a recession in 1937.

3. Summarize the provisions of the second AAA and of the Fair Labor Standards Act and show their relevance for today.

4. Appraise the impact of the New Deal on life in the United States.

Teaching Suggestions This brief section covers the third, and final, two-year phase of the six years of the New Deal. Then, as the text points out, FDR's attention turned increasingly to foreign affairs. The final topic of the section provides an appraisal of the New Deal. Perhaps students should make a reappraisal after they have studied and discussed the next chapter.

• Before discussing the court-packing plan, have students quickly review paragraphs dealing with the Supreme Court on pages 515 and 517.

Here is a good place to correct the common misimpression that the Supreme Court frequently overturns laws passed by Congress. The frequency of such decisions was unusually high in 1935–1936 because of the radical nature of some of the New Deal legislation. The Court strikes down far more state and local laws than it does laws passed by Congress. Also much of the Court's time is spent on interpreting laws where constitutional issues are not at stake or are not paramount.

Plan to incorporate item 5 in *Meeting Our Earlier Selves* (p. 522) in the class discussion of the court-packing plan. Here are other questions and comments that might be used:

1. FDR is considered a master political strategist. What factors might have led him to make, as one historian has put it, "the gravest political miscalculation of his career"? (He interpreted the 1936 landslide election victory as a mandate from the people to overcome obstacles thrown in the path of the New Deal; misjudged public awe of the Court; etc.)

2. What does the Constitution say about the size of the Court? (nothing) Whose responsibility was it to set up the Supreme Court—including determination of its size? (Congress—and presumably Congress could change the size of the Court as it had done in the past) Considering these facts, why the big fuss? (See suggested answer to item 5 in the Chapter Review.)

3. Why was FDR generally pleased with the outcome of his fight with the Court? (the favorable decisions that soon came; the quick chance that he had to appoint two new justices)

4. What had his fight cost him? (much of the good will of Congress; some loss of public confidence in his judgment; etc.)

5. Humorist Finley Peter Dunne once had his "Mr. Dooley" say that "the Supreme Court follows the election returns." To what extent are Supreme Court justices influenced by public opinion? (See a government text like *American Political Behavior*, published by Ginn and Company, on the factors influencing Supreme Court decisions.)

• The film *Storm Over the Supreme Court* (31 min) is a useful supplement.

• In discussing the 1937–1938 recession, you might review the phases of the business cycle (see teaching suggestions for Chapter 14, Section 4) and point out that the recession represented a sharp dip in the upward recovery line.

Various figures from production tables in *Historical Statistics* can be used to show how recovery was halted and then set back. From 1933 to 1937, GNP had been rising $7 billion to $10 billion a year; then in 1938 it fell about $5 billion. Farm cash receipts dropped by $1 billion (over 12%), and the nation's sawmills reduced production by 4 billion board feet (around 17%); etc.

From the text, we can infer that officials were beginning to understand and trying to apply Keynesian theory: reduce government spending to halt or slow down inflation. But the problem was two-sided: inflation (or the threat of inflation) along with still very high unemployment. In recent years the President's economic advisers have been faced with a similar problem: real and very high inflation along with substantial unemployment. Remedies to halt inflation seem bound to aggravate the unemployment problem. Clearly it is difficult to apply Keynesian techniques when both inflation and unemployment are serious concerns.

Tell students that the remedies applied in 1938 helped to lift GNP by $6 billion, or more than enough to bring the economy in 1939 back to its 1937 level.

• In discussing the second AAA you might point out that the first part of the "ever-normal granary" plan (buying surpluses) has always been more popular with farmers than the second part (selling the surpluses in "lean years"). One problem was the near absence of "lean years" as surpluses kept piling up. (Much of the government-owned surplus stockpile was sent abroad in foreign aid programs.) Also, if corn production, for example, fell 10% to 15% below the preceding year, the price of corn would rise—and farmers would want to get the higher price, not have the government depress the price by putting the stored-up corn on the market.

• Ask students, "Which part of the Fair Labor Standards Act (wages or hours) has changed the most since 1938?" (the minimum wage, of course) Over the years, writers have often predicted substantial cuts in the work week. Yet the standard work week in industry has stayed at 40 hours—partly because of the convenience of running three 8-hour shifts when round-the-clock operations are advisable—even while the average work week has gone down somewhat. In business offices the standard work week is often 35 or 37.5 hours. The 1 1/2 pay rate of overtime has not served the objective of "spreading the work" to more people as much as policy makers in 1938 expected. Employers often find the overtime pay less costly than putting extra workers on the payroll and then paying expensive fringe benefits.

The minimum wage did not reach 40 cents an hours until 1945, but that was on the schedule set by the original law in 1938. In 1950 the minimum wage went to 75 cents and in 1956 to $1. Since that time it has more than doubled. Still, the minimum wage has always remained far below the average wage in the nonagricultural part of the economy.

You may want to have students explore and discuss one of the chief issues of the minimum wage: its effect on unemployment, especially teen-age unemployment.

• Here are two points that you might make about the attempted "purge" of conservative Democrats in 1938: (a) It was master politician FDR's second political blunder (after the court-packing plan) in 1938. Or was it? Should the national party leader take high risks to mold the party into a more coherent instrument for making and carrying out policy? The answer depends on one's view of the proper function of parties. (b) FDR intervened in the Democratic primary elections. This was the election, of course, that determined whether the Democratic candidates would be liberal or conservative. But in the "solid South" it also determined the winner of the general election (unless there was a second, "runoff," election), since Republicans offered scarcely any contest.

• Have students (all or a selected number) each find a second appraisal of the New Deal and copy its chief conclusions. In class discussion find out how the various appraisals agree and disagree.

Or read to the class two or three other (somewhat divergent) brief appraisals. After each one is read, have students note points of agreement and disagreement among the various appraisals.

You may want to postpone this appraisal activity until students have completed their study of Chapter 25. Or tell students that after studying Chapter 25, you will ask them to reappraise the New Deal.

CHAPTER REVIEW

Meeting Our Earlier Selves

1. In order of mention in the text the New Deal laws and programs: (a) Emergency Banking Act, (b) Glass-Steagall Act—bank reform, (c) Gold Reserve Act, (d) Securities Exchange Act, (e) Economy Act, (f) legalizing sale of wine and beer, (g) Civilian Conservation Corps, (h) TVA, (i) Home Owners Loan Corporation, (j) National Housing Act—FHA mortgage financing, (k) Resettlement Administration, (l) Wagner-Steagall Act—slum clearance and public housing, (m) AAA, (n) Farm Credit Act, (o) NRA, (p) PWA, (q) CWA, (r) WPA—and NYA, (s) Social Security Act, (t) Revenue Act of 1935, (u) Public Utility Holding Company Act, (v) National Labor Relations Act, (w) Soil Conservation and Adjustment Act, (x) Guffey-Snyder Coal Act, (y) Government Contracts Act of 1936, (z) second AAA—"ever-normal granary" and crop insurance, (aa) Fair Labor Standards Act—wages and hours.

Practically all were experimental or more far-reaching than ever before except the tax legislation. Certain laws and programs, however, had roots in earlier laws: laws dealing with bank reform, the gold standard, the SEC—in earlier regulatory agencies like the ICC and FTC, and aid to agriculture—in the old Federal Farm Board; but in general the New Deal laws went much further.

2. *Workers:* all the programs providing jobs, such as CCC, PWA, CWA, WPA; Social Security Act; National Labor Relations Act; Government Contracts Act; Fair Labor Standards Act.

Consumers: none in the sense that we ordinarily think of consumer legislation; but FDIC (deposit insurance) and SEC protected users—consumers—of bank and stock exchange services.

Owners of businesses: banking laws, mortgage insurance, NRA, Guffey-Snyder Coal Act; all the agricultural legislation protecting farm owners; various programs that helped the construction industry.

3. The first hundred days had been directed mainly toward recovery—of the banks, of business in general (NRA), of employment through various public works programs, of the home mortgage business and the construction industry, etc. There was a reform element in some of these programs but emphasis was on recovery. The second hundred days was directed chiefly toward reform: the various social security programs and labor-management reform especially but also by using the tax laws to redistribute income and by breaking up the powerful public utility systems.

4. Keynes advocated the running of budget deficits (through increased government spending, tax cuts, or both). FDR clung to the prevailing notion that the national government's budget should be balanced. He insisted on the Economy Act and tax increases through early legalization of the sale of beer and wine. He did, however, let budget deficits arise—but on grounds of necessity, not theory. (See comments in Teaching Suggestions for Section 1.)

5. All of the decisions against the New Deal measures: NRA, farm mortgage relief, the AAA, etc. Also decisions against federal and state wage and hour laws. (In fact, the NRA was a failure and probably deserved its fate.)

Opponents of the court-packing plan would attack it as (a) a threat to the check-and-balance system, (b) a dangerous use of presidential power, (c) a sneaky way to accomplish an objective, etc.

6. FDR met increasing opposition because (a) Congress responded to fears that the role of the federal government was growing too fast, (b) the shift from emphasis on recovery to reform was disturbing to interests opposed to reform, (c) the Democratic majority was weaker, (d) conservative Democrats allied themselves with Republicans, (e) once the country was on the road to recovery the Republicans felt no pressure to cooperate.

Questions for Today

1. Social Security—including unemployment insurance and public assistance, farm price supports, the wage and hour law, National Labor Relations Board, mortgage insurance, FDIC, stock market regulation, TVA, grants for public housing, along with other programs not discussed in the text.

2. Assuming the absence of substitutes for the programs provided in the original Social Security Act, students might point out (a) loss of income that their own family now enjoys, (b) greater need to support elderly parents, (c) lack of temporary income when laid off from a job, (d) greater fear of job layoffs, (e) greater need to save for own retirement, (f) more take-home pay because of no Social Security tax deductions.

3. In making comparisons, students should consider FDR's forcefulness, sense of humor, effective use of the media to enlist public support, willingness to listen to expert opinion (Brain Trust), openness to experiment, along with a certain stubbornness as seen in the Court battle.

4. This is a research project. In recent years, however, the federal government has supported various kinds of loan programs with repayment starting after the student takes a job. The NYA was largely a work-study program paying for on-campus jobs for needy students.

CHAPTER 25

Reshaping American Life

Introducing the Chapter In continuing the New Deal, this chapter shifts to a topical approach. Your region and its history might determine the emphasis you place on each of the topics. Yet the drama of the Dust Bowl can be understood by all students, and the New Deal conservation methods still affect us all. The role of the blacks and the attitudes of the New Deal towards them can be evaluated. Eleanor Roosevelt interests students as one of the great women of the twentieth century.

Section 1 (pp. 524–528)
Problems on the Farm

Instructional Objectives Students will be able to

1. List some of the problems faced by farmers in the 1930s.
2. Describe Dust Bowl conditions and effects in the 1930s.
3. Relate New Deal conservation programs to present-day agriculture.
4. Explain the problems of, and New Deal efforts to help, sharecroppers.
5. Tell how the REA improved life in rural America.

Teaching Suggestions Tie the lesson to discussion of the New Deal farm legislation presented in the previous chapter.

• While almost the entire Midwest from Indiana to the Rockies suffered from drought and experienced swirling dust in the early 1930s, and especially 1934, a much smaller area in six or eight Plains states is generally designated the true Dust Bowl—land where topsoil was damaged significantly. To identify this area, have students turn to the vegetation map of the Great Plains on page 321. The area is roughly the "short grass" land from just below the southern edge of the Texas panhandle stretching to Nebraska (some "Dust Bowl" maps include southwest South Dakota). Add to this area a bulge into central Kansas (generally the land in Kansas and Oklahoma shown on the next map with 15–25 inches of annual precipitation).

Students should note that the Dust Bowl was centered in a region of light rainfall that was formerly grassland. High prices for wheat in World War I had encouraged farmers to plow under the grass to make wheat fields on land that normally received barely enough rain for tough-rooted grass to grow. When two or three very dry years followed in succession, there was nothing to hold the top soil when the winds blew. Even where wartime wheat fields had been turned back to grass and were used for grazing cattle, the animals pulverized the soil so that it too was subject to wind erosion.

To the east of the true Dust Bowl there were thousands of farms that suffered little or no wind erosion but still experienced below-average rainfall. Some people from these areas also joined the Dust Bowl migrants.

• Trace the route of migrants from Oklahoma and the Texas panhandle to California. Students can find Interstate 40 (old U.S. Highway 66) on the map on page 630; it was the most widely used route to California.

Ask: "Why did the Okies head west rather than east?" (The drought belt extended well to the east of the "Bowl"; the smaller eastern farms could not provide jobs; West Coast landowners made considerable use of migrant labor.)

Ask: "Why did California try to stop the flow of migrants?" (The state had its own share of unemployed already who were seeking work of any kind; in spite of some relief help from Washington, the state government and localities still had to carry the burden of aiding needy people.)

- If your school is located in or near the 1930s Dust Bowl, encourage students to interview older residents who remember the drought.

- Following the showing of the film *Dust Bowl* (26 min), have students write a one-page review, emphasizing (a) the most impressive scenes, (b) the impact on victims of the dust storms, and (c) lessons to be learned from the Dust Bowl experience.

  Or read aloud a vivid description of a dust storm and its impact on the "Okies" in the first chapter of Steinbeck's *The Grapes of Wrath*. Then encourage students to read the book.

  Other useful audiovisual aids are two sound filmstrips, *The Grapes of Wrath and the 1930s*.

- *Handout lesson:* Have students read *Handout 36*, "Letter from the Dust Bowl." Then have them answer the questions that follow, using the other side of the handout and writing in complete sentences. After they have finished, discuss the responses. Suggested answers include:

1. Handkerchiefs around the face; oiled cloths and gummed strips along the window edges.

2. Cattle were shipped to greener areas to fatten them so that they could be sold at a profit in the market.

3. Abandoned homes; attempts to drill for water; planted trees; gardens now covered with silt.

4. For staying: sentiment; loyalty; refusal to give up; big investment; excellent soil. For leaving: time to put sentiment aside; no improvement in sight; husband already ill. The Hendersons probably stayed; they seem to be courageous people, loyal to their home and region.

- The current or a recent edition of *The United States Government Manual* (a useful reference to have in every high school social studies classroom) provides a two-page description of the Soil Conservation Service. Invite a student to read the account and give highlights of the work performed by this agency. Your school is probably in or near one of the nation's nearly 3000 conservation districts. The student reporting on this agency may be able to contact the Service's district administrator or the county agricultural agent for information on specific activities that affect your locality.

- Have students describe any soil conservation activities that they are familiar with in their locality.

- *Handout lesson competency exercise—map skills:* Have students complete the map on *Handout 37* according to the directions given on the handout. Students can use colored pencils or various kinds of pencil shadings: dark gray, light gray, diagonal lines, checkerboard, etc. The completed maps, of course, will show the highest farm tenancy in the southern cotton-belt states. Answers to question 2 should bring out these points: adaptation of the plantation slave system; one-crop agriculture ruled out self-sufficient farming; poverty conditions made widespread land ownership difficult.

- The topic on "The lot of farm tenants" suggests that the nation's farm problem has two facets: (a) making policy for the commercial farms that produce and market a very high proportion of total farm output; (b) providing some kind of security for people who prefer farm life but whose resources promise little more than subsistence. As the text points out, the AAA programs that helped commercial farmers actually hurt many farm tenants.

  Free-enterprise theory (classical economics) says that the nation is best served when goods are produced most economically: that efficient producers should drive out the inefficient ones. Agriculture—probably the best example of free enterprise in the land despite government subsidies and regulations—has seen a long and continuous decline in the farm population as the less efficient producers (or farmers on the least productive land) have given up the struggle. Yet if some people prefer the farm as long as they can make a modest living and if industry isn't desperate for labor, shouldn't the government help these people too? Aren't they helping the country just by staying off the relief rolls? This kind of argument has long been used to justify programs for subsistence farmers like those carried out by the Farm Security Administration.

  You might point out that the Great Depression interrupted the long and continuous farm-to-city movement. There was actually a brief "back to the farm" migration at the depth of the Depression, for people on the land could at least grow some of their own food.

  Subsistence farming remains a problem. But it was alleviated substantially with wartime and postwar prosperity by a speedup of the exodus from farms, by members of farm families commuting to jobs in the cities, and by the quite new development of factory relocation to rural areas where members of farm families could get jobs and still continue in part-time farming. In 1977 the personal income of farm families from farm sources was $18.3 billion; from nonfarm sources, $24.7 billion (see "Personal Income of the Farm Population" in *Statistical Abstract*.) In 1974, one-half of the 1.7 million farm operators had a principal occupation other than farming.

- Use an overhead projector to show some of the outstanding photographs of sharecroppers, their families, and their living conditions by Walker Evans for the Farm Security Administration. See Agee and Evans's *Let Us Now Praise Famous Men*.

Section 2 (pp. 528–531)
Helping Black Americans

Instructional Objectives Students will be able to

1. List some problems faced by black Americans in the 1930s.

2. Indicate how civil rights were denied to blacks despite the Civil War amendments (13–15).

3. Tell how reformers and leaders worked to create more rights for blacks.
4. Evaluate the relationship between the New Deal and the blacks, including the role of blacks in the administration.
5. Describe the "Black Renaissance" in the arts during the 1930s.

Teaching Suggestions This section will provide a good opportunity for you to review the progress of blacks since the Civil War. The achievements of blacks despite societal restrictions is notable in this period, especially in the arts. You might encourage reports on some of the personalities mentioned in the section and of other prominent black Americans of the 1930s.

• The text indicates that during the depression years about 80 percent of all black Americans were still living in the southern states. There and elsewhere, blacks (and often other minority groups) were "the last to be hired and the first to be fired." In farm areas, blacks often had cash incomes averaging less than $200 a year. In cities, conditions for blacks were usually not much better—especially when food was scarce. In *Native Son*, novelist Richard Wright wrote, "The kitchenette is our prison, our death sentence without a trial." Throughout the nation, blacks constituted one-tenth of the population, but one-sixth of those on relief. After you have related the above, and students have reviewed Section 2 in the text, discuss the following: What living problems did blacks, even more than the whites, face in the 1930s? (greater unemployment; lower incomes; denial of rights; prejudice; poor education; poor housing; inadequate health care)

• You may need to remind students that the authors are using this section, in part, to review and bring up to date the story of how black Americans, after a promising start in obtaining and using political power during Reconstruction, were deprived of political power long before the New Deal. This account helps to put into perspective the relative impotence of the New Deal in contributing to the movement for equal rights for black Americans.

The movement of blacks to the Democratic party is remarkable in that (a) they had been traditionally Republican because of ties to Lincoln and then the Radical Republicans, who had supported equality in Reconstruction, and (b) they perceived southern Democrats as their oppressors.

Use item 2 in *Meeting Our Earlier Selves* (p. 536) in connection with the discussion of the shift of blacks to the Democratic party. Also point out that the blacks who came north became urban blacks who—along with other working-class urbanites—increasingly were identifying with the Democratic party.

• Have an individual or committee report on the Niagara Movement, which was organized in Fort Erie, New York, in 1905. Emphasize the impact of this movement on the progress of civil rights for blacks in the twentieth century. Numerous books deal with black history, such as Franklin's *From Slavery to Freedom,* Hamilton's *The Black Experience in American Politics,* and Quarles's *The Negro in the Making of America.* Hughes, Meltzer, and Lincoln's *A Pictorial History of Black Americans* provides many illustrations. You might give extra credit for the reading of any of the above books.

Or tell the students that the 29 black educators, editors, and professional men from fourteen states who met in Fort Erie under Dr. Du Bois's leadership stated their purposes as (a) opposing the suppression of black rights, (b) the organization of blacks throughout the country to insist on their "rights, industrial opportunity, and spiritual freedom," and (c) the support of the channels of black public opinion.

The next year the group met at Harpers Ferry, Virginia, to pay tribute to John Brown. The meetings provided the impetus for the founding of the National Association for the Advancement of Colored People in 1910.

• Tell students that seven whites and a black, Dr. Du Bois, founded the NAACP to provide a forum for ways to achieve political and racial equality for blacks. As early as 1915, the NAACP was effective in organizing a boycott of the motion picture *The Birth of a Nation* on the grounds that it did not portray blacks truthfully.

Since then, the NAACP has grown in membership to some 450,000 persons, both blacks and whites, with over 1700 branches throughout the country. You might ask: "What are the present-day activities of the NAACP?" (As the most influential civil rights organization in the country, the NAACP argues civil rights cases in the courts. It played a leading role in the 1954 Supreme Court ruling of *Brown* v. *Board of Education of Topeka* that ended segregation in the schools. The NAACP advocates nonviolence in its activities against prejudice and discrimination.)

• Ask a student committee to prepare reports on the contributions of the "Black Cabinet" and other black leaders to the New Deal, beginning with Dr. Will W. Alexander and Mary McLeod Bethune as mentioned in the text. You might also add Arthur W. Mitchell, the first black Democrat to serve in Congress (1934), and Robert C. Weaver of the Housing Authority (appointed in 1966 by President Lyndon B. Johnson as Secretary of the Department of Housing and Urban Development, thus becoming the first black to hold a Cabinet post).

See *A Pictorial History of Black Americans,* page 285, for a group portrait of Roosevelt's "Black Cabinet."

Point out that many school and community libraries have specific reference books that are helpful in researching facts and figures pertaining to black history and biographical information on black personalities. These include: Davis, *The American Negro Reference Book;* Ebony Magazine, *The Negro Handbook;* Ploski, Brown, editors, *Negro Almanac.*

• Tell students that after World War I, New York City's Harlem became the largest black urban community in the world. As the cultural capital of the country, New York attracted the leading black writers, artists, musicians, singers, and actors. The black influence became an important part of the American scene in all aspects of the arts.

To expand the lesson, have students research the contributions to the arts of such leading black writers as Countee Cullen, Langston Hughes, and James Weldon Johnson; musicians Louis Armstrong, Count Basie, Duke Ellington, and Jimmy Lunceford; singers Marian Anderson, Ella Fitzgerald, and Paul Robeson; and artist Aaron Douglas.

• Point out that participation by blacks in the arts—even during the New Deal period—did not come easily. Even in a city like Washington, D.C., blacks could not attend a downtown theater, and no black was permitted to appear on stage in Constitution Hall, owned by the Daughters of the American Revolution.

Even Marian Anderson, considered by many to be the finest singer in the world at the time, was barred from singing in the Hall, prompting Mrs. Roosevelt to resign from the D.A.R. Through the influence of Harold L. Ickes, Secretary of the Interior, Marian Anderson was invited to sing on Easter Sunday 1939 from the steps of the Lincoln Memorial to a huge unsegregated audience. However, another decade passed before the color barrier was ended in the nation's capital.

• Expanding the lesson: Have students or a committee prepare a bulletin board display featuring the contributions to sports of Joe Louis and Jesse Owens, two of the most famous of the black athletes of the 1930s. (Students might seek help from librarians in using the vertical files to seek illustrations suitable for bulletin board display.)

Or tell students that both Louis and Owens as blacks played a significant role in deflating the views of Aryan racial superiority held by some Germans and by Hitler in particular. Known as the "Brown Bomber," Louis knocked out the German champion Max Schmeling in one round in 1938. In the 1936 Olympics in Berlin, Owens won four gold medals in various track events. A furious Hitler left the stadium when Owens and other black athletes stepped forward to receive their medals.

Section 3 (pp. 531–532)
The New Deal and Women

Instructional Objectives Students will be able to

1. Tell about Eleanor Roosevelt, including her role in the New Deal.

2. Explain the increased role of women in the New Deal administration.

3. Describe the status of women in the 1930s and compare it with the present day.

Teaching Suggestions The key figure in this brief section—and among women in the twentieth century—is Eleanor Roosevelt. Although your students may know her only through the textbook, you might broaden their understanding of this remarkable woman by showing a film or having an inclusive report that goes beyond the New Deal period to the time of Mrs. Roosevelt's service as a delegate to the United Nations shortly before her death in 1962.

• Use items 3 and 5 in *Meeting Our Earlier Selves* and item 2 in *Your Region in History* (p. 536) with this lesson. Students who interview elderly women who began their work career in the 1930s should try to elicit impressions that their respondents have about the changes in female employment opportunity today compared with the 1930s.

• As the text points out, women were asked to sacrifice their job ambitions so as not to compete with male "breadwinners." You might follow up this point with questions like these:

1. Why is the prosperity phase of the business cycle the "best time" for an equality movement (women, blacks, Indians, Hispanics, etc.) to push its demands? (deprived groups seen as less threatening if unemployment is relatively low)

2. What are some fallacies in the argument that in hard times women should not take jobs that can be filled by family breadwinners? (Many women are the breadwinners; if the argument is reasonable, then men who are not supporting a family should stand aside for the breadwinners—male or female—and men who are making more than enough to support a family should accept less pay so that a family breadwinner can be hired; men are rarely selected for jobs on the basis of need, so why should that be a factor in female employment; etc.)

3. In a recession today, would you expect female, or any, politicians to call on women to sacrifice their job ambitions to save jobs for "family breadwinners"? (Probably not because (a) more women than ever are the family breadwinners, (b) there are more voting-age females than males, and voter turnout percentages are about equal for males and females—based on 1976 election estimates, (c) women have made gains that they are not willing to give up, and (d) the fallacies in the argument are more widely recognized than in the 1930s.)

• Encourage students to prepare brief reports on the women mentioned in this lesson, other feminists of the 1930s, or other notable women of the 1930s. You might tell students that Frances Perkins was chairperson of the study committee which prepared the report that served as the basis of the Social Security Act.

Section 4 (pp. 533–535)
The Struggles of Labor

Instructional Objectives Students will be able to

1. Tell how the National Labor Relations Act stimulated the growth of labor unions in the 1930s.

2. Explain why the AFL split, resulting in the formation of the CIO.

3. Describe the activities of the CIO and the response of industry.
4. Identify the leading figures in the labor movement of the 1930s.

Teaching Suggestions Student response to this section will depend somewhat on the role that labor unions play in your locality. The dissension in labor's own ranks and labor's confrontation with industry, however, should interest all students, particularly if you ask them to evaluate the viewpoints of each side.

• Students should note that one provision of the National Industrial Recovery Act and then the National Labor Relations Act guaranteed to workers the right to organize and bargain collectively for improvements in wages, hours of work, and working conditions. Have students review two chief functions of the National Labor Relations Board (p. 516): (a) to oversee company elections for union representation and (b) to act on union charges of unfair labor practices by employers.

Even with the help of the Wagner Act, labor's effectiveness in organizing seems remarkable in light of the continuing massive unemployment during the 1930s. Part of the reason for the unions' success lies in the development of the CIO industrial unions. The mass production industries—steel, auto, rubber, etc.—had made a strong comeback from the depths of the depression and wanted to continue operations. To do so, they were forced to accept unionization—by the new CIO unions. The large number of brand new union members helped to swell the ranks of organized labor.

• Point out (or have a student explain) how a big auto or steel company would be organized (a) along craft lines and (b) on the industrial union plan. Discuss the advantages of the industrial union arrangement. Which workers might have favored the craft (or trade) union plan? (skilled workers who believed they might get better terms because of their skills)

• Of the more than 4700 strikes in 1937 the Department of Labor estimated that 82 percent ended in settlements favorable to unions. Students might speculate on reasons for the high success rate. You may need to remind students that the Roosevelt recession began late in 1937 and its effects were felt chiefly in 1938.

• Have a student report on the life and contributions to the labor movement of John L. Lewis. See biographies such as Alinsky's *John L. Lewis: An Unauthorized Biography* or Wechsler's *Labor Baron* for details.

Or tell students that the leonine, six-foot-three-inch Lewis possessed a stentorious voice that made him an impressive physical figure. In addition, though uneducated in the formal sense, he had read the Bible, Shakespeare, and the great philosophers, so that his oratory sounded like the cry of a prophet of old. His was the largest role in the creation of the CIO.

Lewis seemed to have vice-presidential ambitions in 1940, but was ignored by FDR. Lewis then switched his support to Republican presidential candidate Wendell Willkie, whose defeat forced Lewis's resignation as head of the CIO. Later, as will be discussed in Chapter 28, he returned to the national scene in 1948 when he refused to obey a court order to end a coal strike. He died in some eclipse in 1969.

• If students appraised the New Deal after completing the preceding chapter, ask them what new conclusions they have after studying Chapter 25.

CHAPTER REVIEW

Meeting Our Earlier Selves

1. Sharecroppers faced debt bondage to the landowners, loss of tenancy when owners took land out of production under the AAA program, and the income losses resulting from low prices for farm commodities that tenants and owners alike experienced. The New Deal programs (a) hurt when owners took land out of production but (b) helped some croppers with production loans, or mortgage loans, or resettlement on better land.

2. FDR spoke out against lynching and brought more blacks than ever before into the government. While the New Deal programs that promoted business recovery and provided temporary public jobs were not directed particularly at blacks, this minority group did share in the benefits. In some cases the benefits went to blacks in higher proportion than to whites because of the higher unemployment rates for blacks. The New Deal shortcomings included (a) neglect of civil rights, (b) exclusion from housing in TVA model towns, (c) wage inequality under NRA codes, (d) FDR's lack of forthright support for an anti-lynching bill, and (e) failure to provide for equality of treatment under New Deal laws.

3. A women's rights leader might applaud (a) the appointment of a female Cabinet member and of other female federal officials, (b) the influence of Eleanor Roosevelt in public affairs, (c) equality of representation for women on the Democratic Platform Committee, and no doubt other advances not named directly in the text. The rights leaders might regard as a setback the layoffs of women to preserve jobs for men in the depression.

4. Labor used its typical weapon—the strike, adding a new twist in the sit-down strike. Another tactic was the creation of industrial unions—with the AF of L's lukewarm assent at first and then opposition. A third tactic (alluded to in Chapter 24) was the political action, especially lobbying for the favorable labor legislation passed by the New Deal. All were fairly effective in meeting the objectives that were uppermost in each situation.

5. The text says, "She adopted all the nation's unhappy and neglected people as her foster children." Her liberalism epitomized the New Deal.

Questions for Today

1. In an interview the student should raise questions about such things as spending money, part-time work, use of leisure time, responsibility for contributing to the family income, care of siblings, parental restrictions, attitude toward school work, and so on.

2. The most remarkable difference would appear in the rewards available for black athletes, since professional sports apart from boxing were largely closed to black athletes except for all-black teams and "Negro leagues." The range of opportunities for black entertainers has broadened enormously; black actors, for example, are not limited to stereotyped roles. To the extent that there is a greater market for the offerings of black artists and writers, they are better off today; but their position has probably changed the least because artists and writers were not seen as threatening in social relations in the 1930s.

3. The "forgotten Americans" were blacks, women, immigrants, the poor—as listed by the text on page 533 (see also page 519). Some students may suggest that some group that they belong to (youth, ethnic group) are among today's "forgotten Americans" in that they have gotten less attention than some other groups. But they may be hard put to come up with categories who are "forgotten," because of the proliferation of lobbyists or publicists for almost every conceivable group in the land.

CHAPTER 26

Clouds of War

Introducing the Chapter At the outset try to determine student background (from world history or other courses) on the rise of aggressive dictatorships in Europe after World War I. Review American involvement in world affairs from the Senate rejection of the League of Nations to 1933, including the disarmament conferences.

Section 1 (pp. 537–545)
Foreign Affairs, 1933–1939

Instructional Objectives Students will be able to

1. Explain the rise of Mussolini and Hitler as dictators in Europe.
2. Define fascism, nazism, anti-semitism and other terms related to the anti-democratic philosophies of the period.
3. Explain and give examples of the application of the Good Neighbor policy.
4. Describe American neutrality legislation of the 1930s.
5. Tell how war came to Europe on September 1, 1939.

Teaching Suggestions A timetable of events closely connected to the outbreak of World War II is useful. Prepare duplicate copies as a handout. You may want to add or subtract from the list of items below. Events not named specifically in the text narrative are followed by an asterisk. Those that you include in the timetable should be explained briefly, or referred to if you use a film on the background of the war, or be discussed by students who recall the event from a world history course.

1919

Germany Weimar Constitution adopted, providing for an elected president and appointed chancellor (prime minister)*
Scattered Communist uprisings suppressed*

Italy First Fascist group (armed troopers) formed by Benito Mussolini*

1921

Italy Start of repeated clashes between Fascist and Communist groups*

1922

Germany Start of collapse of currency (wild inflation)

Italy Fascists seize control of Communist-held city governments*
Mussolini leads Fascist "March on Rome" (Oct. 28)
King and Italian parliament grant Mussolini dictatorial powers*

1923

Germany Occupation of the Ruhr by French and Belgian troops because of German default on reparations*
Nazis fail in attempt to seize Bavaria (the Munich "Beer Hall Putsch") and Hitler imprisoned

Italy King authorizes formation of a Fascist militia*
Mussolini gets new electoral law making Fascist control of parliament easier*

Spain With king's approval, Primo de Rivera forms military dictatorship

1924

Italy   Fascists gain control of parliament★

1928

Italy   Electorate reduced from almost 10 million to 3 million; all candidates selected by Fascist Grand Council★

1930

Germany   National Socialists (Nazis) rise to second place (after Socialists) in Reichstag★

Italy   Start of almost complete government (Fascist) control of finance and industry as response to depression★

1931

Spain   King Alfonso leaves Spain; republican constitution adopted★

Japan   Japanese troops occupy Manchuria

1932

Germany   Von Hindenburg reelected president over Adolf Hitler★
Hitler refuses to become chancellor without full powers★

Japan   Most of Manchuria set up as independent kingdom of Manchukuo under Japanese protectorate★

1933

Germany   Hitler appointed as chancellor (Jan. 30)
Reichstag building partly burned (Feb. 27); blamed on Communists, and Communist party outlawed
Parliament passes Enabling Act giving Hitler dictatorial powers for four years (Mar. 23)★
National Socialist party declared only political party (July 14)★
National boycott of Jewish businesses and professions, followed by forced retirement of all Jewish government workers★
Withdraws from League of Nations★

Japan   Announces withdrawal from League of Nations over a report critical of Japanese actions in Manchuria

1934

Germany   Hitler visits Mussolini, but Italy opposes German designs on Austria★
Plot against Hitler uncovered and 77 executed including high Nazi leaders★
Nazis assassinate Chancellor Dollfuss of Austria, but Austria resists German takeover★
Hitler becomes head of state as offices of president and chancellor are combined, uses title Der Führer★

1935

Germany   League-held plebiscite in Saar basin returns that region to Germany★

Hitler renounces German disarmament clauses of Versailles treaty★

Italy   Italian troops invade Ethiopia

1936

Germany   German troops reoccupy demilitarized Rhineland
Signs an accord with Italy, setting up Berlin-Rome Axis★
Concludes anti-Communist pact with Japan, thus forming Berlin-Rome-Tokyo Axis★

Italy   Annexes Ethiopia★

Spain   General Franco leads a rebellion against the republican government and gets arms and other support from Germany and Italy

Japan   Signs anti-Communist pact with Germany (see above)
Formation of Cabinet dominated by the military★

1937

Italy   Withdraws from League of Nations

Japan   Begins large-scale aggressive actions in China
Japanese planes bomb U.S. gunboat Panay

1938

Germany   Invades and annexes Austria (March)
Munich Pact dismembers Czechoslovakia (September)

Italy   Introduces "racial" program directed against the Jews★
Takes part in Munich Pact

Japan   National Mobilization Act puts the economy under government control★

1939

Germany   Hitler seizes rest of Czechoslovakia (March)
Annexes Lithuanian port of Memel and makes demands on Poland
Concludes a military alliance with Italy (May)
Hitler arranges nonaggression pact with Stalin (August)
German troops invade Poland (September 1)
Britain and France declare war on Germany (September 3)

Italy   Invasion and annexation of Albania (April)
Military alliance with Germany★
Declares neutrality when Germany invades Poland★

Spain   Civil war comes to end; Franco unchallenged ruler of Spain (March)★

Japan   Renounces anti-Communist pact with Germany when Hitler makes nonaggression treaty with Stalin★

• Students might select particular events from the timetable for brief reports. Urge them to point out links to the outbreak of World War II wherever possible.

Chapter 26

• In conjunction with any explanations of the timetable, use the map on page 544 of the text.

• See the audiovisual list for appropriate titles on the rise of dictatorships and other background for World War II.

• Write these headings on the chalkboard:

BASIC PHILOSOPHY OF FASCISM

Principle *Democratic viewpoint*

Below *Principle,* list the following in a vertical column: (1) Individual exists to serve the state. (2) No criticism of government permitted. (3) Schools teach fascist philosophy and prepare youth for war. (4) Censorship of the press, radio, and films. (5) Individual liberties denied. (6) Women denied political, social, and economic equality. (7) War is the noblest goal of man. Have students write in the appropriate column what they believe are the democratic viewpoints concerning these principles.

After they have finished, discuss the responses to reach a consensus. Then collect the papers for evaluation.

Students may ask: what is the difference between fascism and National Socialism (nazism)? Point out that in addition to the principles listed above, the Nazis added anti-Semitism and the racial view classifying the "Aryan" type of northern Europeans—hence, the Germans—as the "master" race, all others being inferior. But note in the timetable (above) that in 1938 Mussolini aped the Nazis in introducing anti-Jewish restrictions. See Chambers's *This Age of Conflict* or other recent European histories for further definitions and explanation of the Nazi racial theories.

• Students may ask, as have historians before them, how the Germans, with a reputation for culture, scholarship, common sense, and stability could embrace the emotional leadership of Hitler and the cruel barbarism of the Nazis. Point out that explanations are difficult to simplify, but that the following outline may help students categorize the conditions in Germany that paved the way for Hitler:

1. A weak existing democratic government in which the people had little faith.
2. The multi-party system hindered the growth of a strong "center" party.
3. Fear of the Communists (very important).
4. A desire to avenge the defeat suffered in World War I.
5. Unemployment, severe inflation, and depression—all of which the Nazis promised to remedy.
6. Desire of the middle class for stability—even at the sacrifice of liberty (see item 3).
7. No serious opposition from the police and the military high command when the Nazis used strong-armed methods to gain control.

• Ask your students to define anti-Semitism (prejudice against Jews, ranging from dislike to violent hatred). Then point out that Hitler blamed the Jews for Germany's political and economic troubles, even though in 1925 they accounted for only 600,000 persons in a population of over 62 million. You might also define "scapegoat"—one who is blamed for the failure of others and sometimes punished for it.

You might illustrate the plight of the Jews in Germany by having an individual or committee report on the Nuremberg laws of 1935 that deprived the Jews of their citizenship rights, the growth of the concentration camps, and on the "holocaust" whereby millions of Jews were put to death by the Nazis. Shirer's *Rise and Fall of the Third Reich* is a good source.

• Point out that Hitler's *Mein Kampf* is found only in libraries today, but once was required reading in all German schools. Hitler rose from poverty to become rich by collecting royalties from the book. Over 6 million copies were sold by 1940. According to Shirer, ". . . few families felt secure without a copy on the table," and it "was almost obligatory . . . to present a copy to a bride and groom at their wedding." (*Rise and Fall,* page 81.)

• Have students turn to page 544 to locate Ethiopia, the Rhineland, and Spain. Ask: What part did each of these areas play in the steps leading to World War II? (Italy's easy triumph over Ethiopia led Mussolini to be overly confident in joining Hitler's aggression later; the seizure of the Rhineland by the Nazis was a test of French will to resist, leading the Nazis to believe that the French did not want to fight; and Spain's civil war provided a testing ground for equipment and tactics that Hitler would use successfully later against the Allies.)

You might also tell the students that the key issue in Mussolini's war against the Ethiopians was oil, but the excuse was revenge for the defeat inflicted on the Italians by the Ethiopians in 1896. The Italian use of mustard gas in the war was the last use of gas in modern warfare.

The issue creating the Spanish civil war was the conflict between the Fascist-minded rebels, led by General Francisco Franco, and the more liberal followers of the republican government. Despite help from volunteers from all over the world, including the American Abraham Lincoln Brigade, the Spanish government could not withstand General Franco's forces, who were aided by supplies, munitions, and more than 100,000 troops from Italy and Germany. Over a million lives were lost in the war. *For Whom the Bell Tolls* is a vivid portrayal of the Spanish civil war by Nobel-prize winning author Ernest Hemingway.

• Write these headings on the chalkboard:

ROOSEVELT'S GOOD NEIGHBOR POLICY

Action *Significance*

Below *Action,* list the following in a vertical column: Pan-American conference of 1933, Cuban treaty of 1934, Hull-Cardenas settlement. Have students complete the chart by filling in the appropriate spaces, using the text as a guide. After they have finished, discuss the following:

1. Should a country have "the right to intervene in the internal or external affairs of another?" Why?

2. What was the Platt Amendment? If we had not renounced it, is it likely that the Communist regime of Castro would be in power today? Explain.

3. Can the United States ever treat smaller countries as "equals"? Why?

- Point out that one reason why the Japanese paid an indemnity of $2 million for the sinking of the *Panay* was that during the 1930s they did not want to endanger their relations with the nation that was the source of almost all of their scrap iron and steel and two-thirds of their oil. In contrast to the uproar over the sinking of the *Maine* in 1898, according to a 1937 Gallup poll an estimated 72 percent of Americans favored complete withdrawal of our citizens from the Far East rather than going to war over the *Panay* incident.

- *Competency exercise—reading comprehension:* The first two paragraphs of the topic "FDR and neutrality" provide a succinct discussion of the factors that explain the broad public support for U.S. neutrality in the 1930s. Ask students to write five sentences, each of which gives one reason for public support of the neutrality legislation of the 1930s. Have several students each read a sentence until all of the points are mentioned. Then have students suggest revisions until each sentence is a good model. Examples:

1. Some Americans were becoming pacifists.

2. Some people were isolationists who believed that a strong America could ward off any aggressors.

3. Some immigrant Americans did not want to oppose their homeland.

4. Some Americans, including many of Irish descent, disliked England.

5. A small American Nazi party supported German aggression.

6. Some people believed that neutrality would hurt the "real war makers," the arms industry.

- Cartoon interpretation: Use the cartoon on page 541 in conjunction with, or as a substitute for, the competency exercise. Ask: "Which of the opponents of involvement shown in the cartoon are also named in the text narrative in column 1?" (Nazi sympathizers, hate England crowd, isolationists) Then have students give tentative explanation of the other opponents; provide help where needed. (5th columnists were disloyal Americans eager to help "the enemy"; "defeatists" said American intervention wouldn't do any good—and hadn't done any good in W.W. I; point out that there were others besides Irish Americans in the "hate England" crowd; "business as usual" may refer to people who opposed putting the nation on a war footing for the inconveniences it would cause them; "appeasers" were people who applauded the Munich Pact and believed that the dictators' appetite for conquest would soon be satisfied)

Here is a good place to point out that a supporter of neutrality would likely belong to more than one of the groups named in the text and cartoon: a pacifist supporter of the Nye investigation; an isolationist appeaser who disliked England; etc. But some pro-neutrality positions were incompatible: pacifism and American rearmament; isolationist rearmament and acceptance of Nye armament theory; etc.

Continue the cartoon interpretation by having students identify (1) the ropes (neutrality laws) and (2) the menacing figure striding out of the ocean (the aggressors, particularly Hitler).

- Do students find surprising the apparent wide support for a constitutional amendment that would require a war referendum before Congress could declare war? How would such a proposal be greeted today? Why? (Discussion should bring out the point that in this age of undeclared war even Congress has difficulty in deciding when the nation should take part in military activity.) Point out that the proposal, introduced by Congressman Louis Ludlow of Indiana, called for a war referendum except in case of invasion.

- Help students to see that the neutrality legislation of 1935–1937 was designed to accomplish two things: (a) halt any flow of arms from the United States to belligerents and (b) surrender our rights of freedom of the seas in wartime. There was wide recognition, of course, that Wilson's insistence on freedom of the seas had drawn the United States into World War I. Supporters of neutrality were determined not to let that happen again.

Unless students read the text carefully, they may get the wrong impression that the 1937 "cash and carry" law weakened the earlier neutrality laws by permitting belligerents to trade with Americans. But note that the arms embargo remained in force (and other exports could be added to the embargo). The law requiring belligerents to get their own supplies (even of non-armaments) and pay cash was the final surrender of our right to freedom of the seas.

- In discussing the Munich Pact, point out that Hitler said that the Sudetenland was "the last territorial demand that I have to make in Europe." Any promise was heartening to people eager to avoid war. And Hitler's broken promises were easy to overlook. (In 1935 Hitler had said that Germany had no designs on Austria, but then annexed that country early in 1938.) Another factor that made it easier for the appeasers to give in to Hitler was the agitation by Sudeten Germans for union with Germany. Hitler stormed over the "oppression" of these people under Czech rule.

Hitler's seizure of the rest of Czechoslovakia less than six months after Munich finally shattered all hopes that Nazi Germany could be contained short of war. About a month after the Munich conference, Hungary succeeded in getting parts of Czechoslovakia—with the support of Germany and Italy—and then joined Hitler in the seizure of the rest of the country on March 15, 1939, annexing the most eastern region. See the map on page 544. The Munich Pact made Chamberlain "the hero of the hour" in Great Britain and America. He deserved, said the *New York Herald Tribune,* "heartfelt applause." However, Winston Churchill warned that "Britain and France . . . chose dishonor. They will have war." A year later he was right.

- Have students use the map on page 544 to locate the areas affected by the German-Soviet nonaggression pact. Use the text as a guide. Then have students speculate on which side gained the advantage in the secret treaty. Hitler reportedly shouted after the signing: "I have the world in my pocket!"

Point out that Communists throughout the world, including in the United States, changed overnight in their attitudes towards the Nazis after the Soviets signed the nonaggression pact. Now the Nazis were partners rather than enemies! Within two years, the attitude changed again when the Nazis attacked the Soviets.

- On the Nazi movement in the United States, tell students that German Americans in Buffalo, New York, founded the "Bund" (League) in 1936. Various rallies were held, including one that attracted 20,000 persons to Madison Square Garden in New York in 1939. The Nazi swastika hung next to the American flag at the meetings. Members wore uniforms and gave the Nazi salute. The Justice Department estimated actual membership at 7000. This number declined to a very few when the United States went to war. The leader, Fritz Kuhn, went to jail for embezzling Bund money.

Section 2 (pp. 545–550)
The Battlefield Is Everywhere

Instructional Objectives Students will be able to

1. Describe the blitzkrieg tactics of the victorious Nazis in Europe.
2. Identify Billy Mitchell and explain his views on the role of air power in war.
3. Describe the Battle of Britain and how the English won it.
4. Point out highlights of the election of 1940.
5. State the terms of the Lend-Lease Act.

Teaching Suggestions This section provides a careful interweaving of the events in the war with the changing attitudes inside the United States. Technological advances in fighting the war can be the subject of reports. The election of 1940 offers another look at Roosevelt as a masterful campaigner, this time against a determined opponent.

- Have students locate the Maginot line on the map on page 551. This great defensive line of steel and concrete had cost over a half billion dollars and sheltered 300,000 soldiers in a series of underground railroads, power stations, supply depots, and hospitals linked to forts and other defenses along the line. Supposedly impregnable, the Maginot line had huge imbedded guns locked in position and pointed towards Germany. The line was never tested because swift-moving German armor outflanked it.

- Remind students that the startling German-Russian nonaggression treaty of 1939 had promised the Soviet Union a free hand in Finland and in the Baltic republics of Estonia, Latvia, and Lithuania. The Baltic republics quickly made treaties with the Soviet Union after Stalin and Hitler had agreed on the division of Poland (Sept. 29, 1939). These treaties gave the Russians fortified bases and brought these nations effectively into the Soviet orbit; less than a year later they "asked" to be admitted to the USSR. Demands by Russia on Finland for a similar treaty were rejected by the Finns.

Students can use the map on page 544 to find Finland, the Baltic republics, and the line dividing Poland.

In the fall of 1939 many Americans cheered when newsreels showed Finnish victories—in part because this little country was the only one to have paid its World War I war debts to us. A Pulitzer Prize in 1941 went to Robert E. Sherwood's play *There Shall Be No Night,* sympathetic to the Finnish defense against Russian aggression. (Yet the Soviets gained our quick support in 1941 when they were attacked; meanwhile, Finland supported the Nazis.)

Fighting in extreme cold in Finland taught the Soviets much that was later advantageous in fighting the Nazis, including the use of ski troops and mechanized equipment that would not freeze up in sub-zero temperatures.

- A description of the fall of France and the Battle of Britain soon to follow, along with Churchill's stirring speeches, may be heard in the two-record album *The Finest Hours.*

- To students who would like to read more about the fall of France and why it happened so quickly, suggest Shirer's *The Collapse of the Third Republic.* On pages 84–87 you might read or tell to students the story of how General Charles de Gaulle—soon to become the leader of the Free French, and after the war the nation's President—escaped to England.

At the Bordeaux airport in southern France, de Gaulle pretended to walk with a British officer to an Allied plane about to depart for England (meanwhile de Gaulle's luggage had been lashed aboard). Just as agents taking orders from the defeated and Nazi-collaborating French government were about to arrest him, the lanky de Gaulle jumped aboard the small British plane. Seconds later he was rolling down the runway to England and freedom. Several hours later, de Gaulle and Churchill met in the garden of the prime minister's residence to plan de Gaulle's address urging that the French people resist rather than collaborate with the Nazi conquerors and their Vichy government.

A brief explanation of Vichy France (see map, page 551) appears in the next chapter. But you might elaborate now on the division of France into occupied territory and the puppet state which came to be known as Vichy France from the name of its capital city.

- The story of the Battle of Britain begins, in a sense, just before the fall of France when the Belgians surrendered, forcing the evacuation of the British expeditionary force. One of the most dramatic stories of the war is the rescue of some 200,000 British and 140,000 French troops (but the loss of almost all equipment) from the English Channel beaches, chiefly around Dunkirk.

- Have a student report on radar and how it helped English defenses anticipate German air raids. Include (a) explanation of how it works, (b) its background, (c) how it aided the Allies during World War II, (d) how it is used in commercial aviation today, (e) how our Early Warning System protects us today. Explanations of the impact of radar in the Battle of Britain may be found in military histories.

- The surprising nomination of Wendell Willkie in 1940 provides another chance to contrast the nominating process today with the past: today the delegates mostly bound to vote for a particular candidate vs. the large bloc of uncommitted (or weakly committed) delegates in earlier conventions. Point out the influence of the gallery (shouting "We want Willkie") at the 1940 Republican convention in Philadelphia.

In addition to using item 6 in the Chapter Review (p. 553), ask questions like these to guide discussion of the 1940 election:

1. Why was a third term for FDR a major issue?
2. Why did the Republicans make a better showing in 1940 than in 1936?
3. Willkie had a business career, and FDR a political career. How would business experience train one for the Presidency? What advantages come from political experience?

You might tell students that Willkie, in speaking over 500 times with no rest except on Sundays, gradually lost his voice during the campaign, so that no amount of amplification could do more than bring up his voice to a harsh croak. Undoubtedly this handicapped Willkie in competing against the appealing voice and masterful style of FDR.

For students who would like to read more about the campaign, suggest Burns's *Roosevelt: The Lion and the Fox* or biographies of Willkie by Severn and Moscow. Later, Willkie himself wrote *One World* (1943), and served as Roosevelt's personal emissary in visiting various countries, including the Soviet Union. He died in 1944.

- *Handout lesson:* Several key points made by the isolationists and the interventionists appear in *Handout 38* as adapted excerpts from speeches made by Charles Lindbergh and FDR in 1941. The handout can be used in connection with the neutrality legislation (pp. 540–541), or with the 1940 election, or to show that debate over intervention continued after the election and did not come to an end until the attack on Pearl Harbor. Questions like the following can be used to discuss the excerpts:

1. How did Lindbergh want the United States to respond to the war in Europe?
2. Why would some people have called Lindbergh a "defeatist"?
3. FDR proclaimed part of our national policy to be commitment to "all-inclusive national defense." What was the basic difference between Lindbergh's and FDR's notions of "national defense"?
4. What two actions by FDR—one shortly before the 1940 election and one soon afterwards—illustrate his notion of national defense? (Destroyer-for-bases deal; the Lend-Lease proposal)

- In discussing the Lend-Lease Act, you might point out that public opinion polls in January 1941 showed around 70 percent public support for aid to Great Britain even at the risk of war. FDR compared Lend-Lease to lending a garden hose to a neighbor in the event of fire without naming a price first. Senator Robert A. Taft argued, "Lending war equipment is a good deal like lending chewing gum. You don't want it back." Congress voted for the bill by a sizable margin.

- Point out that the meeting at sea between Roosevelt and Churchill was of course highly secret. The President boarded the cruiser *Augusta* off Martha's Vineyard and headed north to Placentia Bay off the southern coast of Newfoundland. Meanwhile, Churchill crossed the Atlantic on the *Prince of Wales*. The two leaders had met briefly once before during World War I.

In *The Grand Alliance,* Churchill vividly describes a Sunday morning church service aboard the *Prince of Wales,* in which the American and British sailors sang hymns—chosen by himself—adding that "It was a great hour to live. Nearly half those who sang were soon to die." (The *Prince of Wales* was sunk by Japanese planes in the Pacific in December 1941.)

Explain that the Atlantic Charter, as an informal statement of ideals, was not a binding alliance (thus resembling Wilson's Fourteen Points). Its major points stated or urged that (1) neither country sought territorial gain; (2) all territorial changes be with the wishes of the people concerned; (3) all peoples should choose their own government; (4) all states, great and small, should have equal access to world trade and raw materials; (5) all states must work together to secure for all persons improved labor standards, economic advancement, and social security; (6) a peace must be established that would allow all persons to live out their lives free from fear and want; (7) the seas and oceans must be open to unrestricted travel for all; and (8) force must be abandoned as an instrument of national policy and the burden of armaments lightened in the search for world security. The Soviet Union joined nine governments-in-exile in endorsing the general principles of the Atlantic Charter in the next few weeks.

Section 3 (pp. 550–553)
War Comes to the United States

Instructional Objectives Students will be able to

1. Describe the spreading of the war in Europe, including the Nazi attack on the Soviet Union.

2. Tell how the convoying of British ships by American vessels brought us closer to war with the Axis Powers.

3. Explain the circumstances of the attack on Pearl Harbor.

Teaching Suggestions The use of text and wall maps will be useful in this section to aid students in locating key war events and estimating the distances involved. You might show a film describing the attack on Pearl Harbor, and have students hear or read Roosevelt's "Day of Infamy" address to Congress asking for a declaration of war.

• The occupation of Greenland (p. 550) came as a result of an agreement with its people to defend Greenland in return for the right to build air and naval bases there. U.S. forces landed in Iceland at the invitation of the Icelandic government, which had recently voted to separate from Denmark, to relieve British troops defending the island. Soon air and naval bases were built there too. The maps of North America on pages 744–745 show Greenland and Iceland.

• Point out that the seizure of German, Italian, and other ships in our ports was to prevent their being sabotaged. The freezing of assets and the closing of consulates was a reply to similar activities by the Axis countries. Such actions are often a prelude to war.

• Have students turn to the map on page 544 to locate the western boundaries of the Soviet Union after the division of Poland in 1939. Then use the map on page 551 to find Leningrad, Moscow, Stalingrad, and Berlin. Estimate the distances separating the cities by air. (approximately 400 miles from Leningrad to Moscow, and 600 miles from Moscow to Stalingrad; from Berlin to the respective Russian cities—800, 1000, and 1500 miles)

Point out that the German objective was to lay siege to and capture each of these three major Russian cities. Along an extensive front from the Baltic Sea to Hungary, a huge German army of some 3 million men with vast numbers of tanks and other mechanical equipment began what seemed an easy conquest as the Germans rolled in blitzkrieg fashion through the flat Ukranian wheatlands (where they were greeted at first as liberators).

For students who would like to read more about the incredible German march into Russia, suggest such books as Carell's *Hitler Moves East 1941–1943* or chapters in such books as Freiden and Richardson's *The Fatal Decisions* or Shirer's *Rise and Fall of the Third Reich*. Various pictorial histories contain many dramatic illustrations, particularly Time-Life's *Russia Besieged*. Then discuss:

1. In view of the historic experience of Napoleon in seeking to conquer Russia, why did Hitler make "his great blunder"? (Against all advice, Hitler was determined to crush communism as well as expand to the East. Also, the inadequacies of the Soviet army in the Finnish campaign convinced Hitler that the Russians could be defeated in a few months. Thus, no winter clothing was issued to the German troops in the fall of 1941.)

2. Why weren't the Russians ready for the German invasion? (Stalin was "not of the opinion that German military successes menaced the Soviet Union and her friendly relations with Germany," according to a German policy paper.)

Explain that at first the Germans seemed unstoppable as they took thousands of prisoners and seized vast stores of Russian war materials and foodstuffs. By October 1941, Hitler informed the German people by radio that "Russia is finished! She will never rise again!" But when the German army could see the gilded church towers of Moscow in the distance, Soviet resistance stiffened.

The early snow and cold caught the Germans by surprise. Without proper clothing or shoes, soldiers suffered from frozen feet and hands. Radiators and boilers froze, and lubricants congealed in guns. The Nazi campaign ground to a halt, and troops struggled to survive as temperatures plummeted to as low as 40 degrees below zero.

• Point out that in 1941 President Roosevelt reportedly tore out a map page from a *National Geographic* magazine, drew a line from southwest Iceland to the Azores to indicate how the United States and Great Britain should divide the defense of the Atlantic. FDR's aide Harry Hopkins took the map to Churchill, who approved the plan. Have students simulate drawing this line.

Thus, in ordering American naval vessels to convoy ships through the western Atlantic, FDR actually brought the U.S. to a war situation anytime the Nazis wanted it. For various reasons—chiefly that he did not care to have the German U-boats face the U.S. too—Hitler ordered caution in confronting U.S. vessels. Even so, as the text indicates, it was hard for us not to become involved.

• Use the map on page 562 to point out Japanese aggression prior to the attack on Pearl Harbor. It consisted chiefly of operations in China plus the obtaining of bases in French Indochina, as the text points out. Korea had been annexed in 1911. In 1920 Japan had received as mandates from the League of Nations Germany's Pacific islands north of the equator—chiefly the Carolines, Marshalls (map, p. 578), and Marianas—so its interests in the Pacific were already far-reaching.

• Students to this day are perplexed that we were attacked by surprise at Pearl Harbor, especially since—as the text indicates—we had broken the Japanese code. One of the answers is that top secret Japanese planning was not shared at the diplomatic level. Thus, their two emissaries in Washington at the time of the attack—Kurusu and Nomura—were merely uninformed decoys in a diplomatic game. So we didn't know exactly when or where an attack would come.

However, it also seems true that the Americans could not believe that an attack would come. Even the commanding officers—General Walter Short and Admiral Husband Kimmel—testified later that neither "considered an attack on Pearl Harbor a possibility."

Yet there were warning signals that were ignored, indicating laxity, or were bungled. For example, a Honolulu lawyer named Royal Vitousek was circling in his private plane early on December 7 when he saw two Japanese Zero planes. On landing, he telephoned army and air corps duty officers and excitedly told them what he had seen. They would not believe him, and did not send out an alert. Also, the American destroyer *Ward* sank a midget Japanese sub inside the Hawaiian defense perimeter. Their report was ignored as possibly being a "false sighting." Two U.S. Army privates, Joseph L. Lockard and George E. Elliott, detected on a portable radar unit the oncoming Japanese planes at a distance of more than 137 miles. Reporting this, they were told by the duty officer to "Forget it—these are probably the B-17s due in from the mainland." An urgent radio message from Chief of Staff General George C. Marshall from Washington to Pearl Harbor failed because of static. The message was sent by commercial channels to Honolulu and given to a boy on a bicycle to deliver. While on the way, he dived into a ditch and stayed there for several hours when he observed the attack.

For students who would like to read more about these events, suggest Farago's *The Broken Seal: The Story of "Operation Magic" and the Pearl Harbor Disaster*, or Chapter 8 in Toland's *The Rising Sun*, Vol. 1.

You might also show the film *December 7, 1941* (27 min).

CHAPTER REVIEW

Meeting Our Earlier Selves

1. Overlooked values include the basic freedoms of all kinds—speech, press, assembly, religion, enterprise; due process rights in criminal trials and in applying government regulations of all kinds; protection of private property; wide career choices for women; respect for minorities; the value of cultural diversity; respect for human life; etc.

2. FDR's policy was basically to be a good neighbor, offering help when asked. TR saw the United States as the community police officer.

3. Actions, including failure to take action, include inadequate pressure to halt the invasion of Ethiopia and remilitarization of the Rhineland, failure to halt outside aid in the Spanish civil war, inadequate pressure against Japanese aggression in China; U.S. absence from League of Nations and U.S. enactment of neutrality laws; the Munich Pact appeasing Hitler—all mentioned or inferred in text. Also weak response of democracies to Hitler's treatment of Jews.

4. Actions include FDR's call for a quarantine of aggressor nations; the repeal of the arms embargo in 1939; ending the commercial treaty with Japan; refusal of Japanese request to end U.S. aid to Chiang Kai-shek; the buildup of U.S. defenses—clearly aimed against the Axis; the destroyer-for-bases deal; the Lend-Lease Act; the secret meeting with Churchill and issuance of Atlantic Charter; occupation of Greenland and Iceland; seizure of Axis shipping in our ports; "freezing" of Axis property; convoying of British ships; order to shoot German subs on sight; arming of merchant ships; etc.

5. Hitler had plans all set to take Polish territory that he wanted for Germany—and to fight France and England if they intervened. He saw that he could bargain with Stalin over Poland and avoid a two-front war if he had to fight France and England. Stalin was glad to get additional Communist territory and an extension of Russia's western border as a buffer zone capable of taking the first blows if Germany should ever decide to attack. The Soviets are said to have been disillusioned by the weakness of earlier French-British responses to German aggression (particularly the Munich Pact) and believed that they could not depend on help from the democracies.

The pact surprised the world because Hitler had risen to power partly on the basis of his anti-Communist views. And the Rome-Berlin-Tokyo Axis was really an anti-Communist pact.

6. At the time, the threat of war with Japan seemed far less likely than war with Germany; Japanese diplomats were in Washington that Sunday morning conferring on arrangements to avoid any outbreak of fighting; our breaking of the Japanese diplomatic and naval codes had, of course, been kept secret; our Pacific defenses seemed formidable; etc. Some historians would later claim that FDR deliberately deceived the American public on the Japanese menace.

Questions for Today

1. The United States is the leader of a great alliance (NATO), has security pacts with nations around the world, has troops and bases around the world, provides heavy economic and military aid to other lands, takes an active role in the UN, etc.

The 1930s demonstrated that powerful aggressors could not be held in check without joint actions by a powerful opposing coalition, that hard times and internal disorder could bring dictators to power, and that neutrality is fruitless if the stakes are very high.

2. Specific answers will depend on the state of the world at the time students are dealing with this question. However, in the 35 years after the end of World War II, individual rights as we understand them were violated in more nations than not.

Intervention is hampered by world opinion and by general practice that one nation may not use force to interfere in the domestic affairs of another where there is no clear threat to security. Resolutions condemning the violation of human rights are passed by the UN General Assembly from time to time. Some countries, including the United States, refuse or cut off foreign aid as a way of protesting the violation of human rights. Etc.

CHAPTER 27

A World Conflict

Introducing the Chapter Encourage each student to become interested in some aspect of the war that can be shared, perhaps through the reading of a book describing an experience or a phase of the war. Another way to develop interest is to read aloud from some of the better-known books describing the war. You might also involve students in the moral issues in Truman's decision to use the atom bomb, and link the dilemma to our possible use of the nuclear bomb today.

Section 1 (pp. 554–558)
Mobilizing for Defense

Instructional Objectives Students will be able to

1. Describe how the United States mobilized for war by means of the draft and a conversion to production for war.
2. Tell about the role of women in our war effort.
3. Explain how blacks and other minority groups played a significant role in the war.
4. Analyze the motivations for the internment of Japanese Americans.
5. State how the United States financed its war effort.
6. List eight or more significant effects of the war on American society.

Teaching Suggestions Collect wartime memorabilia, especially of the home front, for display: ration books or stamps, posters, photos of home-front activities, photos of departing draftees or volunteers, women in uniform, etc. Grandparents of students may be willing to lend items.

- Point out that all men between 18 and 65 had to register for the draft, and all between 18 and 45 (later changed to 36) who were physically fit were liable for military service. By the end of 1942, three-quarters of the undergraduates at Yale had enlisted, and many colleges graduated their students six months early so as to speed up their eligibility for military service.

Conscientious objectors were few, and usually restricted to religious rather than political grounds. Many of these served in noncombat units, particularly in the Medical Corps. About 5000 pacifists were jailed between 1940 and 1945 for refusing to serve in any capacity.

- On rationing: The limits on gasoline probably caused the most widespread inconvenience. Average drivers received an "A" card limiting them to three gallons of gas per week.

One chief objective of food rationing was to curb hoarding. The OPA (Office of Price Administration) issued ration books with point values to households. Grocers collected stamps as well as cash; then turned in the stamps to get credit to buy more groceries for re-sale. Despite complaints, the system worked well, for the Department of Agriculture reported in 1945 that even with the need to supply food to our armed forces and Allies, American civilians were eating better than ever.

- Have students review "Women in the armed forces" in the text. Note that about one in every 70 members of the armed forces was a woman volunteer performing a non-combat role. (There were no women draftees.) Show illustrations of women in uniform from various pictorial histories of the war. Perhaps students can get family photos to display. Then discuss the following:

1. A soldier writing home to a sister thinking of enlisting, asked: "Why can't these gals just stay home and be their own sweet little self, instead of being patriotic?" How would you reply to such a comment today?
2. Should women serve in combat units? Why?
3. If the answer in #2 is "no," what duties should women perform in the military? (in earlier wars, women in uniform served only as nurses)

Tell students that the first commander of the WACs, Colonel Oveta Hobby, would become the first Secretary of the newly created Department of Health, Education, and Welfare in 1958 under President Eisenhower.

Students may be interested in the role of women in the armed forces today. Point out that since the low point of 1947 (about 20,000 enlistees), women in the armed forces have steadily increased in number (about 120,000 in 1978 compared to nearly 2 million men).

- ***Competency exercise—writing opinions:*** Have students go back in time to World War II and write a one-page editorial on "No Color Line in the Foxholes," in which they express their views on racial segregation in the armed forces. Write in complete sentences. Sub-topics might include: (a) how segregation exists, (b) the black contribution to the armed forces, (c) reasons why integration would be desirable.

After they have finished, have several students read aloud their editorials.

- Review the part A. Philip Randolph played in getting the FEPC established. In the 1940 election campaign FDR had made pledges of increased support to black leaders. The prospect of a "march on Washington" probably hurried the fulfillment of the pledges. Several likely reasons may explain his opposition: (a) it would threaten the image of national unity; (b) other groups might apply similar pressure; (c) fear of a backlash that would harm the defense effort and set back what progress blacks had already made.

    Discussion of this incident might lead to consideration of when and for whom a peaceful demonstration is likely to be an effective political technique.

    In 1955 A. Philip Randolph became a vice-president in the AFL-CIO, and in 1963 he helped lead the massive civil rights March on Washington (text page 656). He died in 1979 at age 90.

- Along with ingrained racism, fear of the consequences accounts for the failure to desegregate the armed forces: increase of dissension among the troops; opposition of some Allied units.

    The sound filmstrip "The Negro Fights for the Four Freedoms," in the *History of the American Negro* series, provides a good overview of the situation.

- For those who would like to read more about the contributions of blacks to the war effort, suggest such books as Garfinkel's *When Negroes March,* Lee's *The Employment of Negro Troops,* or descriptions in various pictorial histories, such as Hughes's *A Pictorial History of Black Americans.*

- A useful case study on the West Coast Japanese internment appears in the high school government text *American Political Behavior,* Revised Edition (Ginn), pp. 150–153.

    Fascinating legal analyses of the internment order appear in the opinions written by Supreme Court justices in *Korematsu v. United States* (1944) available in some collections of leading constitutional decisions. The decision was 6–3 upholding the internment program. Justice Hugo Black, writing for the majority, contended that the courts had no business trying to second-guess the executive branch and the military on the reasonableness of the internment order. But then he said that a real danger of invasion of the West Coast did exist when the order was issued and declared that the evacuation order was a reasonable response. Justice Frank Murphy wrote a scorching dissent. He conceded that the military and naval situation in the spring of 1942 was sufficient to generate a real fear of invasion accompanied by sabotage and espionage. "The military command was therefore justified in adopting all reasonable means necessary to combat these dangers." And he said that the Court must not erect too high standards in judging the reasonableness of the measures taken. But then he demonstrated the unreasonableness of the internment order, putting considerable stress on the fact that martial law had not been declared on the West Coast. He concluded by calling the majority decision a "legalization of racism."

- In discussing the tremendous rise in federal tax revenue during the war, you might cite some significant facts and figures:

    — Persons paying income tax (in millions): 1939—3.9; 1941—17.5; 1942—27.6; 1943—40.2; 1944—42.4

    — Individual income tax collected (billions of $): 1939—1.0; 1942—3.3; 1943—6.6; 1945—19.0

    — Total federal tax receipts (billions of $): 1940—5.7; 1942—13.6; 1945—47.6

    — Tax exemption for married couple, no dependents: 1939—$2500; 1941—$1500; 1944–45—$1000

    — Tax rate on lowest bracket of taxable income: 1939—4% on first $4000; 1941—10% on first $2000; 1944—23% on first $2000

    — Tax Payment Act of 1943 provided for income-tax withholding by employers, thus avoiding once-a-year lump payment for most taxpayers—and no doubt catching some people who had previously evaded the tax.

    — Disposable personal income (income after taxes—in billions of $): 1939—70.4; 1941—93.0; 1943—133.5; 1945—150.4

    Conclusion: While the number of taxpayers and the amounts collected grew enormously during the war, the tax burden was hardly oppressive considering that after-tax income doubled from 1939 to 1945.

    In light of the above conclusion, you might ask: Should more of the cost of the war have been paid through taxes and less by borrowing? The answer involves a political judgment of how voters will respond to additional tax increases and an economic judgment of how heavier taxes will affect the willingness of workers and business firms to produce. ("No point in working harder and earning more, since the government will take most of it!" Or is it: "I'll have to work harder to keep my take-home pay from dropping!").

- Have students review the section (or divide the topics among the students) to find and list significant effects of the war on American society. Then list the effects on the board as students respond. Examples:

1. Full employment replaced unemployment, ending the depression.

2. Widespread experience by the public with government regulation.

3. Breakdown of restrictions on use of women in armed forces.

4. Contributions of black servicemen would help to bring desegregation of armed services.

5. Start of legal efforts to end employment discrimination against minorities.

6. Speedup of migration of blacks out of the South.

7. Urbanization of blacks.

8. Racial relations in South increasingly challenged.
9. Improvement (over World War I) in treatment of dissenters—except for Japanese Americans.
10. Rise in job opportunities for women.
11. Decline of black women (and other women, too) in domestic service jobs.
12. Substantial rise in personal income—even after inflation.

For additional items to list and discuss, see "Social Consequences of the War" in Morison's *Growth of the American Republic,* pp. 559–562.

Section 2 (pp. 559–564)
"The End of the Beginning"—1942

Instructional Objectives Students will be able to

1. Describe the naval war with emphasis on use of radar and sonar.
2. Show how American forces contributed to the Allied victory in North Africa.
3. Summarize the role of the Latin American countries in the war.
4. Trace the course of the war in the Pacific from December 7, 1941, to the end of 1942.
5. Show that the turning point in the Allied war effort was reached in 1942.

Teaching Suggestions Be sure that students see, in the section introduction, the overall strategy of fighting two wars on widely separated fronts.

• Have students review the topic "Success in North Africa" (pp. 559–560) and then turn to the map on page 559. Ask students to use the map to explain why the first two weeks of November 1942 were very significant for the Allies. Other questions: (a) Why was stopping the Germans in north-central Egypt so important? (b) Why were Allied landings made on the North African coast opposite Spain? (easy to win support of the French)

If not done earlier, elaborate on the division of France into occupied territory and the puppet state of Vichy France.

You can explain that Italy had won control of Libya (from the Turkish sultans) in 1911–13 before the outbreak of World War I. In 1940–41 there was considerable fighting in North Africa between Italian and British forces, and the British managed to keep the upper hand until heavy German reinforcements came on the scene.

Tell students that the invasion of Sicily and Italy, as shown on the map, is discussed in the next lesson. But they should be able now to speculate on the importance of Tunisia to the Allied cause.

• Tell students that the most colorful and best known of the German generals was Erwin Rommel. Of him, Churchill said in the House of Commons in January 1942: "We have a very daring and skillful opponent against us, and, may I say across the havoc of war, a great general." Another reason Churchill admired the "Desert Fox" was "because, although a loyal German soldier, he came to hate Hitler and all his works." (See *The Grand Alliance,* page 200.) Add that Rommel joined the plot of July 20, 1944, to assassinate Hitler in his secret "Wolf's Lair" hideaway. Four officers died, but Hitler suffered only minor injuries. The Gestapo (secret police) rounded up thousands of suspects—putting 5000 to death. Rommel was given a choice: commit suicide and receive a hero's funeral, or plead not guilty and be killed, along with your wife and son. Rommel committed suicide.

Suggest to interested students that the story is told in Fitzgibbon's *Officers' Plot to Kill Hitler.* See Young's biography and Time-Life's *The War in the Desert* for further information about Rommel's role in the African war—and that of his brilliant opponent, General Montgomery.

• Point out that most of the leading generals of the African campaign moved on to Sicily, Italy, or France as the war progressed, including Rommel, Montgomery, and Americans Eisenhower, Patton, Bradley, and Clark. According to Churchill, the African campaign gave the Americans the combat experience they sorely needed.

• Tell students that when the Americans entered North Africa, the Germans ridiculed our military efforts and our productive capacity. A favorite story relates how Rommel told Hermann Goering, chief of the Luftwaffe (German Air Force), that British fighter bombers had knocked out German tanks with American 40 mm. shells. "Nonsense," scoffed Goering, "nothing but rumors. All the Americans can make are razor blades and refrigerators." Replied Rommel, showing samples of the American shells: "I only wish that we were issued similar razor blades!"

• Have students again locate Stalingrad on the map on page 551. In the winter of 1942–43, an epic struggle for control of the city took place when German General Friedrich Paulus with 330,000 troops faced an equal number of Russians as the bitter winter closed in. For months, fighting building by building, often in hand-to-hand knife and bayonet combat, the troops slaughtered each other. Thousands died each day. "I would not have believed such an inferno could open up on this earth. Men died but they did not retreat," said Russian General Zhukov.

By February 1943, with retreat cut off, Paulus surrendered his last 12,000 men. Later no more than 5000 Germans out of the original 330,000 returned to their homeland. More soldiers died at Stalingrad than the United States lost in all theaters of the war. This is why the Battle of Stalingrad marks the turning point of the war against Germany.

• Point out that there were air attacks on the Philippines as well as at Pearl Harbor on December 7, 1941. The Japanese conquered the Philippines in January 1942 except for American-Filipino defense forces on Bataan and Corregidor under General Douglas MacArthur. The stand there became one of the memorable stories of the war. After retreating to Bataan peninsula on the island of Luzon, about 75,000 American and Filipino troops were forced to surrender on April 9. Almost immediately most of the prisoners had to begin a 60-mile march along hot, dusty roads to Camp O'Donnell. This trek is known as the "Death March." Only a few prisoners escaped along the way. About 20,000 died or were killed during a week of hot sun, lack of water and food, and extreme cruelty by the Japanese. Later, in various primitive compounds, additional thousands died from malnutrition, malaria, and other fevers. After reading the tragic stories of the Death March, Americans everywhere hardened in their determination to defeat the Japanese in the difficult days ahead.

With our loss in Bataan, only Corregidor—a small, rock-like island fortress in Manila Bay with 13,000 defenders—held out against the relentless Japanese attack. But as food and medical supplies ran out and 16,000 artillery shells fell in 24 hours, General Jonathan Wainwright surrendered the last American stronghold in the Philippines on May 6. Meanwhile, by order of President Roosevelt, General MacArthur escaped by patrol boat and plane to Australia to begin planning an Allied comeback.

For students who would like to read more, suggest Hersey's *Men on Bataan* and sections of Toland's *The Rising Sun*, Vol. 1.

• Perhaps earlier use of the map on page 562 was made to point out Japanese aggression prior to the attack on Pearl Harbor. Now have students use the map to see the vastness of post-Pearl Harbor conquests. Remind students that some of the Pacific islands were Japanese mandates from World War I peace settlements. But others were quickly occupied after Pearl Harbor. The Japanese met little resistance and could hold many places with just a handful of troops. But they did fortify strategic places.

Have students use the map to locate Japan's "defensive perimeter" described on page 562.

Do students see the significance of not letting Port Moresby fall to the Japanese? (security of Australia)

• Tell students that Doolittle's 16 B-25 bombers were launched from the aircraft carrier *Hornet* 800 miles from Tokyo (too soon, but they feared that they had been spotted). Flying at treetop level, the planes surprised the Japanese, who had no time to react with their own fighter planes. Bomb hits on planned targets were moderately successful. All planes escaped, but soon used up their gas reserves because of head winds and a storm. One landed in Russia, and the rest crash-landed in Japanese-occupied China; 71 crewmen eventually made their way back to home bases. However, three men died while crash-landing, and eight were captured and brought to Tokyo for trial—and execution.

The Doolittle story is told in Lawson's *Thirty Seconds over Tokyo* and Toland's *The Rising Sun*, Vol. 1. A commercial movie, *Purple Heart,* was made in 1944.

Section 3 (pp. 564–573)
Victory in Europe

Instructional Objectives   Students will be able to

1. Trace U.S. participation in the campaigns in Africa, Sicily, and Italy.

2. Describe the role of air power in the war.

3. Summarize the events of D-Day and the subsequent Allied activities in France and Germany.

4. Give highlights of the election of 1944.

5. Explain why Hitler gambled—and failed—in the Battle of the Bulge.

6. State the purpose and results of the Yalta Conference.

7. Describe the surrender of Germany and the end of the European phase of the war.

Teaching Suggestions   Students by now should have enough background to be able to describe the war situation globally as this section begins in the spring of 1943. Use a wall map and point to various places; then ask students to identify the place and its significance in the war.

• Tell students that the meeting at Casablanca provided an opportunity for Churchill, Roosevelt, and de Gaulle to get together. Neither Churchill nor Roosevelt liked the French leader. Wrote Churchill later of de Gaulle: "I knew he was no friend of England . . . I resented his arrogant demeanor. . . . Yet even when he was behaving worst, he seemed to express the personality of France—a great nation, with all its pride, authority, and ambition." (*The Hinge of Fate,* page 682.)

• Point out that the Allied victory in North Africa meant the fall of what Mussolini dreamed would be a new Roman empire. In three years the Italians had lost African territory ten times the size of their own country. Many of the German prisoners from Africa were brought to prisoner-of-war camps in the U.S. and Canada. By contrast, the more tractable Italian POWs served first as "KPs" (kitchen police) for the American forces in Africa, and later as laborers working for the Allies in Italy.

• Have students use the Mediterranean theater map on page 559 again—this time to follow the fighting in Sicily and Italy. Eisenhower accepted the British-American staff consensus that Sicily had to be taken first in order to clear the Mediterranean of Axis shipping, thus helping insure the success of the pending invasion of Italy.

In Sicily the Axis had 315,000 Italian and 90,000 German troops behind extensive fortifications. An invading force of 250,000 Americans, British, and Canadians in 3000 ships landed successfully amid a joyous reception from Italian civilians. American General George S. Patton and British General Bernard L. Montgomery led their armies to victories by August 17, 1943, with casualties of 167,000 for the Axis and 31,000 for the Allies. However, 60,000 German troops escaped under cover of darkness to mainland Italy, there to await the next invasion.

- Students may be curious about the notorious Patton "slapping" incident in Sicily. Americans at home were shocked to learn that General Patton had slapped an enlisted man in one of the army hospitals in Sicily, meanwhile accusing the soldier of "gold-bricking" (feigning illness to escape military duty). The furor over the incident included cries for Patton's demotion and even dismissal. General Eisenhower soothed angry Americans by ordering Patton to give a personal apology to the soldier and the hospital staff. Later, Patton went on to lead the U.S. 3rd Army to victories in France and Germany. He died in 1945 in a jeep accident in Germany. In 1970 the colorful Patton's role in the war became known to a new generation of Americans through the motion picture *Patton*, starring George C. Scott.

- Students may ask what happened to Mussolini after he was forced to resign on July 25, 1943. Tell them that he was placed under "house arrest" by Marshal Pietro Badoglio's forces—now anti-fascist—and was moved from place to place to avoid rescue attempts by Mussolini's supporters. However, because Hitler still needed Mussolini (to help control northern Italy under Nazi domination), the Germans staged a daring raid in mid-September 1943 by nearly 100 paratroopers. Soon, Mussolini was safe in northern Italy. But he was also now powerless as Hitler's puppet.

- As the Allied armies approached Rome in June 1944, the world wondered what would happen to the Vatican and the great art treasures and buildings of the "Eternal City." Would they be destroyed as the armies clashed? The Germans then announced that Rome would be an "open" city—there would be no fighting. Amid wild celebration, the grateful Italians welcomed the smiling troops of Clark's 88th Division.

- Students should be able to visualize the air war from countless World War II movies and TV shows. But some will be interested in seeing photos and models of World War II bombers and fighters (Allied and Axis).

Point out that by the end of the war the U.S. had produced 296,601 planes, a total that both the Germans and the Japanese had thought impossible of attainment.

The best known of the American planes was probably the Boeing B-17, known as the "Flying Fortress." Heavily armored, armed with .50 caliber machine guns, capable of carrying bomb loads as great as 17,600 pounds and with the aid of the secret Norden bombsight able to bomb with precision at 25,000 feet, the B-17 with its 10-man crew offered maximum performance. It was especially successful in the bombing missions over Germany.

The B-29 Superfortress was used primarily in the war against Japan. Weighing 60 tons and capable of flying nonstop for 16 hours, it became the ultimate weapon of the war (military experts consider the German V-1s and V-2s as having come too late to affect the outcome of the war). As will be described in the next section of the text, the B-29 carried the atom bomb to Hiroshima.

Outstanding fighter planes of the war included the British Spitfire, the German Messerschmitt 109, and the Japanese Zero.

- Have students review "D-Day in France" and locate the Normandy coast on the European theater map on page 571. The film *D-Day* (27 min) will add much vivid detail. With or without the use of the film, you can help students identify advantages of the Allies and of the Germans. Besides the points mentioned in the text, you can mention that the Allies had the advantages (a) of making the earliest landings in darkness, (b) of having well-rested and well-trained troops, and (c) of slow German reaction—Rommel at home attending wife's birthday party, and need to get Hitler's approval. The Germans (a) could fight from protected positions, (b) had numerical superiority and heavier armament at first. Etc.

The story of D-Day is told in many books, the best-known of which is Ryan's *The Longest Day* (made into a popular motion picture in 1962).

- Students will be fascinated by the story of how the Allies alerted the French underground by radio that the invasion was imminent. A first alert was a line from poet Paul Verlaine's *Chanson d'Automne* (Song of Autumn); the second line indicated that the great invasion armada was on its way. Incredibly, German agents knew of these coded messages and informed the German high command. However, no action was taken.

Meanwhile, Eisenhower's dilemma was that the choice of an invasion date was limited to a few days during the summer when there would be an ideal combination of tides and the darkness of a new moon. Thus, continued postponement would have delayed the invasion by at least a month—creating a difficult problem for the many thousands of men waiting at British ports to begin their crossing of the English Channel, and of course jeopardizing security.

- How did the Germans react to D-Day? Point out that a week after D-Day the Germans fired their first "vengeance" (V-1) robot bombs at London. These were really small, pilot-less, jet-propelled small planes with wings that carried a ton of explosives at 350 miles per hour to a pre-set destination. Despite British anti-aircraft ground defenses and the efforts of the Royal Air Force to shoot down the V-1s, about one out of four of the 8000 bombs sent to England reached London, killing 5479, wounding nearly 16,000, and destroying 25,000 buildings. As a terror weapon—it made a horrible "buzz" sound—the V-1 was effective, but it had little impact on the war.

The larger V-2, a true rocket bomb, was another matter. Silent, flying six times faster than any plane at a height of 60-70 miles, the V-2 defied interception. Carrying a ton of explosives, its only warning was the explosion. Fortunately, this bomb was not unleashed until August 1944, and then in limited numbers. In the brief period of its existence, the V-2 killed 8000 Londoners.

After photographic reconnaissance revealed that the V-2

came from underground launching sites in the Kiel Canal area (connecting the Baltic and North seas), relentless Allied bombing attacks destroyed the sites and ended the menace.

- In discussing the fighting after the Normandy invasion, you might point out that General Omar Bradley halted American tanks outside Paris to allow General LeClerc's French 2nd Armored Division the honor of entering first, thereby paying tribute to the French resistance fighters and strengthening the political leadership of General de Gaulle.

    Some historians contend that the Russian halt outside Warsaw was deliberate to discourage the idea of Polish freedom and independence and that the Soviet leaders had no interest in protecting the Polish Jews in Warsaw.

- Students will be interested in descriptions of life under the Nazis in the various conquered countries. For further reading, suggest such books as Frank's *Anne Frank: Diary of a Young Girl*, Steinbeck's *The Moon Is Down*, and Ten Boom's *The Hiding Place*.

    Point out that the resistance of the Dutch to the Nazis provided the background for the classic story of Anne Frank. Hiding out with her family for two years in Amsterdam, meanwhile writing her diary, the teen-age Anne and her family were finally discovered and sent to a concentration camp (along with 200,000 other Dutch Jews). There Anne died; only the father survived in the family. He died in August 1980.

- Point out that with the war going on there was no parade after FDR's fourth inauguration, which took place on a portico of the White House. The President's address was very brief on a cold, gray day. After he finished, he nodded to his son James to get him back inside as quickly as possible. The President had suffered severe chest pains on the portico, and according to Bishop, *FDR's Last Year*, page 246, "... it may have passed across the President's mind that he might be the first President to drop dead at his inauguration."

- Have students turn to the inset map on page 571 to locate the combat area of the Battle of the Bulge. Note where the Meuse River is, and how the Germans, if they had been able to continue their drive, hoped to reach the North Sea. Point out that the Nazis gathered all of their 3000 remaining planes, hundreds of tanks, and 250,000 men for this last desperate gamble. At first, German success was great, aided by troops disguised as American "MPs" who penetrated deeply into Allied lines and by heavy snow and low visibility that hampered Allied planes from attacking the German supply lines. With better weather, and quick movement by Montgomery's and Bradley's troops to close the gap, the Germans suffered staggering losses from which they never recovered. According to Churchill, the Battle of the Bulge was "America's finest battle."

- Have students review "Conferring at Yalta" in the text, and locate Yalta on the map on page 571. Then write these headings on the chalkboard:

THE YALTA CONFERENCE—1945

Beneath this, write *Provisions*. Have students list these, using the text as a guide. Then write *Evaluation of Conference*, and have students list these, again using the text as a guide. Suggested answers include:

Provisions

1. Plans for administration of certain areas of postwar Europe, particularly Poland.
2. Eastern European countries to elect their own governments.
3. Payment of reparations by Germany.
4. Promise by Stalin to declare war on Japan after the defeat of Germany; also, to join the United Nations.
5. Soviets gained Japanese islands and outer Mongolia.

Evaluation of Conference

1. Soviets gained much in terms of postwar control; gave only promises in return.
2. Allies in poor bargaining position because Soviet help was needed to defeat Nazis in Europe, and possibly in Asia to defeat Japan.

- Churchill favored having the Allies take Berlin before the Russians might, while Eisenhower favored by-passing the city. Appoint two committees—one to summarize Churchill's views (in *Triumph and Tragedy*), the other those of Eisenhower (in *Crusade in Europe*). Use the text also as a guide. Discuss what might have been the future of Germany (and our relationships with the Soviets) had Churchill's viewpoint prevailed. Remind students that the control of Berlin became a significant part of the cold war with the Soviet Union—described in the next chapter.

- The circumstances of FDR's death and the worldwide reaction will interest students. You might read to them Churchill's tribute to FDR in Parliament (*Triumph and Tragedy*, Chapter 9). Japanese Prime Minister Suzuki broadcast his condolences to the American people (Toland, *The Rising Sun*, page 869). The German reaction was quite different. Propaganda Minister Goebbels ordered a champagne party and said to Hitler, "I congratulate you! Roosevelt is dead! It is the turning point!" (Shirer, *Rise and Fall*, page 1110)

- Students may inquire about the last days and the deaths of Mussolini and Hitler. Tell them that on April 28, 1945, Mussolini and his mistress were captured in a farm house in northern Italy by anti-Fascists and shot soon thereafter. The next morning, the bodies were dumped in the public square in Milan.

    With the Russian army closing in, Hitler and his new bride Eva Braun committed suicide deep in an underground shelter in Berlin. Hitler's body was then burned. For years thereafter, there was speculation that the death of

Chapter 27

Hitler was a hoax and that he was hiding somewhere in South America. However, on August 2, 1968, the Soviets released conclusive proof (mostly through dental charts) that they had collected the body of the dictator. (See *The New York Times,* August 2, 1968, pages 1, 14.)

• Students might interview veterans of World War II as part of an "oral history" project. In some instances, the experiences of the veterans can be recorded and played back in the classroom. Names of veterans who have dramatic stories to tell may possibly be obtained from a local veterans' organization.

• Tell students that historians rate President Franklin D. Roosevelt as "great," along with Lincoln, Washington, Wilson, and Jefferson. Serving more than three terms—a span denied to Presidents after Truman by the 22nd Amendment—FDR's impact on American history was great because after facing the challenge of the depression, he then became a world leader with our entry into World War II. Supporters assert that his New Deal saved democracy from collapse; critics contend that only the coming of the war brought the country out of the depression. Supporters point to FDR's leadership in planning full production as the key to our victory in the war; critics blame FDR for the disaster at Pearl Harbor and for the Soviet diplomatic victories at Yalta.

Section 4 (pp. 573–578)
The War in the Pacific

Instructional Objectives Students will be able to

1. Explain our "island hopping" strategy in the Pacific.
2. Describe the intensity of the battles of Tarawa, Saipan, and Iwo Jima.
3. Tell about the Battle of Leyte Gulf and MacArthur's triumphant return to the Philippines.
4. Give highlights of the development of the atom bomb.
5. Evaluate Truman's decision to use the atom bomb to end the war against Japan.
6. Evaluate the cost, impact, and significance of World War II.

Teaching Suggestions The war in the Pacific from 1943 to the surrender of Japan in August 1945 is painted in broad brush strokes. Use films and special reports to fill in details of engagements that may interest the class. Some of the following activities also supply further detail.

• Have students turn to the Pacific theater map on page 578 to locate the operations described in "The struggle for the islands." Note the relationship of these islands to the steps necessary to bring Allied forces ever closer to Japan.

• Point out that Tarawa (map, p. 578) consists of coral reefs linked together with shallow lagoons. The Japanese had boasted that a million Americans could not take Tarawa. The defenders were deeply dug in behind thick concrete pillboxes that seemed impervious to heavy bombing attacks. Waves of American marines were caught in a deadly crossfire. Flame-throwers had to be used to reach the enemy. "Terrible Tarawa" cost the U.S. over 1000 dead, but Japan's 3000 marines were wiped out.

Saipan was much the same, but a larger battle. Facing the Americans were nearly 30,000 crack troops, who, as their end drew near, screamed "Banzai" and hurled themselves forward in a last suicidal attack. The Japanese lost almost 24,000 troops; American losses totaled 3426 killed and over 13,000 wounded. When the battle was over, hundreds of civilian Japanese workers hurled their children, and then themselves, off high cliffs to sure death on the rocks below, or cut each other's throats. They believed that to die for their emperor was more honorable than to be captured by the Americans.

Iwo Jima has become a legendary battle in the history of the Marine Corps. A little rock-like island 750 miles from Japan, its possession was considered vital as an emergency landing field and as the "eye" for Superforts on the way to bomb Japan. Some 30,000 American marines stormed the heavily defended island to begin a 26-day battle that ended with over 20,000 American casualties. Again the Japanese refused to surrender, suffering 21,000 killed. Only 200 of their troops surrendered.

Show students the famous photograph of the raising of the American flag by the marines on Mt. Suribachi. One of these was an American Indian named Ira Hayes.

• Students should note that the text's account of Truman's decision to use the atom bomb emphasizes the likely saving of lives—both of Allied troops and of the Japanese people. The excerpt from Truman's memoirs in *Handout 39* tells of other considerations that swayed the President. You may also want to use the film *The Decision to Drop the Bomb* (35 min).

After students have looked at the evidence provided, have them list reasons for dropping the bomb on Japan. Here are reasons often cited:

1. The saving of lives—both of Allied forces and of Japanese.
2. As aggressors the Japanese deserved no special consideration. ("They started the war, didn't they.")
3. The bomb would give the proud Japanese a face-saving reason to end the war immediately.
4. The bomb would permit the United States to determine the peace terms with Japan. (Delay would give the Russians too much influence.)
5. Our ultimatum to the Japanese issued at the Potsdam Conference (July 26, 1945) had brought no reply.

Critics of Truman's decision contend that too little consideration was given to providing the Japanese with a demonstration explosion at some uninhabited or sparsely settled place. Another criticism is that the second bombing (of Nagasaki) could have been delayed to give the Japanese government some additional time to reach a decision on surrendering. You may wish to have students consider these and other criticisms of the decision.

• A touching scene at the Japanese surrender on board the *Missouri* came when General MacArthur asked General Wainwright, who had surrendered at Corregidor, and British General Percival, who had surrendered at Singapore, to step forward to witness the signing. Gaunt and ailing, the two men had endured several difficult years in Japanese prisoner-of-war camps.

• Ask students if we can ever really measure the cost of World War II. Point out that among the millions of persons who died there surely must have been some geniuses in all fields who never had a chance to make their contributions to humankind.

If you want to present more statistics, tell students that the war ended after 2191 days. It involved some 70 million men, of whom some 17 million were killed, and countless civilians—men, women, and children whose lives and deaths will be mostly recalled through the memories of the horrors of the concentration camps. From another viewpoint, fatalities of those in combat were one of every 22 Russians, 25 Germans, 46 Japanese, 150 Italians, 150 English, 200 French, and 500 Americans.

CHAPTER REVIEW

Meeting Our Earlier Selves

1. Two chief sources for the expansion were (a) the vast pool of unemployed not reabsorbed in the work force during the business recovery and (b) women entering the labor force—for both patriotic and economic reasons. In addition some elderly people postponed retirement or returned from retirement to the work force. Somewhat more jobs opened up for young people under age 18 (the draft age). Some workers holding two jobs may have been counted twice. A significant factor in the increase of working-age men and women and draft-age men was that persons born in the World War I and postwar baby boom reached age 18 from about 1934 to 1942.

2. Civilian hardships were probably mostly emotional—family separation, adjustments of moving from place to place, etc. Despite rationing, most civilians saw their standard of living rise during the war years; with shortages of goods and patriotic appeals to buy war bonds, thousands of people were able to accumulate some savings that would be used later to spark the postwar prosperity.

3. Technological advances made warfare highly mobile in contrast to much combat from fixed positions in World War I. (Tanks, trucks, and armored personnel carriers much advanced over those of 1914–1918; larger aircraft aided troop movement and use of paratroopers; etc.) Air power became a decisive factor because of improved aircraft. Property destruction far more widespread—less confined to battlefields—because of bombing from aircraft. Can also mention role of radar and sonar in defense.

4. All the Latin American countries broke diplomatic relations with the Axis powers; most of them eventually entered the war; they served as valuable sources of supply for the Allied cause; etc.

5. The tide turned with (a) victory in North Africa, (b) the stopping of the Germans at Stalingrad, (c) the end of Japanese efforts to take Australia, and (d) the withdrawal of the Japanese from Guadalcanal.

6. The war against Germany required the reoccupation of vast territories seized by the Axis and was chiefly a land war with air support. The war against Japan was more a naval and air war with heavy use of the marines. It was a battle for strategic bases.

Questions for Today

1. Churchill wanted British-American forces in control of all Germany and in the countries bordering the Soviet Union in Eastern Europe to hinder postwar political control of these lands by the Soviet Union. Eisenhower decided to stop short of Berlin to assure the security of his forces scattered throughout Western Europe. Soviet control of East Germany and Eastern Europe has been a source of persistent trouble: periodic tension over the status of Berlin, severe restrictions on human rights, the continued need to maintain strong U.S. or NATO forces in Germany, etc.

2. Among the effects are the nuclear arms race, worries over the possession of "the bomb" by irresponsible leaders, and worries over the disposal of nuclear waste plus other safety hazards. Some people claim good effects of an increase in total energy available to lift world living standards, of the existence of an alternative energy source to replace dwindling fossil fuels, of the availability of radioactive isotopes for use in medicine, and of the restraining influence of "the bomb" on the outbreak of a major war.

Skills to Make Our Past Vivid:

3. (a) The biggest percentage increase in military expenditures was in 1940–1942 (over 1400 percent); in personal consumption, 1940–1946 (about 34 percent; $147.1 - 109.8 = 37.3 \div 109.8 = 34\%$). **(b)** Chiefly because of rising incomes and partly because of inflation: more dollars needed to buy same amount of goods.

CHAPTER 28

Truman: Neither War nor Peace

Introducing the Chapter Begin by reading aloud—or have students read—the unit introduction on page 581. Then have them turn the pages of Chapters 28–30 as another kind of overview. Next call attention to the drawing of the TV set used to start the introduction of each of these three chapters. Ask: "Is the TV set an appropriate symbol for the years 1945–1960?" After students explain why, ask if they can think of some other easy-to-draw and easy-to-recognize artifact that would also be appropriate to symbolize the period.

Having looked quickly through the chapter, can students explain—or guess—the meaning of the chapter title?

Section 1 (pp. 582–587)
Beginnings of the Cold War

Instructional Objectives Students will be able to

1. Show how a new era in the history of the world began with the introduction of nuclear bombs.
2. Describe the background of President Truman.
3. Name and describe the chief United Nations agencies.
4. Explain the dispute over the Security Council's veto power.
5. Show how the Baruch Plan was designed to control atomic energy.
6. Name events that led to a "cold war" with the Soviet Union.
7. Identify the Truman Doctrine, the European Recovery (Marshall) Plan, and the Point Four program.

Teaching suggestions Tell students that the "S" in Truman's name appears both with and without a period. He said he had no middle name other than "S"—therefore, it was not an abbreviation requiring a period.

Collect anecdotes of Truman that show other facets of his character and personality—blunt language, fierce defender of family and friends, poker playing, piano playing.

- If any students have visited the UN buildings in New York City, encourage them to describe their experience.

An interested student might find out how the UN (as originally set up) differed in structure and power from the League of Nations.

Encourage students to look for current news of the UN. Help them analyze the activity to see if it is the kind of thing the UN is equipped to do well or poorly.

- From here to the end of the course there will be several appropriate times to analyze the unfulfilled hopes of the United Nations. But whether you plan for such an analysis here or elsewhere, students need to see now at the outset the crucial importance of the Security Council veto—and what most Americans regard as the misuse of the veto by the Soviet Union.

Some familiarity with the main constituent parts of the UN (General Assembly, Security Council, Secretariat, Social and Economic Council, and the judicial arm—the International Court of Justice, or World Court) seems necessary for (a) understanding the UN's relative impotence and (b) learning to interpret current news relating to the UN.

- A student might volunteer to draw up a fact sheet on the United Nations (as a poster or to be duplicated as a handout) dealing with such matters as current membership size, budget, who pays, chief expenses, and some facts about the UN headquarters.

- The Baruch Plan on atomic-energy control incorporated the principal features of a plan that had been drawn up by a committee headed by Dean Acheson and TVA chairman David Lilienthal, who would become the first head of our own Atomic Energy Commission (pp. 587–588). A United Nations Atomic Energy Commission had already been set up, and Baruch was the U.S. representative on that commission. The plan was designed to give this UN Commission really effective power. And to do so, it proposed that a member of the Security Council could not veto the commission's proposals. This part of the plan was not acceptable at all to the Soviet Union, for the Russians opposed any attempt to weaken its veto power in the Security Council. The second major provision on inspection was rejected by the Soviet Union on grounds that inspection was an invasion of sovereignty. Critics of the Soviet Union said that this sovereignty argument was simply a cover-up for Soviet opposition to outsiders seeing what the Russians were up to. Nine years later the Russians turned down Eisenhower's "open skies" proposal too (p. 607).

Inspection, of course, was a key part of the U.S. proposal. Truman wrote to Baruch, "We should not under any circumstances throw away our gun until we are sure the rest of the world can't arm against us."

- Point out that with the defeat of the Baruch Plan in the UN, the atomic race was on. On September 23, 1949, President Truman announced that the Russians had exploded their first atomic bomb. Then the race for the "super" bomb began, resulting in the creation of the hydrogen bomb by the United States in 1950 and by the USSR in 1953.

The step to the H-bomb was not taken without bitter controversy in the United States. Some scientists, led by J. Robert Oppenheimer, argued against further atomic development. Edward Teller, known as the "father" of the atomic bomb, contended that if we didn't construct the hydrogen bomb, the Soviets surely would. Truman sided with Teller and ordered the building of the bomb. The Soviets followed suit.

- Have students tell what they think Churchill meant by the term "iron curtain." Guide the discussion so that students see that a curtain serves *to keep light out* (democratic ideas, knowledge of the outside world, anything that might show the Communists in a bad light). A curtain also hides from outsiders knowledge of what is going on inside a building (tie to Soviet opposition to inspection). Ask: "Why did he call the curtain iron?" (refers to Soviet Union force to keep the curtain in place, keeping the subject people in line)

  Have students use the map on page 590 and/or the Atlas map of Europe on pages 746–747 to locate the "iron curtain." Communists controlled the territory east of the "curtain" except for Greece and Turkey. Soviet troops were everywhere except for Yugoslavia, where Marshal Tito's Communists were in control, and in 1946 Tito was still under Soviet influence.

  The map on page 590 shows land that had already been annexed by the Soviet Union (following the Hitler-Stalin nonaggression pact of August 1939). Point out that Bulgaria, Romania, and Hungary had formed Communist governments in 1944 when the Russians were pushing the Nazis back into Germany following the Battle of Stalingrad. And East Germany got a Communist government in 1945 but was not established as a nation until 1949 (p. 592). The Soviets would force a Communist government on Czechoslovakia in 1948 (p. 586) and on Poland in 1952.

- The topic "Warnings about Russia" (p. 584) introduces the "containment policy" that would guide American policy in the years to follow. When you are confident that students understand "containment," use item 1 in *Questions for Today* on page 601.

- Students should see that the Truman Doctrine, the Marshall Plan, and Point Four were all foreign-aid proposals/programs. Use the chalkboard for writing responses on how the three programs differed from one another. Probe to see that students understand how each program was designed to protect against the spread of communism.

Section 2 (pp. 587–595)
Dealing with a New World

Instructional Objectives Students will be able to

1. Tell how the nation converted to peacetime with respect to (a) veterans' aid, (b) general employment, (c) labor unrest, and (d) price controls.

2. Summarize the terms of the Atomic Energy Act and the Taft-Hartley Act.

3. Describe Truman's civil rights efforts in 1947–1948.

4. Tell how the National Security Act changed our defense organizations.

5. Describe the problem of the division of Germany, leading to the Berlin blockade by the Russians.

6. Evaluate the Nuremberg trials as a symbolic means to punish the Nazis.

7. Explain the creation of NATO and our role in it.

8. Give highlights of the election of 1948.

Teaching Suggestions After students have read this section, have them tell how their impressions of postwar America in 1946–1948 compare with their impressions of postwar America in 1919–1920. For photos of the postwar scene of the 1940s—to supplement those in the text—see Time-Life's *This Fabulous Century—1940–1950*.

- Is there a Veterans Administration office, or a local veterans' service officer, in your locality? Have a student find out how current provisions of the GI Bill differ from those originally enacted. Also suggest that interested students carry out the activity suggested in item 1 of *Your Region in History* (p. 601).

- The Atomic Energy Commission (AEC) became the Nuclear Regulatory Commission in the 1970s. A student might volunteer to find out specific ways that the AEC spent the $2.5 billion a year mentioned in the text.

- Republican Presidents Eisenhower, Nixon, and Ford each had to deal with a Democratic Congress, but Harry Truman is the only Democratic President since Wilson (1919–1921) whose party did not control Congress. As the text points out, the 80th Congress—elected in 1946 and serving in 1947–1948—had a remarkable record; yet Truman was able to capitalize on its "failures" in the 1948 election. Students should note that its main achievements (unless one regards its refusal to extend the New Deal as an achievement—a quite defensible position) were in the areas of national defense and foreign policy. You might identify some of the key leaders of that Congress.

- *Congress and the Nation, 1945–1964* is a huge reference work published by the Congressional Quarterly Service. It—and later editions—can serve as a valuable resource on the history and provisions of all major congressional legislation since 1945.

- In discussing the Taft-Hartley Act, ask students to identify the New Deal law that had given the unions a tremendous boost in the 1930s (pp. 516–517). Was some balance needed between union power and employer power by 1947? Note on page 588 the postwar labor unrest that was an important factor in getting the Taft-Hartley Act passed. Truman in 1946 had called for even more extreme emergency power than that granted the next year in the Taft-Hartley Act. Yet other features of the law prompted him to veto it.

Over the next thirty odd years the "cooling off" provision would be used on only a few occasions.

In addition to the provisions listed in the text, the Taft-Hartley Act contained a list of eleven unfair union practices that were now banned. Among these were certain kinds of strikes and boycotts to force union recognition, such as the sympathy strike and secondary boycott—by workers of an employer not directly involved in a labor dispute but who is doing business with a strike-bound company. The unfair union practices were among the provisions most bitterly opposed by the unions.

The law's provision allowing states to enact "right-to-work" legislation remained a thorn in labor's side. Invite two students to research and then debate the issue. Unions are the obvious source of pro-union shop arguments. The case for "right-to-work" laws may be obtained from National Right to Work Committee, 8316 Arlington Blvd., Fairfax, VA 22038.

• Debating the two-term limit on Presidents provided by the 22nd Amendment may appeal to students, since the issue requires little research. It is a good topic for "brainstorming." For five minutes or so, have half the class come up with off-the-top-of-the-head arguments for the limitation while the other students suggest opposing arguments. A note-taker for each side should then report the arguments.

On the 1947 change in the presidential succession, call attention to the 25th Amendment (p. 796), which now provides for filling the office of Vice-President when a vacancy occurs. Thus the Speaker is next in line only weeks—not months or years—when the Vice-Presidency is vacant. During all of Truman's first term—almost four years—there was no Vice-President, of course.

• On the chalkboard list the proposed civil rights measures asked of Congress by Truman: (a) anti-lynching law, (b) anti-poll tax law, (c) permanent FEPC, and—not listed in text—(d) a ban on segregation on buses, trains, etc. In an adjacent column list Truman's actions to advance civil rights and the interests of black Americans: (a) set up Committee on Civil Rights, began desegregation of armed forces, (b) appointed black officials (c) strengthened civil rights activities of Justice Department.

After explaining any points that need clarification, invite students to pick out the two or three most significant items—and tell why.

Point out that an estimated 3000 blacks were lynched from the 1880s to the 1960s—with no reported cases since that time.

The 24th Amendment (plus the Voting Rights Act) ended the use of the poll tax as a restriction on voting. In 1952 a poll tax was still collected in 35 states, but only five of these—Arkansas, Alabama, Mississippi, Texas, Virginia—made payment a requirement for voting. (A poll tax is merely a head tax—"poll" means "head"; it was a way of collecting $2 to $5 a year or so from adults who might otherwise pay no direct local taxes. It fell out of use partly because the returns finally brought in little above the cost of collection.)

• Point out that prior to the National Security Act there was a War Department and a Navy Department. The air force was part of the War Department—as the Army Air Corps from 1926 to 1941, then the Army Air Force. One of the purposes of the 1947 legislation was to give the Air Force equal executive status with the Army and Navy. Combining the three branches under a Secretary of Defense seemed preferable to creating a third armed forces Cabinet department. But the new unification law was also designed to reduce squabbling among the branches for appropriations from Congress. The war had also proved the need for clearer coordination among the branches of the armed services. Unification of the departments plus creation of the Joint Chiefs of Staff seemed to be the logical solution.

The National Security Act was also based on the recognition that diplomatic and defense policies needed improved coordination. This would be particularly true in the cold-war era that was already in view in 1947.

• In clarifying any problems that students have with the topics "The problem of Germany" and "The Berlin blockade," have students use the map on page 590 and focus on the four occupation zones of Germany—and of Berlin on the inset map. (Be sure that students do not confuse the three occupation zones of Austria with those of Germany. Fortunately, Austrian unification with a democratic government was accomplished without the severe problems that characterized the issue of Germany.)

The airlift, known as "Operation Vittles," lasted 462 days before the blockade was lifted by the Soviets. In that time, the USAF flew 277,000 missions to Berlin, often from Frankfurt in the American zone, reaching a peak of a plane every 3 1/2 minutes. Later (1961), the construction of the Berlin Wall divided the city into two parts (see Section 2, Chapter 31).

For further reading, suggest Davison's *The Berlin Blockade* or any European history of the period. The film, *Berlin Airlift* (20 min), will be useful.

• On the Nuremberg trials, tell students that four judges—one each from the United States, Russia, Great Britain, and France—headed the International Military Tribunal. The top 24 Nazis—Hitler and Himmler were already dead—were indicted on four counts: conspiracy to commit crimes against peace, crimes against peace, war crimes, and crimes against humanity. The U.S. Army alone provided about twenty carloads of incriminating documents captured from the Germans during the last days of the war. The trials lasted ten months, and when completed totaled 42 huge volumes of transcripts.

The charges were always specific, and supported with evidence and witnesses. The details of the gassing, burning, shooting, freezing, boiling, disemboweling, poisoning, and starving of millions of Jews and other civilian Europeans shocked the civilized world.

Each of the principals pleaded not guilty and sought to blame others. Said Goering, Air Force chief: "It is true that I started the concentration camps. But all I wanted to do was to re-educate political prisoners. From 1934 on, it was Himmler who ran the camps. I had no idea that such terrible things took place." Nonetheless, he and some others received sentences of "Death by the rope!" But Goering would not let the Allies hang him. An hour before his scheduled hanging, he chewed a capsule of potassium cyanide that brought almost instant death.

Point out that the Nuremberg trials have been debated even to the present day as to their value and legality. Jurists ask:

1. Was the Nuremberg court a legal one, since it represented only individual nations and not an international body?

2. Were the judgments political and vengeful rather than based on law? Can a court decree punishment when no law pre-exists?

3. If one's duty is to be loyal and obedient to the state, can one be punished for obeying the orders of the state (and its leader)? Defense attorneys argued that the sole guilty person—Hitler—was not on trial.

Perhaps the American prosecutor, Supreme Court Justice Robert Jackson, spoke for humanity in his reply to criticism of the Nuremberg trials: "If you were to say of these men that they are not guilty, it would be as true to say that there had been no war, there was no slain, there had been no crime."

Have students discuss the above points, particularly this question: "Should one be punished for obeying obnoxious orders of the state?"

For further reading, suggest Bernstein's *Final Judgment: The Story of Nuremberg* or Gilbert's *Nuremberg Diary*. Snyder's *The War*, pages 512–521, contains a succinct summary. There are vivid descriptions in Shirer's *End of a Berlin Diary*.

Point out that, although the trials of the Japanese warlords were overshadowed by the Nuremberg trials, the results were much the same, with certain exceptions. There was evidence that Emperor Hirohito had attended key meetings and knew of the war plans, but he was never brought to trial, being considered too important as a "figurehead" supporting MacArthur's policies in the Allied administration of Japan.

Like Goering, top warlord Tojo sought to commit suicide. He shot himself when American MPs approached his house to arrest him. A Japanese doctor refused to treat him, but American doctors and blood plasma saved him for the trial and subsequent hanging.

For further reading, suggest summaries in Snyder's *The War*, pages 521–523, and Toland's *The Rising Sun*, Vol. 2, pages 1079–1087, or various histories of the period.

The NATO map on page 592—with its unfamiliar polar projection—affords an opportunity to remind students that every flat map of the world—or a sizable section of the world—contains significant distortions. Do students remember the elementary-school demonstration of peeling an orange in sections and pressing the complete peeling flat as a way of understanding the distortions?

Forming alliances and signing mutual defense pacts would become commonplace in the 1950s (as the next chapter points out), but in 1949 the Senate's overwhelming acceptance of a military alliance was remarkable in light of some continuing hopes in the United States that we could return to at least semi-isolation.

• Did you tell students during the discussion of Chapter 24 about the *Literary Digest* poll that predicted a Landon victory over FDR in 1936? That poll contradicted all kinds of other evidence that showed FDR far ahead in public esteem. But public opinion polling had made big strides in the following twelve years, and the polls had made accurate predictions again and again by the time the 1948 campaign was in full swing. A major factor in the 1948 error was that the polling ended too early before the election—just when public support was turning more and more to Truman.

At 7:30 P.M. (CST) of election night, when the editors of the *Chicago Tribune* had to write the headline of the election story for the early morning edition, political analysts were still predicting a Dewey victory on the basis of early returns. In fact, the election was in doubt until early the next morning. But Truman apparently remained confident throughout the campaign. And he particularly enjoyed the *Tribune's* "boner" because that paper was among his loudest opponents.

Another instance that delighted Truman was the wrong election night predictions of radio newscaster H.V. Kaltenborn, a severe Truman critic who kept insisting up to 4 A.M. that Dewey would win. Later, to the nation's amusement, the victorious President gave a humorous imitation of Kaltenborn making his predictions. Truman's imitation, along with speech excerpts from the 1948 campaign, can be heard on Murrow's album *I Can Hear It Now*, Vol. 2.

• *Handout 40* supplies summaries of explanations given by political analysts of Truman's surprise victory in 1948.

Section 3 (pp. 595–601)
President in His Own Right

Instructional Objectives   Students will be able to

1. Show how the growing "red scare" in the United States led to Truman's loyalty check.

2. Tell how the Communist takeover of China affected the United States.

3. Define and describe "McCarthyism."

4. State the terms and impact of the McCarran Internal Security Act and the McCarran-Walter Act.

5. Explain why and how the United States became involved in the Korean War.

6. Point out the causes and the results of the Truman-MacArthur controversy.

Teaching Suggestions This section devotes major space to the "second red scare" and foreign affairs. The summary treatment of the "Fair Deal" seems justified on the ground that most of the legislative enactments provided for extension of, and some improvements in, New Deal programs. A point of major significance is that these programs became so entrenched that when the Republicans regained office under Eisenhower any chances to scuttle the New Deal had passed by. Another significant insight on the Fair Deal is that three of Truman's unsuccessful proposals—on civil rights, health insurance, and aid to education—laid the groundwork for later successes.

• Among the points to cover in a discussion of the "second red scare" are these: (a) against whom was it directed? (b) what situations and events sparked it? (c) what actions were taken to meet the real and assumed threats? (d) who were some of the leading "red hunters"? and finally (e) on the basis of the above analysis, how were the two "red scares" alike and different? (Note the factor of political ambition in both "scares"—Palmer, Nixon, and McCarthy.)

Point out that later Truman regretted his Executive Order setting up the loyalty check, stating that "I have never believed that this government could be subverted or overturned from within by Communists. The security agencies of the government are well able to deal quietly and effectively with any Communists who sneak into the government without invoking Gestapo methods." (Phillips, *The Truman Presidency,* page 357.)

Students may ask that you bring the Hiss case up to date. On being convicted by a second jury, Hiss was sentenced to a 5-year prison term. He gained early release in 1954 for good behavior. Many books have been written about this case—one of the most famous spy stories of modern history—including those by Hiss and Chambers themselves. Seth's *The Sleeping Truth: The Hiss-Chambers Case Reappraised* brings the case up to date.

• Notice that while the account of the fall of China to the Communists seems to interrupt the story of the "red scare," our failed attempts to "save" China added fuel to the "red scare." It is therefore one of the situations accounting for the "scare." This short topic also serves as background for understanding the Korean War (pp. 597–601).

Teacher elaboration of the fall of China might include these points:

1. In 1945 Truman sent Gen. George Marshall (he would become Secretary of State two years later) to mediate with Chiang and Mao. He managed to bring about only a brief truce and then left, angrily denouncing both sides for bad faith. Thereafter further military aid to Chiang proved ineffective.

2. Communist China remained isolated from the world community until the Nixon administration began reconciliation meetings in 1971. (text pp. 686–687)

3. The Carter administration restored formal ties with China in 1979 and ended the Taiwan Defense Treaty.

4. Chiang dominated Taiwan with a 600,000-man army and with protection from Communist attack by our Pacific fleet. U.S. aid and a large measure of free enterprise helped the industrious Taiwanese achieve remarkable economic growth.

• Note that the McCarthy story spans two presidential administrations (and therefore two chapters in the text). You will need to decide whether to postpone major discussion of McCarthy to the next chapter or to bring the material on page 610 into the discussion now.

In any event, you can point out that his importance was great enough to add "McCarthyism" as an *eponym* (the use of a name to identify a way of doing things) to the American vocabulary.

Now or later, have students find definitions of McCarthyism in various dictionaries, including specialized history and political science dictionaries. To their findings you can add ones like these:

— "To many Americans, McCarthyism is Americanism." (radio commentator Fulton Lewis, Jr.)

— "McCarthyism is Americanism with its sleeves rolled up." (McCarthy himself)

— "McCarthy's methods, to me, look like Hitler's." (Eleanor Roosevelt)

— "McCarthyism . . . is a movement around which men of good will and stern morality can unite." (editor and author William F. Buckley, Jr.)

— ". . . inquests into a person's intentions, ideas, associations, and other tests so vague as to guarantee confusion and error." (historian Samuel E. Morison)

• List provisions of the McCarran Act (the Internal Security Act of 1950) on the chalkboard as students identify them from the text. Invite students to express value judgments on each provision. Ask how the provision squares with the spirit and letter of the Bill of Rights.

• Point out that dissatisfaction with the quota system for admitting immigrants—supported by Truman, Eisenhower, and Kennedy—finally resulted in the still-operative Immigration Act of 1965 (p. 665). Since the McCarran-Walter Act no longer applies, there is little point in having students memorize its provisions. Its chief significance here is the links it had with the "second red scare."

• You might point out that in connection with the Truman vetoes of the McCarran Act and the McCarran-Walter Act, the Senate majority leader Scott Lucas of Illinois contended that when a nation faces the threat of Communist subversion, "there is nothing too drastic." Ask students to evaluate this position.

- The succinct yet vivid description of the Korean War needs little elaboration—except where student or teacher interest dictates because of some personal or family connection. The map on page 598, of course, adds immeasurably to following the course of the war.

- Do students appreciate the significance of the Soviet Union's walkout from the Security Council six months before the North Korean attack? Here is another vivid example of the influence of the unexpected on the course of history, a common theme in author Daniel Boorstin's writings (see Epilogue, "The Mysterious Future," and elsewhere in the text).

- On the chalkboard write ten names or terms from the text account of the Korean War as the first column of a matching exercise. Ask students to write brief, informative identifications for the second column. Terms might include the following: 38th parallel, Syngman Rhee, Douglas MacArthur, Yalu River, Inchon, Pusan, Seoul, Chiang Kai-shek, Omar Bradley, Matthew Ridgway, United Nations Command, Security Council.

- *Handout lesson:* Handout 41 focuses on the MacArthur demand that the war be extended to Communist China and not be limited to Korea. The questions at the end can be answered by students on the back of the handout, or used for class discussion, or both.

- Tell students that although "more and more Americans saw that Truman was talking sense" (see text), the immediate emotional response to MacArthur's dismissal was such that (a) Republican House leader Joseph Martin spoke of Truman's impeachment at a press conference, (b) 78,000 telegrams and letters came to the White House, opposing Truman at the rate of 20 to 1, and (c) a Gallup Poll found only 29 percent favored the President's action.

  Later, in one of the most dramatic speeches ever heard in Congress, MacArthur spoke of "closing my fifty-two years of military service," ready at last to "fade away, an old soldier who tried to do his duty as God gave him the light to see that duty." Thereafter, MacArthur continued his triumphant tour and speech-making as "MacArthur for President" buttons appeared throughout the country.

  However, Americans seemed to tire quickly of this hero. MacArthur gave the keynote speech at the 1952 Republican convention, but a new hero—"Ike" Eisenhower—had appeared. Subsequently, MacArthur's "counsel was never invited, his association never encouraged, his name never invoked, and his judgments never embraced." (Hughes, *The Ordeal of Power,* page 34.)

- Point out that MacArthur's role in the Korean War has tended to overshadow his leadership in Japan during the occupation period 1945–1951. As the only Allied occupying power in Japan, the United States through MacArthur brought profound changes: (a) abolition of the cult of the emperor, (b) a written constitution based on American principles of the rights of the individual, (c) the right to vote for women, (d) a program of land redistribution—half the farming families were tenants in 1945, and (e) a revival of industry and business.

- Tell students that historians rate Truman as "near great." In part he may enjoy this high rating because he was a "common American who became an uncommon President." Following FDR, he was expected to be a caretaker President. Yet he had to finish World War II and make the most significant decisions in modern times in employing the atom bomb, fighting the Korean War—soon labeled "Mr. Truman's War" by his critics, and facing the Soviet Union in the cold war. His surprise victory in 1948 brought admiration, even from his foes. Charges of corruption and "5 percenters" in his administration are now largely forgotten.

CHAPTER REVIEW

Meeting Our Earlier Selves

1. Return to isolationism was impossible if one accepts the premise that the Soviet Union was intent on expansion. But even if the Soviet Union had proved its willingness to cooperate with the Western powers after the war, the plan for world peace envisioned in the United Nations Charter demanded the presence of the United States as the strongest military power (with the atom bomb) and the preeminent economic power whose resources would be required in economic reconstruction.

2. Soviet actions included (a) insistence on absolute veto power in the UN Security Council, (b) rejection of the plan for atomic-energy control, (c) violation of the Yalta agreements on free elections in Eastern Europe, (d) support of Communist rebels in Greece, (e) pressure on Turkey, (f) spy rings, (g) reluctance to withdraw troops from Iran, (h) unwillingness to share in postwar reconstruction of Europe, (i) obstruction of peace arrangements for Germany, etc.

3. Foreign aid would help halt the spread of communism because Communists make extravagant promises about economic progress possible under their system and because they seek to exploit unrest. Foreign aid would promote U.S. prosperity by expanding markets for U.S. goods. Loans to foreign countries would be used to buy American products, and gifts of farm products and other goods would remove surpluses that depressed prices.

4. Employers would tend to favor all the provisions cited in the text—although the anti-Communist provisions were recognized as having more political than economic significance. Some union leaders were very opposed to the ban on the closed shop, and union leaders in general opposed the right of states to enact "right-to-work" laws. Any limit on the union shop threatened the growth of union membership. While opposed by union leaders at the time, the provisions on the "cooling off" period and the ban on political contributions turned out to be only minor inconveniences.

5. Responses included Truman's loyalty check, the McCarran Act, certain provisions of the McCarran-Walter immigration act, the vigorous activity of the House Un-American Activities Committee, weak responses to McCarthyism, etc. Ask students to back up their value judgments with reasoned arguments.

6. Accomplishments include a long series of foreign policy decisions (have students cite examples), his support of various measures to maintain and extend New Deal reforms, and his support of a variety of civil rights measures. Failure might include some timidity on opposing fanaticism in the "second red scare," ignoring Communist China's warnings about fighting in North Korea, toleration of cronyism in government, a certain abrasiveness in dealing with the press and with other critics and opponents, etc.

Questions for Today

1. The containment policy is illustrated most clearly in U.S. reaction to the Soviet presence in Afghanistan. Where the Soviets work more subtly to extend Communist influence by sending advisers and other kinds of help to regimes around the world, we can't respond as vigorously because the threat is less imminent and because we engage in similar activities.

2. In civil wars—the most common kind of war since 1945—the UN has been largely ineffectual. In some other situations the UN has helped to arrange an armistice and supplied peacekeeping forces. Students should use a world history text to find examples. The UN's overall failure as a peacekeeping agency rests on fundamental foreign policy differences between the Soviet Union and the Western democracies.

3. Civil rights laws have reduced inequality and promoted the opportunities of minorities. (Have students cite examples.) It also seems unquestionable that the general prosperity of the United States since 1945 rests partly on enormous government spending and provisions of the tax law. This spending is also a major factor in rising inflation. Good and bad effects can be found in most of the major economic legislation of the past fifty years.

CHAPTER 29

Eisenhower: Moderate Republican

Introducing the Chapter Have students speculate on the meaning of "moderate Republican" in the chapter title. .If students need prompting, suggest the term "middle of the road." Probe for the terms "conservative Republican" and "liberal Republican" as other types. Then you might name three or four issues on which conservatives and liberals disagree (issues from the 1950s or today). See if students can identify the stand a conservative would take on the issue—and then the liberal position. The moderate, of course, would be somewhere in between.

After students have read the chapter introduction, point out in relation to paragraph 2 that Moscow was indeed the nerve center for a network of worldwide Communist parties. And the avowed Communist goal of world revolution seemed a reasonable threat in the upheavals after the war—a threat that our foreign-aid programs were designed to alleviate. But Tito's break with Moscow, the Berlin Wall, the Hungarian revolt, and other signs of unrest in the Communist camp showed that "the red network" had weak spots.

Notice that the last sentence of the introduction foreshadows the emergence of a doctrine of co-existence.

Section 1 (pp. 602–608)
The Republicans Return

Instructional Objectives Students will be able to

1. Summarize the election of 1952 and give reasons why Eisenhower won.

2. Describe the background and career of Dwight D. Eisenhower.

3. Summarize the events in Korea that ended the war in a stalemate.

4. Define and evaluate Dulles's "brinkmanship" and "pactomania" policies.

5. Tell how the United States became involved in the war in Indochina.

6. Explain the significance of the CIA and the U-2 incident in our international relations.

Teaching Suggestions Students will be interested in the election of 1952 as the first of the "modern" elections (first to be nationally televised, e.g.). The importance of Eisenhower the man in winning the election can be compared to Stevenson's emphasis on the issues.

• Focus attention on the 1952 election issues (as seen by the Republicans) by pointing out the traditional behavior of the "outs" blaming the "ins" for "the mess the country is in." The Democrats had blamed Hoover and the Republicans for the Great Depression. Have students use the text to show how the Republicans now blamed the Democrats. Notice how each of the terms can be put in terms of "blame": for the fall of China, for the war in Korea, for not "rolling back" communism, for unbalanced budgets and a steeply rising public debt, and for dishonesty in government. You might then have the class consider for which issues, if any, the Democrats deserved blame.

• Point out that Stevenson was not cold and aloof but was somewhat less outgoing than "Ike." Stevenson appears to have been hurt by the "egghead" (intellectual) label. His refusal to promise easy solutions to tough problems led to suspicions of indecisiveness. The Democratic party remained split on the civil rights issue, and Stevenson refused to compromise in order to gain favor in the South. Notice that he lost four important southern states. But his failure to win the Democratic strongholds of the industrial states was even more damaging. A study of UAW members in Detroit indicated that 75 percent with strong union ties voted for Stevenson, but only a little over 50 percent of those with weak union loyalty voted for him.

Tell students that despite his two defeats as a presidential candidate, Adlai Stevenson continued as a prominent figure in American life after being appointed U.S. Ambassador to the UN in 1961 by President John F. Kennedy, a position held until Stevenson's death in 1965.

Examples of Stevenson's eloquent speeches may be found in Peterson's *A Treasury of the World's Great Speeches*, pages 821–826.

• Have students speculate on why a Cabinet representative of the business world would look for things to "stop doing instead of finding new things to do." (rising government activity seen as a burden on business; business managers trained to look at the cost-effectiveness of programs) Ask: "What kinds of programs in particular would business have wanted to cut back in the 1950s?" (rest of chapter gives clues).

• Discuss possible advantages and disadvantages of the chief of staff arrangement that Eisenhower set up for the White House Office. You will need to consider the alternative: half a dozen or so administrative assistants shielding the President. You might point out that every bureaucracy has a chain of command, but the person at the top may allow many exceptions to the general rule of communicating through the boss directly above you.

Adams was forced to resign for accepting small gifts and hospitality from a clothing manufacturer for interceding with two regulatory agencies. Eisenhower then took more direct charge of the White House staff.

- Ask students how the Eisenhower-Dulles foreign policy measured up to Republican platform talk about freeing captive peoples behind the iron curtain.

You will probably need to emphasize that brave talk about "rolling back" instead of merely "containing" communism lost all meaning with cuts in the defense budget. Also link the cuts in the defense budget and the creation of a "strategic mobile reserve" with Dulles's "brinkmanship" policy. (Lacking strong and growing defense forces, how else could the nation respond to Communist threats to the peace except by the threat of massive retaliation?)

- Call attention to the last sentence of the topic "A new foreign policy." Ask students to speculate on what "facts of life" would lead Dulles to "give up these grandiose visions." One of the facts was the cut in defense spending. Another was the need to consult with allies, who might oppose rash action, if you wanted their help in opposing the Communists. A third factor was that the President was a restraining force; he knew the limits of military power. Another fact that would become apparent was that threats of massive retaliation would have little influence on local Communist leaders who did not always dance to Moscow's tune and who could engage in long-term guerrilla warfare. (Note how some of these facts became clear in France's Vietnam War.)

- Have students use the map on page 672 to see (a) the 1945 boundaries of French Indochina, noting its three chief parts—Vietnam, Laos, Cambodia, (b) Dienbienphu, and (c) the demarcation line of 1954. Then discuss the following, using the text as a guide:

1. How did we get involved in France's Vietnam War?

2. How did we help at first?

3. What did Eisenhower refuse to do?

4. How was the Vietnam problem temporarily settled?

5. Did the 1954 settlement represent a "rollback" of communism? (in a sense, since Ho Chi Minh had earlier been recognized as head of a government for the whole of Vietnam; on the other hand, since the Communists never had firm control, their getting half of Vietnam was a loss to the anti-Communist world)

Point out that the 1954 Geneva Conference also provided for the independence of Laos and Cambodia. And— very important—that the United States refused to sign the accords because of unwillingness to share any responsibility for the Communist gains.

- Do you want to give even more attention to the Geneva Conference of 1954 at this time—as background for the second Vietnam War? See the first paragraph on page 653. Notice that the 17th parallel dividing line was viewed —by some conference participants at least—as an armistice line for stopping the civil war, that unification was envisioned through an election, and that the United States would have a share in obstructing the election.

- Avoid memorization of defense treaty members. One would hope, of course, that students would recognize and remember (a) that several defense treaties were regional in scope—western hemisphere; North Atlantic and Western Europe; southeast Asia; Middle East; (b) the names or initials of the regional pacts; (c) that the U.S. was a promoter but not a signatory of METO; (d) that the U.S. made other mutual defense agreements with individual nations; and (e) that West Germany joined NATO.

- Have students open their texts to pages 606–607. Ask them to find in the first three columns three ways that nations try to achieve their foreign policy goals. (war; military or other aid; treaty making)

Then ask: "What is a fourth general foreign policy technique, which is described in the last column?" (espionage)

Ask students to express value judgments (a) on espionage in general and (b) on the specific instances cited on page 607. (Note that secret flights to obtain information is spying—espionage.)

Section 2 (pp. 608–611)
Everybody's New Deal

Instructional Objectives Students will be able to

1. List and evaluate the policies of the Eisenhower administration.

2. Compare the merits of public vs. private power in our American economic system.

3. Tell how Senator Joseph R. McCarthy's impact on the United States reached its peak and then waned.

4. Describe the election of 1956.

Teaching Suggestions This section offers a good opportunity to review the basic philosophy of the New Deal under FDR and Truman and then to make comparisons with the Republican approach under Eisenhower. Students might be encouraged to take sides on the persistent issue of public vs. private power.

- See first paragraph of "Introducing the Chapter" for an activity on analyzing conservative, moderate, and liberal positions on public issues. You can use—or continue— this activity in connection with the domestic issues discussed on pages 608–610, especially the power issue, farm legislation, Social Security amendments, slum clearance and housing, and health insurance. At the same time you may want to have students read about and analyze the National Defense Education Act (pp. 617–618).

- Review any activities from the previous chapter on Senator Joseph R. McCarthy. Tell students that McCarthy received a great ovation at the Republican convention in 1952. Soon afterwards when Ike gave a campaign speech in Wisconsin, McCarthy persuaded him to delete a favorable reference to General George C. Marshall, whom McCarthy had vilified as being part of a Communist conspiracy. President Truman thought that Eisenhower was "badly advised." Later, according to Sherman Adams, "If Eisenhower could have had his own way in dealing with McCarthy, he would have ignored him completely."

Show or make copies of cartoons of the period depicting McCarthy's impact on the American scene. See Butterfield's *The American Past,* Chapter 8. Have students study the cartoons. At this point, you might also show a film about McCarthy. Then discuss the following, using the cartoons, the film, and the text as a guide:

1. Cartoonist Herblock depicted McCarthy with a meat cleaver facing Eisenhower holding a white feather. The President warns, "Have a care, Sir!" Is this cartoon favorable or unfavorable to the President? Explain.

2. Benjamin Franklin once said: ". . . those who would give up essential liberty to purchase a little temporary safety, deserve neither liberty nor safety." Do you agree? Why? How would Senator McCarthy have responded to this statement?

3. Are the authors of the text sympathetic or unsympathetic to McCarthy? What sentences indicate their viewpoint?

4. Do you think that our nation might experience another era of McCarthyism? Under what circumstances?

- Tell students that Eisenhower's heart attack in Denver in September 1955 changed American history in that thereafter the Vice-President has played a greater and more knowledgeable role in presidential affairs. Also, since Eisenhower was 65 years old at the time of his second election, the age and health of the candidates turned out to be a significant consideration for the voters. After a favorable report from his physician, heart specialist Paul Dudley White, Eisenhower called a Cabinet meeting to solicit opinions on a second term. All members favored Ike's renomination. He remained in relatively good health throughout his second term, and died in 1969 at age 79.

Section 3 (pp. 612–615)
The Fight for Equality

Instructional Objectives Students will be able to

1. Explain how the inadequacy of the 1896 Supreme Court *Plessy* v. *Ferguson* decision led to the momentous *Brown* v. *Topeka* school desegregation decision in 1954.

2. Describe reaction in the South to the *Brown* decision and Eisenhower's intervention in Little Rock, Arkansas.

3. Tell how Martin Luther King, Jr., and Rosa Parks became important figures in the quest for black equality.

4. Evaluate the philosophy of nonviolence.

Teaching Suggestions Emphasize the role of the NAACP in getting the Supreme Court to move toward reversal of *Plessy* v. *Ferguson* (p. 529). The NAACP lawyers found what they thought were ideal cases to serve as lawsuits and then provided legal counsel for the plaintiffs. In the 1930s the NAACP began a sustained effort to prove inequality in the schools. They began by suing for equal higher education because southern states had almost no graduate or professional schools for blacks. Moreover, one excuse for separate schools was that they were necessary to avoid violence. But this argument held little weight at the graduate level.

In 1935 the courts of Maryland ordered the state university's law school to admit blacks. To avoid desegregation the state had been granting out-of-state scholarships for blacks seeking a legal education.

The 1938 case alluded to in the text (p. 612, col. 2, para. 4) was a Supreme Court decision that the University of Missouri Law School must furnish the plaintiff (a black student seeking admission) substantially equal facilities within its borders. Missouri did set up a separate black law school —and later a separate journalism school. Another court decision required Kentucky to set up an engineering school for blacks.

On the same day in 1950 that the Court ordered the admission of a black to the University of Texas Law School (p. 612), it ordered the University of Oklahoma to stop segregating a black student who had actually been admitted to work on a doctorate in education. He had been assigned a desk away from the other students, a segregated desk in the library, and separate service in the school cafeteria. (The ax was about to fall on *Plessy* v. *Ferguson*.)

The rising insistence by the Court that separate facilities must be at least roughly equal led many southern school districts in the late '40s and '50s to build new schools for blacks—but the effort came too late.

- A case study of the Montgomery bus boycott appears in the first edition of *American Political Behavior* (Ginn, 1972, 1974), pp. 132–138.

- To aid students in visualizing the racial tensions of the 1950–1960 period, show a film like *The Warren Years: The Great Decisions* (24 min). After the film, discuss what it added to the text.

- Have a panel discussion or debate on the topic "Nonviolence—Is It the Best Way for Black Progress?" Suggest that students research recent articles on this topic (also called *passive resistance*) in the *Readers' Guide to Periodical Literature.* Book titles may be found under "Nonviolence" in the Subject Guide to *Books in Print.*

- Students should note the limited scope of the Civil Rights Acts of 1957 and 1960, chiefly designed to help blacks exercise their voting rights in the South—with the 1960 act going so far as to permit federal judges to register black voters where local officials were putting up obstacles. Have a student read aloud the sentence in the first paragraph of page 615 that tells the significance of the 1957 law. Elaborate, if necessary, on the filibuster technique that had tied up civil rights legislation time after time.

Section 4 (pp. 615–621)
Difficulties Abroad

Instructional Objectives Students will be able to

1. Summarize the international events that made 1956 a difficult year.

2. Trace the development of rockets leading to the beginning of the Space Age.

3. Tell how the shooting down of an American U-2 plane jeopardized our relations with the Soviet Union.

4. Explain how the United States reacted to the coming of power of Castro in Cuba.

Teaching Suggestions The focus of this section is on foreign affairs, missile development, and the start of the Space Age. One of the few significant second-term laws having to do with domestic affairs was the National Defense Education Act (pp. 617–618), which fits neatly into the discussion of Sputnik. You may want to introduce a second major law passed in Eisenhower's second term: the Landrum-Griffin Act, or Labor-Management Reporting and Disclosure Act. (As an alternative, tell students about this law during discussion of the Eisenhower domestic legislation in Section 2.)

The Landrum-Griffin Act grew out of the recommendations of a special Senate committee which for several years had been probing deeply into racketeering and corruption in some labor unions, particularly the Teamsters' Union. An aroused public opinion demanded preventive legislation, and the reform bill passed Congress with an overwhelming majority.

Among the new law's many provisions were the following: (1) Union officials were required to submit detailed financial reports to the Secretary of Labor. (2) Employers were to report on any payments to union officers and to labor-relations consultants. (3) To protect union members who oppose their officers, a labor "bill of rights" guaranteed to members the right to vote in union elections and to speak up against union policies. Unions were required to hold regular elections. (4) Previous legal restrictions on secondary boycotts and blackmail picketing were strengthened.

• Use the map on page 619 to locate the trouble spots in foreign relations in Eisenhower's second term. You might deal with all the crises at one time: Hungary, Egypt, Lebanon, Formosa Strait, Berlin, the U-2 incident, and Cuba. Each of these might be reviewed by using the format suggested in Section Review item 3: (a) causes, (b) participants, (c) results. Summary questions might include the following items:

1. What kind of response did the administration make in each of these situations? Was it suitable? (See item 2 in *Meeting Our Earlier Selves*, p. 622.)

2. The UN peacekeeping mechanism "worked" in the Suez affair. Why? (The Soviet Union and the United States worked together on this occasion, and the other powers involved were not willing to stand up against this combination of forces.)

3. Did the Eisenhower Doctrine provide a new direction for American foreign policy? (It was simply a restatement of the Truman Doctrine with emphasis on the Middle East; it was really the media that elevated the pronouncement to the status of "doctrine.")

4. Should the United States have intervened in Cuba to prevent Castro's rise to power? (Use a question like this to point out, first, that we had given up our declared right to police the Western Hemisphere; and, second, that Castro was hailed as a hero for overthrowing a corrupt regime and had no apparent ties with the Communists. American friendliness turned to hostility—with the expropriation of property a leading factor—and then Castro turned to the Soviet Union for support and adopted the Communist model for his "revolution for social justice.")

• Tell students that the American U-2 shot down by the Russians was a one-man unarmed plane. Instead, it had seven infrared cameras which through portholes could photograph in detail sections of the earth 125 miles wide and 3000 miles long. Enlargement of the film permitted the reading of a newspaper headline nearly 10 miles from the camera!

When shot down, U-2 pilot Francis Gary Powers was carrying curare, a poison which brings instant death. However, after being ejected from his plane, Powers chose not to deny information to the Russians through killing himself. Instead, according to Khrushchev, the pilot made a "complete confession." The U-2 wreckage was displayed in Moscow for propaganda purposes. In a press conference, Khrushchev accused the U.S. of "treachery" and "bandit" acts, and canceled Eisenhower's invitation to visit Russia.

• *Handout lesson:* Use *Handout 42* to show students that the Khrushchev-Nixon "debate" in Moscow was anything but profound. It does show clearly, however, the sensitivity of Soviet leaders about how their goals and their system were shortchanging Russian consumers.

• Have individuals or a committee interested in space science prepare a report on the pioneer days of rocketry, with emphasis on the contributions of Robert H. Goddard. See Ley's *Rockets, Missiles and Men in Space,* Von Braun and Ordway's *History of Rocketry and Space Travel,* and Shelton's *American Space Exploration.* Point out that subsequent stages of our progress in space exploration will be discussed in Section 3, Chapter 31.

You might show the film *The Space Age: From Dr. Goddard to Project Apollo* (27 min).

• To aid students in preparing reports or projects during the study in Chapter 31 of our space program, suggest that they write now to the following address for helpful materials: National Aeronautics and Space Administration, 400 Maryland Avenue, S.W., Washington, D.C. 20546.

• Historians rate President Eisenhower as "average." More than any other President of modern times, he received the trust and affection of the American people. In turn—as related to TV commentator Walter Cronkite—Eisenhower thought that he had created "an atmosphere of greater serenity and mutual confidence" during his tenure. Despite confrontations with the Soviets, he also maintained the peace.

Critics assert that Eisenhower was a caretaker President who refused to provide the dynamic leadership necessary to restrain McCarthyism or to encourage a long overdue civil rights program. Yet the image of a fatherly figure who brought dignity to the nation's highest office remains secure.

CHAPTER REVIEW

Meeting Our Earlier Selves

1. Some policymaking on military matters and in his NATO role, but nothing in a wide range of public affairs; wide administrative experience in the armed services, NATO, and as president of Columbia; diplomatic experience in heading Allied forces in the war and as NATO commander; and his whole career trained him for leadership. Prior to class discussion of this item, have several students pick one other General-President and prepare a brief summary of his background on points pertinent to this question. The others include Washington, Jackson, W. H. Harrison, Taylor, Grant, and Garfield. One or two others might be included but were not known chiefly for their military careers.

2. The line between "threat of force" and diplomacy is not always clear. But forceful might be applied to (a) aid to French in Vietnam—but diplomatic in Geneva Conference, (b) troops to Lebanon, (c) fleet to Formosa Strait in Quemoy-Matsu affair, (d) not withdrawing from Berlin. Diplomatic responses might include (a) Geneva Conference on Indochina; (b) introducing UN resolution condemning USSR on Hungary; (c) supporting UN resolution on Suez crisis. Also point out that to forestall trouble with the Soviet Union the U.S. took "forceful" action in arranging defense treaties and threatening "massive retaliation." We used diplomacy in summit conferences and other meetings with Soviet leaders to ease tensions.

3. A consistently conservative, or "rightist," approach would have alienated liberal Democrats and moderate-to-liberal Republicans, whose support was necessary for getting friendly consideration of proposals most desired by the administration. The presence of a Democratic majority in Congress reminded the administration that the public was not eager to undo the New Deal, whereas continued Republican control would have sent out a different kind of signal.

4. McCarthyism—Ike instituted own security search and tried to stay aloof from McCarthy; desegregation—acted to preserve order but generally failed to enlist his tremendous moral influence on behalf of desegregation; civil rights laws—exerted no great leadership in their behalf; Hungarian affair—protested in UN and supported refugee program. Perhaps other instances—outside the text—can be mentioned.

5. The "relaxation" judgment seems true when the Eisenhower years are compared with what went on before and what would come afterward. It seems more true in the domestic arena in that the New Deal became institutionalized without adding or subtracting major programs. But the domestic scene was not one of relaxation in the civil rights arena. And the 1950s had its share of crises in foreign affairs. Judgments will vary, of course, on the need for periodic "breathing spells." Advocates of reform don't want a "pause that refreshes." Yet sustained public interest in reform seems impossible to achieve. Perhaps the public needs periodic "breathing spells" to revivify energies and to get used to the changes that have come about.

Questions for Today

1. Answers will depend on who is President when students are using the text. There is a tendency, of course, for candidates and platforms to promise more than can be delivered. But some candidates are far more specific than others. A major reason for Jimmy Carter's drastic fall in the public opinion polls was his failure to come anywhere near fulfilling his long list of promises made in the 1976 campaign. In some cases he altered his position; in other cases he held to pre-election positions but could not get support for them.

A major reason that there are changes in position is that candidates fail to appreciate the complexities of certain public issues. Another is that unexpected developments bring new urgencies (taxes may have to be raised instead of cut, e.g.). Another reason is that candidates take inconsistent positions, promising one thing to this group—and something inconsistent to another group.

2. Persistent issues include racial equality, racial imbalance in schools, farm price supports, housing for the needy, health insurance, adequacies of Social Security, the minimum wage, education of the gifted, and issues not directly covered in the chapter.

3. Answers will depend on when students are using the text.

4. Earth satellites are probably being used to achieve the objectives of the "open skies" proposal. But a case can probably be made for inspection at lower altitudes.

CHAPTER 30

Mobile People and Magic Machines

Introducing the Chapter This chapter examines a number of changes taking place in the United States after — and partly because of — World War II. You might review again why we have always been a mobile people. Personalize the chapter title by having students jot down answers to questions like these:

1. In how many communities have you ever lived? (different cities, towns, counties, or neighborhoods in a big city)

2. About how far from your present home was one of your parents born?

3. If possible, estimate the number of places one of your parents lived before your birth.

4. Approximately how many states have you lived in or visited? How many foreign countries?

5. Approximately how far away from your present home have you ever been?

6. In how many states and/or foreign countries do you estimate you have close relatives: grandparents, brothers or sisters, uncles, aunts, cousins?

7. Which of the following forms of transportation have you ever used: airplane, train, intercity bus, ship?

8. What are some machines (mechanical devices) that you have used, or your parents use, that did not exist when your grandparents were teen-agers?

Invite — but do not pressure — students to respond orally. For example, students might show by number of fingers how many places they have ever lived.
Then ask: "What do the answers you have written (and heard) tell about the mobility of Americans? And what do your answers tell about the importance of machines in our lives?"

Section 1 (pp. 623–628)
A Changing People

Instructional Objectives Students will be able to

1. List the ways in which wars bring changes to a society.
2. Summarize the growth and movement of our population.
3. Examine specific aspects of our population shifts.
4. Describe the impact of suburbia on American life.

5. Explain why the average age of our population is increasing.

Teaching Suggestions You might link some of the findings of the 1980 census with the topics explored in this section. Have earlier trends continued — such as the growth of the West and South, the migration of blacks to the cities of the North, the decline in farm population, and the gradual increase in the percentage of our senior citizens?

• Much of this section is a description of our American society during the last quarter century, and you might encourage students to examine your school and community as a microcosm of the country as a whole. Illustrations in pictorial histories, such as Time-Life's *This Fabulous Century—1950–1960* and *1960–1970* will be helpful.

Write these headings on the chalkboard:

DOMESTIC CHANGES CREATED

BY WAR IN AMERICAN LIFE

[Changes   Desirable   Undesirable]

Have students use the text as a guide to list the changes in a vertical column. After they have finished, have them place checks in the adjoining columns to indicate whether they think that the changes listed are desirable or undesirable. Then discuss these to reach a consensus. Some suggested changes: (a) migration, especially to cities; (b) family separations; (c) marriage postponements; (d) mechanical inventions (some destructive, others helpful); (e) medical advances; (f) increased job opportunities.

You might also discuss the following:

1. The great British statesman Edmund Burke, who spoke up for the American colonists in the Revolution, said, "War never leaves where it found a nation." How do you interpret this?

2. Benjamin Franklin once said, "There never was a good war or a bad peace." Do you agree? Why?

3. Are the advances brought by war worth the price in human lives? Explain.

• Use current editions of the *Statistical Abstract of the United States, Information Please Almanac, World Almanac,* and the *Hammond Almanac* (all readily available in most school and community libraries) for the latest census statistics. You might demonstrate the use of these sources by researching the latest population figures for your state and its largest cities.

- Point out that around 10 million Americans speak a language other than English. The largest group speaks Spanish; other languages include Italian, French, German, Polish, Chinese, Greek, Portuguese, Japanese, Korean, and Vietnamese. Have a committee survey your school and/or locality to determine the number of students/residents for whom English is a second language. What services are available to help them learn English?

- *Handout lesson:* Use Handout 43 to give students practice in graphing tabular data and to give visual impact to some of the demographic trends discussed in the text.

Before discussing the content of the graphs, you might call attention to a few points on graphing technique.

1. Notice the "jog" in the vertical scale of the "Population Growth" and "Birth Rates" graphs. Ideally the base line should start at zero, and other horizontal lines should mark off equal quantities. The "jog" shows that some horizontal lines have been omitted to save space. Ask students to visualize how the graphs would look if they were full depth. (The rises and falls in the line would appear somewhat less pronounced.)

2. Point out that ideally the bottom line of the "Big-City Population" graph would be 0% and the top line would be 100% Why? (would show the proportions of big-city and smaller-city populations more graphically)

3. Ask: "Which of these line graphs could just as well be bar graphs?" (All of them) The immigration map, in fact, would be better as a bar graph unless it showed numbers for every year instead of only every fifth year. The line segment between 1965 and 1970 suggests that immigration rose each of the years between 1965 and 1970 at a fairly even pace. In fact, the number rose to 454,000 in 1968, dropped to 359,000 in 1969, and then rose to 373,000 in 1979.

Next ask some questions about the data shown on the graphs:

1. How are the "Population Growth" and "Birth Rates" graphs related?

2. Population growth = number of live births + net number of immigrants − ? Finish the equation. (number of deaths)

3. How is the labor force graph related to the one on population growth? (rising population ordinarily means rise in number of people working and/or seeking work)

4. Which two graphs tell something about population mobility (a "mobile people")? (farm population and big-city population)

5. According to the text, what are some factors that account for the decline of the farm population?

6. Suggest some reasons why big cities had a smaller proportion of our urban population in 1970 than in 1940. Where did many of these people move to?

- *Competency exercise—making graphs:* The *Statistical Abstract* provides other interesting data about postwar population growth and mobility. Have each student prepare an original graph with an appropriate title, using one of the following sets of statistics:

— Four-year college graduates (in thousands): 1940, 187; 1945, 131; 1950, 432; 1955, 286; 1960, 392; 1965, 632; 1970, 792; 1975, 923.

— Admissions to national parks (in millions): 1940, 7.4; 1945, 4.5; 1950, 13.9; 1955, 18.8; 1960, 26.6; 1965, 36.6; 1970, 45.9; 1975, 58.8.

— U.S. overseas travelers (in thousands): 1940, 156; 1945, 117; 1950, 676; 1955, 1,075; 1960, 1,634; 1965, 2,623; 1970, 5,260; 1975, 6,354.

Point out the connections between college attendance and mobility. The other statistics have to do with travel, a kind of mobility. All of the statistics above reflect a growing population, of course.

- Use the map on page 626 for further discussion of population mobility. One of the chief purposes of this map is to remind students that migration is a two-way street after an area has once been settled. Ask questions like these about the map:

1. Which one region gained population at the expense of each of the others? Why? (the West, chiefly because of climate and industrial expansion)

2. Which region had the largest net loss of population resulting from interregional migration? Why? (the North Central—losing 175,000 annually; the drop in farm population was a big factor—with many retired farm people moving South and West and many young people choosing other careers; also faster industrial growth in the South and West)

3. Three regions lost more people than they gained from migration. Does this mean these three regions had a lower total population in 1965 than in 1955? (No! Birth rates are usually more important than migration rates in determining total population. For example, the North Central and Northeast each grew by 5 million and the South by 8 million between 1960 and 1970.)

4. What are some chief reasons that people move from one region to another? (retirees to warm climates; faster industrial growth in some regions than others; college attendance outside of one's own region; job attractions elsewhere for professionals and business managers; etc.)

- Have students turn to the map on page 628. Begin by introducing the term "metropolitan area." Geographers have invented this term to mean any sizable city and the land and people surrounding it. Do your students live in such an area—or close to one? What is it called? (Examples: Chicagoland, Greater New York, Greater Boston, the Capital District—for Washington and Baltimore, the Bay Area—for San Francisco-Oakland, etc.)

Then explain that metropolitan areas are so important in our lives that we want to measure their size and the many things that occur within them. But to measure something we need to know its boundaries. It is possible to measure Denver's population, housing units, factory production, etc., since we can find out its boundary lines. But where are the boundaries of Greater Denver? of Greater Phoenix? of Greater Atlanta? The boundaries are extremely fuzzy. So the Census Bureau has invented a system of standard boundary lines: in general, county boundaries (parishes in Louisiana; boroughs in Alaska; city and town boundaries in New England, where counties are unimportant). So a Standard Metropolitan Statistical Area (SMSA) —a metropolitan area for statistical purposes—is a county or a group of counties containing at least one city of 50,000 population or more. Such a city is called the metropolitan area's central city.

Now students can see on the map that many of the SMSAs have peculiar shapes—because they consist of one or more counties. Notice that county lines in the East and South tend to be more irregular than in the West. Counties in the West also tend to be far larger in area than elsewhere. This point is very important in interpreting the map. Southeastern California and southern Nevada seem to be more urbanized than Wisconsin, but this is not actually true. For example, the Las Vegas, Nevada, SMSA covers more than twice the area as the Little Rock SMSA in central Arkansas, but in the mid-1970s their populations were about the same. Reno's county (SMSA) is very large but is one of the smaller SMSAs in total population. San Bernardino County in southern California is the largest county in the nation—larger than Vermont and New Hampshire combined—but in the 1970s was almost a third smaller in population than the Atlanta SMSA.

Also tell students that most of the large blocks of color on the map represent adjacent SMSAs. There are numerous separate but adjoining SMSAs in the large colored block from northern Massachusetts to Washington, D.C. The large colored block that runs across lower Michigan represents at least eight SMSAs.

With these points in mind, have students locate the colored block that they live in or is nearest to them. Identify one or more SMSAs in that block. Does it consist of one or more than one county? Is there one or more than one central city in their SMSA? Continue with questions like these:

1. How is a community five or ten miles from its central city linked to it? (newspapers, radio, TV, stores, jobs, sports, etc.)

2. Why have many people elected to leave the central city to live in nearby suburbs?

3. What problems has this movement produced for some of our central cities?

• Show the film *The Changing City* (16 min) and/or the flimstrip *The Black Odyssey: Migration to the Cities* to help students visualize some recent population changes in the United States.

Section 2 (pp. 628–634)
Everyday Life Transformed

Instructional Objectives   Students will be able to

1. Describe the growth and characteristics of the American economy since 1945.

2. Give reasons for the long period of postwar prosperity.

3. Explain the economic and social significance of the automobile in contemporary American society.

4. Summarize the impact of machines and new products on American culture.

5. Analyze the role of television in modern life.

Teaching Suggestions   This section continues the opportunity to examine our contemporary society. Students may prefer such topics as automobiles, television, Xerox machines, and computers to defining our GNP or explaining the economic reasons for a rise in prices. Yet all facets can be woven together with a blend of meaningful student discussion and thoughtful teacher analysis.

• Show the class one or more Rube Goldberg cartoons. They were published in the Sunday newspaper comic section for years and represented fantastically complicated ways of performing simple tasks.

Pictures in old mail-order catalogs show mechanical gadgets that fit the authors' observation that American inventors have worked hard to produce gadgetry that saves rather trivial amounts of time and energy. Pictures can also be found in *Those Were the Good Old Days* by Edgar R. Jones (Simon and Schuster, 1959 & 1979), a collection of American advertising from 1880 to 1950. Some modern mail-order houses specialize in gadgetry; use their catalogs for pictures.

Perhaps students can identify kinds of gadgetry (as distinct from immensely useful machines like electric typewriters and power lawnmowers) that made significant contributions to the postwar prosperity: battery-operated tools and toys of all kinds, power windows on cars, electric pencil sharpeners, electric carving knives, electric toothbrushes, etc.

• In discussing GNP, be sure that students understand the reason for making comparisons "in 1958 dollars." Introduce the term constant dollars, meaning dollars having the same purchasing power at different periods.

• You might point out that after the fairly severe postwar recession in 1946–1948, GNP kept rising except for mild setbacks in 1954, 1957–1958, and 1960–1961. The longest continuous stretch of prosperity in our history began in 1961 and lasted for 116 months—almost ten years; this long expansion faltered twice but with no actual decline.

The long stretch of price stability from 1948 to 1965 is truly remarkable. The average annual inflation rate (price rise) of less than 2 percent can be compared with today's rate. Point out that the 1.7 percent average rise meant that some years were a little lower and some a little higher. When the rate reached around 3 percent, there were worries about "creeping inflation." Such a low figure as 3 percent would later appear to be almost a miracle.

Later chapters deal with the inflation of the late 1960s and the 1970s. Here you should probably emphasize the price stability. Students might speculate on the advantages of such a situation.

- Have students compare the impact of the automobile on the post-World War II period with that of the 1920s. (See T.G. activity in Section 4, Chapter 22.)

- Have a panel discussion on "The Future of the Automobile." Students can consult various almanacs and the *Readers' Guide* for helpful resource material. Suggested subtopics might include: (a) trends toward smaller cars, (b) satisfying the need for fuel conservation, (c) meeting the need for pollution controls, (d) meeting competition from foreign car makers, (e) who will be able to afford a car.

- Add these 1978 TV statistics to those given in the text: 99.9 percent of the American homes had one or more of the 138 million sets currently in use. The average American watched over 30 hours of television per week; the family set was turned on more than 6 hours per day. Some 90 million Americans viewed television nightly.

Use the above statistics to stimulate interest in a panel discussion on "The Impact of Television on American Life." Have students use the *Readers' Guide* to locate recent magazine articles on the topic. Suggested questions for discussion include:

1. How is TV watching related to success in school?

2. Is TV more effective than radio or the newspaper in learning about current news? Why?

3. To what extent do TV shows influence the behavior of the impressionable young? Is this good or bad? Why? (See Van Dyke, *Juvenile Delinquency*, Ginn, pages 47–48.)

4. What improvements can be made in TV programming? Should television be used as an educational tool in the school? How?

- Have an individual or committee report on the inventions of Edwin H. Land (Polaroid camera) and Chester F. Carlson (xerography). Emphasize how the copying machine has changed office and business procedures in recent years. See recent encyclopedias and the *Readers' Guide* for helpful background material.

- A number of recent films show the changes brought into our society through automation and the computer. These include *Automation: What It Is and What It Does* (14 min) and *Age of Specialization* (13 min).

- Interesting observations on obsolescence can be found in Lerner, *America as a Civilization*, pp. 867–868, and Boorstin, *The Americans—The Democratic Experience*, Chapter 58, "Flow Technology: The Road to the Annual Model."

Section 3 (pp. 635–636)
Education and Religion

Instructional Objectives Students will be able to

1. Trace the growth of higher education in America in the twentieth century.

2. Evaluate the goals of modern education, particularly "progressive education."

3. Survey the religious scene in contemporary America.

Teaching Suggestions This brief section and the next one can be combined as a single reading assignment. Use any extra available time for work on special reports.

- Have an individual or committee report on the life and contribution to education of John Dewey, with emphasis on his ideas concerning "progressive education." Encyclopedia articles and chapters in histories of education such as Cremin and Borrowman's *Public Schools in Our Democracy* will provide background material.

Or you might tell students that Dewey taught at the Universities of Minnesota, Michigan, and Chicago before his long tenure at Columbia (1904–1930). His influence on American education was great, especially on progressive education, which he conceived to be "learning by doing" and a "continuous reconstruction of living experience based on activity directed by the child." After 1950, the philosophy was criticized for its de-emphasis of academic disciplines. However, much of the American approach to education today—such as stressing the needs of the student rather than subject matter—can still be traced to Dewey's influence.

More recent scholars, such as James Bryant Conant (see text), are less enthusiastic about progressive education and democratic equality in the classroom. In *The American High School Today*, Conant contended, "In all but a few of the schools I visited, the majority of bright boys and girls were not working hard enough" (page 23) and ". . . students should be grouped according to ability . . ." (page 49).

Discuss the above as part of the student report, and relate it to your own school.

- Gather memorabilia of high school education in the 1950s: yearbooks, school newspapers, lists of course offerings, lists of behavior rules, dress codes, etc. Find a current or retired teacher who will provide some recollections of the 1950s (but advise the person that you want *the class* to make comparisons with today). After students have looked at and heard evidence about the 1950s, have them point out differences with today. Do they find any of the 1950 features better? Why? Have them try to account for changes that they identify.

• Use item 4 of *Your Region in History* (p. 639) as a chief vehicle for discussing recent trends in organized religion in America. Try to obtain tape recordings of interviews or class presentations by members of the clergy to use "next year" or with other classes. The tapes should be edited to keep them to a reasonable length.

Section 4 (pp. 636–639)
Art and the Machine

Instructional Objectives   Students will be able to

1. Explain how modern art reflects our contemporary society.

2. List some contemporary American authors and their works.

3. Summarize the impact of books and other cultural forces in our society.

Teaching Suggestions   Cooperation with art instructors and English teachers seems particularly important for planning activities for this brief chapter section. If you feel ill at ease in explaining modern art (or have a bias against it), perhaps a knowledgeable person will prepare a tape recording of commentary on selected reproductions of paintings and photos of sculpture (to save repeated appearances in class). Then you can show the pictures while the recording is played. Sound filmstrips providing explanations are also available.

Of course, plan a trip to a local art museum if that is feasible.

• Ask students who have read any of the authors named on page 638—or others of a comparable stature who have produced fiction since 1945—to review what they have read and point out to the class how the writer reflected the postwar era.

• Have an individual or a committee make a bulletin board display of book jackets, descriptive reviews, and photos of contemporary authors. See the librarian for access to materials in the vertical files.

• Students interested in the theater or modern dance can report on developments since 1945.

CHAPTER REVIEW
Meeting Our Earlier Selves

1. See column 2, page 625, for changes in farming. Some of these changes were under way before 1950, of course. If you live in an agricultural community, students will know about, or be able to find out, numerous specific changes.

2. Expected social changes include (a) rising political conservatism, (b) attempts of younger workers to limit improvements in Social Security and welfare programs that benefit the elderly, (c) more public housing for the elderly, (d) more sharing of big homes by groups of elderly persons, (e) adult education programs aimed at elderly persons, (f) possibly some declines in crime rates, since a high proportion of crimes are committed by youthful offenders, (g) conversion of surplus school houses for programs for the elderly—or just sold off. Note other developments already apparent.

3. Answers will vary according to personal experience and student familiarity with computer technology. One important effect is declining demand for untrained office and factory workers.

4. Again, answers will vary according to personal experience. On the learning of history outside of reading history books, students should recall history learned from movies and TV, stories told by older people, history learned from well-researched historical novels, oral history heard on tapes, visits to historical sites, etc., etc.

5. Answers will depend on personal experience, but students should note the continued vigor of churches and synagogues, the number of religious programs on radio and TV, the flourishing of religious cults, the testimony of religious influence declared by prominent Americans from time to time (President Carter, for example), the legal battle over religious exercises in the schools, the religious arguments used in the abortion debate, and so on.

Questions for Today

1. Generally the student will need to identify gadgetry or other mechanical devices that were not around 20 to 25 years ago. On the matter of improvements in machines over the past twenty years or so, students should point to transistor technology, microcomputers, new synthetic materials, pollution controls, improved paints and lacquers, improved auto tires, etc.

CHAPTER 31

Years of Hope and Promise

Introducing the Chapter Although your students were born after the "thousand days" of John F. Kennedy's Presidency, they will be aware that no President was more respected and admired by young people. Through an overview of Kennedy's life and death, the reading of selected passages from among the many biographies, films, and records, you might recapture some of the spirit of the "New Frontier."

Notice the drawing used with the chapter introductions of this unit: the eagle surrounded by olive branches. Call attention to the text's cover design—or any national symbol showing the eagle clutching arrows in one claw and an olive branch in the other. When students see the "war and peace" symbolism of the drawing, ask them to judge the appropriateness of the drawing for the three chapters of this unit.

A good way to start is to read aloud or play a recording of President Kennedy's Inaugural Address of January 20, 1961, concerning which Speaker of the House Sam Rayburn said, "That speech he made out there was better than Lincoln."

The speech is found in many documentary histories of the period, including *The Annals of America*, Volume 18, 1961–1968. Recordings containing the speech (and many others) include *The Making of the President 1960, John F. Kennedy—The Presidential Years—1960–1963, JFK, John Fitzgerald Kennedy—A Memorial Album*. These albums also contain numerous photographs and descriptive summaries. Your media center may have some of them.

After you have read or played the speech, discuss:

1. Why was the speech widely praised? (inspiring message; placed emphasis on seeking new frontiers after moderate Eisenhower approach; well delivered; eloquent)

2. How would the line "we shall pay any price" be received by youth today?

3. Would you be inspired today by Kennedy's "ask what you can do for your country"? Explain.

Section 1 (pp. 642–646)
John F. Kennedy Wins

Instructional Objectives Students will be able to

1. Summarize the campaign and election of 1960.

2. Trace the background and career of John F. Kennedy.

3. Explain why Kennedy's Inaugural Address was one of history's best.

4. Relate how Kennedy selected his brother Robert for a Cabinet post.

Teaching Suggestions Historians point out that the election of 1960 is one of the most interesting in our history —a hotly contested campaign between two young candidates, a number of significant issues, and a series of TV debates. Use audiovisual materials to re-create the drama of the campaign.

• Have students compare the Kennedy-Nixon debates with the Lincoln-Douglas debates (p. 265). (for the Presidency instead of the Senate; length of speeches; size of audiences; probably fewer issues discussed by Lincoln-Douglas; etc.)

In 1980 two critics of the proposed TV debates between Carter and Reagan proposed that the essential elements of the Lincoln-Douglas debates should be restored by having four or so 90-minute debates, each devoted to a major issue. Each speaker would open with a 3-minute preview statement, and then each would present a 20-minute position statement on the issue. Six alternating rebuttal speeches would follow. Finally each speaker would be allowed five minutes for a conclusion. Have students comment on such a format.

• *Handout lesson:* Use *Handout 44* to focus on Kennedy's views on the religious issue. Have students write answers to the questions on the back of the handout.

• Point out that the election of 1960 was not only one of the most bitterly contested in our history, but also was incredibly close, with Kennedy receiving 49.7 percent of the popular vote to Nixon's 49.6 percent. Later, experts explained the "ifs" of the results: If a combination of 32,500 voters in Texas and Illinois had changed their minds during the last moment of decision, those states would have gone to Nixon, along with the election. Also, the results might have been different if Nixon had not injured his knee (which delayed his campaigning), if President Eisenhower had started campaigning for Nixon a little earlier, and if Nixon had campaigned harder in the big industrial states rather than fulfill his ill-advised promise to visit all 50 states.

E. J. Hughes, an Eisenhower aide, concluded in *The Ordeal of Power* (page 280), "If any one specific and deliberate decision contributed fatally to his [Nixon's] defeat, this was his personal readiness ever to appear in televised debate with Kennedy."

• Have a student report based on Donovan's *P.T.-109*. Or tell students that John F. Kennedy enlisted in the navy (the army rejected him) as a Lt. (j.g.). He became commander of a torpedo boat, *P.T.-109,* which in September 1943 in the South Pacific was sheared in half by a Japanese destroyer, the *Amagiri.* Despite an injury to his back, Kennedy swam for five hours in the dark Pacific, all the while towing with a lifebelt strap a seaman who couldn't swim.

Finally rescued from an island inhabited by friendly natives, Kennedy received the Purple Heart and the Navy and Marine Corps Medal for his heroic feat. Later, ill with malaria, his weight down to 125 pounds, his back in constant pain, he was sent back to the United States to be a naval instructor.

• Students may be interested in reading *Profiles in Courage.* It describes the courage of American statesmen who risked their careers by supporting unpopular issues or voting in opposition to the majority.

As the text indicates, Kennedy himself needed courage to write his book, mostly in a hospital bed. The Library of Congress sent him cartons of books for reference, and his friend Theodore Sorensen did most of the required "legwork."

The book became a bestseller, and was quickly translated into several languages. According to historian James MacGregor Burns, the winning of the Pulitzer Prize meant more to Kennedy than any prize except the Presidency itself.

• There have been a number of sons who followed fathers and/or grandfathers with distinguished political careers, but the Kennedy brothers may be unique. Point out that JFK's older brother, killed in the war, had been the family's hope for a distinguished political career. Besides Robert and Edward, the family was honored by a politically active brother-in-law, Sargent Shriver, who was the Democratic candidate for Vice-President in 1972.

Section 2 (pp. 646–649)
Learning Hard Lessons

Instructional Objectives   Students will be able to

1. Locate Laos, and explain our involvement there.
2. Explain how Kennedy inherited and approved a plan for the invasion of Cuba and why the effort failed.
3. Describe developments in the Berlin problem during the Kennedy administration.
4. Compare Kennedy's "flexible response" to other approaches to international crises.
5. Show how the Alliance for Progress and the Peace Corps fit into the nation's postwar foreign policy.

Teaching Suggestions   This brief section could be combined with the next one as a single reading assignment, particularly since both deal with foreign policy. You might have students prepare a timeline of the events in the two sections.

• Have students locate Laos on the map on page 672. Note that it is a neighbor of China, Vietnam, Cambodia, Thailand, and Burma. Mountainous with dense forests, it is about twice the size of Pennsylvania. Then discuss the following:

1. Why were we involved in Laos? (as part of our global commitment to contain the spread of communism)
2. How did Kennedy avoid the use of American troops in Laos? (through a conference that set up a neutral government, followed by a treaty)

Point out that despite the settlement, the American CIA, the North Vietnamese, and the Chinese remained active in Laos thereafter, including during our subsequent involvement in the Vietnam War. As recently as 1979, 30,000 Vietnamese troops remained in Laos. Laotians would be among the stream of refugees entering the United States following the end of the Vietnam War.

• Point out that Kennedy learned of the planned Bay of Pigs invasion shortly after his inaugural. He was "wary and reserved in his reaction" (Schlesinger), but was assured that all would go well. Also, he was reminded, there wasn't much time to stop the operation because Castro was about to receive warplanes and other supplies from Russia. And the rainy season would soon begin, which would "bog down" the invasion. Under much pressure from CIA director Allen Dulles, who argued that for Kennedy to reject the invasion would be "refusing to allow freedom-loving exiles to deliver their homeland from a Communist dictatorship," Kennedy gave in to the pressure (much to his regret later).

Allen Dulles resigned after the fiasco.

• Despite the tough talk to the President at Vienna, Khrushchev enjoyed chatting with Jacqueline Kennedy. He told her that one of the Soviet space dogs had had puppies. Jokingly, she replied, "Why don't you send me one?" In due time, the Russian ambassador delivered a small, nondescript dog to the Oval Room at the White House. Asked the President: "How did this dog get here?" Replied Jackie, "I'm afraid I asked Khrushchev for it in Vienna. I was just running out of things to say."

• The inset map on page 590 shows the Berlin Wall. It eventually became a 29-mile concrete and wire barrier. The map shows gates—guarded, of course—to permit approved traffic. Since 1963, limited public passage between the two zones has been permitted during selected holidays. Frequent escape attempts have continued over the years despite armed guards, barbed wire, and watch dogs trained to kill.

• On "flexible response" you might ask students if America's postwar response to Communist expansion was ever truly inflexible—despite Dulles's bold talk of "massive retaliation." Students might review the kinds of responses the Truman and Eisenhower administrations had actually made: scattered bases around the globe, defensive alliances, military and economic aid, summit conferences, a small contingent of troops to Lebanon, use of large forces in Korea, fleet contingents to Taiwan, etc. It was probably true, of course, that too much of the defense dollar had come to be devoted to preparation for nuclear warfare and that some change in emphasis was needed.

- In discussing the Alliance for Progress, you might have students review the Marshall Plan (pp. 585–587) and then speculate on reasons why it was such a success while the Alliance for Progress must be counted a failure. The text discussion of the Alliance for Progress supplies a number of inferences. (rebuilding easier than creating modern industrial societies, in large part because of the presence of worker skills and work habits; basic reforms not required in Europe; less feeling of urgency in Latin America; etc.)

Point out that the Alliance for Progress just sort of faded away. The United States began to stress increased trade with Latin America in place of financial aid. Some of the slack in loans was taken up by the World Bank.

- Keep a file of former Peace Corps volunteers in your community. Encourage students to interview a former volunteer. Besides finding out personal details about that person's experience, have the interviewers obtain a reaction to the evaluation provided in the text. Use item 3 in *Meeting our Earlier Selves* and item 3 in *Questions for Today* (p. 659) in the subsequent class discussion. The film *A Mission of Discovery* (28 min) surveys the history and activities of the Peace Corps.

Point out that the Peace Corps continued into the 1980s —with volunteers offering over 300 skills to nations in need of services. In 1971 the agency was taken over by ACTION, which also administered VISTA (Volunteers in Service to America).

Section 3 (pp. 649–653)
Facing Communist Challenges

Instructional Objectives Students will be able to

1. Describe our missile program of the 1960s and efforts towards disarmament.
2. Tell how Kennedy averted war with the Russians over the Cuban missile crisis.
3. Summarize the problems in Vietnam that led to increased American involvement.

Teaching Suggestions The problems discussed in this section should seem almost current to students, since the search for solutions is never ending. You can convey the tensions of the early 1960s through a close examination of the Cuban missile crisis. Films, readings, and records will be helpful as supplementary aids.

- The three topics on the missile gap, disarmament, and the test-ban treaty should probably be consolidated in the class discussion. Help students to see one of the basic issues—a very persistent issue: How important is equality or superiority in long-range nuclear weaponry when each side has the capability (presumably) to destroy the other? (Collect statements and articles on both sides of this issue for students to use in reports or debates.)

Some teachers may want, at this point, to bring in the later developments on arms limitation—the SALT treaties (see index)—to deepen understanding by avoiding a piecemeal approach.

Tell students that, in opposing the test-ban treaty in 1963, nuclear scientist Edward Teller told the Senate, "If you ratify this treaty . . . you will have given away the future safety of this country." Students might speculate on why he wanted the testing program to continue. How would such a statement on nuclear testing be greeted today?

Explanation of the civil defense programs of the early 1960s, particularly the recommendations for bomb shelters, will help students get a sense of public worries over nuclear warfare.

Tell students that the U.S.S. *George Washington* in 1960 was the first submarine to be able to fire a guided missile while submerged. Since then, such submarines no longer are primarily intended to destroy ships at sea, but rather to fire missiles at land targets deep within enemy borders. In theory then, the nation could retaliate even if all of our land missile sites were destroyed.

- The climax of the space exploration story comes in the chapter on the Nixon administration. Consider filling in some gaps in the story between Shepherd's flight and the moon landing via lecture, student report, or film.

You might point out that Kennedy's decision to begin the effort for the moon landing was preceded by little or no public debate. Congress would have to approve—by making appropriations from time to time—but it was the President's decision. In a sense, JFK was issuing a challenge to Congress and the nation: Here is what we are going to do! Are you going to back me on this project? You might ask students to express a value judgment on such a procedure. Encourage students to find out how older relatives and friends reacted to Kennedy's challenge at that time or during the following years of the space program.

- *Handout lesson:* Use *Handout 45* for students to read portions of Kennedy's radio and TV address on the Cuban missile crisis and to consider the four other options—besides the "quarantine"—that were given serious consideration by the President and his advisers. Use the questions at the end of the handout for a written assignment or in class discussion. On item 2, Russell said that "a blockade is too slow, too risky." Kennedy replied that it was "easy to hold those opinions if you did not have the responsibility of action."

- The Cuban missile crisis appears as a case study of presidential decision-making in *American Political Behavior,* Revised Edition (Ginn), pp. 315–323.

- The following account provides an interesting sidelight on the Cuban missile crisis:

    The first real overture came from the Russians when John Scali, an American Broadcasting Company correspondent, was contacted by a Russian friend named Aleksander Fomin at the Soviet Embassy. Would Scali meet him in a Washington restaurant for an urgent message? If the Russians would promise to remove their missiles under UN supervision, would the U.S. promise not to invade Cuba?

    Scali conveyed the message to the State Department. They accepted the offer. The machinery of official communication began, and UN Secretary-General U Thant was notified. Then Khrushchev blustered once more with a new tactic: Would the U.S. also pledge removal of its missiles from Turkey as part of the deal? Kennedy said no. A U-2 plane was shot down over Cuba by the Russians as war still seemed a possibility. The President resisted demands that we bomb the Cuban bases and airfields.

    The United States gave the Russians 24 hours before we would "take military action." At last Khrushchev's answer came in—as the text reports.

Section 4 (pp. 653–656)
A New Frontier

Instructional Objectives   Students will be able to

1. Give examples of the successes and failures of Kennedy's "New Frontier" proposals.

2. Summarize Kennedy's attempts to meet the problem of civil rights.

3. Tell about the "black revolt" of the 1960s, including the attempt to enroll blacks in southern colleges.

4. Describe the "Freedom March" on Washington in 1963.

Teaching Suggestions   The second sentence of the section introduction offers an opportunity to consider this proposition: When the voters elect a President by a decisive majority, they are demanding (giving him a mandate) that he carry out the policies he endorsed or promised.

Discussion should lead to understanding of the variety of reasons that people vote as they do: for a person's good looks or eloquence; because of party loyalty; because they hate the opponent; because of the candidate's stand on one or two issues—not all of them; etc.

Then point out that it is only natural, of course, for "big winners" to interpret their victory as voter approval of their promises and policies.

- Divide available discussion time between JFK's economic policies and the civil rights issue.

    Point out that four significant measures that would later be adopted were proposed by Kennedy or were in the planning stage: general aid to education, Medicare, the war on poverty, and a strong civil rights law.

- Have you discussed or checked on student comprehension of the term *productivity* up to now? It is one of the most important concepts in economics. (See the example in the topic "Controlling the economy.") Unless it gets help from the outside—an undependable circumstance, any society can improve its level of economic welfare only by producing more. More production can come in two ways: (a) by putting more people to work and (b) by workers producing more per hour, day, or year. The latter idea is *productivity:* worker output in a given unit of time. (Productivity is usually measured in *output per worker hour*.)

    Who are the most productive workers? They are the ones who produce the most per hour, day, or week. Should they receive the greater rewards? Why? (Yes! chiefly because if they are not rewarded, why should they put out the extra effort required for their high output?)

    You can discuss productivity in connection with school work. A person who can read with understanding ten pages while another person reads only five is twice as productive. A person who answers correctly one question per minute is more productive than the person who requires two minutes per question. Or the person who writes an excellent composition in half an hour is more productive than the person who writes a poor composition in the same period of time. How do we usually reward the more productive student: with more honors in the way of grades, prizes, praise, etc., and the more productive student has more time to devote to other activities.

    With some kind of background like that provided above, you are now ready to explore the notion of wage-price guidelines like those that the Kennedy administration tried to impose. First, you should find out whether or not students understand that wage levels are the chief component of the prices we pay for most of the goods and services we use. Most of the cost of a loaf of bread, or a haircut, or a refrigerator, or a high school education is wages. Taking our economy as a whole, around three-fourths of the costs of producing goods and services represents wages. The rest represents a return to owners of natural resources and people who have supplied capital. A general rise in wage rates therefore, without a corresponding rise in production, can only result in a rise in prices.

    A second point to make is that wage-price guidelines are extremely difficult to administer. The idea may be admirable when wage hikes are linked to rises in productivity, but how can officials possibly keep track of the thousand upon thousands of wage agreements while at the same time checking up to see if they really are tied to advances in productivity? It seems that wage-price controls or guidelines can have only a temporary influence on inflation without hiring an army of enforcers. And such an effective enforcement program only adds to inflation, since the enforcers have to be paid. Notice that JFK had temporary success in halting a rise in steel prices, but later the steel companies were able to raise their prices without serious objection from the government.

    Perhaps a final point to make is that if wage raises are not tied to productivity then some people are getting more money at the expense of others. If coal miners get higher wages without producing more coal per worker hour, consumers will have to pay more for coal or mine owners will have to accept less. Perhaps some coal mines will shut down because consumers will not pay the higher prices or because mine owners can find better places to invest their money. Then some miners will be laid off because those who are getting higher wages have made coal mining too costly.

- Students should note that the 1960 election was held about the time that the nation was entering a recession—a fairly mild one as it turned out. JFK capitalized on this situation, promising to "get the country moving again." It is notable that now for the first time there was wide support for the Keynesian theory that the national government had an obligation to stimulate the economy to promote prosperity. Congress was willing to go along with measures that boosted spending but balked at a general cut in taxes.

- Tell students that JFK, although attracting more black votes in 1960 than did Nixon, was nonetheless considered by blacks to be somewhat "detached" concerning the need for civil rights. After having breakfast with Kennedy before the 1960 Democratic convention, Martin Luther King said that Kennedy showed a "definite concern but not a 'depthed' understanding." During the campaign, Kennedy stressed that action "to eliminate racial and religious discrimination from American society" might be more successful through "the executive branch without congressional action." He was aware that it would be difficult to pass civil rights legislation in Congress. He had to be satisfied with appointments of blacks to important posts, along with orders protecting civil rights. Kennedy realized that progress would be slow.

Yet for blacks, led by King and other spokesmen, the time had come for change, and the "black revolt" was the result.

- Have an individual or committee report on the experiences of James Meredith and other blacks seeking to enroll in segregated universities. See histories of the period and Meredith's *Three Years in Mississippi,* Lord's *The Past That Would Not Die,* or Dorman's *We Shall Overcome* for details. Then discuss the following:

1. What issues were involved in Meredith's attempt to enroll at the University of Mississippi? (constitutional rights under Article XIV; a federal court order that he be admitted. From Barnett's viewpoint, state vs. federal authority; said Barnett, "We will not surrender to the evil and illegal forces of tyranny.")

2. Do you support the call-out of federal troops? Why? (various answers. Said Kennedy, "We can't take a chance with Meredith's life or let the governor make the federal government look foolish.")

3. In a speech to the nation, Kennedy said, "Our nation is founded on the principle that observance of the law is the eternal safeguard of liberty. . . . Americans are free to disagree with the law, but not to disobey it." Do you agree? Explain.

- Show a film dealing with the civil rights movement and Martin Luther King's role in it during this time.

Your media center may also have helpful sound filmstrips, including the series *The 1960s: A Decade of Hope and Despair* and *The Black American* (Part 5), "Struggle for Civil and Human Rights."

Point out that King's further role in the civil rights movement will be discussed in the next chapter. Encourage now the reading of biographies pertaining to King.

- Tell students that Martin Luther King described Birmingham, Alabama, as "the most segregated city in the United States" in the early 1960s. When JFK saw a newspaper photo of a police dog lunging at a frightened black woman, he said that it made him "sick," adding that "I can well understand why the blacks of Birmingham are tired of being asked to be patient."

Governor George Wallace brought in 700 "deputies" to intimidate the blacks. JFK responded with an order to fly 3000 federal troops to an air base near Birmingham. Wallace withdrew his forces under overwhelming pressure, and cool-headed local black and white leaders restored an uneasy truce to Birmingham.

- Call attention to the picture of the March on Washington on page 657. Play a recording of King's "I Have a Dream" speech or read portions of it to the class. The entire speech appears in *The Annals of America,* volume 18, pp. 156–159. Then raise questions like the following:

1. Has King's dream become a reality?

2. What do you think the March on Washington achieved? (national exposure on TV and in the press, contributing eventually to passage of the Civil Rights Act of 1964)

Section 5 (pp. 657–659)
The Tragic End

Instructional Objectives Students will be able to

1. Give highlights of President Kennedy's assassination and public reaction to his death.

2. Summarize the findings of the Warren Commission.

3. Evaluate the Kennedy years.

Teaching Suggestions As with the death of Lincoln, no future generation can fully re-live the trauma of the death of President Kennedy. The many films, records, and other documentary sources that are available will be most helpful aids. Encourage students to ask older family members to recall their reactions to the news of the assassination.

The film *An American Tragedy—The Death of President Kennedy* (21 min) portrays the incredible event.

For further reading, suggest Manchester's *Death of a President* and Bishop's *The Day Kennedy Was Shot.*

- Point out that the period from Friday, November 22, 1963, when Kennedy was assassinated, to Monday, November 25, when the President was buried in Arlington National Cemetery, was one of deep shock and then grief for the nation. By Sunday, great crowds began to gather in the chilly sunshine. On Monday they waited patiently for the solemn funeral cortege to go by, while millions watched on television. Most of America's daily activities came to a halt.

  Six gray-white horses drew the caisson from the Capitol to the cathedral and then to the cemetery, while bands slowly played funeral marches. Behind the Kennedy family, an assemblage of the world's leaders slowly followed. And finally the martyred President was in his last resting place as the presidential salute of 21 guns reverberated across the Arlington hills. The eternal flame was lit; a Marine guard began his vigil; the silent crowd dispersed in the gathering darkness.

- Some background on Lee Harvey Oswald will interest students. Oswald was born in New Orleans in 1939, two months after the death of his father. At a very young age Oswald was placed in an orphanage by his impoverished mother. His education in New York City was limited. He returned at 17 to New Orleans and joined the Marine Corps. After completing his duty, he became interested in communism and defected to the Soviet Union. There he married Marina Prusakova and decided to return to the United States. He obtained various jobs in the Dallas area, including one with the Texas School Book Depository (from the windows of which shots were fired at President Kennedy).

  Oswald had become involved in a "Fair Play for Cuba" Committee. He purchased a rifle and shot at—without being apprehended—Maj. Gen. Edwin A. Walker, a well-known anti-Communist leader. Oswald knew that the Kennedy motorcade would pass the building where he worked. Later, investigation revealed that the rifle used to kill Kennedy was the one purchased by Oswald.

  The Warren Commission concluded that Oswald's motive for shooting Kennedy included a desire to have a "place in history," and also may have been influenced by the "atmosphere of extreme opposition to President Kennedy that was present in some parts of the Dallas community." The Commission reported that Oswald, acting alone, was not motivated by any membership in a Soviet or Cuban conspiracy organization.

  As the text indicates, the investigation continued. For further reading, suggest Bishop's *The Day Kennedy Was Shot* and abridged versions of the *Report of the President's Commission on the Assassination of President John F. Kennedy.*

- Tell students that historians find it hard to evaluate Kennedy as a President. Said Henry Steele Commager: "We'll never know. But he was a distinguished President. He gave a new vitality to the Presidency, a new excitement." Said Arthur B. Schlesinger, Jr.: "He gave the country back to itself. He accomplished so much in so little time—the new hope for peace." A *Time* magazine essay (November 26, 1965) said that "Kennedy . . . may have made his mark by the magic force of his personality." A Harvard professor remarked that Kennedy was great not for what he did but for "what he was about to do."

CHAPTER REVIEW

Meeting Our Earlier Selves

1. Charm may help a President recruit people to serve in his administration and to "sell" his proposals to decision makers. Charm may help reduce feelings of apathy among citizens. However, charm could be harmful to the extent that it stands in the way of clear analysis. The answer should be, "I'll accept your proposal on its merits, not because I like you personally."

2. Judging from long-term results, Berlin was most successful because the Soviet leaders did not get their way. The solution in Laos merely postponed the Communist takeover. The Bay of Pigs episode in Cuba was a disaster.

3. The Peace Corps succeeded (a) in improving the lives of needy people abroad in small ways, (b) in teaching people in the developing lands ways to help themselves, (c) in creating some good will toward the United States in some places, (d) in broadening the cultural and social outlook of many volunteers, (e) in "lifting the nation's spirit," and (f) in demonstrating the practicality—and problems—of volunteer service programs.

4. Unlike the Korean situation, the Vietnam situation was more clearly a civil war; it involved disregard of agreements made at a peace conference; it began as guerrilla warfare, not the clash of armies; it did not have UN support against the Communists; for a considerable time the United States provided only "advisers" and weapons, not armed forces.

5. Foreign affairs: Cuban missile crisis, nuclear test-ban treaty, Trade Expansion Act, firmness on Berlin, and Peace Corps might be mentioned. Domestic affairs: stepped-up defense program, moon race decision, Area Redevelopment Act, and others might be considered. Some would consider his proposals on civil rights and on poverty as major achievements in that they came to fruition under LBJ.

Questions for Today

1. In 1979 the Soviet presence had been known for some time; it constituted no serious menace; the problem appeared to be a political tempest in a teapot; it quickly disappeared from public attention with nothing accomplished; etc.

2. Attention should focus on tax cuts, wage-price controls or guidelines, size of budget deficits, efforts to balance budget, etc.

3. For the second part of this item, use the *U.S. Government Manual* to see if the agency ACTION still exists; if not, what agency—if any—has replaced it. The history of discontinued agencies appears in the Appendix.

CHAPTER 32

Lyndon B. Johnson—from Success to Failure

Introducing the Chapter After students have read the chapter introduction, have them explain the chapter title: In what broad areas were there successes? Where was there failure?

• Find out if students remember LBJ from an earlier chapter (pp. 613, 615). What do they recall about Johnson from the Kennedy chapter? What impressions do these earlier references give them about Lyndon Johnson? Ask students if they have other impressions of Lyndon Johnson from what they have read and heard.

Section 1 (pp. 660–664)
Taking the Reins

Instructional Objectives Students will be able to

1. Describe the background and career of Lyndon B. Johnson.
2. List the key provisions of the Civil Rights Act of 1964.
3. Name and describe three other major laws enacted in 1964.
4. Summarize the election of 1964, giving reasons for Johnson's landslide victory.

Teaching Suggestions In introducing Lyndon B. Johnson, review the circumstances under which Kennedy chose Johnson to be his running mate in 1960. Note earlier references to LBJ on pages 613 and 615 if you have not already done so.

• In discussing Section Review item 2, "What were Johnson's qualifications for the Presidency?" write student responses on the chalkboard under two headings: Training and Personal Characteristics.

A second approach is to remind students of a President's varied roles: Chief Executive; Commander in Chief; Chief Legislator; Chief Diplomat; Party Chief. You might list these on the board and have students suggest phrases to put under each title. These phrases should deal with both training (experience) and personal characteristics.

Considering all the roles a President must perform, physical vigor would appear to be a significant qualification. (FDR was vigorous, until running for his fourth term, despite being crippled.) LBJ was vigorous, but point out that he had recovered from a severe heart attack suffered in July 1955 while serving as the Senate majority leader. In the long list of desirable attributes of a candidate for President or Vice-President, what rank should voters give to the item "top physical condition"? Students might respond to this question.

• Have students begin a notebook chart on major public laws passed in the Johnson administration, specifying title (when given) and chief provisions.

A second approach is to specify various categories of laws passed, and under each category list the chief accomplishments. Categories might be Civil Rights; Antipoverty Programs; Education; Housing and Urban Development; Social Security and Welfare; Environment; Consumer Protection; Transportation; Miscellaneous.

The authors keep the narrative lively by limiting the number of laws named and described. A major teaching decision will concern which, if any, additional laws to introduce. Are there any that have particular relevance for your community?

• Encourage students to choose one of the domestic laws/programs enacted in the Johnson administration for further study. Were there other significant provisions? What were, or still are, some key issues involved (arguments for and against)? Is the law or program still in effect? Have any changes been made? How well did the law accomplish its objectives? Have there been any adverse side effects? Any unexpected benefits?

• The above kinds of analytical questions, of course, can be used in lecture/class discussion of any particular programs that you want to elaborate on.

• The Civil Rights Act of 1964 serves as a case study of how a bill becomes a law in *American Political Behavior,* Revised Edition (Ginn), pp. 358–370.

• After students have identified the candidates and issues in the 1964 presidential election, use questions like the following for class discussion:

1. What right-wing, or conservative, positions did Goldwater take on the campaign issues? What would be a left-wing, or extreme liberal, position on each of these issues?

2. Goldwater told the Republican convention (and the TV audience): "Extremism in the defense of liberty is no vice." Then he went on to say: "And let me remind you that moderation in the pursuit of justice is no virtue." Why would you expect the delegates to cheer these sentences? (wanted a real conservative this time) Do you agree with these statements? (One can make a strong case for *moderation* as a technique in resolving

public issues. Besides this point, guide students to see that "liberty" and "justice" are glittering generalities; you can't tell whether or not you would agree with Goldwater until you had a fairly clear understanding of what he meant by "liberty" and "justice.")

3. Would you prefer to have "a choice, not an echo"—a conservative facing a liberal as the candidates of the two major parties? Or would you prefer that each major party nominate a "moderate," a middle-of-the roader"? Why?

4. Suppose Kennedy had not been shot and was running for reelection in 1964. Would he have had the same kind of landslide victory over Goldwater? (Use a question like this to have students consider some of Johnson's special advantages in the campaign: sympathy vote for someone cast into the office; no responsibility for the Kennedy failures; credit for getting major bills passed in only a few months as President; etc.)

5. Which were more important in the 1964 election: the issues or the personalities of the candidates? Explain. (Political analysts say that the issues were exceptionally important in this election. Goldwater simply scared too many people with his bold stands.)

6. Why would Johnson get practically all the votes of black Americans? (Goldwater had voted against the Civil Rights Act; his stands on the issues held out little hope for black progress.) Mention that Goldwater's audiences were almost entirely white. Reporter Richard Rovere wrote that in cities like Memphis, Atlanta, and New Orleans, "We would peer beyond the edges of crowds and down side streets to see if we could spot a single black."

You might comment on Richard Nixon's surprising absence from the thick of the fray in the 1964 election after his narrow loss to Kennedy in 1960. In 1962 he ran for governor of California and lost to Pat Brown. Nettled by the long record of press antagonism to him, Nixon announced to the assembled reporters: "You won't have Nixon to kick around anymore because, gentlemen, this is my last press conference."

Section 2 (pp. 664–667)
The Great Society

Instructional Objectives Students will be able to

1. Define "Great Society" and give examples of its programs.
2. Describe how Rachel Carson and others alerted Americans to environmental issues.
3. Explain the role of Ralph Nader in getting laws passed for consumer protection.
4. Show how steeply rising federal spending on social programs and the Vietnam War promoted inflation.

Teaching Suggestions All the laws—or extensions of them—described in this section continue to have an impact today. Examine these effects as you discuss the programs.

• *Handout lesson:* Use *Handout 46* to give students further highlights of LBJ's "Great Society" speech at the University of Michigan. You might point out that from time to time our Presidents have chosen to make significant policy statements away from the White House or Capitol, instead choosing a commencement address or a convention speech to some major interest group as the vehicle. In this case it was a commencement address—as was the case with Secretary of State Marshall's proposal of the Marshall Plan at Harvard in 1947.

Use the questions at the end of the handout for a writing assignment or for class discussion. (1) A brief definition is an adaptation of the first sentence of paragraph 3: "The Great Society is one that provides abundance and liberty for all." (2–3) Answers are obvious. (4) One can cite gains in all three areas—but setbacks as well. Advances in the quality of the environment are perhaps the most visible—affecting both the countryside and the city.

The term "creative federalism" in the last paragraph will likely require some explanation. It refers to cooperative efforts by the federal government and the states to achieve particular social goals. In practice, it has meant the federal government supplying a portion of money—often half or more—for a particular program, along with a set of rules on how it is to be spent, with states or localities paying the rest of the bill. (The federal portions are known as *grants-in-aid*.) A big part of the effort to make the sharing more creative was to supply grants (to state and local agencies and nonprofit groups) for demonstration projects. Mention those you know about in education, including grants to your school district.

• Have students continue the chart of Johnson-supported laws and programs begun in the previous chapter section.

• Students should become aware of the significant differences in Medicare and Medicaid. Medicare is national health insurance for persons age 65 or older. Medicaid is a federal-state welfare program for needy persons under age 65, but the measure of need is hardship in paying medical bills, not the poverty level of other welfare programs. Medicare payments come from a separate Social Security fund financed by the Social Security tax. Medicaid funds come out of general tax revenues. Medicare uses private agencies, chiefly Blue Cross and Blue Shield, to process claims and make payments to hospitals, nursing homes, and physicians. (The private agency contracts with the Social Security Administration to supply this service.) Medicaid suppliers are paid directly by local welfare offices.

You might want to point out that there is a welfare aspect to Medicare in that the earliest beneficiaries had paid nothing into the special health insurance fund. And many later beneficiaries paid only very small amounts. (A similar situation exists in the old-age and disability parts of Social Security in that many beneficiaries receive benefits far beyond the level of their contributions.)

A very significant economic aspect of the two programs is that they boosted demand for medical services but made no direct provision for increasing supply (of physicians, hospital beds, etc.). Therefore, health care costs rose much faster than some other items that are part of the Consumer Price Index.

- Be prepared to help students with facts to carry out activity 1 in *Your Region in History,* or find a volunteer to obtain the information from the Superintendent's office.

Tell students that in signing the Elementary and Secondary Education Act, LBJ said, "I believe deeply that no law I have signed or will ever sign means more to the future of America." Rising amounts of federal aid to education have been the rule since 1965. Use questions like the following in discussing the 1965 law:

1. Should federal aid be limited to public schools? Why? (Note that some kinds of aid to parochial education have won Supreme Court approval—transportation expense, for example—when directed to students, not to the schools.)

2. Should general federal aid to education be based chiefly on the number of poverty-level students in the district? Why? How does such a formula affect your district?

3. Should federal financial aid to the schools be used to further the social objective of achieving racial balance in the schools? Why?

4. General federal aid to education was long opposed on grounds that the federal government would come to control public education. To what extent, if any, have such fears been justified? (Help students identify areas where federal requirements have impinged on local control, such as busing for racial balance, sex equality, administrative paper work, etc.)

5. Has the 1965 education act turned out to be as important as LBJ predicted? (Require students to consider the long-range effects of other Great Society laws and programs.)

- A major problem in dealing with the Johnson administration's environmental laws and programs is their sheer number and scope. There are so many options for lecture, student reports, and films that time may impinge on consideration of other topics. Find out where in the typical high school student's courses she or he will get "ecology" exposure. Then try to determine where the American history class can make a significant contribution.

- Not surprisingly, the senior author, Librarian of Congress Daniel Boorstin, puts unusual emphasis on the power of books in shaping public opinion and thereby influencing policy makers. Ask students if they recall an influential book named in the Kennedy chapter. (Harrington's *The Other America*) It was probably not as widely read by the general public, but it was influential among policy makers. Another book that we have mentioned in this guide is the one in which John Maynard Keynes propounded his theory on the business cycle. It influenced professional economists, who in turn influenced key decision makers.

Students might think of other kinds of media that are influential in shaping public opinion on particular policy issues: a series of newspaper articles, a powerful TV documentary, etc.

Point out that much of Nader's influence on public policy in the years after 1965 came from his formation of a research and lobbying "public interest" group, members of whom were known as "Nader's Raiders."

- Ask students if they can recall what was probably the first example of consumer protective legislation. (The Meat Inspection Act of 1906, followed quickly by the Pure Food and Drug Act the same year) What book and author had tremendous influence in that instance? (*The Jungle* by Upton Sinclair)

A worthwhile student report would be "Consumer Safety Rules and Issues since 1965." For a quick review of the two federal agencies particularly concerned with consumer protection, see *Consumer Product Safety Commission* and *Federal Trade Commission* in the current or a recent edition of the *United States Government Manual.*

The issues on product safety are often explored in consumer journals like *Consumer Reports.* See the *Readers' Guide* for titles of articles that suggest that there may be over-regulation in the field of consumer protection. (If people want to "live dangerously," how difficult should government make it for them to do so? Is a seat-belt warning device enough, or should motorists be unable to drive without fastening the seat belt or having some kind of air-bag restraint?)

- The persistence of serious inflation in the years since 1968 will be discussed again—and again. Review the economic principles as often as necessary.

Section 3 (pp. 667–671)
Black Revolt and Youth Rebellion

Instructional Objectives   Students will be able to

1. Describe the nature of the black revolt and evaluate explanations of its causes.

2. Summarize the provisions of the Voting Rights Act of 1965.

3. Compare the philosophies of Martin Luther King, Malcolm X, and Stokely Carmichael.

4. Survey the social changes in America that affected the outlook of youth and point out some typical ways they reacted in the 1960s.

Teaching Suggestions   Notice a key explanation of the black revolt and the youth rebellion in the section introduction: hopes aroused + lack of quick results = frustration, anger, violence. Return to this explanation after students have read and discussed the section.

- Have students compile a list of frustrations of northern urban blacks in the mid-1960s, starting with the two examples given in the last paragraph on page 667: housing segregation; job discrimination against qualified blacks. Among others, students might mention these: high general unemployment among blacks; extremely high black teen-age unemployment; unsatisfactory public transportation to new factories and offices in the suburbs; unfair treatment by police; low black ownership of businesses in the black community; etc.

Other grievances can be found in the *Report of the Commission on Civil Disorders* (the Kerner Commission Report) or summaries of it.

- Use a film, lecture, or student report(s) to explore the nature of the urban riots of 1965–1968. Notice the frequency of outbreaks starting over some police action (not necessarily brutal), the characteristics of participants, the nature of the violence, the victims, government efforts to control and end the violence, etc.

- Encourage students to give brief reports on several black leaders who rejected Martin Luther King's philosophy and leadership: Malcolm X, Elijah Muhammad, Stokely Carmichael, Eldridge Cleaver, Huey Newton, and others. Ask for emphasis on beliefs and programs.

- Historian Benjamin Quarles points out that "Black Power" spokespersons deemphasized integration (but did not reject it entirely as the Black Muslims did) and called for black leadership of organizations working for black equality. White liberals should "give up policy-making positions and turn their attention to combatting racism among their fellow Caucasians." Carmichael said: "This does not mean we don't welcome help, or friends. But we want the right to decide whether anyone is, in fact, our friend."

A brief lesson on how different people in the 1960s reacted to the term "Black Power" appears in the original edition of *American Political Behavior* (Ginn, 1972, 1974), pp. 112–116. It includes unfavorable responses to the Black Power movement by King and by Roy Wilkins.

Closely associated with "Black Power" was the movement to instill "Black Pride." A favorite slogan was "Black is beautiful," and much emphasis was given to instilling pride in the African heritage.

- Students should add the Voting Rights Act of 1965 to their chart of Johnson administration laws and programs.

- In connection with the "youth rebellion," explore with students the meaning of such terms as *alienation, generation gap,* and *counterculture.* Sociology texts should be useful.

A lesson on *political alienation,* keyed in part to the 1960s, appears in *American Political Behavior,* Revised Edition, pp. 145–155. This lesson reinforces two points made in the history text: the small size of the rebel contingent and the different reactions of the hippies and the militants. One pollster estimated the politically alienated to be 10 percent of young adults in the '60s. Part of these were the political apathetics (hippies and their sympathizers). The others were political activists.

- Alienation, of course, is a matter of degree. The "generation gap" for some young people was much wider than for others. Discuss with students your observations (and the observations of other adults obtained through student interviews) of some milder manifestations of youth rebellion of the late 1960s—particularly in your school and community. What were some signs of rejection of old values? Were students making any "demands"?

- Links between youth rebellion and drug abuse are shown in the topic "Why Do Young Americans Become Involved with Drug Abuse" in Chapter 1 of Van Dyke's *Youth and the Drug Problem* (Ginn).

Section 4 (pp. 672–677)
"The Most Unpopular War"

Instructional Objectives Students will be able to

1. Explain why the Vietnam War became our "most unpopular war."

2. Describe how LBJ widened U.S. involvement in the war.

3. Tell why and how the U.S. intervened in the Dominican Republic.

4. Explain Johnson's "credibility gap" and its political consequences for LBJ.

5. Describe the aftermath of the assassination of Martin Luther King, Jr.

Teaching Suggestions You might review the stages of the Vietnam War leading to the Tonkin Gulf Resolution. If you have students prepare a timeline of the war, have them review the references in Chapters 29 and 31.

- Have students review "The Tonkin Gulf Resolution" in the text, and locate the Gulf of Tonkin on the map on page 672. Note that the gulf is several hundred miles north of the demilitarized zone of the 17th parallel. Then have them write a brief newspaper or TV story headed "LBJ Urges Passage of Tonkin Gulf Resolution." Use complete sentences. Include (a) what powers LBJ sought; (b) why he sought them; (c) who opposed LBJ in the Senate and why. Have several students read aloud their stories. Discuss these. Collect the papers for evaluation. Then discuss the following:

1. Why was the passage of the resolution so popular, since it meant further enlargement of the war? (At this date, most Americans wanted to "contain" communism, forcefully if necessary; LBJ was very persuasive; Goldwater had just accused the Johnson team of "timidity before communism," thus causing LBJ to match Goldwater's militancy.)

2. Why did Senator Morse oppose the resolution? (wanted discussion before voting)

• Students will visualize better LBJ's escalation of the Vietnam War if you write the following on the chalkboard:

AMERICAN TROOPS IN VIETNAM

1963— 16,500
1965— 161,000
1966— 400,000
1967— 475,000

Point out that the peace movement—particularly among college students—and the growing resistance to the draft reached a great intensity by 1967, setting the stage for a "peace" candidate—Senator Eugene McCarthy of Minnesota—as the 1968 presidential campaign approached.

• For a pictorial overview of the war in Vietnam, see Gurney's *A Pictorial History of the United States Army*, pages 768–796. Also well illustrated is the recently issued Boston Publishing's 7-volume series, *The Vietnam Experience*. For the reaction to the war at home, see Time-Life's *This Fabulous Century, 1960–1970*, "Doves and Hawks," pages 200–225.

• Tell students that the Vietnam War was the first war to be extensively televised. Yesterday's military activities could be seen on tonight's news programs. Show a film compiled from these reports, such as National Education Television's *Last Reflections of a War* (44 min) and CBS News's *Vietnam: An Historical Document* (56 min). After showing a film, have students write an evaluation or review. Have several students read aloud their reviews. Collect papers for evaluation.

• Point out that U.S. intervention in the Dominican Republic stirred up some traditional anti-American feeling in Latin America. But this was partly offset by the fear of communism, for Castro had been encouraging left-wing revolutionists throughout the region. The anti-Yankee feelings were also softened a bit when five South American countries sent token units for a peacekeeping force. Juan Bosch's opponent, Balaguer, defeated Bosch by a 3–2 margin in a supervised election in 1966, and then the peace force left.

• Tell students that when Senator Eugene McCarthy announced late in 1967 that as a peace candidate he would challenge LBJ in the spring primaries, he attracted a volunteer army of youthful supporters that critics labeled a "children's crusade." At first, the challenge to LBJ—overwhelming victor in 1964—seemed slight enough. A nationwide Harris poll indicated that McCarthy would lose to the President in the primaries by a 63–17 vote. In New Hampshire, scene of the first primary, Governor John W. King told his people that McCarthy was a "spokesman for surrender."

Yet the energetic McCarthy supporters campaigned on, and almost defeated the President (who did not campaign in the state—see text). Some analysts feel that this omen of defeat prompted Johnson's decision not to seek reelection. However, in *The Vantage Point,* the President says that Lady Bird "did not want me to be a candidate in 1968." Also, he lists various persons to whom he told in confidence that he would not run again. Thereafter, the decision was kept a secret to the last, and the revealing words did not appear on the teleprompter used for LBJ's announcement of withdrawal.

• Have an individual or committee report on the death of Martin Luther King and the subsequent impact throughout America.

Or tell students that King had gone to Memphis to support a strike by the city's sanitation men, most of whom were black. Criticized earlier for staying at a Holiday Inn, King moved to a $13-a-night room at the black-owned Lorraine Motel. While waiting to go to dinner on the evening of April 4, 1968, King went out onto the balcony of the room. From a roominghouse window across the street a sniper fired a single rifle shot that killed King almost instantly. Caught later in London after intensive investigation was a white ex-convict named James Earl Ray, who pleaded guilty to the shooting of King and was sentenced to 99 years in prison.

Ironically, the death of America's most famous spokesman for nonviolence brought violence unparalleled in our history. Washington alone had 10 deaths. At least 2600 fires resulted from the riots; nearly 3000 persons were arrested; over 21,000 injured. To restore order in the cities, 55,000 soldiers were called to duty.

Later, as over 100 million people watched on television, nearly 100,000 mourners followed King's coffin on a farm cart in the slow march to the Georgia grave. On King's monument was inscribed:

Free at last, free at last;
Thank God Almighty, I'm free at last.

CHAPTER REVIEW

Meeting Our Earlier Selves

1. Measures include general aid to education, the Civil Rights Act of 1964, a general tax cut, war on poverty legislation, and medical insurance for the aged. Truman, Eisenhower, and Kennedy had all proposed changes in the immigration law. LBJ's outstanding success can be attributed to sympathy for JFK's efforts, the economic prosperity that suggested that the nation could afford to spread the wealth, the support of southern conservatives in Congress who wanted to see a southern President succeed, a rising moral fervor in the land—sparked by outrage over the treatment of blacks seeking equality, and—perhaps above all—LBJ's skills in influencing members of Congress acquired during his years as majority leader. Special influences on particular measures can also be mentioned.

2. Changes would include the right to be served in places of public accommodation—restaurants, hotels, etc., the end of segregation in the use of tax-supported facilities, fewer obstructions placed on the right to vote, wider availability of jobs, a speeding up of school desegregation, and a consequent improvement in the self-image of southern blacks.

3. *Greater equality* for blacks in the Civil Rights Act of 1964; for poor people in the Equal Opportunity Act; for schools in poverty areas; for the aged in medical care; for Appalachia in development funds; for lower-income people in obtaining housing; for immigrants from areas that formerly had low quotas; etc. *Better environment* in various anti-pollution laws, the Wilderness Act, and highway beautification. *Consumer protection* in the Truth-in-Packaging Act, in safety standards for new cars and tires, in pesticide controls, and in other federal laws not cited specifically in the text.

4. King: blacks should stir the conscience of the nation by nonviolent protest of injustice and thereby win corrective laws. Malcolm X (or Elijah Muhammad): blacks should form a separate society and win political power to run their own affairs. Stokely Carmichael: win political power by having blacks run their civil rights movement and their own institutions. These generalizations, of course, are gross simplifications. King appears to have had the most lasting influence on the civil rights movement—in part because his philosophy was the least antagonistic to people who would have to share power and rewards.

5. Answers, of course, will vary. Stopping aggression and the "domino theory" are closely related. Fighting for "honor" or "reputation" seems the least compelling reason to many people. There are other ways to defend honor and reputation.

6. Antiwar activists gave reasons like these: (a) Undemocratic South Vietnam didn't deserve our help; (b) we had helped to obstruct the decision for Vietnam unification by not signing the agreements made by the Geneva Conference of 1954; (c) a Communist Vietnam was no real menace to the United States; (d) victory would require a much heavier commitment, including perhaps nuclear warfare, with heavy loss of life; (e) U.S. involvement was alienating some of our important allies; (f) the nation had been misled by LBJ and other leaders; etc.

Questions for Today

1. Lessons to be learned include: (a) huge spending programs tend to produce galloping inflation; (b) laws may be passed too fast for proper study and provision for proper administration; (c) a flood of laws increases the likelihood that some will work at cross purposes—conflicting objectives; (d) a rash of laws lifts public expectations beyond reason, and when there are failures, apathy and alienation result; (e) many of the laws are likely to have adverse effects on business—excessive regulation raising the costs of producing goods and services; etc.

2. Answers will depend on the time that students are using this book. It might be pointed out, however, that the number of neglected problems that government has tried to solve by passing laws has rapidly diminished. Thus the opportunities for publishing an influential book that sparks positive government action have probably declined.

3. By 1980, young people were observed to be more career oriented and less politically active. Considerable protest activity, employing the techniques of the 1960s, appeared on the nuclear power issue—and on draft registration when that program was renewed in 1980. Answers will depend on the temper of the times when students are using this text.

4. After Vietnam there appeared to be more reluctance to become actively involved in national struggles where native Communists, or leftists supported by Communists, were trying to seize power. Answers will depend on particular foreign policy issues that are in the news when students are studying this chapter.

CHAPTER 33

The Rise and Fall of Richard Nixon

Introducing the Chapter Have students recall incidents in the career of Richard Nixon up to the 1968 election as reported in their textbook (see index) and as revealed in class discussion. Ask: If a person knew nothing about Nixon as President but had read about his earlier political activities, what are some impressions they might have about him?

Section 1 (pp. 678–681)
Electing the President, 1968

Instructional Objectives Students will be able to

1. Name and describe the leading contenders for President in 1968.
2. Summarize the 1968 election campaign and the results.
3. Explain why Nixon won the election.
4. Identify several controversial decisions of the Supreme Court under Chief Justice Warren and show why they disturbed some Americans.

Teaching Suggestions The turbulent drama of the 1968 election can be conveyed in part through films and magazine illustrations of the period. Encourage the reading of books portraying the campaign. Students may become emotionally involved in the issues; explore these in depth.

- Remind students that back in 1928 no incumbent President was running for election; it was Al Smith against Herbert Hoover. The next time would be 1952: Stevenson against Eisenhower. In 1960 it would happen again: Kennedy against Nixon. When LBJ bowed out, again there was no incumbent President in the field. That added excitement to the nominating process. Help students sense the excitement for the Democratic nomination: two liberal, antiwar Democrats—Robert F. Kennedy and Eugene McCarthy—frantically trying to win delegates in the presidential primaries with liberal Hubert Humphrey standing on the sidelines, hoping and expecting to get the nomination because of loyalty to LBJ. Contrast this race with more recent campaigns when presidential primary elections had become ever more crucial to winning the nomination.

Use pictures, including the one on text page 680, to capture the turbulence of the 1968 Democratic convention. Then use questions like the following to guide discussion:

1. What do you think the result might have been if Robert Kennedy had escaped assassination? (Two antiwar, anti-Johnson candidates against a Johnson supporter, unless they joined forces, might still have meant victory for Humphrey; other possibilities, of course.)
2. Would you expect the behavior of the demonstrators to hurt or to help Humphrey get the nomination?
3. How would the incidents at the Democratic convention hurt Humphrey in the subsequent campaign?
4. Speculate on why Republican conventions seem to be less boisterous than those held by the Democrats.
5. Speculate on how George Wallace affected the election outcome. (Political analysts tend to believe that Wallace took more votes from Humphrey than from Nixon. Many blue-collar workers who ordinarily supported the Democrats appear to have voted for Wallace; it appears to have been a backlash against black militancy and the urban riots. Nixon also benefitted from that backlash.)
6. Why would Wallace hope that the election would be thrown into the House of Representatives?

- Tell students that Senators Eugene McCarthy and Robert F. Kennedy engaged in bitter primary campaigns in which they competed for youthful voters who were opposed to the Vietnam War. When Kennedy entered the race after the New Hampshire primary, McCarthy's supporters felt that their candidate had taken all the political risks (in opposing LBJ), while Kennedy now sought to collect the rewards of victory. McCarthy refused suggestions that he withdraw and throw his support to Kennedy.

After McCarthy won in Oregon, Kennedy needed a victory in California to stay in the race. He got it by a vote of 46 to 42 percent. At the victory party, Kennedy's last words were: "I think we can end the divisions within the United States, the violence."

Point out that subsequently much pressure was placed on 36-year-old Senator Ted Kennedy to accept a draft for either the Vice-Presidency or the Presidency. However, Ted refused, asserting that Nixon would argue "that I was too young, that I had no record in public life strong enough to recommend me for the high office of President."

- Ask students to identify situations in the years immediately preceding the 1968 election campaign which, besides the rise in crime, made "law and order" a hot campaign issue. (urban riots, campus take-overs, protest demonstrations, rising drug abuse, etc.)

Call attention to the fact that the unpopular Supreme Court cases dealing with criminal justice had been handed down in the five years prior to the election. *Escobedo* and *Miranda* aroused far more controversy than did *Gideon* and the death penalty case.

Ask students to identify the controversy aroused by the other cases cited in the text: *Brown,* apportionment of seats in legislatures and Congress, and religious exercises in the public schools.

• Point out some of the disparities in legislative districts that finally prompted the Supreme Court to order reapportionment. In Florida 13 percent of the voters could elect a controlling majority in the legislature. In Georgia three counties had representation equal to one county that had 100 times as many people.

The first case was *Baker* v. *Carr* (1962), dealing with unequal representation in the Tennessee legislature. Its importance was that the Court said that citizens claiming unfair representation could bring a lawsuit into a federal court and then the court could order the legislature to reapportion.

In *Reynolds* v. *Sims* (1964) the Supreme Court said that *both* houses of a state legislature must be apportioned according to population.

Another case in 1964, *Wesberry* v. *Sanders,* led to the ruling that congressional districts must be substantially equal. It involved Georgia, where one district had 823,680 people while another had only 272,154.

• The religious exercise cases cited in the text are *Engle* v. *Vitale* (1962) and *Abington Township School District* v. *Schempp* (1963). The religious exercise controversy has refused to die. For example, the bill setting up the new U.S. Education Department contained a provision supporting voluntary prayer in classrooms, but it was finally deleted by the House-Senate conference committee (Sept. 1980).

Section 2 (pp. 680–688)
Nixon's First Term

Instructional Objectives Students will be able to

1. Describe how President Nixon organized the White House staff.
2. Give highlights of the 1969 *Apollo 11* moon-landing mission.
3. Tell why and how the Vietnam War ended.
4. Describe Nixon's efforts to reduce tensions with Red China and the Soviet Union.
5. Tell how the Nixon administration attempted to deal with inflation.

Teaching Suggestions In assigning the reading for this lesson, you might tell students that Nixon won reelection in 1972 with the largest popular majority in history. Ask them to note accomplishments in the first term that would help to persuade the public that Nixon deserved another four years in the White House.

• The idea that it was hard to discover the "real" Nixon (col. 2, p. 682) served as grist for numerous political cartoons—Nixon peeking out from behind several masks, or selecting from a drawerful of masks the one to wear today, for example. Look for examples in cartoon collections, such as books by Herblock. A popular TV game shown in the Nixon era, "To Tell the Truth," had a panel trying to guess which of three persons was an invited guest. The final line in each case was "Will the real [guest's name] please stand up." Jokesters used this line: "Will the real Richard Nixon please stand up."

• In connection with the topic "The Nixon White House" you might point out that it was considered quite revolutionary when the Administrative Reorganization Act of 1939 gave FDR six administrative assistants. One of the agencies created by FDR, under the authority of that act, was the White House Office. It consisted of these six assistants with their small staffs, the President's own secretaries, and certain other personal aides of the President and First Lady.

The White House Office grew to 238 persons, including secretaries and clerks, by 1950, and to 375 by 1960 under Eisenhower. The 1964 budget set the number at 265. But then it started growing again. The 1978–79 *Government Manual* listed 80 titles and officeholders in the White House Office. Check the current edition for size and for titles of some of the President's personal aides.

• Appoint a committee to create a bulletin board display of the flight of *Apollo 11* to the moon. Use the vertical file of the media center for illustrative material. Students may also have models for display purposes.

• Show the film *America on the Moon—Apollo 11* (9 min). Have students write a summary or review of the film. Collect these for evaluation purposes. For further reading, suggest Armstrong, Collins, and Aldrin's *First on the Moon.*

• If students have begun a timeline of the Vietnam War, have them complete it now. Overall references used include Section 1, Chapter 29; Section 3, Chapter 31; the present section; and Section 3, Chapter 35.

• Help students to see Nixon's apparent strategy in fulfilling his commitment to end U.S. military involvement in the Vietnam War: withdraw ground troops while keeping up—even expanding—the air war as a way of supporting South Vietnam and of putting increasing pressure on North Vietnam to agree to cease-fire arrangements acceptable to the United States.

• In discussing "Moscow and Peking," call special attention to the last sentence on page 686. Have students point out Nixon's "credentials as a fighter against communism." Why did this make his China policy more acceptable than if it had been pursued by a President regarded as "soft on communism"? (public confidence that a hardliner would not be easily fooled)

• Have students review the paragraph on page 652 dealing with the split that had developed between Communist

China and the Soviet Union. Ask them to speculate on how that split made it easier for Nixon and Kissinger to deal with China. (Made China more eager to be friendly. Americans could accept dealings with an enemy of the Soviet Union.) Then ask: Why did a deal with Peking seem to require a deal with Moscow?

• Point out that a second SALT agreement is discussed in Chapter 35.

• Encourage a student to report on U.S.-Chinese relations since 1972.

• An analysis of inflation in 1968–1972 can be found in the annual *Economic Report of the President* of 1973 and later. The 1969–1970 recession was brought on, in part, by restrictive fiscal policy (putting restraints on federal spending) and monetary policy (curbing the rise in the money supply). But, somewhat surprisingly, the ailment (inflation) failed to respond to the medicine (recession). Here was a new phenomenon—continued serious inflation in a recession. It would show up in later recessions as well.

Point out that the measures taken by the Nixon administration, including the wage-price controls (which were not relaxed until 1973), did bring down the inflation rate —for one year. A chief problem with such controls is that they simply hold the lid on pressures that keep building up; they don't get at the malady. Prices rose rapidly the next year.

• *Handout lesson:* Give each student a copy of Handout 47 for a review of some major bills passed in the first term of the Nixon administration. Use in class discussion for further help in answering the question "Why did Nixon win reelection handily in 1972?"

As a writing exercise, tell students to act as text authors and write an additional topic for Section 2 using the information in the handout. Tell them to be selective, not to use all topics. For example, one new topic might be "Promoting public health and safety"; it would mention toy safety, cigarette ads, waste disposal, water pollution, and probably drug control. Another topic, "Helping states and localities," would use revenue sharing, mass transit, airport aid, waste disposal, and water pollution.

• *Handout lesson:* Use Handout 48 to acquaint students with a significant law passed near the end of Nixon's first term— provision for an all-volunteer army. After students have read the excerpts, have them write answers to the comprehension questions.

Follow this exercise with a brief lecture or student report on the successes and failures of the all-volunteer army and of the resumption of draft registration in 1980. Use questions like these to guide discussion:

1. Speculate on reasons why Congress failed to follow the commission's recommendations to have a stand-by draft.

2. What are some incentives besides pay that attract armed forces volunteers in peacetime?

3. What additional incentives can you think of to spur the recruitment of able and energetic volunteers at a reasonable cost?

Section 3 (pp. 688–695)
The Fall

Instructional Objectives   Students will be able to

1. Explain how Nixon and his aides became involved in illegal activities during the 1972 election campaign.

2. Describe the candidates, issues, and results of the 1972 election.

3. Trace the course of the Watergate affair from the break-in to Nixon's resignation.

4. Explain why and how Gerald Ford became Vice-President in 1973.

5. Tell how the United States came to have a gasoline shortage in 1973–1974.

Teaching Suggestions   To get the full dramatic impact of the Watergate story, students should read the entire section at one sitting. Then they can go back and re-read particular topics to answer the Section Review items.

• After students demonstrate understanding of the national security link in Nixon's pursuit of "enemies" (Section Review item 2), you might explore the justification (a) for secrecy in matters of national security and (b) for special limits on civil rights and liberties when national security is at stake.

• Have students compare the 1972 election with another landslide election eight years earlier when Johnson defeated Goldwater. What important element do these two elections have in common? (the extreme positions taken by the losers in each case)

Discuss—or review—accomplishments of Nixon's first term that made him appear to be the moderate in this campaign. (recognition of China and detente with Soviet Union; progress of Vietnam peace talks; efforts to deal with inflation by curbing spending; see also in Handout 47 the moderate nature of laws passed in the first term)

Then ask why conservatives would continue to support Nixon. (Wallace out of race, so Nixon only alternative; Nixon had by no means become a liberal; domestic programs passed in first term were not all Nixon inspired; Nixon continued to stress law and order; etc.)

• A brief account of the Watergate Affair emphasizing the role of the *Washington Post* reporters appears in *American Political Behavior*, Revised Edition (Ginn), pp. 326–329.

• *Handout lesson:* Give each student a copy of Handout 49, which provides a chronology of the Watergate Affair. It can be used to find out what parts of the story students would like to know more about. It also provides a few

Chapter 33

additional names in the cast of characters. Use it with Section Review item 5.

• Compare Nixon's threatened impeachment with the Andrew Johnson impeachment case: motives, accusations, results. Use this occasion to review the impeachment process. Ask students to speculate on the likelihood of a President ever being removed by impeachment. (The Nixon and Agnew resignations suggest that this is the most likely way that any future case would be handled—unless a President really believed the charges were insubstantial or that he was innocent.)

CHAPTER REVIEW

Meeting Our Earlier Selves

1. The sheer growth of federal programs and the far-reaching involvement of the nation in world affairs would demand a larger staff. Equally important is the proliferation of agencies outside the regular Cabinet departments; help in coordinating the work of these agencies is needed. Coordination is also a severe problem throughout the executive branch, because many laws and programs work at cross-purposes or overlap. Modern transportation permits the President great mobility, requiring more help on scheduling time, arranging travel, preparing speeches, etc.

Problems of a large staff: too much authority funneling into hands of one or two people; too much shielding of President from other important decision makers; attention of President to running the White House staff may distract from essential policy making; costs of large staff; etc.

2. The resolution, no doubt, reflected popular opinion that there were insufficient curbs on the President's power to wage war. If the war had been popular, there would not have been this concern.

3. Nixon ruled out (a) a one-sided withdrawal and (b) terms that would amount to a disguised American defeat. In the end, these conditions were not met. The United States withdrew; the North Vietnamese did not. It would be hard to interpret the cease-fire terms as anything but an American defeat—and it soon became obvious that the Communists were the clear victors.

4. Recognition of China was momentous because (a) it overturned a long-standing element of American foreign policy, (b) it paved the way for a second Communist nation to have veto power in the UN Security Council, and (c) it made possible joint U.S.-Chinese efforts to restrain the Soviet Union. Other points might be cited.

Nixon was well suited to bring about this change of policy because of his strong anti-Communist credentials. People who doubted the wisdom of such a move would trust that a hard-liner on communism would not be fooled easily.

5. The resignation of Agnew permitted Nixon to nominate Ford for Vice-President under the provisions of the 25th Amendment; then Nixon's own resignation elevated Ford to the Presidency.

6. Other Watergate by-products: Ford's pardon of Nixon might have been a factor in his defeat in 1976; spurred passage of campaign financing laws; contributed to shake-up of CIA; may have elevated public respect for investigative reporting; gave particular "good guys" in the affair valuable political exposure; etc.

Questions for Today

1. Law and order is likely to be a persistent issue. Watch newspapers and magazines for current remedies. Some recent ones have been (a) mandatory jail terms for certain offenses or for repeaters; (b) supervised work for offenders to repay the victims; (c) treating juveniles as adults for certain crimes; (d) less probation without exacting some kind of punishment; etc.

2. By 1980 all of Indochina had fallen to the Communists, but democratic regimes hardly had a chance in these lands despite the outcome of the Vietnam War. Other lands of Southeast Asia had been able to stay neutral or anti-Communist. Thus, to some extent, the theory may have been both proved and disproved.

3. By 1980 the Nixon policy on China looked remarkably good. China was moving away from rigid positions of the Mao era, trade and cultural relations with the United States were on the upswing, and China was behaving reasonably toward Taiwan. Conditions, of course, could change rapidly.

CHAPTER 34

A New World of Competition

Introducing the Chapter The thrust of this chapter is the struggle for equality. That struggle, as the chapter introduction points out, is inevitably linked with freedom—particularly the freedom to compete.

Students might try to imagine a society where complete equality is the goal. Nobody is allowed to lag behind or get ahead of anyone else: in schooling, in jobs, in income, in housing, even in clothing or other aspects of personal attractiveness. Dull, isn't it? But also there is no freedom.

Then try to imagine a society where complete freedom is the goal. The strongest and most forceful soon manage to take charge. The weakest are left with little or nothing. The strong, of course, will try to maintain their position—and thus even freedom is lost.

Looking at the absolutes in such a way may help students see that a society needs to maintain some kind of balance between freedom and equality.

Section 1 (pp. 699–705)
The Two Traditions

Instructional Objectives Students will be able to

1. Explain Jefferson's idea of a "natural aristocracy," and show that the southern social system excluded vast numbers of people from rising to positions of leadership.
2. Describe inequalities faced by blacks and immigrants in our history.
3. Show that the end of legal school segregation often did not result in racially balanced schools, and tell how the courts tried to achieve racial balance.
4. Define and give examples of "affirmative action."
5. Describe the progress made by blacks in recent decades.

Teaching Suggestions Use the Section Review to find topics students are interested in exploring further.

• Notice what the authors say about Jefferson's understanding of the phrase "all men are created equal"—that is, equal before the law. Point out that the phrase "equal protection of the law" in the Fourteenth Amendment—one of the most important phrases in the Constitution—has much the same meaning.

• De facto segregation, or racial imbalance, in schools remains a sensitive subject. Share your own insights on the problem with students. Collect articles from professional magazines that throw light—not heat—on the subject.

• *Competency exercise—expressing numerical data in sentences:* The following information from a recent edition of the *Statistical Abstract* shows gains by blacks and whites in recent years. (You may wish to update these figures by using the current edition.) Have students use each set of figures to write a sentence. Insist on proper spelling and punctuation.

— Percent of 3 to 5 year olds in nursery school and kindergarten:

1967—whites, 31.8%; blacks, 29.8%

1978—whites, 49.5%; blacks 53.1%

— Median years of school completed by persons 25 and over:

1960—all persons, 10.6; blacks, 8.0

1978—all persons, 12.4; blacks, 11.7

— Percent of high school graduates enrolled in college:

1970—whites, 25.9%; blacks, 19.4%

1978—whites, 24.8%; blacks, 24.2%

— Unemployment rate of males age 16 and over:

1970—whites, 4.4%; blacks, 7.3%

1978—whites, 5.2%; blacks, 10.9%

— Money income of households:

1967—whites, $7,449; blacks, $4,325

1977—whites, $14,272; blacks, $8,422

— Percent of persons below the poverty level:

1966—whites, 11.3%; blacks and others, 39.8%

1977—whites, 8.9%; blacks and others, 29.0%

Example: In 1967 there was a slightly higher percentage of white children enrolled in nursery school and kindergarten, but by 1977 black children had moved ahead—53.1% to 49.5%.

• By 1980 the nation and the Supreme Court had failed to reach a consensus on affirmative action. Notice the 5–4 vote on both the *Bakke* and *Weber* cases. Collect news items of further decisions as they are made. Share with students the arguments of the majority and any dissenters.

The third major affirmative action case, *Fullilove* v. *Klutznick* was decided July 2, 1980, by a 6–3 vote. The case challenged a provision of the Public Works Employment Act of 1977 that required the Department of Commerce to set aside 10 percent of federal public works contracts for construction firms owned by specified minorities. The Court decided that Congress had the power to set quotas to correct past racial injustices. The decision appeared to leave open the question of whether federal agencies on their own could set contract quotas. Dissenters objected on the ground that the equal protection clause of the Fourteenth Amendment clearly and absolutely forbids such type of favored treatment.

Section 2 (pp. 705–709)
Women Seek Equality

Instructional Objectives   Students will be able to

1. Name highlights in the women's equality movement to 1920.

2. Tell how Betty Friedan reawakened the women's rights movement.

3. Identify barriers that women's rights leaders want removed to give women real equality.

4. Provide figures that show the inequality of women.

5. Show how the Civil Rights Act of 1964 has promoted sex equality.

6. List arguments used by supporters and opponents of the proposed Equal Rights Amendment (ERA).

7. Show how the executive and judicial branches of the federal government have aided the women's rights movement.

Teaching Suggestions   Keep a folder of news items and magazine articles on new developments in the women's rights movement. Use the items for lecture notes, bulletin board displays, and student reports.

• Review the list of grievances proclaimed at the Seneca Falls convention in 1848. (See *Handout 17.*) Students should notice that, despite the major attention given thereafter to women's suffrage, women in the mid-19th century had a broad list of grievances.

• Encourage students to prepare brief reports on leaders of, or organizations that are a part of, the current women's rights movement.

• Arrange for a student to interview the manager or personnel director of a business firm that employs a substantial number of both men and women. Find out how, if at all, the firm has had to adapt to government regulations on the hiring, promotion, and pay of female workers. Solicit views on why women—in their own plant or elsewhere—lag behind men in supervisory positions.

• Discuss changes that sex-equality legislation, bureaucratic rulings, and court decisions have brought to your school. First solicit responses from students about changes that they are aware of.

• Point out that federal government pressure on firms holding government contracts and on schools and colleges receiving federal aid in any form was part of the affirmative action activity described in the previous section.

An extremely critical report on the zealousness of the federal bureaucracy in pushing affirmative action appears in "A Little School Against the Big Bureaucracy" in *Reader's Digest,* August 1980, pp. 159–165.

• Tell students that the nation has several million more voting-age women than men and that an estimated 4.5 million more women than men voted in the 1976 presidential election. Ask: (a) What do these figures say about the potential political power of women? (b) How do you account for the difficulties faced in getting ERA ratified and other sex-equality legislation enacted?

These questions can lead to such insights as these: (a) There is no political agenda on which women (or men) are overwhelmingly united. (b) Men still far outnumber women in public office. (c) Some of the goals of the women's rights movement are not attainable through legislation.

• *Handout lesson:* Have students use the data on *Handout 50* to make bar graphs showing changes in the economic position of women. Then have them answer the questions to test their skill in interpreting the graphs. Answers to the interpretive questions follow: (1) four; (2) 1960; (3) those with children under age 6—more than tripled while the other group doubled; (4) after 1970—for the figures shown here; (5) $72; (6) pay, or weekly earnings.

The following questions might then be used to guide discussion:

1. By 1978 about half of all working-age married women were in the labor force compared to only about one-fourth in 1950. What does this situation have to do with the goals of the women's rights movement?

2. What effects, if any, would you expect the big rise in the employment of mothers with young children to have on childrearing?

3. What responsibilities, according to women's rights leaders, does the employment of married women put on husbands?

4. Why is the big rise in professional, technical, and managerial jobs of major significance in the struggle for sex equality?

5. Why has the pay of full-time female workers continued to lag behind that of male workers?

• For further reading on the status of women and the women's liberation movement, you might arrange with your school's librarian to have a special display of books in the library or in your classroom. Helpful titles include Barandall's *America's Working Women*, Degler's *At Odds —Women and the Family in America from the Revolution to the Present*, Landau's *Woman! Woman! Feminism in America*, and *MS* magazine's *The Decade of Women—A History of the Seventies in Words and Pictures*. Extended lists are found in Subject Guide to *Books in Print*.

Section 3 (pp. 710–713)
Spanish-speaking Peoples

Instructional Objectives Students will be able to

1. Identify the chief groups of Spanish-speaking people in the United States and locate their chief areas of settlement.

2. Tell how Cesar Chavez worked to improve the lot of farm laborers.

3. Describe the political relationship of Puerto Rico to the United States.

4. Explain the rise of Cuban immigration in recent years.

Teaching Suggestions If your locality has any sizable numbers of Hispanics, identify them as to origin, residential location if concentrated, chief occupations, extent and types of discrimination, evidence of their particular culture(s) in the locality, etc.

• Remind students that the Immigration Act of 1924 setting up the quota system had put no quota on immigration from the independent nations of the Western Hemisphere (p. 471). This policy had been continued in the McCarran-Walter Act of 1952. Then the Immigration Act of 1965 provided an annual limit of 120,000 persons from Canada and Latin America. (Refugees were an exception to this limit.)

A 1976 amendment to the 1965 law kept the overall limit of 120,000 for the Western Hemisphere but put a limit of 20,000 for any one country. Also instead of admitting these Western Hemisphere immigrants on a first-come, first-served basis, the 1976 law gave preferences to close relatives of U.S. residents and to persons with needed talents and skills.

The effect of both the 1965 law and the 1976 amendments was to put some restraint on Latin American immigration.

• Ask students to name other Hispanics who are well known for their personal achievements (athletes, entertainers, politicians, etc.) or for their leadership in the Hispanic rights movement. Encourage students to prepare a brief written or oral report on one such person.

• Remind students that Hispanics are among the groups favored by affirmative action programs. The *Bakke* case involved a quota for black, Chicano, and Asian American applicants to the medical school where Bakke had applied for admission.

• Keep track of current developments in Puerto Rico's internal conflict over its legal ties with the United States. Students might speculate on advantages and disadvantages of Puerto Rican statehood—both for the United States and for Puerto Rico.

• Have an individual or committee explore the large influx of Cuban refugees in 1980, using the *Readers' Guide* to find pertinent magazine articles.

• Show the film *Mexican Americans: A Quest for Equality* (29 min). Have students write a summary or review. Collect papers for evaluation after several have been read and discussed. See the audiovisual list for other films and filmstrips on Hispanics in the United States.

Section 4 (pp. 713–716)
The American Indians

Instructional Objectives Students will be able to

1. Identify regions having Indian reservations today.

2. Give highlights of government policy toward the Indians over the years.

3. Describe the growth of "Indian Power" in recent decades.

4. Explain the current status of legislation and court rulings related to the American Indian.

Teaching Suggestions Notice that the opening topics review, and then introduce new elements of, government policy toward the Indians.

History of the *termination* policy appears in *Congress and the Nation* (published by Congressional Quarterly Service). As early as 1865, Congress had explored ways of ending federal control. Then termination policy was revived in the Truman administration. But the real push came in 1953 when Congress passed a joint resolution setting forth a policy for congressional committees to follow in proposing specific bills on termination. Between 1953 and 1962 Congress passed 16 bills ending federal controls over some 20,000 Indians.

The laudable objective of "termination" was to remove Indians—when they were ready—from a state of permanent dependency. Interior Secretary Seaton in 1958 said that any plan for termination should have the approval of the people involved.

Most of the larger tribal groups and several national Indian organizations opposed termination. In December 1959 the National Congress of American Indians unanimously adopted a resolution asking for complete repeal of the congressional resolution on termination.

• Have students turn to page 716 to locate federal and state Indian reservations. Tell students that by 1980 the Bureau of Indian Affairs counted about 650,000 Indians residing on or near reservations. The largest group is the Navajo

Chapter 34

(parts of Arizona, New Mexico, and Utah), totaling around 155,000. Other large reservations include the Creek, Cherokee, and Choctaw in Oklahoma; the Southern Pueblos in New Mexico; and the Pine Ridge and Rosebud (Sioux) in South Dakota. You might discuss why these reservations are located where they are (use text index for earlier references). Point out also that according to census reports, several hundred thousand Indians are currently considered "urban dwellers."

• Show the film *The American Indian Speaks*. Have students write a summary or review.

• For further reading, suggest such books as Debo's *A History of the Indians of the United States* and Oswatt's *This Land Was Theirs*. See Subject Guide to *Books in Print* for further titles and *Readers' Guide* for recent articles concerning Indian legislation and court rulings.

• Have students prepare a bulletin board display of Indian life and activities in the present day. Use the vertical file of your school's media center to secure material. The tourism offices of certain states, particularly Arizona, New Mexico, Utah, Oklahoma, Wyoming, Montana, and North and South Dakota, may supply helpful material. See recent almanacs for addresses.

• Keep a current file of news stories on court decisions and other settlements dealing with Indian land claims. Also file stories for lecture notes or student reports on problems arising over use of reservation lands for oil and mineral exploitation.

Section 5 (pp. 716–718)
New Vistas of Equality

Instructional Objectives Students will be able to

1. Explore the current status, legislation, and rights concerning the physically and mentally handicapped.
2. Explain the changing concepts concerning the dominant role of English in the Americanization of immigrants.
3. Survey the status of bilingual education.
4. Explain the problem of the growing membership of tiny countries in the United Nations.

Teaching Suggestions This section illustrates a distinguishing feature of this text: an opportunity to examine aspects of American life not usually studied. The problems and needs of the handicapped can be surveyed, beginning locally with your school. Field trips to institutions for the mentally and physically handicapped might be considered.

• Have students take photographs of ways in which your school and community provide (or noticeably do *not* provide) aids to the handicapped. Make a display of these photographs. Discuss what additional measures might be taken and how these can be achieved. Take account of costs as well as benefits.

• Have a community resource speaker—perhaps a handicapped person—discuss with students the problems of the handicapped in modern society. Are the laws and regulations adequate? What more needs to be done?

• Although it is a sensitive topic, the *cost* of equal treatment for the handicapped can hardly be ignored. It may seem callous to count the dollars, but very large amounts are often involved—particularly in altering existing structures, buses, and so on—for the benefit of relatively small numbers of people. An able student might use the *Readers' Guide* to find available articles dealing with costs.

• Explore "mainstreaming" of handicapped students in your school district.

• At the time this Guide was written, new standards (requirements) on bilingual education were being formulated. Consult professional journals and knowledgeable persons in the superintendent's office to find the basic facts. Use these to stimulate class discussion. Perhaps you can exhibit some materials used in bilingual classes.

• Have students review the founding of the United Nations (p. 583). From a current almanac, read some of the names of the small UN member nations. Locate these on a large world map. Why are some of these nations called "developing" or "underdeveloped"?

CHAPTER REVIEW

Meeting Our Earlier Selves

1. It is believed that lively competition leads to the production of the largest amount of goods and services that buyers want. There is therefore a bigger "pie" for all to share. Competition for social status implies an open society as opposed to one that determines status on the basis of birth. High status in such a society is a reward for achievement. Many of the achievements are things that benefit the society.

Costs of competition for income and status include (a) inequalities—if some get more, others may get less; (b) some competitors suffer emotional disorders; (c) unfair tactics to get ahead seem inevitable, often requiring costly laws and enforcement facilities.

2. Easy acquisition of land plus relatively little restriction on commercial endeavors inhibited the development of an aristocracy. On the frontier, achievement—not "birth"—was what counted. A landed aristocracy developed chiefly in the South but also along the Hudson with the Dutch patroon system. Favored persons received large tracts of land. With so much free land available, the Dutch could not maintain a tenant system. But slavery fastened the landed estate—and aristocracy—on the South. Where indentured servants supplied labor, servitude was regulated by contract and was only temporary.

3. Political equality helps to bring about and maintain other equalities: religious, economic, educational, racial, sexual, etc. The erasing of political inequality will lead the newly enfranchised groups to demand other changes. And where political equality exists, each group will tend to protect other achieved equalities.

4. Laws designed to promote equality: access to public accommodations, school desegregation, equal pay, simple voter registration requirements, income tax, welfare program, public housing, and any others that have the effect of removing political disabilities or of providing special benefits to the poorer classes.

Laws designed to promote competition: antitrust, all the guarantees of personal freedom, any labor laws working against union monopoly, variety in our educational system, laws requiring bidding on government contracts, our whole electoral system, competitive sports in schools, low tariffs, opportunities afforded for advancement in the armed forces and civil service, etc.

Discussion on the value judgment question ought to lead to understanding that persons or groups enjoying competitive advantages continually seek legal means to keep their advantages—to restrict competition. Also, there is the danger that efforts to assure equality will stifle competition.

Questions for Today

1. Examples: (a) airline deregulation opened routes to all airlines and promoted vigorous price competition; a bill to limit importation would restrain worldwide competition.

(b) Guaranteed minimum income is often proposed—to get rid of the worst cases of inequality; student loans based on need tend to equalize opportunities for college education; any "soak-the-rich" taxes seek to redistribute income; any law basing grants or low-cost loans on need (low income) tends to redistribute income; etc.

2. Students should think of such questions as these: Are jobs easier or harder to get because of affirmative action? Has my school had to equalize spending on male and female athletic programs—how has this affected me or my family? Am I getting training in areas that used to be dominated by the opposite sex? What adjustments have my parents made—or resisted making—in the area of sex equality? Is there a handicapped family member who is enjoying new advantages? Etc.

CHAPTER 35

Changing Leaders in Washington

Introducing the Chapter Students will feel a sense of accomplishment as they begin the last chapter of the text. Tell them, however, that although the text must end, our history goes on, as the Epilogue reminds us.

Students will also realize that our recent history is more difficult to appraise than that of earlier periods. The verdict of history takes time! Both Ford and Carter will evoke partisan responses from the students, as will some of the current problems, particularly that of nuclear power.

The concluding chapter(s) of any narrative of chronological history must undergo constant revision. Challenge students to jot down "ideas for revision" as they study this chapter.

Section 1 (pp. 720–726)
Gerald Ford Becomes President

Instructional Objectives Students will be able to

1. Describe the background of President Gerald R. Ford.
2. Explain how Nelson A. Rockefeller became Vice-President.
3. Tell why President Ford pardoned Nixon for any crimes possibly committed while President.
4. Describe laws passed for greater control over the CIA and FBI.
5. Summarize our problems with oil and inflation.
6. Relate how Jimmy Carter won the election of 1976.

Teaching Suggestions In introducing students to the likable Gerald R. Ford, this section illustrates how the Presidency is sometimes attained by chance. Have students react to the moral question facing Ford: Should Nixon have been pardoned?

- Have students review the Twenty-fifth Amendment on pages 796–797. Then discuss the following:

1. By what circumstances does the Vice-President become President? (on the President's death, resignation, or removal from office)
2. Who nominates the new Vice-President when the office is vacant? (the President)
3. Who must confirm the selection? (both houses of Congress)
4. Under what circumstances might the Vice-President be acting President? (when the President signifies that he is unable to discharge his duties or whenever the Vice-President and a majority of the Cabinet attest that the President is unable to perform his duties)
5. How may the President resume his duties thereafter? (by signifying that he is capable of performing his duties again; however, the Vice-President and the Cabinet have four days to object to the President's return; then Congress has 21 days to decide by a two-thirds vote that the President is unable to discharge the duties of the office)
6. If we had not had the Twenty-fifth Amendment in 1974, who would have become President when Nixon resigned? (the Speaker of the House, according to the Succession Act of 1947—see p. 589. In 1974 the Speaker was a Democrat, Carl Albert of Oklahoma)

- Call attention to the pictures of Nelson Rockefeller (1909–1979) on page 721. Tell them that he was the wealthiest man ever to hold high federal office. Nelson served four terms as governor of New York and had held numerous appointive offices.

His unsuccessful attempts to win the Republican nomination for the Presidency in 1960, 1964, and 1968 may be explained in part by resistance to his vast wealth as well as his relatively liberal views.

For further reading see Rodgers's *Rockefeller's Follies* and biographies by Desmond and Morris.

- *Handout lesson:* Use Handout 51 to guide discussion of Ford's pardon of former President Richard Nixon. Suggested answers to the handout questions follow:

1. Ford cited (a) Nixon's health, (b) the long time that would be required for a fair trial, (c) a trial would arouse "ugly passions," (d) the credibility of our free institutions would be questioned—meaning not clear without further examination of what Ford said. See also reasons given in the text.
2. Admission of guilt would have gone a long way in making the pardon more acceptable. Even though both Ford and Nixon knew that acceptance of a pardon implies an admission of guilt, many Americans did not understand this. And even if they did, a forthright statement by Nixon would have helped to calm the "ugly passions" that were still very evident. (It was not a Nixon characteristic to admit wrongdoing—nor to apologize.)
3. Answers will vary. This is a value judgment.
4. Ask students to defend their position with reasoned arguments.

- *Competency exercise—writing opinions:* Have students write a one-page editorial on "Should Draft Evaders Be Pardoned?" Use the text as a guide. Write in complete sentences. Suggest that students compare Ford's and Carter's handling of the draft-evader issue. After students have finished, have several editorials read aloud. Discuss these. Collect papers for evaluation.

- Wiretapping and the use of personal information in the files of government agencies that were brought to light in the Watergate hearings contributed to passage of the Privacy Act of 1974. Tell students that its provisions were as follows:

1. Public disclosure by agencies of any computer bank operation or data collection on individuals.

2. Individuals given right to inspect such files and correct misinformation.

3. Exchange of personal data between agencies restricted.

4. Federal law-enforcement agencies exempt from provisions of the act.

- Notice the emphasis on government spending as an inflation factor in the topic "Problems with the economy" and Ford's efforts to bring spending under control by use of the veto. The 1975 and 1976 editions of the *World Almanac* provide details. Have a student investigate the kinds of measures vetoed by Ford. What kinds of spending increases did he support? Here is an opportunity to discuss priorities in government spending.

Consider the advantages of using the inflation discussion on page 729 in conjunction with the material in this chapter section.

- The topics on "energy" in this chapter section and the next one might also be combined to show the persistent nature of this very contemporary problem and to focus on proposed solutions. Bring later developments into the discussion. On the energy/environment problem as a whole, use questions like these to guide discussion:

1. Before the oil embargo of 1973–1974 the cost of energy in the United States was relatively low—prices would soon double and triple. How did low prices contribute to the energy problem? (failed to encourage energy-saving measures)

2. What are some chief sources of "waste" in the use of energy? (big cars, unnecessary driving, small use of car pools, overheated buildings, poorly insulated buildings, etc.)

3. How do high energy prices help to solve the energy problem? (They encourage conservation efforts and the search for petroleum substitutes.)

4. In 1973 and earlier, gasoline prices in Europe tended to be double those in the United States partly because of very high gasoline taxes. How did this situation help European countries adjust to the oil crisis? (Europeans were less dependent on the automobile and drove smaller, more economical cars.) Point out that a big jump in gasoline taxes is one serious proposal for dealing with our own energy problem—a proposal widely resisted by consumers and politicians. Explore reasons why, but also focus on the economic sense of the proposal.

5. How did rising energy costs contribute to worldwide inflation? (Fuel is a significant cost in almost everything we buy; also many synthetic products are made directly from coal and oil.)

6. How do some "solutions" to environmental problems stand in the way of meeting the energy problem? (auto pollution controls that decrease engine efficiency; strip-mining controls that raise energy costs; closing public land to coal and oil exploration; slowdown on nuclear power development; etc.)

7. What kinds of energy conservation steps are you willing to take in exchange for continued efforts to improve the natural environment? (This question should be faced by students who take a strong pro-environment stance.)

- The significance of the individual vote showed up again in the close election of 1976. While Carter won by a reasonable 2 percent margin of the popular vote, the electoral vote could have resulted in a 269–269 tie—sending the election into the House of Representatives—if fewer than 10,000 votes in Ohio and Delaware had been reversed (for Ford instead of Carter).

- Tell students that Carter decided not to wear formal attire at his "people's inaugural." After the swearing-in ceremony at the Capitol, he surprised the nation by foregoing the use of a limousine and instead walked the mile and a half to the White House with his wife Rosalynn and daughter Amy.

Section 2 (pp. 726–733)
Jimmy Carter: A Campaigner as President

Instructional Objectives Students will be able to

1. Describe the background of President Jimmy Carter.

2. State why Carter's proposals met with opposition from the Congress.

3. Summarize Carter's problems as President, including that of inflation.

4. Explain our current energy problems, and evaluate Carter's proposed solutions.

Teaching Suggestions Bring the description and analysis of the Carter administration up to date. Challenge students to write an account of the 1980 election campaign and the results in a form that might be appropriate for adding to this chapter in a future revision.

- Have students consider Carter's training for the Presidency: naval officer, business executive, state senator, governor. What was missing? (might point to small scale of enterprises he had been associated with; would training in the law have been useful?) How did his background compare with other Presidents? with other recent aspirants to the Presidency?

- Encourage students to have a parent or someone of comparable age read this section—especially through the topic "Presidential weaknesses." Get impressions of how the authors' analysis squares with their own observations and recollections.

- Look for a current issue—a major bill in Congress—where special-interest groups put enormous pressures on members of Congress. Have students help identify the groups involved and their stand on the issue.

  Also look for examples that verify this assertion in the text: "Politicians were attacked or supported not for their general political outlook, but for their stand on a single issue." (Journals or newsletters published by special-interest groups sometimes print information on how particular legislators voted on a bill. You may find examples in the NEA journal or that of your state teachers' association, for example.) On the other hand, other groups like Americans for Democratic Action (ADA) often rate lawmakers on a broad spectrum of issues.

- In the last paragraph on the topic "The problem of inflation," help students see that some of the factors have a direct effect on the price level by making goods more costly to produce. Have students identify these costs. Another set of factors relates to government spending (welfare programs, job creation), helping to produce big budget deficits and subsequent increases in the money supply.

Section 3 (pp. 733–738)
Foreign Affairs under Ford and Carter

Instructional Objectives Students will be able to

1. Describe the role of Henry Kissinger in foreign affairs under Nixon and Ford.
2. Review the ending of the Vietnam War.
3. Explain Carter's relationship with the Russians and the delay in our acceptance of the second SALT agreement.
4. State the terms of our 1977 canal treaty with Panama.
5. Summarize the changing state of international affairs, particularly in the Middle East and Latin America.

Teaching Suggestions This section sets the stage for studying current international problems. Bring problems described in the text up to date.

- Encourage an able student to prepare a comparison of Kissinger with someone who has been Secretary of State since 1976.

- Be sure that students note the outcome of the "two Germanys" problem in 1972. Watch for any subsequent important developments.

- You might remind students that the Arab-Israeli War of 1973 was in a large measure responsible for the energy crisis of 1973–1974, since the Arab states imposed an oil embargo on nations that they said had taken Israel's side in that conflict.

  Follow developments in Israel related to continued occupation of land taken by Israel in the 1973 war—particularly as they relate to American foreign policy.

- Have students review "Dealing with Russia." Add that the major provisions of the SALT II agreement limit both sides (a) to 2400, and later to 2250 bombers and missile launchers and (b) to the creation of one new missile. Programs to improve existing weapons would continue, however. On his return from Vienna in June 1979, Carter warned Congress of possible grave consequences in the future if the Senate did not give its approval to the treaty. Yet a year later this approval had not been given. Continued distrust of the Soviet Union in Congress and the nation was a factor. Then consideration of SALT II approval came to an abrupt halt when the Soviet Union sent troops into Afghanistan in 1980.

- Tell students that the 1981 copyright edition of the text was written before the Soviet Union's invasion of Afghanistan. Ask them to speculate on how the topic "A changing world" would be different if it had been written after the Soviet invasion. Encourage able students to write a two- or three-paragraph topic on the Afghanistan affair, including the Carter administration's response to it.

- Bring the remaining topics in this section up to date—at least to the 1980 election. Suggest to students that the paragraph on the overthrow of the Shah of Iran would be stretched to two or three more paragraphs if the chapter had been written after the storming of the U.S. embassy and the taking of hostages. Ask them what main points they would put in a lengthened topic on Iran.

- A final try at writing textbook narrative could be a topic on the election of 1980. At the least, you might have students suggest main points and sub-points for such a topic. After these have been listed on the board, have students make recommendations for topic sequence for a well-rounded, coherent story.

- A fine review of the 1970s appears in a special report, "How Stormy '70s Reshaped U.S. Future," in *U.S. News & World Report,* December 10, 1979, pp. 49–56. It includes three pages of pictures.

CHAPTER REVIEW

Meeting Our Earlier Selves

1. The presumption for the arrangement is that the Vice-President ought to be someone who can and will work closely with the President—at least to be compatible enough to have the President's confidence so that the Vice-President will be kept informed on essential matters. A safeguard in the arrangement is that the candidate's choice for vice-presidential nominee must be approved by the party convention; yet this is virtually automatic. The President's nomination of a new Vice-President under the 25th Amendment is really safeguarded—by the necessary approval of both houses of Congress.

2. Arguments for clemency: forgiveness is a cherished value resting on religious principles; they were drafted by the luck of the draw—others just as suitable for service escaped the draft by luck; the unpopularity of the war, even its illegality in that war was not declared; costliness of trials and punishment; plan for alternative service would not let offenders off scot-free.

Arguments against: sets a bad example for dealing with future cases of draft evasion and desertion, perhaps even encouraging such action; unfair to those who served honorably; etc.

3. Make this a brainstorming session, since so many points of comparison and contrast are possible.

4. Carter could not possibly accomplish all he promised without having a rubber-stamp Congress. Unfulfilled promises were a factor in the low approval rate shown in public opinion polls in the summer of 1980—the lowest for any President since polling had begun in the 1940s. His many promises also diverted him from concentrating on a few major issues.

5. Hard-to-compromise issues include abortion; numerous ecology issues—strip mining, saving endangered species, etc.; gun control; religious exercises in public schools; neighborhood schools vs. busing; etc. Major parties prefer to avoid such issues because there is no middle ground. A stand on one side or the other will antagonize a particular group of voters.

6. Support: world is unsafe so long as human rights are violated; active concern for fellow humans is a moral imperative; pushing for worldwide human rights puts dictatorial regimes on the defensive; we will win the respect of peoples fighting for human rights and have them on our side when they win; etc.

Attack: self-interest should be the keystone of foreign policy; pushing for human rights threatens our relationships with nations we have to deal with; we have enough imperfections to handle without looking for sinfulness elsewhere; a human-rights campaign diverts our attention from matters affecting our own security; etc.

7. See the topic "A changing world" on pages 736–737.

Questions for Today

1. Answer will depend on developments at the time students are considering this question.

2. Environmentalists favor energy conservation because many forms of energy resource development harm the environment: strip mining, oil spills, wilderness destruction, etc. Many environmentalists also take the position that the industrial nations of the world must slow down on resource use to protect human life in the future.

3. Agencies include the public schools, Internal Revenue Service, Social Security Administration, Selective Service, and possibly the courts and law-enforcement agencies if you have been arrested.

Incorrect information could harm you in seeking employment, in obtaining credit, in criminal penalties if you were falsely listed as a repeat offender, or in your general standing in the community.

See the activities suggested for Section 1 for an item that gives provisions of the Privacy Act.

EPILOGUE

The Mysterious Future

Introduction Notice that the Epilogue surveys the highlights of our past even as it anticipates the future. Do coming events cast their shadows before? If so, suggest that the study of American history through this text has been worthwhile.

Instructional Objectives Students will be able to

1. Point out some highlights of American history that will provide guidelines for our future.

2. State what may be some of the problems that the United States must face in the future.

3. Tell about some of the changes that may take place in our future.

Teaching Suggestions Students may be more interested in their own personal futures than in that of their country. Try to link the individual and the national outlooks.

• Ask students to help you create a list of developments of the past three years (or "since you entered 9th grade"). List responses in three columns under *World, National, Local*. (Have a student copy the list so that you can use ideas with another class or next year.) Then go through each list by having students decide whether the development was *Predictable* or *Unpredictable,* say, 10 years earlier. When most students agree, mark the item *P* or *U*. Otherwise mark it "?".

You might then go through the items marked "P" or "?" after asking, "Which of the *predictable* and *uncertain* items would have been unpredictable 20 years ago?"

Conclude the activity by asking students to try to state some conclusions about making predictions about the future. How is the time factor involved: short-range vs. long-range? What kinds of developments seem most predictable? least predictable? What kinds of happenings upset predictions? In which of the three columns were the developments most predictable? least predictable? Why?

• Remind students of a line graph they have made (or show a graph) that shows changes over a period of ten, twenty, or more years. Then say, "Now let's extend the line for another ten or twenty years into the future. How will we decide how to do this?" (If the existing line shows a definite pattern, it would seem sensible to continue the pattern. Explain the term "extrapolation.") Tell students that many predictions are simply extrapolations. But the careful analyst, while paying close attention to what has happened in the past, looks at other developments that are likely, or are almost certain, to affect the trend.

• Keep a file of news items and magazine articles that predict the future. Distribute these for brief reports. Or use the materials to help students make predictions for the next ten or twenty years.

Be sure to clip any articles you see of predictions made by persons claiming powers of extrasensory perception. Often these appear in December and predict unexpected events of the coming year. Share past predictions and actual results with the class. Are any conclusions possible on the reliability of such predictions?

• Have students begin a list of current problems, using ideas from the second page of the Epilogue. Then add others that seem pertinent. Invite students to predict how some of these problems will look in, say, another twenty years: improved? about the same? worse? What particular kinds of changes? Why? What could be started now to keep the problem from worsening?

• Use an article in *Newsweek* (November 11, 1979) in which prominent Americans give responses to questions about the future: Can we control our world? Will America regain its trust? Educated for what? Will women keep their gains? Is equality possible? Will freedom prevail? Can we cope with technology? Can less be more—can we return to an earlier environment? Can we tame the automobile? Can the world be fed? Is peace with Russia possible?

• Show the film *The Futurists* (25 min) or *Future Shock* (42 min). After the film, have students write summaries or reviews. Have several of these read aloud and discussed. Collect papers for evaluation.

• For further reading about the future, suggest Huxley's *Brave New World* (novel), Orwell's *1984* (novel), Skinner's *Walden II,* and Toffler's *Future Shock*. Give extra credit for reports on any of these books.

General Bibliography

Ahlstrom, Sydney E., *A Religious History of the American People* (1972).

Bailey, Thomas A., *Diplomatic History of the American People* (8th ed., 1969).

Bemis, Samuel F., *A Diplomatic History of the United States* (5th ed., 1965).

Berkhofer, Robert F., Jr., *The White Man's Indian: Images of the American Indian from Columbus to the Present* (1978).

Bining, Arthur C., and Cochran, Thomas C., *Rise of American Economic Life* (4th ed., 1964).

Butts, Freeman, and Cremin, L. A., *A History of Education in American Culture* (1953).

Cochran, Thomas C., and Andrews, Wayne, *Concise Dictionary of American History* (1962).

Commager, Henry S., *The American Mind* (1950).

Cremin, Lawrence A., *American Common School* (1951).

Curti, Merle, *The Growth of American Thought* (1943).

Degler, Carl N., *Out of Our Past: The Forces That Shaped Modern America* (rev. ed., 1970).

Dictionary of American Biography, 20 vols. and index (1928–1937) See also supplements published since 1944.

Dorson, Richard M., *American Folklore* (1959).

Dorson, Richard M., *Buying the Wind: Regional Folklore* (1964).

Flexner, James T., *American Painting*, 3 vols.: *First Flowers of Our Wilderness*, vol. 1; *The Light of Distant Skies*, vol. 2 (1954); *That Wilder Image*, vol. 3 (1962).

Garraty, John A., ed., *Encyclopedia of American Biography* (1974).

Harvard Guide to American History, 2 vols. (rev. ed., 1974).

Historical Statistics of the United States, Colonial Times to 1970.

Hofstadter, Richard M., *The American Political Tradition: And the Men Who Made It* (2nd ed., 1975).

Hofstadter, Richard M., *Anti-Intellectualism in American Life* (1963).

James, Edward T., ed., *Notable American Women, 1607–1950*, 3 vols. (1971).

Johnson, Thomas H., *The Oxford Companion to American History* (1966).

Kazin, Alfred, *On Native Grounds: An Interpretation of Modern American Prose Literature* (1956, reprint 1972).

Lorant, Stefan, *Glorious Burden: The American Presidency* (1968).

Lord, Clifford, and Elizabeth H., *Historical Atlas of the United States* (1953).

McCloskey, Robert G., *The American Supreme Court* (1960).

McLaughlin, Andrew C., *A Constitutional History of the United States* (1935).

Millis, Walter, *Arms and Men: A Study in American Military History* (1956).

Mitchell, Broadus, and Louise P., *Biography of the Constitution* (1964).

Morris, Richard B., *Encyclopedia of American History* (latest edition).

Moyer, A. E., *An Educational History of the American People* (1967).

Parrington, Vernon L., *Main Currents in American Thought*, 3 vols. (1927–1930).

Paullin, Charles O., *Atlas of the Historical Geography of the United States*, John K. Wright, ed. (1932).

Rudolph, Frederick, *The American College and University* (1962).

Schlesinger, Arthur M., Jr., *The Imperial Presidency* (1973).

Schwartz, Bernard, *Reins of Power: A Constitutional History of the United States* (1963).

Steamer, Robert J., *The Supreme Court in Crisis: A History of Conflict* (1971).

Stewart, George R., *American Place-Names: A Concise and Selective Dictionary for the Continental United States of America* (1970).

Stewart, George R., *Names on Land: A Historical Account of Place-Naming in the United States* (3rd ed., 1967).

White, G. Edward, *The American Judicial Tradition: Profiles of Leading American Judges* (1976).

Wilson, Edmund, *Shock of Recognition: Literature in the United States Recorded by the Men Who Made It* (2nd ed., 1955).

Bibliography for Unit 1
Chapters 1–3

* Bakeless, John, *The Eyes of Discovery: The Pageant of North America as Seen by the First Explorers* (1950, reprint 1962).
* Boorstin, Daniel J., *The Americans: The Colonial Experience* (1958).

  Brebner, John B., *Explorers of North America, 1492–1806* (1933).
* Cremin, Lawrence A., *American Education: The Colonial Experience 1607–1783* (1970).
* Davis, David Brion, *The Problem of Slavery in Western Culture* (1966).
* Degler, Carl N., *Out of Our Past: The Forces That Shaped Modern America* (rev. ed., 1970).

  Earle, Alice M., *Child Life in Colonial Days* (1899, reprint 1974).

  Earle, Alice M., *Home Life in Colonial Days* (1898, reprint 1975).
* Flexner, James T., *First Flowers of Our Wilderness*, vol. 1 of *American Painting*.

  Franklin, Benjamin, *Autobiography* (reprint 1970).

  Gibson, Charles, *Spain in America* (1966).

  Jordan, Winthrop D., *White over Black: American Attitudes toward the Negro, 1550–1812* (1968).

  LaFarge, Oliver, *A Pictorial History of the American Indian* (1974).

  Langdon, William C., *Everyday Things in American Life, 1607–1776* (1937).

  Leonard, Jonathan, *Ancient America* (1967).

  Life History of the United States, vol. 1, *The New World* (1963).
* MacGowan, Kenneth, and Hester, Joseph, *Early Man in the New World*.

  Miller, John C., *The First Frontier: Life in Colonial America* (1966).
* Miller, Perry, *Errand into the Wilderness* (1956).
* Miller, Perry, *From Colony to Province* (1953).
* Miller, Perry, *The New England Mind: The Seventeenth Century* (1939, reprint 1961).
* Morgan, Edmund S., *American Slavery—American Freedom: The Ordeal of Colonial Virginia* (1975).
* Morgan, Edmund S., *The Puritan Dilemma: The Story of John Winthrop* (1958).
* Morgan, Edmund S., ed., *The Puritan Family: Religion and Domestic Relations in 17th-Century New England*.
* Morgan, Edmund S., *Visible Saints: The History of a Puritan Idea* (1963).
* Morison, Samuel E., *Admiral of the Ocean Sea* (1942).
* Morison, Samuel E., *The European Discovery of America*, 2 vols.: *The Northern Voyages, AD 500–1600*, vol. 1 (1971); *The Southern Voyages, AD 1492–1616*, vol. 2 (1974).
* Parrington, Vernon L., *The Colonial Mind, 1620–1800* (reprint 1955).
* Priestley, Herbert, *The Coming of the White Man, 1492–1848* (1971).
* Quinn, David B., *England and the Discovery of America, 1481–1620* (1974).

  Reeder, Red, *The French and Indian War* (1972).

  Tunis, Edwin, *Colonial Living* (1976).

  Van Doren, Carl, *Benjamin Franklin* (reprint 1973). An illustrated biography.
* Wertenbaker, Thomas J., *The First Americans: 1607–1690* (1927, reprint 1972).

  Woodward, William E., *The Way Our People Lived* (1968).

  Wright, Louis B., *The Cultural Life of the American Colonies, 1607–1763* (1957).

* Starred items for excellent readers and for special reports.

Bibliography for Unit 2
Chapters 4–6

* Alden, John R., *The American Revolution, 1775–1783* (1954).

  Berkin, Carol, *Women in the American Revolution* (1976).

  Bowen, Catherine D., *John Adams and the American Revolution* (1950).

  Bowen, Catherine D., *Miracle at Philadelphia: The Story of the Constitutional Convention* (1966).
* Butterfield, L. H., et al., *The Book of Abigail and John: Selected Letters of the Adams Family, 1762–1784* (1975).

  Butterfield, Roger, ed., *The American Past* (1966).

  Catton, Bruce, ed., *American Heritage Book of the Revolution* (1965).
* Commager, Henry S., and Morris, Richard B., *The Spirit of 'Seventy Six* (1975).
* Cott, Nancy F., *The Bonds of Womanhood: "Woman's Sphere" in New England, 1780–1835* (1977).

  Cunliffe, Marcus, *George Washington, Man and Monument* (1958).

  Davis, Burke, *Black Heroes of the American Revolution* (1976).

  De Pauw, Linda G., *Founding Mothers: Women of America in the Revolutionary Era* (1975).
* Flexner, James T., *George Washington*, 4 vols. (1965 to 1970).
* Flexner, James T., *Washington: The Indispensable Man* (1979).
* Flexner, James T., *The Young Hamilton: A Biography* (1978).
* Higginbotham, Donald, *The War of American Independence* (1977).
* Jefferson, Thomas, *Family Letters*, Edwin M. Betts and James A. Bear, Jr. eds. (1966).

Life History of the United States, vol. 2, *The Making of a Nation* (1963).
* Malone, Dumas, et al., *The Story of the Declaration of Independence* (1976).
* McDonald, Forrest, *The Formation of the American Republic, 1776–1790* (1965).
* Miller, John C., *The Federalist Era, 1789–1801* (1960).
  Miller, John C., *Sam Adams: Pioneer in Propaganda* (1936).
  Montross, Lynn, *The Reluctant Rebels: The Story of the Continental Congress, 1774–1789* (1950).
* Morgan, Edmund S., *The Birth of the Republic, 1763–1789* (1956).
  Preston, John H., *A Short History of the American Revolution* (1933).
  Quarles, Benjamin, *The Negro in the American Revolution* (1973).
  Schachner, Nathan, *Alexander Hamilton* (1961).
  Shepherd, Jack, *Adams Chronicles* (1976).
* Smith, Page, *John Adams,* 2 vols. (1962).
  Tardiff, Olive, *Molly Stark: Woman of the Revolution* (1976).
  Van Doren, Carl, *The Great Rehearsal* (1948).
* Washington, George, *Basic Selections from Public and Private Writings,* Saul K. Padover, ed. (1955).
* Wills, Garry, *Inventing America: Jefferson's Declaration of Independence* (1978).
* Wood, Gordon S., *The Creation of the American Republic, 1776–1787* (1972).

Bibliography for Unit 3
Chapters 7–9

* Abernethy, Thomas P., *The Burr Conspiracy* (1954, reprint 1968).
* Ammon, Harry, *James Monroe: The Quest for National Identity* (1971).
  Bailey, Thomas A., *Presidential Greatness* (1978).
  Bakeless, John E., *Lewis and Clark: Partners in Discovery* (1947).
  Baker, Nina B., *Pike of Pikes Peak* (1953).
  Beirne, Francis, *The War of 1812* (1949).
* Bemis, Samuel F., *John Quincy Adams and the Union* (1956).
* Boorstin, Daniel J., *The Lost World of Thomas Jefferson* (1960).
  Botkin, B. A., *A Treasury of American Folklore* (1944).
* Brant, Irving, *The Fourth President: The Life of James Madison* (1970).
  Browne, C. A., *The Story of Our National Ballads* (1960).
  Chidsey, Donald B., *Mr. Hamilton and Mr. Jefferson* (1975).
  Cleaves, Freeman, *Old Tippecanoe: William Henry Harrison and His Time* (1939).
* Coit, Margaret, *John C. Calhoun* (1977).
* Coit, Margaret, *The Growing Years, 1789–1829* (1974).
  Curtis, James C., *The Fox at Bay: Martin Van Buren and the Presidency* (1970).
* Dangerfield, George, *The Era of Good Feelings* (1952).
* Davis, David Brion, *The Problem of Slavery in the Age of Revolution, 1770–1823* (1975).
  Desmond, Alice C., *Glamorous Dolly Madison* (1946).
* Eaton, Clement, *Henry Clay and the Art of American Politics* (1957).
  Franklin, John H., *From Slavery to Freedom: A History of American Negroes* (1978).
* Freehling, William, *Prelude to Civil War: The Nullification Controversy in South Carolina, 1816–1836* (1966).
  Green, Constance, *Eli Whitney and the Birth of American Technology* (1956).
* Hammond, Bray, *Banks and Politics in America from the Revolution to the Civil War* (1957).
  Hawke, David F., *Those Tremendous Mountains.* Lewis and Clark expedition.
* Malone, Dumas, *Jefferson and His Time,* 4 vols. (1948–1970).
* Malone, Dumas, *Thomas Jefferson as Political Leader* (1963).
* Meyers, Marvin, *The Jacksonian Persuasion: Politics and Belief* (1960).
  Mirsky, Jeanette, and Nevins, A., *The World of Eli Whitney* (1952).
  Moore, Virginia, *The Madisons* (1979).
* Paterson, Merrill D., *The Jeffersonian Image in the American Mind* (1960).
  Schachner, Nathan, *Aaron Burr: A Biography* (1961).
  Schachner, Nathan, *Thomas Jefferson* (1951).
* Schlesinger, Arthur M., Jr., *The Age of Jackson* (1945).
  Shoemaker, Ervin C., *Noah Webster, Pioneer of Learning* (1936).
  Stone, Irving, *The President's Lady* (1968). Novel about Rachel Jackson.
  Tucker, Glenn, *Tecumseh: Vision of Glory* (reprint 1973).
* Wiltse, Charles M., *The New Nation, 1800–1845* (1961).
  Woodson, Carter G., *The Negro in Our History* (1927).

Bibliography for Unit 4
Chapters 10–12

★ Anderson, Nels, *Desert Saints: The Mormon Frontier of Utah* (1942).

★ Bauer, K. Jack, *The Mexican War, 1846–1848* (1974).

★ Boorstin, Daniel J., *The Americans: The National Experience* (1967).

Botkin, B. A., ed., *Lay My Burden Down: A Folk History of Slavery* (1945).

★ Brooks, Van Wyck, *The Flowering of New England, 1815–1865* (1936).

Buckmaster, Henrietta, *Let My People Go: The Story of the Underground Railroad* (1959).

Burlingame, Roger, *March of the Iron Men: A Social History of Union through Invention* (1938).

★ Cash, W. J., *The Mind of the South* (1960).

Catton, Bruce, *The Coming Fury* (1961).

★ Cochran, Thomas C., and Miller, William, *The Age of Enterprise: A Social History of Industrial America* (1968).

★ Craven, Avery, *The Coming of the Civil War* (1957).

★ Davis, David Brion, *The Problem of Slavery in Western Culture* (1966).

★ De Voto, Bernard, *Year of Decision, 1846* (1961).

★ Duberman, Martin, ed., *The Antislavery Vanguard: New Essays on Abolitionists* (1965).

★ Dumond, Dwight Lowell, *Antislavery Origins of the Civil War in the United States* (1959).

★ Eaton, Clement, *The Freedom-of-Thought Struggle in the Old South* (1964).

★ Eaton, Clement, *The Growth of Southern Civilization, 1790–1860* (1961).

★ Elkins, Stanley M., *Slavery: A Problem in American Institutional and Intellectual Life* (1959).

Filler, Louis, *The Crusade against Slavery, 1830–1860*.

★ Fredrickson, George M., *The Black Image in the White Mind: The Debate on Afro-American Character and Destiny: 1817–1914* (1977).

Fuess, Claude M., *Carl Schurz, Reformer*.

Gara, Larry, *The Liberty Line: The Legend of the Underground Railroad* (1961).

Genovese, Eugene D., *Roll, Jordan, Roll: The World the Slaves Made* (1974).

★ Griffin, Clifford S., *Their Brothers' Keepers: Moral Stewardship in the United States, 1800–1865* (1960).

Haley, Alex, *Roots* (1976). Novel tracing background of American blacks.

★ Harding, Walter, ed., *Henry David Thoreau: A Profile* (1971).

★ James, Marquis, *The Raven* (1977). Life of Sam Houston.

★ Jenkins, W. S., *Pro-Slavery Thought in the Old South* (1959).

Krutch, Joseph W., *Henry David Thoreau* (1974).

Lorant, Stefan, *Lincoln: A Picture Story of His Life* (1952).

Lord, Walter, *A Time to Stand* (1978). The epic of the Alamo.

★ Mannix, Daniel P., *Black Cargoes: A History of the Atlantic Slave Trade, 1518–1865* (1962).

Marshall, Helen E., *Dorothea Dix: Forgotten Samaritan* (1937).

★ Monroe, Paul, *The Founding of the American Public School System* (1971).

★ Moos, Malcolm, *The Republicans: A History of Their Party* (1956).

★ Nevins, Allan, *The Emergence of Lincoln*, 2 vols. (1951).

★ Nevins, Allan, *Ordeal of the Union*, 2 vols. (1947).

★ Nichols, Roy Franklin, *The Disruption of American Democracy* (1962).

★ North, Douglass C., *The Economic Growth of the United States, 1790–1860* (1966).

Oates, Stephen B., *With Malice toward None—The Life of Abraham Lincoln* (1977).

O'Dea, Thomas, *The Mormons* (1964).

Payne, Robert, *The Canal Builders*.

★ Phillips, Ulrich B., *Life and Labor in the Old South* (1929).

★ Potter, David, *Lincoln and His Party in the Secession Crisis* (1962).

★ Potter, David, *The South and the Sectional Conflict* (1968).

★ Rice, C. Duncan, *The Rise and Fall of Black Slavery* (1975).

Richter, Conrad, *The Fields* (1946). Also *The Town* (1950); *The Trees* (1940). Novels of American pioneer life.

Sandburg, Carl, *Abraham Lincoln: The Prairie Years*.

Sherwood, Robert E., *Abe Lincoln in Illinois* (1938). A play.

★ Stampp, Kenneth M., *The Peculiar Institution: Slavery in the Ante-Bellum South* (1963).

Styron, William, *The Confessions of Nat Turner* (1967). Novel about a slave uprising.

★ Taylor, William R., *Cavalier and Yankee: The Old South and American National Character* (1961).

★ Thompson, R. L., *Wiring a Continent: The History of the Telegraph Industry in the United States* (1972).

Tocqueville, Alexis de, *Democracy in America*, 2 vols. (1835, 1840, reprint 1955).

Twain, Mark, *Life on the Mississippi* (1883).

Tyler, Alice F., *Freedom's Ferment: Phases of American Social History to 1860* (1944).

★ Welter, Rush, *The Mind of America, 1820–1860* (1975).

★ Wishy, Bernard, *The Child and the Republic: The Dawn of Modern American Child Nurture* (1968).

Wittke, Carl, *The Irish in America* (1970).

★ Wright, Louis B., and Fowler, Elaine B., *Life in the New Nation, 1787–1860* (1972).

Bibliography for Unit 5
Chapters 13–15

Adams, Andy, *Log of a Cowboy* (1969).
Allen, Gay Wilson, *The Solitary Singer: A Critical Biography* (1962). Life of Walt Whitman.
American Heritage History of the Great West (1965).
American Heritage Picture History of the Civil War, 2 vols. (1960).
American Heritage, *The Confident Years* (1966).
Bakeless, John, *Spies of the Confederacy* (1970).
Benedict, Michael L., *The Impeachment and Trial of Andrew Johnson* (1973).
Berger, Thomas, *Little Big Man* (1964). Novel about the West.
* Berkhofer, Robert F., Jr., *The White Man's Indian: Images of the American Indian from Columbus to the Present* (1978).
* Billington, Ray A., *Westward Expansion: A History of the American Frontier* (4th ed., 1974).
Bishop, Jim, *The Day Lincoln Was Shot* (1964).
Brown, Dee A., *Bury My Heart at Wounded Knee: An Indian History of the American West* (1972).
Buchanan, Lamont, *A Pictorial History of the Confederacy* (1951).
* Buck, Paul H., *The Road to Reunion, 1865–1900* (1959).
Cather, Willa, *My Antonia* (reprint 1961). Novel about pioneer life in Nebraska.
Catton, Bruce, *A Stillness at Appomattox* (1953).
Catton, Bruce, *The Centennial History of the Civil War*, 3 vols.: *The Coming Fury* (1961); *Terrible Swift Sword* (1963); *Never Call Retreat* (1965).
Catton, Bruce, *Gettysburg: The Final Fury* (1974).
Catton, Bruce, *Glory Road: The Bloody Route from Fredericksburg to Gettysburg* (1964).
Catton, Bruce, *Grant Moves South* (1960).
Catton, Bruce, *Grant Takes Command* (1968).
Catton, Bruce, *Mr. Lincoln's Army* (1964).
Catton, Bruce, *Short History of the Civil War* (1963).
Catton, Bruce, *This Hallowed Ground: The Story of the Union Side of the Civil War* (1956).
Chestnut, Mary Boykin, *A Diary from Dixie* (1961).
* Cox, LaWanda, and Cox, John H., *Politics, Principle, and Prejudice, 1865–1866* (1969).
Crane, Stephen, *The Red Badge of Courage* (reprint 1979). Classic Civil War novel.
Dillard, J. D., *American Talk: Where Our Words Came From* (1976).
* Donald, David, *Lincoln Reconsidered* (1956). Essays on the Civil War.
* Eaton, Clement, *A History of the Southern Confederacy* (1954).
Ferber, Edna, *Cimarron* (reprint 1979). Novel about the Oklahoma land rush.
Foley, Rae, *Famous American Spies* (1962).
* Foote, Shelby, *The Civil War: A Narrative*, 3 vols. (1958, 1963, 1974).
Frantz, Joe, and Choate, Julian E., *The American Cowboy: The Myth and the Reality* (1955).

* Freeman, Douglas S., *R. E. Lee: A Biography*, 4 vols. (1934–1935).
Furnas, J. C., *The Americans: A Social History of the United States, 1587–1914* (1969).
* Gard, Wayne, *Frontier Justice* (1949).
* Goetzmann, William H., *Exploration and Empire: The Explorer and the Scientist in the Winning of the American West* (1966).
Grant, Ulysses S., *Personal Memoirs* (reprint 1952).
Horn, Stanley F., *Invisible Empire: The Story of the Ku Klux Klan, 1866–1871* (1969).
Hough, Emerson, *The Story of the Cowboy* (reprint 1936).
Jackson, Helen H., *A Century of Dishonor* (reprint 1972).
Josephy, Alvin M., Jr., *The Patriot Chiefs: A Chronicle of American Indian Resistance* (1969).
Kennedy, John F., *Profiles in Courage* (1964).
Lewis, Lloyd, *Captain Sam Grant* (1950).
Life History of the United States, vols. 5–7: *The Union Sundered* (1963); *The Union Restored* (1977); *The Age of Steel and Steam* (1974).
* Litwack, Leon F., *Been in the Storm So Long: The Aftermath of Slavery* (1979).
Lomax, John A., *Cowboy Songs and Other Ballads* (reprint 1948).
* Loth, David G., *Public Plunder: A History of Graft in America* (1938).
Marshall, Helen E., *Dorothea Dix: Forgotten Samaritan* (reprint 1967).
* McKitrick, Eric L., *Andrew Johnson and Reconstruction* (1960).
* McPherson, James M., *The Abolitionist Legacy: From Reconstruction to the NAACP* (1957).
* McReynolds, Edwin C., et al., *Oklahoma: Past and Present* (rev. ed., 1967).
Meigs, Cornelia, *Louisa May Alcott* (1932).
* Mencken, Henry L., *The American Language* (reprint 1977).
Meredith, Roy. *Mr. Lincoln's Camera Man: Mathew B. Brady* (1974).
Miers, Earl S., *Robert E. Lee*.
Mitchell, Margaret, *Gone with the Wind* (reprint 1976). Novel about the Civil War.
* Nevins, Allan, *The War for the Union*, 4 vols., (1959–1977).
Quarles, Benjamin, *The Negro in the Civil War* (1969).
Randall, J. G., and Donald, David, *The Civil War and Reconstruction* (1961).
Richter, Conrad, *The Sea of Grass* (1937). Novel.
Rolvaag, O. E., *Giants in the Earth* (reprint 1975). Novel of life on the Plains.
Rose, Willie Lee, *Rehearsal for Reconstruction* (1964).
Sandburg, Carl, *Abraham Lincoln: The War Years*, 4 vols.
Simkins, Frances B., and Patton, J. W., *Women of the Confederacy* (1971).
* Smith, Henry Nash, *Virgin Land: The American West as Symbol and Myth* (1950).

* Stampp, Kenneth M., *The Era of Reconstruction 1865–1877* (1965).
  Thomas, Benjamin, *Abraham Lincoln, A Biography* (1957).
  Time-Life, *The Old West*, 26 vols. (1973–1979).
* Turner, Frederick Jackson, *The Frontier in American History* (1893, reprint 1920).
  Wiley, Bell I., *The Life of Billy Yank* (1978); *The Life of Johnny Reb* (1978).
  Williams, Ben A., *A House Divided* (1947). Civil War novel.
* Wilson, Edmund, *Patriotic Gore: Studies in the Literature of the American Civil War* (1962).
* Woodward, C. Vann, *Reunion and Reaction: The Compromise of 1877 and the End of Reconstruction* (1956).
* Woodward, C. Vann, *The Strange Career of Jim Crow* (3rd rev. ed. 1974).
  Woodward, William E., *Meet General Grant* (1946).
* Wright, Edward N., *Conscientious Objectors in the Civil War* (1931).

Bibliography for Unit 6
Chapters 16–18

   Addams, Jane, *Twenty Years at Hull House* (reprint 1966).
* Boorstin, Daniel J., *The Americans: The Democratic Experience* (1974).
* Broehl, W. G., Jr., *The Molly Maguires* (1964).
  Bruce, Robert V., *Bell: Alexander Graham Bell and the Conquest of Solitude* (1973).
  Bruce, Robert V., *Eighteen Seventy-Seven: Year of Violence* (1959).
  Callow, Alexander B., Jr., *The Tweed Ring* (1969).
* Cochran, Thomas C., and Miller, William, *The Age of Enterprise: A Social History of Industrial America* (1968).
* Davis, Allen F., *Spearheads for Reform: The Social Settlements and the Progressive Movement, 1890–1914* (1960).
  Du Bois, W. E., *The Souls of Black Folks* (reprint 1977).
* Garraty, John A., ed., *Labor and Capital in the Gilded Age* (1968).
  Handlin, Oscar, *The Uprooted* (2nd enl. ed., 1973).
  Hawke, David F., *John D. — The Founding Father of the Rockefellers*.
  Higham, John, *Strangers in the Land: Patterns of American Nativism, 1860–1925* (1955).
  Hopkins, H. J., *A Span of Bridges: An Illustrated History*.
* Howard, Ebenezer, *Garden Cities of To-morrow*.
  Howe, George F., *Chester A. Arthur* (1935, reprint 1957).
* Jones, Maldwyn A., *American Immigration* (1960).
  Josephson, Matthew, *Edison: A Biography* (1959).
  Josephson, Matthew, *The Politicos, 1865–1896* (1959).
  Josephson, Matthew, *The Robber Barons* (1962).
* Konvitz, Milton R., and Leskes, L., *A Century of Civil Rights* (1961).
  Leech, Margaret, *The Garfield Orbit* (1978). Recent biography of Garfield.
  Leech, Margaret, *In the Days of McKinley* (1959).
* Litwack, L. F., ed., *The American Labor Movement* (1962).
* Logan, R. W., *The Negro in American Life and Thought: The Nadir, 1877–1901* (1954).
* Morgan, H. W., ed., *The Gilded Age: A Reappraisal* (1963).
  Nevins, Allan, *Grover Cleveland: A Study in Courage*.
  Nevins, Allan, *Hamilton Fish: The Inner History of the Grant Administration* (1936).
  Nevins, Allan, *John D. Rockefeller: The Heroic Age of American Enterprise*.
  Riis, Jacob A., *How the Other Half Lives* (reprint 1972).
  Steffens, Lincoln, *The Shame of the Cities* (reprint 1957).
  Steinman, David B., and Watson, S. B., *Bridges and Their Builders* (1957).
  Stone, Irving, *They Also Ran* (1968).
* Veysey, Laurence R., *The Emergence of the American University* (1965).
  Wall, Joseph F., *Andrew Carnegie* (1970).
  Washington, Booker T., *Up from Slavery* (reprint 1971).
  Weymouth, L., and Glaser, M., *America in 1876: The Way We Were* (1976).
* Wiebe, Robert H., *The Search for Order, 1877–1920* (1967).
  Wittke, Carl, *We Who Built America* (1961).

Bibliography for Unit 7
Chapters 19–21

Adams, Ben, *Last Frontier: Alaska* (1961).
American Heritage, *American Heritage History of World War I* (1964).
Anderson, Maxwell, and Stallings, L., *What Price Glory?* (1924). Play about World War I.
* Bailey, Thomas A., *Woodrow Wilson and the Lost Peace* (1922).
* Baldwin, Hanson W., *World War One: An Outline History* (1964).
* Bass, H. J., *America's Entry into World War One* (1964).
* Blum, John M., *The Republican Roosevelt* (1961).
* Blum, John M., *Woodrow Wilson and the Politics of Morality* (1956).
Borden, Charles A., *Hawaii, Fiftieth State.*
Dierks, Jack B., *Leap to Arms: The Cuban Campaign of 1898* (1970).
Dos Passos, John, *Three Soldiers* (reprint 1964). Novel about World War I.
* Ekirch, Arthur A., Jr., *Progressivism in America: A Study of the Era from Theodore Roosevelt to Woodrow Wilson* (1967).
Faber, Doris, *Petticoat Politics: How American Women Won the Right to Vote* (1967).
* Falls, Cyril, *The Great War, 1914–1918* (1961).
Fredericks, Pierce, *The Great Adventure: America in the First World War* (1960).
* Freidel, Frank, *The Splendid Little War* (1958).
* Garraty, John A., *Woodrow Wilson: A Great Life in Brief* (1977).
Golding, Morton J., *A Short History of Puerto Rico* (1973).
* Goldman, Eric F., *Rendezvous with Destiny: A History of Modern American Reform* (1956).
* Harbaugh, William Henry, *Power and Responsibility: The Life and Times of Theodore Roosevelt* (1961).
* Hays, Samuel P., *The Response to Industrialism: 1885–1914* (1957).
Hemingway, Ernest, *A Farewell to Arms* (1929), reprint 1967). Novel about World War I.
* Hofstadter, Richard, *The Age of Reform: From Bryan to F. D. R.* (1955).
Keller, Allan, *The Spanish-American War: A Compact History* (1969).
* La Feber, Walter, *New Empire: An Interpretation of American Expansion, 1860–1898* (1963).

Leech, Margaret, *In the Days of McKinley* (1959).
Life History of the United States, vols. 8–10: *Reaching for Empire* (1964); *The Progressive Era* (1964); *War, Boom and Bust* (1974).
* Link, Arthur S., *Woodrow Wilson: A Brief Biography* (1972).
* Logan, Rayford W., and Cohen, Irving S., *The American Negro: Old World Background and New World Experience* (1970).
Lorant, Stefan, *The Glorious Burden—The American Presidency* (1976). Pictorial history.
Martin, Ralph G., *Ballots and Bandwagons* (1964).
* May, E. R., *Imperial Democracy* (1961).
McCullough, David, *The Path Between the Seas—the Creation of the Panama Canal, 1870–1914* (1977).
Michener, James A., *Hawaii* (1959). Novel about early life in Hawaii.
* Morison, Samuel E., *"Old Bruin": Commodore Matthew C. Perry* (1967).
Morris, Edmund, *The Rise of Theodore Roosevelt* (1979).
Mowry, George E., *The Era of Theodore Roosevelt, 1900–1912* (1958).
Pringle, Henry F., *Life and Times of William Howard Taft* (1939, reprint 1964).
Pringle, Henry F., *Theodore Roosevelt, a Biography* (1956).
Remarque, Erich M., *All Quiet on the Western Front* (reprint 1978). Novel about World War I from the German viewpoint.
Reynolds, Quentin, *They Fought for the Sky* (1957). Aviators in World War I.
Rickenbacker, Edward, *Fighting in the Flying Circus.* Experiences of a fighter pilot in World War I.
Sandburg, Carl, *Always the Young Strangers* (1953). Autobiographical experiences in the Spanish-American War.
Sinclair, Upton, *The Jungle* (reprint 1971). Novel about Chicago stockyards.
Smith, Gene, *When the Cheering Stopped: The Last Years of Woodrow Wilson* (1964).
Terraine, John, *The Great War: 1914–1918* (1978). A pictorial history.
Tuchman, Barbara, *The Guns of August* (1970). The coming of World War I.
Warren, Sidney, *The Battle for the Presidency* (1968).

Bibliography for Unit 8
Chapters 22–23

Allen, Frederick A., *Only Yesterday: An Informal History of the Nineteen Twenties* (1931).

Allsop, Kenneth, *The Bootleggers and Their Era* (1961).

Anderson, Maxwell, *Winterset* (1935). Play relating to the Sacco-Vanzetti case.

Aymar, Brandt, and Sagarin, Edward, *Laws and Trials That Created History: A Pictorial History* (1974).

Burns, James M., *Roosevelt: The Lion and the Fox* (1970).

Caughey, John W., *Their Majesties, the Mob* (1960).

Chalmers, David M., *Hooded Americanism: The History of the Ku Klux Klan* (1968).

Coffey, Thomas M., *The Long Thirst: Prohibition in America, 1920–1933* (1975).

Dos Passos, John, *Manhattan Transfer* (reprint 1979). Novel about the 1920s.

Dreiser, Theodore, *An American Tragedy* (reprint 1978). Novel about the 1920s.

Durant, John, and Bettman, O. L., *Pictorial History of American Sports* (1965).

Ehrmann, Herbert B., *The Case That Will Not Die: Commonwealth vs. Sacco-Vanzetti* (1969).

Feather, Leonard, *The Book of Jazz* (1976).

Fitzgerald, F. Scott, *The Great Gatsby* (1979). Novel about values in the 1920s.

Furnas, J. C., *Great Times—An Informal Social History of the United States, 1914–1929*.

★ Galbraith, John K., *The Great Crash, 1929* (reprint 1979).

Ginger, Ray, *Six Days or Forever? Tennessee vs. John Thomas Scopes* (1974).

Goldston, Robert, *The Great Depression* (1978).

Hemingway, Ernest, *The Sun Also Rises* (1926). Novel about Americans in postwar Europe.

★ Henri, Florette, *Black Migration, 1900–1920* (1975).

★ Hicks, John D., *Republican Ascendancy, 1921–1933* (1960).

Josephson, Matthew, *Hero of the Cities* (1969). A political portrait of Al Smith.

Lawrence, Jerome, and Lee, R. E., *Inherit the Wind* (1969). Play about the Scopes trial.

★ Leuchtenburg, William E., *The Perils of Prosperity, 1914–1932* (1958).

Lewis, Sinclair, *Babbit* (1949). Novel about business in the 1920s.

Lewis, Sinclair, *Main Street* (reprint 1974). Novel about small-town life in the 1920s.

Life Goes to the Movies (1975). Time-Life.

Lindbergh, Charles A., *The Spirit of St. Louis* (reprint 1953).

Lyons, Eugene, *Herbert Hoover, a Biography* (1964).

Manchester, William, *The Glory and the Dream: A Narrative History of America, 1932–1972* (1974).

Mast, Gerald, *A Short History of the Movies* (1975).

McCoy, Donald R., *Calvin Coolidge* (1967).

★ Moore, Edmund A., *A Catholic Runs for President: The Campaign of 1928* (1956, reprint 1968).

★ Morgan, David, *Suffragists and Democrats: The Politics of Woman Suffrage in America* (1971).

★ Murray, Robert K., *The 103rd Ballot—Democrats and the Disaster in Madison Square Garden* (1976).

★ Murray, Robert K., *Red Scare: A Study in National Hysteria, 1919–1920* (1955).

★ Nevins, Allan, and Hill, F.E., *Ford*, 3 vols. (1976). Henry Ford and his company.

O'Connor, Richard, *The First Hurrah: A Biography of Alfred E. Smith* (1970).

Rice, Arnold S., *The Ku Klux Klan in American Politics* (1972).

Ross, Walter S., *The Last Hero: Charles A. Lindbergh* (1976).

★ Schlesinger, Arthur M., *The Crisis of the Old Order* (1957).

Shipman, David, *The Great Movie Stars* (1970).

Sinclair, Andrew, *Era of Excess: A Social History of the Prohibition Movement* (1964).

Sinclair, Andrew, *The Available Man: The Life Behind the Mask of Warren Gamaliel Harding* (1965).

Smith, Gene, *The Shattered Dream: Herbert Hoover and the Great Depression* (1970).

Sobell, Robert, *The Great Bull Market: Wall Street in the 1920s* (1968).

Spier, Peter, *Tin Lizzie* (1978).

Time-Life, *This Fabulous Century, 1920–1930*; also *This Fabulous Century, 1930–1940* (1969).

Tuttle, William M., Jr., *Race Riot: Chicago in the Red Summer of 1919* (1970).

Williams, Martin T., *The Jazz Tradition* (1970).

★ Wilson, Joan H., *Herbert Hoover: The Forgotten Progressive* (1975).

Bibliography for Unit 9
Chapters 24–27

Agee, James, and Evans, W., *Let Us Now Praise Famous Men* (1960). Depression in the South.
Alinsky, Saul, *John L. Lewis: An Unauthorized Biography* (1970).
Allen, Frederick L., *Since Yesterday* (reprint 1972).
Arnett, Hazel, *I Hear America Singing*. Songs of the 1930s.
Bradley, Omar S., *Bradley: A Soldier's Story* (1978).
★ Brown, Anthony Cave, *Bodyguard of Lies* (1975).
★ Bullock, A. L. C., *Hitler: A Study in Tyranny* (1952).
Burns, James M., *Roosevelt: The Soldier of Freedom* (1970).
Cahn, William, *A Pictorial History of American Labor* (1972).
Carell, Paul, *Hitler Moves East, 1941–1943* (1965).
★ Churchill, Winston S., *The Second World War*, 6 vols.: *The Gathering Storm* (1948; *Their Finest Hour* (1949); *The Grand Alliance* (1950); *Triumph and Tragedy* (1953); *The Hinge of Fate* (1950); *Closing the Ring* (1951).
Clark, Alan, *Barbarossa* (1965). German invasion of Russia.
Collier, Basil, *The Battle of Britain* (1962).
Craig, William, *The Fall of Japan* (1979).
Divine, David, *The Nine Days of Dunkirk* (1959).
Durant, John, *The Heavyweight Champions* (6th ed., 1976).
Eisenhower, Dwight D., *Crusade in Europe* (1948).
Farago, Ladislas, *The Broken Seal: The Story of "Operation Magic" and the Pearl Harbor Disaster*.
★ Feis, Herbert, *The Road to Pearl Harbor: The Coming of the War between the United States and Japan* (1962).
★ Fermi, Laura, *Mussolini* (1966).
Garfinkel, Herbert, *When Negroes March* (1969).
Gurney, Gene, *A Pictorial History of the United States Army* (1978).
Hamilton, Charles V., *The Black Experience in American Politics* (1973).
Hemingway, Ernest, *For Whom the Bell Tolls* (1940). Novel about the Spanish Civil War.
Hersey, John, *Hiroshima* (1946, reprint 1959).
Hingley, Ronald, *Joseph Stalin: Man and Legend* (1974).
★ Holtzman, Abraham, *The Townsend Movement* (1973).
Horan, James D., *The Desperate Years: A Pictorial History of the Thirties* (1962).
Hughes, Langston, et al., *A Pictorial History of Black Americans* (4th rev. ed. 1973).
Lash, Joseph P., *Eleanor and Franklin* (1973); *Eleanor: The Years Alone* (1973).
Laurence, William L., *Dawn over Zero: The Story of the Atomic Bomb* (1972).
Lawson, Ted, and Considine, Bob, *Thirty Seconds over Tokyo* (1953).

★ Leuchtenburg, William E., *Franklin D. Roosevelt and the New Deal, 1932–1940* (1963).
Le Vien, Jack, and Lord, J., *Winston Churchill: The Valiant Years* (1962).
Lewis, Sinclair, *It Can't Happen Here* (1935). Novel about fascist dictator of U. S.
Life History of the United States, vol. 11, *New Deal and Global War* (1964).
Life Picture History of World War II.
Lifton, Robert J., ed., *The Woman in America* (1977).
Loomis, Robert D., *The Story of the U.S. Air Force* (1959).
Manchester, William, *American Caesar: Douglas MacArthur, 1880–1964.*
McKee, Alexander, *Strike from the Sky: The Story of the Battle of Britain* (1971).
★ McWilliams, Carey, *Prejudice: Japanese-Americans, Symbols of Racial Intolerance* (1971).
Merriam, Robert, *Dark December* (1947). Battle of the Bulge.
★ Morison, Samuel E., *The Two-Ocean War: A Short History of the United States Navy in the Second World War* (1963).
★ Nash, Gerald D., *The American West in the Twentieth Century: A Short History of an Urban Oasis* (1977).
Patton, George, *War As I Knew It* (1947).
Perkins, Frances, *The Roosevelt I Know* (1947).
Quarles, Benjamin, *The Negro in the Making of America* (1964).
Roosevelt, Eleanor, *The Autobiography of Eleanor Roosevelt* (1978).
Ryan, Cornelius, *A Bridge Too Far* (1974). Allied invasion of Holland.
Ryan, Cornelius, *The Last Battle* (1966).
Ryan, Cornelius, *The Longest Day* (1975). Allied invasion of Europe.
Schary, Dore, *Sunrise at Campobello* (1958). Play about FDR's triumph over polio.
★ Schlesinger, Arthur M., *The Coming of the New Deal* (1959).
★ Schlesinger, Arthur M., *The Politics of Upheaval* (1967).
Sherwood, Robert E., *There Shall Be No Night* (1940). Play about Russian aggression against Finns in World War II.
★ Shirer, William L., *Berlin Diary: The Journal of a Foreign Correspondent, 1934–1941* (1941).
★ Shirer, William L., *The Collapse of the Third Republic* (1971).
★ Shirer, William L., *The Rise and Fall of the Third Reich* (1960).
★ Snyder, Louis, *The War: A Concise History, 1939–1945* (1960).
Steinbeck, John, *The Grapes of Wrath* (1939, reprint 1976). Novel about Dust Bowl migrants.
Steinbeck, John, *The Moon Is Down* (1942, reprint 1970). Novel about Nazi invasion of Norway.
Taylor, Robert L., *Winston Churchill: The Biography of a Great Man* (1952).

Time-Life, *This Fabulous Century, 1940–1950.*

Time-Life, World War II series; nine volumes (1976–1979).

Toland, John, *The Last Hundred Days* (1966).

Toland, John, *The Rising Sun,* 2 vols. (1970–1971). World War II as experienced by Japan.

Tregaskis, Richard, *Guadalcanal Diary* (1955).

Trevor-Roper, Hugh R., *The Last Days of Hitler* (1962).

Warren, Robert P., *All the King's Men* (1960). Novel about a southern political boss.

Warren, Ruth, *A Pictorial History of Women in America* (1975).

Wechsler, James, *Labor Baron: A Portrait of John L. Lewis* (reprint 1972).

* Williams, T. Harry, *Huey Long* (1969).

Wouk, Herman, *War and Remembrance* (1978).

Young, Desmond, *Rommel, the Desert Fox* (1951).

Bibliography for Unit 10
Chapters 28–30

Baldwin, James, *The Fire Next Time* (1963).

Baldwin, James, *Notes of a Native Son* (1955).

* Bartley, Numan V., *The Rise of Massive Resistance: Race and Politics in the South during the 1950s* (1969).

Coles, Robert, *Children of Crisis: A Study in Courage and Fear* (1967). Civil rights.

* Conant, James, *The American High School Today* (1959).

Cook, Fred J., *The Nightmare Decade: The Life and Times of Senator Joe McCarthy* (1971).

* Cremin, Lawrence A., and Borrowman, M. L., *Public Schools in Our Democracy* (1956).

Davison, W. P., *The Berlin Blockade* (1958).

Eisenhower, Dwight D., *Mandate for Change* (1963).

Eisenhower, Dwight D., *White House Years: Waging Peace, 1956–1961* (1965).

Fehrenbach, Theodore, *This Kind of War* (1963). Describes our role in Korea.

Gilbert, G. M., *Nuremberg Diary.*

Goldman, Eric, *The Crucial Decade and After: America, 1945–1960* (1961).

* Goodrich, Leland M., *The United Nations in a Changing World* (1976).

Halperin, Maurice, *The Rise and Decline of Fidel Castro* (1973).

Haskins, James, *The Life and Death of Martin Luther King, Jr.* (1977).

Higgins, Marguerite, *War in Korea: The Report of a Woman Combat Correspondent* (1951).

* Hoag, Edwin, *American Cities: Their Historical and Social Development* (1969).

* Hook, Sidney, *John Dewey, Philosopher of Science and Freedom* (reprint 1976).

* Hughes, Emmet J., *The Ordeal of Power: A Political Memoir of the Eisenhower Years.* (1975).

* Kennan, George, *American Diplomacy, 1900–1950* (1951).

King, Martin Luther, *Stride Toward Freedom* (1958).

* La Feber, Walter, *America, Russia, and the Cold War, 1945–1975* (3rd ed., 1976).

Larson, Arthur, *Eisenhower: The President Nobody Knew* (1968).

Leckie, Robert, *Conflict: The History of the Korean War, 1950–1952* (1962).

* Leuchtenberg, William E., *A Troubled Feast: American Society since 1945* (1973).

Ley, Willy, *Rockets, Missiles and Men in Space* (1968).

Life History of the United States, vol. 12, *The Great Age of Change (1974).*

* Lomax, Louis E., *The Negro Revolt* (1962).

* Lukacs, John A., *A History of the Cold War* (1970).

Lyon, Peter, *Eisenhower: Portrait of the Hero* (1974).

Manchester, William, *The Glory and the Dream: A Narrative History of America, 1932–1972* (1974).

Meray, Tiber, *That Day in Budapest* (1969). Revolution in 1956 by Hungary against Russian rule.

* Olmstead, Clifton E., *History of Religion in the U.S.* (1960).

* Parmet, Herbert S., *Eisenhower and the American Crusade* (1972).

Phillips, Cabell, *The Truman Presidency* (1966, reprint 1969).

Rae, John B., *The American Automobile: A Brief History* (1965).

* Ransom, Harry H., *The Intelligence Establishment* (1970).

* Rees, David, *Korea: the Limited War* (1964).

Ross, Irwin, *The Loneliest Campaign: The Truman Victory of 1948* (1977).

Rovere, Richard, *Senator Joe McCarthy* (1959).

Russ, Martin, *The Last Parallel* (1973). A marine's war journal about the Korean War.

Seth, Ronald, *The Sleeping Truth: The Hiss-Chambers Case Reappraised* (1968).

* Shirer, William L., *End of a Berlin Diary* (1947, reprint 1961).

Silberman, Charles E., *Crisis in Black and White* (1964).

* Spanier, John, W., *American Foreign Policy since World War II* (rev. ed., 1963).

* Spanier, John W., *The Truman-MacArthur Controversy and the Korean War* (1968).

* Storry, Richard, *A History of Modern Japan* (1960).

Time-Life, *This Fabulous Century—1950–1960* (1970).

Truman, Harry S., *Memoirs,* 2 vols. (1955–1956).

Von Braun, Wernher, and Ordway, F., *History of Rocketry and Space Travel* (1975).

* Williams, William Appleman, *The Tragedy of American Diplomacy* (rev. ed., 1962).

Wise, David, and Ross, T. B., *The U-2 Affair.*

Bibliography for Unit 11
Chapters 31–33

Abel, Elie, *The Missile Crisis* (1968).

Akens, David S., *John Glenn: First American in Orbit* (1969).

Armstrong, Neil, et al., *First on the Moon: The Astronauts' Own Story* (1970).

Bernstein, Carl, and Woodward, R., *All the President's Men* (1976). Nixon's inner circle.

Brink, William, *The Negro Revolution in America* (1969).

Brown, Claude, *Manchild in the Promised Land* (1971). Novel.

★ Brown, Weldon A., *Prelude to Disaster: The American Role in Vietnam, 1940–1963* (1975).

Burns, James M., *John Kennedy: A Political Profile* (1961).

Carson, Rachel, *Silent Spring* (1973).

Chester, Lewis, et al., *An American Melodrama: The Presidential Campaign of 1968* (1969).

Donovan, Robert J., *P.T.—109* (1961). John F. Kennedy in World War II.

Dorman, Michael, *We Shall Overcome* (1964).

Drew, Elizabeth, *Washington Journal: The Events of 1973–1974* (1975).

Ellison, Ralph, *Invisible Man* (1972). Novel.

★ Fall, Bernard B., *The Two Vietnams: A Political and Military Analysis* (2nd rev. ed., 1967).

★ Fitzgerald, Frances, *Fire in the Lake: The Vietnamese and the Americans in Vietnam* (1973).

Frady, Marshall, *Wallace* (1976).

Gallagher, Mary B., *My Life with Jacqueline Kennedy* (1969).

Graham, Frank, Jr., *Since Silent Spring* (1977).

Halberstam, David, *The Best and the Brightest* (1973). The Vietnam War.

★ Harrington, Michael, *The Other America: Poverty in the United States* (1970).

Hart, Gary W., *Right from the Start* (1973). McGovern's 1972 presidential campaign.

★ Heath, Jim F., *Decade of Disillusionment: The Kennedy-Johnson Years* (1975).

Honan, William H., *Ted Kennedy: Profile of a Survivor* (1972).

Johnson, Haynes, et al., *The Bay of Pigs: The Leaders' Story of Brigade 2506* (1964).

Johnson, Lyndon B., *The Vantage Point* (1971).

★ Kearns, Doris, *Lyndon Johnson and the American Dream* (1977).

Kennedy, John F., *Profiles in Courage* (1964).

Kennedy, Robert F., *Thirteen Days* (1971). About the Cuban missile crisis.

★ Leuchtenberg, William E., *A Troubled Feast: American Society since 1945* (1973).

Levine, Suzanne, and Lyons, H., *The Decade of Women*.

Lomax, Louis E., *The Negro Revolt* (1962).

Lord, Walter, *The Past That Would Not Die* (1965, reprint 1967). The story of James Meredith.

Manchester, William, *The Death of a President: November 20–25, 1963* (1977).

★ Martin, David C., *Wilderness of Mirrors* (1980). About the CIA.

Meredith, James, *Three Years in Mississippi* (1976).

Mooney, Booth, *The Lyndon Johnson Story* (1964).

Nader, Ralph, *Unsafe at Any Speed* (1965).

★ Nash, Roderick, *Wilderness and the American Mind* (rev. ed., 1973).

Nixon, Richard M., *Six Crises* (1962).

Nixon, Richard M., *RN: The Memoirs of Richard Nixon*, 2 vols. (1979).

O'Neill, William L., *Coming Apart: An Informal History of America in the 1960s* (1972).

★ *Report of the President's Commission on the Assassination of President John F. Kennedy*.

Saunders, Doris E., ed., *The Kennedy Years and the Negro* (1977).

★ Schell, Jonathan, *The Time of Illusion* (1975). Nixon.

★ Schlesinger, Arthur M., Jr., *A Thousand Days* (1977). Kennedy administration.

★ Schlesinger, Arthur M., Jr., *The Bitter Heritage: Vietnam and American Democracy* (1967).

★ Schlesinger, Arthur M., Jr., *Robert Kennedy and His Times* (1979).

★ Shawcross, William, *Sideshow: Kissinger, Nixon and the Destruction of Cambodia* (1978).

Sidey, Hugh, *John F. Kennedy: Portrait of a President* (1964).

Silberman, Charles E., *Crisis in Black and White* (1964).

Sorenson, Theodore, *Kennedy* (1965).

Szulc, Tad, and Meyer, K. E., *The Cuban Invasion: The Chronicle of a Disaster* (1962).

Time-Life, *This Fabulous Century—1960–1970* (1970).

White, Theodore H., *Breach of Faith: Fall of Richard Nixon* (1975).

White, Theodore H., *The Making of a President, 1960* (1961). Also vols. for 1964, 1968, and 1972.

★ Wills, Garry, *Nixon Agonistes: The Crisis of the Self-Made Man* (1970).

Witcover, Jules, *85 Days: The Last Campaign of Robert Kennedy* (1969).

Woodward, Robert, and Bernstein, C., *The Final Days* (1977). The Nixon administration in its last days.

Bibliography for Unit 12
Chapters 34–35 and Epilogue

* Barber, James D., *The Pulse of Politics: Electing Presidents in the Media Age.*

  Baxardall, Rosalyn, et al., eds., *America's Working Women* (1976).

  Carter, Jimmy, *Why Not the Best?* (1976).

* Debo, Angie, *A History of the Indians of the United States* (1974).

  Eban, Abba, *My Country* (1972). The story of modern Israel.

  Fitzpatrick, J., *Puerto Rican Americans: The Meaning of Migration to the Mainland* (1971).

  Ford, Betty, *The Times of My Life* (1979).

  Ford, Gerald R., *A Time to Heal: The Autobiography of Gerald R. Ford* (1979).

  Friedan, Betty, *The Feminine Mystique* (1977).

  Handlin, Oscar, *Immigration as a Factor in American History* (1959).

  Handlin, Oscar, *The Uprooted* (2nd enl. ed., 1973).

  Huxley, Aldous, *Brave New World* (1979). Novel about the social order of the future world.

  Kennedy, John F., *A Nation of Immigrants* (1964).

  Kissinger, Henry, *The White House Years* (1979).

  Landau, Elaine, *Woman! Woman! Feminism in America* (1964).

  MacDougall, Malcolm D., *We Almost Made It* (1977). Ford election campaign in 1972.

* McWilliams, Carey, *North from Mexico: The Spanish-Speaking People of the United States* (1949).

  Meir, M. S., and Rivera, F., *The Chicano: A History of Mexican-Americans.*

  Miller, William, *Yankee from Georgia* (1978).

  Mollenhof, Clark, *The President Who Failed: Carter Out of Control* (1980).

  Ms Magazine, *The Decade of Women—A History of the Seventies in Pictures.*

  Nava, Julian, *Mexican Americans: A Brief Look at Their History* (1970).

  Orwell, George, *1984* (reprint 1971). Novel about world of the future.

  Reeves, Richard, *A Ford, Not a Lincoln* (1975).

  Schram, Martin, *Running for President, 1976: The Carter Campaign* (1977).

  Shogan, Robert, *Promises to Keep: Carter's First 100 Days* (1977).

  Shoup, Lawrence H., *The Carter Presidency and Beyond* (1979). Power and politics in the 1980s.

  Skinner, B. F., *Walden II* (1961). Novel of the social and cultural revolution of a future America.

  Stroud, Kandy, *How Jimmy Won: The Victory Campaign from Plains to the White House* (1977).

  Ter Horst, J. F., *Gerald Ford: Past . . . Present . . . Future* (1974).

  Terkel, Studs, *Working: People Talk About What They Do All Day and How They Feel About What They Do* (1974).

* Toffler, Alvin, *Future Shock* (1971).

  Wagenheim, Kal, *Puerto Rico, A Profile* (1976).

  Witcover, Jules, *Marathon: The Pursuit of the Presidency, 1972–1976* (1978).

  Wooten, James, *Dasher—The Roots and the Rising of Jimmy Carter* (1978).

HANDOUT 1 Chapter 1

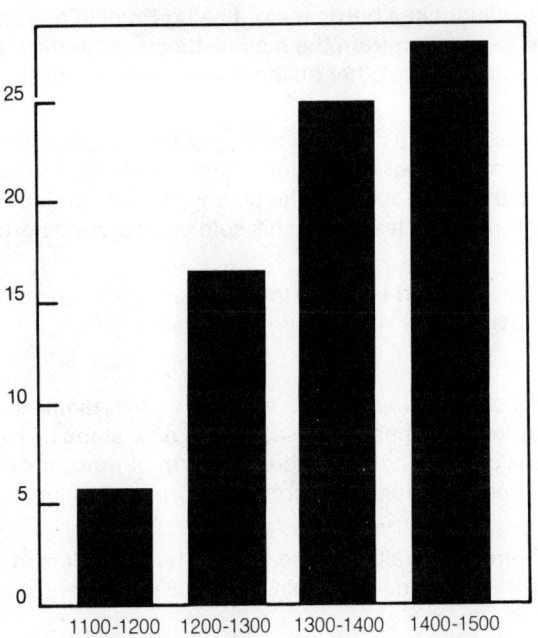

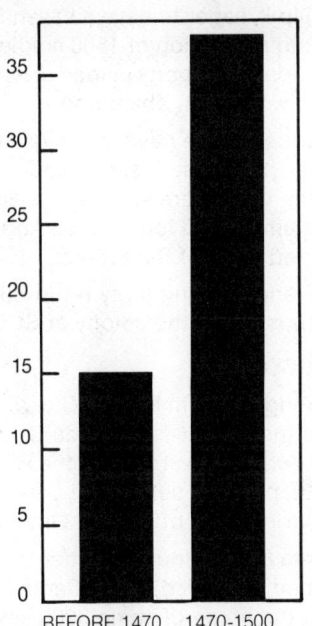

1. How would you describe the growth of European universities and colleges in the four centuries before 1500?

2. What statement can you make to describe the growth of printing houses in Europe during the last three decades of the 1400s?

3. In what ways might these two developments have helped to start and sustain the period of European exploration which began in the 1400s and continued for the next 200 to 300 years?

HANDOUT 2 Chapter 2

A Chronology of Settlements in the Spanish Borderlands

FLORIDA

1559—Philip II, eager to have a haven for Spanish ships caught in a hurricane or fleeing English pirates, arranged for an expedition of 1500 soldiers and colonists to go north from the main settlements in the Caribbean to Florida. One party landed at what is now Pensacola, and the other on the South Carolina coast. Both colonies were soon abandoned.

1565—Alarmed at the news that a group of French Protestants had started a colony at the mouth of the St. John's River (the present site of Jacksonville), Philip II sent another expedition under Pedro Menéndez de Avilés. In the party were some wives and families and 500 African slaves. The colony landed south of the French settlement and founded St. Augustine. From this base the leader and his soldiers marched north and massacred most of the French.

1567—A French raiding party returned to the Jacksonville site and killed all the Spaniards who were holding that outpost. But the colony at St. Augustine managed to survive as a permanent settlement.

NEW MEXICO

1598—Setting out from Mexico City with more than a hundred soldier-settlers, along with their families and African and Indian slaves, Juan de Oñate founded a settlement where El Paso, Texas, now stands. He then proceeded northward along the Rio Grande and took over an Indian village just north of present-day Santa Fe. He named the settlement San Juan, and the settlers built the first permanent Christian church in Spanish territory north of the Rio Grande.

1609—Santa Fe was founded when a new governor, Pedro de Peralta, moved the scattered settlers (most had returned to Mexico) to the Santa Fe site. In twenty years this new capital was the headquarters of 25 missions and the home of some 3000 settlers.

1680—An uprising of the Pueblo Indians led to the killing of 400 settlers, and the rest fled to El Paso.

1697—After five years of fighting, a Spanish military force restored Spanish rule in New Mexico. Several hundred settlers returned to Santa Fe.

1706—Albuquerque founded on the trail from Santa Fe to Mexico.

TEXAS

1598—El Paso founded by Juan de Oñate (see NEW MEXICO above).

1680—Mission Ysleta set up near El Paso.

1718—Hoping to establish missions and forts and thereby drive the French out of Texas, the viceroy at Mexico City sent soldiers and their families to the San Antonio area. A new mission, San Antonio de Valero, later called the Alamo, was set up. By 1731 four other missions were thriving near the Alamo.

1731—Fifteen families arrived and laid out a town that would become San Antonio.

1748—José de Escandon led more than 3200 soldiers and settlers to settle the lower Rio Grande. Fifteen missions and 23 towns were set up on both sides of the river. One of the towns became Laredo.

ARIZONA

1690–1711—Father Eusebio Kino established more than 20 missions in Arizona and Lower California.

1752—Tubac, near Tucson, was made a presidio (fort) to protect miners and farmers in the Santa Cruz Valley against the Indians.

1776—Tucson, the site of an Indian village, became a Spanish fort.

CALIFORNIA

1769—Two expeditions from Lower California (one overland, and one by sea)—led by the governor, Gaspar de Portolá, and Father Junípero Serra—met at San Diego, where a fort and mission were established.

1770—Settlement and mission set up by Portolá at Monterey.

1776—Spanish settlers set up a mission and presidio at Yerba Buena, now San Francisco.

1771–1823—Nearly 20 more missions, one day's walk apart, were set up along the coast, by Father Serra and his associates, from San Diego to Sonoma (north of San Francisco).

1781—A group of families from Mexico founded Los Angeles.

HANDOUT 3 Chapter 2

Writing Historical Inscriptions

Directions: Below is the inscription on a marker honoring an important person in American history. In the space below, write some pertinent facts about a person assigned by your teacher. Then use these facts to write an appropriate inscription as your teacher directs.

PULASKI SKYWAY

In memory of Polish nobleman, Count Casimir Pulaski (1747–1779), who gave his life in the American Revolution. Joined General Washington's Army (1777). Served at Morristown, Brandywine, and Germantown. Supported General Lincoln in South Carolina. Mortally wounded at siege of Savannah (Oct. 9, 1779). Honor to his name in the cause of liberty.

Facts about _____

Now write your inscription in the box below.

HANDOUT 4 Chapter 2

A Chronology for Selected Proprietary Colonies

1624—Dutch settlers from New Netherland build Fort Nassau (now Gloucester, NJ) on Delaware River, but abandon it in 1627.

1632—Sir George Calvert (Lord Baltimore) dies just before getting charter for Maryland. His son Cecil, the second Lord Baltimore, inherits the charter.

1634—Some 200 colonists, including many Catholics, settle at St. Mary's in Maryland. Lord Baltimore stays in England and governs through a deputy (first, Leonard Calvert, his brother).

1638—A Swedish expedition, led by Peter Minuet, a former governor of New Netherland, builds Fort Christina (now Wilmington, Delaware).

1640—A new expedition brings more Swedes and some Finns to Delaware.

1643—New Sweden under Governor Johan Printz (1643–1653) begins building more forts and settlements in Delaware.

1649—Maryland passes Toleration Act, granting religious freedom to all believers in the Trinity.

1653—Settlers from Virginia begin to move into Carolina north of Albemarle Sound and establish Albemarle Colony.

1655—New Netherland Governor Peter Stuyvesant conquers New Sweden and ends Swedish rule in Delaware.

1663—Eight high-ranking Englishmen receive a grant of land comprising present-day North Carolina and South Carolina.

1664—Dutch-held settlements in New Jersey and Delaware come under British rule when England takes New Netherland.

Duke of York grants Jersey to Lord John Berkeley and Sir George Carteret, both of whom were among the eight Carolina proprietors.

1669—The Fundamental Constitutions, written mainly by the philosopher John Locke, sets up an elaborate scheme of government for Carolina, based on a series of landholding classes.

1670—Charles Town (later Charleston, SC) founded; in 1680 relocated to its present site.

1676—Jersey divided into East Jersey (Carteret's land) and West Jersey (now held by four Quakers including William Penn).

1677—Culpeper's Rebellion in Albermarle Colony (North Carolina) led to a brief takeover of the government by people opposing supporters of the proprietors.

1682—Delaware granted to William Penn, but it will have a separate government from Pennsylvania under the Penn family.

1691—Albemarle Colony takes the name North Carolina and has a separate deputy governor.

Maryland becomes a royal colony, but Calverts retain property rights.

1702—Jersey united as a royal colony.

1711–1712—War with Tuscaroras in North Carolina ends with their surrender and removal to New York State.

1721—South Carolina becomes a royal colony.

1729—North Carolina becomes a royal colony.

Carolina proprietors sell their claims.

1751—Maryland charter of 1632 again put into force under fourth Lord Baltimore, now a Protestant.

HANDOUT 5   Chapter 2

Contributions of Selected Languages to English in America

Spanish	French	Dutch	German
bronco	portage	cole slaw	noodle
mustang	toboggan	cookie	pretzel
pinto	voyageur	stoop (porch)	sauerkraut
lasso	cent	spool	loafer
rodeo	dime	boss	phooey
chile con carne	a la mode	patroon	spiel
tamale	bayou	Yankee	nix
sombrero	butte	boodle	kindergarten
cafeteria	crevasse	dumb (stupid)	ouch
patio	levee	Santa Claus	stein
plaza	prairie	snoop	semester
bonanza	sault	spook	delicatessen
calaboose	bureau	cruller	dunk
desperado	depot	pit (seed)	hamburger
vigilantes	shanty	hook (of land)	frankfurter
coyote	lacrosse	pot cheese	stollen
enchilada	picayune	waffle	hex
canyon	rotisserie	caboose	fresh (impudent)
fiesta	sashay	scow	zwieback
hombre	praline	sleigh	liverwurst
marina	pumpkin	logy	scrapple
pronto	caribou*	saw buck	hurrah
tornado		schooner	swindler
stevedore		boor	plunder
filibuster		brandy	poker

*This and some other words from the Indians

©Copyright, 1981, by Ginn and Company (Xerox Corporation).   All Rights Reserved.

Testimony by Benjamin Franklin Before the House of Commons 1766

Subject: American Viewpoint Concerning Taxation by Great Britain

Q. What is your name, and place of abode?

A. Franklin, of Philadelphia.

Q. Do the Americans pay any considerable taxes among themselves?

A. Certainly many, and very heavy taxes.

Q. What are the present taxes in Pennsylvania, laid by the laws of the colony?

A. There are taxes on all estates real and personal, a poll tax, a tax on all offices, professions, trades and businesses, according to their profits; an excise on all wine, rum, and other spirits; and a duty of Ten Pounds per head on all Negroes imported, with some other duties.

Q. For what purposes are those taxes laid?

A. For the support of the civil and military establishments of the country, and to discharge the heavy debt contracted in the last war.

Q. Are not all the people very able to pay those taxes?

A. No. The frontier counties, all along the continent, having been frequently ravaged by the enemy and greatly impoverished, are able to pay very little tax.

Q. Do you think it right that America should be protected by this country (England) and pay no part of the expense?

A. That is not the case. The colonies raised, clothed, and paid during the last war, near 25,000 men, and spent many millions.

Q. Do not you think that people of America would submit to pay the stamp duty, if it was moderated?

A. No, never, unless compelled by force of arms.

Q. What was the temper of America towards Great Britain before the year 1763?

A. The best in the world. They submitted willingly to the government of the Crown, and paid, in all their courts, obedience to acts of Parliament... They had not only a respect, but an affection for Great Britain; for its laws, its customs and manners, and even a fondness for its fashions, that greatly increased the commerce. Natives of Britain were always treated with particular regard; to be an Old-England man was, of itself, a character of some respect, and gave a kind of rank among us.

Q. And what is their temper now?

A. O, very much altered.

Q. To what causes is that owing?

A. To a concurrence of causes; the restraints lately laid on their trade, by which the bringing of foreign gold and silver into the colonies was prevented; the prohibition of making paper money among themselves; and then demanding a new and heavy tax by stamps; taking away, at the same time, trials by juries, and refusing to receive and hear their humble petitions.

Q. Don't you think they would submit to the stamp act, if it was modified, the obnoxious parts taken out, and the duty reduced to some particulars, of small moment?

A. No; they will never submit to it.

Q. What is your opinion of a future tax, imposed on the same principle with that of the stamp-act? How would the Americans receive it?

A. Just as they do this. They would not pay it.

Q. If the act is not repealed, what do you think will be the consequences?

A. A total loss of the respect and affection the people of America bear to this country, and of all the commerce that depends on that respect and affection.

(Adapted from *The Writings of Benjamin Franklin*)

Important Engagements in the American Revolution

1775

B Lexington and Concord (April 19) British destroy colonial supplies at Concord, but suffer heavy casualties on return to Boston.

A Crown Point and Ticonderoga (May 10, 12) Ethan Allen and his Green Mountain Boys capture forts that open invasion route to Canada.

B Bunker Hill (June 17) After three charges and heavy losses, the British force the Americans to retire from the hill for lack of ammunition.

B Quebec (Sept. 12–Dec. 31) American Generals Montgomery and Arnold reach Quebec by land, but are defeated with heavy losses during a blizzard.

1776

A Moore's Creek Bridge (Feb. 27) Patriots defeat Loyalists near Wilmington, NC, and prevent British under Clinton from joining forces with the southern Loyalists.

A Boston (March 17) British siege is lifted when Howe evacuates town and sails with troops to Halifax.

A Charleston (June 28) General Charles Lee leads Patriot defenses and forces British under Clinton to withdraw.

B Long Island (Aug. 27) British General Howe forces Washington to abandon Brooklyn and escape to Manhattan.

B Fall of Fort Washington and Fort Lee (Nov. 16, 18) Washington escapes from forts in New York and New Jersey as British General Cornwallis captures both.

A Trenton (Dec. 26) With a small force, General Washington crosses the Delaware River and surprises the Hessian mercenaries of the British.

1777

A Princeton (Jan. 3) Washington rallies his troops to turn defeat into victory as the British surrender in the college town.

B Ticonderoga (July 5) The British under General Burgoyne recapture the fort shortly before their surrender at Saratoga.

A Oriskany (Aug. 6) General Herkimer defeats the British, forcing them to retreat to Canada.

A Bennington (Aug. 16) American militia inflict heavy losses upon a detachment of General Burgoyne's army.

B Brandywine (Sept. 11) Washington fails to halt General Howe's advance upon Philadelphia, which then falls to the British.

B Germantown (Oct. 4) Washington attempts to surprise British General Howe but is defeated.

A Saratoga (Oct. 17) British General Burgoyne surrenders his army to General Gates in the turning point of the war, leading to France's decision to enter the war as our ally.

1778

A Irish sea raids by John Paul Jones (April 14–24) Successful raids upon British shipping and the seizure of their ships by Jones near English ports.

A British evacuation of Philadelphia (June 18) After occupying the city for seven months, the British depart, bringing joy to Washington at nearby Valley Forge.

I Monmouth (June 28) General Lee disobeys Washington's orders, so that the British cannot be halted on their way to New York.

B Wyoming Valley and Cherry Hill Valley Massacres (July 3, Nov. 11) The most savage raids of the war upon the Americans by the Indians. At Cherry Valley an entire settlement is burned to death.

A Kaskaskia (July 4) General Clark surprises the British and the Indians, giving the Americans a territory as large as France and England combined.

B Savannah (Dec. 29) British land unopposed and rout the Americans.

1779

A Vincennes (Feb. 23) Aided by the French, General Clark overwhelms the British garrison.

B Briar Creek (Mar. 3) British rout Georgia militia as Americans suffer heavy losses.

A Stono Ferry (June 19) General Lincoln's troops attack with heavy losses, forcing the British to retire to Savannah.

A Stony Point (July 15) "Mad Anthony" Wayne successfully storms the British fort.

I Paulus Hook (Aug. 19) "Light Horse Harry" Lee invades British camp protecting the Hudson River, but then has to flee.

1779 (cont.)

A Western New York State (Aug.–Sept.) American General Sullivan removes Indian threat with decisive victories.

A North Sea (Sept. 23) John Paul Jones in *Bonhomme Richard* defeats British *Serapis*.

B Savannah (Sept.–Oct.) Despite the French fleet in the harbor, the British defeat Pulaski's French and American forces.

1780

B Charleston (May 12) The British capture General Lincoln and 5,000 Americans.

B Camden (Aug. 16) General Gates suffers the most crushing American defeat of the war.

A King's Mountain (Oct. 7) American rebels turn the southern war around with a victory.

1781

A Cowpens (Jan. 17) General Morgan captures nine-tenths of the opposing British force.

I Guilford Courthouse (March 15) A major engagement in which American General Greene forces Cornwallis to retreat to the Atlantic coast.

B Cornwallis' Virginia Campaign (May–July) The British march unopposed through Virginia to Yorktown, where Cornwallis assembles over 7,200 men.

A Yorktown (Sept.–Oct. 19) Last major engagement of the war. Cornwallis surrenders his army to Washington and the French.

Winner: **A**-American victory
         B-British victory
         I-Indecisive

HANDOUT 8 Chapter 5

Chief Features of the American Constitutional System

The text of the Constitution of the United States appears on pages 762–797. It is annotated to help you understand each article and section. The charts and text on this handout summarize some of the chief features of our constitutional system.

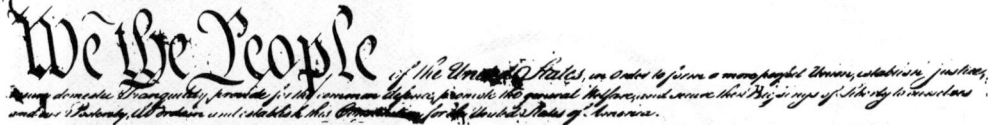

Popular sovereignty. "We the people . . . do ordain and establish this Constitution of the United States." Sovereignty—supreme political authority—rests with the people. Alexander Hamilton wrote, "The fabric of American empire ought to rest on the solid basis of the consent of the people. The streams of national power ought to flow immediately from that pure, original fountain of all legitimate authority."

The principle of popular sovereignty had also been expressed in the Declaration of Independence; ". . . governments are instituted among men, deriving their just powers from the consent of the governed."

In our system the people give their consent by means of written constitutions—both state and national. For many years some Americans argued that the Constitution was simply a compact among the states. But the counter-argument that the Constitution rests on the consent of the people prevailed.

Limited government. Through the Constitution the people granted power to the national government—but with many limitations on the extent and use of this power. The Constitution abounds in the words "no" and "not." The limitations are most obvious in the Bill of Rights. But the original document put some direct limits on both the national government (Art. 1, secs, 9–10) and the states (Art. 1, sec. 10). The Founders chose also to list the powers of Congress in fairly specific terms.

The narrow listing of the powers of the national government helped to persuade the delegates at Philadelphia that the Constitution of the United States need not spell out basic rights and liberties. But the struggle over ratification convinced the First Congress that a Bill of Rights should be added.

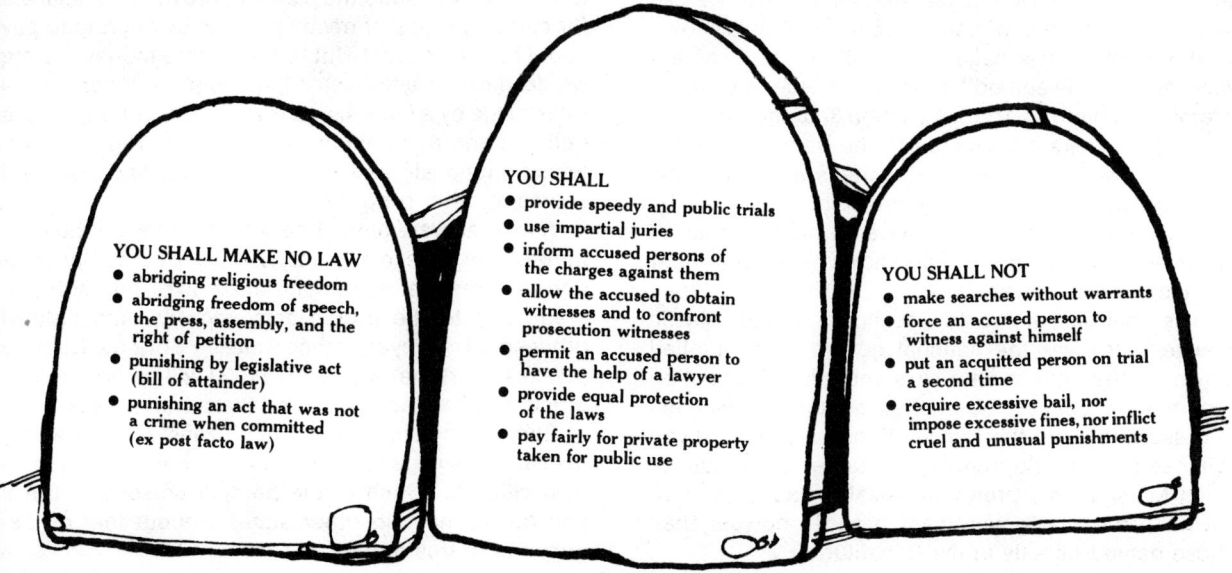

©Copyright, 1981, by Ginn and Company (Xerox Corporation). All Rights Reserved.

FEDERALISM: DIVISION OF POWERS

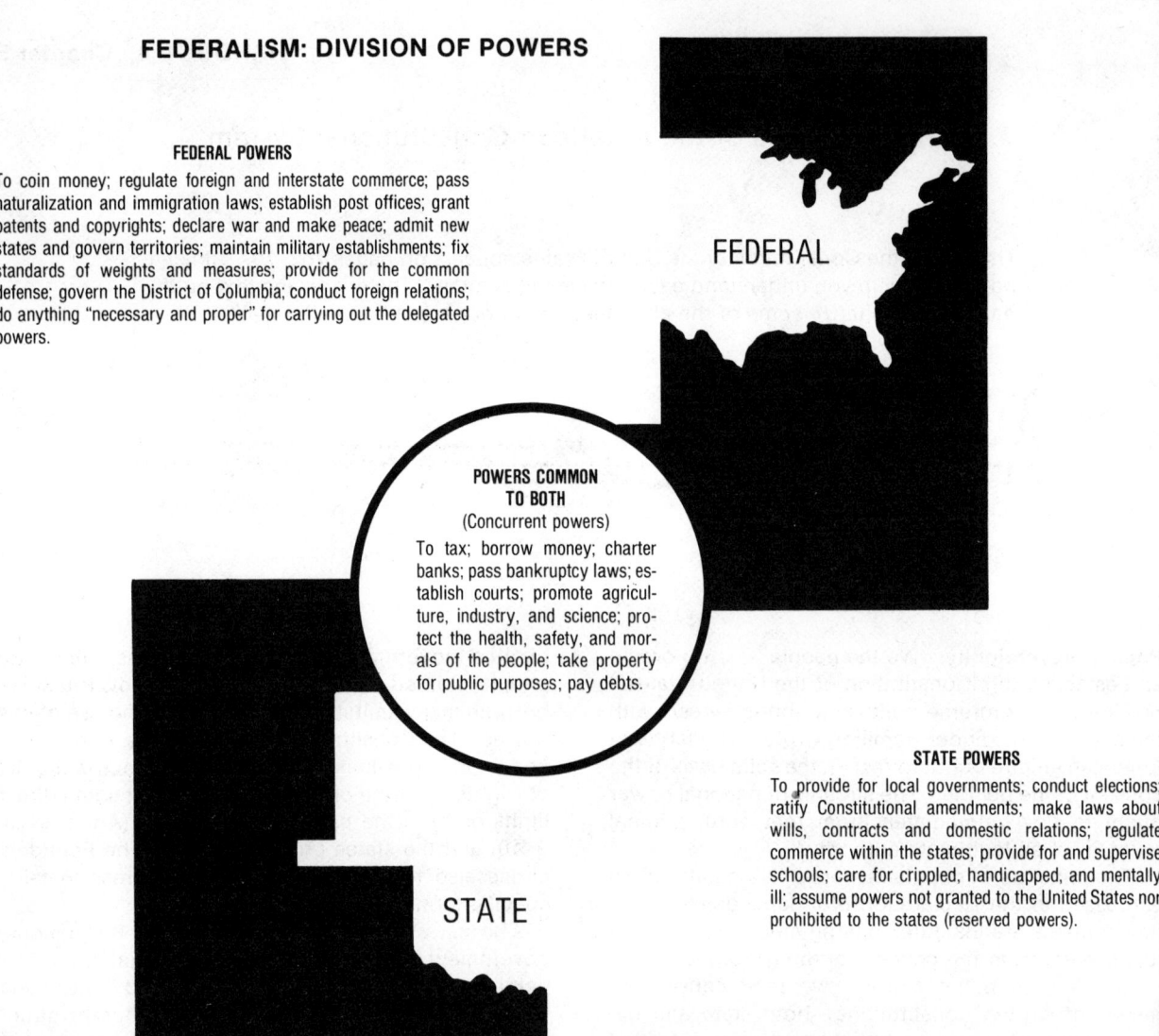

FEDERAL POWERS

To coin money; regulate foreign and interstate commerce; pass naturalization and immigration laws; establish post offices; grant patents and copyrights; declare war and make peace; admit new states and govern territories; maintain military establishments; fix standards of weights and measures; provide for the common defense; govern the District of Columbia; conduct foreign relations; do anything "necessary and proper" for carrying out the delegated powers.

POWERS COMMON TO BOTH
(Concurrent powers)

To tax; borrow money; charter banks; pass bankruptcy laws; establish courts; promote agriculture, industry, and science; protect the health, safety, and morals of the people; take property for public purposes; pay debts.

STATE POWERS

To provide for local governments; conduct elections; ratify Constitutional amendments; make laws about wills, contracts and domestic relations; regulate commerce within the states; provide for and supervise schools; care for crippled, handicapped, and mentally ill; assume powers not granted to the United States nor prohibited to the states (reserved powers).

Federalism. Under a federal system, governmental powers are divided between a sovereign central government and its sovereign subdivisions, which we call *states*. The division of powers in our system is shown in the chart on this page. Our national government has certain "delegated" powers. These are "enumerated," chiefly in Article I, section 8, of the Constitution. All powers not granted to the national government and not prohibited to the states are said to be *reserved powers*. These reserved powers may be exercised by the states. We have no complete list of reserved powers, but the chart shows examples under the label "state powers."

The final part of Article I, section 8, is the "elastic clause." It gives the national government "implied powers," the right to pass laws and take other action that may reasonably be implied by some power expressed directly in the Constitution. In chapter 8 you will see how the Supreme Court under Chief Justice John Marshall interpreted the elastic clause so as to give the national government broader powers than those named directly in the Constitution.

Today hundreds of government programs are joint federal-state activities. In the 1930s, for example, Congress persuaded the states to provide financial aid for certain groups of needy persons by offering to pay about half the costs. But to receive the money, a state would have to administer the program according to rules made by a federal agency. This is the way we are building and maintaining our Interstate Highway system, fighting air and water pollution, and handling scores of other programs.

A federal system must have some rules on the relations of one state to another. Article IV of the Constitution requires that each state must give "full faith and credit . . . to the public acts, records, and judicial proceedings of every other State." So a decision by a Texas court that A owes B $1000 will be honored by officials in Kansas if A moves there from Texas.

Each state also must grant citizens of other states the same privileges and immunities that it grants to its own citizens. Such a rule permits persons to travel and do business in other states without fear of discriminatory treatment.

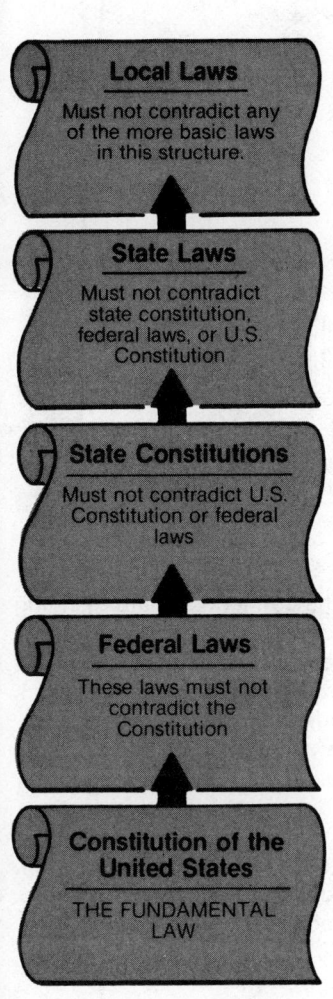

National supremacy. "This Constitution," and the laws and treaties made under its authority, "shall be the supreme law of the land," Article VI proclaims; "and the judges in every State shall be bound thereby. . . ."

In addition, Article VI requires that all officials, state as well as national, "shall be bound by oath or affirmation to support this Constitution."

When a dispute arises over conflicting state law and federal law, the federal courts decide the matter. In the past half century the United States Supreme Court has overturned numerous state laws and local ordinances on the ground that they conflicted with the Constitution's provisions on civil rights and liberties. The Court may also set aside a state law if it is in a field occupied by federal law, leaving no room for state action; or if administration of the state law would interfere with federal activity in that field.

Governor: "I do solemnly swear to uphold and defend . . . the Constitution of the United States."

Judicial review. State and federal law must conform to the Constitution of the United States. But when a conflict arises, who decides it? The Constitution itself did not answer this question directly. But by "reading between the lines," Chief Justice John Marshall in 1803 asserted the Supreme Court's power of judicial review—the power to review and either set aside or uphold an act of Congress or of a state legislature.

Other courts—state and national—also have power to review laws and the actions of government officials. But the United States Supreme Court has the final word.

Far more state and local laws than acts of Congress have been declared unconstitutional by the Supreme Court. Since the late 1930s the Court has used much restraint in overturning federal laws—or parts of laws. Yet, whether the Court exercises its power seldom or often, the principle of judicial review is always at work. Lawmakers and executives constantly raise the question: "But is it constitutional?"

©Copyright, 1981, by Ginn and Company (Xerox Corporation). All Rights Reserved.

The Separation of Powers

The President and other executive officers carry out the laws

Congress enacts the laws

Federal courts apply and interpret the laws

Separation of powers. The Founders believed firmly that separate institutions should exercise the powers of government as protection against tyranny. James Madison wrote in the *Federalist:* "The accumulation of all powers, legislative, executive, and judiciary, in the same hands, whether of one, a few, or many . . . may justly be pronounced the very definition of tyranny."

But Madison also argued that complete separation was neither practical nor desirable. The departments had to be "connected and blended . . . to give to each a constitutional control over the others."

Checks and balances. The connections and blending that Madison recommended are called the check-and-balance system. The President recommends laws for Congress to enact. The Senate can approve or block treaties and major presidential appointments. Congress can remove judges and executive officers if the need should arise. The courts can block illegal or unconstitutional actions of lawmakers and executives. These and other checks are shown in the chart below. Most of them can be found in the Constitution itself. But a few have developed through custom and usage, such as the President's political influence.

THE SYSTEM OF CHECKS AND BALANCES

PRESIDENT — EXECUTIVE

1. Vetoes laws
2. Calls special sessions
3. Sends messages to Congress
4. Leader of party
5. Appeals to the people

1. Nominates judges
2. Grants pardons or reprieves for Federal offenses
3. May refuse to enforce court order

CONGRESS — LEGISLATIVE

1. Overrides veto by two-thirds vote
2. May impeach officials
3. Controls appropriations
4. May reorganize executive departments
5. Can investigate executive departments
6. Senate approves treaties
7. Senate confirms appointments

SUPREME COURT (and lower courts) — JUDICIAL

1. Interprets laws and treaties
2. May rule that the President or other executive officer has acted illegally or misapplied the law

Judicial over Legislative: 1. Interprets laws 2. Interprets treaties 3. Decides on constitutionality of laws

Legislative over Judicial: 1. May impeach judges 2. Senate approves appointments 3. May change size of Supreme Court 4. Sets up new inferior courts and abolishes old ones 5. Regulates the jurisdiction of courts 6. Can propose Constitutional amendments to get around a Court decision

A living, growing Constitution. The delegates at the Philadelphia convention recognized that the Constitution would need to change and grow. The first ten amendments—the Bill of Rights—came quickly in 1791. By 1804 two more had been added—to correct defects in the original articles. Then 60 years went by before the three "Civil War amendments" were added. Only a dozen more amendments came in the next hundred years.

One amazing fact about the amendments as a group is that they added little power to the national government. Yet the Founders would be dumbfounded at the changes in our constitutional government since their day.

By far, the greatest changes in the Constitution have come through *judicial interpretation.* Federal judges—especially those on the Supreme Court—decide the meaning of words and phrases in the Constitution. What is "an establishment of religion" or "equal protection of the laws" or "due process of law"? What does the power of Congress to "regulate commerce . . . among the several States" really mean?

Answers to such questions tell lawmakers and other officials what they may do and must not do. No religious exercises in public schools, for example. Or no separate public schools for black children. For nearly 150 years the courts said that interstate commerce meant the *movement* of goods across state lines. Then in 1937 the Supreme Court said that Congress could regulate labor relations because of their effect on the flow of commerce. Now Congress had the green light to pass other laws dealing with the *production* of goods.

The Constitution also grows as a result of *custom and usage.* Article II describes an indirect method of choosing the President by a body of electors. We follow the required form, but through custom have really turned the election over to the voters operating through political parties. Our whole system of government through political parties, in fact, has developed through custom and usage.

Changes by amendment and by interpretation and usage have kept the Constitution of the United States a living, dynamic framework of government for the American people.

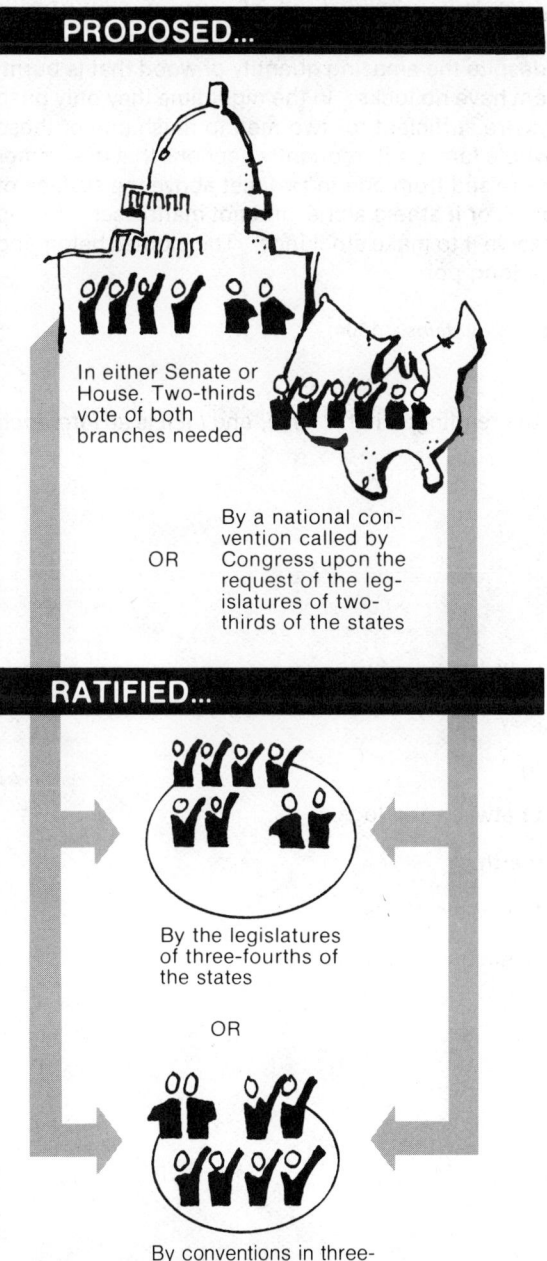

The Amending Process

PROPOSED...

In either Senate or House. Two-thirds vote of both branches needed

OR

By a national convention called by Congress upon the request of the legislatures of two-thirds of the states

RATIFIED...

By the legislatures of three-fourths of the states

OR

By conventions in three-fourths of the states.

HANDOUT 9 Chapter 6

Some Views of the American Frontier by a French Traveler

On the 27th of June (1802) I set out from Lancaster for Shippensburgh. There were only four of us in the stage, which was fitted up to hold twelve passengers. Columbia, upon the Susquehanna River, is the first town we arrived at; it has fifty houses, scattered here and there, and almost all built of wood; at this place ends the turnpike road.

The mode of constructing houses is not the same everywhere. At Philadelphia the houses are built with brick. Elsewhere, of wood, but west of the Allegheny Mountains, one-third of the inhabitants reside in log houses. These dwellings are made with trunks of trees, from twenty to thirty feet in length, about five inches in diameter, placed one upon another, and kept up by notches cut at their extremities. The roof is formed with pieces of similar length, but not quite so thick. Two doors, which often supply the place of windows, are made by sawing away a part of the trunks. The chimney, always placed at one end of the house, is likewise made with the trunks of trees. The back of the chimney is made of clay, about six inches thick, which separates the fire from the wooden walls. The spaces between these trunks of trees is filled up with clay, but so very carelessly, that the light may be seen through every part. These huts are exceedingly cold in winter, despite the amazing quantity of wood that is burnt. The doors move upon wooden hinges, and the greater part of them have no locks. In the night time they only push them shut, or fasten them with a wooden peg. Four or five days are sufficient for two men to finish one of these houses, in which not a nail is used. Two great beds receive the whole family. It frequently happens that in summer the children sleep upon the ground, in a kind of rug. The floor is raised from one to two feet above the surface of the ground, and boarded. They generally make use of feather beds, or feathers alone, and not mattresses. Sheep being very scarce, the wool is very dear; at the same time they reserve it to make stockings. The clothes belonging to the family are hung up round the room, or suspended upon a long pole.

(Adapted from Francois A. Michaux, *Travels to the West of the Allegheny Mountains.* 1804)

Mark each of the following statements *T* if it is *true* according to the reading; *F* if it is *false;* and *I* if it is an *inference* based on the reading.

_____ 1. The stagecoach was packed full of passengers.

_____ 2. The Philadelphia houses were made of brick.

_____ 3. Roofs of the log houses were made of planks.

_____ 4. Sawmills were not available where frontier families built log houses.

_____ 5. Log-house chimneys were made of logs faced with clay.

_____ 6. The fireplace was used for cooking as well as heating.

_____ 7. Much cold air came into the houses through spaces between the logs.

_____ 8. The floor of the log house was simply packed-down earth.

_____ 9. The log house furnished little privacy for individual family members.

_____ 10. The French traveler described log houses west of the Allegheny Mountains.

HANDOUT 10   Chapter 6

During the summer of 1800, the government moved from Philadelphia to Washington. In the letter below, Abigail Adams, wife of President John Adams, describes the new White House residence to her daughter. After you finish reading the letter, answer the questions that follow.

Washington, 21 November, 1800

My dear child,

    I arrived here on Sunday last, and without meeting with any accident worth noticing, except losing ourselves when we left Baltimore, and going eight or nine miles on the Frederick road, by which means we were obliged to go the other eight through the woods, where we wandered two hours without finding a guide, or the path. Fortunately a straggler came up with us, and we engaged him as a guide. Woods are all you see, from Baltimore until you reach the city, which is only so in name. Here and there is a small cottage, without a glass window, interspersed among the forests, through which you travel miles without seeing any human being. In the city there are buildings enough, if they were compact and finished, to accommodate Congress and those attached to it; but as they are, and scattered as they are, I see no great comfort for them. The river, which runs up to Alexandria, is in full view of my window, and I see the vessels as they pass. The house is upon a grand and superb scale, requiring about thirty servants to attend and keep the apartments in proper order. To light the apartments, from the kitchen to parlors and chambers, is difficult indeed. The fires we are obliged to keep to secure us from daily fevers provide cheering comfort. To assist us in this great castle, and render less attendance necessary, bells are wholly wanting, not one single one being hung through the whole house. This is so great an inconvenience! If they will put up some bells, and let me have wood enough to keep fires, I will be pleased. I could content myself almost anywhere three months; but, surrounded with forests, can you believe that wood is not to be had, because people cannot be found to cut and cart it! There is coal available, but we cannot get grates made and set. We have, indeed, come into a new country.

    You must keep all this to yourself, and, when asked how I like it, say that I write you the situation is beautiful, which is true. The house is made habitable, but there is not a single apartment finished. We have not the least fence, yard, or other convenience outside. I use the great unfinished audience room as a drying room for hanging up the clothes! The principal stairs are not up, and will not be this winter. Six chambers are made comfortable, so we may have guests. Upstairs there is the oval room which is designed for the drawing room, and has the crimson furniture in it. If the twelve years, in which this place has been considered as the future seat of government, had been improved, as they would have been if in New England, very many of the present inconveniences would have been removed.

    Since I sat down to write, I have been called down to a servant from Mount Vernon. He has a letter from Mrs. Washington inviting me to Mount Vernon, where, health permitting, I will go, before I leave this place.

(Adapted from *Letters of Mrs. Adams, the Wife of John Adams.* 1848)

---

1. What happened to the Adams family on the way from Baltimore to Washington?
2. What view did Mrs. Adams have from the White House?
3. Why are so many servants needed in the White House?
4. What are Mrs. Adams's complaints about the White House? Why does she want them kept secret?
5. What is used as a place to dry the laundry?
6. How does Mrs. Adams indicate her pride in New England?
7. What invitation does she receive? What are her plans?

HANDOUT 11   Chapter 7

A Senator Opposes the Louisiana Purchase in 1803

Although Jefferson had doubled the size of the country with the purchase of Louisiana, the Federalists opposed him, and sought to defeat the treaty in the Senate, which had to give its approval (and did). Senator Samuel White of Delaware, a Federalist, made the remarks that follow. After you have read them, answer the questions at the end of the handout.

Admitting then, Mr. President, that His Majesty (the King of Spain) is hostile to the cession of this territory to the United States, what reasons have we to suppose that if the Spaniards should interfere, the French Commissioner can give to us peaceable possession of the country? He does not have a single soldier to enforce his orders. I wish not to be understood as predicting that the French not cede to us the actual and quiet possession of the territory. I hope to God they may, for possession of it we must have; I mean of New Orleans, and of such positions on the Mississippi as may be necessary to secure to us forever the complete and uninterrupted navigation of that river.

This I have ever been in favor of; I think it essential to the peace of the United States and to the prosperity of our western country. But as to Louisiana, this new, unbounded world, if it should ever be incorporated into this Union, which I have no idea can be done but by altering the Constitution, I believe it will be the greatest curse that could at present befall us; it may be productive of innumerable evils. Gentlemen on all sides agree that the settlement of this country will be highly injurious and dangerous to the United States. As to removing the Creeks and other nations of Indians from the eastern to the western banks of the Mississippi, and of making the fertile regions of Louisiana a howling wilderness, never to be trodden by the foot of man, it is impracticable.

You had as well pretend to inhibit the fish from swimming in the sea as to prevent the population of that country after its sovereignty shall become ours. To every man acquainted with the adventurous, roving, and enterprising temper of our people, and with the manner in which our western country has been settled, such an idea must be unrealistic. The inducements will be so strong that it will be impossible to restrain our people from crossing the river. Our citizens will be removed to the immense distance of 2,000 or 3,000 miles from the capital of the Union, where they will scarcely ever feel the rays of the general government; their affections will become alienated; they will gradually begin to view us as strangers; they will form other commercial connections, and our interests will become distinct. We do have already territory enough, and $15 million was a most enormous sum to give.

(Adapted from Debates, 8 Congress, pp. 31–35, November 2, 1803)

---

1. What is the Senator's strongest argument? Which is the weakest?
2. How would you answer the argument that although we should have New Orleans and positions on the Mississippi, we should not have the whole Louisiana Territory?
3. What point is the Senator making in his reference to the Constitution?
4. Why does the Senator—as a Federalist—oppose the settling of the Louisiana Territory?
5. From the present-day viewpoint, write a convincing reply to the Senator telling him why the Louisiana Territory was a wise decision.
6. Evaluate the Senator's predictions. Which were fulfilled? Which were unfilled?

HANDOUT 12   Chapter 8

Directions: Reading the following message in which President James Madison asks the nation to go to war in 1812 against Great Britain. Answer the questions that follow before you read the speech by Congressman Randolph.

The conduct of Great Britain has been hostile to the United States as an independent and neutral nation. British cruisers have been in the continued practice of violating the American flag on the great highway of nations, and of seizing and carrying off persons sailing under it.

British cruisers have also violated the rights and peace of our coasts by hovering over and harassing our entering and departing commerce. They have wantonly spilled American blood within our territory. Under pretended blockades, our commerce has been plundered on every sea.

Our attention is also necessarily drawn to the warfare just renewed by the savages on our extensive frontiers—a warfare sparing neither age nor sex and most shocking to humanity. It is difficult not to connect this activity with the cooperation of the British traders and garrisons.

We behold, in short, a state of war against the United States, and, on our side, a state of peace toward Great Britain. Whether we shall remain passive under these accumulating wrongs, or, opposing force in defense of our national rights, is a solemn question which the constitution wisely confides to our Legislature. I am happy in the assurance that their decision will be worthy of a free and powerful nation.

(Adapted from Richardson, *Messages and Papers of the Presidents,* Vol. 1)

Answer the following:

1. What reasons does Madison give to justify our entry into the war?
2. The Senate voted 19-13 and the House of Representatives 79–49 to enter the war. Explain why the vote was so divided.
3. As a member of Congress how would you have voted? Encircle *yes* or *no.* Explain your vote.

Directions: Now read the following excerpt from a speech by Congressman John Randolph of Virginia on the Canadian issue in 1812, and then answer the questions that follow.

This war of conquest, a war for the acquisition of territory and subjects, is to be a holiday campaign—there is to be no expense of blood or treasure on our part! Canada is to conquer herself—she is to be subdued by the principles of fraternity. The people of that country are the first to be lured from their allegiance, and converted into traitors, as preparatory to making them good citizens. I detest this bribery of treason! If they must fall, let it be by the valor of our arms, by fair, legitimate conquest.

Go! March to Canada! Leave the Chesapeake and the whole line of seacoast unprotected! If you take Quebec—have you conquered England? Will you call upon her to leave your ports and harbors untouched, only just till you can return from Canada to defend them? The coast is to be left defenseless, while men of the interior are reveling in conquest and spoil.

While talking of taking Canada, some of us are shuddering for our safety!

(Adapted from *Debates,* 12 Cong., 1 Sess.)

Answer the following:

1. Why is Randolph sarcastic to his War Hawk colleagues?
2. What American attitude does he oppose?
3. Why does he think that our attacking Canada will be dangerous? Give evidence that he was or was not right.
4. Has Randolph's speech changed your war vote in any way? Why?

©Copyright, 1981, by Ginn and Company (Xerox Corporation). All Rights Reserved.

HANDOUT 13 Chapter 9

Andrew Jackson Is Inaugurated

Thousands of people, without distinction or rank, collected in an immense mass round the Capitol, silent, orderly, and tranquil, their eyes fixed, waiting the appearance of the President in the portico. Preceded by the marshals, surrounded by the judges of the Supreme Court, the old man with his gray locks emerged and bowed to the people who greeted him with a shout. Then an almost breathless silence followed, as the crowd became still, listening to catch the sound of Jackson's voice, though it was so low as to be heard only by those nearest to him.

Later, we learned that the crowd had lessened and we might enter the President's house. But what a scene did we witness! The majesty of the people had disappeared, and a rabble, a mob, now scrambled and fought to get into the White House. What a pity! No arrangements had been made, no police officers were on duty, and the whole house had been inundated by the rabble mob. We came too late. The President, after having been literally nearly pressed to death and almost suffocated and torn to pieces by the people in their eagerness to shake hands with Old Hickory, had retreated through the back way and had escaped to his lodgings. Cut glass and china to the amount of several thousand dollars had been broken in the struggle to get refreshments. Punch and other articles had been carried out in tubs and buckets, but had it been in barrels it would have been insufficient. Ice creams and cakes and lemonade for twenty thousand people were provided. Ladies fainted, men were seen with bloody noses. It is almost impossible to describe the confusion—those who got in could not get out again except to scramble out of the windows.

This wild scene had not been anticipated and therefore not provided against. Ladies and gentlemen only had been expected, not the people en masse. But it was the people's day, and the people's President would rule. God grant that one day or other the people do not put down all rule and rulers. I fear, enlightened freemen as they are, they will be found, as they have been in all ages and countries where they get the power in their hands, that of all tyrants, they are the most ferocious, cruel, and despotic.

(Adapted from Mrs. Samuel Harrison Smith, *The First Forty Years of Washington Society.* 1829)

Now answer these questions:

1. How did Jackson's inauguration differ from those of the present day?
2. This was the first inauguration at which spectators became unruly. Why had this not happened before?
3. How would you have arranged to handle the crowd in the White House? How much freedom should visitors have in such a place?
4. The author fears power in the hands of people. Why? Have her fears been justified in later American history? Explain.

HANDOUT 14   Chapter 10

A Railroad Trip from Boston to Lowell, Massachusetts, in 1842

Directions: The famous English novelist Charles Dickens toured the United States in 1842. Below are his impressions of a train ride at that time. After you have finished reading them, answer the questions at the end of the handout.

There are no first- and second-class carriages as with us; but there is a gentlemen's car and a ladies' car; the main distinction between which is that in the first, everybody smokes; and in the second, nobody does. As a black man never travels with a white one, there is also a negro car, which is a great blundering clumsy chest. There is a great deal of jolting and noise.

The cars are like shabby omnibusses, but larger: holding thirty, forty, fifty people. The seats, instead of stretching from end to end, are placed crosswise. Each seat holds two persons. There is a long row of them on each side of the caravan, a narrow passage up the middle, and a door at both ends. In the centre of the carriage there is usually a stove, fed with charcoal or anthracite coal; which is for the most part red-hot. It is insufferably close; and you see the hot air fluttering between yourself and any other object you may happen to look at, like the ghost of smoke.

In the ladies' car, there are a great many gentlemen who have ladies with them. There are also a great many ladies who have nobody with them: for any lady may travel alone, from one end of the U.S. to the other, and be certain of the most courteous and considerate treatment everywhere. The conductor wears no uniform. He walks up and down the car, and in and out of it, as his fancy dictates. A great many newspapers are pulled out, and a few of them are read. Everybody talks to you, or to anybody else who hits his fancy. If a lady takes a fancy to any male passenger's seat, the gentleman who accompanies her gives him notice of the fact, and he immediately vacates it with great politeness.

Except when a branch road joins the main one, there is seldom more than one track of rails, so that the road is very narrow. The train calls at stations in the woods. It rushes across the turnpike road, where there is no gate, no policeman, no signal; nothing but a rough wooden arch, on which is painted "WHEN THE BELL RINGS, LOOK OUT FOR THE LOCOMOTIVE." On it whirls headlong, dives through the woods again, emerges in the light, clatters over frail arches, rumbles upon the heavy ground, and suddenly awakens all the slumbering echoes in the main street of a large town, and dashes on haphazardly down the middle of the road. On and on tears the mad dragon of an engine with its train of cars; scattering in all directions a shower of burning sparks from its wood fire; screeching, hissing, yelling, panting; until at last the thirsty monster stops beneath a covered way to drink, the people cluster round, and you have time to breathe again.

(Adapted from Charles Dickens, *American Notes,* 1842)

1. What customs did Dickens observe that are no longer practiced today?
2. How have the interiors of railroad cars changed from Dickens's day?
3. How was heat provided in the cars? How is it provided today?
4. According to the text, why was there just one track?
5. Why did the train go through the center of town?
6. What role did the train play in the life of the town? How has this changed in the present day?

HANDOUT 15   Chapter 10

A Girl Works in a Lowell, Massachusetts, Factory in 1845

Directions: After you read the testimony given below to a committee of the Massachusetts legislature in 1845, find statements in the testimony or in the text that *agree* or *disagree* with those at the end of the handout.

First to testify was Eliza R. Hemmingway. She had worked 2 years and 9 months in the Lowell Factories; 2 years in the Middlesex, and 9 months in the Hamilton Corporations. Her employment is weaving—works by the piece. . . . She is now at work in the Middlesex Mills, and attends one loom. Her wages average from $16 to $23 a month exclusive of board. She complained of the hours for labor being too many, and the time for meals too limited. In the summer season, the work is commenced at 5 o'clock, A.M., and continued until 7 o'clock, P.M., with half an hour for breakfast and three quarters of an hour for dinner. During eight months of the year, but half an hour is allowed for dinner. The air in the room she considered not to be wholesome. There were 293 small lamps and 61 large lamps lighted in the room in which she worked, when evening work is required. These lamps are also lighted sometimes in the morning. About 130 females, 11 men, and 12 children (between the ages of 11 and 14) work in the same room with her. . . . She thought there was a general desire among the females to work but ten hours, regardless of pay.

(Adapted from *Massachusetts House Document* no. 50, 1845)

From the above testimony or the text, find evidence to *agree* or *disagree* with these statements:

1. Some factory workers were paid according to how much they produced.
2. The length of the work day varied according to the amount of daylight.
3. Fortunately, workers had ample time in which to eat meals.
4. In cold weather, ventilation within the factory was a problem, especially because the lamps consumed much of the oxygen in the air.
5. Children were employed in the factories.
6. Women factory workers would have been pleased with a ten-hour day.
7. It was generally believed that women would not be permanent workers in the factories because within a few years most would leave to marry and raise a family.
8. Northern workers enjoyed being free and yet having security in their jobs.
9. American factory workers, although specialized, had to serve an apprenticeship of several years to learn how to use their machines.
10. American factory towns were generally cleaner than those in England.

HANDOUT 16   Chapter 10

Directions: Complete the graph below. The bars for immigration in the 1820s have been completed. Fill in similar bars for the 1830s, 1840s, and 1850s.

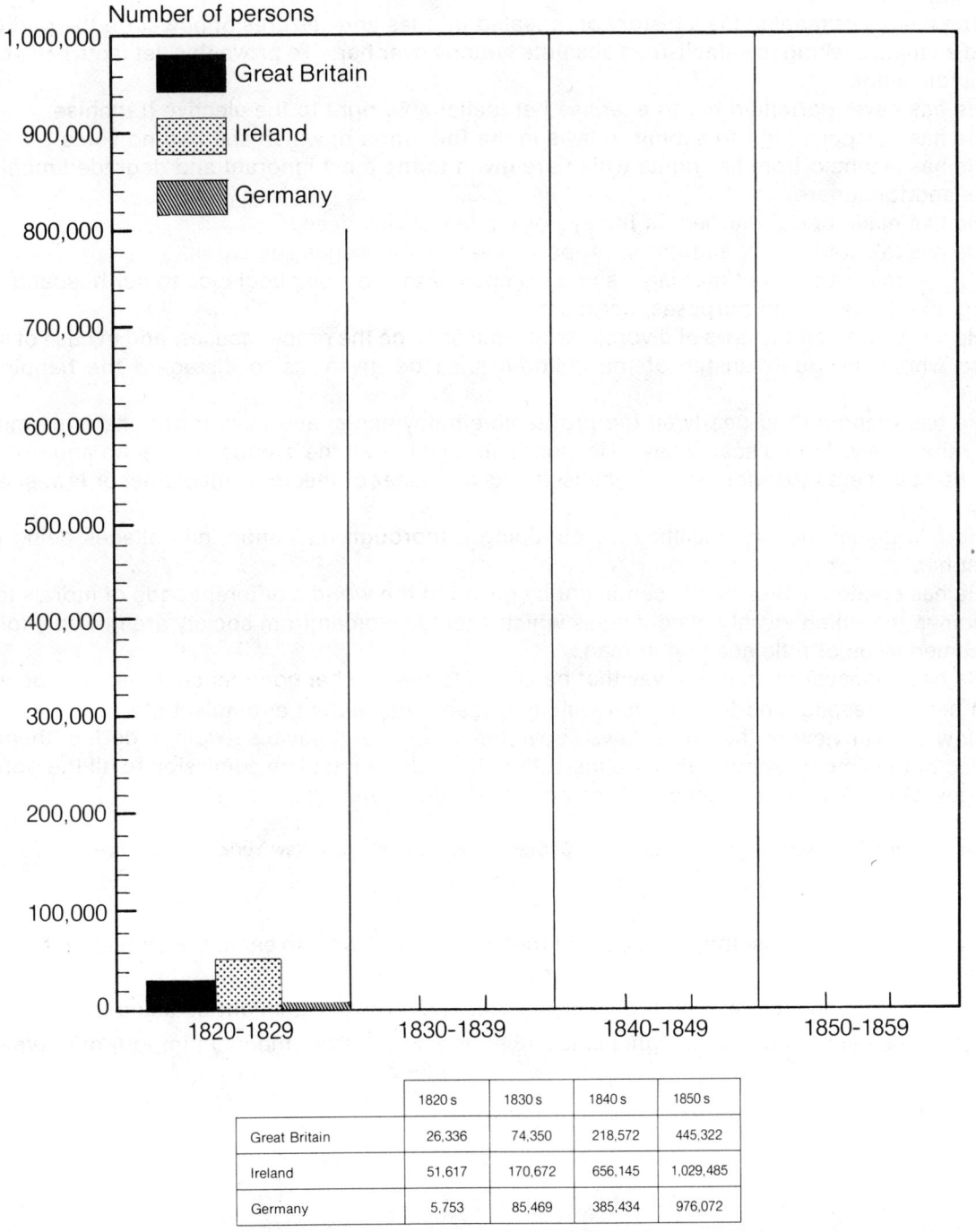

U.S. Immigration from Great Britain, Ireland, and Germany, 1820-1859

	1820s	1830s	1840s	1850s
Great Britain	26,336	74,350	218,572	445,322
Ireland	51,617	170,672	656,145	1,029,485
Germany	5,753	85,469	385,434	976,072

©Copyright, 1981, by Ginn and Company (Xerox Corporation). All Rights Reserved.

HANDOUT 17   Chapter 11

Directions: Below is a slightly shortened and adapted version of the Seneca Falls Declaration of Women's Rights. Read it, and then answer the questions that follow.

The Seneca Falls Declaration of Women's Rights

We hold these truths to be self evident: that all men and women are created equal; that they are endowed by their Creator with certain inalienable rights; that among these are life, liberty, and the pursuit of happiness. . . .

The history of mankind is a history of repeated injuries and seizures of power on the part of man toward woman, seeking to establish an absolute tyranny over her. To prove this, let facts be submitted to a candid world.

He has never permitted her to exercise her inalienable right to the elective franchise.

He has compelled her to submit to laws in the formation of which she had no voice.

He has withheld from her rights which are given to the most ignorant and degraded men—both natives and foreigners.

He has made her, if married, in the eye of the law, civilly dead.

He has taken from her all right in property, even to the wages she earns.

. . . In the covenant of marriage, she is compelled to promise obedience to her husband, he becoming, to all intents and purposes, her master. . . .

He has so framed the laws of divorce, as to what shall be the proper causes, and in case of separation, to whom the guardianship of the children shall be given, as to disregard the happiness of women. . . .

He has monopolized nearly all the profitable employments, and from those she is permitted to follow, she receives but a scanty pay. He closes against her all the avenues to wealth and distinction which he considers most honorable to himself. As a teacher of theology, medicine, or law, she is not known.

He has denied her the facilities for obtaining a thorough education, all colleges being closed against her.

He has created a false public sentiment by giving to the world a different code of morals for men and women, by which moral delinquencies which exclude women from society are not only tolerated but deemed to be of little account in man.

He has endeavored, in every way that he could, to destroy her confidence in her own powers, to lessen her self-respect and to make her willing to lead a dependent and abject life.

Now . . . in view of the unjust laws above mentioned, and because women do feel themselves deprived of their most sacred rights, we insist that they have immediate admission to all the rights and privileges which belong to them as citizens of the United States. . . .

(Adapted from *History of Woman Suffrage,* Elizabeth C. Stanton, et al., eds., Vol. I, New York, 1881, pp. 70–73.)

1. In a vertical column, list the grievances of the declaration. Next to each, state whether it is *valid* or *invalid* today.
2. If this declaration were written today, what additional grievances might be listed by women?
3. What three gains in women's rights since 1848 do you consider the most important? Why?

HANDOUT 18   Chapter 11

A Day on the Oregon Trail in 1843

More than a thousand pioneers with their 5000 cattle gathered at Independence, Missouri, in the spring of 1843 to make a journey of 2000 miles to Oregon. They would travel to Fort Laramie, cross the Rockies to Ford Bridger, and then head northwest along the Snake and Columbia rivers. (See map on page 240 to follow this route.)

A cattleman, Jesse Applegate, kept a diary, from which the following is an excerpt. After you read it, answer the questions that follow at the end of the handout.

Our 1,000 migrants had about 120 wagons, drawn by six ox teams each. Because our group was so large, we separated into two columns which traveled in supporting distance of each other. Later, when all danger from the Indians was past, we broke up into small parties better suited to the narrow mountain paths. I stayed with the cow columns, and I will describe the journey for just a single day.

It is 4 A.M. The sentinels on duty discharge their rifles to signal us the hours of sleep are over. The night tenants pour out of every wagon and tent. Soon smoke from breakfast fires rises on the morning air. Sixty men start for the corral to round up the cattle that form a huge semicircle around the encampment. By 5 A.M. the herders get the well-trained animals moving slowly toward camp. Some of the oxen are driven into the corral to be yoked. The corral is a large circle of wagons fastened together by their tongues and ox chains. In case of an attack by the Sioux we would have a strong defense.

From 6 to 7 A.M. is a busy time. Breakfast is to be eaten, the wagons loaded, and the teams yoked to their respective wagons. All drivers know that at 7 A.M. they must be ready; otherwise at the signal to march they must take their place at the dusty rear for the day. The women and children have taken their place in the wagons. About fifteen young hunters leave the line of march to go out on a buffalo hunt. They may have to ride twenty miles to reach the buffalo, for the unfriendly Sioux have driven the buffalo out of the Platte region.

At the stroke of 7, a trumpet sounds in the front of the line. With a cracking of whips and loud commands to oxen, the line begins to move through its long day across the grassy bluffs. The air is so clear that a rifle report can be heard for a few hundred yards, but the smoke of the discharge can be seen for miles. An object thought to be two hours away may require a day's journey.

The morning hours pass by quickly. At noon, the caravan stops, and all eat and rest. Friends get together. The animals graze at convenient watering places near the bank of the Platte. When the bugle sounds, the westward journey slowly begins again. Soon, with the high sun, drowsiness falls on man and beast, and even the children nap inside the wagons.

As the sun gets low in the west, the circle of wagons must begin to form the necessary fortification for the night. As each wagon is brought into position, the team is unyoked and driven out to pasture. Everyone is busy: preparing fires of buffalo chips; cooking the evening meal; pitching tents; repairing wagons. A noble man, Dr. Marcus Whitman, ministers to the sick. Armed guards are posted; there will be four watches for the night. A violin makes lively music, but as darkness falls, the camp becomes quiet. We have accomplished twenty miles of the journey. Sleep comes easily underneath the broad expanse of the stars.

(Adapted from *Transactions of the Fourth Annual Re-Union of the Pioneer Association;* for 1876, Salem, Ore., 1877, pp. 57–65.)

Now respond to the following:

1. List what you think were some of the reasons the migrants wanted to go to Oregon.
2. Why was the caravan so large? List the advantages and disadvantages of this mode of travel.
3. In the diary, Applegate explains that the caravan had its own governing body that made rules and acted as a court. Why was this necessary?
4. What was the purpose of forming a circle of wagons each evening?
5. How was some of the food obtained? What kinds of food could be stored without refrigeration?
6. What were some lessons that children might learn during the journey?

HANDOUT 19 Chapter 12

Word Recognition and Sentence Writing

Below are listed twenty less-familiar words found in Chapter 12. Each of these words can replace an underlined word or phrase in the sentences that follow. In the answer space write the listed word that can replace the underlined word or phrase.

anarchy	defy	inevitable	patronage	servile
avenge	forebodings	involuntary	prejudice	sovereignty
concoct	fugitive	martyr	rational	travesty
dilemma	incitement	optimist	reckoning	wary

_____ 1. The sheriff caught the *runaway* ten miles from home.

_____ 2. He couldn't *come up with* a new plan.

_____ 3. He said he would *pay back* the injury done to his sister.

_____ 4. He was very *suspicious* as he watched the stranger.

_____ 5. The victim of his own *bias,* he spoke against equality.

_____ 6. The slave's need to work long hours was often *against his wishes.*

_____ 7. Lincoln was a *level-headed* thinker.

_____ 8. When the mob took over the government, *chaos* resulted.

_____ 9. The Americans objected to British *governmental authority.*

_____ 10. Douglas faced a *problem* in seeking to please both the North and the South.

_____ 11. The *arousal* of a proslavery mob led to the death of Lovejoy.

_____ 12. By John Brown's *calculation,* thousands of slaves would join him.

_____ 13. He decided to *challenge* the order of the court.

_____ 14. Abolitionists felt that the war was *unavoidable.*

_____ 15. She was willing to be a *sufferer* in the cause of freedom.

_____ 16. The newspapers carried grim *predictions* of war.

_____ 17. He was a *cheerful person* who did not believe that there would be a Civil War.

_____ 18. To the North, the Dred Scott decision was a *misrepresentation* of justice.

_____ 19. His *fawning* obedience was scorned by other slaves.

_____ 20. The *influence* of Jackson secured his appointment.

Now write ten original sentences using one of the listed words correctly in each sentence. Use the back of the paper to write your sentences.

HANDOUT 20   Chapter 12

Abe Lincoln Is Nominated for the Presidency

After losing to Stephen Douglas in 1858 in the race for the United States Senate, Lincoln was not a favorite candidate for the Presidency in 1860 when the Republican convention met in Chicago. Observers thought that either Senator William H. Seward of New York or Governor Salmon P. Chase of Ohio would win. Yet as the balloting began, the race seemed to be between Seward and Lincoln. A reporter for the *Cincinnati Commercial* described the scene:

About a thousand confident Seward men marched as usual from the Richmond House to the Convention Hall by following their brilliantly uniformed band. However, by circling a little too far around the city, they were tardy in arriving at the wigwam, and were not all able to get inside, where there was not a square foot unoccupied. Tens of thousands of people milled around outside.

After Seward's nomination, the applause was enthusiastic. Lincoln's name brought a prodigious response, rising and raging far beyond the Seward shriek. Then the seconding of Seward gave his men another chance. The effect was startling. Hundreds of persons stopped their ears in pain. The shouting was absolutely frantic, shrill and wild. Looking from the stage over the vast amphitheatre, I could see below thousands of black hats flying with the velocity of hornets over a mass of human heads.

Now the Lincoln men had another try upon his seconding, and the uproar was unbelievable. It sounded like a score of big steam whistles, accompanied by a stamping that made every plank and pillar in the wooden building quiver. One man leaped upon a table, and, swinging hat and cane, performed like an acrobat. During this demonstration, the Seward men sat in silence with whitened faces.

As the voting began, it was apparent that Seward did not have as much strength as anticipated. Some of the New England states gave part of their votes to Lincoln, but New York cast 70 votes for Seward. However, in a surprise, Virginia gave Seward but 8 votes and Lincoln 14, causing the New Yorkers to look at each other in alarm. When Indiana gave 26 votes to Lincoln, it seemed evident that Lincoln, Cameron, and Bates had the combined strength to defeat Seward. At the end of the first ballot, Seward was ahead of Lincoln, 173½ to 102, but still short of a majority.

The Convention proceeded to a second ballot, as the delegates rose to a high pitch of excitement. At the end of the ballot, Seward had 184½ and Lincoln 181. With the third ballot, a fatal defection from Seward in New England to Lincoln was noticed, and it was whispered about: "Lincoln will be nominated on this ballot." Then Carter of Ohio got the floor, and all seemed to know what he was about to do. He cried, "I rise, Mr. Chairman, to announce the change of four votes from Mr. Chase to Mr. Lincoln." The deed was done. Lincoln had the nomination. There was a moment of silence.

Then the nerves of the thousands broke and there was a noise in the wigwam like the rush of a great wind. Thousands cheered with the energy of insanity. At a sky-light on the roof over the stage, a man fired a salute to announce to the crowd waiting outside that Lincoln had won. Nearby, cannon were fired, and the smell of gunpowder drifted through the air. Soon, with bands playing, great processions marched jubilantly through the city, led by "Old Abe" men carrying rails.

That night, as I went home on the night train, I saw that late as it was there were tar barrels burning, drums beating, and guns firing at every station. Every boy seemed to be carrying a split rail.

(Adapted from Murat Halstead, *Caucuses of 1860: A History of the National Political Conventions.* Columbus, 1860, pp. 143–154.)

Now answer the following questions:

1. What reasons help explain why some delegates switched from Seward and other candidates to Lincoln?
2. Find out why some states have more delegates than others.
3. How did the crowd outside the Convention Hall learn of Lincoln's victory? How would the crowd get the news today?
4. Since Lincoln's day, what changes have taken place in the behavior of delegates inside the Convention Hall?
5. How have the victory celebrations changed from Lincoln's day to the present?

HANDOUT 21   Chapter 13

The Military Draft in the Union and the Confederacy

The Union

1. The United States Conscription Act was passed March 1863. All men 20–45 years of age had to register for military service. Later, with quotas established for the various states, there were four drafts from July 1863 to December 1864.
2. The states were given credit for previous enlistments, and these were subtracted from the quotas. The western states had the highest percentage of volunteers.
3. Service could be "commuted" (evaded) on payment of $300 to procure a substitute. Exemption was given for the entire war if the substitute enlisted for 3 years (even if he died within the month or deserted, perhaps the day after enlistment). This provision, of course, was unfair to the poor, and it led to working-class draft riots in New York City in 1863.
4. In the first draft (July 1863), married men over 35 were not drafted until all other possible draftees in a district had been called. This provision was dropped in later drafts.
5. Exemptions were also given to sole supporters of aged parents and to eldest brothers in large families of young children, but not to supporters of families as such. The chief cause of exemption was physical disability.
6. Religious conscientious objectors were also exempt, but had to serve in some noncombatant branch.
7. Bounties were paid to volunteers upon enlistment. This practice encouraged "bounty jumpers" to enlist and desert. Sometimes they would repeat the experience several times before being caught.

The Confederacy

1. Men 18–35 were subject to the draft. This source was important because volunteer enlistments were for a term of 12 months.
2. Exemptions were given to ministers, conscientious objectors, railway employees, postmen, druggists, and teachers. Added later were millers, blacksmiths, editors, printers, and plantation overseers (at the rate of 1 to every 20 slaves).
3. Substitutes could be provided, but this practice was stopped at the end of 1863 when the price of a substitute reached $6000 in depreciated currency.
4. In 1864, exemptions were reduced, and military service was extended to include men from 17 to 50.
5. There were no draft riots, but deserters formed roving gangs that terrorized cities, requiring army detachments to control them. By June 1863, absentees in the army reached 30 percent.

---

1. Why was conscription (the draft) necessary in both the North and the South during the Civil War?
2. Historians seem to agree that conscription in the Civil War, particularly in the North, provided relatively few draftees, but was useful in securing "an enormous number of volunteers." For what reasons would men volunteer rather than wait to be drafted?
3. A common saying in both the North and the South was that the conflict was "a rich man's war and a poor man's fight." Do you agree or disagree? Explain.
4. In all American wars, we have given exemptions to conscientious objectors for religious reasons. Why do you favor or oppose this practice? Should these persons be required to fulfill noncombat duties, such as medical service? Explain.
5. Give reasons why you favor or oppose occupational deferments or exemptions from military service. Why were these given, especially in the Confederacy?
6. In an evaluation of the draft laws of the Union and Confederacy, which aspects seem fair or unfair to you? Explain.

HANDOUT 22 Chapter 13

President Lincoln Delivers the Gettysburg Address

The invitation notified Lincoln that the National Soldiers' Cemetery at Gettysburg, where thousands had fallen in the greatest battle ever to take place on American soil, would be dedicated on November 19, 1863. The finest orator of the day, Edward Everett, would deliver the principal address. Would Lincoln make a "few appropriate remarks"?

The President accepted the invitation. However, worried about the success of the Union armies on the fighting fronts and the grave illness of his young son Tad, he had little time to prepare his speech, and had to finish it on the late afternoon train from Washington to Gettysburg. The next morning, Lincoln rode on horseback with the procession to the cemetery. There a crowd of 15,000 waited patiently for the ceremonies to begin, while the bands played patriotic marches and peddlers sold souvenirs from the battlefield.

The eloquent Everett spoke for two hours until at last he came to his closing words: ". . . in the glorious annals of our common country there will be no brighter page than that which relates to the battles of Gettysburg." The weary crowd applauded, then listened to the Baltimore Glee Club sing an ode. Knowing that his time had come to speak, the somber President put on his steel-rimmed spectacles, unfolded a single sheet of paper, and nodded as he was introduced. He spoke in a clear, high-pitched voice. Perhaps only a small portion of the large crowd heard the 268 words destined to become one of the immortal masterpieces of the English language:

"Four score and seven years ago, our fathers brought forth upon this continent a new nation, conceived in liberty, and dedicated to the proposition that all men are created equal. Now we are engaged in a great civil war, testing whether that nation, or any nation so conceived and so dedicated, can long endure. We are met on a great battlefield of that war. We are met to dedicate a portion of it as the final resting place of those who here gave their lives that that nation might live. It is altogether fitting and proper that we should do this. But in a larger sense we cannot dedicate—we cannot consecrate—we cannot hallow this ground. The brave men, living and dead, who struggled here, have consecrated it far above our poor power to add or detract. The world will little note, nor long remember, what we say here, but it can never forget what they did here. It is for us, the living, rather to be dedicated here to the unfinished work that they have thus far so nobly advanced. It is rather for us to be here dedicated to the great task remaining before us, that from these honored dead we take increased devotion to that cause for which they here gave the last full measure of devotion; that we here highly resolve that these dead shall not have died in vain; that this nation, under God, shall have a new birth of freedom, and that government of the people, by the people, shall not perish from the Earth."

Lincoln was finished almost before the crowd realized that he had begun. The tardy applause caused him to believe that his speech was a failure. He was therefore cheered the next day by a message from Everett: "I should be glad if I could flatter myself that I came as near to the central idea in two hours as you did in two minutes."

Now answer the following questions:

1. What do you think is the central idea of the Gettysburg Address that Everett referred to?
2. Using no more than 100 words, summarize the address in your own words. Use complete sentences.

HANDOUT 23 Chapter 14

The Impeachment Trial of President Andrew Johnson

After President Johnson ignored the Tenure of Office Act in removing Secretary of War Stanton against the wishes of Congress, Radicals in the House decided to impeach the President. This was voted by the House, and the charges were then tried by the Senate, with the Chief Justice presiding. The following is a description of the trial by one of Johnson's military aides.

When, from my seat in the gallery, I looked down on the Senate chamber, I had a moment of almost terror. It was not because of the great assemblage; it was rather in the thought that one could feel in the mind of every man and woman there that for the first time in the history of our country a President was on trial for more than his life.

There was a painful silence when the counsel for the President filed in and took their places. (The President was not present.) The prosecution managers were already in their seats. Benjamin Butler arose to make the opening address. It was a violent attack on the President.

The trial lasted three weeks. The President never appeared. He remained absolutely calm through it all, doing routine work in the White House. As the trial proceeded, the conviction grew with me that the weight of evidence and of constitutional principle lay with the defense. The prosecution showed much personal feeling and prejudice rather than proof. Every appeal that could be made to the passions of the time was utilized.

But the legal struggle was hardly the contest that counted. The debate was for the benefit of the country at large; while the legal lights argued, the enemies of the President were working in other ways. The Senate was thoroughly canvassed, personal argument and influence were in constant use. Every personal motive, good or bad, was played upon. Long before the final ballot, it became known how most of the men would probably vote. Toward the end the doubtful ones had narrowed down to one man—Senator Edmund G. Ross of Kansas.

Kansas was, from inception and history, abolitionist and radical, and it was supposed that Senator Ross would vote with the Radicals. But it became known that he was doubtful; it was charged that he had been subject to personal influence—feminine influence. His cohorts in the Senate and the House bore down upon him with party discipline and then ridicule. Ross refused to make an announcement of his policy.

On May 16, 1868, the vote was taken. The floor and galleries were crowded. The Chief Justice directed that the roll be called. The clerk called out: "Mr. Anthony." The Chief Justice called out: "Mr. Anthony, how say you? Is the respondent, Andrew Johnson, President of the United States, guilty or not guilty of a high misdemeanor as charged in this article?"

"Guilty," answered Mr. Anthony. A sigh passed over the crowd. A two-thirds vote of 36 to 18 was necessary to convict. The same form was maintained with each Senator in turn. Senator Ross was the sphinx; no one knew his position.

The tension grew as Ross was reached. When the clerk called it, and the Senator stood forth, the crowd held its breath. "Not guilty!" called the Kansas Senator.

It was like the boiling over of a caldron. The Radicals turned to Ross in rage. When the vote was over—35 to 19—there was a wild outburst, chiefly groans of anger and disappointment. The President's friends were in a minority.

(Adapted from Margarita Spalding Gerry, Ed., *Through Five Administrations: Reminiscences of Colonel William H. Crook.* New York, 1910, 124–134.)

Now answer the following questions:

1. Had President Johnson been removed from office by impeachment, what would have been the impact upon future American history?
2. Should the trial have been closed to the public? Why?
3. Had Johnson been impeached, who would have become President?
4. What are the *advantages* and *disadvantages* of impeachment as a means of removing a President from office? What other ways might be alternatives?

A Grand Jury Condemns the Ku Klux Klan

Despite the Fourteenth Amendment, various secret societies attempted to restore white supremacy in the South. Most active was the Ku Klux Klan. Below is a portion of a federal grand jury report addressed to the United States Circuit Court.

We have investigated crimes committed by the Ku Klux Klan by gathering evidence from the victims and the members themselves. The jury has been shocked beyond measure at the number and character of the atrocities committed, producing a state of terror and a sense of utter insecurity among a large portion of the people, especially the black population. We have established the following:

1. That the Klan, or "Invisible Empire of the South," embraces in its membership a large proportion of the white population, every profession and class, and includes many prominent citizens.
2. That the Klan is bound together by an oath taken at initiation that binds them to secrecy, the violation of which is death.
3. That the members must furnish themselves with a pistol, a Ku Klux gown (white recommended), and a signal instrument. Many of the operations of the Klan were executed at night, and were directed against both black and white persons who were members of the Republican party by warnings to leave the country, by whippings, and by murder.
4. That in large portions of the counties, the civil law has been set at defiance and ceased to afford any protection to the citizens.
5. That the Klan, in carrying out the purposes for which it was organized and armed, inflicted cruel vengeance on the black citizens by breaking into their houses at the dead of night, dragging them from their beds, torturing them in the most inhuman manner, the reason being their political affiliations.

The jury has been appalled as much at the number of outrages as at their character, it appearing that 11 murders and over 600 whippings have been committed in York County alone. We believe from the testimony that an equal number has been committed in other counties.

We are of the opinion that the most vigorous prosecution of the parties implicated in these crimes is imperatively demanded; that without this there is great danger that these outrages will be continued, and that there will be no security to our fellow citizens of black descent.

We would say further that unless the strong arm of the government is interposed to punish these crimes committed upon this class of citizens, there is every reason to believe that an organized and determined attempt at retaliation will be made, which can only result in a state of anarchy and bloodshed too horrible to contemplate.

(Adapted from *42 Congress, 2 Session, House Report No. 22*, pp. 48–49)

Now answer the following questions:

1. Why was the Klan called the "Invisible Empire"?
2. What reasons would motivate even prominent citizens to join the Klan?
3. Why was the Klan most active at night?
4. How did the Klan intimidate blacks?
5. Why didn't the local officers of the law prevent the activities of the Klan?
6. What does the jury fear will happen unless the Klan is stopped? Did this happen?

HANDOUT 25   Chapter 15

Views on Indian Policy

Directions: Below are statements reflecting different viewpoints concerning the Indian problem in the United States during the nineteenth century. After reading them, answer the questions that follow.

When you first came we were very many, and you were few; now you are many, and we are getting very few, and we are poor. You are here told that we are traders and thieves, and it is not so. We have given you nearly all our lands, and if we had any more land to give we would be very glad to give it. . . .

At the mouth of Horse Creek, in 1852, the Great Father made a treaty with us by which we agreed to let all that country open for fifty-five years for the transit of those who were going through. We kept this treaty; we never treated any man wrong; we never committed any murder or depredation until after the troops were sent into that country, and the troops killed our people and ill-treated them, and thus war and trouble arose. . . .

I have sent a great many words to the Great Father, but I don't know that they ever reach the Great Father. The words would never come to him, so I thought I would come and tell you myself.

(From speech of Chief Red Cloud in New York on July 16, 1870.)

If they—the Indians—stand up against the progress of civilization and industry, they must be relentlessly crushed. The westward course of population is neither to be denied nor delayed for the sake of all the Indians that ever called this country their home. They must yield or perish. . . .

Whenever the time shall come that the roving tribes are reduced to a condition of complete dependence and submission, the plan to be adopted in dealing with them must be substantially that which is now being pursued in the case of the more tractable and friendly Indians.

(Adapted from *Report of the Commissioner of Indian Affairs,* Washington, 1873, pp. 391–401.)

To recognize the Indian ownership of the limitless prairies and forests of this continent—that is, to consider the dozen squalid savages who hunted at long intervals over a territory of 1,000 square miles as owning it outright—necessarily implies a similar recognition of the claims of every white hunter, squatter, horse thief, or wandering cattleman. . . .

In fact, the mere statement of the case is sufficient to show the absurdity of asserting that the land really belonged to the Indians. The different tribes have always been utterly unable to define their own boundaries. . . . Their claims all conflicted with one another . . . they were always willing to sell land to which they have merely the vaguest title.

(Theodore Roosevelt, *The Winning of the West,* Vol. I, New York, 1910, Appendix A.)

1. What three basic points are made by Chief Red Cloud?
2. What reason does the Commissioner of Indian Affairs give for saying that the Indians "must yield or perish"?
3. Why does ex-President Roosevelt feel that the Indian claims to land are meaningless?
4. Prepare a brief statement *agreeing* or *disagreeing* with any one of the viewpoints expressed above.

HANDOUT 26 Chapter 15

A Kansas Homesteader Builds a Sod House in 1877

Thousands of settlers built sod houses, usually with help from their neighbors, before they could afford the more costly, permanent frame houses. The house described below cost Howard Ruede $10.05, including ridgepole, rafters, nails, hinges, a window, and firewood.

The sod wall is about 2 feet thick at the ground, and slopes off to about 14 inches at the top. The roof is composed of a ridge pole and rafters of rough split logs, on which are laid corn stalks, sorghum, willow switches, or anything that will prevent the two layers of sod on the roof from falling between the rafters. The roof has a very slight pitch, for if it had more, the sod would wash off when there is a heavy rain.

Sod is the only material the homesteader has at hand, unless he happens to be one of the fortunates who secured a creek claim with timber suitable for house logs.

Sometimes there is a "bee," and the neighbors gather around and put up the house in a day. Of course there is no charge for labor. The women come too, and while the men lay up the sod walls, they prepared dinner for the crowd, and have a very sociable hour at noon. A house put up this way is very likely to settle and get out of shape.

When the prairie is thoroughly soaked by rain or snow is the best time for breaking sod for building. The regulation thickness is 2½ inches. The slices are cut in 12-inch furrows by a plow and a team of horses. Then they are cut into 18-inch pieces with a sharp spade. The wall rises rapidly even when the builders are green hands. The door and window frames are set in place first and the wall built around them. Building such a house is hard work.

When the top of the walls is reached, the crotches (forks of a tree) are set at the ends and in the middle of the house and the ridge pole—usually a single tree trunk the length of the building—is raised to its place by sheer strength of arm, it being impossible to use any other power. Then rails are laid from the ridge log to the walls and covered with the available material. If the builder is able, he has sawed cottonwood rafters and a pine or cottonwood board roof covered with sod.

At first these sod houses are unplastered, but such a house is somewhat cold in the winter, as the crevices between the sods admit some cold air; so some of the houses are plastered with a kind of "native lime," made of sand and a very sticky native clay. This plaster is very good unless it happens to get wet. In a few of the houses this plaster is whitewashed, which helps the looks very much. Some sod houses are mighty comfortable places to go into in cold weather, and it doesn't take much fire to keep them warm.

(Adapted from *Sod-House Days: Letters from a Kansas Homesteader, 1877–78* by Howard Ruede, edited by John Ise. Copyright, 1937 Columbia University Press. Used by permission of Columbia University Press.)

HANDOUT 27 Chapter 16

Andrew Carnegie Visits Oil Creek

Born in Scotland, Andrew Carnegie came with his family to Pittsburgh in 1848, where he became a telegrapher and railroad superintendent before investing in iron manufactures. At age 26, he visited the newly discovered oil wells at Oil Creek. Later he recorded his observations in his *Autobiography*.

There had been such a rush to the oil fields that it was impossible for all to obtain shelter. This, however, to the class of men who flocked thither, was but a slight drawback. A few hours sufficed to build a shanty, and it was surprising in how short a time they were able to surround themselves with many of the comforts of life. They were men above the average, men who had saved considerable sums and were able to venture something in the search for fortune.

What surprised me was the good humor which prevailed everywhere. It was a vast picnic, full of amusing incidents. Fortunes were supposedly within reach; everything was booming. The adaptability of the American was never better displayed than in this region. Order was soon evolved out of chaos. It would be safe to wager that a thousand Americans in a new land would organize themselves, establish schools, churches, newspapers, and brass bands—in short, provide themselves with all the appliances of civilization—and go ahead developing their country before an equal number of British would have discovered who among them was the highest in hereditary rank and had the best claims to leadership owing to his grandfather. There is but one rule among Americans—the tools to those who can use them.

Not long ago, Oil Creek furnished a few barrels of oil every season, gathered with blankets from the surface of the creek by the Seneca Indians. The oil was then bottled in Pittsburgh and sold at high prices as medicine—a dollar for a small vial. It had general reputation as a sure cure for rheumatic tendencies. As it became plentiful and cheap its virtues vanished. What fools we mortals be!

Today, Oil Creek has a thousand inhabitants, with refineries and millions of dollars in capital. At first, its oil production was of the crudest character. When the oil was obtained it was run into flat-bottomed boats which leaked badly. Water ran into the boats and the oil overflowed into the river. In this way the Allegheny River became literally covered with oil. The loss involved in transportation to Pittsburgh was estimated at fully a third of the total quantity, and before the boats started it is safe to estimate that another third was lost by leakage.

More recently, we obtained an option to purchase a well on the Storey farm. We made a lake of oil by excavating a pool sufficient to hold a hundred thousand barrels (the waste to be made good every day by running streams of oil into it, and to hold it for the not far distant day when, as we then expected, the oil supply would cease). We abandoned the reserve. We did not think then of Nature's storehouse below which still keeps on yielding many thousands of barrels per day without apparent exhaustion.

(Adapted from *AUTOBIOGRAPHY OF ANDREW CARNEGIE*. Copyright 1920 by Louise Whitfield Carnegie. Used by permission of Houghton Mifflin Company.)

Now answer the following:
1. What type of Americans were attracted to the oil fields?
2. How does Carnegie compare the Americans and the British?
3. What was the early use of the rock oil gathered by the Indians?
4. What pollution problem is described by Carnegie?
5. What mistake did Carnegie make in estimating the underground supply of oil?

HANDOUT 28   Chapter 16

Naming Causes and Results

Directions: For each statement below, write a CAUSE or a RESULT as directed. In a number of instances the event or development may have had several causes or results. In each case choose one you think is most significant.

1. Rockefeller arranged with the railroads to get rebates on his oil shipments.
   Result: _____

2. By the 1890s the owners of major business firms had no personal interest in the workers.
   Cause: _____

3. By the 1870s labor strikes in America were becoming frequent.
   Cause: _____

4. In the 1880s business combinations known as trusts were formed in a number of major industries.
   Result: _____

5. The price of western land rose substantially between 1870 and 1900.
   Cause: _____

6. In the early days of railroading, long-distance freight might be reloaded several times.
   Cause: _____

7. Gompers stressed "bread and butter" unionism—higher wages, shorter hours, and safer working conditions.
   Result: _____

8. William Sellers designed standard machine bolts and screws.
   Result: _____

9. Farm families were now able to buy a large selection of goods.
   Cause: _____

10. Frederick Taylor designed 15 different shovels for use in the Bethlehem Iron Company.
    Result: _____

©Copyright, 1981, by Ginn and Company (Xerox Corporation). All Rights Reserved.

HANDOUT 29 Chapter 17

European Immigration, 1821-1920

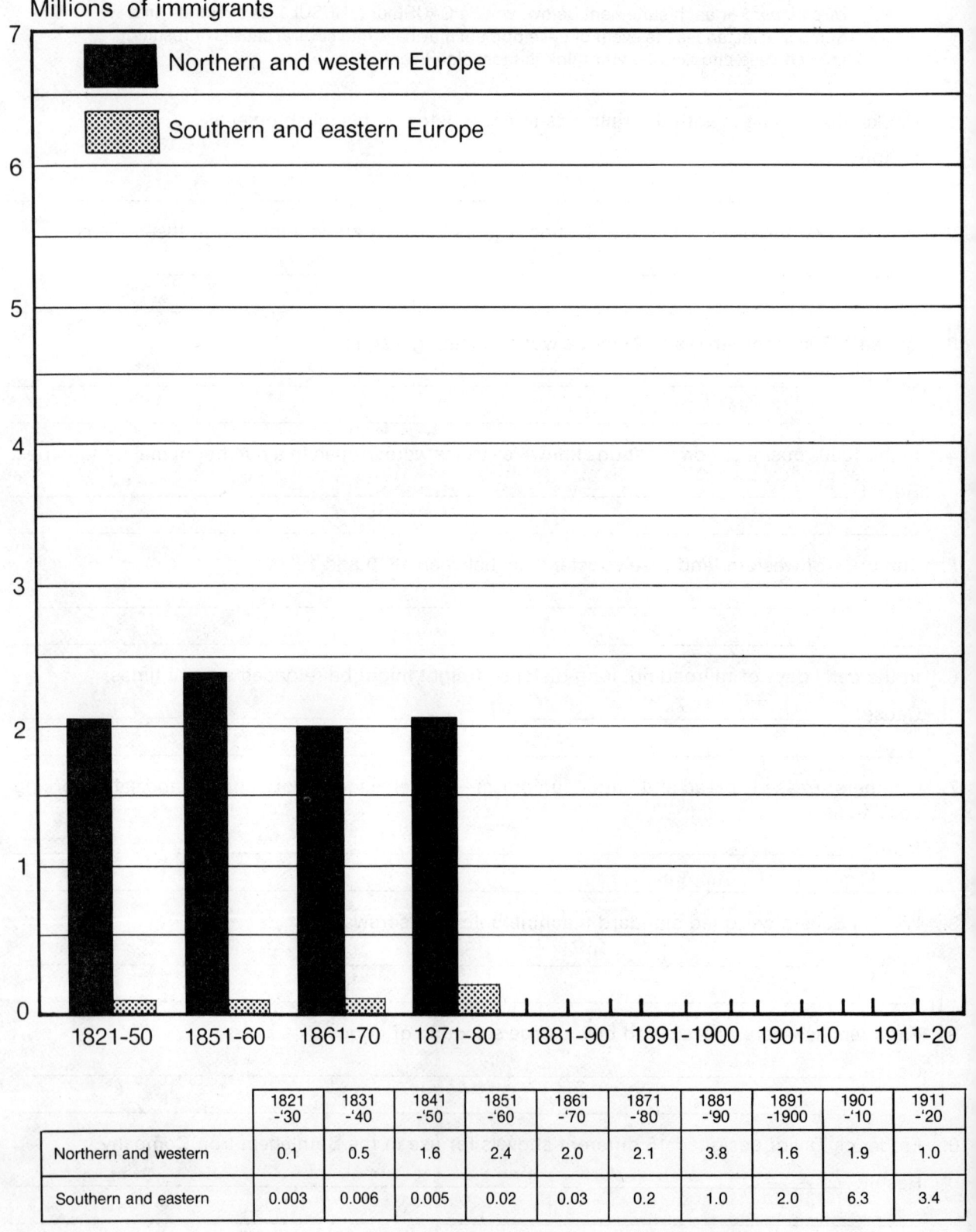

	1821-'30	1831-'40	1841-'50	1851-'60	1861-'70	1871-'80	1881-'90	1891-1900	1901-'10	1911-'20
Northern and western	0.1	0.5	1.6	2.4	2.0	2.1	3.8	1.6	1.9	1.0
Southern and eastern	0.003	0.006	0.005	0.02	0.03	0.2	1.0	2.0	6.3	3.4

©Copyright, 1981, by Ginn and Company (Xerox Corporation). All Rights Reserved.

HANDOUT 30 Chapter 17

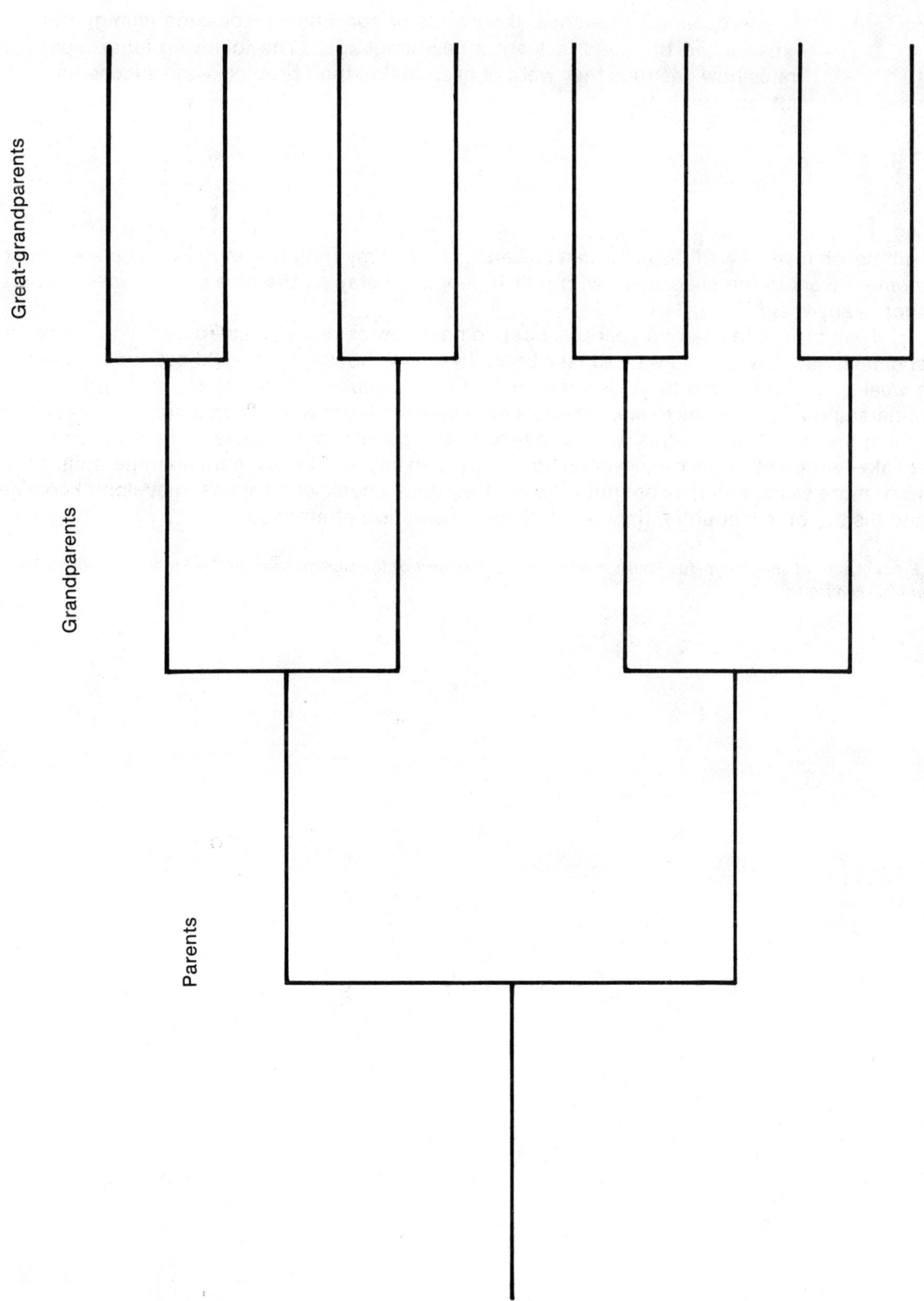

HANDOUT 31   Chapter 17

Letter from a Polish Immigrant

In coming to America, thousands of non-English-speaking immigrants experienced the need to learn a new language. The following letter illustrates how desirous they were of overcoming their problems and succeeding in their new land.

I am polish man. I want be american citizen. . . . But my friends are polish people—I must live with them—I work in the shoesshop with polish people—I stay all the time with them—at home—in the shop—anywhere.

I want live with american people, but I do not know anybody of american. I go 4 times to teacher and must pay $2 weekly. I wanted take board in english house, but I could not, for I earn only $5 or 6 in a week. . . . Better job to get is very hard for me, because I do not speak well english and I cannot understand what they say to me. The teacher teach me—but when I come home—I must speak polish and in the shop also. In this way I can live in your country many years—like my friends—and never speak—write well english—never be good american citizen. I know here many persons, they live here 10 or more years, and they are not citizens, they don't speak well english, they don't know geography and history of this country, they don't know constitution of america.

(From "Letter of an Anonymous Polish Immigrant. . .," *Report of the Commission on the Problem of Immigration in Massachusetts,* 1914.)

HANDOUT 32 Chapter 18

The Election Campaign of 1896

An English journalist, G. W. Steevens, came to the United States in 1896 to observe the presidential candidates. Here are his impressions of William Jennings Bryan, the Democratic candidate who was campaigning in Washington, D.C.

I walked to the park where the great meeting was to be held, and mingled with the crowd. The speakers' platform was built in front of a large stage, which was draped with bunting, flags on every corner, and festooned with hundreds of incandescent lights. From a nearby stand a band punctuated the speeches with "The Battle Cry of Freedom" and other airs. In front of the platform was massed the crowd, about ten thousand strong.

A speaker was declaiming with vigor and eloquence from the platform, but the crowd took not the least notice. They were not there to hear arguments; they were there to hear Bryan. Suddenly the band crashed out "See the Conquering Hero Comes." Instantly the whole park awoke with the waving of a forest of little American flags. When Bryan appeared on the platform, ten thousand hats flew in the air. A little girl in silver tripped along the platform rail, and presented a bunch of silver roses.

Bryan waved his arm above his head, and gradually the crowd became silent. He began in a plain, hoarse but very rich voice. He was glad to see once more those with whom he had spent four years of official life [in Congress].

As for the speech, why trouble to inquire about it? It reads well in this morning's newspaper, though I thought it smacked of platitude [a dull remark delivered profoundly]. But no matter—the crowd had come to see and hear, but not to reason.

Steevens visited Canton, Ohio, to observe Republican candidate William McKinley conduct his front-porch campaign:

If you want to see the presidential candidate, you ring the bell and walk in. I rang and walked in. Mr. McKinley was sitting on a rocking-chair in a little office not ten feet from the door. He wore a frockcoat and loosely-tied brown slippers. He also was not unmindful of the spittoon.

He is gifted with a kindly courtesy that is plainly genuine and completely winning. His personality presents a rare combination of strength and charm. But when I sought to interview him, the answer was no.

Soon a delegation of people, all wearing something yellow—badges, flowers, or caps—came marching down the road from the railroad platform.

When Mr. McKinley came forward to speak, the place was like a field of buttercups leaping into the air and yelling themselves hoarse. His speech was not long, and, to tell the truth, it was not interesting. He is no orator as Bryan is. Indeed he is almost the least effective speaker I have heard here. There was neither argument nor eloquence. I suppose he could not help remembering that he had said much the same thing before, and would repeat it in a few hours to the next group.

(Adapted from G. W. Steevens, *The Land of the Dollar,* Edinburgh and London, 1897, pp. 80–87.)

HANDOUT 33 Chapter 21

The Sinking of the Lusitania

Below are three historic items that relate to the sinking of the British Cunard liner *Lusitania*.

The following advertisement appeared in the Washington, D.C., newspapers on April 22, 1915:

NOTICE!

TRAVELLERS intending to embark on the Atlantic voyage are reminded that a state of war exists between Germany and her allies and Great Britain and her allies; that the zone of war includes the waters adjacent to the British Isles; that, in accordance with formal notice given by the Imperial German Government, vessels flying the flag of Great Britain, or any of her allies, are liable to destruction in those waters and that travellers sailing in the war zone on ships of Great Britain or her allies do so at their own risk. IMPERIAL GERMAN EMBASSY

On the same day, German submarine Captain Schwieger made these notations in his sea log:

Right ahead appeared four funnels and two masts of a steamer. Clean bow-shot from 700-meter range. Shot hits starboard side right behind bridge. An unusually heavy detonation follows. . . . Life-boats being cleared and lowered to water. Many boats crowded, come down bow first or stern first in the water and immediately fill and sink. The ship blows off. In the front appears the name *Lusitania* in gold letters. . . . I submerge to 24 meters and go to sea.

The following appeared on the front page of The Evening Telegram *in New York on Friday, May 7, 1915:*

EXTRA! LUSITANIA BLOWN UP BY GERMANS: LOSS OF LIFE REPORTED SLIGHT

The *Lusitania,* the largest and fastest steamship in passenger service, was torpedoed by a German submarine off the coast of Ireland at two o'clock this afternoon. An official announcement given out in London this evening says the vessel remained afloat "at least twenty minutes" after the explosion.

A despatch from London says it is believed "there was no great loss of life." The passengers numbered 1,253 and the crew about 750. Late this afternoon it was stated that about twenty of the *Lusitania's* boats were afloat near where the steamship sank and that a Greek steamship, several patrol boats, and two motor fishing boats were standing by the small boats.

HANDOUT 34 Chapter 22

During the 1920s sociologists Robert and Helen Lynd studied Muncie, Indiana, to determine the effects of modern inventions and leisure on contemporary life. In 1929 they published their findings in *Middletown*. Below are adapted extracts from this book.

The Automobile in the 1920s

No one questions the use of the auto for transporting groceries, getting to one's place of work or to the golf course, or in place of the porch for "cooling off after supper" on a hot summer evening; however much the activities concerned with getting a living may be altered by the fact that a factory can draw from workmen within a radius of forty-five miles . . . these things are hardly major issues. But when auto riding tends to replace the traditional call in the evening parlor as a way of approach between the unmarried, "the home is endangered," and all-day Sunday motor trips are a "threat against the church"; it is in the activities concerned with the home and religion that the automobile occasions the greatest emotional conflicts.

Group-sanctioned values are disturbed by the inroads of the automobile upon the family budget. . . . According to an officer of a Middletown automobile financing company, 75 to 90 percent of the cars purchased locally are bought on time payment, and a workingman earning $35 a week frequently plans to use one week's pay each month as payment for his car.

The automobile has apparently unsettled the habit of careful saving for some families. "Part of the money we spend on the car would go to the bank, I suppose," said more than one working-class wife. . . . The "moral" aspect of the competition between the automobile and certain accepted expenditures appears in the remark of another businessman, "An automobile is a luxury, and no one has a right to one if he can't afford it. I haven't the slightest sympathy for anyone who is out of work if he owns a car." . . .

Meanwhile, advertisements pound away at Middletown people with the tempting advice to spend money for automobiles for the sake of their homes and families: "Hit the trail to better times!" says one such advertisement.

Another depicts a gray-haired banker lending a young couple the money to buy and proffering the friendly adivce: "Before you can save money, you first must make money. And to make it you must have health, contentment, and full command of all your resources. . . . I have often advised customers of mine to buy cars, as I felt that the increased stimulation and opportunity of observation would enable them to earn amounts equal to the cost of their cars."

Many families feel that an automobile is justified as an agency holding the family group together. "I never feel as close to my family as when we are all together in the car," said one mother. . . . But this centralizing tendency of the automobile may be only a passing phase. . . . The fact that 348 boys and 382 girls in the three upper years of the high school places "use of the automobile" fifth and fourth respectively in a list of twelve possible sources of disagreement between them and their parents suggests that this may be an increasing decentralizing agent.

(Abridged from *MIDDLETOWN* by Robert S. and Helen M. Lynd, copyright 1929 by Harcourt Brace Jovanovich, Inc.; renewed 1957 by Robert S. and Helen M. Lynd. Reprinted by permission of the publisher.)

Income Distribution in the United States

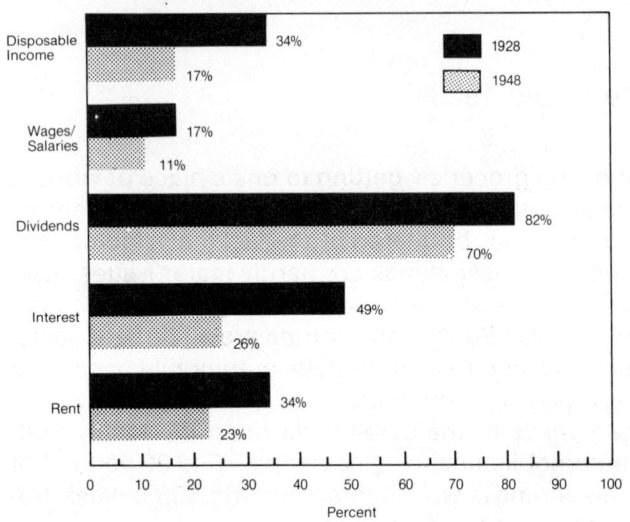

Share of Total Income Going to Top 5 Percent of Population, 1928 and 1948

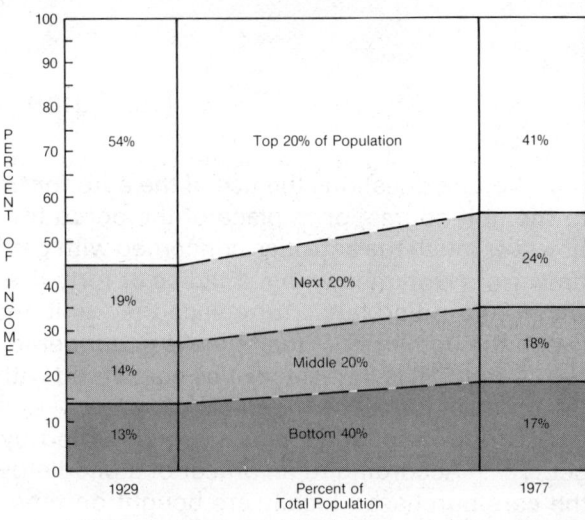

Distribution of Family Income, 1929 and 1977*

* 1977 figures not strictly comparable with 1929.

1. How, according to the text, did the lopsided distribution of income help to bring on the depression?

2. *Disposable income* is income after taxes. Between 1928 and 1948 what probably happened to taxes on high incomes? Explain.

3. In the graph on the left, which of the items represent income from property?

4. Why did so much of the dividend income go to the top 5% of the population?

5. Many people who are not wealthy earn some income from interest and rent. Name some specific sources of interest and rental income.

6. What do both graphs show about changes in income distribution after the late 1920s?

7. Does our society benefit in any way by having 20% of the population receive around 40% of the income?

8. What benefit, if any, would you expect our society to reap if the bottom 40% were to get a substantially larger share of the total income?

HANDOUT 36 Chapter 25

For 27 years Caroline A. Henderson and her husband were successful farmers in Oklahoma. But for five years there was drought, and then came the dust storms. Below are parts of a letter to a friend. After reading them, answer the questions that follow.

LETTER FROM THE DUST BOWL

June 30, 1935

Dear _____:

... Wearing our shade hats, with handkerchiefs tied over our faces ..., we have been trying to rescue our home from the accumulations of wind-blown dust which penetrates wherever air can go. It is an almost hopeless task, for there is rarely a day when at some time the dust clouds do not roll over. "Visibility" approaches zero and everything is covered again with a silt-like deposit which may vary in depth from a film to actual ripples on the kitchen floor. I keep oiled cloths on the window sills and between the upper and lower sashes. They help just a little to retard or collect the dust. Some seal the windows with the gummed-paper strips used in wrapping parcels, but no method is fully effective. ...

Early in May, with no more grass or even weeds on our 640 acres than on your kitchen floor, and even the scanty remnants of dried grasses from last year cut off and blown away, we decided, like most of our neighbors, to ship our cattle to the central part of the state. ... Whether this venture brings profit or loss depends on whether the cattle make satisfactory gains during the summer and whether prices remain reasonable or fall back. ...

... a good many people have left this country either temporarily or permanently. ... And they were not merely "drifters," as is frequently alleged. ... The list [includes] 109 persons in 26 families, [some of whom have been here] as long as forty years. In these families there had been two deaths from dust pneumonia. ... On a sixty-mile trip yesterday to procure tractor repairs we saw many pitiful reminders of broken hopes and apparently wasted effort. Little abandoned homes where people had drilled deep wells for the precious water, had set trees and vines, built reservoirs, and fenced in gardens—with everything now walled in or half buried by banks of drifted soil. ...

Naturally you will wonder why we stay where conditions are so extremely disheartening. Why not pick up and leave as so many others have done? It is a fair question, but a hard one to answer.

Recently I talked with a young university graduate of very superior attainments. He took the ground that in such a case sentiment could and should be disregarded. He may be right. Yet I cannot act or feel or think as if the experiences of our twenty-seven years of life together had never been. ... To leave voluntarily ... seems like defaulting on our task. We may *have* to leave because we can't hold out indefinitely without some return from the land. ...

... Our soil is excellent. We need only a little rain ... to make it productive. ... We have spent so much in trying to keep our land from blowing away that it looks foolish to walk off and leave it. ...

... The dust has been particularly aggravating to [Will's] bronchial trouble, but he keeps working on. A great reddish-brown dust cloud is rising now in the southeast, so we must get out and do our night work before it arrives. Our thoughts go with you.

(Adapted from "Letters from the Dust Bowl" by Caroline Henderson. Copyright © 1936, by The Atlantic Monthly Company, Boston, Mass. Reprinted with permission.)

Now use the other side of this handout to answer the following questions:

1. What means were used to keep from breathing the dust and to keep it out of the house?
2. What was done with the cattle? Why?
3. What signs of the drought were seen along the sixty-mile trip?
4. List Mrs. Henderson's reasons for staying and for leaving. What do you think was her final decision? Why?

HANDOUT 37   Chapter 25

Directions: Below is an alphabetical list of states showing the percentage of farmers who were tenants in 1930. Use the figures to complete the map below. Use four different colors or map shadings for the categories shown in the map legend.

Ala.	64.7	Ga.	68.2	Maine	4.5	Nebr.	47.1	Ohio	26.3	Tex.	60.9
Ariz.	16.4	Idaho	25.3	Md.	26.5	Nev.	12.9	Okla.	61.5	Utah	12.2
Ark.	63	Ill.	43.1	Mass.	5.6	N. H.	5.3	Ore.	17.8	Vt.	9.7
Calif.	18	Ind.	30.1	Mich.	15.5	N. J.	15.6	Pa.	15.9	Va.	28.1
Colo.	34.5	Iowa	47.3	Minn.	31.1	N. M.	20.2	R. I.	12.5	Wash.	17
Conn.	6.2	Kan.	42.3	Miss.	72.2	N. Y.	13.2	S. C.	65.1	W. Va.	18.6
Del.	33.8	Ky.	35.9	Mo.	34.8	N. C.	49.2	S. Dak.	44.6	Wis.	18.2
Fla.	28.4	La.	66.6	Mont.	24.5	N. Dak.	35.1	Tenn.	46.2	Wyo.	22

1. Which section of the country had the *highest* percentage of farm tenants in the 1930s? _____

2. What were some reasons for the high farm tenancy here? _____

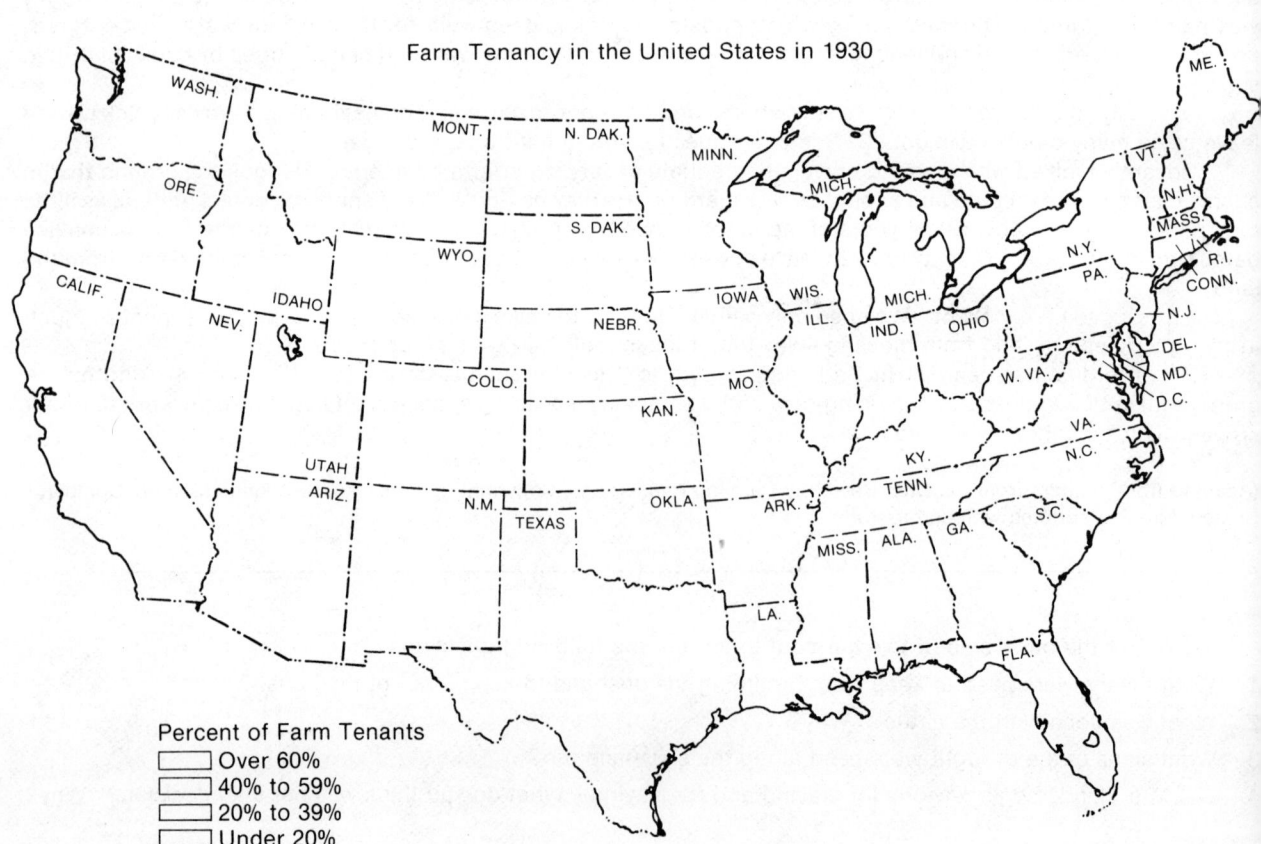

Farm Tenancy in the United States in 1930

Percent of Farm Tenants
- Over 60%
- 40% to 59%
- 20% to 39%
- Under 20%

When Europe went to war in 1939, the United States became much divided over the issue of remaining isolated from the war or aiding the Allies. Below are excerpts from speeches representing both points of view.

The Isolationists: America First

It is now obvious that England is losing the war. I believe this is realized even by the British government. But they have one last desperate plan remaining. They hope that they may be able to persuade us to send another American Expeditionary Force to Europe and to share with England militarily as well as financially the fiasco of this war. . . .

From the standpoint of aviation, I have been forced to the conclusion that we cannot win this war for England, regardless of how much assistance we extend. I ask you to look at the map of Europe today and see if you can suggest any way in which we could win this war if we entered it. . . .

[Yet] there is a policy open to this nation that leaves us free to follow our own way of life and to develop our own civilization. . . . It is based upon the belief that the security of a nation lies in the strength and character of its own people. It recommends the maintenance of armed forces sufficient to defend this hemisphere from attack by any combination of foreign powers. . . . Practically every difficulty we would face in invading Europe becomes an asset to us in defending America. Our enemy, and not we, would then have the problem of transporting millions of troops across the ocean and landing them on a hostile shore. . . .

[But] even in our present condition of unpreparedness no foreign power is in a position to invade us today. If we concentrate on our own defenses and building the strength that this nation should maintain, no foreign army will ever attempt to land on American shores.

(Adapted from speech by Charles A. Lindbergh in New York, April 23, 1941.)

The Interventionists: Aid for Our Allies

Our national policy is this:

First, by an impressive expression of the public will and without regard to partisanship, we are committed to all-inclusive national defense.

Second, we are committed to full support to all those resolute peoples, everywhere, who are resisting aggression and are thereby keeping war away from our Hemisphere. By this support, we express our determination that the democratic cause shall prevail, and we strengthen the defense and security of our own nation.

Third, we are committed to the proposition that principles of morality and considerations for our own security will never permit us to acquiesce in a peace dictated by aggressors and sponsored by appeasers. We know that enduring peace cannot be bought at the cost of other people's freedom.

In the recent national election there was no substantial difference between the two great parties in respect to that national policy. . . . Let us say to the democracies, "We Americans are vitally concerned in our defense of freedom. We are putting forth our energies, our resources, and our organizing powers to give you the strength to regain and maintain a free world."

(Adapted from Franklin D. Roosevelt, *Annual Message to Congress,* January 6, 1941.)

HANDOUT 39   Chapter 27

The greatest decision of World War II had to be made by President Truman. In the excerpts below, he explains what happened.

Truman Decides to Use the Atomic Bomb

April 12, 1945 . . . That first meeting of the Cabinet was short, and when it adjourned . . . Secretary [of War Henry] Stimson . . . asked to speak to me about a most urgent matter. Stimson . . . wanted me to know about an immense project that was under way—a project looking to the development of a new explosive of almost unbelievable destructive power. That was all he felt free to say at the time, and his statement left me puzzled. It was the first bit of information that had come to me about the atomic bomb, but he gave me no details. It was not until the next day that I was told enough to give me some understanding of the almost incredible developments that were under way and the awful power that might soon be placed in our hands.

. . .

April 25 . . . At noon I saw Secretary of War Stimson. . . .

He explained . . . the revolutionary changes in warfare that might result from the atomic bomb and the possible effects of such a weapon on our civilization.

. . . [It] would be certain to have a decisive influence on our relations with other countries. And if it worked, the bomb, in all probability, would shorten the war.

[Secretary of State James] Byrnes had already told me that the weapon might be so powerful as to be potentially capable of wiping out entire cities and killing people on an unprecedented scale. . . . And . . . the bomb might well put us in a position to dictate our own terms at the end of the war. Stimson, on the other hand, seemed at least as much concerned with the role of the atomic bomb in the shaping of history as in its capacity to shorten this war. As yet, of course, no one could positively know that all the gigantic effort that was being made would be successful. . . . He . . . suggested that I designate a committee to study and advise me of the implications of this new force.

. . . [The committee recommended] that the bomb be used against the enemy as soon as it could be done. They recommended further that it should be used without specific warning and against a target that would clearly show its devastating strength. I had realized, of course, that an atomic bomb explosion would inflict damage and casualties beyond imagination. On the other hand, the scientific advisers of the committee . . . [concluded] that no technical demonstration they might propose, such as over a deserted island, would be likely to bring the war to an end. It had to be used against an enemy target.

The final decision of where and when to use the atomic bomb was up to me. . . . I regarded the bomb as a military weapon and never had any doubt that it should be used. . . . and when I talked to Churchill he unhesitatingly told me he favored the use of the atomic bomb if it might aid to end the war.

. . . I wanted it dropped on a military target. . . as nearly as possible upon a war production center of prime military importance.

. . .

Four cities were finally recommended as targets: Hiroshima, Kokura, Niigata, and Nagasaki. . . .

—Adapted from *Memoirs of Harry S. Truman: Year of Decision*, Vol. 1, Doubleday & Company. Copyright © 1955 by Time Inc. Used by permission of Time Inc.

Reasons for Truman's Surprise Victory in 1948

A summary of the explanations given by political analysts follows:

- Seizing the initiative and going to the attack, Truman did not have to defend the weaknesses or the problems of his administration. Instead, he attacked the Republican Congress for its failure to enact needed legislation.

- Truman appealed successfully to the various special interest and minority groups, conveying the impression that the Republican party represented only big business and Wall Street. Even the traditionally Republican midwestern farmers believed Truman when he told them: "Vote for yourselves! Vote for your farms! Vote for the standard of living that you have won under a Democratic administration!"

- The foreign aid program was considered to be one of the strongest points in favor of the Truman administration. When in the summer of 1948 the Communists closed the access routes to the free city of Berlin, the U.S. response was the "Berlin Airlift," a massive effort to supply the beleagured city by air. Truman received the credit for acting decisively in this crisis.

- The vote-getting powers of Roosevelt and the appeal of the New Deal carried over to Truman's "Fair Deal" program. Repeatedly Truman urged the voters to remember the "benefits of the New Deal."

- The polls may have been misleading in that they did not reflect an apparent trend to Truman in the closing weeks of the campaign. The prestigious Elmo Roper organization stopped its poll-taking during the 2nd week of September, asserting that "Thomas Dewey is almost as good as elected." This attitude—also reflected in the press—lulled the Republican party into a false sense of security.

- Although the Republican campaign was a model of efficiency, it did not create any warmth or emotional involvement towards the candidate. Meanwhile, Dewey dealt in platitudes and generalities rather than in specific issues, and conveyed such an air of overconfidence that many otherwise uncommitted voters turned in sympathy to Truman as the underdog.

- The Democrats had become the majority party, and not enough of them were willing to abandon the New Deal philosophy for the restraint and conservatism promised by Dewey, who in turn remained unconvincing to the voters.

- Truman proved that as a man of the people he displayed characteristics that the people admired. Even the Republican *New York Sun* admitted: "You just have to take off your hat to a beaten man who refuses to stay licked!"

HANDOUT 41   Chapter 28

After you read the following, review the map and the references to the Korean War in the text. Then answer the questions at the end of the handout.

The Korean War: Should We Have Invaded Red China?

For

In December 1950, after Red China's entry into the Korean War, the Joint Chiefs of Staff ordered General MacArthur to contain the war to Korea and not to order his troops to cross the Yalu River into China. MacArthur disagreed, favoring also: (1) a naval blockade of China; (2) bombardment of Chinese bases and military centers; (3) employment of Chinese Nationalist troops in Korea; (4) assaults on Chinese coastal areas from Taiwan.

MacArthur publicized his views further in another statement: "The enemy, therefore, must by now be painfully aware that a decision of the UN to depart from its tolerant effort to contain the war to the area of Korea, through an expansion of our military operations to its coastal areas and interior bases, would doom Red China to the risk of imminent military collapse."

In a letter to Congressman Joseph W. Martin, MacArthur wrote: "It seems strangely difficult for some to realize that here in Asia is where the Communist conspirators have elected to make their play for global conquest, and that we have joined the issue thus raised on the battlefield; . . . that if we lost this war to Communism in Asia the fall of Europe is inevitable; win it and Europe most probably would avoid war and yet preserve freedom. As you point out, we must win. There is no substitute for victory."

In 1954, MacArthur said: "It was in our power to destroy the Red Chinese Army and Chinese military power. And probably for all time."

Against

In Senate hearings, General Marshall opposed MacArthur's views: "He would have us risk the involvement not only in an extension of the war with Red China, but in an all-out war with the Soviet Union."

Secretary of State Acheson also felt that an invasion of Red China would lead to war with the Soviet Union. "Russian self-interest in the Far East and the necessity of maintaining prestige in the Communist sphere make it difficult to see how the Soviet Union could ignore a direct attack upon the Chinese mainland."

In reply to those who contended that we could defeat Red China without invading their soil, General Bradley said: "I do not believe you could get any decision by naval and air action alone."

In the British House of Commons, Churchill argued: " . . . the Soviet plan would evidently be to get the United States and the United Nations . . . involved as deeply as possible in China. . . . the United Nations should avoid by every means in their power becoming entangled . . . in a war with China."

1. Why did MacArthur want to invade Red China?
2. In ordering MacArthur to contain the war to Korea, the Joint Chiefs of Staff favored a limited war. However, in wanting to invade Red China, MacArthur stated, "We must win. There is no substitute for victory." Do you agree? Why?
3. Could the UN forces under MacArthur have defeated both Red China and the Soviet Union? Why?
4. Which statement impresses you the most? Why?
5. Would you have favored our going to war against Red China in 1950–1951? Why?

HANDOUT 42   Chapter 29

The Nixon-Khrushchev "Debate"

Vice-President Richard M. Nixon and Russian Premier Nikita Khrushchev became involved in 1959 in an impromptu "debate" at the American National Exhibition in Moscow. This took place as the two leaders paused to examine the well-stocked kitchen. Annoyed at Nixon's remark that most U.S. workmen could afford a similar kitchen, Khrushchev sharply replied:

You think that Russians will be dumbfounded by this exhibit. But the fact is that all newly built Russian homes will have this equipment. You need dollars in the U.S. to get this house, but here all you need is to be born a citizen. If an American citizen does not have dollars, he has the right to . . . sleep on the pavement. And you say we are slaves of Communism!

N.: We don't think this fair will astound the Russian people, but it will interest them just as yours interested us. To us diversity, the right to choose, the fact that we have a thousand different builders, that's the spice of life. We don't want to have a decision made at the top by one government official saying that we will have one type of house. That's the difference . . .

K.: On political differences, we will never agree . . .

N.: Isn't it better to be talking about the relative merits of our washing machines than the relative strength of our rockets? Isn't this the kind of competition you want?

K.: Yes, that's the kind of competition we want, but your generals say they are so powerful they can destroy us. We can also show you something so you will know the Russian spirit. We are strong, we can beat you . . .

N.: To me, you are strong and we are strong. In some ways, you are stronger than we are. In others, we are stronger . . .

The leaders moved on to a table of California wines. Someone handed a glass to Khrushchev. He proposed a toast: "To peace and the elimination of all military bases on foreign lands."

N.: Let us just drink a toast to peace.

A Russian in the group proposed: "One hundred years to Premier Khrushchev!"

N.: I will drink to that. We may disagree with your policy, but we want you to be of good health. May you live to be one hundred years old.

K.: At ninety-nine years of age we shall discuss these questions further. Why should we be in haste?

N.: You mean that at ninety-nine, you will still be in power, with no free elections?

©Copyright, 1981, by Ginn and Company (Xerox Corporation). All Rights Reserved.

HANDOUT 43 Chapter 30

Directions: Use the data provided to make appropriate line graphs.

Demographic Trends after World War II

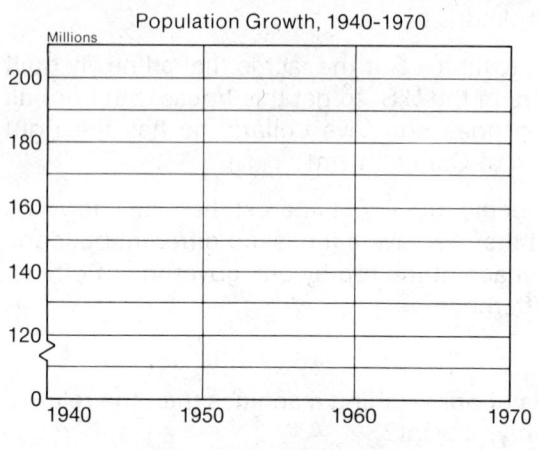
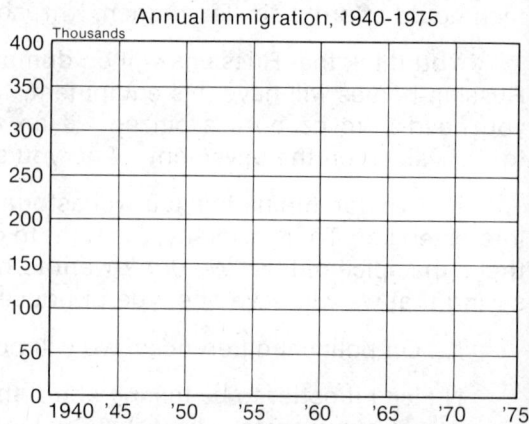
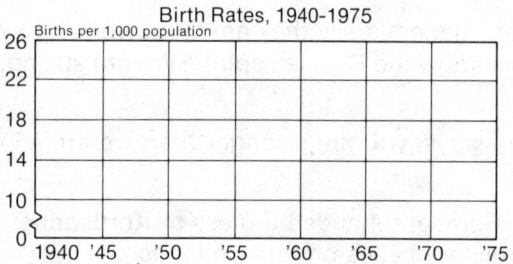

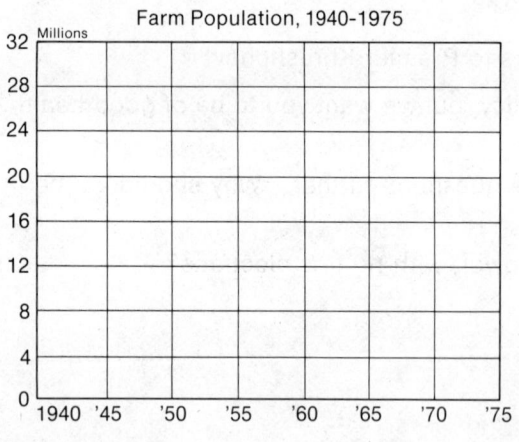
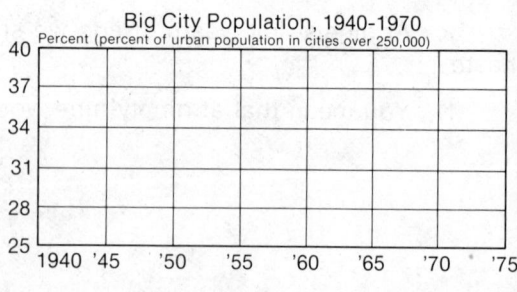

	1940	1945	1950	1955	1960	1965	1970	1975
Population (in millions)	131.7	—	150.7	—	179.3	—	203.2	—
Birth rates (births per 1,000 population)	19.4	20.4	24.1	25.0	23.7	19.4	18.4	13.8
Immigration (annual totals in thousands)	71	38	249	238	265	297	373	386
Civilian labor force (total, in thousands)	55.6	53.9	62.2	65.0	69.6	74.5	82.7	92.6
Civilian labor force (females, in thousands)	—	15.0	18.4	20.5	23.2	26.2	31.5	37.0
Farm population (in millions)	30.5	24.4	23.0	19.1	15.6	12.4	9.7	8.9
Population of cities over 250,000 (percent of urban pop.)	38.6	—	36.1	—	31.4	—	28.2	—

©Copyright, 1981, by Ginn and Company (Xerox Corporation). All Rights Reserved.

HANDOUT 44   Chapter 31

As a Roman Catholic, Democratic candidate John F. Kennedy in 1960 knew that in 1928 Alfred E. Smith had been badly beaten by Hoover partly because of the religious issue. So Kennedy decided to meet the problem head-on, and early in the campaign spoke to a group of Protestant ministers in Houston, Texas. After you read highlights from the speech, answer the questions that follow.

John F. Kennedy Speaks on the Religious Issue

Because I am a Catholic, and no Catholic has ever been elected President, the real issues in this campaign have been obscured. So it is apparently necessary for me to state once again, not what kind of church I believe in, but what kind of America I believe in.

I believe in an America where the separation of church and state is absolute—where no Catholic prelate would tell the President, should he be a Catholic, how to act, and no Protestant minister would tell his parishioners for whom to vote; where no church or church school is granted any public funds of political preference; and where no man is denied public office merely because his religion differs from the President who might appoint him or the people who might elect him.

I believe in an America that is officially neither Catholic, Protestant, nor Jewish; where religious liberty is so indivisible that an act against one church is treated as an act against all.

For, while this year it may be a Catholic against whom the finger of suspicion is pointed, in other years it has been, and may someday be again, a Jew—or a Quaker—or a Unitarian—or a Baptist. It was Virginia's harassment of Baptist preachers, for example, that helped lead to Jefferson's Statute of Religious Freedom. Today I may be the victim, but tomorrow it may be you.

Finally, I believe in an America where religious intolerance will someday end; where all men and all churches are treated as equal; where every man has the same right to attend or not attend the church of his choice.

This is the kind of America I believe in—and this is the kind of America I fought for in the South Pacific and the kind my brother died for in Europe. No one suggested then that we might have a "divided loyalty," that we did "not believe in liberty" or that we belonged to a disloyal group that threatened "the freedoms for which our forefathers died."

I ask you tonight to follow in that tradition—to judge me on the basis of fourteen years in the Congress—on my declared stands against an ambassador to the Vatican, against unconstitutional aid to parochial schools, and against any boycott of the public schools—which I attended myself.

I am not the Catholic candidate for President. I am the Democratic Party's candidate for President who happens also to be a Catholic. I do not speak for my church on public matters—and the church does not speak for me.

(Adapted from speech, September 12, 1960, Houston, Texas.)

Now answer the following questions:
1. Why does Kennedy believe that he must speak on the religious issue?
2. Do you agree with Kennedy that no church or church school should be granted public funds? Why?
3. How does Kennedy link the religious issue to his Protestant audience?
4. How does Kennedy relate the religious issue to his war service?

HANDOUT 45   Chapter 31

On October 22, 1962, as the world tensely awaited the outcome of the confrontation between the United States and the Soviet Union over the missile threat in Cuba, President John F. Kennedy addressed the nation—and the Russians—via radio and television. Parts of his speech follow:

President Kennedy's Response to the Missile Threat

"It shall be the policy of this nation to regard any nuclear missile launched from Cuba against any nation in the Western Hemisphere as an attack by the Soviet Union on the United States requiring a full retaliatory response upon the Soviet Union. . . .

"Any hostile move anywhere in the world against the safety or freedom of people to whom we are committed—including in particular the brave people of West Berlin—will be met by whatever action is needed. . . .

"I call upon Chairman Khrushchev to halt and eliminate this clandestine, reckless and provocative threat to world peace and to stable relations between our two nations. I call upon him further to abandon this course of world domination and to join in an historic effort to end the perilous arms race and transform the history of man."

*****

Prior to the decision by Kennedy to "quarantine" (blockade) the Russian supply vessels approaching Cuba, various proposals were advanced by the President's advisers. These included:

1. Low level flights—harassing the Soviets with flares and the threat of air strikes.
2. Action inside Cuba—leaflet drops by planes to intimidate Castro and seek to stir up the people against him.
3. Air strike—bombing of the missile launching sites.
4. Invasion—full scale use of American troops.

Now answer the following questions:
1. Would you have supported any of the above proposals rather than the blockade? Why?
2. Senators Russell and Fulbright of the Armed Forces Committee favored invasion as the "only acceptable solution." What reasons might they have given?
3. What reasons might explain why the Russians "backed off"?
4. What do you suppose President Kennedy thought would have happened if we had invaded Cuba?

HANDOUT 46   Chapter 32

On May 22, 1964, President Lyndon B. Johnson outlined his goals for America in a speech to students at the University of Michigan. After you read *highlights* from the speech, answer the questions that follow.

The Great Society

I have come today from the turmoil of our Capitol to the tranquility of your campus to speak about the future of our country. The challenge of the next half century is whether we have the wisdom to use [our] wealth to enrich and elevate our national life and to advance the quality of American civilization.

Your imagination, your initiative, and your imagination will determine whether we build a society where progress is the servant of our needs or a society where old values and new visions are buried under unbridled growth.

The Great Society rests on abundance and liberty for all. It demands an end to poverty and racial injustice, to which we are totally committed in our time. But that is just the beginning. The Great Society is a place where every child can find knowledge to enrich his mind and to enlarge his talents. It is a place where leisure is a welcome chance to build and reflect, not a feared cause of boredom and restlessness. It is a place where the city of man serves not only the needs of the body and the demands of commerce but the desire for beauty and hunger for community.

So I want to talk to you today about three places where we begin to build the Great Society—in our cities, in our countryside, and in our classrooms.

It is harder and harder to live the good life in American cities today. The catalog of ills is long: there is the decay of the centers and the despoiling of the suburbs. There is not enough housing for our people or transportation for our traffic. Our society will never be great until our cities are great.

A second place where we begin to build the Great Society is in our countryside. We have always prided ourselves on being not only America the strong and America the free but America the beautiful. Today that beauty is in danger. The water we drink, the food we eat, the very air that we breathe are threatened with pollution.

A third place to build the Great Society is in the classrooms of America. There your children's lives will be shaped. Our society will not be great until every young mind is set free to scan the farthest reaches of thought and imagination. We are still far from that goal. Today, 8 million adult Americans, more than the entire population of Michigan, have not finished five years of school. Nearly 54 million, more than one-quarter of all America, have not even finished high school.

These are three of the central issues of the Great Society. The solution to these problems does not rest on a massive program in Washington, nor can it rely solely on the strained resources of local authority. They require us to create new concepts of cooperation, a creative federalism, between the [national] government and the leaders of local communities. . . .

---

1. How does Johnson define the "Great Society"?
2. In what three areas must the Great Society be built?
3. Give an example of at least one problem in each of these areas.
4. In which of these three areas, in your judgment, have we made the most progress since Johnson's time? Explain.

©Copyright, 1981, by Ginn and Company (Xerox Corporation). All Rights Reserved.

HANDOUT 47   Chapter 33

Numerous laws passed during the Nixon administration's first term simply provided funds, and sometimes alterations, for established programs. Some other major laws are listed below.

91st Congress, 1969–1970

Toy safety: added electrical, mechanical, and heat hazards to previous bans placed on hazardous toys sold in interstate commerce.

Cigarette ads: forbade cigarette advertising on radio and television.

Voting rights: extended the Voting Rights Act of 1965 for five more years, put a 30-day limit on residency requirements for voting in presidential elections, and banned literacy tests.

Postal service: dropped the Post Office Department as an executive (Cabinet) department and created the United States Postal Service as an independent agency with power to set postal rates, services, etc.

Drug control: reduced penalties on drug use but increased penalties on sale of drugs; provided 300 more narcotics agents; expanded drug-abuse programs.

Mass transit aid: provided federal aid for building and improving urban area bus and subway lines.

Airport modernization: authorized spending of $5 billion for automated navigational aids and airport modernization other than passenger terminals—to be paid with higher passenger taxes and airport fees.

Waste disposal: authorized $463 million over three years for aid to states and cities to plan and build systems for the disposal and recovery of solid wastes.

92nd Congress (1971–1972)

Revenue sharing: provided $30 billion, spread over five years, for states and localities to spend on a variety of public programs with a minimum of federal control.

Water pollution: passed over Nixon's veto, the law authorized nearly $25 billion over three years to clean up rivers and lakes—chiefly through state and local grants for sewage treatment plants.

Campaign spending: put limits on amounts presidential and congressional candidates could spend in election campaigns and set requirements for reporting contributions and expenditures.

Drug control: authorized $1 billion for coordination of federal anti-drug programs including aid to state and local programs; led to establishment of Drug Enforcement Administration in the Justice Department.

HANDOUT 48 Chapter 33

In 1969 President Nixon created the Gates Advisory Commission to develop a plan for ending military conscription and creating an all-volunteer army. Subsequently, Congress passed a bill ending the draft. The new law took effect on January 27, 1973. Below are excerpts from the Gates report. After you read them, answer the questions that follow.

An All-Volunteer Army

We unanimously believe that the nation's interests will be better served by an all-volunteer force, supported by an effective stand-by draft, than by a mixed force of volunteers and conscripts; that steps should be taken promptly to move in this direction; and that the first indispensable step is to remove the present inequity in the pay of men serving their first term in the armed forces.

The United States has relied through history on a voluntary armed force except during major wars and since 1948. A return to an all-volunteer force will strengthen our freedoms, remove an inequity now imposed on the expression of the patriotism that has never been lacking among our youth, promote efficiency of the armed forces and enhance their dignity.

In recent years, about 500,000 men a year have volunteered only because of the threat of the draft; the best estimates are that at least half—about 250,000 men—are "true volunteers." Such men would have volunteered even if there had been no draft, and they did volunteer in spite of an entry pay that is roughly 60 per cent of the amount that men of their age, education, and training could earn in civilian life.

The often ignored fact, therefore, is that our present armed forces are made up predominantly of volunteers. The return of voluntary means of raising and maintaining our armed forces should be seen in this perspective. With true volunteers now providing some 250,000 enlisted men annually, a fully volunteer force of 2.5 million men can be achieved by improving pay and conditions of service sufficiently to induce approximately 75,000 additional young men to enlist each year from the 1.5 million men who will annually turn 19 and who will meet the physical, moral, and mental requirements.

(Source: *Congressional Record,* 91 Cong., 2 Session, February 24, 1970)

---

1. What did the commission recommend as protection in case not enough volunteers could be recruited?
2. What did they say was the first necessary step to get more volunteers?
3. The commission found about half of all volunteers at that time to be "true volunteers." Who were in the other half?
4. How many volunteers altogether did the commission estimate would be needed each year to keep the armed forces at the 2.5 million level?

HANDOUT 49 Chapter 33

Chronology of Watergate

Some of the significant events leading to the decision of President Richard Nixon to resign from office rather than face impeachment include the following:

June 17, 1972 — Arrest of five men in a break-in of the Democratic headquarters at Watergate in Washington, D.C.

June 19 — White House denies involvement.

June 20 — Discussion by Nixon and aide H.R. Haldeman concerning Watergate; 18½-minute gap in a tape of this conversation.

August 26 — Money traced from Committee to Re-elect the President to Watergate burglars.

January 1973 — Senator Sam Ervin heads committee to investigate Watergate. Hearings are televised.

April 30 — Nixon announces resignations of aides Haldeman, Erlichman, and Attorney General Kliendienst; also dismisses aide John Dean.

June 25–29 — In testifying before Watergate Committee, Dean accuses Nixon of complicity in Watergate affair.

July 3 — Aide Alexander Butterfield reveals existence of White House taping system.

October 12 — U.S. Court of Appeals upholds Judge Sirica's orders that tapes must be surrendered by Nixon.

October 21 — "Saturday Night Massacre" — Cox fired; Richardson and Ruckelshaus resign.

March 1, 1974 — Grand jury indicts White House aides Haldeman, Erlichman, Mitchell, Mardian, Colson, Strachan, and Parkinson in the Watergate cover-up. Nixon is named an unindicted co-conspirator.

April 18 — Special Prosecutor Leon Jaworski subpoenas tapes.

April 19 — Nixon supplies "edited" transcripts of the tapes.

July 24 — U.S. Supreme Court rules that Nixon must turn over original tapes to Jaworski.

July 27 — House Judiciary Committee passes first article of impeachment of Nixon, charging him with obstruction of justice in attempting to cover-up the Watergate break-in.

July 29 — Two additional articles of impeachment are passed.

August 8 — Nixon announces resignation rather than face impeachment.

August 9 — Gerald R. Ford becomes President.

HANDOUT 50 Chapter 34

The Changing Employment Scene for Women

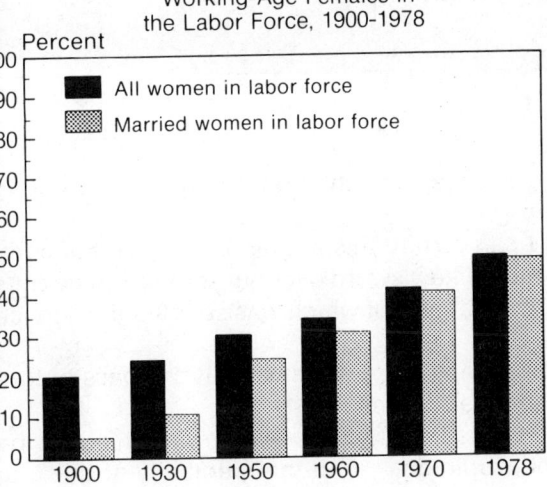

Working-Age Females in the Labor Force, 1900-1978

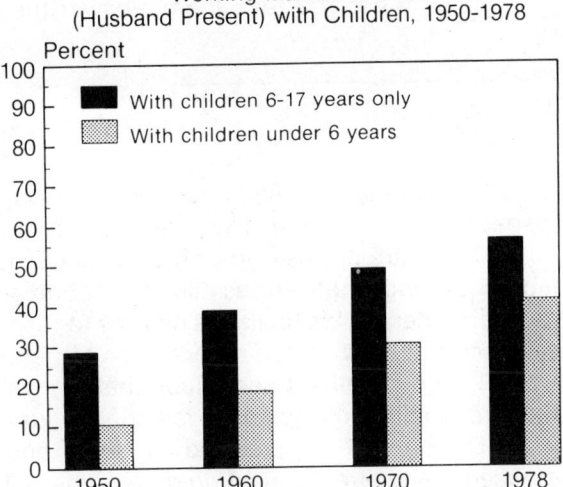

Working Married Women (Husband Present) with Children, 1950-1978

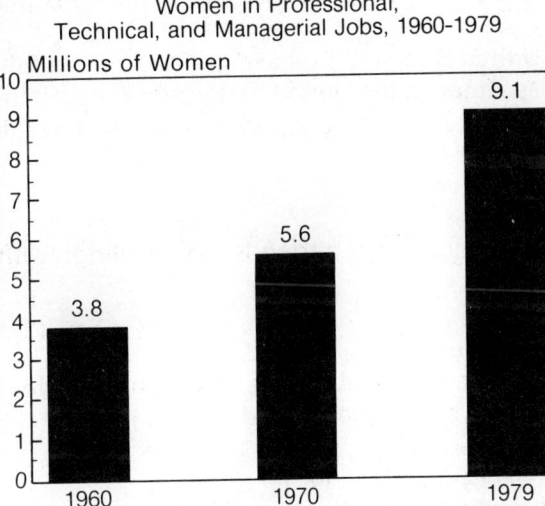

Women in Professional, Technical, and Managerial Jobs, 1960-1979

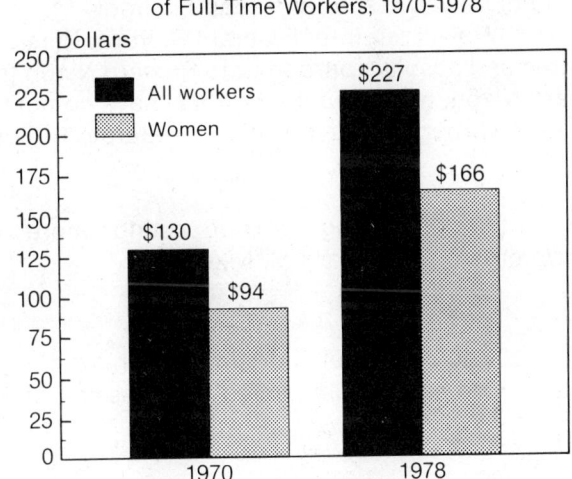

Median Weekly Earnings of Full-Time Workers, 1970-1978

1. Between 1930 and 1978 the percentage of women who were in the labor force doubled, and the percentage of married women who were in the labor force went up over—?—times.

2. In which year was the percentage of married working women with children age 6 to 17 a little more than twice as high as for working mothers with children under age 6?

3. Between 1950 and 1978 which rose faster: the number of working mothers with children under age 6 or those with children over age 6 only?

4. In which years did women make the fastest gains in getting professional, technical, and managerial jobs: before 1970 or after 1970?

5. Between 1970 and 1978 the median pay of all full-time workers went up $97, but the median pay of full-time women workers went up only—?—.

6. Looking at all four graphs, one might reasonably conclude that women have made bigger gains in job opportunities than in —?—.

©Copyright, 1981, by Ginn and Company (Xerox Corporation). All Rights Reserved.

HANDOUT 51   Chapter 35

Directions: Below are statements made by the principals and others on the pardon of former President Richard M. Nixon by President Gerald R. Ford. After you read them, answer the questions that follow.

On the Pardon of Nixon by Ford

". . . I have . . . searched my own conscience . . . to determine the right thing for me to do in respect to . . . Richard Nixon, and his loyal wife and family. . . .

"There are no historic or legal precedents to which I can turn in this matter. . . . But it is common knowledge that serious allegations and accusations hang like a sword over our former President's head, threatening his health as he tries to reshape his life, a great part of which was spent in the service of his country and by the mandate of its people. . . .

"I am compelled to conclude that many months and perhaps more years will have to pass before Richard Nixon could obtain a fair trial by jury . . . in the United States. . . .

"During this long period of delay and protracted litigation, ugly passions would again be aroused. And our people would again be polarized in their opinions. And the credibility of our free institutions of government would again be challenged at home and abroad. . . .

"My conscience tells me clearly and certainly that I cannot prolong the bad dreams that continue to reopen a chapter that is closed. My conscience tells me that only I, as President, have the constitutional power to shut and seal this book. . . .

"Now, therefore, I, Gerald R. Ford, President of the United States, . . . have granted . . . a full, free and absolute pardon unto Richard Nixon for all offenses against the United States which he, Richard Nixon, has committed or may have committed or taken part in during the period from January 20, 1969, through August 9, 1974."—Gerald R. Ford, September 8, 1974.

*****

"I was wrong in not acting more decisively and more forthrightly in dealing with Watergate."—Richard M. Nixon.

*****

"You do not put conditions on an act of mercy." (Ford aide Phil Buchen when asked by reporters why Ford had not demanded a confession of guilt by Nixon as a condition of the pardon.)

*****

". . . I cannot in good conscience support your decision to pardon former President Richard Nixon even before he has been charged with the commission of any crime. . . . [I]t is impossible to conclude that the former President is more deserving of mercy than persons of lesser stations in life whose offenses have had less effect on our national well-being."—Jerald ter Horst, in resigning as Ford's Press Secretary.

Now answer the following questions:
1. What reasons does Ford give for pardoning Nixon?
2. In accepting the pardon, Nixon made no admission of guilt. Should he have? Why?
3. Do you support ter Horst's statement? Why?
4. If you were President, would you have pardoned Nixon? Why?

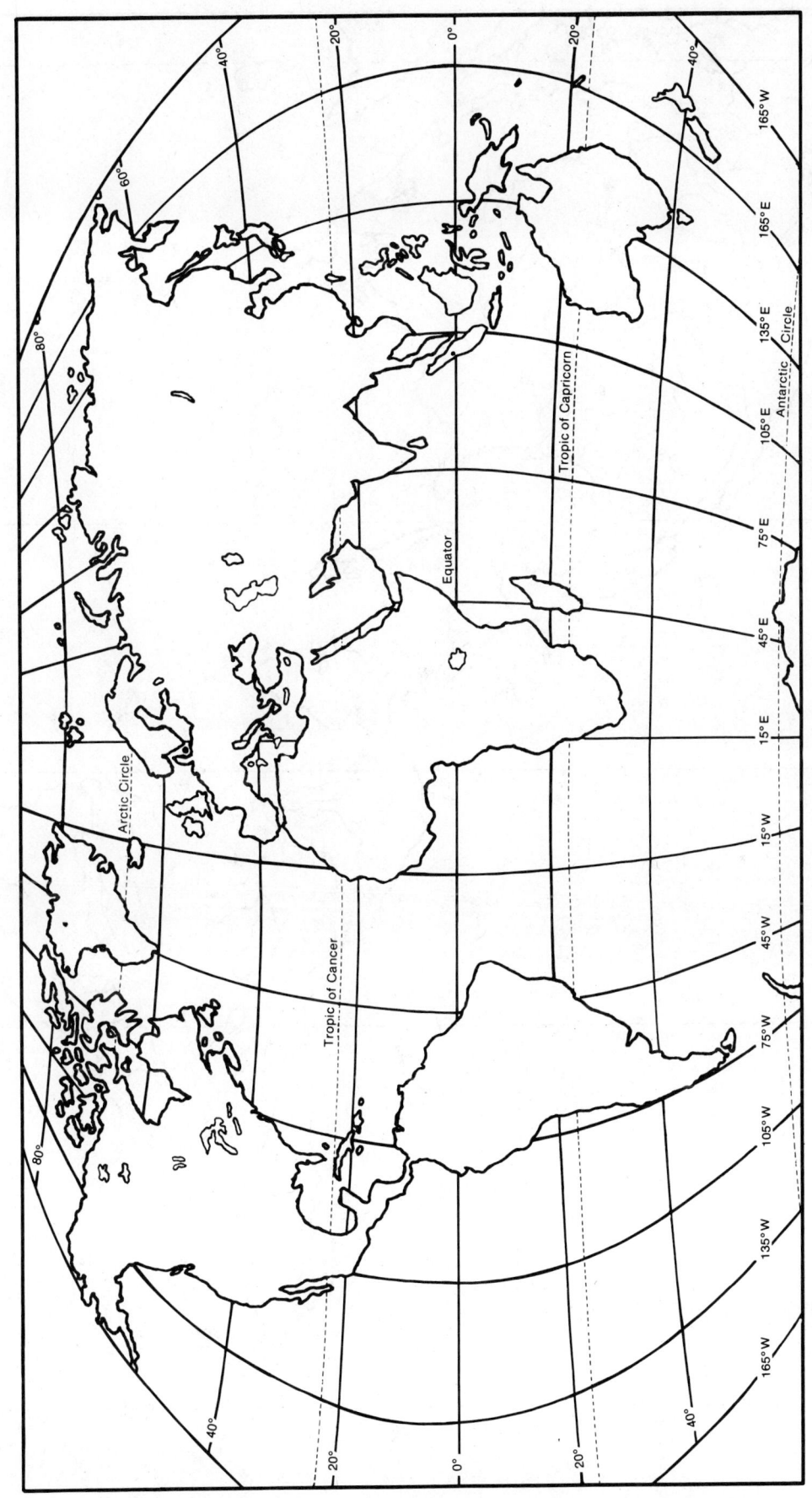

Outline Map 1 World   271

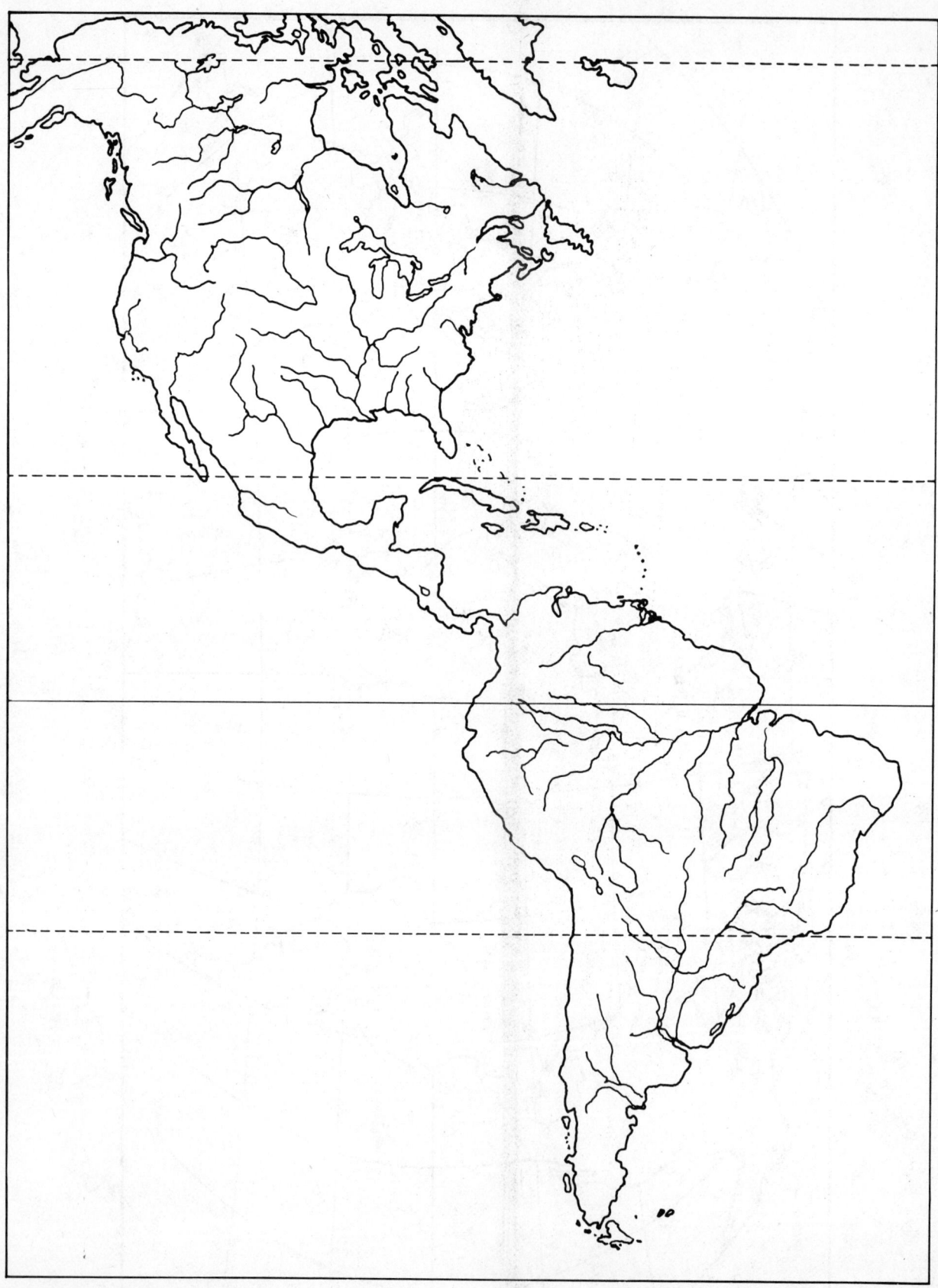

Outline Map 3 North America

Outline Map 4 United States

Outline Map 5　　Eastern United States

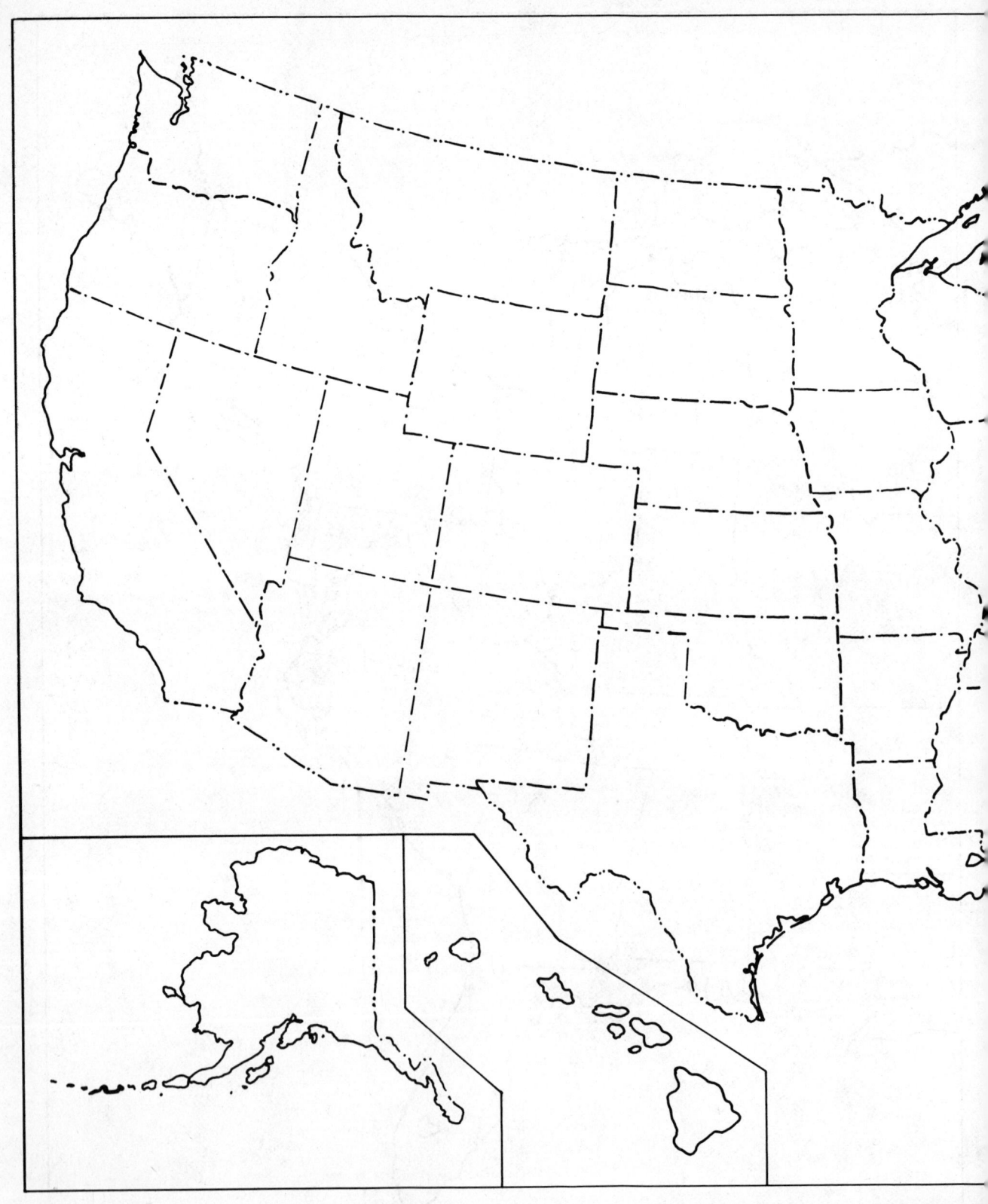

Outline Map 6 Western United States

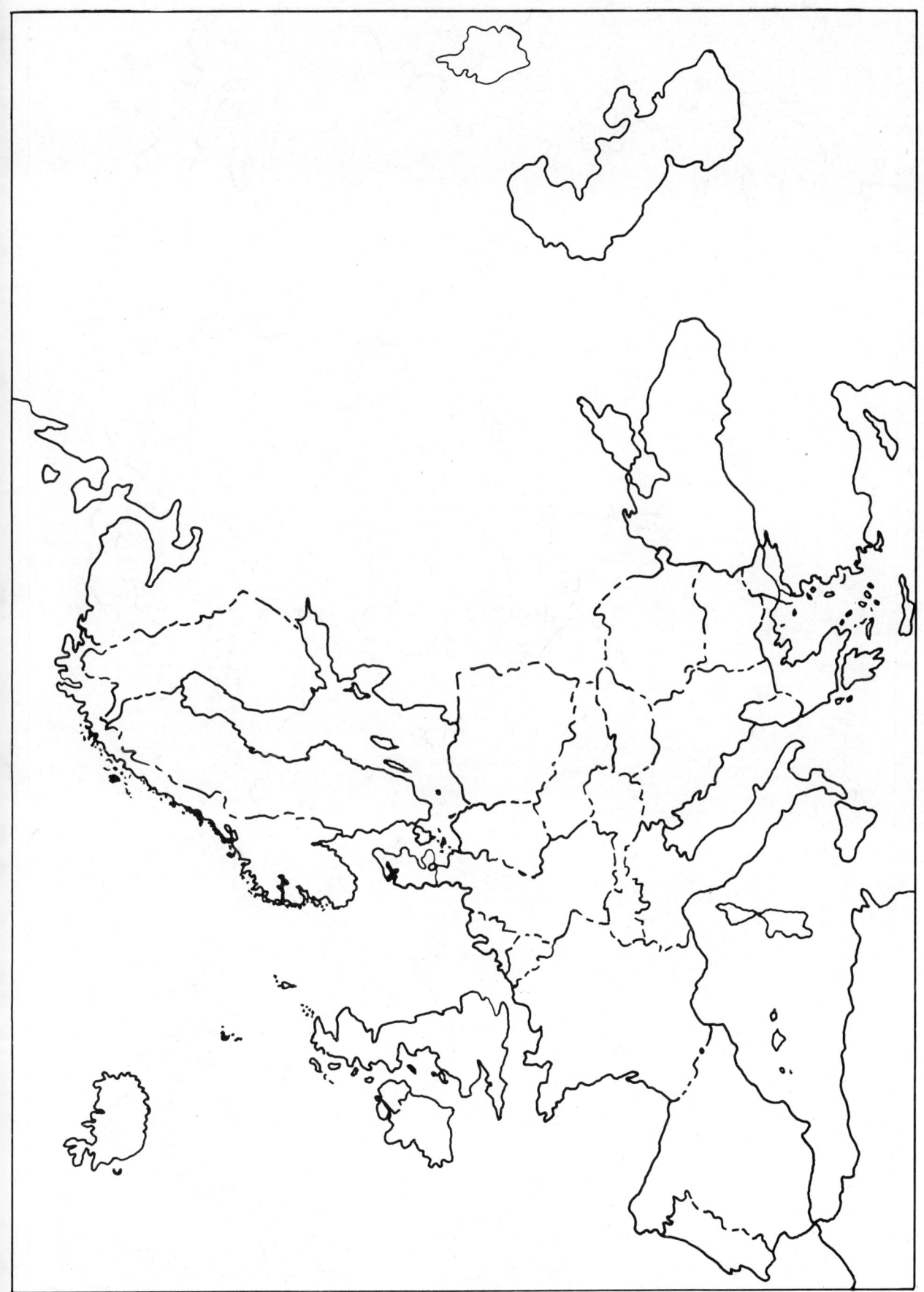

Outline Map 7　Europe

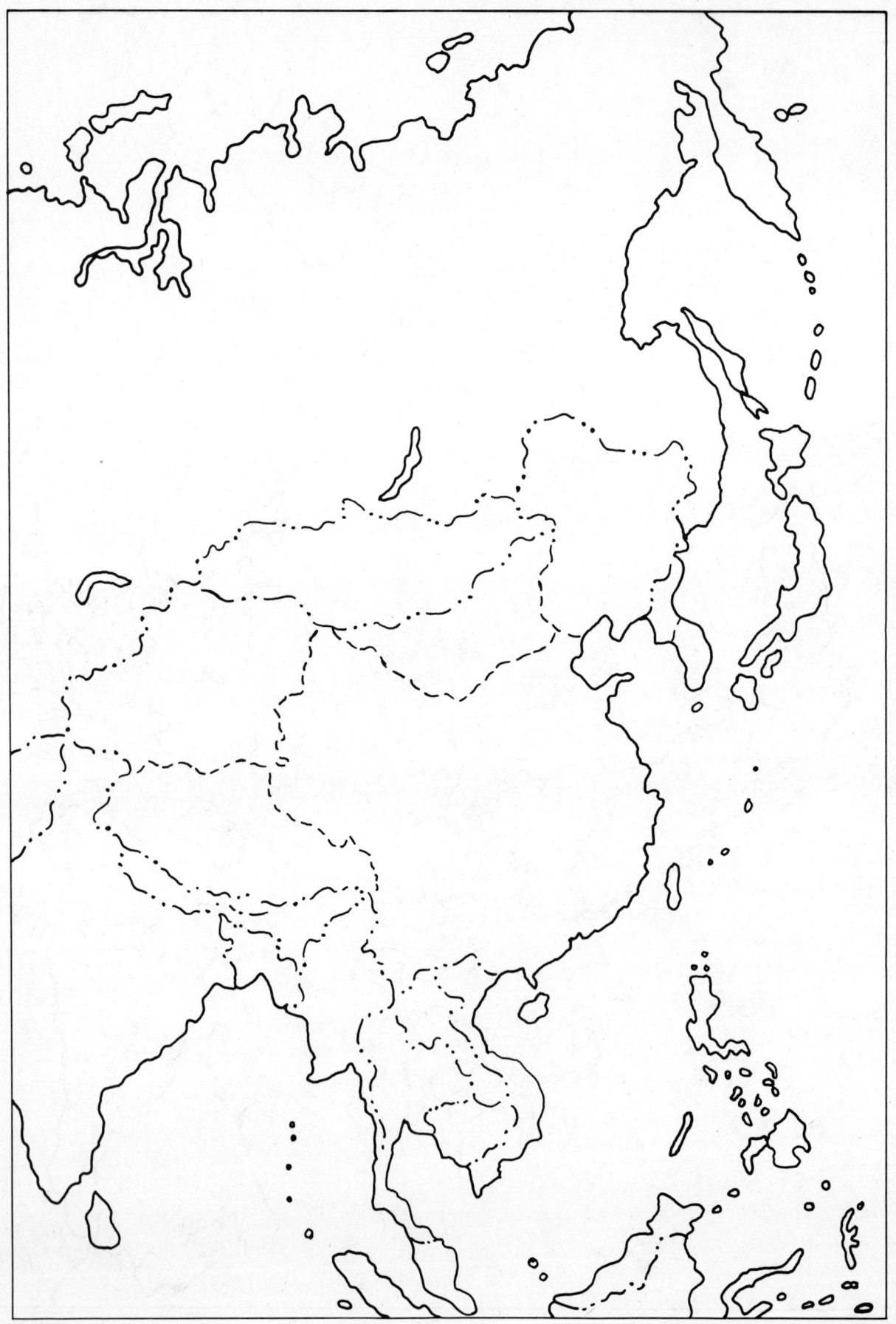

Outline Map 8 Eastern Asia

REPORT ON OUTSIDE READING

Author _____

Book or
Magazine
Title _____

Title of
Chapter
or Article _____

Date of
Magazine _____

Brief summary of the chapter or article:

How did it add to your understanding of the subject matter of this unit? What particular points did it illustrate?

Unit 1 Test   THE MAKING OF AMERICANS

Part A   Select the *one best answer* and put its letter in the answer space.

_____ 1. Our best guess is that the first Indians arrived on the American continent (A) 5,000 (B) 25,000 (C) 100,000 (D) 500,000 years ago.

_____ 2. The strongest and most centralized government seen by the white explorers in the New World was created by the (A) Mayas (B) Incas (C) Aztecs (D) Anasazi.

_____ 3. Of the United States today, the largest early concentration of Indians was found in (A) New York (B) Texas (C) Alaska (D) California.

_____ 4. The event that opened European eyes to the riches of the East was the (A) Crusades (B) discovery of America (C) Norse voyages to Iceland (D) invention of the compass.

_____ 5. Columbus finally received financial support for his voyage from (A) Portugal (B) France (C) Spain (D) Italy.

_____ 6. Spanish is the language of all South American countries except (A) Argentina (B) Brazil (C) Chile (D) Peru.

_____ 7. Balboa was the first European to (A) discover California (B) discover Florida (C) go up the Mississippi (D) see the Pacific.

_____ 8. The explorer who proved that the world was round was (A) Drake (B) Prince Henry the Navigator (C) Magellan (D) Vasco da Gama.

_____ 9. A book that excited the minds of western Europeans was about the adventures in China of (A) Christian missionaries (B) Bartholomew Dias (C) the Crusaders (D) Marco Polo.

_____ 10. The first explorer to sail in behalf of England to the New World was (A) Leif Ericsson (B) Henry Hudson (C) John Cabot (D) Sir Francis Drake.

_____ 11. Entry into the St. Lawrence River to establish French claims in the region was made by (A) Cartier (B) Verrazano (C) La Salle (D) Champlain.

_____ 12. Religious conversion of Indians was a chief feature of colonization policy of (A) English and Dutch (B) English and French (C) French and Spanish (D) all Europeans.

_____ 13. The policy of having colonies produce raw materials for the homeland and buy manufactured goods from it is called (A) free trade (B) mercantilism (C) triangular trade (D) exploitation.

_____ 14. Where was enslavement of Indians most successful? (A) New Spain (B) New France (C) New Netherland (D) New England.

_____ 15. The term *mestizo* refers to Spanish settlers who (A) were cowboys (B) owned property (C) had mixed blood (D) lived in missions.

_____ 16. Besides the English ships, the Spanish Armada's worst enemy was (A) smallpox (B) wind (C) fire (D) wet gunpowder.

_____ 17. Queen Elizabeth gave the first English colonial charter to (A) Sir Walter Raleigh (B) John Smith (C) Sir Humphrey Gilbert (D) John Winthrop.

_____ 18. A rescue party sent to Roanoke Island found (A) a thriving settlement (B) a mysterious sign (C) a starving remnant (D) signs of a massacre.

_____ 19. The number of women in the first expedition to Jamestown was (A) none (B) 9 (C) 31 (D) 58.

_____ 20. Which product most helped the Virginia colony to succeed? (A) rice (B) fish (C) lumber (D) tobacco.

_____ 21. Which term *fails* to describe the Pilgrim's relation to the Church of England? (A) dissenters (B) Independent (C) Separatist (D) conformist.

_____ 22. Another term for *land grant* in colonial days was (A) mortgage (B) patent (C) copyright (D) franchise.

_____ 23. Which colony had the largest population by 1650? (A) Virginia (B) New York (C) Massachusetts Bay (D) Pennsylvania.

_____ 24. What religious dissenter from Massachusetts Bay founded Rhode Island? (A) John Winthrop (B) Anne Hutchinson (C) Miles Standish (D) Roger Williams.

_____ 25. The Dutch claim to New Netherland rested on the explorations of (A) Peter Stuyvesant (B) Peter Minuet (C) Henry Hudson (D) the Duke of York.

_____ 26. The log cabin was introduced to America by the (A) Swedes (B) French (C) English (D) Dutch.

_____ 27. The first legislative act of religious toleration in the American colonies was passed by (A) Georgia (B) New Jersey (C) New York (D) Maryland.

_____ 28. By 1765 the colony with the largest *mix* of population from various European countries was (A) Massachusetts Bay (B) Pennsylvania (C) the Carolinas (D) Delaware.

_____ 29. The Huguenots came to the colonies after being deprived of religious freedom in (A) Germany (B) Holland (C) Spain (D) France.

_____ 30. The signing of an indenture made an immigrant a (A) landowner (B) slave (C) servant (D) tenant.

_____ 31. Which of these colonies depended most on direct two-way trade with England for survival? (A) New York (B) Massachusetts (C) Virginia (D) Pennsylvania.

_____ 32. Women in the colonies could not (A) practice law (B) publish newspapers (C) hold office (D) run plantations.

_____ 33. The first colony to require schools was (A) Massachusetts Bay (B) New York (C) Virginia (D) Pennsylvania.

_____ 34. John Peter Zenger won a pioneer case involving freedom of (A) worship (B) press (C) speech (D) assembly.

_____ 35. A colonial artist would most likely specialize in (A) landscapes (B) seascapes (C) portraits (D) still lifes.

_____ 36. The term "salutary neglect" refers to England's (A) neglect in sending royal governors (B) failure to trade with the colonies (C) neglect in supplying protection against the Indians (D) weak enforcement of the Navigation Acts.

_____ 37. A legally licensed pirate was sometimes called a (A) navigator (B) privateer (C) mercantilist (D) protectionist.

_____ 38. By 1700 England's chief rival for supremacy in North America was (A) Spain (B) Holland (C) France (D) Germany.

_____ 39. The sponsor of the Albany Plan of Union was (A) William Pitt (B) Jonathan Edwards (C) Edmund Andros (D) Benjamin Franklin.

_____ 40. By the Peace of Paris in 1763 most of the French land in North America (A) was kept by France (B) was ceded to Great Britain (C) was divided between Great Britain and Spain (D) became part of an even bigger New France.

Part B Three of the items in each of the following series are related to the introductory phrase in *italics*. In the answer space write the letter of the one item which *does not belong* in the group.

_____ 41. *Early Indian groups from Mexico to Peru:* (A) Mayas (B) Aztecs (C) Hohokams (D) Incas.

_____ 42. *Modern foods introduced by the Indians:* (A) corn (B) oranges (C) potatoes (D) tomatoes.

_____ 43. *Known to the Indians before the arrival of the Spanish:* (A) dogs (B) horses (C) buffalo (D) deer.

_____ 44. *Consumed by the Indians before the arrival of the Europeans:* (A) alcohol (B) corn (C) squash (D) tobacco.

_____ 45. *Sites of Spanish missions:* (A) California coast (B) Santa Fe region (C) eastern Kansas (D) Tucson region.

_____ 46. *Known to Marco Polo:* (A) China (B) silk (C) printing press (D) spices.

_____ 47. *Promoters of English settlements in America in late 1500s:* (A) Hakluyt (B) Gilbert (C) Raleigh (D) Hudson.

_____ 48. *Nations founding colonies in the New World:* (A) Sweden (B) Netherlands (C) France (D) Germany.

_____ 49. *Proprietary colonies:* (A) Rhode Island (B) Carolinas (C) Pennsylvania (D) Georgia.

_____ 50. *Offshoots of Massachusetts Bay colony:* (A) Connecticut (B) Maine (C) Vermont (D) New Hampshire.

_____ 51. *Things opposed by Quakers:* (A) taking part in government (B) use of bishops and ministers (C) war (D) ceremonial worship.

_____ 52. *Persons welcomed in Rhode Island:* (A) Puritan dissenters (B) Roman Catholics (C) Quakers (D) Jews.

_____ 53. *Chief exports of southern colonies:* (A) fish (B) rice (C) sugar (D) tobacco.

_____ 54. *Colonial artisans and craftsmen:* (A) Myer Myers (B) Paul Revere (C) Jonathan Edwards (D) John Goddard.

_____ 55. *Officers in French and Indian Wars:* (A) George Washington (B) William Pitt (C) James Wolfe (D) Edward Braddock.

Part C In the answer space write the name of the person identified. Use TEN of the following twelve names:

Amherst · Brent · de Champlain · Ponce de Leon · Drake · Ericsson · Hutchinson · Montcalm · Oglethorpe · Penn · Revere · Stuyvesant

_____ 56. Searched for but failed to find the fountain of youth.

_____ 57. Banished from Massachusetts, she was killed by the Indians.

_____ 58. A French Huguenot descendant who was a silversmith.

_____ 59. He founded a colony for his fellow Quakers.

_____ 60. She ran Lord Baltimore's estates but was denied the right to vote.

_____ 61. British general who helped defeat the French.

_____ 62. A "sea dog" who helped destroy the Spanish fleet.

_____ 63. He may have preceded Columbus to the New World.

_____ 64. He surrendered a Dutch colony to the British.

_____ 65. He founded a colony for criminals and the poor.

Part D In the space below begin your answer to whatever essay question or questions your teacher may ask.

Unit 2 Test FORMING A NEW NATION

Part A

1. The big problem facing the British after the French and Indian War was (A) guerrilla warfare by the French-Canadians (B) quarrels with Spain over Florida (C) Indian uprisings west of the Appalachians (D) getting the colonies to form a united government.
2. The Royal Proclamation of 1763 forbade (A) smuggling (B) westward expansion beyond the Appalachians (C) trade with French, Spanish, and Dutch sugar islands (D) the importation of molasses.
3. The Sugar and Stamp acts were designed chiefly (A) to raise funds for the defense of the colonies (B) to prove the right of Parliament to tax the colonies (C) to enrich the British upper class (D) to reduce colonial consumption of sugar and paper.
4. In the Declaratory Act, Parliament declared that (A) it would seek colonial assent for any new taxes (B) it could pass laws on any matters affecting the colonies (C) the colonies would have to provide their own defense (D) new taxes would be imposed.
5. A chief colonial objection to the Quebec Act was that it (A) cut off colonial trade with Canada (B) canceled the western land claims of several colonies (C) made Quebec the capital of all the British colonies in North America (D) abolished colonial assemblies.
6. The Boston man who did the most to fan the flame of rebellion against the British was (A) Thomas Hutchinson (B) George Washington (C) John Hancock (D) Samuel Adams.
7. Edmund Randolph declared that, next to King George, the man most responsible for the Declaration of Independence was (A) Thomas Paine (B) Silas Deane (C) William Prescott (D) Alexander Hamilton.
8. "The country is safe," said Washington after hearing of the battle of (A) Lexington (B) Concord (C) Fort Ticonderoga (D) Bunker Hill.
9. During the first two years of the Revolutionary War, the Americans were most dependent upon the French for (A) clothing (B) ships (C) gunpowder (D) food.
10. Foreign soldiers hired by the British were known as (A) loyalists (B) mercenaries (C) rabble in arms (D) militia.
11. After independence, the new state constitutions weakened the power of the (A) legislature (B) governor (C) courts (D) people.
12. In Shays's Rebellion, the rebels were largely (A) debt-ridden farmers (B) angry merchants (C) investors in western lands (D) whiskey distillers.
13. The compromise plan which broke the deadlock between the small and the large states provided that in Congress (A) both houses would be based on population (B) there would be only one house with one vote for each state (C) one house would be based on population and the other on equality (D) both houses would be based on equality.
14. States were persuaded to ratify the Constitution by the promise of (A) a bill of rights (B) low taxes (C) a national court system (D) national assumption of state debts.
15. The bargain over the site of the national capital involved the issue of (A) the national bank (B) assumption of state debts (C) a protective tariff (D) paying off foreign loans.
16. The followers of Jefferson favored (A) protective tariffs (B) a national bank (C) strong state governments (D) a strong national government.
17. President Washington reacted to Britain's war against the French Republic by (A) supporting Genêt's appeal for funds (B) issuing a Proclamation of Neutrality (C) ordering a boycott of French goods (D) sending warships to France.
18. The Whiskey Rebellion arose over (A) a tax on whiskey (B) efforts to halt the sale of whiskey (C) a ban on whiskey advertising (D) restrictions on using corn to make whiskey.

_____ 19. The Alien and Sedition Acts were passed (A) to suppress Republican opposition to the Federalists (B) to help the French in their war against the British (C) to help the Republicans elect Jefferson (D) to do none of the above.

_____ 20. The opening of most of the Ohio country to white settlement was achieved by (A) Jay's Treaty (B) the Treaty of Paris of 1783 (C) Pinckney's Treaty (D) the Treaty of Greenville.

Part B Three of the items are related to the introductory phrase in *italics*. In the answer space write the letter of the one item that *does not belong*.

_____ 21. *Colonial responses to the Stamp Act:* (A) boycotting British goods (B) terrorizing tax collectors (C) declaring independence (D) forming the Sons of Liberty.

_____ 22. *Provisions of the Townshend Acts:* (A) duties on numerous colonial imports (B) penalties for boycotting British goods (C) reorganization of the customs service (D) pressure on New York to provide supplies for British troops stationed there.

_____ 23. *Provisions of the Intolerable Acts:* (A) suspension of the Massachusetts Assembly (B) closing of the port of Boston (C) suspension of New England town meetings (D) quartering of British troops in private homes.

_____ 24. *Reasons for American victory in the Revolution:* (A) Washington's leadership (B) superior equipment and training (C) miscalculations of the British (D) aid by the French.

_____ 25. *Provisions of the Treaty of Paris:* (A) acknowledgment of American boundaries (B) Mississippi open to both British and Americans (C) property restored to Loyalists (D) right of Americans to fish in Newfoundland waters.

_____ 26. *Powers of the central government under the Articles of Confederation:* (A) to deal with foreign governments (B) to declare war (C) to coin money (D) to lay and collect taxes.

_____ 27. *States that ceded western land claims:* (A) Maryland (B) Massachusetts (C) Virginia (D) North Carolina.

_____ 28. *Members of Washington's Cabinet:* (A) Hamilton (B) Madison (C) Jefferson (D) Randolph.

_____ 29. *Generals who fought the Indians in the Northwest:* (A) Harmar (B) Wayne (C) Pinckney (D) St. Clair.

_____ 30. *Authors of the Federalist Papers:* (A) Adams (B) Madison (C) Jay (D) Hamilton.

Part C Write the letter of the person who said or wrote each of the following quotations.

_____ 31. "Our repeated petitions have been answered only by repeated injury."

_____ 32. "Millions for defense, but not one cent for tribute."

_____ 33. "These are the times that try men's souls."

_____ 34. "There is scarcely any part of my conduct that may not hereafter be drawn into precedent."

_____ 35. "Jefferson is to be preferred. He is by far not so dangerous a man; and he has pretensions to character."

A. Washington
B. Franklin
C. Hamilton
D. John Marshall
E. Paine in the *Crisis*
F. Madison
G. Jefferson in the *Declaration of Independence*

Part D If you drew a line connecting the three places in each group below, which place would be in the middle? Put its letter in the answer space.

_____ 36. (A) Providence   (B) Boston   (C) New York

_____ 37. (A) Detroit   (B) Quebec City   (C) Montreal

_____ 38. (A) Trenton   (B) Saratoga   (C) Yorktown

_____ 39. (A) Montreal   (B) Fort Ticonderoga   (C) Albany

_____ 40. (A) Lake Erie   (B) Lake Michigan   (C) Lake Ontario

Part E Show that you understand the cause-effect relationship of the items listed below by putting the letter of the "cause" in the answer space.

_____ 41. (A) Kentucky and Virginia Resolutions (B) Alien and Sedition Acts
_____ 42. (A) Intolerable Acts (B) Boston Tea Party
_____ 43. (A) Declaration of Independence (B) Articles of Confederation
_____ 44. (A) acceptance of Articles of Confederation (B) surrender of western land claims
_____ 45. (A) depression after War of Independence (B) Shays's Rebellion

Part F In the answer space write the missing key word or phrase.

_____ 46. The colonists demanded "No ___?___ without representation."
_____ 47. Supporters of the new Constitution were called ___?___
_____ 48. Jefferson and his followers demanded ___?___ construction, or interpretation, of the Constitution.
_____ 49. In 1790 our largest city was ___?___
_____ 50. The ___?___ of 1798 provided for the deportation of foreigners considered dangerous to national security.
_____ 51. The attempt of French secret agents to collect a bribe for Talleyrand was known as the ___?___
_____ 52. The three-fifths compromise concerned the counting of ___?___ for determining representation in Congress.
_____ 53. The political supporters of Jefferson and Madison were called ___?___
_____ 54. ___?___ was a black man killed in the Boston Massacre.
_____ 55. The ___?___ names six purposes for establishing the Constitution.
_____ 56. Under the ___?___ system the three independent branches of the government exercise restraints on each other.
_____ 57. Treaties with foreign nations must be approved by the ___?___
_____ 58. The lawmaking branch of the national government is known as ___?___

Part G Arrange each series of events in the order in which they occurred. Then in the answer space put the letter of the event which happened *second*.

_____ 59. (A) Olive Branch Petition (B) Yorktown (C) Battle of Saratoga
_____ 60. (A) Intolerable Acts (B) Boston Tea Party (C) Bunker Hill
_____ 61. (A) Constitutional Convention (B) Bill of Rights adopted (C) Annapolis meeting
_____ 62. (A) Shays's Rebellion (B) Boston Massacre (C) Whiskey Rebellion
_____ 63. (A) Washington's Farewell Address (B) Naval War with France (C) XYZ Affair
_____ 64. (A) Washington winters at Valley Forge (B) Declaration of Independence signed (C) First Continental Congress meets
_____ 65. (A) Bank of the United States established (B) Northwest Ordinance passed (C) Washington picks Hamilton for Secretary of the Treasury

Part H On the back, answer whatever essay questions your teacher may ask.

Unit 2 Test ©Copyright, 1981, by Ginn and Company (Xerox Corporation). All Rights Reserved.

Unit 3 Test   BUILDING A STRONG NATION

Part A In the answer space write the letter of the person who made the statement.

_____ 1. "Don't give up the ship."
_____ 2. "The power to tax is the power to destroy."
_____ 3. ". . . Liberty *and* Union, now and forever, one and inseparable."
_____ 4. "Our Union, it must be preserved."
_____ 5. "The Union—next to our liberties, most dear."
_____ 6. "We have met the enemy and they are ours."

(A) James Monroe
(B) Andrew Jackson
(C) James Lawrence
(D) John C. Calhoun
(E) Daniel Webster
(F) James Madison
(G) John Marshall
(H) Oliver H. Perry

Part B Select the *one best answer* and put its letter in the answer space.

_____ 7. Two envoys who received Napoleon's offer to sell Louisiana were (A) Madison and Monroe (B) Monroe and Livingston (C) Madison and J. Q. Adams (D) Clay and Adams.

_____ 8. Lewis and Clark reached the Rockies by following (A) the Oregon Trail (B) Indian trails (C) the Platte River (D) the Missouri River.

_____ 9. What led Burr to challenge Hamilton to the fatal duel? (A) Burr's failure to win the governorship of New York (B) insults about Burr's wife (C) the failure of the Burr conspiracy (D) Burr's trial on charges of treason.

_____ 10. European nations and the United States had paid the Barbary States (A) for guiding their ships through the Strait of Gibraltar (B) for protection against Spanish pirates (C) as a cheap substitute for war (D) for providing ship-repair services.

_____ 11. Jefferson had doubts about the Louisiana Purchase because (A) the Constitution did not authorize it (B) the price was too high (C) new states formed from it would favor the Federalists (D) the land was useless.

_____ 12. The chief significance of the Louisiana Purchase *in 1803* was (A) its low cost (B) its scenic beauty (C) its assurance of American control of the Mississippi (D) its strengthening of the Republican party.

_____ 13. Burr was acquitted on the charge of treason because (A) Jefferson took his side (B) Burr won the sympathy of the jury (C) the judge declared a mistrial (D) the prosecution failed to produce two witnesses to a treasonable act.

_____ 14. The first case in which the Supreme Court pronounced a law unconstitutional and assumed the power of judicial review was that of (A) *McCulloch* v. *Maryland* (B) the *Dartmouth College Case* (C) *Martin* v. *Hunter's Lessee* (D) *Marbury* v. *Madison*.

_____ 15. What was a "cause" of the War of 1812 supported chiefly on the western frontier? (A) British incitement of the Indians (B) impressment of seamen (C) trade blockade by Britain (D) buildup of British forts along the Mississippi.

_____ 16. Opponents of the War of 1812 included (A) James Madison (B) western frontiersmen (C) eastern merchants (D) Henry Clay and his friends.

_____ 17. The British burned the White House because (A) the Americans had burned York (Toronto) in Canada (B) Dolley Madison had insulted the British ambassador (C) Fort McHenry had refused to surrender (D) snipers had killed a British general.

_____ 18. Jackson's victory at New Orleans (A) led the British to ask for an armistice (B) gave the Americans the advantage in the peace treaty (C) took place after the peace treaty was signed (D) saved the Louisiana Territory for the United States.

_____ 19. Calhoun's Bonus Bill would have provided (A) pensions for veterans of the War of 1812 (B) funds for internal improvements (C) free land for western settlers (D) payment of the Treasury surplus to the states.

20. The *Gibbons* v. *Ogden* "steamboat case" was significant in that it (A) limited the taxing power of the states (B) prevented states from impairing the obligation of contracts (C) permitted the states to regulate coastal trade (D) broadened federal power over commerce.

21. Monroe's Era of Good Feelings ended because of (A) his death (B) another war (C) sectional rivalries (D) the Hartford Convention.

22. The Monroe Doctrine was proclaimed in order (A) to check British naval supremacy (B) to halt independence movements in South America (C) to help Britain defeat Napoleon (D) to prevent European powers from helping Spain regain its American colonies.

23. Although remembered mostly for his dictionary, Noah Webster also made important contributions to (A) spelling (B) arithmetic (C) geography (D) oratory.

24. The "Corrupt Bargain" was between (A) Monroe and J. Q. Adams (B) Clay and Adams (C) Jackson and Clay (D) Monroe and Jackson.

25. The *strongest* suffrage trend in the Jackson era was to give the vote to (A) women (B) free blacks (C) white males under 21 (D) propertyless white males.

26. A guiding political principle of President Andrew Jackson was that (A) politicians are corrupt (B) the spoils do not belong to the victors (C) to the victors belong the spoils (D) government jobs should go to specially trained people.

27. What two issues were central to the Webster-Hayne debate? (A) tariff and the national bank (B) the slave trade and immigration restrictions (C) Jackson's vetoes and the Marshall Court's decisions (D) the price of western land and nullification.

28. What was our Indian policy in the Jackson administration? (A) set up reservations on Indian homelands (B) integrate Indians into American society (C) by treaty or force move Indians to west of the Mississippi (D) establish Florida as Indian territory.

29. Which of these was NOT part of Jackson's financial policies? (A) veto the recharter of the national bank (B) provide a uniform national currency (C) deposit federal money in state banks (D) distribute the Treasury surplus to the states.

30. Jackson's statement that "John Marshall has made his decision; now let him enforce it" was made in reference to (A) the tariff controversy (B) jurisdiction over Indian lands (C) the Fugitive Slave Act (D) rechartering the national bank.

Part C In the answer space write the name of the person identified. Use TEN of the twelve names:

J. Q. Adams · Calhoun · Chase · Clay · Harrison · Jackson · Key · L'Enfant · Pike · Stuart · Tecumseh · Wilkinson

31. Was implicated in Burr's conspiracy.

32. A Supreme Court justice who was impeached and acquitted.

33. Drew the plan for the city of Washington.

34. Formed a confederacy to drive settlers from the Northwest Territory.

35. This "great compromiser" became Secretary of State but failed to become President.

36. Explored the central part of the Louisiana Territory.

37. His ideas formed the Monroe Doctrine.

38. A barrel of hard cider helped elect him President.

39. He wrote "The Star-Spangled Banner."

40. He painted famous portraits of Washington.

Part D In the answer space write the letter of the one item that *does not belong* in the group.

_____ 41. *Members of the Virginia dynasty of Presidents:* (A) Washington (B) Adams (C) Jefferson (D) Madison.

_____ 42. *Evidence that the White House was built before 1812:* (A) occupied by Jefferson (B) burned by the British (C) painted white (D) laundry dried in the East Room by Abigail Adams.

_____ 43. *Federalist laws/programs dropped when Jefferson became President:* (A) Bank of the United States (B) excise tax on whiskey (C) 14-year waiting period for naturalization (D) Sedition Act.

_____ 44. *Provisions of the Missouri Compromise:* (A) Missouri to enter Union as a slave state (B) Maine to enter as a free state (C) gradual emancipation of slaves in Missouri (D) no slavery in Louisiana Territory north of 36° 30" line.

_____ 45. *Voting procedures before the Civil War:* (A) use of secret ballots (B) use of printed ballots (C) voice voting (D) use of hand-written ballots.

Part E In the answer space write the letter of a cause that goes with the event.

	Event	*Cause*
_____ 46.	War of 1812	(A) Hartford Convention
_____ 47.	"Corrupt Bargain" charge	(B) Specie Circular
_____ 48.	Death of Federalist party	(C) Southern demands for more slave territory
_____ 49.	Missouri Compromise	(D) Violation of American rights at sea
_____ 50.	Panic of 1837	(E) Rise of grand hotels
_____ 51.	Sale of Louisiana Territory to U.S.	(F) Clay appointed Secretary of State
_____ 52.	*Marbury* v. *Madison* case	(G) The Peggy Eaton affair
_____ 53.	Acquisition of Florida	(H) Appointment of "midnight judges"
_____ 54.	Rising popularity of political conventions	(I) French failure to subdue Haiti
_____ 55.	Formation of "Kitchen Cabinet"	(J) Spanish failure to control Indians

Part F In the answer space write *Yes* if the person or group favored the issue on the right. If not, write *No*.

	Person or group	*Issue*
_____ 56.	Thomas Jefferson	56. A nation of shops and factories
_____ 57.	Shipowners and merchants	57. Embargo Act
_____ 58.	John Marshall	58. Judicial review by the Supreme Court
_____ 59.	New England Federalists	59. The War of 1812
_____ 60.	James Madison	60. Calhoun's Bonus Bill
_____ 61.	Cherokee Indians	61. Jackson's Indian policy
_____ 62.	Henry Clay	62. Jackson's election in 1824
_____ 63.	Directors of the "pet" banks	63. Western land speculation
_____ 64.	South Carolina's legislature	64. Nullification of the tariff
_____ 65.	Martin Van Buren	65. Limit on working day for federal workers

Part G On the back, answer whatever essay questions your teacher may ask.

Unit 4 Test SECTIONALISM AND EXPANSION

Part A Match the persons on the right with the achievements on the left.

_____ 1. Invention of the telegraph
_____ 2. Laying of the Atlantic cable
_____ 3. Waltham labor system
_____ 4. Use of interchangeable parts
_____ 5. Building of clipper ships
_____ 6. Steamboat building
_____ 7. Promoting Erie Canal

(A) DeWitt Clinton
(B) Cyrus W. Field
(C) Robert Fulton
(D) Francis Cabot Lowell
(E) Donald McKay
(F) Samuel F. B. Morse
(G) Eli Whitney

_____ 8. Leading slaves to freedom
_____ 9. *Essay on Duty of Civil Disobedience*
_____ 10. Reform of public education
_____ 11. Crusade for mental hospitals
_____ 12. Religious revival meetings
_____ 13. Publishing abolitionist newspaper
_____ 14. Organizing Women's Rights Convention

(H) Dorothea Dix
(I) Charles G. Finney
(J) William Lloyd Garrison
(K) Horace Mann
(L) Lucretia Mott
(M) Henry David Thoreau
(N) Harriet Tubman

_____ 15. Defending the Alamo
_____ 16. Opening the Oregon Trail
_____ 17. Leading Mormons to Utah
_____ 18. Opening Santa Fe Trail
_____ 19. Attracting settlers to Texas
_____ 20. Founding mission in Oregon

(O) Stephen Austin
(P) William Becknell
(Q) William Travis
(R) Marcus Whitman
(S) Nathaniel Wyeth
(T) Brigham Young

Part B Put the letter of the *one best answer* in the answer space.

_____ 21. Around 1815 a horse-drawn loaded wagon could travel from Massachusetts to South Carolina in about (A) 10 days (B) 3 weeks (C) 10 weeks (D) 6 months.
_____ 22. New York became the nation's commercial metropolis because of (A) the Erie Canal (B) the transcontinental railroad (C) interstate turnpikes (D) the steamboat.
_____ 23. The two chief sources of immigration in 1820–1860 were (A) Russia and Italy (B) France and Scandinavia (C) Scotland and Wales (D) Ireland and Germany.
_____ 24. Settlers to the Far West traveled in large wagon trains (A) for safety (B) to share supplies (C) to reduce expenses (D) to get experience in self-government.
_____ 25. "Fifty-four forty or fight!" refers to the dispute over (A) Alaska (B) Texas (C) Oregon (D) California.
_____ 26. Which of the following would an abolitionist oppose most strongly? (A) Fugitive Slave Act (B) Compromise of 1850 (C) Wilmot Proviso (D) Kansas-Nebraska Act.
_____ 27. "Beecher's Bibles" were (A) maps of escape routes for slaves (B) antislavery propaganda pamphlets (C) "tickets" for the Underground Railroad (D) rifles for antislavery settlers.
_____ 28. The slavery issue getting most attention in Congress from 1820 to 1860 was (A) stopping the importation of slaves (B) emancipation of slaves (C) humane treatment of slaves (D) extension of slavery into the western territories.

_____ 29. In their 1860 national convention the Democrats split over the issue of (A) support for slavery in the territories (B) the protective tariff (C) land grants to railroads in the West (D) emancipation.

_____ 30. The position of Stephen Douglas on the issue of slavery in the territories was that (A) the Missouri Compromise should not be changed (B) the voters of a territory should decide the issue (C) the number of slaves in any territory should be limited (D) slavery should be abolished west of the Mississippi.

_____ 31. Douglas broke with Buchanan over the latter's attempt to (A) admit Kansas as a free state (B) withdraw official patronage from Illinois (C) disregard the Lecompton Constitution (D) deprive Kansas of popular sovereignty.

_____ 32. The Kansas-Nebraska Act (A) repealed the slavery restriction of the Missouri Compromise (B) provided for slavery in Kansas (C) abandoned the principle of popular sovereignty (D) was vigorously resisted by proslavery men.

_____ 33. The belief that the enlargement of the United States to its natural continental boundaries was clear and certain was called (A) the moving frontier (B) territorial expansion (C) aggressive annexation (D) manifest destiny.

_____ 34. The man who was almost beaten to death for his fierce verbal attack on slavery supporters was Senator (A) Douglas (B) Butler (C) Brooks (D) Sumner.

_____ 35. About what percent of the popular vote did Lincoln win in 1860? (A) 28% (B) 39% (C) 47% (D) 56%.

_____ 36. In which territory was the most blood spilled over the issue of slavery in the 1850s? (A) Kansas (B) Nebraska (C) Iowa (D) Utah.

_____ 37. Who was President when most of the land just west of the Louisiana Territory came into the Union? (A) Polk (B) Tyler (C) Fillmore (D) Buchanan.

Part C In the answer space put the letter of the source of the quotation.

Quotation

_____ 38. "In the United States, a man builds a house in which to spend his old age, and he sells it before the roof is on."

_____ 39. [Slavery is] "the most safe and stable basis for free institutions in the world."

_____ 40. "... if it is deemed necessary that I should mingle my blood ... with the blood of millions in the slave country ... I say let it be done."

_____ 41. [The insane confined] "in cages, closets, cellars, stalls, pens!"

_____ 42. [It is] "our manifest destiny to overspread and to possess the whole continent."

_____ 43. "... neither slavery nor involuntary servitude shall ever exist in any part of the territory" acquired from Mexico.

_____ 44. [The abolitionists have] "produced nothing good or valuable in their operations for twenty years."

_____ 45. [Concerning Harriet Beecher Stowe:] "Is this the little woman whose book made such a great war?"

Source

(A) Dorothea Dix
(B) Wilmot Proviso
(C) John L. O'Sullivan
(D) Daniel Webster
(E) Abraham Lincoln
(F) John Brown
(G) Alexis de Tocqueville
(H) John C. Calhoun

Part D Three of the items are related to the introductory phrase in *italics*. In the answer space write the letter of the one item that *does not belong*.

_____ 46. *Features of early American railroads:* (A) single set of tracks (B) light, speedy engines (C) stable, firm roadbeds (D) government and private financing.

_____ 47. *Early features of Waltham labor system:* (A) pleasant living environment (B) assurance of long-term jobs (C) hiring of unmarried women (D) provision of cultural attractions.

_____ 48. *Advantages of balloon-frame construction:* (A) little use of scarce lumber (B) minimal building skills required (C) easy dismantling and reassembling (D) strength and durability.

_____ 49. *Points made in Dred Scott decision:* (A) Missouri Compromise was void (B) slaves were not citizens (C) Congress could not restrict slavery in the territories (D) a slave taken into a free state became free.

_____ 50. *Responses in the North to the Fugitive Slave Act:* (A) passage of Personal Liberty laws (B) nullification conventions (C) support of the Underground Railroad (D) mass protest meetings.

_____ 51. *Active abolitionists:* (A) Henry Clay (B) Angelina Grimké (C) Elijah Lovejoy (D) James G. Birney.

_____ 52. *Leaders of the women's rights movement:* (A) Elizabeth Cady Stanton (B) Harriet Tubman (C) Sojourner Truth (D) Susan B. Anthony.

_____ 53. *Provisions of the Compromise of 1850:* (A) strong Fugitive Slave Act (B) California admitted as free state (C) Utah and New Mexico territories opened to slavery (D) slavery abolished in District of Columbia.

_____ 54. *States or parts of states carved out of the Oregon country:* (A) Idaho (B) Washington (C) Utah (D) Oregon.

_____ 55. *Lincoln's views on slavery in 1860:* (A) was morally wrong (B) must not be extended (C) should be abolished at once (D) no interference where already established.

Part E In each exercise one item is a *cause,* another is a *result,* and a third item is *not related* to the other two. Write the letter of the *cause* in the answer space.

_____ 56. (A) broadening of women's rights (B) growth of mental hospitals (C) Seneca Falls Convention

_____ 57. (A) founding of Liberia (B) formation of American Colonization Society (C) Ostend Manifesto

_____ 58. (A) Indians protecting their lands (B) wagon trains forming a government (C) Mormons moving to Utah

_____ 59. (A) Crittenden amendments (B) abolitionists' petitions to Congress (C) "gag rule"

_____ 60. (A) U. S. war with Mexico (B) acceptance of 49th parallel as Oregon boundary (C) Fugitive Slave Act

_____ 61. (A) Kansas-Nebraska Act (B) Underground Railroad (C) railroad expansion in west

_____ 62. (A) Buchanan picked as Democratic presidential candidate in 1856 (B) "Bleeding Kansas" (C) Gadsden Purchase

Part F In the answer space write *Yes* if the person or group favored the issue on the right. If not, write *No.*

_____ 63. President James Buchanan   63. Lecompton Constitution
_____ 64. Great Britain   64. Independence of Texas
_____ 65. Stephen A. Douglas   65. Popular sovereignty
_____ 66. Antislavery Northerners   66. Dred Scott decision
_____ 67. Henry David Thoreau   67. The Mexican War
_____ 68. Slaveholders   68. Crittenden amendments
_____ 69. Border slave states   69. Support for Lincoln in 1860
_____ 70. Daniel Webster   70. Compromise of 1850

Part G On the back, answer any essay questions your teacher may ask.

Unit 4 Test

Unit 5 Test ROCKY ROAD TO UNION

Part A In the answer space write the letter of the person quoted.

Source

_____ 1. "If I could save the Union without freeing any slave, I would do it."
_____ 2. "Give me 5000 fresh men and I will be in Washington tomorrow."
_____ 3. "Find out where your enemy is. . . . Strike him as hard as you can."
_____ 4. "War is cruelty and you cannot refine it."
_____ 5. "Go West, young man!"
_____ 6. "Money was as plenty as dust."
_____ 7. "I am Denver City."

(A) Ulysses S. Grant
(B) Robert E. Lee
(C) Thomas J. Jackson
(D) Abraham Lincoln
(E) William T. Sherman
(F) Mark Twain
(G) Horace Greeley
(H) William Larimer

Part B Select the *one best answer* to each sentence and put its letter in the answer space.

_____ 8. At the time of the Civil War, blacks constituted what percent of the total population of the country? (A) 5 (B) 15 (C) 25 (D) 35.

_____ 9. Civil War battle deaths totaled more than (A) 6,000 (B) 60,000 (C) 600,000 (D) 6,000,000.

_____ 10. The Union population was how many times greater than that of the Confederacy? (A) 2 (B) 3 (C) 4 (D) 5.

_____ 11. Lincoln's delay in freeing the slaves was due mainly to (A) opposition in the North to confiscation of property (B) fear of losing the loyalty of the border states (C) fear that it would not be approved abroad (D) the belief that emancipation was unconstitutional.

_____ 12. Blacks were used in the armed forces in the Civil War (A) chiefly by the Union (B) mainly by the Confederacy (C) equally by both sides (D) by neither side.

_____ 13. The standard infantry weapon in the Civil War was the (A) flintlock musket (B) rifle (C) automatic pistol (D) machine gun.

_____ 14. The term "conda" in the North referred to a (A) type of army horse (B) slang term for a tent (C) blockade of the South (D) network of railroads.

_____ 15. Lincoln gave first priority to (A) saving the Union (B) upholding national honor (C) freeing the slaves (D) avoiding bloodshed.

_____ 16. The battle between the *Monitor* and the *Merrimac* was *most significant* because (A) neither ship won (B) large 11-inch guns were used for the first time (C) the era of wooden naval ships was over (D) new battle tactics were used.

_____ 17. On surrendering to Grant, Lee said, "This will have a very happy effect upon my army." He was referring to (A) relief that the war was over (B) Grant's allowing retention of swords and horses (C) Grant's tribute to the Confederate army (D) Grant's promise of continued white supremacy.

_____ 18. Leaders of the "Radicals" in Congress were (A) Clay and Davis (B) Tilden and Seymour (C) Stevens and Sumner (D) Blaine and Brooks.

_____ 19. "Black Codes" referred to (A) military intelligence codes (B) secret agreements by blacks to overthrow white rule (C) rules of conduct for southern blacks (D) signals used by blacks to ridicule white "enemies."

_____ 20. The most important work of the Freedmen's Bureau in aiding southern blacks was to provide (A) a means for education (B) forty acres and a mule to each family (C) protection from the KKK (D) voting rights.

_____ 21. The real reason for Johnson's impeachment was (A) his drinking and cursing (B) his firing of Stanton (C) his obstruction to the Radicals' Reconstruction bills (D) his attachment to the Democratic party.

_____ 22. In *Plessy* v. *Ferguson* the Supreme Court (A) ruled "Jim Crow" laws illegal (B) upheld the legality of sharecropping (C) approved separate but equal public facilities for blacks (D) denounced the Ku Klux Klan.

_____ 23. If you flew straight from Vicksburg to Gettysburg, you would pass closest to (A) Chattanooga (B) Charleston (C) Mobile (D) Richmond.

_____ 24. Which of these slave-holding states joined the Confederacy? (A) Maryland (B) Kentucky (C) Tennessee (D) Missouri.

_____ 25. Regarding the political status of the Confederate states, Lincoln believed that they (A) should be put under military rule (B) had never legally left the Union (C) must beg for forgiveness (D) should be treated as territories.

Part C Three of the items are related to the introductory phrase in *italics*. In the answer space write the letter of the item that *does not belong*.

_____ 26. *Why the South thought it would win the Civil War:* (A) lack of unity of the North (B) belief that Britain and France would break the Union blockade (C) belief in superiority of Confederate troops (D) knowledge of superior Confederate industrial resources.

_____ 27. *Favors promised to Southerners by Rutherford B. Hayes to win Presidency in 1877:* (A) withdrawal of last federal troops from South (B) support of "Jim Crow" laws (C) appointment of a Southerner to Cabinet (D) generous spending for internal improvements in South.

_____ 28. *Effects of the "war in the West" in 1862–1863:* (A) brought fighting to an end in Tennessee (B) brought U. S. Grant into prominence (C) closed the Mississippi to Confederates (D) showed that the war could not be won quickly.

_____ 29. *Provisions of the Fourteenth Amendment:* (A) citizenship for blacks (B) equal protection of the laws (C) reduction of representation in Congress for not allowing adult male blacks to vote (D) requirement that Confederate war debts must be paid.

_____ 30. *Steps taken by the Union to finance the war:* (A) taxing excess profits of corporations (B) taxing individual incomes (C) issuing paper money (D) borrowing.

_____ 31. *Use of buffalo by Plains Indians:* (A) food (B) shelter (C) transportation (D) clothing.

_____ 32. *Problems faced by Plains Indians after the Civil War:* (A) buffalo slaughter (B) homesteading by white settlers (C) lack of horses and weapons (D) railroad development encouraging settlement.

_____ 33. *Factors in ending the open range for cattle ranchers:* (A) start-up of more and more ranches (B) shutdown of Indian reservations (C) growth of barbed wire fencing (D) bad weather.

_____ 34. *Problems faced by farmers on Great Plains:* (A) overcrowding (B) extremes of temperature (C) lack of timber (D) drought.

_____ 35. *Cow towns:* (A) Abilene (B) Cripple Creek (C) Laramie (D) Dodge City.

Part D Match the person or term on the right with the explanation on the left.

_____ 36. Indecisive commander of the peninsular campaign

_____ 37. Designer of the "anaconda" plan

_____ 38. Led the march from Atlanta to the sea

_____ 39. Seized New Orleans for the Union

_____ 40. Led Union forces at Gettysburg

(A) David G. Farragut
(B) U. S. Grant
(C) George McClellan
(D) George G. Meade
(E) Winfield Scott
(F) William T. Sherman

Unit 5 Test

_____ 41. Victor at Bull Run, he was known as "Stonewall"
_____ 42. Surrendered Confederate forces at Appomattox
_____ 43. President of the Confederacy
_____ 44. Fought Grant at Vicksburg
_____ 45. Led Confederates at Pittsburg Landing (Shiloh)

(A) Jefferson Davis
(B) Thomas J. Jackson
(C) Albert S. Johnston
(D) Joseph E. Johnston
(E) Robert E. Lee
(F) John C. Pemberton

_____ 46. Eastern end of the Pony Express
_____ 47. First state to secede from Union
_____ 48. Reconstruction ended first in this state
_____ 49. Site of Custer's last stand
_____ 50. Comstock Lode and Virginia City
_____ 51. Gold rush in the Black Hills
_____ 52. Original home of the longhorn cattle
_____ 53. Land rush of 1889

(A) Alabama
(B) Missouri
(C) Montana
(D) Nevada
(E) Oklahoma
(F) Pennsylvania
(G) South Carolina
(H) South Dakota
(I) Tennessee
(J) Texas

_____ 54. Provided farmland for western settlers
_____ 55. Attempted to "Americanize" the Indians
_____ 56. Provided postwar aid in the South
_____ 57. Outlined congressional plan for Reconstruction
_____ 58. Involved misuse of funds by railroad officials

(A) Civil Rights Act of 1866
(B) Crédit Mobilier
(C) Dawes Act
(D) Freedman's Bureau Act
(E) Homestead Act
(F) Wade-Davis bill

_____ 59. Built Abilene into a cow town
_____ 60. Started a cattle trail from Texas to Wyoming
_____ 61. Made a fortune from silver mining
_____ 62. Publicized the sad plight of the Indians
_____ 63. Leader in the slaughter of the buffalo
_____ 64. His cartoons stirred public opinion against Boss Tweed
_____ 65. Collapse of his investment house led to the panic of 1873
_____ 66. Impeached as Grant's Secretary of War for accepting bribes
_____ 67. Loser in the disputed election of 1876
_____ 68. Leader of the Radical Republicans
_____ 69. Assassinated President Lincoln
_____ 70. Founder of the American Red Cross

(A) Clara Barton
(B) W. W. Belknap
(C) John Wilkes Booth
(D) Mathew Brady
(E) William Cody
(F) Jay Cooke
(G) Charles Goodnight
(H) Joseph G. McCoy
(I) John W. Mackay
(J) Thomas Nast
(K) Thaddeus Stevens
(L) Samuel Tilden
(M) Sarah Winnemucca

Part E In the space below begin your answers to whatever essay questions your teacher may ask.

Unit 6 Test   THE NEW INDUSTRIAL AGE

Part A Match the quotation with the writer or speaker by putting the correct letter in the answer space.

_____ 1. "Under scientific management, the answer to [a] question is not a matter of anyone's opinion; it is a question for accurate, scientific investigation."

_____ 2. "I am a Stalwart, and Arthur is President now."

_____ 3. ". . . farmers [should] raise less corn and more Hell."

_____ 4. "You shall not crucify mankind upon a cross of gold."

(A) W. J. Bryan
(B) Charles Guiteau
(C) Mark Hanna
(D) Mary Lease
(E) F. W. Taylor

Part B In the answer space put the letter of the industry or business field that the person was associated with.

_____ 5. James Bogardus
_____ 6. Andrew Carnegie
_____ 7. Edwin L. Drake
_____ 8. James B. Eads
_____ 9. Thomas A. Edison
_____ 10. Elisha G. Otis
_____ 11. John D. Rockefeller
_____ 12. Washington Roebling
_____ 13. Richard Sears
_____ 14. A. T. Stewart

(A) Bridge construction
(B) Building construction
(C) Electric industry
(D) Merchandising
(E) Petroleum industry
(F) Steel industry

Part C Select the *one best answer* to each sentence and put its letter in the answer space.

_____ 15. Big business organized *pools* (A) for recreation for workers (B) to boost worker efficiency (C) to fix prices (D) to collect funds for supporting colleges.

_____ 16. The site of the first commercial oil wells was (A) Pennsylvania (B) Texas (C) Michigan (D) Oklahoma.

_____ 17. Coal miners organized a secret society known as (A) the Knights of Labor (B) the United Coal Diggers (C) the Undergrounders (D) the Molly Maguires.

_____ 18. A chief reason for the growth of the American Federation of Labor was its emphasis on (A) the overthrow of capitalism (B) higher pay and shorter hours (C) electing union supporters to public office (D) social clubs for workers.

_____ 19. The big majority of immigrants after the Civil War settled (A) on farms in the Midwest (B) in the cities (C) on the Great Plains (D) in the South.

_____ 20. The Immigration Restriction League emphasized a reduction in immigration through (A) quotas for each country (B) a literacy test (C) age limits (D) skill requirements.

_____ 21. The Morrill Act of 1862 created (A) bonuses for veterans (B) land grants for railroads (C) land-grant colleges (D) national parks.

_____ 22. An enterprise shared by Leland Stanford, John D. Rockefeller, and Matthew Vassar was (A) the financing of settlement houses (B) the endowment of colleges (C) the founding of oil companies (D) railroad building.

_____ 23. Republican bosses who opposed civil service reform called themselves (A) Populists (B) Mugwumps (C) Spoilers (D) Stalwarts.

_____ 24. The only President to serve two separate terms was (A) Harrison (B) Grant (C) Cleveland (D) Arthur.

_____ 25. Business corporations formed trusts chiefly (A) to influence legislation (B) to control prices (C) to win public confidence (D) to attract workers.

_____ 26. Some corporations obtained an advantage over their rivals by getting railroads (A) to offer rebates (B) to give up their land grants (C) to boycott other companies (D) to build standard-gauge track.

_____ 27. The new mail-order houses were like the new department stores in that both (A) sold chiefly to farm families (B) relied on the Post Office for orders and deliveries (C) were operated by the same companies (D) provided a wide range of goods to people at varied income levels.

_____ 28. A chief difference between the Knights of Labor and the A F of L was that only the Knights of Labor (A) demanded higher wages (B) worked for the eight-hour day (C) tried to enroll all workers in one union (D) were involved in strikes.

_____ 29. Between 1860 and 1915 the nation's population (A) grew in the cities and declined on the farms (B) grew in cities and rural areas but much faster in the cities (C) grew only because of immigration (D) stopped growing.

_____ 30. Between 1870 and 1900 the number of cities over 100,000 more than doubled. Most of these new big cities were in the (A) Far West (B) South (C) Northeast and Midwest (D) Great Plains.

_____ 31. West Coast efforts to restrict immigration were directed chiefly against people from (A) Mexico (B) Hawaii and the Philippines (C) Ireland (D) China and Japan.

_____ 32. On the issue of progress for black Americans, W. E. B. Du Bois rejected Booker T. Washington's emphasis on (A) political action (B) gradualism and industrial training (C) voting rights for blacks (D) emigration of blacks to Africa.

_____ 33. In the thirty years after the Civil War the general level of prices (A) declined substantially (B) kept rising (C) remained steady (D) rose and fell sharply about every five years.

_____ 34. What effect does a big increase in money supply tend to have on the general level of prices? (A) raise it (B) lower it (C) keep it steady (D) force it up and down.

Part D Three of the items are related to the introductory phrase in *italics*. In the answer space write the letter of the item that *does not belong*.

_____ 35. *Effects of railroad building in the West:* (A) drop in land prices near the railways (B) rise in population of West (C) reduction in coast-to-coast travel time (D) adoption of standard gauge track.

_____ 36. *Fears aroused by giant business corporations:* (A) little control of management by stockholders (B) their lack of efficiency (C) little contact between workers and owners (D) power of big business to influence governmental decisions.

_____ 37. *Factors promoting immigrant colonies in American cities:* (A) public schools (B) foreign language newspapers (C) churches and synagogues (D) old-country stores and shops.

_____ 38. *Proposals to increase money supply in the late 19th century:* (A) preserve gold standard (B) issue more greenbacks (C) coin more silver (D) force Treasury to buy silver.

_____ 39. *Planks in Populist party platform:* (A) increase in money supply (B) high tariff (C) income tax (D) government ownership of railroads.

_____ 40. *Major political issues in 1870–1900:* (A) tariff (B) antitrust laws (C) "cheap" vs. "sound" money (D) extension of slavery.

Part E Match the person on the right with his/her achievement on the left.

_____ 41. Devised ways to make factory work more efficient.
_____ 42. Bought and merged steel companies to form the U. S. Steel Corporation.
_____ 43. Organized a company chiefly to invent and perfect new products.
_____ 44. Organized the American Federation of Labor.
_____ 45. Pointed out the importance of the frontier in the shaping of American institutions.
_____ 46. Establishment of settlement houses.
_____ 47. Helped develop "garden cities."
_____ 48. Led movement to limit the use of alcoholic beverages.
_____ 49. Promoted organizations for black Americans.
_____ 50. Sponsored bill requiring Treasury to buy and coin silver.
_____ 51. Led the Stalwarts in Congress.
_____ 52. Sponsored the bill for civil service reform.
_____ 53. Led the fight for the Interstate Commerce Act.
_____ 54. Known as "Czar" of the House of Representatives.
_____ 55. Started the Granger societies.
_____ 56. Ran as Populist candidate for President in 1892.

(A) Jane Addams
(B) Richard Bland
(C) Roscoe Conkling
(D) Jacob Coxey
(E) Shelby M. Cullom
(F) Thomas A. Edison
(G) Samuel Gompers
(H) Mark Hanna
(I) Oliver H. Kelley
(J) J. P. Morgan
(K) Frederick Olmstead
(L) George Pendleton
(M) Thomas B. Reed
(N) Frederick W. Taylor
(O) Frederick J. Turner
(P) James B. Weaver
(Q) Ida Wells-Barnett
(R) Frances Willard

Part F Arrange the events in each series in the proper time order. Then in the answer space put the letter of the event that occurred *last*.

_____ 57. (A) Garfield assassination (B) passage of civil service reform law (C) Hayes-Conkling battle over patronage.
_____ 58. Inauguration of (A) Benjamin Harrison (B) Rutherford B. Hayes (C) James A. Garfield.
_____ 59. (A) Interstate Commerce Act (B) Sherman Antitrust Act (C) Wilson-Gorman tariff bill passed.
_____ 60. (A) Farmers' Alliances organized (B) Populist party formed (C) Patrons of Husbandry organized.

Part G In the space below begin your answers to whatever essay questions your teacher may ask.

Unit 7 Test DEMOCRATIC REFORMS AND WORLD POWER

Part A In the answer space print the letter of the person who is identified.

    1. Pushed the Open Door policy
    2. Mexican President opposed by Wilson
    3. Made Panama Canal Zone safe from yellow fever
    4. Led Filipino revolt against U. S. rule
    5. Headed Food Administration in World War I
    6. Reform governor of Wisconsin
    7. Led Senate fight against the Versailles Treaty
    8. Head of U. S. Forest Service
    9. Headed War Industries Board in 1918
  10. Wrote on the influence of sea power in history
  11. Defeated Spanish fleet at Manila in 1898
  12. Democratic candidate for President in 1904
  13. Democratic candidate for President in 1920
  14. Published shocking pictures of city slums
  15. Cruel Spanish general sent to put down Cuban revolt
  16. Helped stamp out yellow fever in Cuba
  17. Head of United Mine Workers in 1902
  18. Military governor of Cuba, 1899–1902
  19. "Yellow Press" publisher in 1890s
  20. Opened Japan to U.S. trade

(A) Emilio Aguinaldo
(B) Bernard M. Baruch
(C) William E. Borah
(D) James M. Cox
(E) George Dewey
(F) William Gorgas
(G) John Hay
(H) Herbert Hoover
(I) Victoriano Huerta
(J) Robert M. La Follette
(K) Alfred Thayer Mahan
(L) John Mitchell
(M) Alton B. Parker
(N) Matthew C. Perry
(O) Gifford Pinchot
(P) Joseph Pulitzer
(Q) Walter Reed
(R) Jacob Riis
(S) Valeriano Weyler
(T) Leonard Wood

Part B In the answer space put the letter of the *best* answer for each statement.

21. Which did the United States obtain before 1890? (A) Virgin Islands (B) Puerto Rico (C) Philippines (D) Alaska.

22. The problem known as the "*Alabama* claims" involved (A) Indian land claims in Alabama (B) loss of union vessels to Confederate commerce raiders (C) Alabama's Confederate war debt (D) mining claims in Alabama.

23. The incident involving an attack on U.S. sailors in Chile was significant in that (A) the dispute was settled by arbitration (B) our response was widely praised throughout Latin America (C) our response was a setback to good relations with Latin America (D) Spain regained control of Chile.

24. The Venezuelan boundary dispute was significant in that (A) we gained important oil lands (B) we tried to protect a small Latin American nation from a major world power (C) it led to war with Spain (D) Great Britain lost British Guiana.

25. How did the United States obtain Hawaii? (A) by purchase (B) as part of the settlement of the Spanish-American War (C) by arbitration (D) by a revolution engineered by American settlers and officials.

26. Best known of the American military units in the Spanish-American War were the (A) Raiders (B) Rangers (C) Commandos (D) Rough Riders.

_____ 27. The Spanish-American War was won chiefly by (A) the U. S. Navy (B) the Cuban revolutionaries (C) Roosevelt's cavalry regiment (D) General Shafter's brilliant strategy.

_____ 28. The Spanish-American War proclaimed that the United States (A) would help independence movements all over the world (B) favored settlement of disputes by arbitration (C) had joined the race for empire (D) had the strongest armed forces in the world.

_____ 29. In order to win control in the Philippines the United States had to (A) put down a Filipino rebellion (B) guarantee its future independence (C) promise a huge aid program (D) drive out the Japanese.

_____ 30. A U. S. promise to respect the sovereignty of Cuba was made in the (A) Platt Amendment (B) Ostend Manifesto (C) Teller Amendment (D) Monroe Doctrine.

_____ 31. To get U. S. troops out of Cuba, its government had to agree to the terms of the (A) Platt Amendment (B) Ostend Manifesto (C) Teller Amendment (D) Monroe Doctrine.

_____ 32. Our chief purpose for proposing the Open Door policy in China was (A) to obtain a sphere of influence there (B) to promote democracy in China (C) to get more workers from China (D) to assure U. S. trade rights in China.

_____ 33. The Boxer Rebellion took place in (A) China (B) Japan (C) Philippine Islands (D) Korea.

_____ 34. Sinclair's novel *The Jungle* influenced the passage of the (A) Hepburn Act (B) Pure Food and Drug Act (C) Employers' Liability Act (D) Meat Inspection Act.

_____ 35. Theodore Roosevelt's position on the Sherman Antitrust Act was that it should (A) be enforced vigorously against all trusts (B) be used to break up "bad" trusts (C) be repealed (D) be ignored.

_____ 36. A chief reason for Wilson's election victory in 1912 was that (A) the voters had tired of Progressive reforms (B) women had won the right to vote (C) Taft and T. Roosevelt split the Republican vote (D) Wilson had the most political experience.

_____ 37. The Clayton Act strengthened the Sherman Antitrust Act by (A) outlawing specific monopolistic practices (B) ordering particular trusts to be dissolved (C) providing financial aid for small business firms (D) creating Federal Reserve banks.

_____ 38. The chief reason for building the Panama Canal was (A) to force transcontinental railroads to reduce their rates (B) to increase the efficiency of the U. S. Navy (C) to broaden U. S. control over Latin America (D) to reduce travel time between New York and California.

_____ 39. The Roosevelt Corollary to the Monroe Doctrine was a statement in defense of (A) Roosevelt's method of obtaining canal rights in Panama (B) the purchase of the Virgin Islands (C) the right of Latin American republics to run their own affairs (D) the right of the U.S. to intervene in Latin America.

_____ 40. The term "dollar diplomacy" is associated with the Presidency of (A) McKinley (B) T. Roosevelt (C) Taft (D) Wilson.

_____ 41. President Wilson responded to the outbreak of World War I by (A) proclaiming U. S. neutrality (B) sending aid to Britain and France (C) condemning Germany (D) offering his services as a mediator.

_____ 42. Wilson's Fourteen Points were a statement of (A) peace agreements made by the Allies (B) America's war aims (C) our reasons for entering the war (D) our conditions for dropping out of the war.

_____ 43. The text authors say that the worst feature of the Versailles Treaty was (A) the absence of provision for a League of Nations (B) the creation of new European republics (C) the heavy reparations imposed on Germany (D) the Allied takeover of German colonies.

_____ 44. A chief reason for the Senate's refusal to approve the Versailles Treaty was that (A) it was too favorable to Germany (B) the Peace Conference had ignored Wilson's advice (C) the U. S. had received no territory (D) Wilson had failed to secure the advice of congressional leaders in drafting the treaty.

Part C Three of the items are related to the introductory phrase in *italics*. In the answer space write the letter of the item that *does not belong*.

_____ 45. *Factors bringing the United States into war with Spain in 1898:* (A) demand of newspapers for sensational news (B) Spain's violation of the Monroe Doctrine (C) American sympathy for the Cubans (D) imperialist sentiment of some politicians and businessmen.

_____ 46. *Lands coming under U. S. control as a result of the Spanish-American War:* (A) Puerto Rico (B) Guam (C) the Philippines (D) Samoa.

_____ 47. *Provisions of the Hepburn Act:* (A) cancelled railroad land grants (B) extended Interstate Commerce Commission control over other transportation facilities besides railroads (C) forbade railroad rebates (D) gave ICC the power to force railroads to charge fair rates.

_____ 48. *Conservation efforts under Theodore Roosevelt:* (A) big increase in national forests (B) reforestation of cut-over land (C) building dams for irrigation of desert land (D) stopping all mining on public lands.

_____ 49. *Reform measures providing for more "direct" democracy:* (A) workmen's compensation (B) initiative (C) referendum (D) recall.

_____ 50. *Muckrakers:* (A) Ida Tarbell (B) Samuel "Golden Rule" Jones (C) Frank Norris (D) Lincoln Steffens.

_____ 51. *How Taft disappointed the Progressives:* (A) supported Payne-Aldrich tariff (B) sided with Ballinger against Pinchot (C) took a go-slow position on reform measures (D) failed to enforce the Sherman Antitrust Act.

_____ 52. *Progressive reforms under President Taft:* (A) income-tax amendment (B) passage of stronger antitrust law (C) growth of national forests (D) federal control of minerals in public land sold to private buyers.

_____ 53. *Areas of major reform in Wilson's first term:* (A) tariff revision (B) currency and banking (C) conservation of natural resources (D) strengthening of antitrust law.

_____ 54. *Purposes of Federal Reserve Act:* (A) to bring state banks under federal control (B) to provide an elastic currency (C) to help prevent "runs" on banks (D) to serve as "bankers' banks."

_____ 55. *British violations of international law in 1914–1915:* (A) maintaining a blockade far from German coast (B) seizing vessels bound for neutral countries (C) sinking neutral vessels without warning (D) enlarging the list of contraband to include even food.

_____ 56. *Reasons for U. S. entry into World War I:* (A) desire for share of Germany's colonies (B) unrestricted submarine warfare by Germany (C) Zimmermann note (D) desire to prevent defeat of Britain and loss of British sea power.

_____ 57. *New features of warfare in World War I:* (A) heavy dependence on trenches (B) use of poison gas (C) wide use of machine guns and automatic rifles (D) heavy bombing by airplanes.

_____ 58. *Home-front activities designed to help win the war:* (A) drafting of women for jobs in war industries (B) voluntary food conservation (C) war bond drives (D) government takeover of railroads.

_____ 59. *Effect of World War I on American labor:* (A) substantial wage increases (B) opening of industrial jobs to blacks and women (C) increase in the length of the working day (D) rise in union membership.

_____ 60. *Efforts to enlist support of the war:* (A) punishing resistance to the war (B) winning loyalty of German Americans by promoting German language and culture (C) hiring writers and speakers to create war propaganda (D) controlling foreign-language newspapers.

Part D On the back, answer whatever essay questions your teacher may ask.

Unit 8 Test FROM BOOM TO BUST

Part A In the answer space put the letter of the person who is identified.

1. Co-author of a treaty renouncing war as an instrument of national policy
2. Cabinet officer convicted in Harding scandals
3. Progressive party candidate in 1924 presidential election
4. Democratic candidate in 1924 election
5. Illustrator of 1920s "flaming youth"
6. Black musician of the '20s
7. Defeated by Al Smith in 1928 convention
8. Author of poetic work, *The Waste Land*
9. Secretary of the Treasury under Harding, Coolidge, and Hoover
10. Perfected automobile assembly line
11. Playwright of the 1920s
12. Secretary of State under Hoover
13. Attorney General during the "Red Scare"
14. Ambassador who helped settle oil problem in Mexico
15. Journalist who poked fun at American follies

(A) John W. Davis
(B) T. S. Eliot
(C) John Held, Jr.
(D) Albert Fall
(E) Henry Ford
(F) Earl "Fatha" Hines
(G) Frank Kellogg
(H) Robert M. La Follette
(I) William G. McAdoo
(J) Andrew Mellon
(K) H. L. Mencken
(L) Dwight W. Morrow
(M) Eugene O'Neill
(N) A. Mitchell Palmer
(O) Henry Stimson

Part B In the answer space put the letter of the *best* answer to the statement.

16. What happened to total nonfarm employment and total union membership from 1921 to 1929? (A) both grew rapidly (B) both rose but jobs much faster (C) jobs rose but union membership declined (D) only slight growth for both.

17. The Palmer raids of 1918–1920 were designed to (A) crush the "new" Ku Klux Klan (B) round up and deport "subversive" aliens (C) find witnesses for the Sacco-Vanzetti trial (D) catch bootleggers.

18. The Sacco-Vanzetti case aroused widespread concern over the (A) return of the payroll money (B) fairness of the trial (C) persecution of Italian Americans (D) question of whether or not they were really anarchists.

19. What two long-sought reforms were realized in 1919–1920? (A) prohibition and women's suffrage (B) the eight-hour day and abolition of child labor (C) old-age insurance and health insurance (D) voting rights for blacks and anti-lynching law.

20. Corruption pervaded the Harding administration because (A) the President was dishonest (B) rapid social change characterized the postwar era (C) Prohibition made lawbreaking respectable (D) Harding made unwise appointments.

21. A chief result of the Fordney-McCumber tariff was that (A) Japan became the world leader in trade (B) the prices of U. S. farm products doubled (C) European nations raised their tariffs (D) tariffs all over the world were lowered.

22. Teapot Dome and Elk Hills are names associated with (A) bootlegger hideouts (B) the veterans' bonus bill (C) labor unrest in 1919 (D) the Harding scandals.

23. Federal regulation of business in the 1920s was characterized by (A) encouragement of cooperation among business firms (B) strict enforcement of the antitrust laws (C) repeal of the antitrust laws (D) a "hands off" policy—neither regulation nor help.

_____ 24. Congress tried to help farmers in the early 1920s with a bill providing for (A) new homesteads in the West (B) federal purchase of crop surpluses (C) price controls on farm machinery (D) direct payments to cover losses.

_____ 25. In the 1928 election Al Smith's chief support came from (A) the big cities (B) the rural South and Midwest (C) the Ku Klux Klan (D) supporters of Prohibition.

_____ 26. Lindbergh became a national hero by becoming the first (A) to fly a single-wing airplane (B) to make a goodwill trip to Mexico (C) to fly across the Atlantic (D) to make a solo nonstop flight across the Atlantic.

_____ 27. The stock market boom of the late 1920s was characterized by the entry of many buyers seeking (A) control of corporations (B) gains from rising stock prices (C) safe investments (D) income from dividends.

_____ 28. The 1920s stock market boom was fueled by (A) house-to-house selling campaigns (B) TV advertising (C) widespread borrowing by stock buyers (D) the encouragement of speculation from the White House.

_____ 29. By 1932 about one worker in four was jobless, making total unemployment about (A) 4 million (B) 8 million (C) 12 million (D) 16 million.

_____ 30. The depression in 1930 was aggravated by a (A) big rise in prices (B) wave of strikes (C) big jump in immigration (D) major farm-belt drought.

_____ 31. Hoover responded to European difficulties in paying their war debts by (A) declaring a one-year postponement on payments (B) cutting the interest rates in half (C) getting Congress to cancel the debts (D) sending surplus food to Europe.

_____ 32. In signing the Kellogg-Briand Pact some 65 nations agreed to (A) lower their tariffs (B) renounce offensive war (C) reduce armaments (D) provide a security force for the League of Nations.

_____ 33. In 1931–1932 the hopes for world peace were shattered by (A) the collapse of the League of Nations (B) the sending of U. S. troops to Central America (C) attacks by Japan on China (D) Germany's takeover of its former colonies.

_____ 34. The Hoover administration took a strong position on the Monroe Doctrine by (A) announcing the Hoover Corollary (B) insisting on friendly governments in Latin America (C) sending Marines to Nicaragua (D) renouncing the Roosevelt Corollary.

_____ 35. The chief issue in the 1932 election was (A) how to deal with the depression (B) whether to end Prohibition (C) payment of the war debts (D) the tariff.

Part C Three of the items are related to the introductory phrase in *italics*. In the answer space write the letter of the item that *does not belong*.

_____ 36. *Forces contributing to the Red Scare of 1919–1920:* (A) Communist revolution in Europe (B) election of Communists to public office in several states (C) urban race riots (D) bombings and bomb scares.

_____ 37. *Signs of anti-foreign prejudice in early 1920s:* (A) the appearance of "new" Ku Klux Klan (B) passage of National Origins Act (C) Sacco-Vanzetti case (D) urban race riots.

_____ 38. *Characteristics of labor-management relations in 1919:* (A) orderly strikes ending in peaceful settlements (B) widespread strikes accompanied by violence (C) clashes brought on by lifting of the wartime ban on strikes (D) labor demands to keep benefits won in wartime.

_____ 39. *Features of immigration laws passed in 1921 and 1924:* (A) limits on total annual immigration (B) quotas set for various countries (C) quotas favoring countries of northern and western Europe (D) ban against Latin American immigrants.

_____ 40. *Persons harassed by Ku Klux Klan of 1920s:* (A) blacks (B) Jews (C) Protestants (D) Roman Catholics.

____ 41. *Treaty provisions from Washington Conference of 1921:* (A) a ratio of 5:5:3 in capital ships for Great Britain, the United States, and Japan (B) creation of a security force to enforce the treaties (C) respect for Open Door in China (D) limits on building naval bases in the Pacific.

____ 42. *Factors promoting prosperity in the 1920s:* (A) buying of autos and radios (B) installment buying (C) rising prices of farm products (D) improvements in factory production.

____ 43. *"Causes" of the Great Depression:* (A) rapid slowdown of government spending in 1928–1929 (B) the stock market crash (C) big inequalities of wealth and income (D) disruptions in international trade from war debts and tariffs.

____ 44. *Hoover administration steps to deal with the Great Depression:* (A) lending money to business through Reconstruction Finance Corporation (B) stepping up of public works spending (C) supporting farm prices (D) creating one million public-service jobs.

____ 45. *Famous athletes of the '20s:* (A) Babe Ruth (B) Wilt Chamberlain (C) Bobby Jones (D) Jack Dempsey.

Part D Each of the events or quotations below is associated with the person or Presidency of Harding, Coolidge, or Hoover. Put the initials of the right person in the answer space:

     WGH—Warren G. Harding   *CC*—Calvin Coolidge   *HH*—Herbert Hoover

____ 46. "There is no right to strike against the public safety by anybody, anywhere, anytime."

____ 47. "I have no trouble with my enemies. It is my friends who keep me walking the floors at night."

____ 48. "The fundamental business of the country . . . is on a sound and prosperous basis."

____ 49. Was Secretary of Commerce before becoming President.

____ 50. Was governor of a state before becoming President.

____ 51. Served in U. S. Senate before becoming President.

____ 52. Twice vetoed the McNary-Haugen farm bill.

____ 53. Washington Conference and naval limitation treaties.

____ 54. Settlement of oil-property problem with Mexico.

____ 55. Made goodwill trip to Latin America.

____ 56. Signed bill creating Reconstruction Finance Corporation.

____ 57. "The business of America is business."

____ 58. Signed the Fordney-McCumber Tariff Act.

____ 59. His corrupt associates brought shame to his administration.

____ 60. Signed Hawley-Smoot Tariff Act.

Part E Begin your answer to any essay questions your teacher may ask.

Unit 9 Test DEPRESSION AT HOME AND AGGRESSION ABROAD 1933–1945

Part A In the answer space put the letter of the person who is identified.

1. Chief Justice when FDR attacked the Supreme Court
2. Administered WPA and other work relief programs
3. Main force behind the organization of the CIO
4. Radio-priest opponent of F. D. Roosevelt
5. Secretary of Labor in the New Deal
6. Secretary of State who promoted Good Neighbor policy
7. Director of NYA's Division of Negro Affairs
8. Conducted a Senate investigation of arms industry
9. Louisiana politician who proposed "Share the Wealth" program
10. Head of the National Recovery Administration
11. Urged the creation of strong, separate air force
12. "The only thing we have to fear," he said, "is fear itself."
13. Wrote a famous novel about Dust Bowl migrants
14. Joking about the depression, he said, "We are the first nation . . . to go to the poorhouse in an automobile."
15. Head of Porters union who organized a black march on Washington
16. Secretary of Agriculture and later Vice-President
17. Author and sponsor of the National Labor Relations Act
18. New Deal critic who proposed an expensive old-age pension plan
19. "Conscience of the New Deal" who worked to get women into government

(A) Mary McLeod Bethune
(B) Charles E. Coughlin
(C) Harry Hopkins
(D) Charles E. Hughes
(E) Cordell Hull
(F) Hugh Johnson
(G) John L. Lewis
(H) Huey Long
(I) Billy Mitchell
(J) Gerald P. Nye
(K) Frances Perkins
(L) A. Philip Randolph
(M) Will Rogers
(N) Eleanor Roosevelt
(O) F. D. Roosevelt
(P) John Steinbeck
(Q) Francis Townsend
(R) Robert Wagner
(S) Henry A. Wallace

Part B One step in evaluating the New Deal is to identify measures that had a lasting effect on American life and the economic system. Below are some aspects of the American system today. If the item had its *origin* in the New Deal (1933–1938), mark it YES; if not, mark it NO.

20. Firms doing business with the federal government must make good faith efforts to employ women and members of certain minorities.
21. Most banks provide deposit insurance.
22. Many localities have public housing for low-income persons.
23. Graduated income and inheritance taxes help to redistribute wealth.
24. A corporation offering stock for sale must provide detailed information to prospective buyers.
25. A federal agency makes and enforces health and safety requirements for employers to follow.
26. School districts may not provide separate facilities for black children.
27. Dams in the Tennessee River system contribute to the prosperity of the region.
28. A "green belt" of trees from the Dakotas to Texas helps prevent dust storms on the Great Plains.
29. Unemployment insurance provides temporary income for many laid-off workers.

_____ 30. Most Americans over age 65 are enrolled in a health insurance program.
_____ 31. Workers in business and industry are guaranteed the right to join unions and to bargain collectively.
_____ 32. Most employers must pay not less than a specified minimum wage.
_____ 33. Food processors must provide informative labels on packages.
_____ 34. Nearly all farm families have electric power available.
_____ 35. Large areas of the West are productive because of irrigation dams.

Part C Identify the part played in World War II by each person on the right by putting the letter in the proper answer space.

_____ 36. Led British troops to victory in North Africa
_____ 37. Supervised atomic energy experiment at Chicago
_____ 38. Commanded U. S. naval forces in the Pacific
_____ 39. Led first U. S. air raid on Tokyo
_____ 40. Commanded Germany's *Afrika Korps*
_____ 41. Developed the blood bank for storing blood plasma
_____ 42. Led U. S. Third Army in breakthrough of German lines after D-Day
_____ 43. Returned in triumph to the Philippines

(A) James B. Doolittle
(B) Charles Drew
(C) Enrico Fermi
(D) Douglas MacArthur
(E) Bernard Montgomery
(F) Chester Nimitz
(G) George Patton
(H) Erwin Rommel

Part D In the answer space put the letter of the best answer.

_____ 44. Which phrase best describes FDR's approach to the economic problems when he took office? (A) conservative and cautious (B) bold and experimental (C) dedicated to socialism (D) timid and indecisive.

_____ 45. The 1933 money crisis, according to FDR's advisers, was that (A) the abundance of dollars was causing inflation (B) the scarcity of dollars resulted in low wages and prices (C) foreigners would not accept our low-value dollars (D) lenders were getting back less than they had loaned.

_____ 46. John Maynard Keynes argued that in a depression the national government should (A) balance the budget (B) raise taxes and cut spending (C) cut taxes and increase spending (D) let nature take its course.

_____ 47. Which of these early New Deal measures was the wrong depression medicine according to modern economic thinking? (A) work relief programs (B) the Economy Act (C) dollar devaluation (D) rise in public works spending.

_____ 48. How did FDR devalue the dollar? (A) by reducing the amount of gold that backed each dollar (B) by substituting silver for the gold backing (C) by abandoning the gold standard entirely (D) by having the Mint coin smaller dollars.

_____ 49. Why did FDR devalue the dollar? (A) to raise prices (B) to lower prices (C) to keep the price level steady (D) to balance the budget.

_____ 50. What was FDR's role in ending Prohibition? (A) none (B) signing the 21st Amendment (C) signing a bill to legalize the sale of beer and wine (D) ordering the Justice Department not to prosecute bootleggers.

_____ 51. What two New Deal agencies administered programs designed specifically for young adults? (A) HOLC and FHA (B) PWA and CWA (C) SEC and AAA (D) NYA and CCC.

_____ 52. How was the National Industrial Recovery Act (NIRA) related to the federal antitrust laws? (A) no relationship (B) antitrust laws, in effect, were suspended by NIRA (C) both designed to promote vigorous competition (D) both aimed at promoting labor-management cooperation.

_____ 53. Which election did FDR win most decisively? (A) 1932 (B) 1936 (C) 1940 (D) 1944.

_____ 54. In order to stop Supreme Court interference with the New Deal, FDR urged Congress to (A) draft legislation more carefully (B) impeach and remove conservative judges (C) increase the size of the Court (D) initiate changes in the Constitution to overcome the Court's objections.

_____ 55. The course of business recovery from 1933 to 1939 (A) was steadily upward (B) was up one year and down the next (C) peaked in 1935 (D) was upward until hit by a recession in 1937–1938.

_____ 56. The chief destination of migrants from the Dust Bowl was (A) California (B) Florida (C) Oklahoma (D) Illinois.

_____ 57. The Committee for Industrial Organization was formed chiefly to (A) disband the NRA (B) lobby for the Wagner Act (C) promote sit-down strikes (D) organize new unions to serve both skilled and unskilled workers.

_____ 58. From 1933 to 1939 Congress responded to war and threats of war in the world by (A) ordering the arming of American merchant vessels (B) putting limits on the sale of arms to belligerents (C) insisting on freedom of the seas (D) stopping manufacture of armaments.

_____ 59. Hitler set Germany on a course of aggression with the stated goal of (A) wiping out Communist regimes (B) uniting surrounding people of "German blood" with Germany (C) conquering Europe (D) uniting Germany and Italy.

_____ 60. The Munich Pact provided for the dismemberment of (A) Italy (B) Poland (C) Austria (D) Czechoslovakia.

_____ 61. World War II began in September 1939 when German troops invaded (A) Poland (B) Hungary (C) Denmark (D) Austria.

_____ 62. The response of Congress in 1939 to the outbreak of war in Europe was to (A) keep the Neutrality Act of 1937 intact (B) repeal the arms embargo (C) strengthen the neutrality law (D) send U. S. troops to Europe.

_____ 63. A key factor in the Battle of Britain was that the British (A) could decode German secret messages (B) had more planes than the Germans (C) had the more skillful pilots (D) had the best planes.

_____ 64. Before entering the war the United States aided Britain in all the following ways EXCEPT (A) providing destroyers (B) convoying merchant ships (C) blockading German ports (D) lending and leasing war supplies.

_____ 65. Blacks served in our armed services in World War II (A) only in noncombat positions (B) in all branches except the Air Force (C) chiefly in segregated units (D) in a larger proportion to their numbers than whites.

_____ 66. After our entry into the war, British-U. S. efforts to defeat Germany were first concentrated in (A) Italy (B) the Netherlands (C) southern Russia (D) North Africa.

_____ 67. Our *early* war strategy in the Pacific (1942) was (A) to hold existing bases (B) to blockade and starve out Japan (C) to recapture Indochina (D) to retake the Philippines.

_____ 68. At Yalta, Stalin promised all of these EXCEPT (A) to permit free elections in Poland and other East European nations (B) to supply aid for the rebuilding of Germany (C) to join the war against Japan (D) to join the United Nations.

_____ 69. After the invasion of Germany, Eisenhower's most crucial decision was (A) to set up military government in western Germany (B) to put Nazi war criminals on trial (C) to stop 50 miles west of Berlin (D) to install De Gaulle as president of France.

_____ 70. Truman's justification for using the atomic bomb against Japan was that (A) it would keep Russia from taking Japan (B) it would avenge Japanese atrocities (C) the bomb had to be tested in actual combat (D) it would actually save lives.

Part E On the back of this page start your answer to any essay questions your teacher may ask.

Unit 10 Test   POSTWAR PROBLEMS 1945–1960

Part A   In the answer space put the letter of the person who is identified.

_____ 1. Warned, ". . . an iron curtain has descended across the Continent"
_____ 2. Served many years as UN Under Secretary
_____ 3. Served as first UN Secretary-General
_____ 4. Succeeded Marshall as Secretary of State
_____ 5. Proposed containment policy from his diplomatic post in Moscow
_____ 6. Investigated for spying by House Un-American Activities Committee
_____ 7. Commanded Eighth Army in Korea
_____ 8. Democratic candidate for President in 1952 and 1956
_____ 9. Was fired as Secretary of Commerce for opposing the administration's foreign policy
_____ 10. Eisenhower's White House chief of staff
_____ 11. Early U. S. developer of rocket engines
_____ 12. Sparked a black bus boycott in Alabama
_____ 13. Headed U. S. rocket research after World War II
_____ 14. Wrote the novel *Ship of Fools*
_____ 15. Invented xerography, a copying process

(A) Dean Acheson
(B) Sherman Adams
(C) Ralph Bunche
(D) Chester F. Carlson
(E) Winston Churchill
(F) Robert H. Goddard
(G) Alger Hiss
(H) George F. Kennan
(I) Trygve Lie
(J) Rosa Parks
(K) Katherine Anne Porter
(L) Matthew B. Ridgway
(M) Adlai Stevenson
(N) Wernher Von Braun
(O) Henry A. Wallace

Part B   Mark the item *HST* if it refers to Harry Truman or his administration; mark it *DDE* if it refers to Dwight Eisenhower or his administration; write BOTH if it applies to both.

_____ 16. First President to be limited to two terms by 22nd Amendment.
_____ 17. "Last night the moon, the stars, and all the planets fell on me."
_____ 18. Served as first commander of NATO forces.
_____ 19. Rose in office with help of Pendergast political machine.
_____ 20. Signed executive order to get rid of "disloyal" federal workers.
_____ 21. Armistice achieved in Korean War.
_____ 22. His Point Four program began economic aid to developing nations.
_____ 23. Appointed first black federal judge.
_____ 24. Had to work with a Congress of the opposite party.
_____ 25. Signed two Civil Rights Acts, the first since Reconstruction.
_____ 26. Took part in the Potsdam Conference.
_____ 27. Began nation's first space exploration program.
_____ 28. Proposed U. S. and Soviet aerial photography to inspect each other's defenses.
_____ 29. Security pacts and mutual defense treaties were arranged.
_____ 30. Peace treaty signed with Japan.

Part C In the answer space put the letter of the place associated with the listed event.

_____ 31. Trial of Nazi war criminals
_____ 32. Overthrow of an unfriendly premier with CIA help
_____ 33. Bus boycott led by Martin Luther King, Jr.
_____ 34. United Nations charter signed
_____ 35. NATO supreme headquarters set up
_____ 36. Attempt by governor to stop school desegregation
_____ 37. Start of MacArthur's offensive drive in Korea
_____ 38. Communist Chinese shelling of Nationalist-held island
_____ 39. Meeting of Eisenhower and Khrushchev to relax the cold war
_____ 40. Meeting of Truman, Stalin, and Churchill

(A) Camp-David
(B) Inchon
(C) Iran
(D) Little Rock
(E) Montgomery
(F) Nuremberg
(G) Paris
(H) Potsdam
(I) Quemoy
(J) San Francisco

Part D Put the letter of the *best* answer in the answer space.

_____ 41. In organizing the United Nations a major issue dividing the Soviet Union and the United States was (A) the location of the permanent headquarters (B) the use of the veto in the Security Council (C) the size of the General Assembly (D) naming a Secretary-General.

_____ 42. In which UN body are all member nations represented? (A) General Assembly (B) Security Council (C) Economic and Social Council (D) International Court of Justice.

_____ 43. Effective international control of atomic energy was blocked by (A) French demands for the atomic bomb blueprints (B) Russia's refusal to stop atomic weapons research (C) fears over the U. S. monopoly on uranium ore (D) Russia's demand for veto power in the world atomic energy agency.

_____ 44. What broken Yalta promise poisoned U. S.-Soviet Union relations in 1946? (A) To allow free elections in Eastern Europe (B) to join the United Nations (C) to enter the war against Japan (D) to take part in the postwar occupation of Germany.

_____ 45. Truman adopted the policy that Communist regimes in the world had to be (A) crushed (B) contained (C) appeased (D) "democratized."

_____ 46. What Communist activity led directly to proclamation of the Truman Doctrine? (A) spying in Canada (B) setting up a Communist regime in Poland (C) undermining the anti-Communist government in Greece (D) growth of the Communist party in Turkey.

_____ 47. The Truman Doctrine proclaimed that the United States would (A) suspend the Monroe Doctrine (B) aid reconstruction of war-torn Europe (C) break diplomatic relations with Communist governments everywhere (D) help free peoples who were resisting threats to their freedom.

_____ 48. A chief goal of the Marshall Plan was (A) to end worldwide poverty (B) to restore democratic governments in Eastern Europe (C) to halt the growth of Communist parties in Western Europe (D) to provide arms to anti-Communist governments.

_____ 49. Under the Presidential Succession Act of 1947 the person next in line to the Presidency after the Vice-President would be the (A) President pro tem of the Senate (B) Speaker of the House (C) Secretary of State (D) Secretary of Defense.

_____ 50. The Soviet Union set up the Berlin blockade to prevent the Western powers from (A) making Berlin the capital of West Germany (B) setting up a separate West German government (C) sending Marshall Plan aid to Eastern Europe (D) forming a unified government for Berlin.

_____ 51. In joining NATO the U. S. made a major shift in foreign policy in that (A) we had joined the first peacetime alliance in our history (B) Congress lost the power to declare war (C) we were committed to defending anti-democratic governments (D) most U. S. troops would be stationed in Europe.

_____ 52. The McCarran Act of 1950 and McCarran-Walter Act of 1952 were both inspired by fear of (A) postwar recession (B) overpopulation (C) Communist subversion (D) rapid inflation.

_____ 53. The United Nations could take immediate action against aggression in Korea because (A) UN armed forces had been set up a few months earlier (B) Russia was boycotting the Security Council (C) most nations were UN members (D) Communist China urged UN action.

_____ 54. Truman's removal of MacArthur from command in Korea was significant in that it (A) reaffirmed civilian control over the military (B) brought a quick ceasefire (C) induced China to withdraw its troops (D) led the Republicans to nominate a general—Eisenhower—for President in 1952.

_____ 55. The terms "massive retaliation" and "brinkmanship" were used to describe the early foreign policy views of (A) Dean Acheson (B) George Marshall (C) Ezra Taft Benson (D) John Foster Dulles.

_____ 56. In the long run the Eisenhower administration's impact on New Deal-Fair Deal programs was (A) to close them down (B) to continue them and provide for moderate expansion and improvements (C) to allow them to continue but with drastic cuts in support (D) to replace them with costly new programs.

_____ 57. What new Cabinet department was set up in Eisenhower's Presidency? (A) Defense (B) Transportation (C) Health, Education, and Welfare (D) Energy.

_____ 58. In the late 1950s southern politicians and governments generally responded to desegregation decisions with (A) a policy of "massive resistance" (B) eager acceptance (C) a determination to proceed "with all deliberate speed" (D) new threats of secession.

_____ 59. Eisenhower responded to the Suez War of 1956 by (A) sending aid to Israel (B) joining Russia in a UN demand for a cease-fire (C) supporting our French and British allies (D) remaining aloof.

_____ 60. In which decade did the U. S. "baby boom" reach a peak? (A) 1930s (B) 1940s (C) 1950s (D) 1960s.

Part E Three of the items are related to the introductory phrase in *italics*. In the answer space write the letter of the item that *does not belong*.

_____ 61. *U. S. population characteristics, 1945–1970:* (A) rural-to-city movement of blacks (B) rapid growth of suburbs (C) rising proportion of elderly (D) growth chiefly from immigration.

_____ 62. *Major "growth industries," 1945–1970:* (A) electronics (B) computers (C) railroads (D) construction.

_____ 63. *Provisions of Taft-Hartley Act:* (A) outlawing of closed shop (B) empowering President to halt certain strikes temporarily (C) forbidding strikes by public employees (D) requiring union officials to sign non-Communist affidavits.

_____ 64. *Prominent American novelists, 1945–1970:* (A) James Jones (B) Eudora Welty (C) Helen Frankenthaler (D) Ralph Ellison.

_____ 65. *Influential religious voices, 1945–1970:* (A) Mark Rothko (B) Norman Vincent Peale (C) Billy Graham (D) Fulton J. Sheen.

Part F Begin your answer to any essay question your teacher may ask.

Unit 11 Test TURBULENT TIMES 1961–1974

Part A In the answer space put the letter of the person who is identified. Two names are not used.

_____ 1. Wrote *The Other America* and made poverty an issue
_____ 2. Republican candidate for President in 1964
_____ 3. Governor Barnett tried to stop this person's enrollment in the state university
_____ 4. First black Cabinet member
_____ 5. Publicized danger of pesticides in *Silent Spring*
_____ 6. Fought for racial equality as a Black Muslim
_____ 7. Led campaign for auto safety rules
_____ 8. First black Supreme Court justice
_____ 9. Headed commission to investigate President Kennedy's assassination
_____ 10. Alabama governor and third-party candidate for President in 1968
_____ 11. Made first U.S. space flight
_____ 12. Resigned as Vice-President in 1973
_____ 13. Appointed Chief Justice by President Nixon
_____ 14. Defeated for President by Nixon landslide in 1972
_____ 15. Headed first moon-landing mission

(A) Spiro Agnew
(B) Neil Armstrong
(C) Warren Burger
(D) Rachel Carson
(E) Barry Goldwater
(F) Michael Harrington
(G) Malcolm X
(H) Thurgood Marshall
(I) Eugene McCarthy
(J) George McGovern
(K) James Meredith
(L) Ralph Nader
(M) Dean Rusk
(N) Alan B. Shepherd
(O) George Wallace
(P) Earl Warren
(Q) Robert Weaver

Who played each of these roles in the Watergate affair? Put the letter in the answer space.

_____ 16. Headed Senate investigation of 1972 campaign, including Watergate
_____ 17. Special Prosecutor discharged under Nixon's orders
_____ 18. Break-in of his office started the affair
_____ 19. Wrote news stories that kept the case in the public eye
_____ 20. Resigned as Attorney General when ordered to fire Special Prosecutor

(A) Archibald Cox
(B) John Ehrlichman
(C) Sam Ervin
(D) Leon Jaworski
(E) Laurence O'Brien
(F) Elliot Richardson
(G) Robert Woodward

Part B Each of the events or quotations below is associated with the person or Presidency of Kennedy, Johnson, or Nixon. Put the initial of the right person in the answer space:

K—Kennedy   J—Johnson   N—Nixon

_____ 21. Medicare added to the social security system.
_____ 22. Arabs responded to U. S. aid to Israel with oil embargo.
_____ 23. Laws passed for highway beautification and wilderness preservation.
_____ 24. His performance in a TV debate helped bring him victory.
_____ 25. Reversed American foreign policy by supporting Red China's membership in UN.
_____ 26. Two Supreme Court appointees rejected by the Senate.
_____ 27. Departments of Transportation and of Housing and Urban Development created.
_____ 28. ". . . ask not what America will do for you—ask what you can do for your country."
_____ 29. Stepped up space exploration with pledge to land a man on the moon before 1970.

_____ 30. "We have talked long enough . . . about civil rights. . . . It is time . . . to write it in the books of law."

_____ 31. Elementary and Secondary Education Act tied school aid to community poverty levels.

_____ 32. The decision to remove 150,000 more troops from Vietnam "means that we finally have in sight the just peace we are seeking."

_____ 33. The Alliance for Progress was a kind of Marshall Plan for Latin America.

_____ 34. U.S. participation in Vietnam War reached a peak.

_____ 35. Trade Expansion Act gave the President power to cut tariffs up to 50 percent.

Part C In the answer space put the letter of the *best* answer.

_____ 36. J.F. Kennedy's chief handicap as a presidential candidate in 1960 was his (A) age (B) record in Congress (C) wealth (D) religion.

_____ 37. The Bay of Pigs incident involved an attempted invasion of (A) Cambodia (B) Cuba (C) Laos (D) Vietnam.

_____ 38. The Berlin Wall was built (A) to fortify the city against attack (B) to keep East Germans from fleeing to the West (C) to halt the flow of West German refugees to East Germany (D) to preserve the rights of all four occupation powers.

_____ 39. Defense Secretary McNamara called for armed forces capable of a "flexible military response" in order to (A) respond to Russian efforts to set up Communist regimes in former colonial areas (B) reduce U.S. dependence on NATO (C) cut the defense budget (D) reduce U.S. overseas troop strength.

_____ 40. The chief mission of volunteers in the Peace Corps was (A) to teach English as a second language (B) to provide training in democracy for newly independent peoples (C) to help people in developing lands set up self-help projects (D) to demonstrate peaceful ways of resolving conflict.

_____ 41. The name *Nautilus* was given to our first (A) nuclear-powered submarine (B) intercontinental ballistic missile (C) space vehicle (D) nuclear-powered aircraft carrier.

_____ 42. Kennedy responded to Soviet resumption of nuclear testing in the atmosphere in 1961 by (A) protesting to the UN (B) matching Russia's atmospheric testing (C) inviting Khrushchev to Camp David (D) ordering underground nuclear testing.

_____ 43. What action did Kennedy take to resolve the Cuban missile crisis? (A) negotiated for a U.S. missile site on Turkey's border with Russia (B) ordered an air strike on Cuban missile bases if Russia did not respond in 72 hours (C) ordered a naval blockade of offensive military equipment under shipment to Cuba (D) turned the entire matter over to the UN.

_____ 44. L.B. Johnson called his domestic proposals the (A) New Frontier (B) Great Society (C) Crusade for Justice (D) New Freedom.

_____ 45. Which of these background features was shared by Presidents Kennedy, Johnson, and Nixon? (A) service as Vice-President (B) service in both houses of Congress (C) father's political prominence (D) wealthy family.

_____ 46. VISTA was set up as a (A) tutoring service for visually handicapped children (B) job training program (C) domestic Peace Corps (D) college aid program.

_____ 47. The chief measure in LBJ's "war on poverty" was the (A) Economic Opportunity Act (B) Civil Rights Act (C) 10 percent income-tax surcharge of 1967 (D) Urban Development Act.

_____ 48. The urban riots of 1965–1967 can be explained in part as black frustration over (A) the slow pace of lawmaking under LBJ (B) the ineffectiveness of new laws in meeting the high hopes that had been raised (C) the unusually hot weather (D) the injustice of the Vietnam War.

_____ 49. Compared to the youth of the 1950s, those of the 1960s tended to be (A) smaller in numbers (B) more concerned about careers (C) more practical and less idealistic (D) more critical of traditional behavior and the established order.

_____ 50. Which of these youth categories or groups of the 1960s showed the least interest in public affairs? (A) Students for a Democratic Society (B) civil rights marchers (C) Yippies (D) hippies.

_____ 51. Under the Tonkin Gulf Resolution the President (A) had to get specific congressional approval to use the armed forces (B) had broader legal power to wage war (C) had to withdraw U.S. troops from Vietnam (D) was directed to seek an armistice in Vietnam.

_____ 52. A Defense Department study called "The Pentagon Papers" was made to explore (A) our role in Vietnam (B) the use of U.S. troops in the Dominican Republic (C) CIA activities in Latin America (D) the "missile gap."

_____ 53. What was unusual about the 1968 Democratic convention in Chicago? (A) the hot, muggy weather (B) the riots in the city's black neighborhoods (C) the youth demonstrations in downtown Chicago (D) the nomination of a Republican for Vice-President.

_____ 54. Nixon's program for winding down the war in Vietnam was interrupted by (A) the 1968 election (B) a raid on Cambodia (C) peace talks in Paris (D) mass desertions of South Vietnamese troops.

_____ 55. The Watergate affair grew out of efforts of Nixon's associates (A) to tighten security of classified defense documents (B) to reduce Henry Kissinger's influence (C) to assure Nixon's reelection in 1972 (D) to get water rights on land leased to them in California.

Part D Three of the items are related to the introductory phrase in *italics*. In the answer space put the letter of the item that *does not belong*.

_____ 56. *Provisions of Civil Rights Act of 1964:* (A) desegregation of hotels, restaurants, and other facilities serving the public (B) ban on sale of private housing to "whites only" (C) ban on racial discrimination in use of federal funds (D) creation of a Community Relations Service.

_____ 57. *Provisions of the Immigration Act of 1965:* (A) abolished the quota system (B) put limit of 120,000 yearly from Western Hemisphere countries (C) skilled workers and relatives of Americans favored (D) immigrants from newly independent nations favored.

_____ 58. *Reasons for the U.S. presence in Vietnam:* (A) to prevent the fall of other Southeast Asian nations to the Communists (B) to stop aggression (C) to support a UN resolution for help to South Vietnam (D) to make our promises of help against Communist aggression believable.

_____ 59. *Chief issues in the 1968 presidential campaign:* (A) immigration reform (B) Vietnam (C) law and order (D) urban unrest and black progress.

_____ 60. Supreme Court cases on criminal justice: (A) *Gideon* v. *Wainwright* (B) *Escobedo* v. *Illinois* (C) *Brown* v. *Board of Education* (D) *Miranda* v. *Arizona*.

Part E Begin your answers to whatever essay questions your teacher may ask.

Unit 12 Test   THE UNITED STATES LOOKS AHEAD

Part A   In the answer space put the letter of the person who is identified.

_____ 1. Headed Indian Affairs in Interior Department
_____ 2. Served as Secretary of State under Nixon and Ford
_____ 3. Headed two Cabinet departments under Carter
_____ 4. Ford's chief rival for nomination in 1976
_____ 5. Organized farm workers in California
_____ 6. Long-time governor of Puerto Rico
_____ 7. Reawakened the women's rights movement with *The Feminine Mystique*
_____ 8. Headed Carter's White House staff
_____ 9. Picked by Ford to fill vacant Vice-Presidency
_____ 10. Vice-President in Carter's administration

(A) Cesar Chavez
(B) Betty Friedan
(C) Forrest J. Gerrard
(D) Patricia R. Harris
(E) Hamilton Jordan
(F) Henry Kissinger
(G) Luis Muñoz Marin
(H) Walter Mondale
(I) Ronald Reagan
(J) Nelson Rockefeller

Part B   In each series two of the items are closely related. In the answer space write the letter of the item that is NOT.

_____ 11. (A) Le Duc Tho   (B) Menachem Begin   (C) Anwar el-Sadat.
_____ 12. (A) Rickover   (B) nuclear submarines   (C) Phnom Penh.
_____ 13. (A) Yom Kippur War   (B) Khmer Rouge   (C) Arab oil embargo.
_____ 14. (A) Susan B. Anthony   (B) Elizabeth Cady Stanton   (C) Romana A. Bañuelos.
_____ 15. (A) American Indian Movement   (B) Know-Nothing party   (C) Immigration Restriction League.

Part C   In the answer space put the letter of the *best* answer or completion.

_____ 16. In the United States the ideal of *equality* has generally been understood as (A) the equalizing of income and status for everyone (B) the equalizing of opportunity (C) foolish because it goes against human nature (D) the key to economic progress.

_____ 17. Jefferson believed that government should be in the hands of a "natural aristocracy" composed of those persons who (A) were the most talented and industrious (B) came from the "best families" (C) had the most wealth (D) owned the natural resources.

_____ 18. In which of these areas has equality been most nearly achieved in the United States? (A) housing (B) voting rights (C) income (D) land ownership.

_____ 19. In the 19th century (the 1800s) immigration discrimination showed up chiefly in (A) immigration quotas favoring certain countries (B) requiring immigrant children to learn English before entering public school (C) bars on land ownership by immigrants (D) unfair treatment of Newcomers by the Oldcomers.

_____ 20. Which of these organizations promoted *fair* treatment of immigrant newcomers? (A) Know-Nothing party (B) Ku Klux Klan (C) Hull House (D) American Protective Association.

_____ 21. By the 1970s the chief issue in school desegregation was (A) the continuance of laws barring black students in white schools (B) the absence of black teachers in predominantly white schools (C) federal court orders to bus students to achieve racial balance (D) the larger class size in predominantly black schools.

_____ 22. In dealing with blacks and certain other minorities, a business with an *affirmative action* policy promises (A) to pay the minorities higher wages (B) to treat them exactly like whites (C) to favor minority businesses when purchasing supplies (D) to give them preferences in hiring and promotion.

_____ 23. By the 1970s blacks had made the *least* progress in which of these areas? (A) education (B) teen-age employment (C) elective and appointive positions in government (D) business jobs for trained and educated persons.

_____ 24. By the 1970s which of these was the most important barrier to full female equality? (A) custom and tradition (B) collapse of the women's rights movement (C) legal barriers (D) affirmative action programs.

_____ 25. By the 1970s in which of these areas did females have a *majority* status? (A) elective offices (B) total population (C) business management (D) representation on U.S. stamps and coins.

_____ 26. The largest numbers of Spanish-speaking people in the fifty states have come from (A) Spain (B) Cuba (C) Puerto Rico (D) Mexico.

_____ 27. Discrimination against Hispanics is most evident in which of these areas? (A) unequal voting rights (B) lack of access to public schools (C) low-paying jobs (D) immigration barriers.

_____ 28. "Operation Bootstrap" refers to efforts to promote economic progress in (A) Cuba (B) Mexico (C) Puerto Rico (D) barrios in U.S. cities.

_____ 29. A high proportion of Cuban Americans (A) are political refugees (B) have settled in the Midwest (C) are migrant farm workers (D) support the Castro regime in Cuba.

_____ 30. In which of these areas did American Indians make the greatest progress in the 1970s? (A) voting rights (B) winning compensation for broken treaties (C) election or appointment to political office (D) obtaining off-reservation industrial jobs.

_____ 31. In promoting equal rights for the handicapped the term "mainstreaming" refers to (A) removing employment barriers (B) fixing public facilities for easier use (C) including the handicapped in affirmative action programs (D) getting handicapped students into regular classrooms and school activities.

_____ 32. Which of these reasons did President Ford give for pardoning Richard Nixon? (A) Nixon's innocence (B) to heal the nation's wounds (C) to satisfy public opinion (D) to save the Treasury the cost of the trials.

_____ 33. To earn clemency under Ford's plan, Vietnam deserters and draft evaders would have to (A) work for two years in a public service job (B) serve a term in the Peace Corps (C) serve in the armed forces for two years (D) join the National Guard.

_____ 34. The Privacy Act of 1974 gave citizens the right to (A) be free from telephone tapping (B) stop unfavorable newspaper publicity (C) examine collected government information about themselves (D) hold private meetings with federal officials.

_____ 35. Which of these *increases* were most responsible for the steep inflation of the 1970s? (A) teen-age unemployment and farm surpluses (B) foreign auto imports and crime rates (C) union wage rates and female employment (D) oil prices and government spending.

_____ 36. The majority of OPEC nations are in (A) the Middle East (B) Latin America (C) Southeast Asia (D) Europe.

_____ 37. The letter *E* in OPEC stands for (A) Enterprise (B) Exporting (C) Educational (D) European.

_____ 38. The Carter administration's response to the financial crisis facing the Social Security system was (A) to cut benefits (B) to raise the retirement age (C) to raise Social Security taxes (D) to cut out disability benefits.

_____ 39. Following the fall of South Vietnam in 1975 the Vietnamese (A) brought the rest of Indochina under Vietnamese control (B) fought other Communist factions in neighboring lands (C) received massive economic aid from the United States (D) agreed to accept Chinese Communist controls.

_____ 40. In 1979 in which two countries were leaders friendly to the United States overthrown? (A) Egypt and Israel (B) Syria and Lebanon (C) Mexico and Nigeria (D) Iran and Nicaragua

Part D If the item below is associated with Gerald Ford or his administration, mark it **F**; with Carter, mark it **C**; with both, mark it **B**.

_____ 41. Worked for detente with the Soviet Union.
_____ 42. Played for the All-Stars in a football game.
_____ 43. Supported new canal treaties with Panama.
_____ 44. Made human rights a chief issue in dealing with other countries.
_____ 45. Mediated a peace treaty between Israel and Eygpt.
_____ 46. Vetoed bills requiring strip miners to restore land.
_____ 47. Ran the federal government with big budget deficits.
_____ 48. Served over 20 years in the U.S. House of Representatives.
_____ 49. Graduated from the United States Naval Academy.
_____ 50. Set up the Intelligence Oversight Board to monitor the CIA.

Part E Begin your answers to whatever essay questions your teacher may ask.

Final Test A HISTORY OF THE UNITED STATES

Part A Thirty American Presidents are listed on the right. In the answer space put the **bold-face** initials of the person who is described or quoted.

1. Purchased land that doubled the nation's area.
2. Moved funds from Bank of the U.S. to "pet" state banks.
3. Put down rebellion of western farmers over a whiskey tax.
4. Charged with making a "corrupt bargain" with Henry Clay to win the Presidency.
5. His fight over Reconstruction led to his impeachment.
6. Signed Alien and Sedition acts and appointed "midnight judges."
7. Withdrew last Union troops to end Reconstruction.
8. Gave in to demands of War Hawks for war with Britain.
9. Asked Congress to declare war after the "enemy" had given in to most of our demands.
10. "The business of America is business."
11. Acquired most of the land west of Texas and the Rockies.
12. Asked the nation to bind up its wounds: "With malice toward none, with charity for all."
13. Corruption by Cabinet members and other officials marred the ad-
14. ministrations of these *two* Presidents.
15. Vetoed pension bills and plugged the drain on gold.
16. His term was marred by the Great Stock Market Crash.
17. His motto was "Speak softly and carry a big stick."
18. This "cold war" fighter began a "containment policy" toward the Soviet Union.
19. "The world must be made safe for democracy."
20. Persuaded the Russians to dismantle missile sites in Cuba.
21. "The only thing we have to fear is fear itself."
22. His flood of bills included a "war on poverty."
23. Helped the leaders of Egypt and Israel negotiate a peace treaty.
24. Became Vice-President and President without winning a popular election.
25. Used troops to stop opposition to school desegregation in Arkansas.

G Washington
J Adams
T Jefferson
J Madison
J Monroe
JQ Adams
A Jackson
JK Polk
J Buchanan
A Lincoln
A Johnson
US Grant
RB Hayes
CA Arthur
G Cleveland
W McKinley
T Roosevelt
WH Taft
W Wilson
WG Harding
C Coolidge
HC Hoover
FD Roosevelt
HS Truman
DD Eisenhower
JF Kennedy
LB Johnson
RM Nixon
GR Ford
J Carter

Part B In the answer space put the letter of the person's *major field of achievement*.

(A) Abolition/black equality
(B) Business organization
(C) Diplomacy
(D) Discovery/exploration
(E) Education
(F) Labor organization
(G) Lawmaking (Congress)
(H) Science/invention
(I) Social work/reform
(J) Supreme Court
(K) Women's rights

_____ 26. Jane Addams
_____ 27. Warren Burger
_____ 28. John C. Calhoun
_____ 29. Cesar Chavez
_____ 30. Dorothea Dix
_____ 31. Frederick Douglass
_____ 32. Betty Freiden
_____ 33. Samuel Gompers
_____ 34. John Hay
_____ 35. Charles E. Hughes
_____ 36. Frank Kellogg
_____ 37. Henry Kissinger
_____ 38. Meriwether Lewis
_____ 39. Elijah Lovejoy
_____ 40. Horace Mann
_____ 41. John Marshall
_____ 42. J. P. Morgan
_____ 43. Samuel Morse
_____ 44. Zebulon Pike
_____ 45. George Pullman
_____ 46. Walter Reed
_____ 47. Richard Sears
_____ 48. Daniel Webster
_____ 49. Frances Willard

Identify each person's major field of artistic achievement.

(A) Craft work   (B) Literature   (C) Music   (D) Painting

_____ 50. Thomas H. Benton
_____ 51. John S. Copley
_____ 52. Richard H. Dana
_____ 53. Theodore Dreiser
_____ 54. Helen Frankenthaler
_____ 55. Earl Hines
_____ 56. Myer Myers
_____ 57. Jackson Pollock
_____ 58. Eudora Welty

In the answer space put the letter of the war for which each person is most noted.

(A) French and Indian War
(B) Revolutionary War
(C) War of 1812
(D) Mexican War
(E) Civil War
(F) Spanish-American War
(G) World War I
(H) World War II

_____ 59. George Dewey
_____ 60. Nathanael Greene
_____ 61. Andrew Jackson
_____ 62. Thomas J. Jackson
_____ 63. George McClellan
_____ 64. Chester Nimitz
_____ 65. George Patton
_____ 66. John J. Pershing
_____ 67. Von Steuben
_____ 68. Zachary Taylor
_____ 69. Tecumseh
_____ 70. James Wolfe

Part C In each exercise one item is a *cause*, another is a *result*, and a third is *not directly related* to the other two. Write the letter of the *result* in the answer space.

_____ 71. (A) Stamp Act (B) Intolerable Acts (C) Boston Tea Party.
_____ 72. (A) Western land claims ceded (B) Shays's Rebellion (C) Articles of Confederation ratified.
_____ 73. (A) Promise of a Bill of Rights (B) ratification of the Constitution (C) District of Columbia picked for federal capital.
_____ 74. (A) Impressment of American seamen (B) Hartford Convention (C) Napoleonic Wars.
_____ 75. (A) Monroe Doctrine (B) struggle for independence in Latin America (C) *Chesapeake* affair.
_____ 76. (A) Tariff of Abominations (B) Jackson veto of bill to recharter the Bank of the United States (C) Calhoun's doctrine of nullification.
_____ 77. (A) XYZ Affair (B) Personal Liberty laws passed (C) Fugitive Slave Law passed.
_____ 78. (A) FDR's currency devaluation (B) moratorium on European war debts (C) low wage and price levels in 1933.
_____ 79. (A) *Brown v. Board of Education of Topeka* (B) 100 members of Congress sign a "Southern Manifesto" (C) televised McCarthy-Army hearings.

Final Test

Part D In the answer space write the *postal abbreviation* for the state (colony) described or most closely associated with the item.

AL (Ala)	FL	KY	MO	NC	TN (Tenn)
AK (Alaska)	GA	LA	MT (Mont)	ND	TX
AZ (Ariz)	HI	ME	NE (Neb)	OH	UT
AR (Ark)	ID (Ida)	MD	NV (Nev)	OK	VT
CA (Cal)	IL	MA (Mass)	NH	OR	VA
CO (Colo)	IN	MI (Mich)	NJ	PA	WA (Wash)
CT (Conn)	IA (Iowa)	MN (Minn)	NM	RI	WV
DE (Del)	KS (Kan)	MI (Miss)	NY	SC	WI (Wisc)
				SD	WY (Wyo)

_____ 80. Farmers in the western part of their state staged a "Whiskey Rebellion."

_____ 81. Four of our first five Presidents came from here.

_____ 82. Founded as a haven for Roman Catholics from England.

_____ 83. Discovery of gold at Sutter's Mill started a gold rush.

_____ 84. Colonists protecting a supply of arms touched off the War of Independence.

_____ 85. Known for many years as the Indian Territory.

_____ 86. "Custer's Last Stand" climaxed the Indian wars.

_____ 87. Lincoln debated Douglas for a seat in the Senate.

_____ 88. Acquired by purchase from Russia.

_____ 89. Annexation and a boundary dispute brought war with Mexico.

_____ 90. Here Franklin proposed a plan of union for the colonies.

_____ 91. Progressive reforms under La Follette provided a "laboratory for democracy."

_____ 92. Brigham Young led a stream of settlers to a new homeland.

_____ 93. Sherman marched to the sea, burning the capital on the way.

_____ 94. Overthrow of a queen led to annexation.

95–100. Now write two appropriate original items for your state.

_____

_____

_____

_____

ANSWER KEY TO TESTS

Unit 1

1. B	29. D
2. B	30. C
3. D	31. C
4. A	32. C
5. C	33. A
6. B	34. B
7. D	35. C
8. C	36. D
9. D	37. B
10. C	38. C
11. A	39. D
12. C	40. B
13. B	41. C
14. A	42. B
15. C	43. B
16. B	44. A
17. C	45. C
18. B	46. C
19. A	47. D
20. D	48. D
21. D	49. A
22. B	50. C
23. C	51. A
24. D	52. B
25. C	53. A
26. A	54. C
27. D	55. B
28. B	
56. Ponce de Leon
57. Hutchinson
58. Revere
59. Penn
60. Brent
61. Amherst
62. Drake
63. Ericsson
64. Stuyvesant
65. Oglethorpe

Unit 2

1. C	24. B
2. B	25. C
3. A	26. D
4. B	27. A
5. B	28. B
6. D	29. C
7. A	30. A
8. D	31. G
9. C	32. D
10. B	33. E
11. B	34. A
12. A	35. C
13. C	36. A
14. A	37. C
15. B	38. A
16. C	39. B
17. B	40. A
18. A	41. B
19. A	42. B
20. D	43. A
21. C	44. B
22. B	45. A
23. A	
46. taxation
47. Federalists
48. strict
49. Philadelphia
50. Alien Act
51. XYZ Affair
52. slaves
53. Republicans
54. Crispus Attucks
55. Preamble
56. checks & balances
57. Senate
58. Congress 63. C
59. C 61. A 64. B
60. A 62. A 65. C

Unit 3

1. C	16. C
2. G	17. A
3. E	18. C
4. B	19. B
5. D	20. D
6. H	21. C
7. B	22. D
8. D	23. A
9. A	24. B
10. C	25. D
11. A	26. C
12. C	27. D
13. D	28. C
14. D	29. B
15. A	30. B
31. Wilkinson
32. Chase
33. L'Enfant
34. Tecumseh
35. Clay
36. Pike
37. J. Q. Adams
38. Harrison
39. Key
40. Stuart
41. B 54. E
42. C 55. G
43. A 56. No
44. C 57. No
45. A 58. Yes
46. D 59. No
47. F 60. No
48. A 61. No
49. C 62. No
50. B 63. Yes
51. I 64. Yes
52. H 65. Yes
53. J

Unit 4

1. F	36. A
2. B	37. A
3. D	38. G
4. G	39. H
5. E	40. F
6. C	41. A
7. A	42. C
8. N	43. B
9. M	44. D
10. K	45. E
11. H	46. C
12. I	47. B
13. J	48. A
14. L	49. D
15. Q	50. B
16. S	51. A
17. T	52. B
18. P	53. D
19. O	54. C
20. R	55. C
21. C	56. C
22. A	57. B
23. D	58. A
24. A	59. B
25. C	60. A
26. A	61. C
27. D	62. B
28. D	63. Yes
29. A	64. Yes
30. B	65. Yes
31. D	66. No
32. C	67. No
33. D	68. Yes
34. D	69. No
35. B	70. Yes

Unit 5

1. D	36. C
2. C	37. E
3. A	38. F
4. E	39. A
5. G	40. D
6. F	41. B
7. H	42. E
8. B	43. A
9. C	44. F
10. A	45. C
11. B	46. B
12. A	47. G
13. B	48. I
14. C	49. C
15. A	50. D
16. C	51. H
17. B	52. J
18. C	53. E
19. C	54. E
20. A	55. C
21. C	56. D
22. C	57. F
23. A	58. B
24. C	59. H
25. B	60. G
26. D	61. I
27. B	62. M
28. A	63. E
29. D	64. J
30. A	65. F
31. C	66. B
32. C	67. L
33. B	68. K
34. A	69. C
35. B	70. A

Unit 6

1. E	31. D
2. B	32. B
3. D	33. A
4. B	34. A
5. B	35. B
6. F	36. A
7. E	37. A
8. A	38. B
9. C	39. B
10. B	40. D
11. E	41. N
12. A	42. J
13. D	43. F
14. D	44. G
15. C	45. O
16. A	46. A
17. D	47. K
18. B	48. R
19. B	49. Q
20. B	50. B
21. C	51. C
22. B	52. L
23. D	53. E
24. C	54. M
25. B	55. I
26. A	56. P
27. D	57. B
28. C	58. A
29. B	59. C
30. C	60. B

Unit 7

1. G	31. A
2. I	32. D
3. F	33. A
4. A	34. D
5. H	35. B
6. J	36. C
7. O	37. A
8. C	38. B
9. B	39. D
10. K	40. C
11. E	41. A
12. M	42. B
13. D	43. C
14. R	44. D
15. S	45. B
16. Q	46. D
17. L	47. A
18. T	48. D
19. P	49. A
20. N	50. B
21. D	51. D
22. B	52. B
23. C	53. C
24. B	54. A
25. D	55. C
26. D	56. A
27. A	57. D
28. C	58. C
29. A	59. C
30. C	60. B

ANSWER KEY TO TESTS

Unit 8

1. G
2. D
3. H
4. A
5. C
6. F
7. I
8. B
9. J
10. E
11. M
12. O
13. N
14. L
15. K
16. C
17. B
18. A
19. A
20. D
21. C
22. D
23. A
24. B
25. A
26. D
27. B
28. C
29. C
30. D
31. A
32. B
33. C
34. D
35. A
36. B
37. D
38. A
39. D
40. C
41. B
42. C
43. A
44. D
45. B
46. CC
47. WGH
48. HH
49. HH
50. CC
51. WGH
52. CC
53. WGH
54. CC
55. HH
56. HH
57. CC
58. WGH
59. WGH
60. HH

Unit 9

1. D
2. C
3. G
4. B
5. K
6. E
7. A
8. J
9. H
10. F
11. I
12. O
13. P
14. M
15. L
16. S
17. R
18. Q
19. N
20. No
21. Yes
22. Yes
23. No
24. Yes
25. No
26. No
27. Yes
28. Yes
29. Yes
30. No
31. Yes
32. Yes
33. No
34. Yes
35. No
36. E
37. C
38. F
39. A
40. H
41. B
42. G
43. D
44. B
45. B
46. C
47. B
48. A
49. A
50. C
51. D
52. B
53. B
54. C
55. D
56. A
57. D
58. B
59. B
60. D
61. A
62. B
63. A
64. C
65. C
66. D
67. A
68. B
69. C
70. D

Unit 10

1. E
2. C
3. I
4. A
5. H
6. G
7. L
8. M
9. O
10. B
11. F
12. J
13. N
14. K
15. D
16. DDE
17. HST
18. DDE
19. HST
20. Both
21. DDE
22. HST
23. HST
24. Both
25. DDE
26. HST
27. DDE
28. DDE
29. Both
30. HST
31. F
32. C
33. E
34. J
35. G
36. D
37. B
38. I
39. A
40. H
41. B
42. A
43. D
44. A
45. B
46. C
47. D
48. C
49. B
50. B
51. A
52. C
53. B
54. A
55. D
56. B
57. C
58. A
59. B
60. C
61. D
62. C
63. C
64. C
65. A

Unit 11

1. F
2. E
3. K
4. Q
5. D
6. G
7. L
8. H
9. P
10. O
11. N
12. A
13. C
14. J
15. B
16. C
17. A
18. E
19. G
20. F
21. J
22. N
23. J
24. K
25. N
26. N
27. J
28. K
29. K
30. J
31. J
32. N
33. K
34. J
35. K
36. D
37. B
38. B
39. A
40. C
41. A
42. D
43. C
44. B
45. B
46. C
47. A
48. B
49. D
50. D
51. B
52. A
53. C
54. B
55. C
56. B
57. D
58. C
59. A
60. C

Unit 12

1. C
2. F
3. D
4. I
5. A
6. G
7. B
8. E
9. J
10. H
11. A
12. C
13. B
14. C
15. A
16. B
17. A
18. B
19. D
20. C
21. C
22. D
23. B
24. A
25. B
26. D
27. C
28. C
29. A
30. B
31. D
32. B
33. A
34. C
35. D
36. A
37. B
38. C
39. B
40. D
41. B
42. F
43. B
44. C
45. C
46. F
47. B
48. F
49. C
50. F

Final Test

1. TJ
2. AJ
3. GW
4. JQA
5. AJo
6. JA
7. RBH
8. JM
9. WM
10. CC
11. JKP
12. AL
13. USG
14. WGH
15. GC
16. HCH
17. TR
18. HST
19. WW
20. JFK
21. FDR
22. LBJ
23. JC
24. GRF
25. DDE
26. I
27. J
28. G
29. F
30. I
31. A
32. K
33. F
34. C
35. J
36. C
37. C
38. D
39. A
40. E
41. J
42. B
43. H
44. D
45. B
46. H
47. B
48. G
49. I or K
50. D
51. D
52. B
53. B
54. D
55. C
56. A
57. D
58. B
59. F
60. C
61. C
62. E
63. E
64. H
65. H
66. G
67. B
68. D
69. C
70. A
71. B
72. C
73. B
74. A
75. A
76. C
77. B
78. A
79. B
80. PA
81. VA
82. MD
83. CA
84. MA
85. OK
86. MT
87. IL
88. AK
89. TX
90. NY
91. WI
92. UT
93. GA
94. HI